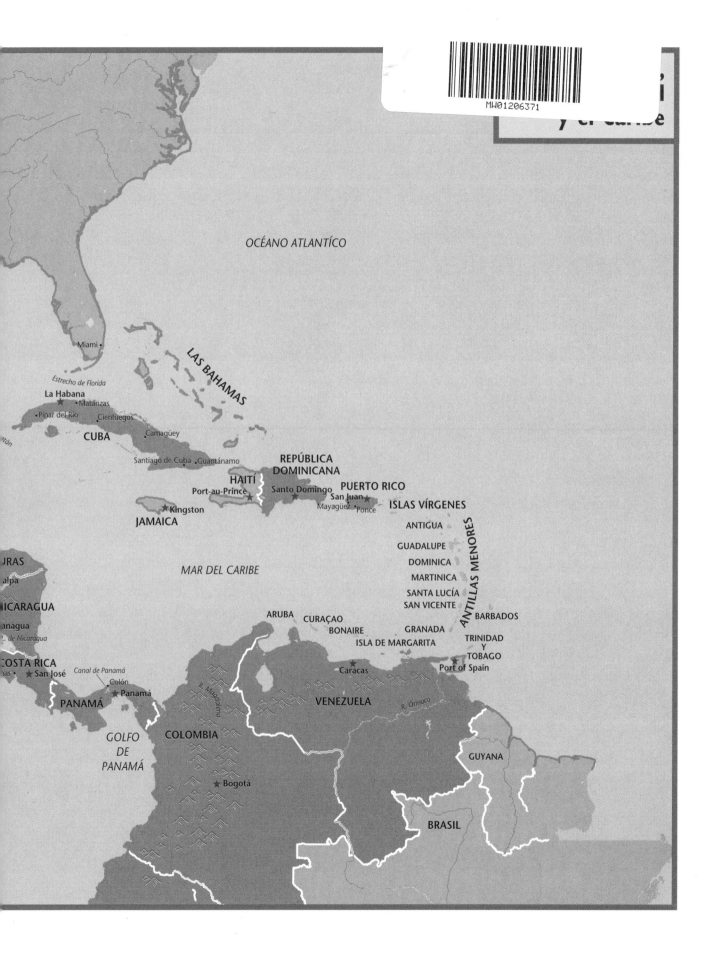

y el caribe

OCÉANO ATLANTÍCO

Miami

Estrecho de Florida

LAS BAHAMAS

La Habana ★ • Matanzas
• Pinar del Río • Cienfuegos
CUBA • Camagüey
Santiago de Cuba • Guantánamo

REPÚBLICA
DOMINICANA

HAITÍ
Port-au-Prince ★ • Santo Domingo • San Juan ★ PUERTO RICO
Mayagüez • • Ponce ISLAS VÍRGENES
★ Kingston
JAMAICA

ANTIGUA

GUADALUPE

DOMINICA

MARTINICA

SANTA LUCÍA
SAN VICENTE

MAR DEL CARIBE

ANTILLAS MENORES

BARBADOS

JRAS
alpa

NICARAGUA
anagua
L. de Nicaragua

ARUBA CURAÇAO
BONAIRE GRANADA
ISLA DE MARGARITA
TRINIDAD
Y
TOBAGO
Port of Spain

COSTA RICA
nas • ★ San José
Canal de Panamá
Colón
PANAMÁ ★ Panamá

Caracas

VENEZUELA
R. Orinoco

R. Magdalena

COLOMBIA

GOLFO
DE
PANAMÁ

GUYANA

★ Bogotá

BRASIL

4th EDITION

POCO A

POCO

4th EDITION

POCO A POCO

James M. Hendrickson
Guiomar Borrás A.

Thunderbird–American Graduate School of
International Management

INSTRUCTOR'S ANNOTATED EDITION

HEINLE & HEINLE PUBLISHERS
Boston, Massachusetts 02116, U.S.A.
A Division of International Thomson Publishing, Inc.
The ITP logo is a trademark under license.

Boston • Albany • Bonn • Cincinnati • Detroit • Madrid • Melbourne • Mexico City
New York • Paris • San Francisco • Singapore • Tokyo • Toronto • Washington

The publication of **Poco a poco, Fourth Edition** was directed by the members of the Heinle & Heinle College Foreign Language Publishing Team:

Wendy Nelson, Editorial Director
Tracie Edwards, Market Development Director
Gabrielle B. McDonald, Production Services Coordinator
Amy Jennings, Associate Development Editor

Also participating in the publication of this program were:

Publisher: Vincent P. Duggan
Managing Editor: Beth Kramer
Project Manager: Angela Castro
Compositor: Circa 86, Red Bank, NJ
Photo/Video Specialist: Jonathan Stark
Associate Editor: Beatrix Melauner
Associate Market Development Director: Rosella Romagnoli
Production Assistant: Lisa LaFortune
Manufacturing Coordinator: Wendy Kilborn
Photo Coordinator: Lisa LaFortune
Illustrator: David Sullivan
Interior Designer: Circa 86, Red Bank, NJ
Cover Illustrator: Marta M. Kaldenbach
Cover Designer: Sue Gerould/Perspectives

Library of Congress Cataloging-in-Publication Data

Hendrickson, James M.
    Poco a Poco / James M. Hendrickson, Guiomar Borrás A.—4th ed.,
    instructor's annotated ed.
        p.   cm.
    ISBN 0-8384-7843-3
    1. Spanish language—Textbooks for foreign speakers—English.
  I. Title.
  PC4129.E5H46 1997
  468.2'421—dc21

                                    97—31617
                                    CIP

Manufactured in the United States of America

ISBN: 0-8384-7843-3 student text
0-8384-7852-2 instructor's text
10 9 8 7 6 5 4 3 2 1

Table of Contents to the Instructor's Guide

PREFACE

Teaching for Communicative Proficiency

Poco a poco, 4th edition, is an introductory language program whose primary purpose is to help beginning-level students become functionally proficient in the Spanish language and familiar with common Hispanic customs and traditions.

The materials in the *Poco a poco* program are designed and organized around the three principles of communicative proficiency: function, content, and accuracy. In this program, students use language in realistic contexts (function), communicate with each other on topics relevant to their own lives and interests (content), and develop their skill in using phonological, lexical and grammatical features of Spanish (accuracy). The entire program meets or exceeds the new National Standards in Foreign Language Education in the five goal areas of communication, culture, connections, comparisons, and communities. These standards were sponsored by the American Council on the Teaching of Foreign Languages (ACTFL).

Poco a poco provides a carefully sequenced series of integrated materials for developing linguistic and communicative competence in Spanish. The pronunciation, vocabulary and grammar sections in the program focus on language as it is used by native speakers of Spanish in everyday situations. Because functional language proficiency is a primary outcome of *Poco a poco,* its themes focus on communicating in Spanish in real-life contexts. For example, students learn to greet people, exchange personal information, make invitations, order a meal in a restaurant, understand a radio commercial, respond to apartment advertisements, and express their opinions on a wide variety of topics.

What's New in the Fourth Edition?

Based on extensive feedback from many users of the third edition of *Poco a poco,* we have made the following changes in this fourth edition to make the program even more useful and enjoyable for students and their instructors.

- The completely new *Poco a poco* video program was designed specifically for the *Poco a poco* program. In addition, viewing activities have been included in the *síntesis* section at the end of each chapter in the student textbook, making the video easier to work with, and more relevant to other in-class instruction.

- Additional literary reading selections were added to the *En contexto* sections of the student textbook, to better prepare students for reading authentic texts.

- Task-based *Internet Activities* are presented in the *Síntesis* section of each chapter and are designed to stimulate students' interest in using the World Wide Web to expand their knowledge of the cultures of the Spanish-speaking world, while engaging them in a fun task that challenges them to use the functional language they've acquired in the classroom. All *Internet Activities* are level appropriate.

- The **Workbook** contains a short self-quiz, called the *Autoprueba,* which appears at the end of each chapter so that students can evaluate their own progress in learning both the Spanish language and Hispanic cultures before they are tested formally in class.

Other changes:

- Several *Gramática funcional* sections were resequenced. Formal commands appear earlier, and the introduction to the imperfect tense appears somewhat later so that students have more opportunities to practice the preterite tense. In addition, the explanations of how native Spanish speakers use these two tenses were rewritten based on recent research and reviewer feedback.

- An expanded exercise sequence following *Vocabulario útil* and *Gramática funcional* provides greater flexibility and more opportunities for controlled and meaningful practice.

- Brief dialogues open the *Gramática funcional* sections to contextualize the grammatical principals taught in those sections.

- Pronunciation activities were consolidated and are now conveniently placed in the **Laboratory Manual.**

- The information in the *Notas culturales* sections was revised and updated.

- The *Para escribir mejor* sections were rewritten and reorganized in a more pedagogically sound sequence.

- References to **Atajo,** the writing assistant software program, now appear in English for easier reference by students.

- The *¡Escuche!* sections now appear in the **Laboratory Manual.**

How does *Poco a poco*

Poco a poco, Fourth Edition was written to encourage your students to begin using Spanish fast. Developed to meet the requirements of the ACTFL National Standards for Foreign Language Learning, this new edition of *Poco a poco* features more cultural input and diversity, more opportunities for students to actively explore the Spanish-speaking world, and a greater emphasis on developing students' own insights into the nature of language and culture.

En contexto sections utilize a story-line to introduce new structures, vocabulary and culture. As students follow the experiences of several travelers, they acquire new language in context.

En contexto sections are also recorded on the laboratory tape program so that students can practice the dialogs before coming to class.

> "I like the way **Poco a poco** presents culture through the eyes—or diary—of young travelers, people with whom our students can identify."
>
> **Carmen Vigo-Acosta,**
> Mesa Community College

> "I still find **Poco a poco** to be a terrific blend of "traditional" grammar and "communicative" activities. It's also a flexible text. Most chapters can be organized in a variety of ways."
>
> **Sandra Rosenstiel,**
> University of Dallas

EN CONTEXTO

Play Lab Tape

Have students form pairs and act out this conversation together.

Hoy es miércoles el veintiséis de septiembre. Ahora Carlos Suárez está en una cabina telefónica en el Zócalo.(1) Está hablando con su amiga Anita Camacho, que está en casa.

ANITA: Bueno.(2)
CARLOS: ¡Hola, Anita! Habla Carlos.
ANITA: Carlos, ¿qué tal?
CARLOS: Muy bien, gracias. Y tú, ¿cómo estás?
ANITA: Bastante bien. ¿Qué hay de nuevo?
CARLOS: Oye,(3) Anita, hay un concierto esta noche en Bellas Artes.(4) ¿Quieres ir?°
ANITA: Ay, Carlos... no puedo.° Esta noche voy a° comer con mi familia en la Zona Rosa(5) y luego vamos al cine.°
CARLOS: ¡Qué interesante! Bueno, ¿quieres salir° conmigo el domingo? Voy al Parque de Chapultepec.(6)
ANITA: El domingo... el domingo... ¡Claro que sí! Me gusta mucho Chapultepec. ¿A qué hora vamos?
CARLOS: Por la tarde... paso por ti° a la una. Vamos en el metro(7) y luego comemos en el Museo de Antropología.(8) ¿Qué te parece?°
ANITA: ¡Perfecto! Muchas gracias por la invitación, Carlos. Eres muy simpático.
CARLOS: De nada.° Hasta el domingo, Anita.
ANITA: Hasta el domingo.

Do you want to go?
I can't/I'm going
to the movies
to go out

I'll pick you up
What do you think?

You're welcome

Notas de texto

1. *El Zócalo* is considered to be at the exact center of Mexico City. It is the former site of important Aztec temples, pyramids, and religious ceremonies. Today visitors can see the ruins of this ancient civilization as well as the National Cathedral and several government buildings that contain giant murals that depict the history of Mexico.

1. Use your knowledge and experience to add more information to these cultural notes.
2. If you have audio-visual materials to accompany these notes, use them in class to reinforce this information.

teach language?

ach of *Poco a poco's* 18 chapters is organized around manageable communicative goals. Your students acquire vocabulary, grammar structures, and communicative functions through both practice and open-ended activities, always within the context of the unit's geographical location.

Para leer mejor (presenting and practicing strategies) and **¡A leer!** (recycling strategies) develop reading skills as students explore authentic documents, realia, and the rich literary tradition of the Spanish-speaking world. Students are taught valuable reading strategies to minimize their frustration as they read authentic materials and to increase their linguistic comprehension and their cultural appreciation.

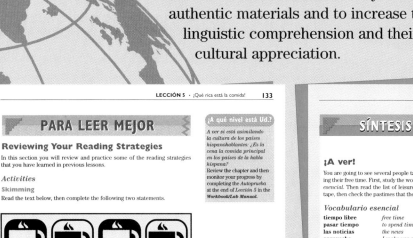

PARA LEER MEJOR

Reviewing Your Reading Strategies

In this section you will review and practice some of the reading strategies that you have learned in previous lessons.

Activities

Skimming

Read the text below, then complete the following two statements.

¡A qué nivel está Ud.?
A ver si está asimilando la cultura de los países hispanohablantes: ¿Es la cena la comida principal en los países de la habla hispana? Review the chapter and then monitor your progress by completing the *Autoprueba* at the end of *Lección 5* in the *Workbook/Lab Manual.*

Lo positivo y lo negativo del café

El café es una de las bebidas más populares en todo el mundo, pero pocas personas saben realmente lo que una taza de café significa. Como contiene cafeína es un estimulante del sistema nervioso, cardiovascular y muscular. Es diurético y estimula la digestión. En cantidades normales, una o dos tazas al día estimula además la actividad intelectual y física, así como la lentitud cardiaca y digestiva, pero en cantidades elevadas provoca taquicardia y como descontrola el sistema nervioso, puede ocasionar temblores. Es preferible que se abstenga de tomarlo si tiene úlcera, hipertensión, insomnio o padece de los nervios. Si es así, prefiera el que viene descafeinado y no abuse, para que pueda saborearlo siempre.

Source: "El café, lo positivo y lo negativo de esta bebida", Buenhogar, Año 23, No. 11, Mayo 17, 1988, página 11.

1. This reading is about . . .
   a. the intricacies of the human nervous system.
   b. the complexities of the human digestive system.
   c. the advantages of drinking decaffeinated coffee.
   d. the benefits and disadvantages of drinking coffee.

Answers: 1. d   2. a

SÍNTESIS

¡A ver!

You are going to see several people talk about some activities they enjoy during their free time. First, study the words and their meaning in the *Vocabulario esencial*. Then read the list of leisure-time activities. Third, watch the videotape, then check the pastimes that the people mention during their interviews.

Vocabulario esencial

tiempo libre	*free time*
pasar tiempo	*to spend time*
las noticias	*the news*
aprovecho	*I make use of*

_____ leer	_____ hacer ejercicio
_____ ir al cine	_____ ver la televisión
_____ jugar fútbol	_____ jugar a las cartas
_____ ir al parque	_____ salir con los papás
_____ ir de compras	_____ ver películas en video

Answers: leer, ir al cine, jugar fútbol, ir al parque, hacer ejercicio, ver la televisión, salir con los papás

What gestures of affection between the family members did you notice as you watched the video segment? Make a list of them in English.

¡A leer!

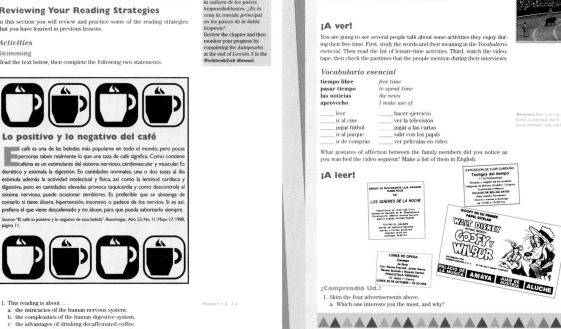

¡Comprendió Ud.?

1. Skim the four advertisements above.
   a. Which one interests you the most, and why?

Poco a poco is unique in its development of writing skills (increasingly valuable in an Internet-accessed world). **Para escribir mejor** activities present and practice targeted writing strategies in each chapter, while **¡A escribir!** activities, based on the chapter's theme, recycle both the strategies of the current chapter and revisit those of earlier chapters. These activities guide students through the writing process, from the organization of ideas to sequencing paragraphs to writing for different genres.

"I applaud the…grammar presentation. It appears less ambiguous and gives students more time to 'acquire' a structure before going on to more complex structures."

Julia Aguilar,
University of Pennsylvania

PARA ESCRIBIR MEJOR

Writing Topic Sentences

Your ability to write clear, concise topic sentences is essential to writing well. A good topic sentence has the following features:

- It comes at the beginning of a paragraph.
- It states the main idea of the paragraph.
- It focuses on only one topic of interest.
- It makes a factual or personal statement.
- It is neither too general nor too specific.
- It attracts the attention of the reader.

Activities

A. Listed below are five possible topic sentences for an opening paragraph about Hispanic families. Discuss the sentences with a classmate. Which sentence do you think is most appropriate to begin the paragraph? Why? Your classmate may have several different opinions; there is no one correct answer.

1. Cada año hay más divorcios en las familias hispanas.
2. Por lo general, las familias hispanas son muy unidas.
3. Muchas veces los abuelos viven en la casa de sus nietos.
4. La mujer hispana tiene muchas responsabilidades con su familia.
5. Normalmente, la familia hispana no incluye animales domésticos.

B. First, write a topic sentence for an opening paragraph about a description of your family. Second, write five or six sentences to develop the idea stated in your topic sentence. Third, exchange your paragraph with a classmate. Read each other's paragraph and discuss how you might improve its topic sentence; use the questions below to help you do so.

Does the topic sentence . . .
1. come at the beginning of the paragraph? ___ yes ___ no
2. state the main idea of the paragraph? ___ yes ___ no
3. focus on only one topic of interest? ___ yes ___ no
4. make a factual or personal statement? ___ yes ___ no
5. seem neither general nor too specific? ___ yes ___ no
6. attract the attention of the reader? ___ yes ___ no

¿A qué nivel está Ud.?

*¡A ver si puede resolver este rompecabezas!
Si Pancho está soltero, pero su hermana Josefina está casada con Guillermo, entonces Guillermo es el __ de Bernado e Isabel (que son los padres de Pancho, y los __ de Guillermo). Por fin, Pancho es el __ de Guillermo.*
Review the chapter and then monitor your progress by completing the *Autoprueba* at the end of *Lección 4* in the ***Workbook/Lab Manual.***

You could expand this activity to have students select one of the topic sentences and then, with a partner, write a paragraph that fits the topic sentence. Afterwards, students could write these paragraphs on the chalkboard or on an overhead transparency to compare them.

Atajo

Functions:
Writing an introduction; describing people; talking about the present; stating a preference

Vocabulary:
Family members; people; up-bringing; senses; personality

Grammar:
Verbs: *estar, tener,* progressive tenses; Adjectives position

---

SÍNTESIS

¡Comprendió Ud.?

1. ¿Cuándo es el cumpleaños de la bebé?
2. ¿En qué fecha es su bautismo? ¿Dónde es?
3. ¿Cuál es el nombre completo de la bebé?
4. ¿Cómo se llaman los padrinos de ella?
5. ¿Dónde viven Lucía y su familia?

¡A escribir!

En uno o dos párrafos describa a su familia, específicamente...

1. quiénes son (nombre y cuántos años tienen).
2. dónde viven (ciudad, casa o apartamento).
3. dónde trabajan o estudian.
4. sus pasatiempos y deportes favoritos.

¡A conversar!

Charle con otro(a) estudiante.

1. Bring to class some photographs of your family to share with a classmate. Describe your family as well as you can in Spanish.
2. Describe one of your favorite relatives in Spanish to a classmate. Use the vocabulary you have learned up to now; do not use a dictionary.

Lucía

Nací en la Ciudad de Mexico, D.F. el día 28 de julio de 1997 y me bautizaron el día 8 de diciembre del mismo año en la Parroquia del Verbo Encarnado (La Sagrada Familia)

Mis Padres:
Gonzalo Aguilar Abarca
Y
Norma M. de Aguilar

Mis Padrinos:
Marcelo Maldonado A.
Y
Josefina R. de Maldonado

Answers:
1. Su cumpleaños es el 28 de julio.
2. Su bautismo es el 8 de diciembre. Es en la Parroquia del Verbo Encarnado (La Sagrada Familia).
3. Su nombre completo es Lucía Aguilar M.
4. Sus padrinos se llaman Marcelo y Josefina Maldonado.
5. Viven en México, D.F. (la Ciudad de México).

This activity reinforces orally what students have done in writing in the ¡A escribir! activity above.

Atajo

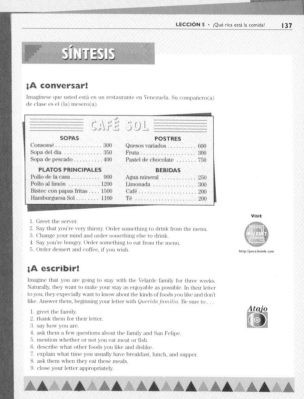

SÍNTESIS

¡A ver!

You are going to listen to two Hispanic men speaking about *taquerías*. Then you will watch two Mexican women going out for lunch in a restaurant. First, study the words and phrases and their meaning in the *Vocabulario esencial*. Second, read the sentences in the two activities below. Third, watch the videotape, then complete the sentences by checking the appropriate words and phrases in the activities.

Vocabulario esencial

la farolada	*corn tortilla with meat and melted cheese*
doble ración	*double serving*
variedad muy grande	*a wide variety*
comida de paso	*fast food*
buen sabor	*good flavor*
huele riquísima	*it smells delicious*
¡Provecho!	*Enjoy your meal!*
sabroso	*delicious*

A. En la taquería.

1. Tres platos típicos que se sirven en la taquería son...
   ____ tacos ____ bistec ____ chuletas
   ____ huevos ____ pescado ____ ensaladas

2. Muchas personas comen en la taquería porque...
   ____ la comida está rica.
   ____ se sirve comida rápida.
   ____ los precios son económicos.

3. La taquería es...
   ____ formal
   ____ informal

B. En el restaurante.

1. Laura come...
   ____ sopa ____ ensalada
   ____ tacos ____ chuletas

2. La amiga de Laura come...
   ____ sopa ____ pollo
   ____ queso ____ mariscos

Answers:
A. 1. tacos, bistec, chuletas 2. se sirve comida rápida 3. informal
B. 1. ensalada 2. sopa 3. bueno 4. bueno 5. formal

Poco a poco's completely new **text-tied video** combines with the **¡A ver!** activities found in the *Síntesis* sections of the textbook to make video easy to integrate into your syllabus and a valuable source of aural input for your students.

SÍNTESIS

¡A conversar!

Imagínese que usted está en un restaurante en Venezuela. Su compañero(a) de clase es el (la) mesero(a).

CAFÉ SOL

SOPAS		POSTRES	
Consomé	300	Quesos variados	600
Sopa del día	350	Fruta	300
Sopa de pescado	400	Pastel de chocolate	750

PLATOS PRINCIPALES		BEBIDAS	
Pollo de la casa	900	Agua mineral	250
Pollo al limón	1200	Limonada	300
Bistec con papas fritas	1500	Café	200
Hamburguesa Sol	1100	Té	200

1. Greet the server.
2. Say that you're very thirsty. Order something to drink from the menu.
3. Change your mind and order something else to drink.
4. Say you're hungry. Order something to eat from the menu.
5. Order dessert and coffee, if you wish.

Visit
http://poco.heinle.com

¡A escribir!

Imagine that you are going to stay with the Velarde family for three weeks. Naturally, they want to make your stay as enjoyable as possible. In their letter to you, they expecially want to know about the kinds of foods you like and don't like. Answer them, beginning your letter with *Querida familia*. Be sure to . . .

1. greet the family.
2. thank them for their letter.
3. say how you are.
4. ask them a few questions about the family and San Felipe.
5. mention whether or not you eat meat or fish.
6. describe what other foods you like and dislike.
7. explain what time you usually have breakfast, lunch, and supper.
8. ask them when they eat these meals.
9. close your letter appropriately.

Atajo

¡A conversar! activities encourage students to make the transition from learning about the language to learning to *use* the language through information-gap activities, pair and group activities, and role-plays found in the *Síntesis* section at the end of each chapter.

" I found these (text-specific video activities) intriguing. I like to use video in class and students really enjoy seeing actual scenes. I liked the types of activities that accompany the videos... the whole concept seems extremely useful."

Crista Johnson,
University of Delaware

GRAMÁTICA FUNCIONAL

Describing more past experiences

—¿Qué hicieron Julio y su hijo?
—**Se divirtieron** en el restaurante.
—Bueno, ¿qué pasó después?
—Juan Carlos **pidió** un refresco y su papá le **sirvió** una Coca.

Preterite with stem-vowel changing verbs

Spanish *-ir* verbs that have a stem-change in the present tense also have a stem change in the *usted / él / ella* and *ustedes / ellos / ellas* forms of the preterite tense: *e* becomes *i* and *o* becomes *u*.

servir

Present (e → i)	Preterite (e → i)
sirvo	serví
sirves	serviste
sirve	sirvió
servimos	servimos
servís	*servisteis*
sirven	sirvieron

divertirse

Present (e → ie)	Preterite (e → i)
me divierto	me divertí
te diviertes	te divertiste
se divierte	se divirtió
nos divertimos	nos divertimos
os divertís	*os divertisteis*
se divierten	se divirtieron

dormir

Present (o → ue)	Preterite (o → u)
duermo	dormí
duermes	dormiste
duerme	durmió
dormimos	dormimos
dormís	*dormisteis*
duermen	durmieron

Ex. A. Answers:
pidieron, pedí, pidieron, pedimos,
Durmieron, dormí, durmieron,
durmió;
Se divirtieron, me divertí, se
divirtió, te divertiste

Practiquemos

A. Una llamada telefónica. Gloria está hablando con Bienvenida, su suegra que vive en San Juan, Puerto Rico. Complete la conversación entre Gloria y Bienvenida con formas apropiadas de los verbos indicados.

pedir
—¿Qué _____ ustedes en el restaurante anoche?
—Pues, yo _____ un bistec. Julio y Juan Carlos _____ pescado. Después, nosotros _____ queso y fruta como de postre.

dormir
—¿_____ ustedes bien?
—Yo _____ muy bien. Los niños _____ muy bien, pero Julio _____ mal. Ahora está mejor, gracias a Dios.

Gramática funcional and **Vocabulario útil** sections, praised for their clarity and ease of use, make producing accurate Spanish easier for students.

New! The **Autoprueba**, a short self-quiz in the *Workbook/Lab Manual*, allows students to evaluate their own progress in learning both language and culture before they are tested formally in class. **Autopruebas** are designed to make your students accountable for what they learn and to inspire them to take an active role in the learning process.

How does *Poco a poco* teach culture?

Poco a poco presents culture through contextualized activities, *Notas culturales*, Internet activities, text-tied video, and readings selected from authentic literary and non-literary sources. This rich variety of cultural inputs provides both valuable background for language acquisition, and an incentive to explore the Spanish-speaking world.

Each **Paso** (containing three chapters) is placed in a particular geographic area, including: Mexico, Venezuela, Spain, Chile, and the United States.

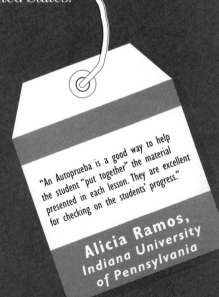

"An Autoprueba is a good way to help the student "put together" the material presented in each lesson. They are excellent for checking on the students' progress."

Alicia Ramos,
Indiana University
of Pennsylvania

Within each chapter, **Notas culturales**, often accompanied by photos, art, or realia, provide succinct cultural insights targeted to the chapter's lesson.

New chapter-by-chapter **Internet activities** encourage personalized exploration of authentic culture through task-based activities. Students have an opportunity to put their Spanish to use in the "real world."

New **text-tied video** shot on location in Spain, Puerto Rico, and Mexico, offers students an authentic view of cultures within an appropriate linguistic framework.

How does *Poco a poco* develop students' analytical and cognitive skills?

Vocabulario útil sections help your students explore the nuances of the Spanish language while demonstrating the close link that exists between language and culture.

Notas culturales link your students to the varied cultures of the Spanish-speaking world, encouraging them to see the similarities and differences that exist between the those cultures and their native cultures.

Internet activities ask students to analyze and compare processes and outcomes in their native culture with similar activities in a Spanish-speaking country (for example, renting an apartment in Chile after visiting various web-sites).

How does *Poco a poco* connect students to the wider world?

Internet activities encourage students to use their new language both within and beyond the school setting. Your students will learn to work independently, using the World Wide Web to complete real-life tasks, and learning to become life-long learners who use the language for personal enjoyment and enrichment.

Geographically-contextualized chapters provide a strong grounding in geography and culture for all language acquisition. Students studying with *Poco a poco, Fourth Edition*, take the language they learn in the classroom and apply it towards real-life objectives. The goal of *Poco a poco* is to show that the Spanish language is a lot more than what is printed on the textbook pages, that their is a vibrant, diverse Hispanic world that is much closer to each of us every day.

HOW POCO A POCO, 4/E WORKS

Component	Description	Usage	Skills developed/practiced	More information
Student Text	Full color; hard cover	Daily, in class and at home	Reading, vocabulary, listening, speaking, culture, grammar, writing	Introductory lesson, plus 18 lessons divided into 6 units, each representing a different Spanish-speaking country or region
Instructor's Annotated Edition	Full color; teaching tips and expansion of activities	Daily, in class	Teaching Spanish and Hispanic cultures especially for new teacher	Many pedagogical suggestions as well as suggested syllabi for varying course schedules and correlations to *Atajo* and *Poco a poco* video
Poco a poco Internet Activities	Task-based activities using the Worldwide Web	Optional	Develops reading skills, listening skills, writing skills and teaches Spanish and Hispanic cultures	Additional extension activities; accessible to any computer linked to Worldwide Web; found at http://poco.heinle.com
Poco a poco Video	Fully integrated with textbook; approximately 5–10 minutes per lesson; correlated to *Síntesis* section of textbook	Optional	Listening, vocabulary, culture, speaking	Variety of native speakers; short dialogues and interviews. For purchase only
Workbook	Combined with **Lab Manual**	Daily, at home	Vocabulary and grammar; guided and open-ended compositions in every lesson	Correlated with *Atajo* software; answers in separate answer key (Packaged with **Workbook/Lab Manual** at your request)
Lab Manual	Combined with **Workbook**	Weekly, in language lab or at home	Listening comprehension, vocabulary, and pronunciation	Many prelistening hints for students; answers in separate answer key
Lab Tape Program	Approximately 30 minutes per lesson; many interactive activities	Weekly, use with **Lab Manual**	Listening comprehension, vocabulary, and pronunciation	Variety of native speakers; available for duplication; sets of 10 or more; tapescript available
Computerized Test Bank	Ready-to-use tests, I quiz per lesson, I test per *Paso*. Speaking tests also provided for each lesson.	Optional	Tests reading, vocabulary, listening, speaking, culture, grammar, writing	Answer key included; checklist of *Paso* objectives available on IBM or MAC format for CD ROM
Transparencies	Full color; boxed separately	Optional	Vocabulary, functions, speaking	Correlated to specific activities; recycled to integrate with text
Instructor's Manual	Teaching tips and suggestions; separate component	Optional	For new teachers and and new users of *Poco a poco*	Lesson plans and laboratory tapescript
Atajo: Writing Assistant for Spanish Software	Word processing; bilingual Spanish-English dictionary; examples of how words and phrases are used; reference grammar with 250,000 conjugated verb forms; hard-to-define idiomatic expressions	Optional	Develops writing skills through task-based writing activities	Runs on most networks; correlated with activities in the **Workbook** and **Student Text** For purchase only
Electronic Study Guide Software	Vocabulary and grammar practice activities; specific feedback for wrong answers; self-test mode	Optional	Grammar, vocabulary	Available for DOS and Macintosh platforms. 3 1/2 inch disk drive. 4MB RAM

CHAPTER ORGANIZATION

SECTION/Subsection	Function	In/Out of Class
Lesson goals and contents	*Lesson overview*	*Out*
EN CONTEXTO	Lesson storyline: reading/listening	Out
Notas de texto	Cultural comments	Out
¿Comprendió Ud.?	Comprehension check	In
VOCABULARIO ÚTIL	Vocabulary presentation	Either
Practiquemos	Vocabulary practice	Both
GRAMÁTICA FUNCIONAL	Grammar presentation	Either
Practiquemos	Grammar practice	Either
Charlemos	Speaking practice	In
PARA LEER MEJOR	Reading strategy and practice	Out
¿Comprendió Ud.?	Comprehension check	In
PARA ESCRIBIR MEJOR	Writing strategy and practice	Out
NOTAS CULTURALES	Culture presentations and practice	Either
(in appropriate places)		
SÍNTESIS	Additional communication practice	
¡A ver!	Listening, Culture	In
¡A leer!	Reading	Out
¡A escribir!	Writing	Out
¡A conversar!	Speaking	In
VOCABULARIO	Lesson vocabulary lists	Out

SUGGESTED SYLLABI

The authors of the fourth edition of the *Poco a poco* program understand that you and your students vary considerably in the amount of time you devote to the language teaching-learning process. For this reason, the syllabi that follow are only suggested. Feel free to choose those materials that you find most useful to serve the needs and interests of your students.

The following syllabi assume that your students have read and studied each section of the textbook thoroughly before coming to class. This procedure will minimize your explanations of vocabulary, grammar, culture, and directions–and will maximize your students' use of Spanish.

CONFIGURATION A:
Two-semester sequence

	Semester 1		Semester 2
Week: 1	Introduction Lección Preliminar	16	Review Lección 10
2	Lección 1	17	Lección 10
3	Lección 1 Lección 2	18 19	Lección 11 Lección 11
4	Lección 2 Lección 3	20	Lección 12 Lección 12
5	Lección 3 Review		Review
6	Lección 4	21	Lección 13
7	Lección 4 Lección 5	22	Lección 13 Lección 14
8	Lección 5	23	Lección 14
9	Lección 6	24	Lección 15
10	Lección 6 Review	25	Lección 15 Review
11	Lección 7	26	Lección 16
12	Lección 7 Lección 8	27	Lección 16 Lección 17
13	Lección 8 Lección 9	28	Lección 17 Lección 18
14	Lección 9 Review	29	Lección 18 Review
15	Semester Exam	30	Semester Exam

3 hours weekly   4 hours weekly   5 hours weekly

Workbook/Lab Manual	Workbook/Lab Manual **Atajo**	Workbook/Lab Manual **Atajo** **Poco a poco video**

CONFIGURATION B:
Three-semester sequence

		Semester 1		Semester 2		Semester 3
Week:	1	Introduction Lección Preliminar	16	Review Lección 10	31	Review
	2	Lección 1	17	Lección 7	32	Lección 13
	3	Lección 1	18	Lección 7	33	Lección 13
	4	Lección 2	19	Lección 8	34	Lección 14
	5	Lección 2	20	Lección 8	35	Lección 15
	6	Lección 3	21	Lección 9	36	Lección 15
	7	Lección 3 Review	22	Lección 9 Review	37	Lección 15 Review
	8	Lección 4	23	Lección 10	38	Lección 16
	9	Lección 4	24	Lección 10	39	Lección 16
	10	Lección 5	25	Lección 11	40	Lección 17
	11	Lección 5	26	Lección 11	41	Lección 17
	12	Lección 6	27	Lección 12	42	Lección 18
	13	Lección 6	28	Lección 13	43	Lección 18
	14	Review	29	Review	44	Review
	15	Semester Exam	30	Semester Exam	45	Semester Exam

These syllabi assume that you will use the lessons and their related ancillaries, including the **Workbook/Lab Manual, Atajo,** and the **Poco a poco video.**

CONFIGURATION C:
Three-quarter sequence

		Quarter 1		Quarter 2		Quarter 3
Week:	1	Introduction Lección Preliminar	11	Review	21	Review
	2	Lección 1	12	Lección 7	22	Lección 13
	3	Lección 1	13	Lección 7	23	Lección 13
	4	Lección 2		Lección 8	24	Lección 14
	5	Lección 2	14	Lección 8	25	Lección 14
	6	Lección 3		Lección 9	26	Lección 15
	7	Lección 3 Review	15	Lección 9 Review	27	Lección 15 Review
	8	Lección 4	23	Lección 10	38	Lección 16
	9	Lección 4	24	Lección 10	39	Lección 16
	10	Lección 5	25	Lección 11	40	Lección 17
	11	Lección 5	26	Lección 11	41	Lección 17
	12	Lección 6	27	Lección 12	42	Lección 18
	13	Lección 6	28	Lección 13	43	Lección 18
	14	Review	29	Review	44	Review
	15	Quarter Exam	30	Quarter Exam	45	Quarter Exam

3 hours weekly	4 hours weekly	5 hours weekly
Workbook/Lab Manual	Workbook/Lab Manual **Atajo**	Workbook/Lab Manual **Atajo** **Poco a poco video**

TO THE TEACHER

Teaching Spanish Successfully

Welcome to *Poco a poco!* This program was carefully conceived and produced to help students communicate in Spanish and become familiar with Hispanic cultures beginning on the first day of class. It was also designed to help you teach your students successfully whether you are a beginning or a veteran instructor of foreign language. The abundant information in the *Instructor's Manual* and the numerous marginal notes in this annotated edition of the students' textbook will help you become a more successful manager of learning. The authors recommend a three-prong approach to selecting the activities, exercises, and suggestions offered in the *Poco a poco* program: adopt, adapt, or omit them according to your students' communicative needs and to your personal teaching style.

- **Adopt according to needs and styles.** This program provides many listening, speaking, reading, writing, and cultural activities that fulfill the communicative needs of students whose learning styles vary considerably. As their instructor, you are in the best position to know those needs and styles, and to select the materials that will most efficiently and effectively help your students to communicate within a Hispanic community. Choose an activity or an exercise depending, for example, on your students' interest in its topic and their ability to complete the stated task successfully. Similarly, adopt the pedagogical suggestions based on your own teaching style and on your experience as an instructor.

- **Adapt according to needs and styles.** A key feature of *Poco a poco* is its eclectic approach to second language acquisition and instruction. The activities, exercises, and suggestions are not "carved in stone." Feel free to modify any of them according to your students' communicative needs, thematic interests, and proficiency level as well as your own preferences. Trust your imagination and experiment with your creativity; you and your students may be well rewarded.

- **Omit according to needs and styles.** Do not feel fearful or guilty about omitting any activity, exercise, or suggestion in *Poco a poco.* You may wish to disregard some of them for different reasons such as lack of time, irrelevance to your course goals or objectives, or simply because you or your students do not like them. This program contains a supermarket of abundant varied materials and information for creating an atmosphere of teaching-learning that is most conducive to your student clients and to your own instructional approach.

The authors and editors of this extremely popular program wish you success in teaching Spanish and Hispanic culture . . . *poco a poco.*

SUPPLEMENTS TO POCO A POCO, 4/E

The textbook for *Poco a poco, Fourth Edition* is accompanied by a rich ancillary package of mutually supportive materials.

- The *Workbook/Laboratory Manual,* which is carefully integrated with the textbook, provides additional practice in developing vocabulary and grammar usage, listening comprehension, reading skills, and writing skills. The *Laboratory Manual* (and accompanying tape program) is designed to improve students' oral proficiency, with emphasis on learning strategies to understand and reproduce authentic oral discourse in Spanish. Presented throughout the *Laboratory Manual* are several margin hints to the student that suggest areas to recall or review. Students may find them useful when completing the corresponding activities. A separate Workbook Answer Key is provided free to the instructor and is available with the workbook upon request.

- The *Laboratory Tape Program* accompanies the *Laboratory Manual* and consists of approximately 30 minutes of listening practice per lesson. The tapes provide a variety of listening comprehension exercises and activities, in addition to pronunciation practice for the first ten lessons, which students respond to in the *Laboratory Manual.* The themes and functions are practiced with creative and meaningful listening tasks suitable for first-year students. The *En contexto* sections of the textbook are recorded on the Laboratory Tape Program, indicated by the tape symbol in the margin. A complete transcript for the Laboratory Tape Program is included in the *Instructor's Resource Manual.*

- The *Instructor's Annotated Edition (IAE)* is an annotated version of the student textbook. The numerous margin notes suggest ways to modify or expand specific exercises and activities, provide suggestions for instruction, and supply answers to the closed-ended exercises in the text. The IAE also presents suggested syllabi for several types of course settings, including two-semester, three-semester, and three-quarter sequences and a lesson organization chart including those activities best suited for in-class or out-of-class work.

- The *Instructor's Resource Manual* materials includes the Laboratory Tapescript and an instructor's manual.

- The *Computerized Test Bank* is designed to test linguistic and communicative competence for each lesson in the *Poco a poco* program. There are 19 lesson tests and six cumulative *Paso* tests, with a corresponding Answer Key and speaking situations. New in the Testing Program are checklists available for instructors to distribute to their students to help them prepare for the cumulative *Paso* exams. A teacher note at the end of every *Paso* reminds instructors that these checklists are available for review. The tests are available in word processing documents in IBM or MAC format on CD ROM.

- The *Overhead Transparency Program* contain full-color transparencies, including maps of all the Spanish-speaking countries as well as vocabulary displays and pictorial situations which help students practice corresponding grammar, vocabulary, and functions presented in the text. Specific cross-references to the transparency program are provided in the margins of the Instructor's Annotated Edition.

- The *Poco a poco Video Program* *is* completely new and features Hispanic cultures and people performing a variety of language functions in context. Video-based exercises are found in the *Síntesis* section at the end of each chapter.

- *Atajo* is a computerized writing assistant for Spanish that helps students practice their writing skills. The program contains a bilingual dictionary, a verb conjugator, a grammar reference, an index to functional phrases and a thematic dictionary. This software is specifically correlated to *Poco a poco* with corresponding writing activities in the textbook and workbook.

- The *Poco a poco* homepage, which can be accessed via the Worldwide Web at http://poco.heinle.com links students to Spanish-language web sites throughout the world and asks students to perform engaging tasks that build on their in-class experience.

- *Poco a poco Electronic Study Guide* software offers students abundant activities to practice vocabulary and grammar presented in the *Poco a poco* textbook. Specific feedback to wrong answers helps guide students to figure out the correct answers. A self-test mode allows students to do a final check on how well they've learned the new material before formal testing in-class.

Desk Copy Information

If you decide to adopt the *Poco a poco* program, you will receive free upon request:

- An *Instructor's Annotated Edition* of *Poco a poco, 4th edition*, which includes numerous margin notes, suggested syllabi for three different configurations of semester/quarter sequences; a chapter organization chart, and an introduction to the instructor

- A *Workbook/Laboratory Manual*

- A set of color transparencies

- A *Computerized Test Bank* with written and speaking tests for each of the 19 lessons and a comprehensive written test for each Paso

- A *Workbook/Laboratory Manual Answer Key*

- An *Instructor's Resource Manual* containing chapter-by-chapter lesson plans, correlations to the video and software programs, a textbook answer key, and a tapescript for the Laboratory Tape Program

You may also purchase:

- The *Poco a poco Video*, to accompany *Poco a poco, 4th edition*. Each segment of the video is cross-referenced in the textbook.

- *Atajo: Writing Assistant for Spanish* software

- *Poco a poco* Electronic Study Guide software

If you decide to adopt *Poco a poco, 4th edition,* your students may purchase:

- A Student Textbook

- A Workbook/Laboratory Manual

- Workbook/Laboratory Manual Answer Key

- *Poco a poco* Electronic Study Guide software

- *Atajo: Writing Assistant for Spanish* software

For more information, write to Heinle & Heinle Publishers, Inc., 20 Park Plaza, Boston, MA 02116.

4th EDITION

POCO A POCO

James M. Hendrickson
Guiomar Borrás A.

Thunderbird–American Graduate School of
International Management

HEINLE & HEINLE PUBLISHERS
Boston, Massachusetts 02116, U.S.A.
A Division of International Thomson Publishing, Inc.
The ITP logo is a trademark under license.

*Boston • Albany • Bonn • Cincinnati • Detroit • Madrid • Melbourne • Mexico City
New York • Paris • San Francisco • Singapore • Tokyo • Toronto • Washington*

The publication of **Poco a poco, Fourth Edition** was directed by the members of the Heinle & Heinle College Foreign Language Publishing Team:

Wendy Nelson, Editorial Director
Tracie Edwards, Market Development Director
Gabrielle B. McDonald, Production Services Coordinator
Amy Jennings, Associate Development Editor

Also participating in the publication of this program were:

Publisher: Vincent P. Duggan
Managing Editor: Beth Kramer
Project Manager: Angela Castro
Compositor: Circa 86, Red Bank, NJ
Photo/Video Specialist: Jonathan Stark
Associate Editor: Beatrix Melauner
Associate Market Development Director: Rosella Romagnoli
Production Assistant: Lisa LaFortune
Manufacturing Coordinator: Wendy Kilborn
Photo Coordinator: Lisa LaFortune
Illustrator: David Sullivan
Interior Designer: Circa 86, Red Bank, NJ
Cover Illustrator: Marta M. Kaldenbach
Cover Designer: Sue Gerould/Perspectives

Library of Congress Cataloging-in-Publication Data

Hendrickson, James M.
    Poco a Poco / James M. Hendrickson, Guiomar Borrás A.—4th ed.,
    instructor's annotated ed.
       p.   cm.
    ISBN 0-8384-7843-3
    1. Spanish language—Textbooks for foreign speakers—English.
    I. Title.
    PC4129.E5H46 1997
    468.2'421—dc21

                                    97—31617
                                        CIP

Manufactured in the United States of America

ISBN: 0-8384-7843-3 student text
0-8384-7852-2 instructor's text
10 9 8 7 6 5 4 3 2 1

To the Memory of
my Mother and Father
—*James M. Hendrickson*

I would like to dedicate this work to my mother, Gisela; to my son, Santiago; to my brother, Tommy; to my family and to my students.

I would like to thank my friend, Stephen Frail, for thinking of me when this project came up. I would also like to thank Wendy Nelson, Amy Jennings, James M. Hendrickson, and Angela Castro for their guidance and help with this project.

Special thanks go to my students in Venezuela and in the United States since they have always been my source of encouragement and inspiration.

—*Guiomar Borrás A.*

CONTENTS

LECCIÓN PRELIMINAR • ¡Mucho gusto! 2

COMMUNICATIVE GOALS: You will be able to greet others, introduce yourself, and share some basic information about yourself.

Objetivos funcionales

Language Functions:
Greeting others
Introducing yourself
Saying where you are from
Exchanging addresses
Exchanging telephone
 numbers
Telling your age
Saying good-bye
En contexto

Vocabulario y comunicación útil

Vocabulario útil:
Greetings
Personal introductions
Numbers 0-30
Farewells
Gramática funcional:
Subject pronouns
Present tense of the verb **ser**
Sentence negation
The verb form **hay**

Cultura

Notas culturales:
Addressing others:
 tú and **usted**
Meeting and greeting
 others

Paso I ▸ Entre amigos ▸ México

PASO STORY LINE: Carlos Suárez and Anita Camacho meet each other in their English class at the Universidad Nacional Autónoma de México. Later, Carlos meets Anita's family who lives in a fashionable neighborhood of Mexico City. One day Carlos invites Anita to spend a Sunday afternoon with him at Chapultepec Park.

LECCIÓN I • ¿Qué estudias aquí? 22

COMMUNICATIVE GOALS: You will be able to become better acquainted with your classmates and describe your life at school.

Objetivos funcionales

Language Functions:
Identifying people and things
Indicating relationships
Telling time
Describing school-related
 activities
Describing everyday
 activities
En contexto

Vocabulario y comunicación útil

Vocabulario útil:
Classmates and friends
Academic courses
Telling time
Days of the week
Gramática funcional:
Gender and plural of nouns
Definite and indefinite
 articles
Present tense of regular
 -ar verbs
The contractions **al** and **del**
Me gusta + infinitive

Cultura

Notas culturales:
24-hour system of time
Education in Latin
 America and Spain

Síntesis

¡A ver!:
Video: Meeting Students
 at the Universidad
¡A leer!
¡A escribir!

LECCIÓN 2 • ¡Aquí tienes tu casa! 44

COMMUNICATIVE GOALS: You will be able to describe yourself, describe your friends and family, and describe what you do at home.

Objetivos funcionales

Language Functions:
Describing people and things
Describing daily activities
Indicating ownership
Defining relationships
En contexto

Vocabulario y comunicación útil

Vocabulario útil:
Nuclear family members
House pets
Numbers 31-99
Colors
Gramática funcional:
Agreement with descriptive adjectives
Present tense of the verb *tener*
Possessive adjectives
Possession with *de(l)*
Present tense of regular *-er* and *-ir* verbs
Present tense of *hacer*

Cultura

Notas culturales:
Hand gestures
Conversational customs

Síntesis

¡A ver!:
Video: A Mexican Family Lunch
¡A leer!
¡A escribir!

LECCIÓN 3 • ¿Quieres salir conmigo? 70

COMMUNICATIVE GOALS: You will be able to discuss how you, your friends, and your family spend your free time.

Objetivos funcionales

Language Functions:
Making invitations
Expressing likes and dislikes
Expressing plans and intentions
Describing leisure-time activities
Accepting and declining invitations
En contexto

Vocabulario y comunicación útil

Vocabulario útil:
Pastimes and sports
Months of the year
Gramática funcional:
Present tense of the verb *ir* + *a(l)*
Present tense of other irregular *yo* verbs
Personal *"a"*
The verb *gustar* + infinitive

Cultura

Notas culturales:
Sports in the Spanish-speaking world

Síntesis

¡A ver!:
Video: Hispanic Pastimes
¡A leer!
¡A escribir!

LECCIÓN 6 • ¡Felicidades, Beti! 139

COMMUNICATIVE GOALS: You will be able to comment on the weather and describe your daily routines.

Objetivos funcionales	Vocabulario y comunicación útil	Cultura	Síntesis
Language Functions: Describing people, Describing the weather, Specifying dates, Expressing opinions, Describing daily routines, Comparing and contrasting, Expressing preferences **En contexto**	**Vocabulario útil:** Weather expressions, Idioms: **tener frío, calor**, Seasons of the year, Numbers 100–1,000, Parts of the body **Gramática funcional:** Reflexive verbs and pronouns, Comparatives and superlatives, The verbs **ser** versus **estar** (summary)	**Notas culturales:** The *quince años* celebration, The centigrade system, Climate in Spanish-speaking countries	**¡A ver!:** Video: Daily Routines **¡A leer!** **¡A escribir!**

Paso 3 ▸ Día tras día ▸ Los Estados Unidos

PASO STORY LINE: Julio and Gloria Sepúlveda are a young Puerto Rican couple who now live in New York City. Shortly before Christmas, they go shopping for clothing with their two small children at Macy's department store. On December 24th, Julio's mother arrives in New York and has several unfortunate experiences on the way from the airport to her son's apartment.

LECCIÓN 7 • ¡Julio, es hora de levantarte! 170

COMMUNICATIVE GOALS: You will be able to describe where you live, your household chores, and what activities you and others did recently.

Objetivos funcionales	Vocabulario y comunicación útil	Cultura	Síntesis
Language Functions: Describing one's personal residence, Expressing preferences, Describing one's household chores, Discussing past activities, Specifying how long ago, Communicating more smoothly **En contexto**	**Vocabulario útil:** Rooms of a house, Furniture and appliances, Household chores **Gramática funcional:** Preterite of regular verbs, The verb form **hace** + time (ago), Direct object pronouns	**Notas culturales:** Housing in Latin America and Spain, Gender roles in Hispanic cultures	**¡A ver!:** Video: Finding a Roommate **¡A leer!** **¡A escribir!**

Paso 4 ▶ ¡A pasarlo lo máximo! ▶ España

PASO STORY LINE: Elena Navarro is a single parent who lives in Barcelona with her six-year old daughter, Rita. They go grocery shopping in speciality stores, look for bargains in a department store, and visit the island of Mallorca with several relatives.

LECCIÓN 10 • ¿En qué puedo servirle? 246

COMMUNICATIVE GOALS: You will be able to talk and write about common foods and describe how life was when you were younger.

Objetivos funcionales	Vocabulario y comunicación útil	Cultura	Síntesis
Language Functions: Expressing opinions Specifying preferences Stating grocery needs Expressing likes and dislikes Communicating more smoothly Describing past experiences **En contexto**	**Vocabulario útil:** Specialized food stores Fruits and vegetables **Gramática funcional:** Double object pronouns Imperfect tense	**Notas culturales:** Shopping for groceries Hispanic markets	**¡A ver!:** Video: Planning Something Special **¡A leer!** **¡A escribir!**

LECCIÓN 11 • Aquí vendemos de todo 270

COMMUNICATIVE GOALS: You will be able to ask questions and express your opinions in department stores and non-food specialty shops.

Objetivos funcionales	Vocabulario y comunicación útil	Cultura	Síntesis
Language Functions: Giving advice Making requests Stating reasons Asking for information Naming non-food items Expressing preferences **En contexto**	**Vocabulario útil:** Jewelry and writing materials Electronic gadgets and photo supplies Shopping expressions **Gramática funcional:** The prepositions *por* and *para* Adverbs	**Notas culturales:** Department stores Specialized non-food stores	**¡A ver!:** Video: Making Purchases **¡A leer!** **¡A escribir!**

LECCIÓN 12 • ¿Qué van a comer? 293

COMMUNICATIVE GOALS: You will be able to order a meal in a restaurant and describe some of your past experiences.

Objetivos funcionales	Vocabulario y comunicación útil	Cultura	Síntesis
Language Functions:	**Vocabulario útil:**	**Notas culturales:**	**¡A ver!:**
Naming tableware items	Table setting	Restaurant customs	Video: In the Tapas Bar
Ordering a meal	Restaurant expressions	*Tapas* bars	**¡A leer!**
Making requests	**Gramática funcional:**		**¡A escribir!**
Stating preferences	Present perfect		
Expressing opinions	indicative		
Describing recent activities	Preterite and imperfect		
Narrating childhood	(summary)		
experiences			
En contexto			

Paso 5 ▶ ¡Que se diviertan Uds.! ▶ Chile

PASO STORY LINE: We first meet Luis and Jorge as they vacation in the resort community of Viña del Mar. Back home in Santiago, the two university students learn that a young woman they saw at the beach has been selected as queen of an international song festival. Later, Jorge and his girl friend attend the festival queen's wedding, where they have a good time.

LECCIÓN 13 • ¡Que les vaya bien! 316

COMMUNICATIVE GOALS: You will be able to describe your outdoor activities and a short vacation trip.

Objetivos funcionales	Vocabulario y comunicación útil	Cultura	Síntesis
Language Functions:	**Vocabulario útil:**	**Notas culturales:**	**¡A ver!:**
Giving advice	Beach resort	Viña del Mar	Video: Outdoor
Expressing wants	Country outing	The history of Viña	Pastimes
Persuading others	**Gramática funcional:**	del Mar	**¡A leer!**
Making invitations	Present subjunctive		**¡A escribir!**
Expressing intentions	following **querer**		
Making recommendations	Present subjunctive		
Describing weekend	following other verbs of		
activities	volition		
En contexto			

LECCIÓN 18 • Viaje a las islas encantadas   431

COMMUNICATIVE GOALS: You will be able to discuss health-related matters and describe hypothetical situations.

Objetivos funcionales	Vocabulario y comunicación útil	Cultura	Síntesis
Language Functions: Expressing opinions Giving recommendations Giving advice on health Making speculations Describing impressions Explaining medical problems Stating factual information **En contexto**	**Vocabulario útil:** Common illnesses and treatments The human body (review) **Gramática funcional:** "If" clauses Infinitive and subjunctive uses (summary) Indicative and subjunctive uses (summary)	**Notas culturales:** Medical advice for travellers Medical assistance abroad	**¡A ver!:** Video: A Visit to the Doctor **¡A leer!** **¡A escribir!**

TO THE STUDENT

Learning Spanish Successfully

Welcome to *Poco a poco!* This program was carefully designed with you in mind. It contains many different components which are all integrated to help you learn Spanish successfully, efficiently, and enjoyably. Being proficient in two or more languages can be rewarding to you personally and professionally. But learning to communicate in a language other than your native language takes patience, concentration, and practice.

Be patient. It takes time and patience to learn another language, so take your time and be patient with yourself as you learn to communicate in Spanish. At first, you may feel that spoken Spanish sounds "faster" than English (it isn't) or that some sounds of Spanish seem a bit "strange" to your ear. But as you become accustomed to listening to Spanish in class and on the *Poco a poco* tapes, that "strange" feeling will fade away. And remember that nobody is perfect! Because you are a beginning student of Spanish, your instructor won't expect you to speak with native-like pronunciation, to write grammatically perfect sentences, or to always use the most appropriate words to express your thoughts and feelings. Making errors is a normal part of learning any skill for the first time, especially communicating in another language. So be tolerant of your mistakes, laugh at them, and learn from them. And most importantly—be patient with yourself!

Concentrate on the message. Research shows that good language learners focus their attention on understanding the meaning of a message. Rather than concentrating on individual words or translating word for word, try to get the gist or general idea of the speaker or writer. As you listen to or read Spanish, focus your attention on what the speaker or writer is trying to express. For example, ask yourself: "What is the most important information that he or she wants me to understand?" Your ability to understand spoken or written Spanish also depends on your personal motivation. Most of the exercises and activities in the *Poco a poco* program were written to encourage you to share personal information with your classmates. For instance, you will talk and write about your family and friends, how you spend your free time, what foods you like and dislike, and where you plan to take your next vacation.

Practice, practice, practice! A major goal of the *Poco a poco* program is to help you become more proficient in Spanish. You will have plenty of opportunities to practice listening, speaking, reading, and writing Spanish in the same ways that Hispanics use the language in everyday situations: to meet each other, to talk with friends, to order a food in a restaurant, to read the newspaper, to write a letter to a friend, to listen to the radio, and so forth. Of course, you should try to practice Spanish outside of class whenever you can with your classmates, with international students on your campus, and with other native speakers in your community. If your area has a Spanish-language radio station, listen to it frequently even if you understand very little at first. If you have access to Spanish-language television programs, watch the soap operas and children's programs because they are easier to understand than many of the other programs. Many Spanish-language movies are now available on videocassette; watching one or two of them every week will significantly improve your proficiency in Spanish.

With patience, concentration, and practice, you will become more proficient in Spanish . . . *poco a poco.*

You will have several tools to help you accomplish the goals of ***Poco a poco:***

The ***Student Textbook,*** which balances formal functional vocabulary and grammar instruction with skill development in listening, speaking, reading, writing and Spanish and Hispanic cultures.

The ***Workbook/Lab Manual,*** which is carefully integrated with the textbook, provides additional practice in developing vocabulary and grammar usage, listening comprehension, reading skills, and writing skills. The ***Laboratory Manual*** offers hints in the margin to help you recall or review new and previously learned material.

You may wish to use ***Atajo: Writing Assistant for Spanish,*** a computerized writing support program that will help you practice writing skills. The program contains a bilingual dictionary, a verb conjugator, a grammar reference, an index to functional phrases and a thematic dictionary. You will find useful correlations to the ***Atajo*** program in your textbook and workbook.

The ***Poco a poco*** homepage, found at http://poco.heinle.com, will contain additional task-based activities to help you explore the Spanish language resources found on the World Wide Web.

PREFACE

Teaching for Communicative Proficiency

Poco a poco, 4th edition, is an introductory language program whose primary purpose is to help beginning-level students become functionally proficient in the Spanish language and familiar with common Hispanic customs and traditions.

The materials in the *Poco a poco* program are designed and organized around the three principles of communicative proficiency: function, content, and accuracy. In this program, students use language in realistic contexts (function), communicate with each other on topics relevant to their own lives and interests (content), and develop their skill in using phonological, lexical and grammatical features of Spanish (accuracy). The entire program meets or exceeds the new National Standards in Foreign Language Education in the five goal areas of communication, culture, connections, comparisons, and communities. These standards were sponsored by the American Council on the Teaching of Foreign Languages (ACTFL).

Poco a poco provides a carefully sequenced series of integrated materials for developing linguistic and communicative competence in Spanish. The pronunciation, vocabulary and grammar sections in the program focus on language as it is used by native speakers of Spanish in everyday situations. Because functional language proficiency is a primary outcome of *Poco a poco,* its themes focus on communicating in Spanish in real-life contexts. For example, students learn to greet people, exchange personal information, make invitations, order a meal in a restaurant, understand a radio commercial, respond to apartment advertisements, and express their opinions on a wide variety of topics.

What's New in the Fourth Edition?

Based on extensive feedback from many users of the third edition of *Poco a poco,* we have made the following changes in this fourth edition to make the program even more useful and enjoyable for students and their instructors.

* The completely new *Poco a poco* video program was designed specifically for the *Poco a poco* program. In addition, viewing activities have been included in the *síntesis* section at the end of each chapter in the student textbook, making the video easier to work with, and more relevant to other in-class instruction.

* Additional literary reading selections were added to the *En contexto* sections of the student textbook, to better prepare students for reading authentic texts.

* The *Workbook* contains a short self-quiz, called the *Autoprueba,* which appears at the end of each chapter so that students can evaluate their own progress in learning both the Spanish language and Hispanic cultures before they are tested formally in class.

Other changes:

- Several *Gramática funcional* sections were resequenced. Formal commands appear earlier, and the introduction to the imperfect tense appears somewhat later so that students have more opportunities to practice the preterite tense. In addition, the explanations of how native Spanish speakers use these two tenses were rewritten based on recent research and reviewer feedback.

- An expanded exercise sequence following *Vocabulario útil* and *Gramática funcional* provides greater flexibility and more opportunities for controlled and meaningful practice.

- Brief dialogues open the *Gramática funcional* sections to contextualize the grammatical principals taught in those sections.

- Pronunciation activities were consolidated and are now conveniently placed in the **Laboratory Manual.**

- The information in the *Notas culturales* sections was revised and updated.

- The *Para escribir mejor* sections were rewritten and reorganized in a more pedagogically sound sequence.

- References to **Atajo,** the writing assistant software program, now appear in English for easier reference by students.

- The *¡Escuche!* sections now appear in the **Laboratory Manual.**

Acknowledgements

We wish to express our sincere appreciation to the following people who contributed to the *Poco a poco* program: Charles Heinle, president of Heinle & Heinle Publishers, who supported the project; Stan Galek, Vice President of English as a Second Language who initiated the project; Vince Duggan, Vice President of Foreign Languages, who encouraged the publication of its fourth edition; Wendy Nelson, Editorial Director, and Amy Jennings, Associate Developmental Editor, who supervised the project with expertise and diligence; Gabrielle McDonald, Production Services Coordinator, and Angela Castro, Project Manager, whose meticulous work is reflected in a product of extremely high quality. We would also like to thank Paul Hoff, co-author of the Laboratory Manual and author of the Testing Program. Many thanks to the photographers; Circa 86, the designer; and David Sullivan, the illustrator, for making this program visually attractive, yet functionally practical.

We are deeply indebted to the many reviewers of this fourth edition of *Poco a poco:*

Poco a poco reviewers

Julia Aguilar
University of Pennsylvania

Ruth Bell
University of Delaware

Jennifer Eddy
Drew University

Herschel Frey
University of Pittsburgh

Crista Johnson
University of Delaware

Patricia L. MacGregor-Mendoza
New Mexico State University

Alicia Ramos
Middlebury College

Fernando Rivas
St. Mary's University

Sandra Rosenstiel
University of Dallas

Carmen Vigo Acosta
Mesa Community College

Joe Wieczorek
University of Maryland

We are also indebted to several expert reviewers, Sandra Rosenstiel of the University of Dallas, Janice Wright of the University of Kansas, and Montserrat Vilarrubla of Illinois State College, who assisted in the review of the cultural information in *Poco a poco.*

Many thanks also to the reviewers and other professionals who contributed to the first, second, and third editions of *Poco a poco.*

Some information in the *Notas culturales* sections of the textbook in all four editions was adapted and updated from two Learning Aids which were produced and published by Brigham Young University: *España* and *Latin America*. These and other cultural materials are currently available from the David M. Kennedy Center for International Studies, 280 HRCB, Provo, UT, 84602. We would like to express our appreciation to Deborah L. Coon, Manager of Publication Services at the Center, for granting permission to adapt and reprint this cultural information.

Finally, we wish to express our deepest appreciation to the tens of thousands of colleagues and students who have used the *Poco a poco* program. Their tremendous support has made it possible for us to continue sharing our love of the Spanish language and Hispanic culture to heights far beyond the perimeters of our dreams. *¡Un millón de gracias a todos!*

COMMENTS: We are very interested in receiving your comments on and your reactions to the *Poco a poco* program. Your viewpoints and experiences using the program in the classroom will be extremely helpful. Please address your ideas to us in care of: Heinle & Heinle Publishers, Inc., 20 Park Plaza, Boston, MA, 02116.

James M. Hendrickson
Guiomar Borrás A.

Preliminar

¡Mucho gusto!

▶ COMMUNICATIVE GOALS

You will be able to greet others, introduce yourself, and share some basic information about yourself.

▶ LANGUAGE FUNCTIONS

Greeting others
Introducing yourself
Saying where you are from
Exchanging addresses
Exchanging telephone numbers
Telling your age
Saying good-bye

http://poco.heinle.com

▶ VOCABULARY THEMES

Greetings
Personal introductions
Numbers 0–30
Farewells

▶ GRAMMATICAL STRUCTURES

Subject pronouns
Present tense of the verb *ser*
Sentence negation
The verb form *hay*

▶ CULTURAL INFORMATION

Addressing others: *tú* and *usted*
Meeting and greeting others

EN CONTEXTO

 **Play Lab Tape**

Carmen Fuentes García(1) es profesora de español. Ahora° ella está hablando con su° estudiante en una sala de clase en Las Cruces, Nuevo México.(2)

Now
speaking with her

CARMEN: ¡Buenos días, señor!(3)

KEITH: ¡Buenos días, profesora!

CARMEN: ¿Cuál es su nombre?

KEITH: Mi nombre es Keith Howe. Y usted, ¿cómo se llama?

CARMEN: Me llamo Carmen Fuentes Ortega. Mucho gusto,° Keith.

Nice to meet you

KEITH: El gusto es mío.° ¿De dónde es usted, profesora?

My pleasure

CARMEN: Soy de Guadalajara, México.(4) ¿Y usted?

KEITH: Soy de los Estados Unidos... de Miami, Florida.

CARMEN: Ah, de Miami, ¿eh? Hay° muchos cubanos en Miami, ¿verdad?°

There are / aren't there?

KEITH: Sí. Hay mucha gente° hispana allí.° Hay cubanos, puertorriqueños y mexicanos. También° hay muchas personas de la América Central y de la América del Sur.(5)

people / there
Also

CARMEN: Sí, lo sé,° Keith. Miami es una ciudad internacional.(6)

I know (it)

Included on Laboratory Tape Program.

1. One purpose of the *En contexto* section is to provide a realistic language sample of how native speakers actually use Spanish in daily conversation.
2. Ask students to practice this dialogue in pairs.

These notes give students additional information about Hispanic cultures and the Spanish language. Feel free to expand on the commentary here, based on your own knowledge and experience.

Note #1: For a detailed explanation on how Spanish surnames are formed, see page 108 in *Lección 4*.
Note #2: Ask students to name other American towns and cities that have Spanish names. Write those names on the board, or on an overhead transparency, and have students guess what the names mean in English.

Notas de texto

1. Many native speakers of Spanish have a double surname. For example, Carmen's first surname (Fuentes) is from her father, and her second surname (García) is from her mother's maiden name.
2. Dozens of American cities and towns as well as a few states bear Spanish names; for example: Los Angeles, San Diego, Santa Fe, Las Vegas, El Paso, Nevada, Colorado. These names are an indication of the rich Hispanic heritage of the United States.

3. Note that in Spanish an inverted exclamation mark is placed at the beginning of an exclamation, and an inverted question mark is placed at the beginning of a question.
4. Guadalajara is the second largest city in Mexico with a population of five million people.
5. Miami, Florida, has a huge Spanish-speaking population as a result of large-scale immigration from Latin America. Millions of Hispanic-Americans also live in San Diego, Los Angeles, San Antonio, Chicago, and New York City.
6. Miami is a very cosmopolitan city where people from all over the world have settled.

¿Comprendió Ud.?

Answers: 1. mexicana 2. Guadalajara 3. estudiante 4. los Estados Unidos (Miami, Florida) 5. Nuevo México 6. español 7. muchos (muchos hispanos)

1. ¿Es Carmen Fuentes mexicana o cubana? / Es _____ .
2. ¿De qué ciudad es la profesora? / Es de _____ .
3. ¿Es Keith Howe estudiante o profesor? / Es _____ .
4. ¿De dónde es Keith? / Es de _____ .
5. ¿Estudia en Florida o en Nuevo México? / Estudia en _____ .
6. ¿Qué estudia Keith, inglés o español? / Estudia _____ .
7. ¿Hay muchos o pocos hispanos en la Florida? / Hay _____ .

VOCABULARIO ÚTIL

Useful vocabulary

A saludar y a conocer a la gente
(Greeting and meeting people)

In this section you will learn how to greet people, introduce yourself, and use the numbers 0–30 in Spanish.

Teach the gesture for ¡Adiós!

Adiós.[1]	*Good-bye.*	**Bastante bien.**	*Rather well.*
Hasta luego.	*See you later.*	**(Muy) bien.**	*(Very) well.*
Hasta mañana.	*See you tomorrow.*	**Más o menos.**	*So-so.*

Encantado.	*(men say this)*	*Nice to meet you.*
Encantada.	*(women say this)*	*Nice to meet you.*
Mucho gusto.	*(men and women say this)*	*Nice to meet you.*

---

[1]*Adiós* carries a more definitive sense of "good-bye" than does *hasta luego.* Use *adiós* when you do not expect to see the other person(s) for a while, such as much later in the day or the following day.

VOCABULARIO ÚTIL

Have students act out these short dialogues in pairs.

Situaciones formales

Note: The questions *¿Cómo está usted?*, *¿Y usted?*, *¿Cómo se llama usted?* and *¿De dónde es usted?* are usually used with people whom you address on a last-name basis.

Títulos personales

The following personal titles and their abbreviations are used in formal interactions between people. There is no standard Spanish equivalent for Ms.; use *señorita* or *señora*, as appropriate.

Point out that *señor, señora, señorita, don,* and *doña* are not capitalized unless they begin a sentence.

señor	**(Sr.)**	*Mr., sir*
señora	**(Sra.)**	*Mrs., ma'am*

señorita (Srta.) *Miss*

Some Spanish speakers use the titles *don* and *doña* when speaking or referring to a highly esteemed or older person. These two titles are used with the first name of a man *(don)* or a woman *(doña)* to convey a feeling of affection and respect, while maintaining formality.[1]

---

[1]If you wish, explain that the word *don* comes from *D* = de, *O* = origin, *N* = noble; therefore, *don* = "of noble origen."

Buenos días, don Pablo.	*Good morning, Pablo.*
Buenas tardes, don José.	*Good afternoon, José.*
Buenas noches, doña Carmen.	*Good evening/night, Carmen.*

Let's practice

Practiquemos

A. ¡Mucho gusto, profesor(a)! Your instructor is going to greet you, ask your name, and where you are from. Answer him or her, using the following example and phrases appropriately.

The *Practiquemos* section contains a series of carefully sequenced convergent or close-ended (one possible answer) exercises designed to practice grammatical structures that have just been presented. The exercises can be practiced orally in class, then assigned for written practice at home. This section always ends with a writing activity.

Ex. A. The example and the model are provided here to guide you and your students. After speaking with several students, you may want to modify the model.

Have students act out these short dialogues in pairs.

Ejemplo:　　—Buenas tardes. Soy Javier Gómez. ¿Cómo se llama usted?

　　　　　　—Me llamo Kristina Haskell.

　　　　　　—Encantado.

　　　　　　—Mucho gusto, profesor.

　　　　　　—El gusto es mío. ¿De dónde es usted, Kristina?

　　　　　　—Soy de Seattle, Wáshington.

PROFESOR(A): **Buenos(as) _____ . Soy _____ . ¿ _____ ?**

USTED: 　　　Me llamo _____ .

PROFESOR(A): 　_____ .

USTED: 　　　Mucho _____ , profesor(a).

PROFESOR(A): 　_____ . ¿De dónde _____ ?

USTED: 　　　Soy de _____ .

Situaciones informales

Note: The questions *¿Qué tal?, Y tú, ¿cómo estás?, ¿Cómo te llamas?, ¿De dónde eres?*, and the farewell expression *chao* are used with classmates, friends, and other people whom you address on a first-name basis.

Practiquemos

B. En clase. Speak with several of your classmates by modifying the following conversations. Don't forget to shake hands when meeting each other.

Ex. B. Follow-up activity: Divide the class in half. One half stands in a reception line while the other half waits to go through the line. One by one, students greet one another and introduce themselves. Remind them to shake hands when meeting each other. For example: —¡Hola! Me llamo Kevin. —Amy Taylor. ¡Mucho gusto! (They shake hands.) If your class is large, have students form two or more reception lines.

1. A: ¡Hola! ¿Qué tal?
   B: _____ . ¿Y tú?
   A: _____ , gracias.

2. A: ¡Hola! Me llamo _____ . ¿Y tú?
   B: Me llamo _____ .
   A: _____ .

3. A: ¿De dónde eres?
   B: Soy de _____ . ¿Y tú?
   A: _____ .

4. A: ¡Hasta mañana!
   B: _____ .
   A: _____ .

5. Introduce two of your classmates to each other, using the following example.

   KELLY: Hillary, quiero presentarte a° Keith.
   HILLARY: ¡Hola, Keith!
   KEITH: ¡Hola! Mucho gusto, Hillary.
   HILLARY: Encantada.

   I want to introduce you to

   A: _____ , quiero presentarte a _____ .

   B: ¡Hola, _____!

   A: ¡_____! _____ , _____ .

C. ¿Qué tal? Carry on a longer conversation with a classmate whom you don't know, using the incomplete dialogue below. Afterwards, one of you introduces the other person to a different classmate.

   A: ¡Hola! ¿Cómo estás?
   B: _____ . Y tú, ¿qué tal?
   A: _____ , gracias. Me llamo _____ . ¿Cómo te llamas?
   B: _____ . ¡Mucho gusto!
   A: _____ . ¿De dónde eres, _____?
   B: _____ .
   A: ¡Qué interesante!°
   B: ¿De dónde eres tú, _____?
   A: _____ . _____ , quiero presentarte a _____ .
   B: _____ .
   C: _____ . ¿De dónde _____?
   B: _____ .
   C: _____ .

   How interesting!

NOTAS CULTURALES

Addressing Others: *tú* and *usted*

When Spanish speakers address one person, they express the word *you* in one of two ways: *tú* or *usted*. The following guidelines, however, should be helpful to you.

Tú is an informal form of address. In general, use *tú* with someone with whom you are on a first-name basis. For example, Spanish speakers use *tú* when addressing a relative, a close friend, a person of the same age or social position, a classmate, a small child, and a pet.[1] You will be using the *tú* form when speaking to a classmate while participating in the oral activities of *Poco a poco*.[2]

Usted (abbreviated *Ud.*) is a formal form of address. In general, use *usted* when speaking or writing to a person with a title such as *señorita, doctor, profesora*, and so forth. Spanish speakers use *usted* when addressing a stranger, a casual acquaintance other than a child, a person much older than themselves, and a person in a formal position or in a position of authority such as a supervisor, a store clerk, or a police officer. When you are unsure about whether to use *tú* or *usted*, it is wiser to use *usted*.

[1] In Guatemala children usually address their parents using *usted*.

[2] In Argentina, Uruguay, Paraguay, in some parts of Chile, Ecuador, and Colombia, and in most of Central America, most Spanish speakers use *vos* instead of *tú*. If you wish, briefly explain the use of *vos*. You will be understood perfectly, however, when you use *tú* in those countries.

Answers: *1. usted 2. tú 3. tú 4. usted 5. tú 6. usted*

¿Tú o usted?

How would *you* address the following people?

1. your Spanish instructor
2. a pen pal from Costa Rica
3. Pepe Ramírez, an eight-year old boy
4. Doctor Ramírez, the boy's father
5. an exchange student from Spain
6. doña Rosa, the student's mother

Los números 0–30

You can use numbers in Spanish for many purposes such as understanding page numbers in class, counting, adding and subtracting, and saying your address, telephone number, and age.

0 **cero**	11 **once**	22 **veintidós**
1 **uno**	12 **doce**	23 **veintitrés**
2 **dos**	13 **trece**	24 **veinticuatro**
3 **tres**	14 **catorce**	25 **veinticinco**
4 **cuatro**	15 **quince**	26 **veintiséis**
5 **cinco**	16 **dieciséis**[3]	27 **veintisiete**
6 **seis**	17 **diecisiete**	28 **veintiocho**
7 **siete**	18 **dieciocho**	29 **veintinueve**
8 **ocho**	19 **diecinueve**	30 **treinta**
9 **nueve**	20 **veinte**	
10 **diez**	21 **veintiuno**[4]	

Activities:
1. Have students repeat the numbers after you.
2. Have students make flashcards with numbers from 0 to 30. Then they show them to a partner who says the number in Spanish.
3. Point out the differences in writing the numbers 1 and 7 in Spanish.
4. If you wish, tell your students that the number seven represents good luck in the Spanish-speaking world; for example, in Spanish and Latin American literature, cats have seven, not nine, lives.

[3] The numbers 16 to 19 and 21 to 29 can be written either as one world (e.g., *dieciséis*) or as three words (e.g., *diez y seis*). In most Spanish-speaking countries, people prefer to use the single word.

[4] The number *veintiuno* changes to *veintiún* before a plural masculine noun; for example: *Somos veintiún estudiantes.* (We are twenty-one students).

Practiquemos

D. ¿Cuántos estudiantes somos? *(How many students are we?)*
Vamos a contar *(to count)* el número de estudiantes en la clase.

Ejemplo: *Uno... dos... tres...*

Ex. D. Begin the count off by counting yourself: *Uno...* (then point to the first student who should say *dos*, etc., around the class).

E. Problemas de matemáticas. Complete los problemas con otro(a) estudiante.

Ex. E. Follow-up activity: Send two students to the board, and ask the others to take out paper and pencil. Say some numbers between 0–30 in random order and ask students to write them down (e.g., 9, 15, 25). Then point to the numbers that the two students wrote on the board, and ask the class to read them aloud in Spanish.

+ más   – menos

Ejemplos: $2 + 2 = ?$ Estudiante A: *¿Cuántos son dos más dos?*
Estudiante B: *Cuatro.*

$3 - 1 = ?$ Estudiante A: *¿Cuántos son tres menos uno?*
Estudiante B: *Dos.*

$3 + 3 = ?$	$8 - 3 = ?$	$11 + 4 = ?$	$16 + 10 = ?$
$6 - 2 = ?$	$7 + 3 = ?$	$14 + 5 = ?$	$25 - 11 = ?$
$4 + 2 = ?$	$9 - 1 = ?$	$15 - 4 = ?$	$22 + 7 = ?$
$6 + 1 = ?$	$4 - 7 = ?$	$16 - 3 = ?$	$30 - 9 = ?$

F. Información personal. Converse con otro(a) estudiante.

1. KEITH: ¿Cuál es tu número de teléfono? *(What's your phone number?)*
   KELLY: 239-4971 (dos, tres, nueve..., cuatro, nueve, siete, uno).
   ¿Y el tuyo? *(And yours?)*

   A: ¿Cuál es tu número de teléfono?
   B: _____ . ¿Y el tuyo?
   A: _____ .
   B: Muchas gracias.

2. KEITH: ¿Cuál es tu dirección? *(What's your address?)*
   KELLY: Camino Linda Vista, número 3547 (tres, cinco, cuatro, siete); apartamento número 11 (once).
   A: ¿Cuál es tu dirección?
   B: _____ . ¿Y la tuya?
   A: _____ .
   B: Muchas gracias.

3. KELLY: ¿Cuántos años tienes? *(How old are you?)*
   KEITH: Tengo veintitrés años. *(I'm 23 years old)* ¿Y tú?
   KELLY: Diecinueve.

   A: ¿Cuántos años tienes?
   B: Tengo _____ . ¿Y tú?
   A: _____ .

Ex. F.
1. Point out the difference between *tú* (you) (with an accent mark) as a subject pronoun and *tu* (your) (without an accent mark) as a possessive adjective.
2. Point out that Spanish speakers say the name of their street first, then their house number. Demonstrate this with several examples before students begin this activity.
3. If your students ask, give them the Spanish equivalents of the following words: road = *camino*, street = *calle*, avenue = *avenida*, boulevard = *bulevar*, route = *ruta*, drive = *paseo*, highway = *carretera*, freeway = *autopista*.
4. Tell students that in Spanish-speaking countries, streets are often named after historical dates (e.g., *Cinco de Mayo*), saint's names (e.g., *San Antonio*), and famous people (e.g., *Generalisimo Castro*).
5. Remind students that *veintiuno* changes to *veintiún* before a masculine plural noun; for example: *Tengo veintiún años.*
6. Tell students your office telephone number in Spanish, as well as your home address and phone number, if you wish.

NOTAS **CULTURALES**

Meeting and Greeting Others

Being warm, friendly, and affectionate are traits of Spanish-speaking cultures. In social situations, Spanish speakers usually exchange physical hellos and good-byes; for example, Hispanic men and women often shake hands when greeting each other and when saying good-bye. Simple handshakes, however, may not convey enough warmth among relatives and close friends. Men who know each other well often follow a handshake by a hug and several pats on the back.

Often, when close male friends have not seen each other for a long time, they give one another an *abrazo,* which is a hearty embrace accompanied by several slaps on the back. Spanish-speaking teenage girls, adult women, and a male and female who are good friends often greet one another by placing their cheeks lightly together and kissing the air.

When being introduced in Spanish-speaking countries, men and women always shake hands, and two young females or a young male and female may kiss lightly on the cheek. A nod of the head, a wave of the hand, or saying *¡Mucho gusto!* are not enough. In fact, if you do not shake hands when introduced to a Spanish speaker, he or she may think you are unfriendly or ill-mannered.

Conversación

Write a short conversation in Spanish for each photograph below.

Estas dos amigas, que son estudiantes universitarias, se encuentran en un parque y se saludan con un beso.

Estos tres señores se conocen en la Universidad de México en México, D.F., donde hay una reunión de arquitectos latinoamericanos hoy.

En México, Distrito Federal (capital de la República Mexicana), estos dos amigos se saludan con un abrazo.

GRAMÁTICA FUNCIONAL

Identifying people and indicating where they are from

—¿De dónde **eres**, Kelly?
—**Soy** de los Estados Unidos.

—Mi familia **es** de Toronto.
—¡Mi papá **es** de Montreal!
—Usted y yo **somos** canadienses.

Where are you from, Kelly?
I'm from the United States.

My family is from Toronto.
My Dad is from Montreal!
You and I are Canadian.

Subject pronouns and present tense of the verb *ser*

What are subject pronouns and verbs?

A verb is a word that expresses action (e.g., run) or indicates a state of being (e.g., is). A subject pronoun identifies who does the action of a verb. Study the Spanish subject pronouns along with the present tense forms of the verb *ser*. Then read how they are used in the example conversations above.

ser *(to be)*

Singular

(yo)	soy	I am
(tú)	eres	you (informal) are
(usted, él, ella)	es	you (formal) are; he/she is

Plural

(nosotros/nosotras)	somos	we are
(vosotros/vosotras)	sois	you (informal) are[1]
(ustedes, ellos/ellas)	son	you are; they are

1. In *Poco a poco*, the *vosotros/vosotras* verb forms are included in the verb paradigms for the sake of completeness and so that students could recognize their meaning if they heard or read the verb forms. No exercises or activities, however, are included in the program. Students will have no difficulty in learning these verb forms for productive use (i.e., speaking and writing), if necessary. You might like to use *vosotros* forms when speaking to your class; if you do this consistently throughout the term, your students will acquire the *vosotros* forms for receptive use (i.e., listening and reading comprehension).
2. Have students act out these short dialogues in pairs.
3. Point out the difference between *él* (he) (with an accent mark) as a subject pronoun and *el* (the) (without an accent mark) as a definite article.

[1] In most of Spain, the plural form of *tú* is *vosotros* (referring to males only or to a mixed group of males and females) and *vosotras* (referring to females only).

you are   *vosotros* ⎫
              } *sois*
you are   *vosotras* ⎭

—Alicia y Regina, ¿de dónde **sois?**

—De Madrid. **¿Sois** vosotras de Cuba?

Note: In ***Poco a poco***, the verb forms for *vosotros/vosotras* will be provided in italics so that you will recognize their meaning when your hear or read them.

How to use subject pronouns

1. In Latin America, *ustedes* is the plural form for both *tú* and *usted*.

2. *Ellos* can refer to males or to a group of males and females; *ellas* refers to a group of females only.

3. Since Spanish verb endings usually indicate the subject of a sentence, subject pronouns (e.g., *yo, ella, ustedes*) are used less often than in English. However, Spanish speakers do use subject pronouns to clarify or to emphasize the subject of a sentence.

—¿Son **ustedes** de México?	*Are you from Mexico?*
—No, señor. Somos de la América Central. **Ella** es de Nicaragua y **él** es de Honduras.	*No, sir. We are from Central America. She is from Nicaragua, and he is from Honduras.*

How to make a sentence negative

To negate a Spanish sentence, place the word *no* in front of the verb.

Kelly **no es** del Canadá; ella es de los Estados Unidos.	*Kelly isn't from Canada. She is from the United States.*

The verb form *hay*

A useful Spanish verb form is *hay*, which means **there is** and **there are** (or **is there** and **are there** in questions). Use *hay* to indicate the existence of people, places, and things; *hay* may be followed by a singular or plural noun.

—¿Cuántas personas **hay** en tu clase de español?	*How many persons are there in your Spanish class?*
—**Hay** una profesora y veintisiete estudiantes.	*There is a teacher and twenty-seven students.*

The *Practiquemos* section contains a series of carefully sequenced convergent or closed-ended (one possible answer) exercises designed to practice grammatical structures that have just been presented. The exercises can be practiced orally in class, then assigned for written practice at home. This section always ends with a writing activity.

Ex.A. Answers:
1. *Sí. Sandra Bullock es actriz.*
2. *No. Edward Kennedy no es actor.*
3. *No. Courtney Cox no es dentista.*
4. *Sí. Daisy Fuentes es reportera.*
5. *No. Robin Williams no es estudiante.*
6. *No. Al Gore no es presidente.*
Statements 7 and 8 are open-ended; therefore, the answers will vary.

Practiquemos

A. ¿Sí o No? Say whether you agree or disagree with the statements below.

Ejemplos: Meryl Streep es actriz. → *Sí. Meryl Streep **es** actriz.*

Meryl Streep es profesora. → *No. Meryl Streep **no es** profesora.*

1. Sandra Bullock es actriz.
2. Edward Kennedy es actor.
3. Courtney Cox es dentista.
4. Daisy Fuentes es reportera.
5. Robin Williams es estudiante.
6. Al Gore es presidente.
7. Mi papá es profesor.
8. Mi mamá es siquiatra.

B. ¿Quiénes son? *(Who are they?)* Complete the sentences below with appropriate names and the correct verb form: *es* or *son*.

Ejemplo: _____ → un actor famoso
Kevin Costner es un actor famoso.

Personas		Profesiones
1. _____	→	el líder de Cuba
2. _____	→	dos actores famosos
3. _____	→	artistas[1] importantes
4. _____	→	profesores excelentes
5. _____	→	el presidente de los Estados Unidos

C. ¿De dónde son? Say where the following people are from, using appropriate forms of the verb *ser + de*.

Ejemplo: Keith _____ → los Estados Unidos
Keith es de los Estados Unidos.

1. Nelson Mandela	→	Soweto en África
2. Isabel Allende	→	Chile en Sud América
3. Indira y Mahatma Gandhi	→	la India
4. Keith, tú	→	de Miami, Florida
5. Mi papá y mi mamá	→	_____
6. Yo	→	_____

Ex. C. Answers:
1. *Nelson Mandela es de Soweto en África.*
2. *Isabel Allende es de Chile en Sud América.*
3. *Indira y Mahatma Gandhi son de la India.*
4. *Keith, tú eres de Miami, Florida.*
5. and 6. [open]

D. ¿Y usted? Write the following sentences on a separate sheet of paper adding information that applies to you and your parents.

Me llamo _____ . Yo soy de _____ . Mi papá se llama _____ y mi mamá se llama _____ . Mi papá es de _____ y mi mamá es de _____ .

Charlemos

E. Dos estudiantes. Converse con otro(a) estudiante.

Estudiante A

1. ¡Hola! Me llamo _____ .
3. _____ ¿De dónde eres?
5. _____ . ¿ _____ estudiante?

Estudiante B

2. Me llamo _____ . ¡Encantado(a)!
4. Soy de _____ . ¿Y tú?
6. Sí, yo _____ estudiante de español.

Let's chat

The *Charlemos* section contains a series of carefully sequenced oral communication activities that are progressively more open-ended (more than one possible answer).

Ex. E. Poco a poco has many "teeter-totter" activities such as this one. Show students how to act out this dialogue in pairs (Student A covers the right column, student B covers the left column). Model the activity with one or two students so your class understands how to practice it. While students are doing this activity, walk around the classroom and check to see that they have covered their partner's written cues.

---

[1] Explain that *artista* can refer to a painter or sculptor, or even an actor. Here *artistas* is intended to refer to artists in general.

F. ¿Hay o no hay? Exprese sus ideas y opiniones con otro(a) estudiante.

1. En mi universidad hay/no hay...

   a. profesores buenos.
   b. clases de Swahili.
   c. una cafetería buena.
   d. estudiantes liberales.
   e. muchas computadoras IBM.

2. En mi clase de español hay/no hay...

   a. un televisor Sony.
   b. un mapa de México.
   c. muchos estudiantes.
   d. personas interesantes.
   e. computadoras MacIntosh.

Ex. G. Videotape several role plays, then replay the videotape and have students evaluate themselves.

G. Una conversación final. Role-play a conversation with a classmate, using the cues below to guide you.

1. Greet each other appropriately.
2. Introduce yourselves and shake hands.
3. Find out where each other is from.
4. Ask how old the other person is.
5. Say good-bye to one another.

Reading better

List other Spanish-English cognates on the board or on an overhead transparency. Then ask students to guess their English meaning. For example:

Cognates	False Cognates
teléfono	*éxito*
importante	*grado*
universidad	*dirección*

PARA LEER MEJOR

Recognizing Cognates

Spanish and English share many words that are identical or very similar in spelling and meaning. These related words are called *cognates*. Your ability to recognize cognates and guess their meaning will help you read Spanish efficiently.

Activity

1. Write down as many cognates as you can find on the business cards on the next page. Then write the English meaning of each cognate; don't be afraid to guess!
2. Work with another student and compare the meaning of the cognates you found.

A word of caution

You probably had little or no difficulty understanding the essential information printed on the business cards because they contain many cognates. But some cognates are *false cognates* such as the boldface words in the following sentences.

- Carlos **molesta** a María.
- La **lectura** es interesante.
- Mi profesora está **embarazada.**
- El español es mi **idioma** favorito.

The verb *molestar* means to **bother,** not to molest; *lectura* means **reading,** not lecture; *embarazada* means **pregnant,** not embarrassed; and *idioma* means **language,** not idiom.[1]

---

[1]The actual equivalents of these English words are as follows: molest = *importunar,* lecture = *conferencia* (another false cognate!), embarrassed = *avergonzada,* idiom = *modismo.*

In the **Poco a poco** program, you will read and hear many Spanish-English cognates. The more of them you understand, the more quickly and easily you will learn Spanish.

Writing better

PARA ESCRIBIR MEJOR

Using a Bilingual Dictionary

A bilingual dictionary is a useful tool that, when used properly, can enhance the quality and accuracy of your writing in Spanish. Here are some suggestions to help you.

1. When you look up the Spanish equivalent of an English word, you will often find several meanings of it listed like this:

   wall: *pared; muro; muralla*

2. In larger dictionaries, the Spanish equivalents may appear in a phrase or sentence to clarify their meaning and use.

   wall: *pared (de casa); muro (de jardín, de campo); muralla (de ciudad, de fortaleza)*

3. If your dictionary has no example phrases or sentences, look up each new Spanish word in the Spanish-English section.

   pared: wall, *entre cuatro paredes*
   muro: wall, *muro de contención* = retaining wall
   muralla: wall, rampart which surrounds a place

4. It is even better, however, to check the meaning of a word in a Spanish-Spanish dictionary.

   pared: *obra de fábrica levantada a plomo con queso, longitud y altura proporcionados para cerrar un espacio o sostener las techumbres*
   muro: *paredón, barbacana, barrera, defensa*
   muralla: *fábrica que ciñe y encierra para su defensa una plaza*

5. Looking up many words in a bilingual dictionary is inefficient. It is wiser to use the words and phrases you already know in Spanish as much as possible. You will learn new ones as you continue reading and listening to the language.

Visit

http://poco.heinle.com

Activity

1. Look up the following English words in a bilingual dictionary, and write their Spanish equivalents.
   a. exit (e.g., in a building)
   b. direction (e.g., on a street)
   c. grade (e.g., on a test)
2. Look up the Spanish words in a Spanish-Spanish dictionary.
3. Compare your findings with those of a classmate.

¿A qué nivel está Ud.?

¿Qué tal?, *¿De dónde es Ud.?*, *¿Cómo se llama?*
Can you answer these often asked questions?
Review *Lección preliminar* and then monitor your progress by completing the *Autoprueba* at the end of the chapter in the **Workbook/Lab Manual.**

VOCABULARIO

Sustantivos (Nouns)

la ciudad *city*
la clase *class*
el español *Spanish (language)*
los Estados Unidos *United States*
el (la) estudiante *student*
la gente *people*
el (la) líder *leader*
la mamá *mother (Mom)*
el papá *father (Dad)*

Profesiones (Professions)

el actor *actor*
la actriz *actress*
el (la) autor(a) *author*
el (la) dentista *dentist*
el (la) profesor(a) *instructor, professor, teacher*
el (la) presidente *president*
el (la) reportero(a) *reporter*

Cómo saludar (How to greet)

¡Buenos días! *Good morning!*
¡Buenas tardes! *Good afternoon!*
¡Buenas noches! *Good evening!*
¡Hola! *Hi! (informal)*
¿Qué tal? *How's everything? (informal)*
¿Cómo estás? *How are you? (informal)*
¿Cómo está usted? *How are you? (formal)*

Cómo contestar (How to answer)

Bastante bien. *Rather well.*
Más o menos. *So-so.*
¡(Muy) bien! *(Very) well!*
¡(Muchas) gracias! *Thank you (very much)!*
¿Y tú? *And you? (informal)*
¿Y usted? *And you? (formal)*

Cómo despedirse (How to say good-bye)

¡Adiós! *Good-bye!*
¡Chao! *Bye! (informal)*
¡Buenas noches! *Good night!*
¡Hasta luego! *See you later!*
¡Hasta mañana! *See you tomorrow!*

Presentaciones (Introductions)

¿Cómo se llama usted? *What's your name? (formal)*
¿Cómo te llamas? *What's your name? (informal)*
¿Cuál es tu nombre? *What's your name? (informal)*
Me llamo... *My name is . . .*
Mi nombre es... *My name is . . .*
Encantado(a). *Nice to meet you.*
¡Mucho gusto! *Nice to meet you.*
El gusto es mío. *My pleasure.*
Quiero presentarte a... *I want to introduce you to . . . (informal)*

Cómo pedir información (How to ask for information)

¿Cuál es tu dirección? *What's your address? (informal)*
¿Cuál es tu número de teléfono? *What's your telephone number? (informal)*
¿De dónde es usted? *Where are you from? (formal)*
¿De dónde eres tú? *Where are you from? (Informal)*

Títulos personales (Personal titles)

señor (Sr.) *Mr., sir*
señora (Sra.) *Mrs., ma'am*
señorita (Srta.) *Miss*

Los números (Numbers)

cero *zero*
uno *one*
dos *two*
tres *three*
cuatro *four*
cinco *five*
seis *six*
siete *seven*
ocho *eight*
nueve *nine*
diez *ten*
once *eleven*

doce *twelve*
trece *thirteen*
catorce *fourteen*
quince *fifteen*
dieciséis *sixteen*
diecisiete *seventeen*
dieciocho *eighteen*
diecinueve *nineteen*
veinte *twenty*
treinta *thirty*

Palabras interrogativas (Question words)

¿Cómo? *How?*
¿Cuántos(as)? *How many?*
¿De dónde? *Where from?*
¿Qué? *What?*
¿Quién? *Who?*

Verbos (Verbs)

hablando *speaking*
hay *there is, there are*
lo sé *I know (it)*
ser *to be*
tengo (19 años) *I am (19 years old)*

Adverbios (Adverbs)

ahora *now*
allí *there*
aquí *here*
más *plus*

menos *minus*
también *also, too*

Pronombres (Pronouns)

él *he*
ella *she*
ellas *they*
ellos *they*
nosotros(as) *we*
tú *you (informal)*
usted *you (formal)*
ustedes *you (formal, plural; informal in Latin Amer.)*
vosotros(as) *you (informal, plural in parts of Spain)*
yo *I*

Otras palabras (Other words)

a *at, to*
bien *well, fine*
con *with*
de *from, of*
mi *my*
otro(a) *another*
sí *yes*
su *her, his*
y *and*

Expresiones idiomáticas (Idiomatic expressions)

¿verdad? *isn't that right?*
¡Qué interesante! *How interesting!*

Only the new words and phrases that are practiced actively in this lesson appear in the *Vocabulario*. For additional words and phrases see the Glossary at the end of this book.

UNITED STATES

Tijuana

Isla
Cedros

Gulf of
California

North
Pacific
Ocean

Islas
Marías

MEXICO

Durango

Xalapa

Mexico City

Acapulco

Gulf of Mexico

Bahía de
Campeche

Isla de
Cozumel

Golfo de
Tehuantepec

MEX

MEXICO

Entre amigos
México

Carlos Suárez and Anita Camacho meet each other in their English class at the Universidad Nacional Autónoma de México. Later, Carlos meets Anita's family who lives in a fashionable neighborhood of Mexico City. One day Carlos invites Anita to spend a Sunday afternoon with him at Chapultepec Park.

1

¿Qué estudias aquí?

▶ COMMUNICATIVE GOALS

You will be able to become better acquainted with your classmates and describe your life at school.

▶ LANGUAGE FUNCTIONS

Identifying people and things
Indicating relationships
Telling time
Describing school-related activities
Describing everyday activities

▶ VOCABULARY THEMES

Classmates and friends
Academic courses
Telling time
Days of the week

▶ GRAMMATICAL STRUCTURES

Definite and indefinite articles
Gender and plural of nouns
The contractions *al* and *del*
Present tense of regular *-ar* verbs
***Me gusta* + infinitive**

▶ CULTURAL INFORMATION

24-hour system of time
Education in Latin America and Spain

http://poco.heinle.com

If you wish to obtain free information in English or Spanish on Mexico, call the Mexican Government Tourist Office via their toll-free telephone number: 800 44-MEXICO.

EN CONTEXTO

 Play Lab Tape

Me llamo Anita Guadalupe Camacho Ortega. Soy estudiante de la UNAM. (1) En la UNAM estudio turismo, sicología, inglés y alemán.° Estudio en el turno matutino.

German

Mi nombre es Carlos Javier Suárez Chac. También soy estudiante de la UNAM en el turno matutino. Estudio física, cálculo, computación° e inglés. (2)

Point out that Carlos' second surname (Chac) is Mayan. Hispanic names are described in *Lección 4* on page 108.

Computer Science

Es lunes.° Son las nueve de la mañana. Ahora Carlos y Anita están hablando en su clase de inglés.

Monday

CARLOS: ¡Hola! ¿Qué tal? Me llamo Carlos Suárez. ¿Cómo te llamas?
ANITA: Anita Camacho. Mucho gusto.
CARLOS: El gusto es mío. ¿De dónde eres, Anita?
ANITA: Soy de aquí... de México.(3) ¿Y tú, Carlos?
CARLOS: Soy de Mérida, Yucatán.(4) ¿Qué estudias aquí?
ANITA: Turismo, sicología, geografía, francés, alemán e inglés.
CARLOS: Ah, eres estudiante de lenguas, ¿verdad?
ANITA: Sí. Quiero ser intérprete. Y tú, ¿qué estudias, Carlos?
CARLOS: Inglés, física, cálculo y computación. Quiero ser ingeniero nuclear.
ANITA: ¡Qué interesante! ¿Son difíciles tus cursos?
CARLOS: Física, cálculo y computación°... no. Pero... el inglés, ¡sí! El inglés no es fácil° para mí,° Anita.
ANITA: Bueno,(5) compañero. Tengo° una idea. ¿Por qué° no estudiamos inglés en la biblioteca?° Para mí, el inglés es muy fácil.
CARLOS: ¡Bueno!

easy / for me
I have / Why
library

Notas de texto

1. *La Universidad Nacional Autónoma de México (la UNAM),* located in Mexico City, is one of the largest universities in Latin America with a student population of over 400,000 students who attend classes in buildings located in different areas of the city. The UNAM is called a *Ciudad Universitaria* which has large parking lots, many bus stops, and even its own subway station. Because the university has so many students, it operates on two shifts called *turnos.* The morning session *(turno matutino)* starts at 7:00 a.m. and the evening session *(turno vespertino)* begins at 5:00 p.m.

2. The word *y* becomes *e* before a word beginning with *i* or *hi. (Comprendo español e inglés. Estudio literatura e historia).* The conjunction *o* (or) becomes *u* before a word beginning with *o* or *ho* (¿Es tu nombre Omar *u Óscar? ¿Practica usted tenis u hockey?).* Both of these changes occur for pronunciation reasons.

1. Tell students that another term for *turno matutino* is *horario diario.* Also, explain that many universities in Spain also operate on shifts as follows: *turno de mañana* (8:00 a.m.-1:00 p.m.), *turno de tarde* (3:00-6:00 p.m.), *turno de noche* (5:00-8:00 p.m.).
2. If you have photographs of the UNAM and/or of Mexico City, show them to your students, and describe each picture in very simple Spanish.
3. Note #2: These minor spelling changes are explained here very early in the book for recognition in speech and writing.
4. Use a large map to point out the location of the State of Yucatán and its capital, Mérida.

3. People who are from Mexico City usually say they are from *México* or *D.F.* rather than from *la Ciudad de México* when they are speaking in their country.
4. Mérida is the capital of the Mexican state of Yucatán, located 955 miles (1,537 kilometers) southeast of Mexico City in the Yucatán Peninsula.
5. In Mexico, *bueno* has several equivalents in English: good, great!, okay, and well . . . among others. The context of the sentence will help you understand which meaning of *bueno* the speaker wants to convey.

1. The purpose of this exercise is to check students' overall comprehension of the reading selection.
2. Answers:
1. a. *Sí* b. *No* c. *No* d. *Sí*
e. *No* f. *Sí* g. *No*
2. a. *Carlos, Anita,* [open]
b. *turismo, psicología, geografía, francés, alemán,* [open]; *cuatro, física, cálculo, computación, inglés,* [open];
c. *nueve,* [open]

¡Comprendió Ud.?

1. Lea cada *(Read each)* oración, luego responda **sí** o **no.**
   a. Anita y Carlos son mexicanos.
   b. Ellos son profesores de la UNAM.
   c. Anita estudia inglés, pero Carlos no.
   d. Anita y Carlos son compañeros de clase.
   e. Para Carlos el inglés es bastante fácil.
   f. Los dos estudiantes estudian en el turno matutino.
   g. La clase de inglés de Carlos y de Anita es por la tarde.

2. Complete las siguientes oraciones.
   a. El compañero de clase de Anita se llama _____ . La compañera de clase de Carlos se llama _____ . Un compañero de mi clase se llama _____ , y una compañera de mi clase se llama _____ .
   b. Anita tiene seis clases. Ella estudia _____ , _____ , _____ , _____ , _____ e inglés. Carlos tiene _____ clases solamente. Él estudia _____ , _____ , _____ e _____ . Yo tengo (una clase/ _____ clases). Estudio _____ .
   c. Carlos y Anita estudian inglés a las _____ de la mañana. Yo estudio español a la(s) _____ de la _____ (mañana/tarde/noche).

VOCABULARIO ÚTIL

In this section you will learn to describe some people you know, describe your class schedule, and tell time.

Los amigos

el amigo	*friend*	**la amiga**	
el novio	*boyfriend/girlfriend*	**la novia**	
el compañero de clase	*classmate*	**la compañera de clase**	
el compañero de cuarto	*roommate*	**la compañera de cuarto**	

Practiquemos

A. Mis amigos. Complete las siguientes oraciones. Luego léaselas a un(a) compañero(a) de clase.

Ejemplo: Mi compañera de clase se llama _Mónica_.
                Ella es _modesta_.

> **¡CUIDADO!** *(Be careful!)* Adjectives ending in *-o* refer to males, and adjectives ending in *-a* refer to females; adjectives ending in other letters can refer to both males and females. Adjective agreement will be explained formally in *Lección 2*.

1. Mi compañero de clase se llama _____ .
   Él es (tímido / modesto / cómico).
2. Mi compañera de clase se llama _____ .
   Ella es (sincera / tímida / modesta)
3. Mi compañero(a) de cuarto se llama _____ .
   Él/Ella es (paciente / responsable / interesante).
4. Tengo un amigo que se llama _____ .
   Él es _____ (liberal / conservador).
5. Tengo una amiga que se llama _____ .
   Ella es _____ (inteligente / independiente / generosa).
6. Mi novio(a) se llama _____ . (No tengo novio/novia.)
   Él/Ella es (romántico[a] / sincero[a] / generoso).

B. Otras personas importantes.
Complete las siguientes oraciones con palabras de la lista y otras palabras que usted sabe *(know)*.

Ejemplo: Mi profesor favorito se llama _Everett Lyons_.
                Él es _interesante_.

bilingüe	importante	serio(a)	estudioso(a)
multilingüe	interesante	cómico(a)	organizado(a)

1. Mi mamá se llama _____ . Ella es _____ . (No tengo mamá.)
2. Mi papá se llama _____ . Él es _____ . (No tengo papá.)
3. Mi esposo(a) se llama _____ . Él/Ella se llama _____ . (No tengo esposo/esposa).
4. Mi profesor(a) de español se llama _____ . Él/Ella es _____ .
5. Mi doctor(a) se llama _____ . Él/Ella es _____ . (No tengo doctor[a]).
6. Me llamo _____ . Soy _____ .

C. Personas ideales.
Exprese sus opiniones, completando las siguientes oraciones con palabras que usted sabe.

Ejemplos: El amigo ideal es _inteligente y generoso_.
                 La novia ideal es _romántica y paciente_.

1. El amigo (La amiga) ideal es...
2. El novio (La novia) ideal es...

Ex. A. This activity reinforces the notion of recognizing and using cognates at a very early level of language acquisition for the purpose of communication. It also builds students' confidence in using Spanish communicatively. The activity also provides an early introduction of adjective-noun agreement without having introduced it formally.

The directions are given in Spanish to begin building students receptive (e.g., reading) vocabulary.

At this time, do not give a detailed explanation of how the verb *llamarse* is conjugated. Students should be able to recognize the meaning of *se llama* based on their background knowledge from *Lección preliminar* (e.g., *¿Cómo se llama usted?*), the example provided here, and the context of these sentences.

Ex. B. This activity reinforces the notion of adjective-noun agreement in a communicative format, without having introduced the notion formally.

At this point, you could introduce the words for some family members such as *hermano, hermana, abuelo, abuela, hijo, hija*. These words are presented and practiced in *Lección 1* and *Lección 2*.

Ex. C. The purpose of this activity is to give students an opportunity to use Spanish adjectives that they have learned in a communicative format.

Follow-up activities: 1. Have
students exchange and read each
other's descriptions. 2. Ask students
to tell you the characteristics of an
ideal spouse. Write the adjectives
on the board, then have students
vote on the three most important
characteristics of an ideal spouse.

Have students repeat the Spanish
name of each category and course
after you.

Only the most common academic
subjects are included here to limit
the amount of vocabulary
introduced in this lesson. If you
wish, however, tell students the
names of other subjects that they
are studying but are not listed here.

Tell students that another word for
"language" is *(el) idioma*. In Spain,
the word for "computer science" is
(la) informática.

3. El presidente (La presidenta) ideal es...
4. El profesor (La profesora) de español ideal es...

Los cursos

> **¡CUIDADO!** Academic courses are not capitalized in Spanish.

Practiquemos

Ex. D.
1. Point out the use of *para* = for a
   purpose: *para una clase de lenguas.*
2. Add several more titles of books
   to extend this exercise, if you
   wish. Answers: *Es para una clase
   de...* 1. *ciencias naturales*
   2. *letras* 3. *física* 4. *bellas artes*
   5. *estudios profesionales* 6. *lenguas*
   7. *ciencias sociales*

D. Libros para clases. Identifique para qué clase se usan los siete libros de texto *(textbooks)* de la lista.

Ejemplo: *Poco a poco*
Es para una clase de lenguas.

Libros de texto	Clases
1. *Plantas raras de Costa Rica*	Letras
2. *Los poemas de Gabriela Mistral*	Lenguas
3. *Las teorías de Albert Einstein*	Bellas artes
4. *El período azul de Pablo Picasso*	Física
5. *Medicina moderna: la cardiología*	Ciencias sociales
6. *Historia de la gramática española*	Ciencias naturales
7. *Problemas socioeconómicos de México*	Estudios profesionales

E. Mis estudios y mis libros. ¿Qué estudia usted y cómo se llaman sus libros?

Ejemplo: Estudio *español.* Mi libro de *español* se llama *Poco a poco.*

1. Estudio _____ . Mi libro de _____ se llama _____ .
2. Estudio _____ . Mi libro de _____ se llama _____ .
3. También estudio _____ . Mi libro de _____ se llama _____ .

¿Qué hora es? *(What time is it?)*

This question can be answered in three ways, depending on the time.

On the hour

Es la una.   **Son las siete.**

On the quarter or the half-hour

Son las siete y cuarto.   **Son las siete y media.**   **Son las ocho menos cuarto.**

Minutes before and after the hour

Es la una y diez.   **Son las ocho menos diez.**

Additional information

1. Use *es* to tell time between 12:31 and 1:30. Otherwise, use *son* because it refers to more than one hour (plural).

   —¿Qué hora **es**?   *What time is it?*
   —**Es** la una menos cuarto.   *It's 12:45.*
   —No. **Son** las diez y veinte.   *No. It's 10:20.*

2. After a specific time, use *de la mañana* (in the morning/a.m.) from midnight until lunchtime, *de la tarde* (in the afternoon/p.m.) until it gets dark, then *de la noche* (in the evening/p.m.).

   —Mi clase de computación es a **las nueve de la mañana** y mi clase de música es a **las dos de la tarde.**

   My computer science class is at nine o'clock in the morning and my music class is at two o'clock in the afternoon.

3. To ask or tell when an event occurs, use the word *a*.

—¿**A** qué hora vas a clase?   *What time do you go to class?*
—**A** las diez de la mañana.   *At ten o'clock in the morning.*

Practiquemos

F. ¿Qué hora es? Dígale *(Say)* la hora a otro(a) estudiante.

Ejemplo: —¿*Qué hora es?*
               —*Son las ocho menos diez.*

1.   2.   3.   4.

5.   6.    7.    8.

G. ¡A escuchar! Your instructor is going to read aloud Kelly's class schedule for today. As you listen, fill in the time beside each of her classes.

Ejemplo: español *9:00 a.m.*

1. biología _____
2. inglés   _____
3. álgebra _____
4. piano   _____

Los días de la semana *(The days of the week)*

lunes	*Monday*
martes	*Tuesday*
miércoles	*Wednesday*
jueves	*Thursday*
viernes	*Friday*
sábado	*Saturday*
domingo	*Sunday*

> **¡CUIDADO!** The days of the week are not capitalized in Spanish. Also, the first day of the week is Monday in Spanish-speaking countries, rather than Sunday.

H. Mis clases. Dígale a otro(a) estudiante los días y las horas de las clases que usted tiene.

Ejemplo: *Tengo mi clase de biología los* (on) *martes y los jueves. La clase es a las nueve de la mañana.*

1. Tengo mi clase de _____ los _____ . La clase es a la(s) _____ .
2. Tengo mi clase de _____ los _____ . La clase es a la(s) _____ .
3. Tengo mi clase de _____ los _____ . La clase es a la(s) _____ .

NOTAS CULTURALES

24-hour System of Time

The 24-hour system of telling time, sometimes called "military time," is commonly used for plane, train, and bus schedules, radio and television programs, formal invitations, and announcements of official events. To use the 24-hour system, simply count hours consecutively beginning with midnight.

Official Use (24-hour system)		**Conversational Use** (12-hour system)
10:00 diez	→	las diez de la mañana
13:00 trece	→	la una de la tarde
23:00 veintitrés	→	las once de la noche

In Spain and Latin America many scheduled meetings or events such as business and doctor appointments, religious services, funerals, and bullfights begin on time. When you are invited to a **social** function, however, many guests arrive a half-hour to an hour after the specified time. When in doubt, you can ask the time and add ¿en punto? (on the dot?).

I. ¿Qué hay en la televisión? Anita is looking at some television listings in a Mexican TV guide. Answer her questions, using the 12-hour system of telling time.

Ejemplo: —¿A qué hora es "La Familia Robinson"?
—*Es a las dos y media.*

1. ¿A qué hora es el "Cine Club"?
2. ¿A qué hora es "Hablando de Fútbol"?
3. ¿A qué hora es la serie "Los Pequeños Muppets"?
4. ¿A qué hora es "Los Comediantes Desaparecidos"?
5. ¿A qué hora es la telenovela "Cuando llega el amor"?

Hora	Programa
14:00	Laura, la pequeña niña de la pradera
14:30	La Familia Robinson
15:00	Los Pitufos
15:30	Desafío
16:00	Corre G.C., Corre
16:30	XWiAh Radio Aventura!
17:00	El Pájaro Loco
17:30	El Mago de Oz
18:00	Los Pequeños Muppets
18:30	Los Super Amigos

Hora	Programa
19:00	Noticiero
19:25	Milo Cruz en el Fútbol
19:30	Extravagancias
20:00	Hablando de Fútbol
21:00	Nova: Una cara normal
22:00	Imevisión informa
22:30	El Show de Benny Hill
23:30	Cine Club
01:00	Imevisión Informa

Hora	Programa
19:00	Cuando llega el amor
20:00	Chespirito
21:00	Yo compro esa mujer
21:30	Balada por un amor
22:00	Los Comediantes Desaparecidos
22:30	24 Horas
23:00	Película

Ex. H.

1. Before students do this activity, have them repeat the days of the week after you. At this point, you could introduce the word *hoy* in order to say *Hoy es...* + today's day, followed by *Mañana es...* + tomorrow's day.
2. Tell students how to specify a particular day of the week in Spanish; for example: *el martes* = **on** Tuesday / *los martes* = **on** Tuesdays.
3. Follow-up activity: Ask several students about their class schedules. Examples: *¿En qué días tiene su clase de inglés? ¿En qué días no tiene usted clase?* Expect one-word answers.

1. Show students some realia using the 24-hour system of time. Examples: schedules, formal invitations, official announcements.
2. Have students convert the following 24-hour times into 12-hour times: 16:30, 13:55, 20:00, 19:20, 23:15.

Ex. I.

1. Answers: *1. Es a las once y media de la noche. 2. Es a las ocho de la noche. 3. Es a las seis de la tarde. 4. Es a las diez de la noche. 5. Es a las siete de la noche.*
2. Follow-up activity: Ask students what their favorite TV program is, as well as the day and time the program is on. Begin this activity by telling them your own preference.

GRAMÁTICA FUNCIONAL

Identifying people, places, and things

—La UNAM es una universidad enorme, ¿verdad, Anita?
—Sí, Carlos. Hay muchos estudiantes aquí.

Definite and indefinite articles

A noun names a person *(Carlos, amigo)*, a place *(Mérida, ciudad)*, a thing *(libro, computadora)*, or a concept *(clase, español)*. In Spanish, all nouns are classified as having a **gender**—either masculine or feminine.[1] A noun is often preceded by a definite article: *el, la, los, las* (the), or by an indefinite article: *un, una* (a, an), *unos, unas* (some).

How to determine gender of nouns

1. In Spanish, nouns referring to males and most nouns ending in -*o* are masculine. Nouns referring to females and most nouns ending in -*a* are feminine. Definite and indefinite articles must match the gender (masculine or feminine) of the nouns they modify.

   Es **el/un** amig**o**.   Es **la/una** amig**a**.
   Es **el/un** teléfon**o**.   Es **la/una** bibliotec**a**.

2. Most nouns ending in -*l* or -*r* are masculine, and most nouns ending in -*d* or -*ión* are feminine.

   Es **el/un** españo**l**.   Es **la/una** universida**d**.
   Es **el/un** acto**r**.   Es **la/una** lecc**ión**.

3. Some nouns do not conform to the rules stated here. One way to remember the gender of these nouns is to learn the definite articles and the nouns together: for example, *la clase, el día* (day), *el mapa* (map), and *la mano* (hand).

How to form the contractions al *and* del

The definite article *el* combines with the words *a* (to, at) and *de* (of, from) to form the words *al* and *del*.

Guatemala está **al** sur de México.   *Guatemala is to the south of Mexico.*

El español es una lengua **del** mundo.   *Spanish is a language of the world.*

1. Have students make color-coded flashcards to learn the gender of each new noun introduced in this book: blue ink for masculine nouns, pink ink for feminine nouns. This concept is used in Superlearning and Suggestopedia approaches to second language acquisition and has been validated by research conducted at the University of Indiana.
2. Emphasize the importance of learning the gender of nouns that either have no rules for gender or that are exceptions to the rules stated here. Tell students to learn definite articles and nouns together; for example, *el nombre* and el *día.*

---

[1]Spanish speakers do not consider nouns as being male or female (except when referring to people or animals). Therefore, the terms "masculine" and "feminine" are simply labels for classifying nouns.

> **¡CUIDADO!** Do not contract *a* or *de* with *el* when the definite article is capitalized. Compare: Lima es la capital *del* Perú. / San Salvador es la capital *de El* Salvador.

Practiquemos

A. ¿Qué son? Identifique los objetos.

Ejemplo: Guitarra
Es una guitarra.

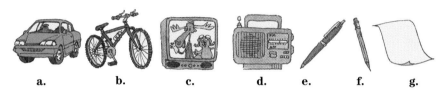

a.   b.   c.   d.   e.   f.   g.

B. ¿Sabe usted? Complete las siguientes oraciones con el artículo indefinido apropiado y la palabra apropiada entre paréntesis.

Ejemplo: Carlos Suárez es... (industria / persona).
Carlos Suárez es *una persona.*

1. México es... (país / mapa).
2. El español es... (lengua / libro).
3. Guadalajara es... (ciudad / estado).
4. El Yucatán es... (península / océano).
5. La UNAM es... (compañía / universidad).

C. ¿Qué o quién es? Lea las oraciones con el artículo definido apropiado (**el**, **la**).

Ejemplo: Pilar Camacho: Es *la* mamá de Anita.

1. Jorge Suárez: Es _____ papá de Carlos.
2. intérprete: Es _____ profesión futura de Anita.
3. computación: Es _____ curso favorito de Carlos.
4. Dr. Méndez: Es _____ profesor de Anita y Carlos.
5. Mérida: Es _____ ciudad de la familia Suárez.
6. la UNAM: Es _____ universidad de Anita y Carlos.

D. El Ecuador. Escriba otra vez (*Rewrite*) el siguiente párrafo con artículos definidos e indefinidos apropiados. Use las contracciones **al** y **del** cuando sea necesario.

_____ Ecuador es _____ país que está situado _____ sur de Colombia en Sud América. En _____ parte _____ Ecuador están Los Andes. _____ capital _____ país es Quito, _____ ciudad maravillosa. _____ lengua oficial _____ Ecuador es _____ español, pero muchas personas hablan el quechua, que es _____ lengua indígena.

> ### *How to make nouns plural*
>
> In Spanish, all nouns are either singular or plural. Definite and indefinite articles must match the number (singular or plural) of the nouns they modify.
>
> To make Spanish nouns plural, add -*s* to nouns ending in a vowel (*a, e, o*). Otherwise, add -*es*.[1]
>
> | **Singular** | **Plural** | **Singular** | **Plural** |
> |---|---|---|---|
> | el amigo | → **los** amigo**s** | una clase | → **unas** clase**s** |
> | la amiga | → **las** amiga**s** | un profesor | → **unos** profesor**es** |

Practiquemos

E. Lógicamente. Complete las oraciones lógicamente y correctamente con las palabras de la columna.

Ejemplo: El alemán y el francés son...
El alemán y el francés son lenguas.

Ex. E. Answers: 1. compañeros de clase 2. novios 3. universidades 4. saludos 5. días de la semana 6. cursos 7. países

1. Carlos y Anita son...   país
2. Romeo y Julieta son...   novio
3. Harvard y la UNAM son...   curso
4. "¡Hola!" y "¿Qué tal?" son...   saludo
5. El domingo y el viernes son...   día
6. El derecho y los negocios son...   universidad
7. Los Estados Unidos y México son... compañero de clase

F. Dos compañeros. Escriba el párrafo con los artículos definidos e indefinidos apropiados.

Ex. F. Answers: los, la, una, la, una, Una, las, la

Uno de _____ compañeros de Anita se llama Carlos Suárez. Él es de Mérida en _____ Península Yucateca, que es _____ ciudad interesante. Ahora Carlos estudia en _____ UNAM, que es _____ universidad enorme. _____ de _____ clases de Carlos y de Anita es el inglés. Para ella _____ clase es fácil, pero para él es un poco difícil.

Charlemos

G. ¿Qué hay? Exprese sus ideas y opiniones a otro(a) estudiante.

1. En mi universidad hay...
   a. una cafetería buena.   d. un centro de estudiantes.
   b. una biblioteca enorme.   e. unos estudiantes hispanos.
   c. una estación de radio.   f. unos estudiantes asiáticos.

Allow students to do these activities in pairs. Expect students to make many grammatical errors at this early stage of language acquisition, but do not correct them at this time. Instead, jot down the most serious errors, then point them out after the practice session, using brief explanations and several examples written on the chalkboard or an overhead transparency.

---

[1]Here are two additional rules for making nouns plural:
1. Nouns ending in -*án*, -*és*, or -*ión*: drop the accent mark before adding -*es*.
   el/un alem**án**   el/un japon**és**   la/una lecc**ión**
   los/unos alem**anes**   los/unos japon**eses**   las/unas lecc**iones**
2. Nouns ending in -*z*: drop the -*z*, then add -*ces*.
   la/una actri**z**   las/unas actri**ces**

2. En mi clase de español hay...
   a. una guitarra.
   b. un(a) profesor(a).
   c. un mapa de Sud América.
   d. un televisor a colores.
   e. unos exámenes difíciles.
   f. unos estudiantes japoneses.

H. Información personal. Pregúntele a otro(a) estudiante.

Use *tú* since you are asking your classmate . . .

1. cómo se llama.
2. de dónde es.
3. cuántos años tiene.
4. qué estudia aquí.
5. en qué días estudia español y a qué hora.
6. cuántas horas estudia español y dónde.
7. si (*if*) el español es una lengua fácil o difícil.

Ex. H. Remind students to use *tú* verb forms when asking each other these questions.

NOTAS CULTURALES

Education in Latin America and Spain

In Latin America and Spain, an elementary school is sometimes called *escuela básica, escuela primaria,* or simply *escuela* or *primaria* which lasts six years. A high school has many names: *liceo, bachillerato, instituto, escuela superior, escuela secundaria* or *secundaria* which lasts five or six years. A *colegio* is generally a private school for children up to the age of about seventeen years old. The Spanish word *colegio* is a false cognate in English; the word for "college" is *universidad.*

After completing the *primaria,* Latin Americans and Spaniards enter the labor force, enroll in a technical school *(politécnico),* or study for several more years in a *secundaria.* There are few junior or community colleges in Spanish-speaking countries. After completing the *secundaria,* some students enroll in a university.

Competition for acceptance at public universities is intense. Because all government-run universities are free, students who wish to enroll in one must pass rigorous entrance examinations *(pruebas).* Once accepted by a university, the students pursue a degree *(título)* in a highly-structured program with few or no elective courses.

Few universities have student residence halls as in the United States and Canada. Students usually live in their homes with their parents, in boardinghouses *(pensiones),* or in private homes. Universities in Spain and Latin America have a political and social function as well as an educational one. They are usually autonomous and can determine their own policies and teaching staff with little or no interference from the government as long as they abide by the national curriculum established for students' basic education.

1. Emphasize that the Spanish word for college is *universidad,* not *colegio.*
2. Tell students that in Spanish-speaking countries, parents can choose from many different types of private primary and secondary schools.
3. Write to several universities in Spain or Latin America for information about courses and programs for foreign students interested in the Spanish language as well as Hispanic literature and culture. Share this information with your students. More information is available on the Internet (http://www.studyabroad.com).

I. Un anuncio. Lea el siguiente anuncio, luego conteste las preguntas.

PREUNIVERSITARIO
Estudiantes de Chile

Considere la mejor alternativa para la preparación de las pruebas de Aptitud Académica y de Conocimientos Específicos.

Material de apoyo sin cargo, experiencia, actividades culturales y recreativas, computación.

Valor del Curso: $ 5.000 al año.
Matrícula hasta el 19 de Abril.

EN EL CAMINO HACIA LA UNIVERSIDAD

CENTRO DE ESTUDIOS PREUNIVERSITARO ESTUDIANTES DE CHILE

CARMEN 35

1. What is this advertisement about?
2. Who would be interested in reading the ad?
3. What does the owl seem to symbolize in Chilean culture?

GRAMÁTICA FUNCIONAL

Describing everyday activities

—¿A qué hora regresas a casa, Carlos?
—Regreso a las seis de la tarde.
—Y luego, ¿descansas un poco?
—Sí, tomo una siesta. Luego estudio.

Present tense of regular -ar verbs

How to form the present tense

An infinitive is a nonpersonal verb form; for example, *hablar*. Spanish infinitives end in either *-ar*, *-er*, or *-ir*. All Spanish infinitives have two parts: a stem and an ending.

To form the present tense of Spanish infinitives ending in *-ar*, drop the infinitive ending from the verb and add a personal ending to the stem.

habl-*ar* *(to speak, to talk)*

(yo)	habl**o**	*I speak*
(tú)	habl**as**	*you (informal) speak*
(usted, él/ella)	habl**a**	*you (formal) speak, he/she speaks*
(nosotros/nosotras)	habl**amos**	*we speak*
(vosotros/vosotras)	habl**áis**	*you (informal) speak*
(ustedes, ellos/ellas)	habl**an**	*you (formal) speak, they speak*

How to use the present tense

Spanish speakers use the present tense to express (1) what people do over a period of time, (2) what they do habitually, and (3) what they intend to do at a later time.

1. Carlos **estudia** inglés en la UNAM.
   Carlos is studying English at the UNAM.
2. **Estudia** mucho por la noche.
   He studies a lot in the evening.
3. Mañana **estudia** con Anita.
   Tomorrow he's studying with Anita.

In this lesson, you have already seen some *-ar* verbs. Study these useful verbs with the example phrases:

tomar exámenes	*to take tests*
llegar a clase	*to arrive at class*
regresar a casa	*to return home*
escuchar las cintas	*to listen to tapes*
trabajar por la noche	*to work at night*
descansar por una hora	*to rest for an hour*
hablar español en casa	*to speak Spanish at home*
estudiar en la biblioteca	*to study in the library*

Practiquemos

A. Carlos y yo. Complete el siguiente párrafo de Anita, usando apropiadamente los verbos de la lista.

somos   hablamos   estudiamos
tomamos   regresamos   descansamos

Carlos y yo _____ compañeros. _____ una clase de inglés en la UNAM. Nosotros _____ inglés en la biblioteca para nuestro examen los viernes por la mañana. Luego _____ en la cafetería donde _____ de nuestras actividades. Por la tarde _____ a casa.

B. Carlos y sus padres. Complete los siguientes párrafos de Carlos con la forma apropiada de los verbos entre paréntesis.

1. **(hablar)** Me llamo Carlos Suárez. (Yo) _____ español, maya y un poco de inglés. Mi papá y mi mamá _____ español y maya. Nosotros _____ maya en casa.
2. **(trabajar)** (Yo) _____ en un restaurante en México, D.F. Mi papá _____ en una gasolinera *(gas station)* en Mérida y mi mamá _____ en casa. Mi familia y yo _____ mucho.
3. **(descansar)** (Yo) _____ los domingos cuando no tengo clases. Los días de trabajo mi papá y mi mamá _____ por una hora en la tarde. Los domingos ellos _____ un poco más.

C. Una amiga de Anita. Complete el párrafo con la forma correcta de los infinitivos.

ser   hablar   escuchar
tomar   llegar   trabajar

¡Hola! Me llamo Beatriz Martínez. Yo __*soy*__ una amiga de Anita Camacho. Ella y yo _____ un curso de francés en la UNAM. Anita _____ bien el francés, pero para mí la lengua _____ difícil. Anita y yo _____ a clase a las once de la mañana. La profesora _____ francés muy bien, pero ella _____ rápidamente. Los miércoles mis compañeros de clase y yo _____ cintas en francés en el laboratorio de lenguas y _____ exámenes los viernes. La profesora, mis compañeros y yo _____ mucho, pero la clase _____ interesante.

D. Querida Anita... Imagine that Anita Camacho is your pen pal. Write a letter to her in Spanish beginning with *Querida* (Dear) *Anita*, and say . . .

1. where you are from
2. in which school you are a student
3. how many classes you are taking
4. what subjects you are studying

Charlemos

Ex. E.
1. In this activity, students simply choose to combine *Me gusta* or *No me gusta* with infinitive verb phrases, according to their personal preferences. We introduce the use of *(no) me gusta* + infinitive here for several purposes: to teach students how to express their likes and dislikes, to practice the new vocabulary in a personalized, communicative format, and to introduce *gusta* + infinitive construction which is explained in more detail in *Lección 3*.
2. Follow-up activity: You could introduce the construction *A* + name *(no) le gusta* + infinitive, then have students work in groups of four in which they tell what their conversation partner likes and does not like to do.

E. Mis preferencias. Tell a classmate what you like to do (*Me gusta* + infinitive) and what you don't like to do (*No me gusta* + infinitive).

1. tomar exámenes

2. escuchar la radio

3. hablar por teléfono

4. estudiar con amigos

5. trabajar por la noche

6. descansar en la biblioteca

Ejemplos: *Me gusta hablar por teléfono.* (I like to talk on the phone.)
No me gusta tomar exámenes. (I don't like to take tests.)

Me gusta... (I like . . .)
No me gusta... (I don't like . . .)

F. ¿Sí o No? Pregúnteles a unos compañeros de clase.

Ejemplo: estudiar en la biblioteca
—*¿Estudias en la biblioteca?*
—*Sí.*
—*Escribe tu nombre aquí, por favor.*

Nombre

1. hablar español con amigos   _____
2. estudiar en la biblioteca   _____
3. escuchar la radio en casa   _____
4. trabajar mucho en la clase   _____
5. tomar un curso de sicología   _____

G. Entrevista. (*Interview*) Pregúntele a otro(a) estudiante.

1. ¿Estudias más los sábados o los domingos? ¿Qué estudias?
2. ¿Hablas poco o mucho por teléfono? ¿Con quién hablas?
3. ¿Escuchas música clásica o música moderna? ¿Qué escuchas?
4. ¿Llegas a la universidad en auto, en autobús, en bicicleta, en motocicleta o a pie *(on foot)?*
5. Cuando regresas a casa, ¿estudias, trabajas o descansas?

H. Charla final. Hable con un(a) compañero(a) de clase.

Tell your conversation partner . . .

- when you arrive at school (days, times).
- your class schedule (classes, days, times).
- when you get home from school (days, times).
- something about your work (place, days, times).

PARA LEER MEJOR

Recognizing Spanish Affixes

An affix is added to the beginning (prefix) or to the end (suffix) of a word stem to create a new word. Knowing the meaning of Spanish affixes can significantly increase your ability to read Spanish efficiently.

Activities

A. Write the English equivalent of the following Spanish prefixes and suffixes, using the example words to help you.

Ex. F.
1. This is a signature activity in which students stand up and mingle with each other as they would at a cocktail party. Before you begin the activity, carefully explain what students are supposed to do, and provide several examples to reinforce your explanation. This activity works best in groups of 5–6 students. Do not explain how to form *tú* commands (e.g., *Escribe*) at this point; students should simply use the command here as a formulaic expression such as *por la mañana.*
2. Point out the idiomatic use of *por* here: *por favor* = please.

Ex. G. Follow-up activity: Have students ask you these questions, using *usted* verb forms.

Ex. H. Remind students to cover their partner's role before they begin this teeter-totter activity.

This exercise enhances students' confidence and motivation in learning Spanish.
1. Point out that this is only a partial list of Spanish-English correspondences.
2. Read aloud each Spanish word and ask students to guess its meaning in English.
3. Explain that many Spanish prefixes can be added to words to change them to their opposite meaning (for example: *posible* → *imposible*).

A. *bi-* (two), *tri-* (three), *im-* (not), *in-* (not), *-ed*, *-ous*, *-ty*, *-sion/-tion*

Spanish	English	Examples
Prefix		
mono-	*mono- (one)*	**mono**lingüe, **mono**polio, **mono**riel
bi-	_____	**bi**lingüe, **bi**cicleta, **bi**mestre
tri-	_____	**tri**lingüe, **tri**ángulo, **tri**mestre
im-	_____	**im**posible, **im**paciente, **im**parcial
in-	_____	**in**necesario, **in**mortal, **in**creíble
Suffix		
-mente	*-ly*	especial**mente**, rápida**mente**
-ado, -ada	_____	ocup**ado**, motoriz**ado**, divorci**ada**
-oso, -osa	_____	maravill**oso**, gener**oso**, fabul**osa**
-dad, -tad	_____	oportuni**dad**, ciu**dad**, liber**tad**
-ción, -sión	_____	conversa**ción**, ac**ción**, televi**sión**

B. 1. It advertises a computer course.
2. They are located in Madrid, Spain.
Addresses: Alcalá, 30. 28014 Madrid and Dr. Esquerdo, 160 28007 Madrid.
3. a. school   f. laboratory
   b. methods   g. April
   c. ministry   h. product
   d. existing   i. construction
   e. requirements
4. a. *oficialmente*
   b. *prácticamente*
   c. *diseño de sistemas expertos*
   d. *sólidos conocimientos de programación*

B. Use your knowledge of Spanish affixes to help you understand the following advertisement.

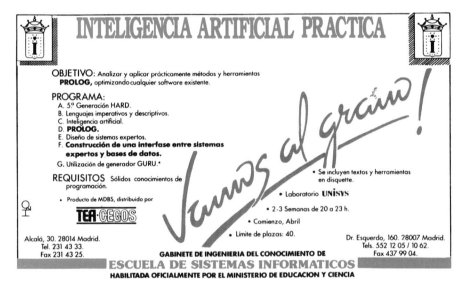

1. What is this advertisement about?
2. Where are these two schools located? Write the addresses of each one.
3. Write the English equivalents for the following words.

   a. escuela   d. existente   g. abril
   b. métodos   e. requisitos   h. producto
   c. ministerio   f. laboratorio   i. construcción

4. Write the Spanish equivalents for the following words and phrases.

   a. officially   c. design by system experts
   b. practically   d. solid knowledge of programming

PARA ESCRIBIR MEJOR

Organizing Your Ideas

A good way to improve your writing is to organize the ideas you want to express.

Activity

1. Look at the chart below and familiarize yourself with the information about Anita Camacho.

Nombre	Anita Camacho	Compañero(a)	Usted
Nación	México		
Lengua	español		
Edad *(Age)*	19 años		
Escuela	UNAM		
Cursos	turismo inglés alemán sicología		
Compañero(a)	Carlos Suárez		

2. Now read the following description of Anita Camacho and note how the information in the chart above was used in this paragraph.

   Anita Camacho es de México. Ella habla español. Anita tiene diecinueve años. Estudia en una universidad. Se llama la Universidad Nacional Autónoma de México. Anita estudia turismo, inglés, alemán y sicología. Estudia con un compañero de clase. Se llama Carlos Suárez.

3. Fill in the chart with information about one of your classmates. Then write a similar descriptive paragraph about him or her.
4. Now fill in the chart with information about yourself. Then write a paragraph describing yourself.
5. Exchange both of your paragraphs with a classmate. Check each other's work for errors, and correct any you find. Discuss the results together, then return his or her paragraph.

Atajo

Functions:
Describing people; introducing; talking about the present

Vocabulary:
Countries; languages; studies; arts; numbers 0–20

Grammar:
Verbs: *ser;* Prepositions: *de;* Personal pronouns: *él, ella;* Articles: indefinite *un, una*

¿A qué nivel está Ud.?

¿Sí o no? In an Hispanic country, if you are invited to a party that begins at 8 p.m. are you expected to arrive on time?
Review the chapter and then monitor your progress by completing the *Autoprueba* at the end of *Lección 1* in the **Workbook/Lab Manual.**

SÍNTESIS

¡A ver!

Adriana and Olga are students at the *Universidad Intercontinental* in Mexico City. You will see them speaking with an interviewer about the courses they are taking this semester. First, study the words and their meaning in the *Vocabulario esencial*. Then read over the activity and watch the interviews. You may not understand every word that Adriana and Olga say, but you will be able to grasp the most important information. Finally, check your comprehension by doing the activity.

Vocabulario esencial

materia	*course*
me gusta más	*I like most*
me gusta menos	*I like least*

Answers: 1. b 2. c 3. a 4. a 5. b 6. c

1. Adriana tiene...
   a. 20 años   b. 21 años   c. 23 años
2. A Adriana le gusta estudiar...
   a. derecho   b. computación   c. publicidad
3. A Adriana no le gusta estudiar...
   a. filosofía   b. biología   c. geología
4. Olga tiene...
   a. 20 años   b. 21 años   c. 23 años
5. Olga está en el _____ semestre.
   a. primer   b. segundo   c. tercer
6. A Olga le gusta estudiar...
   a. turismo   b. negocios   c. derecho civil

¡A leer!

Visit

http://poco.heinle.com

Read the advertisement on page 41, then answer the questions about it.

¿Comprendió Ud.?

1. This ad is aimed at . . .
   a. adults.
   b. children.
   c. professional people.
   d. all of the people mentioned in a, b, and c.

SÍNTESIS

2. According to the ad, in which countries could people learn English?

3. What kinds of accomodations are available for these students?

4. What sorts of instructional programs are offered in the ad?

5. How can people obtain more information about these programs?

Answers: 1. d 2. United States, Canada, England 3. dormitories, hotels, family homes 4. moderate to intensive lessons, small groups and individual sessions, all instructional levels, specialized English for different professions 5. Call one of the two telephone numbers given.

¡A conversar!

Imagine you are at a party sponsored by the International Club at your school. A Mexican student (role-played by your partner) sits down next to you. Do the following in Spanish:

1. Greet each other appropriately.
2. Introduce yourselves and shake hands.
3. Ask and tell each other where you are from.
4. Talk briefly about . . .
   a. your school life (your courses, the names of your instructors).
   b. your work (where you work, which days, what time you get there).
5. Now introduce your new friend to another student (a classmate) and say something interesting you learned in your first conversation.

Atajo

¡A escribir!

Write a short paragraph about some things you do during the day. Try to use only the Spanish you already know; do *not* use any dictionaries. Here is the beginning of a sample paragraph:

Me llamo Joyce Arvin. Soy estudiante de Georgetown College en Kentucky. Voy° a la universidad en bicicleta. Llego a las ocho de la mañana. Voy a la biblioteca y estudio por dos horas...

If you wish, give students additional vocabulary such as: *mirar la televisión / videos, tomar un refresco / café / una cerveza, tocar la guitarra, caminar, bailar.*

I go

VOCABULARIO

Sustantivos

el apartamento *apartment*
el auto *car*
la biblioteca *library*
la bicicleta *bicycle*
el bolígrafo *ballpoint pen*
la cinta *tape, tape recording*
la compañía *company*
el día *day*
la escuela *school*
el estado *state*
el examen *test*
la fiesta *party*
la guitarra *guitar*
la hora *hour*
el lápiz *pencil*
el libro *book*
la mano *hand*
el mapa *map*
la motocicleta *motorcycle*
el océano *ocean*
el país *country*
el papel *paper*
la península *peninsula*
el radio *radio*
la semana *week*
el teléfono *telephone*
el televisor *TV set*
la universidad *university*

La gente
(People)

el (la) amigo(a) *friend*
el (la) compañero(a)
  de clase *classmate*
el (la) compañero(a)
  de cuarto *roommate*
la novia *girlfriend*
el novio *boyfriend*

Los cursos
(Courses)

el alemán *German (language)*
el álgebra *Algebra*
el baile *Dance*
la biología *Biology*
el cálculo *Calculus*
la ciencia *Science*
la computación *Computer Science*
la economía *Economics*
el francés *French (language)*
la geografía *Geography*
la geología *Geology*
la geometría *Geometry*
la historia *History*
el inglés *English (language)*
las lenguas *Languages*
la literatura *Literature*
la música *Music*
la pintura *Painting*
la química *Chemistry*
la sicología *Pyschology*

Estudios profesionales
(Professional studies)

la computación *Computer Science*
el derecho *Law*
el turismo *Tourism*
la medicina *Medicine*
la educación *Education*
la ingeniería *Engineering*
los negocios *Business*
el periodismo *Journalism*

Profesiones
(Professions)

el (la) intérprete *interpreter*
el (la) ingeniero(a) *engineer*

Los días de la semana
(Days of the week)

el lunes *Monday*
el martes *Tuesday*
el miércoles *Wednesday*
el jueves *Thursday*
el viernes *Friday*
el sábado *Saturday*
el domingo *Sunday*

Verbos

descansar *to rest*
escuchar *to listen*
estudiar *to study*
hablar *to speak, to talk*
llegar *to arrive*
(no) me gusta + infinitive
  I (don't) like
regresar *to return*
quiero *I want*
saber *to know*
tengo *I have*
tomar *to take*
trabajar *to work*
voy *I go*

Artículos
(Articles)

el, la, los, las *the*
un(a) *a, an*
unos(as) *some*

VOCABULARIO

Palabras interrogativas (Question words)

¿Cómo? *How?*
¿Cuándo? *When?*
¿Dónde? *Where?*
¿Por qué? *Why?*

Otras palabras

difícil *difficult*
fácil *easy*
para mí *for me*
pero *but*
por *for (duration of time)*
solamente *only*

Cómo pedir la hora

¿A qué hora? *At what time?*
¿Qué hora es? *What time is it?*

Expresiones idiomáticas

a pie *on foot*
¡Bueno! *Great!, Okay!, well*
¡Cuidado! *Be careful!*
de (por) la mañana *in the morning*
de (por) la tarde *in the afternoon*
de (por) la noche *in the evening*
en casa *at home*
por favor *please*

2

¡Aquí tienes tu casa!

▶ COMMUNICATIVE GOALS

You will be able to describe yourself, describe your friends and family, and describe what you do at home.

▶ LANGUAGE FUNCTIONS

Describing people and things
Describing daily activities
Indicating ownership
Defining relationships

▶ VOCABULARY THEMES

Nuclear family members
House pets
Numbers 31–99
Colors

▶ GRAMMATICAL STRUCTURES

Agreement with descriptive adjectives
Present tense of the verb *tener*
Possessive adjectives
Possession with *de(l)*
Present tense of regular *-er* and *-ir* verbs
Present tense of *hacer*

▶ CULTURAL INFORMATION

Hand gestures
Conversational customs

http://poco.heinle.com

Atajo

EN CONTEXTO

Es sábado. Son las seis de la tarde. Carlos Suárez está en la casa de su amiga Anita Camacho en la Colonia del Valle.(1) Ahora ella le presenta a Carlos a su familia.

ANITA: Papá, quiero presentarte a un amigo. Se llama Carlos Súarez.
CARLOS: Encantado, señor.
JOSÉ: José Camacho. Mucho gusto.
CARLOS: El gusto es mío.
ANITA: Y mi mamá...
PILAR: Encantada. Aquí tienes tu casa, Carlos.(2)
CARLOS: Muchas gracias, señora.
ANITA: Carlos y yo estudiamos inglés en la UNAM.
PILAR: Ah, ¿sí? ¿Es difícil el inglés, Carlos?
CARLOS: Sí, señora, pero Anita es una buena profesora.
ANITA: Gracias, Carlos.
JOSÉ: Aquí en la casa hablamos un poco de inglés. Es una lengua bastante importante hoy día,° ¿verdad?(3)
CARLOS: ¡Claro que sí!°
(Entra un perro° en la casa.)
CARLOS: ¡Ah! Ustedes tienen° un perro. ¿Cómo se llama?
ANITA: Bandido.° Tenemos un gato° también... se llama Café,° por su color. Tiene cuatro años. Es de mi hermana° Sara. Ahora ella y mi hermano° Raúl están en el Parque Alameda con unos amigos de la familia.

nowadays
Of course!
dog
have
Bandit / cat / Brown(y)
sister / brother

Notas de texto

1. Mexico City is divided up into neighborhoods called *colonias.* In other areas of the Spanish-speaking world, the word for *colonia* may be *zona, barrio, sector, comuna,* or *urbanización.*

2. When one translates word for word from one language into another, the meaning of a phrase or sentence can often be distorted. For example, the expression *Aquí tienes tu casa* literally means "Here you have your house"; in this context it means "Make yourself at home."

3. In Spanish-speaking countries, many people value English highly because a good working knowledge of English is an asset for getting a job, getting a promotion, and traveling abroad.

¡Comprendió Ud.?

1. Escriba el nombre de las cinco personas de la familia de Anita.

2. Carlos Suárez es...
   a. un amigo de José.   c. un amigo de Anita.
   b. el padre de Sara.   d. un hermano de Raúl.
3. Sara tiene...
   a. un perro de cuatro años.   c. una madre difícil.
   b. dos hermanas idénticas.   d. un gato de cuatro años.
4. El nombre del perro es...
   a. Bandido.   c. Alameda.
   b. Colonia.   d. Café.
5. En la casa de Anita se habla...
   a. mucho español y mucho inglés.
   b. mucho español y un poco de inglés.
   c. mucho español y un poco de alemán.
   d. español, inglés y un poco de francés.

TRANSPARENCY No. 9: Family Tree

VOCABULARIO ÚTIL

In this section you will learn to describe your family, your friends, and some of your possessions.

La familia

Mi **padre** se llama José y tiene cincuenta y un años.

Mi **madre** es Pilar y tiene cuarenta y cinco años.

Tengo un **hermano,** Raúl y una **hermana** que se llama Sara.

Nuestro **perro** se llama Bandido y nuestro **gato** se llama Café.

Otros parientes (relatives)

el padrastro	*stepfather*	la madrastra	*stepmother*
el hermanastro	*stepbrother*	la hermanastra	*stepsister*

Los números 31–99

30	**treinta**	y uno
40	**cuarenta**	y dos
50	**cincuenta**	y tres
60	**sesenta**	y cuatro
70	**setenta**	y cinco
80	**ochenta**	y seis
90	**noventa**	y siete
		y ocho
		y nueve

CARLOS: ¿Cuántos años tiene tu papá?
ANITA: Tiene cincuenta y un años.
CARLOS: ¿Y tu mamá?
ANITA: Cuarenta y cinco.

Practiquemos

A. ¿Quiénes son? Complete las oraciones con la relación correcta de las siguientes personas y los siguientes animales.

Ejemplo: Sara es *la hermana* de Raúl y Anita.

1. Café es _____ de Sara.
2. José es _____ de Sara, Anita y Raúl.
3. Raúl es _____ de Anita y Sara.
4. Bandido es _____ de la familia.
5. Sara es _____ de Raúl y Anita.
6. Pilar es _____ de Sara, Raúl y Anita.

B. ¿Cuántos años tienen? Escuche a su profesor(a) de español y escriba la edad *(age)* de las siguientes personas de la familia de Anita.

Ejemplo: José Camacho ___51___

Pilar Camacho	_____	Lupe Ortega	_____
Ramiro Camacho	_____	Francisco Ortega	_____
Ángela Camacho	_____	Margarita Gómez	_____

C. Mi familia. Complete las siguientes oraciones. Luego léale las oraciones a otro(a) estudiante.[1]

1. Mi familia es _____ . (intelectual/tolerante/próspera).
2. Mi papá se llama _____ . Él es (reservado/paciente/artístico).
3. Mi mamá se llama _____ . Ella es (intuitiva/adaptable/sincera).
4. Mi hermana se llama _____ . Ella es (inteligente/atlética/buena).
5. Mi hermano se llama _____ . Él es (ambicioso/honesto/generoso).

---

[1] Remember that adjectives ending in -*o* refer to males, and adjectives ending in -*a* refer to females. Adjectives ending in other letters can refer to both males and females. Adjective agreement will be explained formally later in this lesson.

D. ¿Y tu familia? Hable con un(a) compañero(a) de clase.

Estudiante A

1. ¿Cuántos años tiene tu papá?
3. ¿Y tu mamá?
5. Mi mamá tiene _____ años y mi papá _____ . Y tú, ¿cuántos años tienes?
7. _____ . ¿Tienes hermanos?

9. Tengo _____ . (No tengo _____ .)
11. Sí, tengo _____ . (No,...) ¿Y tú?

Estudiante B

2. Tiene _____ .
4. _____ . ¿Y tus padres?
6. Yo tengo _____ . ¿Y tú?
8. Sí, tengo _____ hermano y _____ hermana. (No, no tengo hermanos.) ¿Cuántos hermanos tienes tú?
10. ¿Tienes animales en tu casa?
12. Sí, ... (No,...)

Los colores[1]

amarillo	*yellow*	**marrón**[2]	*brown*
anaranjado	*orange*	**negro**	*black*
azul	*blue*	**rojo**	*red*
blanco	*white*	**rosado**	*pink*
gris	*gray*	**verde**	*green*

Practiquemos

E. ¿De qué color es? Indique el color de los objetos.

1.   2.   3.

4.   5.   6.

_____

[1] To express the meaning of light or dark with most colors, use *claro* or *oscuro*, respectively.
azul claro   light blue   *azul oscuro*   dark blue

[2] Other words for the color brown are *pardo(a)*, *café* (for eyes), and *castaño(a)* (for hair). In Cuba, Puerto Rico, and several other areas of the Spanish-speaking world, the word *moreno(a)* is used to denote dark or brown skin. In other Spanish-speaking countries, however, *moreno(a)* refers to a person with dark hair or eyes.

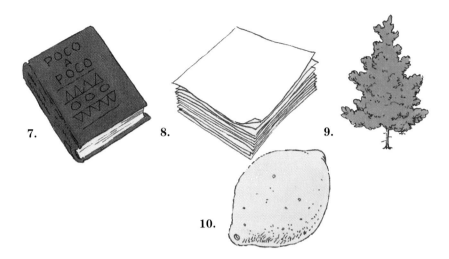

7.   8.   9.

10.

E. Los colores. Lea las siguientes oraciones y después hable con otro(a) estudiante.

1. Mi color favorito es _____ . Otro color que me gusta es _____ . No me gusta el color _____ .
2. El color exterior de la casa (del apartamento) de mi familia es _____ .
3. En mi casa (apartamento) hay un teléfono _____ , un radio _____ y un televisor _____ .
4. Tengo un perro _____ y un gato _____ . (No tengo perro/gato.)
5. El color de mi auto (bicicleta/motocicleta) es _____ . (No tengo auto/bicicleta/motocicleta.)

NOTAS CULTURALES

Los gestos°

Los españoles y los latinoamericanos usan muchos gestos con las manos cuando hablan. Por ejemplo, hay gestos para expresar "tacaño°", "¡Cuidado!" y "¡Un momento!" Es posible tener una breve conversación con las manos.

Los turistas de otros países necesitan tener mucho cuidado con los gestos cuando visitan España o Latinoamérica. ¿Por qué? Porque todos° los gestos no son iguales en todas las culturas. Por ejemplo, Los norteamericanos usan algunos gestos que no tienen equivalentes en la cultura hispánica y algunos que pueden ser ofensivos. Aquí tiene usted algunos gestos del mundo° hispano.

gestures

stingy

all

world

¡No!   Vamos a beber.   Un momento.   dinero

Tell students that another word Spanish speakers use for *tacaño* is *codo* (literally, "elbow").

!Cuidado!   ¡Fantástico!   ¡Estás loco(a)!   tacaño

¿Comprendió Ud.?
Indique cierto o falso.

Answers: 1. *Cierto* 2. *Falso* 3. *Cierto* 4. *Falso*

	Cierto	Falso
1. Es importante comprender los gestos cuando se visita Latinoamérica o España.	_____	_____
2. No es posible tener una breve conversación con el uso de los gestos hispánicos.	_____	_____
3. Los hispanos tienen gestos para expresar una variedad de conceptos.	_____	_____
4. Todos los gestos norteamericanos son los mismos que los gestos hispánicos.	_____	_____

GRAMÁTICA FUNCIONAL

Describing people and things

—¡Julieta, mi Julieta! ¡Eres joven! ¡Eres bonita! ¡Eres simpática!

—¡Romeo, mi Romeo! ¡Eres muy dramático!

Agreement with descriptive adjectives

Adjectives are words that describe nouns or pronouns. In Spanish, descriptive adjectives must match the gender (masculine or feminine) and number (singular or plural) of the noun or pronoun they describe.

How to match adjectives with their nouns

1. Adjectives ending in *-o* change to *-a* to indicate feminine gender, and add *-s* to indicate plural.

	Singular	**Plural**
Masculine	amigo generos**o**	amigos generos**os**
Feminine	amiga generos**a**	amigas generos**as**

2. Adjectives ending in *-e* do not change to make gender agreement. For plural, add *-s*.

Singular	**Plural**
amig**o** (amig**a**) inteligent**e**	amig**os** (amig**as**) inteligent**es**

3. Adjectives ending in a consonant add *-a* to agree with feminine nouns. For plural, add *-es* to masculine adjectives and *-s* to feminine adjectives.

	Singular	**Plural**
Masculine	amigo español	amigos español**es**
	amigo trabajado**r**	amigos trabajador**es**
Feminine	amiga español**a**	amigas español**as**
	amiga trabajado**ra**	amigas trabajador**as**

Where to place adjectives

1. Most Spanish adjectives follow the nouns they describe, as shown in the examples above.

2. Spanish adjectives of **quantity** precede the nouns they describe, as in English.

—¿**Cuántas hermanas** tienes?   *How many sisters do you have?*
—Tengo **una hermana gemela.**   *I have a twin sister.*

Las características físicas

alto   bajo   delgado   gordo

joven   anciana   guapo   feo

bonito[1]	*pretty*		
grande	*large, big*	**pequeño**	*small, little*
nuevo	*new*	**viejo**[2]	*old*

La personalidad

bueno	*good*	**malo**	*bad*
simpático	*nice*	**antipático**	*unpleasant*
trabajador	*hardworking*	**perezoso**	*lazy*

---

[1] The adjective *guapo* is used to describe a good-looking person, ususally a male. The adjective *bonito* is used to describe a pretty person, usually a female, and to describe places and things; for example: *Es un auto bonito.* In summary:

Male persons: *guapo / guapos*
Female persons: *guapa / guapas; bonita / bonitas*
Places and things: *bonito / bonita / bonitos / bonitas*

[2] The adjective *viejo* is usually used to describe things and places; it may have a derogatory connotation when it refers to people.

Practiquemos

A. ¿Quién es? Mire *(Look at)* las ilustraciones que su profesor(a) va a describir. Escuche la descripción de la persona o del animal. Luego diga su nombre.

B. ¿Cómo es? Complete las siguientes oraciones, usando el vocabulario nuevo de esta sección, como en el ejemplo.

Ejemplo: Carlos no es feo; es *guapo.*

1. Anita no es fea; es _____ .
2. Carlos y Anita no son perezozos; son _____ .
3. Raúl y Sara no son antipáticos; son _____ .
4. José no es muy alto; es un poco _____ .
5. Pilar no es perezosa; es _____ .
6. La madre de doña Pilar no es joven; es _____ .
7. Bandido no es malo; es _____ .
8. Café no es delgado; es _____ .
9. La casa de la familia Camacho no es nueva; es _____ .
10. La casa de los Camacho no es pequeña; es _____ .

C. La familia Camacho. Complete el siguiente párrafo usando los adjetivos de la lista. ¡Cuidado con las terminaciones de los adjetivos!

gordo	grande	pequeño	perezoso	trilingüe
joven	blanco	mexicano	bilingüe	trabajador

Ex. A.
1. Read each description twice. Then ask students: ¿Cómo se llama? The answers appear here in parenthesis.
2. Follow-up: Students work in pairs describing each drawing in Spanish.
   1. Es muy gordo y un poco antipático. Tiene cuatro años. (Café)(6)
   2. Es joven, muy guapa y estudiosa. Habla tres lenguas. (Anita)(3)
   3. Es muy simpática y relativamente joven; ella tiene solamente 45 años. (Pilar)(2)
   4. Es un poco bajo y muy simpático. Estudia para ser ingeniero. (Carlos)(4)
   5. Es pequeño, blanco y muy bueno. (Bandido)(5)
   6. Es alto y un poco gordo. Tiene 51 años y es dentista. (José)(1)
3. Follow-up activity: Students work in pairs describing each drawing in Spanish.

Ex. B. Answers: 1. bonita/guapa 2. trabajadores 3. simpáticos 4. bajo 5. trabajadora 6. anciana 7. bueno 8. gordo 9. vieja 10. grande

Ex. C. Answers: mexicanos, grande, trabajadora, trabajador, trilingüe, perezosa, jóvenes, blanco y pequeño (pequeño y blanco), gordo

Los miembros de la familia Camacho son residentes de la Ciudad de México; son _____ . Ellos tienen una casa _____ en la Colonia del Valle. La madre de Anita es arquitecta. Pilar trabaja en casa diez horas al día; es muy _____ . El señor Camacho es dentista; José es _____ también.

Anita es estudiante de la UNAM; habla español, alemán e inglés. Es _____ Ella no es _____ porque estudia mucho. Anita tiene un hermano y una hermana. Raúl tiene diez años, y Sara tiene ocho años; ellos son _____ .

En la casa hay dos animales: Bandido que es un perro _____ y _____ , y Café que es un gato muy _____ .

Ex. D. Answers: 1. *trabajadores* 2. *simpática* 3. *perezoso* 4. *gemelas* 5. *trabajador/trabajadora*

D. ¿Cómo son? Describa a las siguientes personas.

Ejemplo: Doña Pilar es una señora *simpática.* (simpático)

1. Doña Pilar y don José son _____ . (trabajador)
2. Anita es una persona _____ . (simpático)
3. Carlos no es un estudiante _____ . (perezoso)
4. Carlos tiene dos hermanas _____. (gemelo)
5. Mi profesor(a) de español es _____ . (trabajador)

Ex. E.
1. Read the following description two or three times. Afterwards, go over the answers with your students. *¡Hola! Me llamo Carlos Suárez. Soy de Mérida en la península de Yucatán. Tengo veintitrés años y ahora soy estudiante de la UNAM. Quiero ser ingeniero nuclear. Somos seis en mi familia: mi papá y mi mamá, mi hermano, mis dos hermanas y yo. Mi papá se llama Jorge y tiene cincuenta y siete años. No es muy joven pero trabaja diez u once horas al día en una gasolinera. Somos buenos amigos, mi papá y yo. Mi mamá se llama María y tiene cuarenta y seis años. Trabaja en casa donde cuida a mis dos hermanas gemelas, Clarisa y Marisa, que tienen cuatro años. Normalmente ellas son muy simpáticas, pero a veces no. También tengo un hermano que es mayor que yo. Ricardo tiene veinticinco años y ahora trabaja con su esposa Luisa en un hotel de Cancún.*
2. Answers: Father: Jorge, age 57, works 10–11 hours in a gas station; mother: María, age 46, cares for her two daughters at home; brother: Ricardo, age 25, is married to Luisa, he works at a hotel in Cancún; sisters: Marisa and Clarisa, age 4, twin sisters, sometimes they are good, other times they are not very nice

E. La familia de Carlos. Su profesor(a) va a leer una descripción de Carlos y su familia. Escuche la descripción y complete el cuadro con la información apropiada.

La familia de Carlos Suárez

	Nombre	Edad	Otra información
	Carlos	23	Estudia ingeniería en la UNAM, su papá y él son buenos amigos
Padre	_____	____	_____
Madre	_____	____	_____
Hermano	_____	____	_____
Hermanas	_____	____	_____

F. ¡Hola, Carlos! Imagine that you have received a letter from Carlos Suárez in which he asked you some questions. Answer his letter and tell him about yourself. Be sure to include information about school, your likes and dislikes, your physical description, and your family members.

Ex. G. Have your students share their paragraph with one or more classmates. Afterwards, they could briefly share this information orally with the class.

G. Una persona especial. Write a short paragraph describing a person you know or would like to know. Use adjectives you learned in this lesson.

Ejemplos: *Mi novio se llama Mark. Es alto y guapo, pero no es muy trabajador. Tiene veinte años... etc.*

Laura es simpática, ... etc.

Charlemos

H. Opiniones personales. Hable con otro(a) compañero(a) de clase.

1. ¿Es nuestra escuela (universidad) bonita o fea? ¿Es nueva o vieja?
2. ¿Cómo son los estudiantes aquí? ¿jóvenes o ancianos? ¿simpáticos o antipáticos?
3. Y los profesores aquí, ¿son conservadores o liberales?
4. ¿Es la clase de español pequeña o grande? ¿Es buena o mala?
5. Y tú, ¿eres un(a) estudiante trabajador(a) o perezoso(a)?

I. Mi familia y yo. Converse con un(a) compañero(a) de clase. Use los adjetivos de personalidad y de características físicas en la página 52.

Ejemplo: A: *Soy joven. No soy perezosa. ¿Y tú?*
            B: *Soy trabajador. No soy muy alto.*

A: Soy _____ . No soy _____ . ¿Y tú?
B: Soy _____ . No soy muy _____ .

A: Mi padre es _____ y un poco _____ . ¿Y tus padres?
B: Mi papá es muy _____ y un poco _____ . (No tengo padre.)

A: Mi mamá es _____ , pero no es muy _____ . ¿Y tu mamá?
B: Mi madre es _____ , pero no es _____ . (No tengo madre.)

A: Mi hermano es _____ y muy _____ . ¿Cómo es tu hermano?
B: Es _____ y un poco _____ . (No tengo hermanos.)

A: Mi hermana es _____ . Ella no es _____ . ¿Cómo es tu hermana?
B: Ella es _____ y un poco _____ . (No tengo hermanas.)

Ex. I. Remind students that they could use the following step family words, if they wish: *el padrastro, la madrastra, el hermanastro, la hermanastra.*

GRAMÁTICA FUNCIONAL

Describing ownership and relationships

—¿Qué tienes en la mano, Raúl?
—Tengo un radio pequeño, mamá.
—¿De quién es el radio?
—Es de mi amigo Pablo.

Present tense of *tener*

One way to indicate ownership or relationships is to use the verb *tener*, meaning **to have**.[1] Its present tense forms are as follows:

Remind students that Spanish speakers use the verb *tener* to ask about or state someone's age.

---

[1] Recall that in *Lección preliminar*, you learned to use *tener* to ask your classmates' age and to say your age in Spanish: —*¿Cuántos años tienes? —Tengo veintidós años.*

tener

(yo)	**tengo**	*I have*
(tú)	**tienes**	*you (informal) have*
(usted, él/ella)	**tiene**	*you (formal) have; he/she has*
(nosotros/nosotras)	**tenemos**	*we have*
(vosotros/vosotras)	***tenéis***	*you (informal) have*
(ustedes, ellos/ellas)	**tienen**	*you have; they have*

Possessive adjectives

Another way to indicate ownership or relationships is to use possessive adjectives.

How to match possessive adjectives with their nouns

In Spanish, possessive adjectives must match the gender (masculine or feminine) and number (singular or plural) of the nouns they describe.

1. The possessive adjectives *mi*, *tu*, and *su* have two forms: singular and plural.

	Singular	**Plural**
my	**mi** amigo(a)	**mis** amigos(as)
your (informal)	**tu** profesor(a)	**tus** profesores(as)
his, her, its, your (formal), their	**su** familia	**sus** familias

2. The possessive adjective *nuestro* has four forms: masculine, feminine, singular, and plural.[1]

	Masculine	**Feminine**	
our	nuestro hermano	nuestra familia	**Singular**
	nuestros hermanos	nuestras familias	**Plural**

---

[1] Like *vosotros*, *vuestro* (your) is used in many parts of Spain when addressing more than one person in an informal way; in Latin America, *su* would be used instead. Like *nuestro*, the possessive adjective *vuestro* also has four forms: masculine, feminine, singular, and plural.

Singular	*vuestro hermano*	*vuestra familia*
Plural	*vuestros hermanos*	*vuestras familias*

How to use possessive adjectives

1. The possessive adjectives *su* and *sus* are equivalent to English *his, her, its, your, their.* Usually, the context of the sentence clarifies their meaning.

—Aquí tiene usted **su** diccionario, profesora. Gracias.	*Here is your dictionary, professor. Thank you.*
—Y aquí tiene **sus** exámenes, Anita. Son excelentes.	*And here are your tests, Anita. They're excellent.*
—Gracias. ¡Ah! Magda está en el hospital, pero aquí tiene **su** trabajo.	*Thank you. Oh! Magda is in the hospital, but here is her work.*

2. You can clarify or emphasize the meaning of *su* and *sus* by using the word *de* with a subject pronoun *(de él, de ella, de usted, de ellos, de ellas, de ustedes).*

Pilar es la mamá **de ella**, no **de él**.   *Pilar is **her** Mom, not **his**.*

3. English speakers express possession by attaching an **'s** to a noun. Spanish speakers show this same relationship by using *de* with a noun.

Es el gato **de** Sara.   *It is Sara's cat.*

Ask students to guess the meaning of *su* and *sus* in this conversation.

Remind students of the contraction *de + el = del*; for example: *Es el auto del señor Camacho.*

Practiquemos

A. ¿Qué tienen? Diga qué tienen estas personas, usando **tengo, tienes, tiene, tenemos** o **tienen.**

Ejemplo: Carlos *tiene* una amiga simpática.

1. José y Pilar _____ una familia pequeña.
2. La familia Camacho _____ una casa grande.
3. Anita, tú _____ muchos amigos, ¿verdad?
4. Sara _____ un gato que se llama Café.
5. Mis amigos y yo _____ muchas fiestas.
6. Y yo _____ ...

Ex. A. Answers: 1. *tienen* 2. *tiene* 3. *tienes* 4. *tiene* 5. *tenemos* 6. *tengo*

B. Entre amigos. Complete el diálogo con los adjetivos **mi(s), tu(s), su(s)** o **nuestro(a/os/as).**

CARLOS: ¿Es grande _____ familia, Anita?
ANITA: No, _____ familia es pequeña. Somos cinco personas en casa.
CARLOS: En _____ casa somos seis: _____ padres, _____ hermano, _____ dos hermanas gemelas y yo.
ANITA: _____ hermanas gemelas, ¿cómo se llaman?
CARLOS: Clarisa y Marisa.

Ex. B.
1. Do in class as oral pair work.
2. Answers: *tu, mi (nuestra), mi (nuestra), mis, mi, mis, Tus*

C. Álbum de fotos. Complete la conversación con las formas apropiadas del verbo **ser + del, de la, de los** o **de las.**

Ex. C. Answers: *Son de las, es del, Es de la, Es del, son del*

Ejemplo: CARLOS: ¿De quién es el auto rojo?
                      ANITA: *Es del* hermano de mi papá.

CARLOS: ¿De quiénes son los gatos?
ANITA: _____ amigas de mi mamá.
CARLOS: ¿Y el perro
                 pequeño?
ANITA: El perro _____
                 padre de mi papá.
CARLOS: ¿De dónde es el
                 padre de tu papá?
ANITA: _____ ciudad de
                 Guaymas.
CARLOS: ¿Y la familia aquí
                 en tu casa?
ANITA: _____ hermano de mi mamá.
CARLOS: Aquí hay una foto de dos amigos.
ANITA: Sí, _____ Colegio Juárez.

D. ¿Quiénes son? Identifique quiénes son estas personas.

Ejemplo: Carlos / amigo / Anita
                      *Carlos es el amigo
                      de Anita.*

1. **José**

2. **Sara**

3. **Pilar**

4. **Anita**

5. **Raúl**

1. Carlos / amigo / la familia Camacho
2. Marisa y Clarisa / hermanas gemelas / Carlos
3. Don José y doña Pilar / padres / Anita
4. María / madre / Carlos y / esposa / Jorge
5. Ricardo / hermano / Carlos, Clarisa y Marisa

E. ¿De quién es? Identifique de quiénes son las cosas de las ilustraciones.

Ejemplo: *Es el gato de Sara.*

F. En su opinión... Escriba oraciones para expresar sus opiniones sobre nuestro país. Use palabras de cada *(each)* columna u otras palabras que usted sabe.

Ejemplos: *Nuestra sociedad es progresiva.*
Nuestra sociedad no es progresiva.

	país		**bueno**
Nuestro	**autos**		**viejo**
Nuestra	**sociedad**	**es (no es)**	**moderno**
Nuestros	**ciudades**	**son (no son)**	**violento**
Nuestras	**presidente**		**trabajador**
	televisión		**progresivo**

Ex. E. Answers:
1. *Es la guitarra de José (don José / del señor Camacho).*
2. *Es la bicicleta de Pilar (doña Pilar / de la señora Camacho).*
3. *Es el perro de Anita.*
4. *Es el radio de Raúl.*

Charlemos

G. Hablando de familias... Pregúntele a otro(a) estudiante.

1. En tu opinión, ¿es importante tener una familia grande? ¿Es tu familia pequeña o grande? ¿Cuántos son ustedes?
2. ¿Cuántos hermanos tienes? ¿Cómo se llaman? ¿Cómo son?
3. ¿Quién es el "bebé" de tu familia? ¿Cuál es su nombre? ¿Cómo es?

H. ¿Cómo son? Pregúntele a un(a) compañero(a) de clase sobre las siguientes personas y los siguientes lugares. Responda con oraciones como las del ejemplo.

Ejemplo: casa
A: ¿Cómo es tu casa?
B: *Mi casa es pequeña.*
A: ¿De qué color es?
B: *Es blanca.*

1. casa
2. escuela
3. familia
4. padres
5. hermanos
6. amigos

Ex. H. Encourage your students to talk about themselves as much as possible, using words, phrases, and grammatical structures introduced and practiced in *Lección preliminar* and *Lección 1*.

I. Charla final. Pregúntele a un(a) compañero(a) de clase.

En tu casa

1. ¿Cuántas personas hay en tu familia?
2. ¿Cuántos hermanos(as) tienes? ¿Cómo se llama(n) y cuántos años tiene(n)? ¿Tienes un(a) hermano(a) gemelo(a)?
3. ¿Tienes un perro o un gato? (¿Sí? ¿Cómo se llama?)

Tus amigos

1. ¿Cómo se llama tu mejor (*best*) amigo(a)? ¿Cuántos años tiene? ¿Cómo es tu amigo(a)? Por ejemplo, ¿es alto(a), guapo(a), simpático(a)?
2. ¿Tienes un(a) compañero(a) de cuarto? (¿Sí? ¿Cómo es él/ella?)
3. ¿Tienes novio/novia ahora? (¿Sí? ¿Cómo es él/ella?)

En tu escuela

1. ¿Cuántas clases tienes?
2. ¿Qué clases tienes?
3. ¿Cuál es una clase que te gusta mucho?
4. ¿Cómo se llama tu mejor profesor o profesora? ¿Cómo es él/ella?

Ask students the following questions: 1. How do you usually greet: a. a friend you often see at school? b. one of your instructors? c. a good friend you haven't seen for a year? d. a six-month-old baby you've just met? 2. What is different about conversational customs in Spanish-speaking countries and your country? What customs are similar?

If you wish, provide students with several sentences and their English meaning for beginning conversations in Spanish. Examples: *Me gusta su ciudad. ¡Qué niña más bonita tiene usted! ¿Cuánto tiempo ha vivido usted en esta linda casa?*

NOTAS CULTURALES

Conversational Customs

It is important to greet Spanish speakers with a handshake or, among close friends, a hug or a kiss on each cheek before beginning and often ending a conversation with them.

During a conversation, Spanish speakers tend to stand closer to one another than English speakers. As a result, an English speaker's reaction may be to back away to reach a comfortable speaking distance. However, the Spanish speaker will probably react by stepping forward to regain his or her own preferred conversational distance.

For a Spanish speaker, direct eye contact during conversation indicates interest and sincerity. Often, a Spanish speaker may touch the arm, shoulder or lapel of a friend during a conversation. It is not uncommon for women to walk arm in arm, especially mothers and daughters, and teenage girls who are close friends. It is also socially acceptable for a young man to put his arm around the shoulder of a male friend as they walk along and talk.

J. Un conflicto cultural. Anita and Carlos meet Kelly, an American exchange student, at a party. They greet her, introduce themselves, and ask her where she is from. They also ask her age, how many brothers and sisters she has, and if she has a boyfriend. Anita and Carlos stand quite close to Kelly while they are talking with her, but soon they begin to feel that something is wrong with Kelly because every time they look directly at her, she seems uncomfortable when she answers their questions.

1. What is wrong here?
2. What should Anita, Carlos, or Kelly do?

GRAMÁTICA FUNCIONAL

Describing daily activities

—¿Dónde vives aquí en México, Carlos?
—Vivo en un apartamento en la Colonia Roma.
—¿Qué haces los domingos por la tarde?
—Descanso y leo periódicos.

Present tense of regular -er and -ir verbs

To form the present tense of Spanish infinitives ending in -er and -ir, add a personal ending to their verb stem.

Point out how *deber* is used with an infinitive for expressing "ought to do something." Write several examples on the chalkboard to illustrate your explanation.

Emphasize that the verb *leer* retains the *le* in its present tense conjugation: *leo, lees,* etc.

	com + er	**viv + ir**
(yo)	com**o**	viv**o**
(tú)	com**es**	viv**es**
(usted, él/ella)	com**e**	viv**e**
(nosotros/nosotras)	com**emos**	viv**imos**
(vosotros/vosotras)	*com**éis***	*viv**ís***
(ustedes, ellos/ellas)	com**en**	viv**en**

Study these useful -er and -ir verbs with the example phrases:

aprender mucho	*to learn a lot*
beber café	*to drink coffee*
comer en casa	*to eat at home*
comprender bien	*to understand well*
deber estudiar	*ought to study*
escribir una carta	*to write a letter*
leer un periódico	*to read a newspaper*
recibir un abrazo	*to receive a hug*
vivir en una casa	*to live in a house*

Present tense of *hacer*

The present tense of *hacer* (to do, to make) is formed exactly like regular verbs ending in -er, except the *yo* form.

	hac + er
(yo)	ha**go**
(tú)	hac**es**
(usted, él/ella)	hac**e**
(nosotros/nosotras)	hac**emos**
(vosotros/vosotras)	*hac**éis***
(ustedes, ellos/ellas)	hac**en**

Practiquemos

Ex. A. Encourage your students to provide their own solutions for the problems if they are able to do so in Spanish.

A. Problemas y soluciones. Lea los problemas de unos amigos de Carlos y Anita. Luego diga una solución apropiada.

Ejemplo: Luisa no come por la mañana;...
    *Luisa no come por la mañana; **debe** comer un poco de fruta.*

Problemas	Soluciones
1. Beto no tiene trabajo ahora;	comer un poco de fruta.
2. Pilar no comprende a su madre;	estudiar sus lecciones.
3. María trabaja mucho día y noche;	descansar los domingos.
4. Pablo tiene problemas emocionales;	hablar con un siquiatra.
5. Ramona no es una buena estudiante;	charlar con ella en casa.
6. Félix no tiene muchos amigos;	hacer amigos en la escuela.
	tomar clases en una escuela.

Ex. B. No. 10: Remind students how two Spanish verbs can be placed together; the first verb *(debes)* is conjugated, and the second verb *(hacer)* is an infinitive.

B. Charla con un amigo. Anita habla con su amigo Carlos. ¿Qué dice él?

Ejemplo: ANITA: ¿Dónde vives? (Colonia Roma)
    CARLOS: *Vivo en la Colonia Roma.*

Anita	Carlos
1. ¿Con quién vives, Carlos?	con un compañero de cuarto
2. ¿A qué hora comes?	a las 2:00 de la tarde
3. ¿Qué comes normalmente?	sándwiches
4. ¿Bebes mucha Coca-Cola?	No,... mucho café
5. ¿Aprendes mucho en la UNAM?	Sí... ¿Y tú?
6. ¿Dónde lees normalmente?	en la biblioteca
7. ¿Escribes mucho también?	Sí,... en una computadora
8. ¿Qué haces los domingos?	No ____ mucho los domingos.
9. ¿Qué haces mañana?	muchas actividades
10. Pero ¿qué debes hacer?	estudiar para un examen

Ex. C. Answers: 1. *vivimos, vive, viven* 2. *recibimos, recibe, recibo, recibir* 3. *como, come, comemos, come* 4. *leemos, lee, leo* 5. *hacemos, hace, hago*

C. Compañeros de cuarto. Complete los siguientes párrafos con las formas apropiadas de los verbos entre paréntesis para saber un poco de Carlos y su compañero de cuarto.

1. **(vivir)** Mi compañero de cuarto se llama Tomás Rodríguez. Tomás y yo _____ en un apartamento en Colonia Roma. La familia de Tomás _____ en Oaxaca en el sur de México. Sus hermanos son jóvenes y _____ en casa.
2. **(recibir)** Tomás y yo _____ cartas de nuestras familias. Tomás _____ muchas y yo _____ pocas. Debo _____ más cartas de mi familia, ¿verdad?
3. **(comer)** Por la tarde yo _____ en la cafetería de la UNAM. Tomás _____ en el hotel donde trabaja. Por la noche _____ juntos en nuestro apartamento. Los domingos Tomás _____ con la familia de su novia Lupita.
4. **(leer)** Tomás y yo _____ mucho por la noche. Tomás _____ periódicos políticos y yo _____ mis libros de texto.
5. **(hacer)** Los sábados y domingos Tomás y yo _____ diferentes actividades. Tomás _____ actividades con Lupita y yo _____ actividades con mis compañeros de la universidad.

D. Dos compañeros. Complete el párrafo con la forma correcta de los infinitivos.

ser	comer	estudiar
tener	vivir	aprender
beber	hablar	comprender

¡Hola! Me llamo Anita. *Vivo* en México, D.F. _____ estudiante de la UNAM donde _____ para ser intérprete. _____ mucho en mis clases. _____ un amigo que se llama Carlos Suárez. _____ un compañero en la clase de inglés. Cuando nuestro profesor _____ rápidamente en inglés, Carlos no _____ bien. Mi amigo _____ mucho pero el inglés _____ difícil. Carlos y yo _____ en la cafetería donde también _____ café y _____ sándwiches.

E. Diálogo escrito. José Camacho, Anita's father, wants to know more about his daughter's new friend, Carlos Suárez. Write a dialogue between José and Carlos, using the cues below and the infinitives in parenthesis to guide you. Search through this lesson and the previous one to find the information you need for Carlos' responses. Use *usted* verb forms when Carlos speaks to José, and *tú* verb forms when José speaks to Carlos.

José wants to know . . .

- where Carlos is from. **(ser de)**
- what his family is like. **(ser)**
- where he lives now. **(vivir)**
- what he is studying at school. **(estudiar)**
- how many classes he is taking. **(tomar)**

F. Actividades diarias. Diga lo que usted y otras personas hacen y no hacen.

Ejemplos: *No bebo Coca-Cola en clase.*
    Mi familia bebe Coca-Cola en casa.

¿Quién?	**¿Qué?**	**¿Dónde?**
(yo)	comer nachos	en casa
mi familia	leer literatura	en clase
amigo(a), tú	beber Coca-Cola	en la escuela
mis compañeros	aprender español	en la cafetería
mis amigos y yo	escribir en inglés	en la biblioteca

G. Entrevista. Pregúntele a un(a) compañero(a) de clase.

1. ¿Dónde vives ahora? ¿Con quién vives? ¿Cuál es tu dirección?
2. ¿Tienes muchas o pocas clases? ¿Cuántas? ¿Son difíciles o fáciles?
3. ¿Aprendes mucho o poco en nuestra clase de español? ¿Debes estudiar mucho para nuestros exámenes? En general, ¿eres un(a) estudiante bueno(a) o malo(a)?
4. ¿Lees mucho o poco? ¿Qué lees frecuentemente? ¿Lees novelas históricas o novelas románticas?
5. Por la tarde, ¿comes en la cafetería o en casa? ¿Comes mucho o poco, normalmente? ¿Comes sándwiches? ¿Bebes café?
6. ¿Qué haces los sábados y domingos?

PARA LEER MEJOR

Skimming and Scanning

Two useful reading strategies are skimming and scanning. When skimming reading material, we read it quickly to get the gist or general idea of its content. Often we reread the same material and scan it to find specific information.

Activities

A. Skim the four descriptions below to get a general understanding of what they are about. Then answer the following questions.

1. What are these descriptions about?
2. What do you suppose their purpose is?
3. Where do you think they were published?

Nombre: Marco Luis Corona
Dirección: Egido 624, Apt. 2, entre Paula y San Usidro, Habana Vieja, CUBA
Edad: 20 años
Pasatiempos: Escuchar música, leer, coleccionar fotos de artistas y hacer amistades.

Nombre: Noelia Barrera Alba
Dirección: El Miramar, Apartado 3 Norte, C.P. 4300 Durango, Dgo. MÉXICO
Edad: 16 años
Pasatiempos: Tocar instrumentos musicales, salir, leer poemas e intercambiar correspondencia con chicos y chicas de todo el mundo.

Nombre: Rosario Inés Arias
Dirección: Calle Variante No. 3, Código Postal 4150, Mirimire, Edo. Falcón, VENEZUELA
Edad: 17 años
Pasatiempos: Coleccionar postales, billetes, calcomanías, monedas y todo lo referente a mis ídolos Chayane, Luis Miguel y Patrick Swayze. También me gusta leer, escuchar música, escribir, escalar montañas e ir a los ríos y playas.

Nombre: Susana Prado Rivera
Dirección: Calle Guadalajara No. 5-2475, Panamá, REPÚBLICA DE PANAMÁ
Edad: 18 años
Pasatiempos: Coleccionar postales, estampillas y todo lo relacionado con Chayanne, leer libros, oír música variada, aprender todo lo referente a las ciencias, especialmente la medicina, mantener correspondencia con chicos de otros países y practicar deportes.

B. Scan the descriptions to find the information asked for in the following questions.

1. What is the first name of the oldest person described?
2. Who enjoys . . .
   a. collecting stamps?
   b. listening to music?
   c. climbing mountains?
   d. collecting postcards?
   e. playing musical instruments?
   f. music by the rock star Chayanne?
3. Which person would you like to have as a pen friend, and why?

PARA ESCRIBIR MEJOR

Learning Spanish Word Order

Word order refers to the meaningful sequence of words in a sentence. The order of words in Spanish sentences differs somewhat from English word order. Some common rules of Spanish word order are:

- Definite and indefinite articles precede nouns.
  Los gatos *y* **los perros** *son animales.*
  Tengo **un gato** *y* **un perro.**
- Subjects usually precede their verbs in statements.
  Mi gato es *negro.*
- Subjects usually follow their verbs in questions.
  *¿***Tiene usted** *animales en casa?*
- Adjectives of quantity usually precede nouns.
  *¿***Cuántos animales** *tienes en casa?*
- Adjectives of description usually follow nouns.
  El **perro marrón** *se llama Bandido.*
- Possession is often expressed by using *de* with a noun.
  Café **es el gato de Sara.**

Activity

1. Unscramble the words in the following sentences, then rewrite them in their correct sequence. Be sure to capitalize the first word of every sentence and to end each one with a period.

Example: es Anita Camacho de México
           Anita Camacho es de México.

   a. es Anita una universitaria estudiante
   b. Carlos Suárez su clase compañero se llama de
   c. Carlos un poco y Anita hablan de inglés
   d. años tienen cuántos ellos ¿?
   e. Carlos veintitrés tiene y tiene diecinueve Anita
   f. tiene Anita hermanos ¿?

2. Now work with a classmate. Compare your sentences and check for errors in word order, spelling, capitalization, and punctuation.

Atajo

Functions:
Writing a letter (informal); introducing; describing people

Vocabulary:
Family members; numbers; animals: domestic; colors; university

Grammar:
Verbs: *ser, tener;*
Possession with *de;*
Adjectives: agreement, position

¿A qué nivel está Ud.?

Veo Veo, ¿Qué cosita ves? In order to play this game you need to know the vocabulary for colors: Which color do you associate with a school bus?
Review the chapter and then monitor your progress by completing the *Autoprueba* at the end of *Lección 2* in the *Workbook/Lab Manual.*

SÍNTESIS

¡A ver!

You are going to see a typical scene of two grandparents who visit their relatives and have lunch with them. First, study the words and phrases and their meaning in the *Vocabulario esencial*. Then read the seven statements in the activity. Third, watch the videotape, then indicate whether the statements are true *(cierto)* or false *(falso)*.

Vocabulario esencial

abuela	*grandmother*
abuelo	*grandfather*
¿Qué tal la escuela?	*How's school?*
A ver.	*Let's see.*
llevar a los niños al parque	*to take the children to the park*
Como tu quieras.	*As you wish.*

	cierto	falso
1. Pepito tiene una hermana.	——	——
2. La abuela es muy simpática.	——	——
3. El esposo de Laura es anciano.	——	——
4. Hay un perro negro en la casa.	——	——
5. El abuelo es el padre de Laura.	——	——
6. Marcos y Laura tienen tres niños.	——	——
7. Hay mucho amor (love) en esta familia.	——	——

Visit

http://poco.heinle.com

¡A leer!

¿Comprendió Ud.?

1. Scan the zodiac chart that follows to locate the signs and descriptive adjectives for the following people, and decide whether or not the descriptions are accurate in your opinion.

a. yo
b. mi papá
c. mi mamá
d. mi hermano
e. mi hermana
f. mi amigo(a)

SÍNTESIS

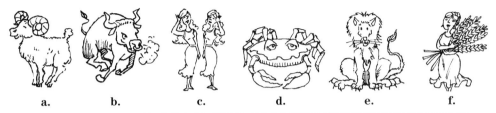

a.   b.   c.   d.   e.   f.

ARIES: rápidos, ágiles, impacientes, impulsivos.
TAURO: sensibles, sensuales, artísticos, exuberantes.
GEMINIS: curiosos, observadores, adaptables, habladores.
CANCER: sensitivos, ingeniosos, tímidos, cambiantes.
LEO: extrovertidos, voluntariosos, exigentes, generosos.
VIRGO: analíticos, intolerantes, autocríticos, aprensivos.
LIBRA: estéticos, refinados, conciliadores, cooperadores.
ESCORPION: compulsivos, magnéticos, posesivos, leales.
SAGITARIO: ambiciosos, entusiastas, francos, alegres.
CAPRICORNIO: conservadores, juiciosos, reservados.
ACUARIO: excéntricos, independientes, humanitarios.
PISCIS: delicados, imaginativos, intuitivos, soñadores.

g.   h.   i.   j.   k.   l.

2. Skim the Gemini horoscope to get the gist of the information it contains.
   Then answer the questions that follow.

---

géminis

Amor: Estará muy bien aspectado, disfrútalo. **Amigos:** Estarás rodeada de ellos y serás el centro de atención. **Casa:** Tus padres depositarán su confianza en ti, y tendrás más libertad. **Un consejo:** Un triunfo no significa la victoria, esfuérzate. **No te pases con:** Los gritos. **Suerte en:** Los grupos. **Bien con:** Sagitario y Acuario.

---

a. In general, is the horoscope positive or negative?
b. Does it describe someone you know? If so, is he or she a Gemini?
c. How does it compare to the adjectives given in the zodiac chart for Gemini?

SÍNTESIS

¡A conversar!

Role-play the following situations in Spanish with a classmate.

Follow-up activities:
1. Ask students to report at least two things they learned about their conversation partner. 2. Have students write an original dialogue based on this activity. 3. Students could play the role of reporters. Provide them with a tape recorder and have them use it to interview their classmates. 4. Invite students to create their own scenario or skit based on information they used in this activity; you could give students extra credit for doing so.

Estudiante A

1. Greet your classmate.

3. Respond, then ask the same question.

5. Respond appropriately, then introduce yourself.

7. Answer, then ask the same question.

9. Acknowledge the comments. Then say something about the people you live with.

11. Answer the question, if you wish. Then ask the same questions.

Estudiante B

2. Answer appropriately, then ask how he or she is.

4. Answer the question, then introduce yourself.

6. Respond, then ask your friend where he or she is from.

8. Respond, then say where you live and describe the people you live with.

10. Find out your friend's age.

12. Answer the questions, if you think they aren't too personal.

Atajo

¡A escribir!

Write a short letter to a classmate you don't know well.
In your letter, . . .

1. write an appropriate greeting.
2. introduce yourself, stating your name and age.
3. say where you live and include your address and phone number.
4. briefly describe yourself, your parents, your brothers and sisters, your instructors, your classmates, and your friends.
5. end with an appropriate leave-taking expression.

VOCABULARIO

Sustantivos

el (la) bebé *baby*
la carta *letter*
la edad *age*
el parque *park*
el periódico *newspaper*

La familia

la hermana *sister*
la hermanastra *stepsister*
el hermanastro *stepbrother*
el hermano *brother*
la madrastra *stepmother*
la madre *mother*
el padrastro *stepfather*
el padre *father*
los padres *parents*

Los animales

el gato *cat*
el perro *dog*

Las características físicas

alto *tall*
anciano *elderly*
bajo *short (in height)*
bonito *pretty*
delgado *thin*
feo *ugly*
gordo *fat*
grande *large, big*
guapo *good-looking*
joven *young*
nuevo *new*
pequeño *small, little*
viejo *old*

La personalidad

adaptable *adaptable*
ambicioso *ambitious*
antipático *unpleasant*
artístico *artistic*

bueno *good*
dramático *dramatic*
generoso *generous*
honesto *honest*
intelectual *intellectual*
inteligente *intelligent*
intuitivo *intuitive*
malo *bad*
paciente *patient*
perezoso *lazy*
próspero *prosperous*
reservado *reserved*
simpático *nice*
sincero *sincere*
tacaño *stingy*
tolerante *tolerant*
trabajador *hardworking*

Los colores

amarillo *yellow*
anaranjado *orange*
azul *blue*
blanco *white*
gris *gray*
marrón *brown*
negro *black*
rojo *red*
rosado *pink*
verde *green*

Adjetivos posesivos

mi(s) *my*
nuestro(a,os,as) *our*
su(s) *his, her, your (formal), its*
tu(s) *your (informal)*

Otros adjetivos

atlético *athletic*
bilingüe *bilingual*
español *Spaniard, Spanish*
gemelo *twin*
mejor *best*
mexicano *Mexican*

Preguntas

¿Cuál? ¿Cuáles? *What? Which one(s)?*
¿De quién? ¿De quiénes? *Whose?*

Verbos

aprender *to learn*
beber *to drink*
comer *to eat*
comprender *to understand*
deber (+ infinitive) *ought to, should*
escribir *to write*
hacer *to do, to make*
leer *to read*
recibir *to receive*
tener *to have*
vivir *to live*

Los números

cuarenta *forty*
cincuenta *fifty*
sesenta *sixty*
setenta *seventy*
ochenta *eighty*
noventa *ninety*

Expresiones idiomáticas

¡Claro que sí! *Of course!*
hoy día *nowadays*

¿Quieres salir conmigo?

▶ COMMUNICATIVE GOALS

You will be able to discuss how you, your friends, and your family spend your free time.

▶ LANGUAGE FUNCTIONS

Making invitations
Expressing likes and dislikes
Expressing plans and intentions
Describing leisure-time activities
Accepting and declining invitations

▶ VOCABULARY THEMES

Pastimes and sports
Months of the year

▶ GRAMMATICAL STRUCTURES

Present tense of the verb *ir* + *a(l)*
Present tense of other irregular *yo* verbs
Personal *a*
The verb *gustar* + infinitive

▶ CULTURAL INFORMATION

Sports in the Spanish-speaking world

http://poco.heinle.com

Atajo

VIDEO

EN CONTEXTO

 Play Lab Tape

Have students form pairs and act out this conversation together.

Hoy es miércoles el veintiséis de septiembre. Ahora Carlos Suárez está en una cabina telefónica en el Zócalo.(1) Está hablando con su amiga Anita Camacho, que está en casa.

ANITA: Bueno.(2)

CARLOS: ¡Hola, Anita! Habla Carlos.

ANITA: Carlos, ¿qué tal?

CARLOS: Muy bien, gracias. Y tú, ¿cómo estás?

ANITA: Bastante bien. ¿Qué hay de nuevo?

CARLOS: Oye,(3) Anita, hay un concierto esta noche en Bellas Artes.(4) ¿Quieres ir?° *Do you want to go?*

ANITA: Ay, Carlos... no puedo.° Esta noche voy a° comer con mi familia en la Zona Rosa(5) y luego vamos al cine.° *I can't/I'm going / to the movies*

CARLOS: ¡Qué interesante! Bueno, ¿quieres salir° conmigo el domingo? Voy al Parque de Chapultepec.(6) *to go out*

ANITA: El domingo... el domingo... ¡Claro que sí! Me gusta mucho Chapultepec. ¿A qué hora vamos?

CARLOS: Por la tarde... paso por ti° a la una. Vamos en el metro(7) y luego comemos en el Museo de Antropología.(8) ¿Qué te parece?° *I'll pick you up / What do you think?*

ANITA: ¡Perfecto! Muchas gracias por la invitación, Carlos. Eres muy simpático.

CARLOS: De nada.° Hasta el domingo, Anita. *You're welcome*

ANITA: Hasta el domingo.

Notas de texto

1. *El Zócalo* is considered to be at the exact center of Mexico City. It is the former site of important Aztec temples, pyramids, and religious ceremonies. Today visitors can see the ruins of this ancient civilization as well as the National Cathedral and several government buildings that contain giant murals that depict the history of Mexico.

1. Use your knowledge and experience to add more information to these cultural notes.
2. If you have audio-visual materials to accompany these notes, use them in class to reinforce this information.

2. Spanish speakers use different expressions to answer the telephone, depending on the country they are from. Mexicans say *Bueno,* Cubans say *Oiga,* Spaniards say *Dígame,* and people from other Spanish-speaking countries say *Aló* or *Hola.*

3. *Oye* (literally "hear") is an expression that Spanish speakers use to signal someone to listen carefully. It is the equivalent of English "listen" as in the statement: "Listen, I want to tell you something."

4. *El Palacio de Bellas Artes* is a concert hall where performances of the famous *Ballet Folklórico de México* are held. The hall also contains an excellent collection of paintings by renowned Mexican artists such as Tamayo, Orozco, and Siqueiros.

5. *La Zona Rosa* or "The Pink Zone" is a fashionable shopping district in the heart of Mexico City where you can find chic boutiques, elegant hotels, and a wide variety of ethnic restaurants. Also located there is the *Instituto Mexicano Norteamericano de Relaciones Culturales,* where Mexicans study English and people from many countries study Spanish.

6. *El Parque de Chapultepec* is a large and impressive park located in the center of Mexico City. It is named in honor of the Aztec Indian god, Chapultepec, meaning "grasshopper" in the Náhuatl language. There are many attractions in the park, including the *Museo de Arte Moderno* and the famous *Museo Nacional de Antropología e Historia de México.* Atop a hill overlooking Mexico City is Chapultepec Castle, which was once an ancient Aztec fortress, and was later converted into an official residence for the presidents of Mexico. The *Parque de Chapultepec* also has a large lake where visitors can rent rowboats and paddleboats to spend a pleasant afternoon.

El metro es un medio de transporte importante en México, D.F. porque millones de personas lo usan diariamente. La estación de Bellas Artes está en el centro de la ciudad, muy cerca del Palacio de Bellas Artes y de algunos museos interesantes.

7. Mexico City has a clean, efficient, and inexpensive subway system that millions of people use daily to commute to and from work and school and to visit many attractions that the capital has to offer. Each subway station has a different symbol representing its name so that people who cannot read can easily identify the station they are looking for.

8. The *Museo Nacional de Antropología e Historia de México* has a first-class restaurant where visitors can enjoy a refreshment or have lunch indoors or on the outdoor terrace. The servers dress in colorful regional costumes of Mexico.

¿Comprendió Ud.?

Correct the following false statements, based on your comprehension of the conversation above and the cultural notes that follow it.

1. Hay un concierto en el Zócalo.
2. Anita sale con Carlos esta noche.
3. Ahora Anita está en Bellas Artes.
4. No hay restaurantes en la Zona Rosa.
5. Carlos invita a Anita y a su familia.
6. Los dos compañeros van a Chapultepec a pie.
7. El sábado Carlos y Anita salen para el parque.
8. No hay restaurantes en el Parque de Chapultepec.

TRANSPARENCY No. 8A:
Leisure Activities

1. Ask your students to bring large color photographs of the pastimes presented here. Two excellent sources are magazines and brochures. Laminate the photographs, then use them to teach pastimes and to review the names of colors.
2. Tell students that another word for *cartas* is *(los) naipes.* You might also teach them *el juego de cartas (naipes)* = card game.
3. The verb *salir* is introduced and practiced in this section in its infinitive form as well as *tú* form. Students will learn the irregular *yo* form *(salgo)* later in this lesson.

VOCABULARIO ÚTIL

Cómo conversar sobre pasatiempos

In this section you will learn to describe some leisure activities that you and others enjoy, and to make, accept, and decline invitations.

—¿Qué te gusta hacer?
—Me gusta...

Los pasatiempos

ir al cine   **ir de compras**   **bailar en las fiestas**   **salir con los amigos**

mirar la televisión   **ver películas en video**   **sacar fotos**   **jugar a las cartas en video**

> **¡CUIDADO!** The verb *jugar* means to play a game or a sport, and the verb *tocar* means to play a musical instrument, a stereo, a radio, or a tape recorder.

visitar a los abuelos   **tocar la guitarra y cantar**

4. The infinitive *jugar* and its verb forms will be followed by the preposition *a* throughout the **Poco a poco** program (except when Latin Americans are speaking in a dialogue) as is common in Spain.

5. The word *abuelos* is introduced here for the first time. Tell students the meaning of *abuelo* and *abuela*, and have them guess the meaning of *abuelos*. You might like to review the words for other family members: *padre, padrastro, madre, madrastra, hermano, hermanastro, hermana, hermanastra.*

6. Teacher talk: Use the drawings to describe what these people like to do; for example: *A José y a Pilar les gusta ir al cine.* Your students will understand you even though they have not studied this formally because they have already learned *Me gusta* and *Te gusta.*

Ex. A.

1. This activity recycles the *(no) me gusta* + infinitive construction.

2. Point out the differences between *el televisor* vs *la televisión*, and *el radio* vs *la radio*.

3. Encourage your students to continue this activity using the *-ar, -er,* and *-ir* verbs with words they learned in previous lessons.

Ex. B.

1. No. 8: Students use only the regular *tú* form *(sales)* of *salir* to ask the question; the answer will be either *sí* or *no.* The irregular *yo* form *(salgo)* is introduced later in this lesson.

2. Once the data has been gathered, you could poll the class.

Ex. C.

1. No. 1: Students should be able to guess the meaning of the cognate *discos compactos* (compact disks or CDs).

2. No. 2: If you wish, give names of other musical instruments; for example: *el saxofón, la trompeta, el clarinete, la flauta, el órgano, el violoncello, la armónica.*

3. You may want to ask your students whether they would like to do some of these activities; for example: *¿Le (te) gustaría tocar un instrumento musical?*

1. Emphasize that the months of the year are **not** capitalized in Spanish.

2. Tell students that some Spanish speakers spell *septiembre* without the *p: setiembre.*

3. Point out that Spaniards use the cardinal number *uno* with dates, except in business transactions in which case they use *primero.*

A. Preferencias. Exprese sus preferencias con un(a) compañero(a) de clase.

Ejemplos: *Me gusta ir al cine frecuentemente.*
                 No me gusta cantar cuando escucho la radio.

	ir al cine frecuentemente
	cantar cuando escucho la radio
	salir con mis amigos los viernes
Me gusta...	mirar la televisión por la noche
No me gusta...	escuchar música rock en la radio
	jugar a las cartas con mi familia
	ver películas violentas en la tele
	hablar por teléfono con mis amigos
	ir de compras los días que no trabajo

B. ¿Sí o No? Pregúnteles a sus compañeros de clase sobre sus pasatiempos.

Ejemplo: bailar en las fiestas
                —*¿Bailas en las fiestas?*
                —*Sí.*
                —*Escribe tu nombre aquí, por favor.*

Nombre

1. bailar en las fiestas _____
2. leer novelas románticas _____
3. sacar fotos de tus amigos _____
4. tocar un instrumento musical _____
5. descansar los fines de semana _____
6. ver muchas películas en video _____
7. escuchar música *rap* en la radio _____
8. salir con tus amigos frecuentemente _____

C. ¿Te gusta la música? Pregúntele a otro(a) compañero(a) de clase.

1. ¿Te gusta escuchar la música? ¿Qué tipo de música te gusta escuchar más: música clásica o jazz? ¿Tienes pocas o muchas cintas de música? ¿Tienes muchos o pocos discos compactos?

2. ¿Tocas la guitarra, el piano, el violín u otro instrumento musical? ¿Qué instrumento quieres aprender a tocar: la guitarra, el piano, el violín u otro instrumento?

Los meses del año

> **¡CUIDADO!** In Spanish, the months of the year are **not** capitalized.

English speakers usually use ordinal numbers (first, second, third) to express dates with days of the month (e.g., second of October). But Spanish speakers use ordinal numbers only to refer to the first day of the month; for example: *el primero de enero* = January 1st. Otherwise, they use cardinal numbers *(dos, cinco, quince)* with dates; for example: *el dos de octubre* = October 2nd. To say what happens **on** a certain date, use *el* with the date; for example: *el cinco de mayo* = on May 5th.

enero	febrero	marzo	abril
L M M J V S D	L M M J V S D	L M M J V S D	L M M J V S D
1 2	1 2 3 4	1 2	1 2 3
3 4 5 6 7 8 9	7 8 9 10 11 12 13	6 7 8 9 10 11 12	4 5 6 7 8 9 10
10 11 12 13 14 15 16	14 15 16 17 18 19 20	13 14 15 16 17 18 19	11 12 13 14 15 16 17
17 18 19 20 21 22 23	21 22 23 24 25 26 27	20 21 22 23 24 25 26	18 19 20 21 22 23 24
24/31 25 26 27 28 29 30	28	27 28 29 30 31	25 26 27 28 29 30

mayo	junio	julio	agosto
L M M J V S D	L M M J V S D	L M M J V S D	L M M J V S D
1	1 2 3 4 5	1 2 3	1 2 3 4 5 6 7
2 3 4 5 6 7 8	6 7 8 9 10 11 12	4 5 6 7 8 9 10	8 9 10 11 12 13 14
9 10 11 12 13 14 15	13 14 15 16 17 18 19	11 12 13 14 15 16 17	15 16 17 18 19 20 21
16 17 18 19 20 21 22	20 21 22 23 24 25 26	18 19 20 21 22 23 24	22 23 24 25 26 27 28
23/24 25 26 27 28 29 /30/31	27 28 29 30	25 26 27 28 29 30 31	29 30 31

septiembre	octubre	noviembre	diciembre
L M M J V S D	L M M J V S D	L M M J V S D	L M M J V S D
1 2 3 4	1 2	1 2 3 4 5 6	1 2 3 4
5 6 7 8 9 10 11	3 4 5 6 7 8 9	7 8 9 10 11 12 13	5 6 7 8 9 10 11
12 13 14 15 16 17 18	10 11 12 13 14 15 16	14 15 16 17 18 19 20	12 13 14 15 16 17 18
19 20 21 22 23 24 25	17 18 19 20 21 22 23	21 22 23 24 25 26 27	19 20 21 22 23 24 25
26 27 28 29 30	24/31 25 26 27 28 29 30	28 29 30	26 27 28 29 30 31

Cómo invitar

—Voy a tener una fiesta.	*I'm going to have a party.*
—¿En qué fecha?	*On what date?*
—El treinta de noviembre.	*On November 30th.*
—Ay, no puedo ir.	*Gee, I can't go.*
—¿Quieres ir al cine?	*¿Do you want to go to the movies?*
—¿Cuándo?	*When?*
—Esta noche.	*Tonight.*
—No puedo ir hoy.	*I can't go today.*
—Vamos este fin de semana.	*Let's go this weekend.*
—Bien. Gracias.	*Okay. Thanks.*
—De nada.	*You're welcome.*

Practiquemos

D. Los días festivos. Complete las frases con los meses y las fechas apropiados.

1. El Día del Trabajo es en ___(mes)___ .
2. El Día del Padre es en ___(mes)___ .
3. El Día de la Madre es en ___(mes)___ .
4. El Día de San Patricio es en ___(mes)___ .
5. El Día de Dar Gracias es en ___(mes)___ .
6. El Día del Año Nuevo es el ___(#)___ de ___(mes)___ .
7. El Día de San Valentín es el ___(#)___ de ___(mes)___ .
8. El Día de la Independencia de los Estados Unidos es el ___(#)___ de ___(mes)___ .

E. Una invitación. Imagínese que usted está hablando con un(a) compañero(a) de clase por teléfono. Complete la siguiente conversación y luego practíquela con otro(a) estudiante.

TRANSPARENCY No. 8B:
Sports

1. Activity: Pantomime the following sports, and ask your students to say aloud the name of each one: *nadar, pescar, correr, esquiar, patinar, hacer ejercicio, montar a caballo, montar en bicicleta, jugar al básquetbol.*
2. Additional sports are: *las artes marciales, el básquetbol, (el baloncesto), el béisbol, el juego de boliche (bolos), las carreras, el ciclismo, la equitación, el esquí (acuático), el fútbol, el fútbol norteamericano, el rugby, la gimnasia, el golf, el trote, la lucha, la natación, el paracaidismo, el tenis, la vela, el vólibol, el yoga.*

Estudiante A

1. ¿Aló?

3. _____ . Y tú, ¿cómo estás?

5. ¿Una fiesta? ¿Cuándo?

7. ¿A qué hora?

9. Perfecto, gracias, (nombre).

11. _____ .

Estudiante B

2. ¡Hola, _____ (el nombre de su amigo/a)! Habla _____ . ¿Qué tal?

4. _____ . Oye, ¿quieres ir a una fiesta?

6. El (#) de mes.

8. A la(s) _____ . ¿Qué te parece?

10. De _____ . ¡ Hasta _____ !

Los deportes

¿Qué te gusta hacer?

hacer ejercicio   jugar al tenis   montar en bicicleta   nadar en la piscina

correr en el parque   caminar el domingo   pescar   esquiar

patinar   montar a caballo

Practiquemos

F. Preferencias. Dígale a un(a) compañero(a) de clase unos deportes que a usted le gustan. Los tres puntos (...) indican otras posibilidades que usted prefiere comunicar.

Me gusta...
correr por la mañana (por la tarde / ...)
montar en mi bicicleta roja (azul / ...)
hacer ejercicio en un gimnasio (en casa / en ...)
pescar con mis amigos (con mi hermano[a] / con ...)
esquiar en Colorado (en el Canadá / en Vermont / en ...)
jugar al béisbol (al básquetbol / al vólibol / al ...)

G. Deportes favoritos. Pregúntele a otro(a) estudiante.

1. ¿Cuál es tu deporte favorito? ¿Qué otro deporte te gusta mucho?
2. ¿Esquías? (¿Sí? ¿Dónde esquías? ¿Con quién esquías? ¿En qué meses esquías?)
3. ¿Nadas bien o mal? ¿Dónde y con quién te gusta nadar? ¿Cuándo nadas?
4. ¿Pescas frecuentemente o no? (¿Dónde pescas? ¿En qué meses?)
5. ¿Montas a caballo? (¿Sí? ¿Es fácil o difícil montar a caballo? ¿Es más fácil montar a caballo o montar en bicicleta?)
6. ¿Haces mucho o poco ejercicio? ¿Qué tipo *(kind)* de ejercicio haces? ¿Dónde haces ejercicio normalmente?

H. ¡A nadar! Hable con un(a) compañero(a) de clase.

Estudiante A	**Estudiante B**
1. ¿Quieres ir a nadar?	2. ¿Dónde?
3. _____.	4. ¿Cuándo?
5. El (#) de (mes).	6. Ay, no puedo. ¿Es posible el (#) de (mes)?
7. ¿Qué día de la semana es?	8. _____.
9. ¡Sí, puedo ir!	

No me gustan ni los pasatiempos ni los deportes. Me gusta descansar en mi hamaca.

3. If you wish, introduce *patinar sobre hielo* (to ice skate) and *patinar sobre ruedas* (to roller skate).
4. Tell students that in Mexico the word for *piscina* is *alberca*.

Ex. G. No. 6. Remind students of the irregular form *hago*, which they learned in *Lección 2*. The present tense forms of *hacer* are reviewed and practiced later in this lesson.

Two related topics that you might like to discuss with your students are: (1) the large number of professional baseball players on U.S. teams, and (2) the Hispanic Baseball Association.

to begin

praise
with whom
on the contrary
in regard / work

to avoid / comparisons
between

NOTAS CULTURALES

Al comenzar° una conversación

Las personas de Latinoamérica y de España muchas veces comienzan una conversación con una frase de elogio° sobre el país, la ciudad o el pueblo de la persona con quien° hablan. También, las personas hacen preguntas sobre la familia de la persona. De lo contrario,° en los Estados Unidos y en Canadá, los estadounidenses y los canadienses muchas veces hacen preguntas con respecto° al trabajo° que hace la persona, por ejemplo: ¿En qué trabaja Ud.?

Es importante, al comenzar una conversación, de evitar° comparaciones° políticas o económicas entre° su país y el país de la persona con quien Ud. habla.

¿Qué dice usted? Conteste las siguientes preguntas.

1. ¿Qué deportes son populares en su ciudad, estado o provincia?
2. ¿Qué deportes son especialmente importantes en su escuela o universidad?

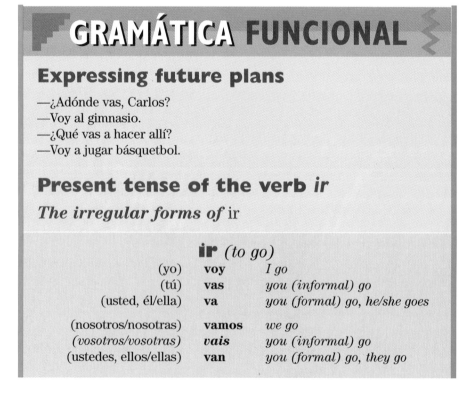

GRAMÁTICA FUNCIONAL

Expressing future plans

—¿Adónde vas, Carlos?
—Voy al gimnasio.
—¿Qué vas a hacer allí?
—Voy a jugar básquetbol.

Present tense of the verb *ir*

The irregular forms of ir

	ir *(to go)*	
(yo)	**voy**	*I go*
(tú)	**vas**	*you (informal) go*
(usted, él/ella)	**va**	*you (formal) go, he/she goes*
(nosotros/nosotras)	**vamos**	*we go*
(vosotros/vosotras)	***vais***	*you (informal) go*
(ustedes, ellos/ellas)	**van**	*you (formal) go, they go*

Uses of these forms

1. To tell where people are going, use a form of the verb *ir* plus the preposition *a*, followed by a destination.

—¿Adónde **van** ustedes?	*Where are you going?*
—**Voy a la piscina.**	*I'm going to the pool.*
—Y yo **voy al parque.**	*And I'm going to the park.*

Remember: The definite article *el* (the) combines with the preposition *a* (to) to form the word *al* (to the), as in the second example above.

2. To express future plans, use a form of the verb *ir* plus the preposition *a*, followed by an infinitive.

| —¿Qué **vas a hacer** ahora? | *What are you going to do now?* |
| —**Voy a jugar** al tenis. | *I'm going to play tennis.* |

Tell students that the *ir a* + infinitive construction functions exactly like the *deber* + infinitive construction: the first verb is conjugated, and the second verb retains its infinitive form. Example: *Debo estudiar ahora. / Voy a estudiar ahora.*

Practiquemos

A. Una invitación. Complete esta conversación, usando **ir, voy, vas, va, vamos** y **van.** Luego practique la conversación con un(a) compañero(a) de clase.

Ex. A. Answers: *vas, Voy, ir, vamos, vas, Voy, ir, van, Van, Vamos, va*

ANITA: ¡Hola, Carlos! ¿Adónde _____ ahora?

CARLOS: (Yo) _____ al cine. ¿Quieres _____ conmigo?

ANITA: No puedo. Mi hermana y yo _____ al parque.

CARLOS: ¿Qué _____ a hacer este fin de semana, Anita?

ANITA: ¡(Yo) _____ a una fiesta! ¿Quieres _____ ?

CARLOS: Bueno, gracias. ¿Quiénes _____ con nosotros?

ANITA: _____ mi amiga Ramona y su novio Tomás.

CARLOS: ¿_____ (nosotros) en auto o en metro?

ANITA: En auto. La fiesta _____ a ser en otra ciudad.

B. ¿Adónde van? Complete las oraciones con formas del verbo **ir** + **al, a la, a los,** o **a las.**

Ex. B. Answers: 1. *van al* 2. *van a los* 3. *va a la* 4. *vas al* 5. *van a las,* 6. *Vamos* + [open] 7. *Voy* + [open]

Ejemplo: Carlos *va a la* biblioteca para leer.

1. Carlos y Anita _____ cine en la Zona Rosa.
2. José y sus amigos _____ juegos de fútbol.
3. Anita _____ casa de sus abuelos esta noche.
4. Carlos, ¿tú _____ gimnasio para hacer ejercicio?
5. José y Pilar _____ ciudades de Puebla y Jalapa.
6. Mis amigos y yo...
7. Y yo...

C. Mis planes. Escriba usted qué va a hacer y cuándo.

Ejemplos: *Esta noche voy a descansar.*
Voy a una fiesta el primero de enero.
En diciembre voy a esquiar en Colorado.

Esta noche voy a _____. Mañana voy a _____. Este fin de semana voy a _____ y _____. Voy a _____ el sábado, y el domingo voy a _____ mucho.

En diciembre voy a _____ y el primero de enero voy a _____. En _____ voy a _____. En junio o julio voy a _____.

Charlemos

D. Este fin de semana. Pregúntele a otro(a) estudiante qué va a hacer este fin de semana.

Ejemplo: A: *Este fin de semana, ¿vas a estudiar mucho o poco?*
                 B: *Voy a estudiar poco.*

Este fin de semana...

1. ¿vas a estudiar mucho o poco?
2. ¿vas al cine o a una fiesta?
3. ¿vas a salir con amigos o vas a trabajar?
4. ¿vas a hacer ejercicio o vas a descansar?
5. ¿vas a mirar la televisión o escuchar la radio?

E. Durante la semana. Dígale a un(a) compañero(a) adónde va usted durante la semana.

Ex. E. If you wish, give students additional words for places that they go to during the week such as *el supermercado, el centro comercial, el correo, el banco, la iglesia, la sinagoga.*

TRANSPARENCY No. 6:
Seasons

GRAMÁTICA FUNCIONAL

Describing leisure-time activities

—¿Qué haces los domingos, Carlos?
—Leo un poco y hago ejercicio. ¿Y tú, Anita?
—Frecuentemente salgo con mis amigos.
—¿Quieres salir conmigo el domingo?
—Bueno, ¿qué hacemos, compañero?
—Vamos a comer en la Zona Rosa. ¿Está bien?
—Sí, gracias.

Present tense of other verbs with irregular yo forms

How to form irregular verbs

1. Some common Spanish verbs have irregular *yo* forms in the present indicative tense.

yo *form*

hacer	*to do, to make*	**hago**	**Hago** mucho ejercicio.
salir	*to leave, to go out*	**salgo**	**Salgo** todos los sábados.
poner	*to put, to put on*	**pongo**	**Pongo** música rock en casa.

You may want to introduce *llevar* (to take; to carry; to take along) and contrast it with *traer* (to bring) by writing on the board several sentences using each verb. Afterwards, you could begin using these two verbs in your teacher talk.

traer	to bring	**traigo**	**Traigo** mi disco compacto.
dar	to give	**doy**	**Doy** una fiesta el viernes.
saber	to know (how)	**sé**	**Sé** jugar bien al béisbol.
conocer	to know, to meet	**conozco**	**Conozco** a Carlos Suárez.

2. The other present tense forms of these verbs are regular.

hacer	**saber**	**conocer**	**dar**
hago	sé	conozco	doy
hac**es**	sab**es**	conoc**es**	d**as**
hac**e**	sab**e**	conoc**e**	d**a**
hac**emos**	sab**emos**	conoc**emos**	d**amos**
*hac**éis***	*sab**éis***	*conoc**éis***	*d**ais***
hac**en**	sab**en**	conoc**en**	d**an**

How to use saber *and* conocer

As you see above, the verbs *saber* and *conocer* both mean "to know," and they have irregular *yo* forms *(sé/conozco)*. These verbs represent two different kinds of knowledge. Here is how to use them:

1. Use the verb *saber* to express knowing something (information) or knowing how to do something.

—¿**Sabes** jugar al tenis?   *Do you know how to play tennis?*

—No, pero **sé** jugar al golf.   *No, but I know how to play golf.*

—¿**Sabes** qué? ¡Me gusta el golf!   *Do you know what? I like golf!*

2. Use the verb *conocer* to express being acquainted with a person, place, or thing. Spanish speakers use the preposition *a* immediately before a direct object that refers to a specific person or persons.[1]

—¿**Conoces** la Ciudad de México?   *Do you know Mexico City?*

—No, pero **conozco** Acapulco.   *No, but I know Acapulco.*

—¿Quieres **conocer** a mi amiga?   *Do you want to meet my friend?*

—Ya **conozco** a tu amiga Luisa.   *I already know your friend Luisa.*

---

[1] The direct object of a verb is the person or thing that receives the action of the verb. For example, in the sentence "I know Carlos," **Carlos** is the direct object. The "personal *a*," which has no English equivalent, is usually repeated before each noun or pronoun; however, it is usually not used with the verb *tener* even when the direct object is a person.

Conozco **a** Carlos.	*I know Carlos.*
Conozco **a** Carlos y **a** Anita.	*I know Carlos and Anita.*
Carlos y Anita tienen muchos amigos.	*Carlos and Anita have many friends.*

Practiquemos

A. ¿Sabe usted?
Diga qué o a quiénes Carlos y Anita conocen, según *(according to)* la información que usted sabe de ellos.

Ejemplos: *Carlos conoce a Anita Camacho.*
Anita no conoce Mérida, Yucatán.

Carlos...	Anita...
1. Anita Camacho.	1. Carlos Suárez.
2. los Camacho.	2. Mérida en el Yucatán.
3. el perro de los Camacho.	3. la familia de Carlos.
4. los abuelos de Anita.	4. su profesor de inglés.
5. el Parque de Chapultepec.	5. la biblioteca de la UNAM.

Ex. A. Answers:
Carlos: 1. *conoce a Anita Camacho.*
2. *conoce a los Camacho.* 3. *conoce el perro de los Camacho.* 4. *no conoce a los abuelos de Anita.* 5. *conoce el Parque de Chapultepec.*
Anita: 1. *conoce a Carlos Suárez.*
2. *no conoce Mérida en el Yucatán.*
3. *no conoce a la familia de Carlos.*
4. *conoce a su profesor de inglés.*
5. *conoce la biblioteca de la UNAM.*

B. Entrevista.
Practique con otro(a) estudiante.

Ejemplo: A: ¿(Saber) _____ jugar al golf?   B: Sí, (saber) _____ jugar bien.
¿Sabes jugar al golf?   *Sí, sé jugar bien.*

Ex. B.
1. Be sure students cover their partner's column to make this exercise more spontaneous.
2. Answers: 1. *Haces* 2. *Hago* 3. *Das* 4. *Doy* 5. *Sales* 6. *salgo* 7. *Tienes* 8. *tengo* 9. *Conoces* 10. *conozco*
3. Have one student role-play *Estudiante A* ask you the questions, using the *usted* forms of the verbs in parenthesis.

Estudiante A   **Estudiante B**

1. ¿(**Hacer**) _____ mucho ejercicio?   2. ¿Mucho? No. (**Hacer**) _____ un poco.
3. ¿(**Dar**) _____ muchas fiestas?   4. ¡Sí! (**Dar**) _____ muchas en casa.
5. ¿(**Salir**) _____ mucho los lunes?   6. ¿Los lunes? No, (**salir**) _____ poco.
7. ¿(**Tener**) _____ clase los jueves?   8. Sí, (**tener**) _____ tres clases.
9. ¿(**Conocer**) _____ a mis profesores?   10. No, no (**conocer**)_____a tus profesores.

C. ¡Hola, Mamá!
Escriba la carta de Carlos a su mamá. Use las formas apropiadas de los infinitivos dados.

Ejemplo: Mis estudios *van* más o menos bien.

Ex. C. Answers:
Paragraph 1: Salgo, tenemos, hacemos, voy, va, sé, conocen, es, tiene, vamos, Van, va, trae, traigo
Paragraph 2: hago, hago, pongo, tengo, salimos, voy

ir	dar	tener	saber	poner
ser	salir	hacer	traer	conocer

Querida Mamá,

[Yo] _____ mucho con mis amigos de la UNAM, especialmente los fines de semana cuando [nosotros] _____ más tiempo. Mis amigos y yo _____ muchas actividades. Por ejemplo, el primero de julio [yo] _____ con dos amigos a una fiesta que Luisa Gómez _____ a dar en su casa. Yo _____ que ustedes no _____ a Luisa, pero ella _____ muy simpática y _____ una casa con una piscina grande. El domingo por la tarde mi amiga Anita y yo _____ al Parque de Chapultepec. ¿_____ ustedes al parque con frecuencia como nosotros? Cuando Anita _____ al parque conmigo, ella _____ sándwiches y yo _____ fruta.

En casa [yo] _____ mucho ejercicio. Cuando [yo] _____ ejercicio, [yo] _____ música rock en la radio. Al momento [yo] no _____ novia, pero Anita y yo _____ mucho. Ahora [yo] _____ a descansar un poco.

Abrazos de tu hijo, Carlos

Charlemos

D. ¿Qué hacen Carlos y usted? Complete las siguientes oraciones de una manera personal.

Ejemplo: Carlos conoce a muchas personas, y yo _____ a (pocas / muchas) personas.
Carlos conoce a muchas personas, y yo conozco a pocas (muchas) personas.

1. Carlos hace mucho ejercicio, y yo _____ (poco / mucho) ejercicio. [No _____ ejercicio.]
2. Cuando él hace ejercicio, pone música rock; cuando yo _____ ejercicio, _____ (música rock / jazz / clásica). [No _____ música.]
3. Él tiene muchos amigos, y yo _____ (pocos / muchos) amigos. [No _____ amigos.]
4. Carlos sale con sus amigos los fines de semana, y yo _____ con mis amigos (los fines de semana / frecuentemente). [No ——— con amigos.]
5. Carlos da pocas fiestas, y yo _____ (pocas / muchas) fiestas. [No _____ fiestas.]
6. Él sabe jugar al fútbol, y yo _____ jugar al (fútbol / básquetbol / béisbol / vólibol / tenis / golf). [No _____ deportes.]

E. ¿Qué sabe usted? Pregúntele a otro(a) estudiante, usando una forma del verbo **saber** o **conocer**. Su compañero(a) debe responder apropiadamente.

Ejemplo: A: *¿Sabes cuántas lenguas habla Anita?*
B: *Sí. Ella habla tres lenguas.*

¿Sabes... / ¿Conoces...
1. la música mexicana?
2. la Ciudad de México?
3. el Parque de Chapultepec?
4. qué estudia Anita en la UNAM?
5. dónde vive la familia Camacho?
6. a la familia de Anita Camacho?
7. cantar en español como Carlos?
8. el nombre del gato de Sara Camacho?
9. cómo se llaman las hermanas de Carlos?
10. un poco a Carlos Suárez, el amigo de Anita?

F. Los pasatiempos. Pregúntele a otro(a) estudiante.

1. ¿Sales con tus amigos con mucha o con poca frecuencia? ¿Adónde van y qué hacen?
2. ¿Adónde vas de compras, y con quién vas?
3. ¿Vas al cine con mucha frecuencia o con poca frecuencia?
4. ¿Con quién vas a las fiestas? ¿Qué traes a las fiestas? ¿Bailas en las fiestas?
5. ¿Cuál es tu programa de (televisión/radio) favorito?
6. ¿Haces mucho o poco ejercicio? ¿Cuándo haces más ejercicio, por la mañana, por la tarde o por la noche? ¿Dónde haces ejercicio?

7. ¿Qué deportes sabes jugar? ¿Con quién te gusta jugar a los deportes?
8. ¿Qué haces los fines de semana?

Ahora su compañero(a) de clase va a hacerle las preguntas a usted.

G. ¿Quieres conocer a mi familia? Bring some photographs of your family to class. Show these pictures to several classmates and tell them who the people are *(ser)*, what skills they know how to do *(saber)*, and what interesting persons and places they are familiar with *(conocer)*. Jot down a few notes for each picture before sharing them.

GRAMÁTICA FUNCIONAL

Expressing likes and dislikes

—¿Qué te gusta hacer?
—Me gusta ir al cine.
—A mi mamá le gusta ir al
   cine también.

What do you like to do?
I like to go to the movies.
My Mom likes to go to the
   movies, too.

The verb *gustar* + infinitive

1. Expect students to use *me/te gusta* + infinitive in communicative speaking and writing activities. The other indirect object pronouns appear here because you will be using them in your teacher talk, and your students will want to understand what you are saying. The use of *gustar* + noun(s) is introduced in *Lección 5*.
2. If you wish, point out that these are indirect object pronouns (which are introduced formally in *Lección 8*).

To express likes and dislikes, Spanish speakers often use the verb *gustar* (to be pleasing to someone).

To express to whom something is pleasing, use one of the following pronouns with the verb form *gusta* plus an infinitive.

me	*to me*
te	*to you (informal)*
le	*to you (formal)*
le	*to him*
le	*to her*
nos	*to us*
os	*to you (informal)*
les	*to you*
les	*to them*

+ **gusta** + *infinitive*

As you see in the chart above, the pronouns *le* and *les* have more than one meaning. To clarify to whom something is pleasing, specify the person or persons with *a* (to) such as *a Carlos* and *a tus amigos*, and remember to include the pronoun *le* or *les*.

—¿**A Carlos le** gusta nadar?
—Sí. También **le** gusta pescar.
—¿**Les** gusta pescar **a tus amigos?**
—No, pero **les** gusta esquiar.

Does Carlos like to swim?
Yes. He also likes to fish.
Do your friends like to fish?
No, but they like to ski.

Practiquemos

A. Los gustos. Lea los gustos de Carlos, de su familia y de sus amigos, usando **le** o **les.**

1. A Carlos _____ gusta visitar Chapultepec.
2. A Sara _____ gusta jugar con su gato Café.
3. A Anita y a Carlos _____ gusta caminar en el parque.
4. A las hermanas gemelas de Carlos _____ gusta nadar.
5. A la familia Camacho _____ gusta comer en la Zona Rosa.
6. A los abuelos de Carlos _____ gusta recibir sus cartas.
7. A un compañero de Carlos _____ gusta ir al cine con su novia.

B. Los fines de semana. Complete la conversación, usando **me, te, le, nos, les.**

ANITA: ¿Qué _____ gusta hacer los fines de semana, Carlos?
CARLOS: _____ gusta correr en el Parque de Chapultepec.
ANITA: ¿Verdad? A mi amiga Ramona _____ gusta correr allí también.
CARLOS: ¿Qué _____ gusta hacer los fines de semana a ustedes?
ANITA: _____ gusta ir de compras y comer en un restaurante.

C. ¿Qué les gusta hacer a ustedes? Escriba un párrafo sobre los pasatiempos que les gusta hacer a usted y a sus amigos.

Charlemos

D. ¿Y a tu familia? Pregúntele a otro(a) estudiante.

Ejemplo: a tu papá / jugar al tenis
            A: *¿A tu papá le gusta jugar al tenis?*
            B: *Sí, le gusta.* (o: *No, no le gusta.*)

1. a tu papá / ir de compras
2. a tu mamá / mirar la televisión
3. a tus padres / jugar a las cartas
4. a tu hermano(a) / patinar con sus amigos
5. a tus abuelos / montar en bicicleta en un parque

E. ¿Qué hay en la tele? Converse con otro(a) estudiante.

Estudiante A

1. ¿Te gusta mirar la tele?

3. ... Me gusta mirar un programa que se llama _____.
5. Es el (día) a la(s) _____ de la (mañana / tarde / noche).

Estudiante B

2. ... Mi programa favorito es _____. ¿Miras mucho o poco la tele?
4. ... ¿En qué día es?
6. Ah, sí. En mi opinión, es un programa (bueno / malo).

F. Charla final. Hable con un(a) compañero(a) de clase a quien usted no conoce bien.

1. Say "hello" to each other.
2. Talk about what you are going to do this weekend.
3. Discuss what activities you enjoy doing.
4. Say when you like to do them (time, days, or months).
5. Now tell each other what pastimes you dislike.

Pre-reading activities: 1. Have students point out the cognates in this realia pieces and say their English equivalents. 2. Have students point out other words that they can guess from context.

PARA LEER MEJOR

Using Context to Predict Content

Efficient readers use effective strategies for guessing the meaning of unfamiliar words and phrases in a reading selection. For example, they rely on what they already know about the reading topic (background information), they guess what the reading will be about (prediction), and they use ideas they understand in the passage (context). In this section you will practice using these three reading strategies.

Answers:
A. 1. They are both movie stars.
2. In the entertainment section of magazines and newspapers.

B. [open]

Activities

A. Background information
   1. What do Clint Eastwood and Sigourney Weaver have in common?
   2. Where do people usually read about them?

B. Prediction
   1. First, look at the reading and read the large, boldface type word at the top center. Second, read the subtitles in smaller boldface type. Third, look at the photograph.
   2. What do you suppose the descriptions are about?

Answers:
C. 1. a. *Favorable opinion* b. [open]
2. a. **Los imperdonables:** *recomendable, polifacético, un espléndido western, una dimensión enorme,* (last sentence of the first film), *buena;* 1492...: *una superproducción, de una manera mucho más afortunada, aspectos sobresalientes, el espléndido trabajo fotográfico, el reparto de lo mejor, un convincente Depardieu, deja constancia de su capacidad histriónica, muy buena.*
b. "1492..." c. Britain, France, Spain

C. Context
   1. Skim the reading without stopping to understand the gist of its content.
      a. In general, what is the author's opinion of these movie reviews?
      b. Which movie would you prefer to see, and why?
   2. Scan the reading to complete the following tasks.
      a. Underline the words and phrases that indicate the author's favorable opinion of these two films.
      b. Name the film that the author likes best.
      c. Name the three countries in which the second film was produced.

Desde la Butaca
Cineguía

EZEQUIEL BARRIGA CHAVEZ

LOS IMPERDONABLES. De Clint Eastwood, con Clint Eastwood, Gene Hackman, Morgan Freeman, Richard Harris. Recomendable filme del polifacético Eastwood que nos ofrece en esta ocasión un espléndido western. El asunto gira en torno de un grupo de pistoleros que van en busca de un par de maleantes, para cobrar la recompensa. Naturalmente, en manos de este director la trama adquiere una dimensión enorme. Los fanáticos del Western y del buen cine por nada del mundo se deben perder esta cinta. (Adolescentes) Buena.

1492 **LA CONQUISTA DEL PARAISO.** De Ridley Scott, con Gerard Depardieu, Armand Assante y Sigourney Weaver. Se trata de una superproducción británico-francesa-española en que su autor recrea la hazaña de Colón, de una manera mucho más afortunada que la versión "oficial" que dirigió el señor Glenn. En esta costosa producción hay aspectos sobresalientes como la recreación de época, el espléndido trabajo fotográfico, la musicalización de Vangelis, y el reparto de lo mejor, encabezado por un convincente Depardieu que deja constancia de su capacidad histriónica. (Todo publico) Muy buena.

PARA ESCRIBIR MEJOR

Combining Sentences

In this section you will learn to improve your writing style by combining sentences. Here are three Spanish words you can use to combine sentences and parts of sentences:

y   *and*
pero   *but*
que   *that, which, who*

Atajo

Functions:
Writing a letter (informal);
describing people; talking
about the present; inviting,
accepting & declining

Vocabulary:
Sports; leisure; board
games; family members;
animals: domestic;
university

Grammar:
Verbs: *ser, tener;* Article:
contractions *al, del*

B. Answers:
  *1. Tengo cuatro profesores que son
  realmente maravillosos. 2. Carlos es
  inteligente, pero el inglés es difícil
  para él. 3. Carlos quiere ser ingeniero
  y vivir en Mérida. 4. Paso mucho
  tiempo con Carlos, que estudia inglés
  conmigo. 5. Carlos es mi compañero
  que le gusta mucho jugar fútbol. 6.
  Un día voy a los Estados Unidos,
  pero ahora es difícil para mí.*

Activities

A. Read Anita's letter to her American pen pal, and circle all the sentence connectors.

Querida Diane:

¿Qué tal? ¿Cómo está la familia?

Mis estudios en la UNAM van bien. Tomo cuatro cursos: sicología, turismo, inglés y alemán. Mis profesores son excelentes y aprendo mucho de ellos.

Ahora paso mucho tiempo con mi amigo Carlos Suárez, que estudia en la UNAM también. Carlos tiene veintitrés años, es guapo, inteligente y es muy simpático. Nos gusta salir los fines de semana. Aquí tienes una foto de nosotros dos en el Zócalo, que está en el centro de mi ciudad.

Un día quiero ir a los Estados Unidos, pero ahora no puedo porque tengo mis clases. Diane, ¿por qué no regresas a México en julio o agosto? Vamos a bailar, ir de compras y visitar unos museos de la ciudad. ¡Aquí tienes tu casa!

Bueno, en pocos minutos va a llegar una de mis estudiantes, que aprende francés. ¿Sabes? Doy clases de francés e inglés aquí en casa. Espero recibir tu carta pronto.

Tu amiga,
Anita

B. Combine the following sets of sentences using *y*, *pero*, and *que* appropriately.

Example: Estudio en la UNAM. No es fácil.
                Estudio en la UNAM, pero no es fácil.

1. Tengo cuatro profesores. Son realmente maravillosos.
2. Carlos es inteligente. El inglés es difícil para él.
3. Carlos quiere ser ingeniero. Quiere vivir en Mérida.
4. Paso mucho tiempo con Carlos. Estudia inglés conmigo.
5. Carlos es mi compañero. Le gusta mucho jugar fútbol.
6. Un día voy a los Estados Unidos. Ahora es difícil para mí.

C. Using Anita's letter as a model, write in Spanish to one of your classmates about yourself, your family, pets, and friends, and your activities and studies. This is an excellent way to start meeting your new classmates.

SÍNTESIS

¡A ver!

You are going to see several people talk about some activities they enjoy during their free time. First, study the words and their meaning in the *Vocabulario esencial*. Then read the list of leisure-time activities. Third, watch the videotape, then check the pastimes that the people mention during their interviews.

Vocabulario esencial

tiempo libre	*free time*
pasar tiempo	*to spend time*
las noticias	*the news*
aprovecho	*I make use of*

_____ leer   _____ hacer ejercicio
_____ ir al cine   _____ ver la televisión
_____ jugar fútbol   _____ jugar a las cartas
_____ ir al parque   _____ salir con los papás
_____ ir de compras   _____ ver películas en vídeo

Answers: *leer, ir al cine, jugar fútbol, ir al parque, hacer ejercicio, ver la televisión, salir con los papás*

What gestures of affection between the family members did you notice as you watched the video segment? Make a list of them in English.

¡A leer!

SERGIO DE BUSTAMANTE LILIA ARAGON
RUBEN ROJO
EN

LOS SEÑORES DE LA NOCHE

Espectáculo de: José Luis Cruz
basado en Macbeth de W. Shakespeare
Escenografía: Gilberto Aceves Navarro
Música original: Antonio Russek

TEATRO EL GALEON
Detrás del Auditorio Nacional
Jueves y Viernes 20:30 hrs.
Sábados 19:00 hrs.
Domingos 18:00 hrs

EXPOSICION DE FLOR GARDUÑO
Testigos del tiempo
71 FOTOGRAFIAS
Rituales y religión de los pueblos
indígenas de Bolivia, Ecuador, Uruguay,
Guatemala y México
PALACIO DE BELLAS ARTES
Sala Justino Fernández
Abierto: martes a domingo
de 10:00 a 18:00 hrs.

GOOFY EN SU PRIMER
PAPEL ESTELAR
WALT DISNEY
PICTURES PRESENTA
GOOFY Y WILBUR
DISTRIBUIDA POR
WARNER ESPAÑOLA, S.A.
© THE WALT DISNEY COMPANY
PALACIO DE LA MUSICA   AMAYA   JUAN DE AUSTRIA   ALUCHE

LUNES DE OPERA
Carmen
de Bizet
Con: Norma Eternod, Judith Sierra,
Renato Buchelli y Ricardo Santini
PINACOTECA VIRREINAL
Dr. Mora 7, Centro
LUNES 26 DE OCTUBRE / 19:30 HRS.

¿Comprendió Ud.?

1. Skim the four advertisements above.
   a. Which one interests you the most, and why?

SÍNTESIS

Visit

http://poco.heinle.com

   b. Anita Camacho wants to have fun with her sister Sara (8 years old) and her brother Raúl (10 years old). Where do you suppose she might take them, and why?

2. Scan the ads to locate the following information.
   a. What's going on at the Palace of Fine Arts? When can the public see this exhibition?
   b. Which performance will appeal most to fans of Shakespeare?
   c. When and where is the opera *Carmen* being held? How many performances are scheduled?
   d. Where is the cartoon being shown? Who produced it?

¡A conversar!

Create and role-play short dialogues with a classmate based on the situations below. Try to use words and phrases that you have learned.

1. Your Mexican-American friend calls you on the phone to invite you to a football game (mention the date and time). You are unable to accept the invitation. Say so tactfully.
2. Friends of yours, a family from El Salvador who live in your town, send you an invitation to a party at their home (the invitation should include the date and time). You call them to accept the invitation.
3. Your Cuban-American friend invites you to go fishing with her family for the weekend (mention the date and time). Think about your schedule, then decide whether or not to accept the invitation. Call your friend and communicate your decision.

¡A escribir!

Write a short letter to Anita and Carlos. In the first paragraph of your letter, tell them about some leisure activities you, your family, and your friends enjoy. In the second paragraph, invite them to visit you when you are not in school (mention which months). Tell them what there is to see and do in your community. Do not use a bilingual dictionary to look up words you do not know; rather, use only the Spanish you have learned.

Atajo

VOCABULARIO

Sustantivos

los abuelos *grandparents*
el cine *movie theater*
el concierto *concert*
el deporte *sport*
el disco compacto *compact disk (CD)*
la fecha *date*
la fiesta *party*
el gimnasio *gymasium*
el juego *game*
el mes *month*
el metro *subway*
el museo *museum*
el parque *park*
el pasatiempo *pastime, leisure-time activity*
la piscina *swimming pool*
el primero *first*
el tipo *kind, type*

Los meses del año
(Months of the year)

enero *January*
febrero *February*
marzo *March*
abril *April*
mayo *May*
junio *June*
julio *July*
agosto *August*
septiembre *September*
octubre *October*
noviembre *November*
diciembre *December*

Los pasatiempos
(Leisure activities)

bailar *to dance*
ir al cine *to go to the movies*
ir de compras *to go shopping*
jugar (a las) cartas *to play cards*

mirar (la) televisión *to watch television*
sacar fotos *to take pictures*
tocar la guitarra *to play the guitar*
ver películas en video *to see movie videos*

Los deportes
(Sports)

caminar *to walk*
correr *to run, to jog*
esquiar *to ski*
el fútbol *soccer*
hacer ejercicio *to exercise*
jugar (al) tenis *to play tennis*
montar a caballo *to go horseback riding*
montar en bicicleta *to go bicycling*
nadar *to swim*
patinar *to skate*
pescar *to fish*

Verbos

cantar *to sing*
conocer *to know (a person or place), to meet (someone)*
dar *to give*
gustar *to be pleasing, to like*
invitar *to invite*
ir *to go*
pasar (por) *to pick up (someone)*
poder (puedo) *to be able (I can)*
poner *to put, to put on (music)*
saber *to know (something, how to)*
salir *to go out, to leave*
traer *to bring*
visitar *to visit*

Adverbios

este fin de semana *this weekend*
esta noche *tonight*
hoy *today*

Preposiciones

conmigo *with me*

Expresiones idiomáticas

de nada *you're welcome*
¿Qué hay de nuevo? *What's new?*
¿Qué te parece? *What do you think?*

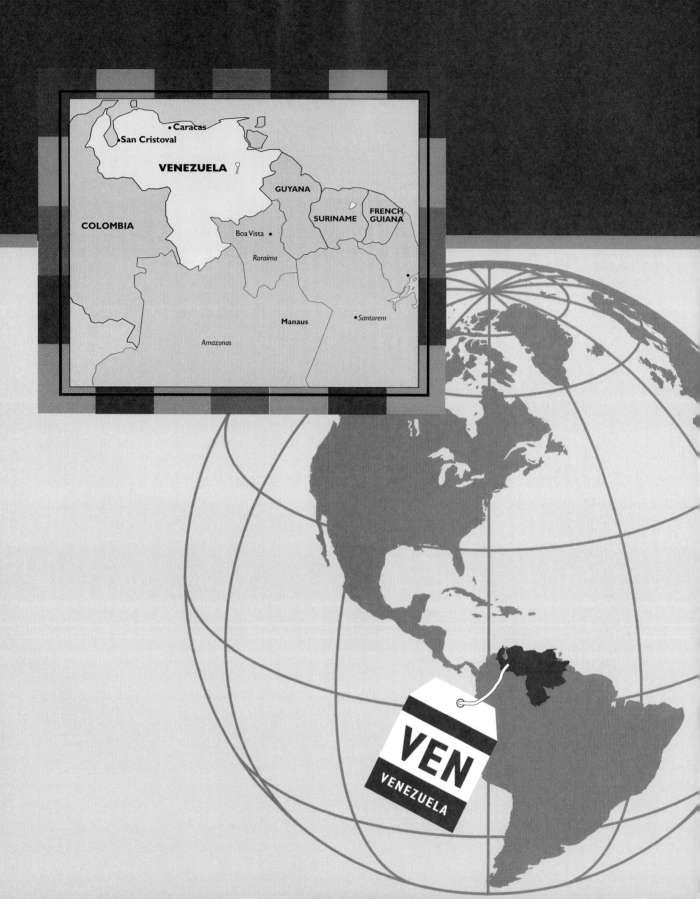

VENEZUELA

Caracas

San Cristoval

COLOMBIA

GUYANA

SURINAME

FRENCH
GUIANA

Boa Vista

Roraima

Manaus

Santarem

Amazonas

VEN

VENEZUELA

¡Saludos a la familia!

▶ *Venezuela* ◀

Lorena Velarde lives with her large, closely-knit family in San Felipe, Venezuela. We join them for lunch, learn about their daily activities, and celebrate the important fifteenth birthday of Lorena's sister Beti.

4

Abuelita, ¡cómo te gustan las telenovelas!

▶ COMMUNICATIVE GOALS

You will be able to describe your family and other relatives and to describe what you and they do.

▶ LANGUAGE FUNCTIONS

Identifying family members
Describing family members
Describing actions in progress
Expressing wants and preferences
Stating intentions
Describing states of mind
Describing physical conditions

http://poco.heinle.com

▶ VOCABULARY THEMES

Family members
Marital status

▶ GRAMMATICAL STRUCTURES

Present tense of stem-changing verbs (e→ie)
Present tense of the verb *estar*
The verb *estar* with adjectives
Idioms: *tener ganas de, celos, miedo, prisa, razón, sueño*
Present progressive tense

▶ CULTURAL INFORMATION

Hispanic families
Hispanic names

If you wish to obtain free information on Venezuela, write: Venezuela Tourist Office, 20 North Wacker Drive, Room 750, Chicago, IL 60606 telephone: (312) 236-9655.

 **LAB TAPE**

Have students role-play this conversation in small groups of three members.

Hoy es jueves, el primero de marzo. Esta noche toda la familia Velarde está en su apartamento en San Felipe.(1) Lorena está estudiando sus lecciones del politécnico donde toma una clase de hotelería.(2) Tomás está hablando por teléfono con su novia Ceci, y Beti está jugando con su sobrino° Memo. Los otros están mirando la televisión.

nephew

BETI: Tía,° ¿qué hora es?   *Aunt*

ELENA: Pues,° son las nueve menos cinco. ¿Por qué, Beti?   *Well*

BETI: Porque quiero mirar un programa de deportes a las nueve.

ELENA: Pero a las nueve comienza° la telenovela *Por este país*.(3)   *starts*

MATILDE: Ay, ¡qué bueno! Es mi telenovela favorita.

BETI: Abuelita, ¡cómo te gustan las telenovelas!(4) ¿Pero por qué te gusta *Por este país*?

MATILDE: Porque esa° telenovela siempre° presenta y explica los   *that / always* problemas de nuestro país.

ELENA: Y también adoras al actor Alejandro Carrillo, ¿verdad, Matilde?

MATILDE: Pues, claro que sí. Alejandro Carrillo es un hombre° simpático y   *man* es muy buen actor.

BETI: Sí, abuelita, tienes razón.° Los actores de *Por este país* son muy   *you're right* buenos.

MATILDE: Claro, niña y también me gustan las soluciones que dan a los problemas.

BETI: Sí, abuelita, las soluciones son interesantes y muy prácticas.

Notas de texto

1. *San Felipe* is the capital of the state of Yaracuy located west of Caracas, the capital of Venezuela.

Ask your students if they watch soap operas on television. If they do, ask which ones they like, why they like them, and who the main characters are. Also, ask them the names of the soaps that they dislike, and why.

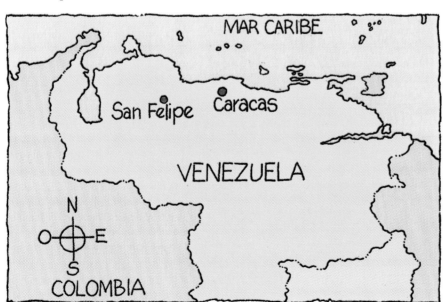

2. A *politécnico* is a type of vocational school where adult students learn specific trades such as tourism *(el turismo)*, hotel management *(la hotelería)*, carpentry *(la carpintería)*, and bookkeeping *(la contabilidad)*.

3. *Telenovelas* (soap operas) such as *Por este país* (Around This Country) are very popular in Spanish-speaking countries among people of all age groups except the very young. Venezuela, with its thriving movie and television industry, has become one of the most important producers of the soaps. Many television companies in Spanish-speaking countries, the United States, and Canada telecast Venezuelan soap operas.

4. The names *abuelito* (grandpa), *abuelita* (grandma), *papá* or *papi* (dad), and *mamá* or *mami* (mom), carry strong feelings of affection among Spanish speakers.

¡Comprendió Ud.?

1. Skim the dialogue once to get the gist of it. Then read all the *Notas de texto*.
   a. ¿Dónde están hablando Beti y doña Matilde?
   b. ¿De qué están hablando ellas?

2. All of the statements below are false. Scan the reading to locate the true facts, then rewrite the statements.
   a. Beti es la prima de Elena.
   b. La telenovela comienza a las diez.
   c. Juan y Rosa Velarde están comiendo.
   d. Tomás es el hermano mayor de Ceci.
   e. Alejandro Carrillo es profesor de drama.
   f. *Por este país* es una novela histórica.
   g. Lorena es estudiante de la universidad.
   h. A doña Matilde no le gustan las telenovelas.

3. ¿Conoce usted a una persona como doña Matilde? (¿Sí? ¿Cómo se llama él/ella? Es una mujer [*woman*], un hombre, una niña o un niño? ¿Cómo es su personalidad? ¿Dónde vive ahora?)

Answers:
1. *a. Están hablando en su apartamento. 2. Están hablando de los programas de televisión.*
2. *a. Beti es la sobrina de Elena*
   b. La telenovela comienza a las nueve.
   c. Juan y Rosa Velarde están mirando la televisión.
   d. Tomás es el novio de Ceci.
   e. Alejandro Carrillo es actor.
   f. Por este país es, una telenovela.
   g. Lorena es estudiante del politécnico.
   h. A doña Matilde le gustan las telenovelas.
3. *[open]*

TRANSPARENCY No. 9: Family Tree

VOCABULARIO ÚTIL

Cómo conversar de la familia[1]

In this section you will learn to describe your immediate and extended family.

—Me llamo Lorena Luisa Velarde Salinas. Tengo veintitrés años. Vivo con mi familia aquí en San Felipe, Venezuela. Soy secretaria bilingüe y estudio hotelería por la noche.

---

[1] In Spanish-speaking countries, the word *familia* can include close friends who do not necessarily live together or have blood kinship ties.

—*Mi nombre es Juan Antonio Velarde Molinas, y mi esposa se llama Rosa María. Soy el papá de Lorena. Trabajo en un banco de San Felipe.*
—*Soy Rosa María Salinas de Velarde. Tengo cuarenta y seis años. Mi marido Juan y yo tenemos cuatro niños: Roberto, Lorena, Tomás y Beti.*

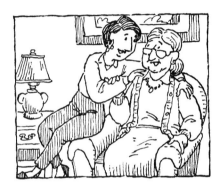

—*Me llamo Elena María Velarde de Muñoz. Juan es mi hermano mayor;°*   older
el tiene cuarenta y ocho años y yo tengo treinta y cuatro. Estoy divorciada. No tengo niños.
—*Soy Matilde Catalina Figueroa de Salinas. Tengo setenta y ocho años y soy viuda. Rosa María es mi hija.*

—*Me llamo Silvia Marcela Rodríguez de Velarde y tengo veintisiete años. Mi marido Roberto y yo tenemos un hijo de cinco años, que se llama Memo.*
—*Mi nombre es Roberto Javier Velarde Salinas. Soy el hermano mayor de Lorena. Tengo veintiocho años y estoy casado con Silvia.*

—*Soy Beti Angélica Velarde Salinas. Soy la "bebé" de la familia porque tengo catorce años. Asisto a un colegio en San Felipe.*
—*Me llamo Tomás Bernardo Velarde Salinas y soy el hermano menor° de*   younger
Lorena. Tengo dieciocho años y estudio en la universidad. Tengo una novia que se llama Ceci.

1. Before assigning this section, brainstorm with your students about their own families by asking such questions as *¿Tiene usted una familia grande o pequeña? ¿Cuántas personas hay en su familia? ¿Cómo se llama su papá/mamá? ¿Cuántos años tiene? ¿Dónde viven sus padres?*
2. Use these self-descriptions as the basis for short or long dictations. A great deal of research indicates that giving dictations at regular intervals is a very useful pedagogical technique for improving students' listening comprehension proficiency.

Ex. A. Answers: *Rodrigo = abuelo, Carmen = abuela, Pedro = abuelo, Matilde = abuela, Elena = tía, Juan = padre, Rosa = madre, Silvia = cuñada, Roberto = hermano, Tomás = hermano, Beti = hermana, Memo = sobrino*

Follow-up activities:
1. Work with your class to recreate Lorena's family tree either on the chalkboard or on an overhead transparency. Include the names of her relatives as well as their ages, marital status, and relationships to each other.
2. Afterwards, expand the family tree by inventing information about Lorena's other relatives and telling it to your students. A good way to do so is to create short anecdotes about these relatives and their activities, using vocabulary that your students have learned from previous lessons.

Los parientes *(relatives)*[1]

el marido	*husband / wife*	**la esposa**
el hijo	*son / daughter*	**la hija**
el abuelo	*grandfather / grandmother*	**la abuela**[2]
el nieto	*grandson / grandaughter*	**la nieta**
el tío	*uncle / aunt*	**la tía**
el sobrino	*nephew / niece*	**la sobrina**
el primo	*male cousin / female cousin*	**la prima**
el suegro	*father-in-law / mother-in-law*	**la suegra**
el yerno	*son-in-law / daughter-in-law*	**la nuera**
el cuñado	*brother-in-law / sister-in-law*	**la cuñada**

El estado civil *(marital status)*

Es...		Está...	
soltero(a).	*single*	**casado(a).**	*married*
viudo(a).	*widowed*	**divorciado(a).**	*divorced*

Practiquemos

A. La familia de Lorena Velarde. Scan the captions on pages 96–97 to complete the family tree below. Write each family member's name on the line and their relationship to Lorena in the parenthesis. A heart (♥) symbolizes marriage, and a cross (†) symbolizes a deceased person.

La familia de Lorena

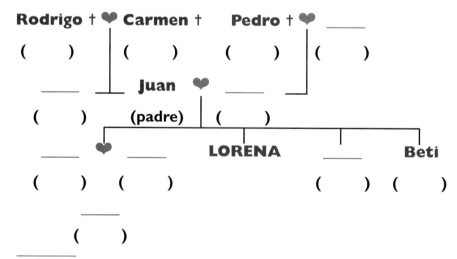

[1] In Spanish-speaking countries, the following people are part of the family, in addition to those listed here: *el bisabuelo* (great-grandfather), *la bisabuela* (great-grandmother), *el padrino* (godfather), and *la madrina* (godmother). In Hispanic cultures, the father and the godfather refer to each other as *compadre*, and the mother and godmother refer to each other as *comadre*.

[2] The masculine plural forms are used to refer to both genders of relatives. For example, *abuelos* can mean grandfathers or grandparents; *padres* can mean fathers or parents; *hermanos* can mean brothers or brothers and sisters; *tíos* can mean uncles or aunts and uncles. The intended meaning of each plural form depends upon its context.

B. ¡Qué familia! Complete las siguientes oraciones, mirando la ilustración en el Ejercicio A.

Ejemplo: Silvia es *la cuñada* de Lorena.

Ex. B Answers: 1. *el suegro* 2. *la suegra* 3. *el sobrino* 4. *el tío* 5. *la cuñada* 6. *la nuera* 7. *el yerno* 8. *la abuela* 9. *el nieto* 10. *la hija*

Parientes

1. Rodrigo es _____ de Rosa.
2. Matilde es _____ de Juan.
3. Memo es _____ de Beti.
4. Tomás es _____ de Memo.
5. Elena es _____ de Silvia.
6. Silvia es _____ de Juan y Rosa.
7. Juan es _____ de Matilde.
8. Matilde es _____ de Roberto.
9. Tomás es _____ de Matilde.
10. Lorena es _____ de Juan y Rosa.

tío	**abuela**
nieto	**suegra**
hija	**suegro**
nuera	**cuñada**
yerno	**sobrino**

C. En la casa de los Velarde. Diga el estado civil de estas personas.

Ejemplo: Lorena es *soltera*.

Ex. C. Answers: 1. *soltero* 2. *casada* 3. *divorciada* 4. *casada* 5. *viuda* 6. *casado* 7. *soltera* 8. *casado*

1. Tomás es _____.
2. Silvia está _____.
3. Elena está _____.
4. Rosa está _____.
5. Matilde es _____.
6. Roberto está _____.
7. Beti es _____.
8. Juan está _____.

D. Mis parientes. Complete las oraciones con el nombre del pariente apropiado.

Ejemplo: El hermano de mi papá es mi *tío*.

Ex. D.
1. Answers: 1. *tío* 2. *hermana* 3. *prima* 4. *tía* 5. *hermano (a)* 6. *abuelos*
2. Follow-up oral activity: First, divide your class into teams of 3–4 students. Second, ask students in each team to write sentences similar to those they completed in Activity C. Third, distribute the sentences to opposing team members who read them, then say the definitions or have teams quiz each other orally. Award points and/or prizes, if you wish.

Parientes

1. El padre de mis primos es mi _____
2. La hermana de mi hermano es mi _____.
3. La hija de mis tíos es mi _____.
4. La esposa de mi tío es mi _____.
5. Mi sobrino es el hijo de mi _____.
6. Soy el (la) nieto(a) de mis _____.

tío	**hermano**
tía	**hermana**
prima	**abuelos**
padres	**sobrinos**

E. Preguntas personales. Pregúntele a otro(a) estudiante.

Ex. E. Have students ask you these questions, using *usted* verb forms.

1. ¿Estás casado(a) o eres soltero(a)?
2. ¿Tienes niños? ¿Sí? ¿Cómo se llama(n)?
3. ¿Quién está casado en tu familia? Pues, ¿cuántos niños tiene(n)? ¿Cuántos cuñados tienes?
4. ¿Quién está divorciado en tu familia? ¿Dónde vive(n) ahora?
5. ¿Cuántos tíos tienes? ¿Cómo se llaman tus tíos? ¿y tus tías? ¿Dónde viven tus tíos? ¿Cómo se llama tu tío favorito? ¿y tu tía favorita?
6. ¿Eres tío(a)? ¿Sí? ¿Cómo se llaman tus sobrinos? ¿Cuántos años tienen?
7. ¿Tienes pocos o muchos primos? Pues, ¿dónde viven ellos?
8. ¿Cuántos abuelos tienes? ¿Cómo se llama(n)? ¿Cuántos años tiene(n)?

NOTAS CULTURALES

Familias hispanas

social unit

includes

united / any / member / needs

contributes

away

few times / elderly

En la cultura hispana la unidad social° más importante es la familia. Además del padre, de la madre, de los hermanos, la familia incluye° a los abuelos, los tíos, los primos y los sobrinos.

Las familias hispanas son muy unidas.° Cuando algún° miembro° de la familia necesita° ayuda, la familia da ayuda material y emocional. Muchas veces, en una familia hay dos o más generaciones que viven en una casa. Los abuelos viven con sus hijos y así contribuyen° a la educación de los nietos y ayudan a los padres que trabajan afuera° de la casa. Muy pocas veces,° los abuelos viven en casas de ancianos.° Los abuelos son un elemento muy importante dentro de la unión y la tradición familiar.

Write the following questions on the board. Then ask your students to work in pairs and discuss their answers in English. Afterwards, bring the class together and discuss your students' responses to the questions. 1. What does the word "family" mean to you? 2. What advantages are there to being part of a family? What disadvantages are there, if any? 3. If you have pets at home, are they treated as animals or more like family members? Explain your answer.

Ex. F.
1. Be sure students do this activity with a different partner from the one with whom they spoke when doing Activity D. Activity D recycles the language function of asking about family members, but it is a more open-ended activity than Activity E.
2. Students could also write out this activity.

F. Entrevista. Converse con otro(a) compañero(a) de clase.

Find out . . .

1. the names of your classmate's parents, and their age.
2. how many brothers and sisters he or she has, if any.
3. what their names and ages are, and where they live.
4. where these immediate family members study or work.

G. Mi familia. Dibuje su árbol familiar *(Draw your family tree)*. Después, escriba una descripción de su familia. Luego, usando su descripción, hable de su familia con un(a) compañero(a) de clase, que debe hacerle a usted preguntas apropiadas.

H. Un(a) pariente especial.

1. Write a description of a relative whom you like very much. Here are some guidelines for your description.

Escriba...

- su nombre completo.
- cuántos años tiene.
- su estado civil.
- dónde vive ahora.

- sus características físicas.
- su personalidad.
- sus actividades preferidas.
- otra información interesante.

2. Bring a photograph of this relative to class and read your description to a classmate.

Ex. H. Have students exchange their written descriptions, read them, correct the errors in them, then discuss the errors with a classmate.

GRAMÁTICA FUNCIONAL

Describing wants and preferences

—¿Qué quieres hacer mañana?
—Tengo ganas de ir de compras.
—Yo prefiero ir al cine.

What do you want to do tomorrow?
I feel like going shopping.
I prefer to go to the movies.

Present tense of verbs with stem-vowel change: e → ie

A stem is the part of an infinitive to which one adds personal endings. For example, the stem of *hablar* is **habl-**. Several types of vowel changes occur in the stem of some Spanish infinitives in the present tense.

The following verbs change their stem vowel from *e* to *ie*, except in the *nosotros(as)* and *vosotros(as)* forms.

comenzar	**pensar**	**querer**	**preferir**
(to begin)	*(to think)*	*(to want, to love)*	*(to prefer)*
comienzo	pienso	quiero	prefiero
comienzas	piensas	quieres	prefieres
comienza	piensa	quiere	prefiere
comenzamos	pensamos	queremos	preferimos
comenzáis	*pensáis*	*queréis*	*preferís*
comienzan	piensan	quieren	prefieren

Teach students how to use prepositions with these two verbs: *comenzar a* + infinitive and *pensar en* + infinitive.

Remind students that they already learned the present tense forms of *tener* in *Lección 2*.

Two *e* → *ie* verbs have an irregular *yo* form.

tener   **venir**

(to have)   *(to come)*

ten**go**   ven**go**
tienes   **vie**nes
tiene   **vie**ne
tenemos   venimos
tenéis   *venís*
tienen   **vie**nen

To express what people feel like doing, use the expression *tener ganas de* + an infinitive.

—¿Qué **tienes ganas de hacer**?   *What do you feel like doing?*
—Me gustaría hacer ejercicio.   *I would like to exercise.*

Point out that the *me gusta* + infinitive and the *me gustaría* + infinitive constructions function exactly alike. Explain that *me gusta* refers to the general enjoyment of an activity while *me gustaría* suggests a desire to engage in an activity.

Practiquemos

A. Preferencias personales. Complete las siguientes conversaciones con **quiero, quieres, prefiero** o **prefieres**.

Ex. A. Answers:
Conversation 1: *Prefieres, prefiero, quiero*
Conversation 2: *Quieres, quieres, Quiero*
Conversation 3: *Quieres, prefieres, prefieres, Prefiero*

SILVIA: Roberto, ¿_____ ir al parque o al cine con Memo?
ROBERTO: Pues, _____ ir al parque; _____ jugar con él.

TOMÁS: ¡Hola, Ceci! ¿_____ salir conmigo el sábado?
CECI: Bueno, sí. ¿Qué _____ hacer, Tomás?
TOMÁS: _____ montar a caballo. ¿Qué te parece?
CECI: ¡Perfecto! Muchas gracias, Tomás.
TOMÁS: De nada, Ceci.

BETI: ¿_____ ver una película en video, Tomás?
TOMÁS: Sí, pero ¿qué _____ un video de rock o una comedia?
BETI: Pues, no sé. ¿Qué _____ tú?
TOMÁS: _____ ver una comedia. ¿Qué te parece, Beti?
BETI: Bueno, una comedia está bien conmigo.

Ex. A. and **Ex. B.** After you have discussed the answers to these two exercises, have students role-play the dialogues.

B. Entrevista con doña Matilde. Raquel Navarro es reportera. Ella quiere escribir un artículo sobre la gente anciana. En este momento ella está hablando con doña Matilde. Complete su conversación, usando la forma apropiada de los siguientes verbos: **pensar, preferir, querer, tener, venir.**

Ex. B. Answers: *tiene, tengo, Tiene, tengo, vienen, vienen, Prefiero, Tiene, piensa, prefiero*

RAQUEL: ¿Cuántos años _____ usted, doña Matilde?
MATILDE: Pues, _____ 78 años, señorita.
RAQUEL: ¡Qué bien! ¿_____ usted muchos nietos?
MATILDE: Sí, _____ nueve. Cuatro de ellos viven aquí conmigo.
RAQUEL: Y los otros... ¿_____ a visitarla frecuentemente?
MATILDE: Bueno, no _____ frecuentemente porque viven en Caracas.

RAQUEL: Sé que usted no trabaja ahora. ¿Qué hace durante el día?

MATILDE: Me gusta mirar la tele. (Yo) _____ ver telenovelas.

RAQUEL: ¿_____ usted una telenovela favorita, doña Matilde?

MATILDE: Claro que sí, señorita. Se llama *Por este país.*

RAQUEL: ¡Qué interesante! ¿Y qué _____ usted de las telenovelas venezolanas, doña Matilde?

MATILDE: Bueno, pues... me gustan mucho, pero (yo) _____ las telenovelas mexicanas porque son bastante melodramáticas.

C. ¡Uy! ¡Los lunes! Imagínese que hoy es lunes. Diga qué planes tienen las siguientes personas.

Ejemplo:

¿Qué piensa hacer Beti ahora?

Piensa ir al colegio.

O: *Piensa ir a la escuela.*

1. **¿Qúe piensa hacer Elena esta mañana?**

2. **¿Qué no tiene ganas de hacer Roberto hoy?**

3. **¿Qué prefieren hacer doña Matilde y Memo por la tarde?**

4. **¿Qué quiere hacer Juan ahora?**

D. Mis actividades.

1. Primero, complete la tabla con sus obligaciones y deseos para mañana.

Ejemplo:

Hora	Obligación	Deseo
8:00	tomar un examen	jugar al tenis
15:00	trabajar en Sears	descansar en casa
21:00	estudiar español	mirar la televisión

Hora	Obligación	Deseo
_____	_____	_____
_____	_____	_____
_____	_____	_____

Ex. D. If you wish, you could introduce the expression *tener que* + infinitive at this point; for example: *Tengo que tomar un examen.* Then have students express what they have to do today, tonight, tomorrow, and so forth.

2. Luego escriba un párrafo, usando la información de su tabla.

Ejemplo: *A las ocho de la mañana voy a tomar un examen, luego quiero jugar al tenis. A las tres de la tarde voy a trabajar en Sears, luego voy a descansar en casa. A las nueve de la noche voy a estudiar español, luego pienso mirar la televisión.*

Charlemos

Ex. E. Encourage your students to continue this activity by saying additional activities that they feel like doing today or would like to do tomorrow. You might like to list some of these activities on the chalkboard.

E. Mis deseos. Dígale a un(a) compañero(a) de clase sus deseos para hoy y mañana.

Ejemplos: *Hoy tengo ganas de descansar en casa.*
Mañana me gustaría hacer ejercicio.

1. Hoy tengo ganas de...
   a. trabajar mucho.
   b. ir de compras.
   c. descansar en casa.
   d. comer en un restaurante.
   e. caminar un poco.

2. Mañana me gustaría...
   a. ir al cine.
   b. hacer ejercicio.
   c. salir con mis amigos.
   d. comer en un restaurante.
   e. visitar a un(a) amigo(a).

TRANSPARENCY No. 8A and 8B: Leisure Activities and Sports

F. ¿Qué prefieres? Pregúntele a un(a) compañero(a) de clase qué prefiere hacer.

Ejemplos: ¿esquiar o patinar?
A: *¿Prefieres esquiar o patinar?*
B: *Prefiero esquiar.*

1. ¿jugar al tenis o al básquetbol?
2. ¿montar en bicicleta o a caballo?
3. ¿correr en el parque o nadar en la piscina?
4. ¿escribir cartas o leer un libro?
5. ¿escuchar la radio o mirar la televisión?
6. ¿ir al cine o ver películas en video?
7. ¿salir con amigos o visitar a los abuelos?

Ex. G. Have students ask you these questions, using *usted* verb forms.

G. Familia y casa. Pregúntele a otro(a) compañero(a) de clase.

1. ¿Es tu familia pequeña o grande? ¿Cuántos son ustedes? ¿Quiénes son? ¿Cuántos años tienen?
2. ¿Hay unas personas divorciadas en tu familia? ¿Quiénes son?
3. Y tu casa o apartamento: ¿es grande? ¿De qué color es?
4. ¿Dónde quieres vivir en cinco años? ¿Prefieres vivir en una casa o en un apartamento?
5. ¿Cuántos niños tienes ahora? ¿Cuántos niños quieres tener? ¿Piensas que es una buena idea tener pocos o muchos niños?

GRAMÁTICA FUNCIONAL

Stating locations and describing feelings

—¿Dónde está Lorena, mamá?
—Está en el politécnico, Beti.
—Ella está muy ocupada, ¿verdad?
—Sí, Lorena siempre tiene prisa.
—¿Está contenta Lorena, mamá?
—Pues, claro que sí, mi hija.

Present tense of the verb *estar*

estar *(to be)*

(yo)	**estoy**	*I am*
(tú)	**estás**	*you (informal) are*
(usted, él/ella)	**está**	*you (formal) are, he/she is*
(nosotros/nosotras)	**estamos**	*we are*
(vosotros/vosotras)	***estáis***	*you (informal) are*
(ustedes, ellos/ellas)	**están**	*you, they are*

Two uses of estar

1. To state where people are, use *estar en* + a location.
    —¿Dónde está papá?   *Where is Dad?*
    —**Está en el banco.**   *He's at the bank*

2. To describe how people are feeling, use *estar* + an adjective.
    —¿Cómo estás, Elena?   *How are you, Elena?*
    —**Estoy muy cansada.**   *I'm very tired.*

Here are some adjectives you can use with *estar*:

triste	*sad*	**contento(a)**	*happy*
enfermo(a)	*sick*	**enojado(a)**	*angry*
ocupado(a)	*busy*	**preocupado(a)**	*worried*

Idioms with tener

To describe how people are feeling, you can also use the verb *tener* + a noun.

—**¿Tienes sueño,** mamá?   *Are you sleepy, Mom?*
—Sí, **tengo mucho sueño.**   *Yes, I'm very sleepy.*

Note: To express **very** with the *tener* expressions, use a form of the adjective *mucho*, which must match the gender (masculine or feminine) and number (singular or plural) of its noun, as in the example above.

Some uses of *ser* and *estar* are summarized and practiced in *Lección 6 beginning* on page 158.

At this point, you could explain the use of *ser* and *estar* + physical appearance and/or emotional state; for example, *Es bonita* vs. *Está bonita* and *Es nervioso* vs. *Está nervioso*.

If you wish, tell students other adjectives they could use with *estar* such as *aburrido(a)* and *interesado*.

1. At first, students will often use adjectives to express these concepts, as they do in English. With practice, however, students will use these *tener* expressions confidently and accurately.
2. Collect photographs that depict these emotional states and use the photos to practice and review this new vocabulary.

Review the idiomatic use of *tener años: ¿Cuántos años tiene usted? ¿Cuántos años tiene su padre? Y su madre, ¿cuántos años tiene ella?*, etc.

Here are some expressions you can use with *tener:*

tener sueño	*to be sleepy*	**tener celos**	*to be jealous*
tener prisa	*to be in a hurry*	**tener miedo**	*to be afraid*
tener razón	*to be right*	**tener paciencia**	*to be patient*

Practiquemos

Ex. A. Answers: estás, estoy, Estás, está, Está, está, Están, está

A. Conversación con Amanda. Complete la conversación entre Lorena y su amiga Amanda, usando formas del verbo **estar.**

AMANDA: ¡Hola, Lorena! ¿Cómo _____?
LORENA: Pues, _____ más o menos bien.
AMANDA: ¿ _____ preocupada, niña?
LORENA: Un poco. Mi abuelita _____ en el hospital.
AMANDA: Ay, no. ¿ _____ muy enferma?
LORENA: No, ella _____ un poco enferma. Es anciana, ¿sabes?
AMANDA: Ah, sí... comprendo. ¿ _____ tus padres con tu abuela?
LORENA: Bueno, mi mamá _____ con ella en este momento.

Ex. B. Some of these items have more than one correct answer; therefore, no answers are provided here.

B. Conclusiones. Complete las siguientes oraciones con una conclusión lógica.

Ejemplo: Roberto tiene una esposa; él *está casado.*

> **triste**
> **enojado(a)**
> **cansado(a)**
> **ocupado(a)**
> **contento(a)**
> **preocupado(a)**

1. Beti tiene miedo de un examen; ella está...
2. Memo tiene mucho sueño; el niño está muy...
3. La novia de Tomás no tiene celos; Ceci está...
4. Elena tiene mucha prisa hoy; ella está...
5. Tomás tiene problemas emocionales; él está...
6. Matilde tiene pocos problemas; ella está...

C. La familia Velarde. Mire el dibujo, luego conteste las preguntas en español.

1. ¿Dónde está la familia Velarde esta noche?
2. ¿Está ocupado Memo en este momento?
3. ¿Cómo están el niño y sus padres?
4. ¿Cómo está doña Matilde esta noche?
5. ¿Está enferma doña Matilde?
6. ¿Cómo están Beti y Tomás?
7. ¿Qué tal Juan en este momento?
8. ¿Y su esposa Rosa?
9. ¿Qué tiene Elena?
10. ¿Qué pasa con Lorena ahora?

D. ¿Cómo están? Complete las siguientes oraciones, usando la forma correcta de **tener años, tener celos, tener miedo, tener prisa, tener razón, tener sueño, tener ganas de.**

Ejemplo: LORENA: Mi sobrino Memo *tiene* cinco *años.*

MATILDE: Me llamo Matilde Figueroa y yo _____ 78 _____.

ROBERTO: Mi papá trabaja ocho horas al día en el banco, luego camina un kilómetro a nuestro apartamento. Cuando llega a casa, descansa en el sofá porque _____.

CECI: Tomás, tú _____ de mí porque recibo cartas de un amigo alemán, pero no debes _____ porque sus cartas no son románticas.

ROSA: _____ porque mi marido va a pescar con dos amigos y él no sabe nadar.

BETI: Abuelita, _____: las telenovelas mexicanas son dramáticas, pero interesantes.

TOMÁS Beti y yo tenemos una clase a las 8:30. Ahora son las 8:20, pero salimos de casa en un minuto. ¡Uy! Esta mañana nosotros _____.

USTED: Y esta (mañana/tarde/noche) yo _____.

Charlemos

Ex. E. Follow-up activity: Students join another pair and ask them questions, using these items as cues; for example, *Cuando ustedes están enojados, ¿qué hacen?*

E. ¿Qué hace usted? Dígale a un(a) compañero(a) qué hace usted en las siguientes situaciones. Los tres puntos (...) indican otra posibilidad.

1. Cuando estoy enojado(a),
   a. ir al cine.
   b. hacer ejercicio.
   c. escuchar la radio.
   d. ...

2. Cuando tengo miedo,
   a. leer un libro.
   b. tocar la guitarra.
   c. visitar a unos amigos.
   d. ...

3. Cuando estoy contento(a),
   a. dar una fiesta.
   b. me gustar bailar.
   c. ir de compras.
   d. ...

4. Cuando tengo prisa,
   a. no comer mucho.
   b. no trabajar bien.
   c. querer descansar.
   d. ...

Ex. F. Demonstrate exactly what students are expected to do; many students learn better from observing a demonstration than from reading instructions.

F. ¡Adivínelo! Form groups of three or four persons. Each student writes two sentences that 1) describe where a person *(tú)* is right now or how a person is feeling, and 2) can be acted out. Put all the sentences in a container. One student takes a sentence, reads it silently, then acts it out. The other group members try to guess what the sentence says.

Ejemplos: *Estás en la biblioteca.*
Tienes mucho sueño.
Estás muy preocupado(a).

Mention to your students that women in the middle classes who have been to the university and are working keep their last names.

NOTAS CULTURALES

Apellidos° hispanos

En la tradición hispana, los niños reciben° más de un nombre, por ejemplo: María Rebeca, Tomás Enrique. Algunas veces, los niños reciben el nombre del santo o de la santa° dependiendo° del día en que nacen°; por ejemplo, el 25 de julio es el día de Santiago Apóstol, así que el nombre del niño va a ser Santiago. Muchas veces, los padres escogen° el nombre del niño o de la niña para honrar° a otro miembro de la familia.

Los hispanos usan sobrenombres°; por ejemplo, Natividad se transforma° en Nati, Guillermo en Memo, Teresa en Tere y los nombres compuestos° se abrevian°; María Teresa se transforma en Maritere y María del Carmen se transforma en Maricarmen. Los sobrenombres más comunes terminan° en -*ita* para niñas: Cristina=Cristinita, Isabel=Isabelita; y en -*ito* para niños: Miguel=Miguelito, Rafael=Rafaelito.

Los hispanos tienen dos apellidos. El primero° es el apellido del padre y el segundo° es el apellido de la madre: Olga González Alvarez. A veces solamente se usa el apellido del padre y se abrevia el apellido de la madre: Olga González A. Los dos apellidos se necesitan para propósitos legales.°

last names

receive

saint / depending /are born

choose / to honor

nicknames / is transformed
compound / are shortened

finish

first / second

legal

Cuando una mujer se casa, ella toma el apellido de su esposo. Por ejemplo, si Olga González Alvarez se casa con Ernesto Castro Ramírez, entonces su nombre es Olga González de Castro. Para propósitos legales, sus papeles son archivados° bajo el apellido de su padre.

filed

▲ ▲ ▲ ▲ ▲ ▲ ▲ ▲ ▲ ▲

G. ¿Cómo se llama? Put the following names in alphabetical order as they would appear in a telephone directory.

Ana María Ross Múñoz
Juan Carlos Mendoza Farías
Marvin Luis Murillo Loría
Josefina del Carmen Orozco Méndez
Luis Alberto Alvarado Ramírez
Miguel Angel Rivera Fernández
Marta Mercedes González de Darce

Write your full name according to the Hispanic system of names.

1. Write the full name of a man and a woman on the board or on an overhead transparency. Then show students how Hispanic names change over three generations originating from the husband and wife.
2. Tell students that some Spanish speakers give their friends nicknames based on some personal characteristic; for example: *Flaco, Gordo, Gordita, Negrita, Morena.* These nicknames may seem offensive to English speakers, but they are not so intended.

GRAMÁTICA FUNCIONAL

Describing actions in progress

—¿Qué estás haciendo, Lorena?
—Estoy estudiando para un examen.

Present progressive tense

How to form the present progressive

Use a present tense form of *estar* plus a present participle, which is formed by adding *-ando* to the stem of *-ar* verbs and *-iendo* to the stem of *-er* and *-ir* verbs.[1]

$$\left.\begin{array}{l} \text{estoy} \\ \text{estás} \\ \text{está} \\ \text{estamos} \\ \textit{estáis} \\ \text{están} \end{array}\right\} + \left\{\begin{array}{ll} \text{estudi\textbf{ando}} & \textit{(studying)} \\ \text{com\textbf{iendo}} & \textit{(eating)} \\ \text{escrib\textbf{iendo}} & \textit{(writing)} \end{array}\right.$$

How to use the present progressive

Spanish speakers often use the simple present tense to describe routine actions. They use the present progressive tense to describe what is

1. Emphasize that the present participle always ends in *-o*. This is because present participles are not adjectives.
2. Point out that the present progressive tense is never used to express future actions, conditions, or events.

---

[1] Two irregular present participles are: *leyendo* (reading) and *trayendo* (bringing).

happening right now—at this very moment. Compare the two captions in the following illustrations.

Happens habitually

Generalmente, Lorena **come** *(eats)* con su familia en casa.

Happening right now

Pero en este momento Lorena **está comiendo** *(is eating)* en una cafetería.

Practiquemos

A. ¿Aló? Lorena está hablando por teléfono con unos amigos. ¿Qué preguntas les hace Lorena, y qué responden ellos?

Ejemplo: Miguel, ¿estudiar?   no, descansar
                      —*Miguel, ¿estás estudiando?*   —*No, estoy descansando.*

Lorena	**Amigo(a)**
1. Daniel, ¿trabajar mucho?	no, leer una novela
2. Carlitos, ¿estudiar ahora?	no, tocar el piano
3. Señora Piñero, ¿comer?	no, escribir una carta
4. Usted, ¿escuchar la radio?	no, mirar una telenovela
5. Sr. Bermúdez, ¿hacer ejercicio?	sí, jugar con mis nietos

B. ¿Qué están haciendo? Describa qué están haciendo estas personas.

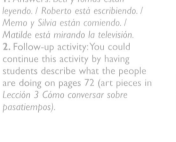   

Beti y Tomás...   Roberto...   Matilde...
                                              Memo y Silvia

C. Situaciones. Lea cada situación, luego escriba una o dos oraciones sobre lo que usted piensa que está ocurriendo.

1. Lorena está en la oficina de su profesor de hotelería. Mañana ella tiene un examen importante. ¿Qué está haciendo Lorena en la oficina? ¿y su profesor?
2. Elena, la tía de Lorena, está con dos clientes en su boutique pequeña. ¿Qué está haciendo Elena? ¿y sus clientes?
3. En este momento Roberto y Silvia Velarde están en una fiesta en la casa de unos amigos. ¿Qué están haciendo Roberto y Silvia? ¿y sus amigos?
4. Ahora doña Matilde está con su nieta Beti. A la abuelita le gusta mirar telenovelas. ¿Qué está haciendo doña Matilde? ¿y Beti?
5. Memo es el bebé de la familia Velarde. En este momento el niño está en el sofá con su abuela Rosa María. Son las seis de la tarde. ¿Qué está haciendo Memo? ¿y su abuelita?

D. Conversaciones. Escriba una carta breve a su amigo(a) en la que describe lo que está pasando en estos momentos.

Charlemos

E. ¡Adivínelo! Hable con otro(a) estudiante y adivinen qué están haciendo las siguientes personas en este momento.

Ejemplo: su abuelo
            Ahora mi abuelo está trabajando.

1. su padre o madre
2. su hermano o hermana
3. su mejor amigo o amiga
4. su actor o actriz favorito(a)
5. el autor de su texto ***Poco a poco***
6. el presidente de los Estados Unidos

F. Charadas. En diferentes hojas de papel, escriba varias acciones usando el presente progresivo. Su profesor(a) va a corregir sus oraciones. Luego usted y sus compañeros van a escoger unos papeles y van a actuar lo que dice en el papel. Los otros estudiantes tienen que adivinar lo que el actor o la actriz están haciendo o actuando.

Ejemplos: *Estás comiendo en casa.*
             Estás mirando la televisión.

PARA LEER MEJOR

Using Text Organization to Predict Content

The way in which a text is organized can help you predict what you will read. Of course, it is important to understand the main ideas in a reading passage. One way of doing so is to read it several times.

Activities

A. Look at how this greeting card is laid out and printed.

  1. What do you think is the main purpose of the poem?
  2. What do you expect its central theme is about?

---

*Para Una Abuelita
Muy Especial*

*A veces no nos damos cuenta
Del amor que compartimos
en familia,
Y muy pocas veces,
Hablamos de este amor...*

*Pero llega tu cumpleaños
y es muy importante
expresarte todo
Ese amor que sentimos
hoy y siempre
Por ti, querida abuelita*

¡Feliz cumpleaños!

B. Skim the poem to get the gist of its content. Do not stop to look up unfamiliar words in a dictionary.

  1. For whom is this poem intended?
  2. From whom is the poem sent?
  3. What is the tone of the poet?

  ____ formal   ____ informal
  ____ happy   ____ sad

C. Scan the poem to locate specific information.

  1. List the words from the poem that you associate with love.
  2. Write the words whose meaning you could guess from context.
  3. Write the words that seriously impeded your comprehension.

D. Read the poem again to improve your understanding of its meaning.

PARA ESCRIBIR MEJOR

Writing Topic Sentences

Your ability to write clear, concise topic sentences is essential to writing well. A good topic sentence has the following features:

- It comes at the beginning of a paragraph.
- It states the main idea of the paragraph.
- It focuses on only one topic of interest.
- It makes a factual or personal statement.
- It is neither too general nor too specific.
- It attracts the attention of the reader.

Activities

A. Listed below are five possible topic sentences for an opening paragraph about Hispanic families. Discuss the sentences with a classmate. Which sentence do you think is most appropriate to begin the paragraph? Why? Your classmate may have several different opinions; there is no one correct answer.

1. Cada año hay más divorcios en las familias hispanas.
2. Por lo general, las familias hispanas son muy unidas.
3. Muchas veces los abuelos viven en la casa de sus nietos.
4. La mujer hispana tiene muchas responsabilidades con su familia.
5. Normalmente, la familia hispana no incluye animales domésticos.

B. First, write a topic sentence for an opening paragraph about a description of your family. Second, write five or six sentences to develop the idea stated in your topic sentence. Third, exchange your paragraph with a classmate. Read each other's paragraph and discuss how you might improve its topic sentence; use the questions below to help you do so.

Does the topic sentence . . .

1. come at the beginning of the paragraph?   ___ yes   ___ no
2. state the main idea of the paragraph?   ___ yes   ___ no
3. focus on only one topic of interest?   ___ yes   ___ no
4. make a factual or personal statement?   ___ yes   ___ no
5. seem neither general nor too specific?   ___ yes   ___ no
6. attract the attention of the reader?   ___ yes   ___ no

You could expand this activity to have students select one of the topic sentences and then, with a partner, write a paragraph that fits the topic sentence. Afterwards, students could write these paragraphs on the chalkboard or on an overhead transparency to compare them.

Atajo

Functions:
Writing an introduction; describing people; talking about the present; stating a preference

Vocabulary:
Family members; people; up-bringing; senses; personality

Grammar:
Verbs: *estar, tener*; progressive tenses; Adjectives position

SÍNTESIS

¡A ver!

You are going to meet Miguel and Laura who will introduce themselves and talk about their families. First, study the words and sentences and their meaning in the *Vocabulario esencial*. Second, read the two paragraphs below to know what information you need to listen for. Third, watch the videotape, then write in the missing numbers and words in the paragraphs.

Vocabulario esencial

traductor	*translator*
el tercero	*third*
Me encanta la lectura.	*I like to read.*
país	*country*
hijos	*children*
medio	*half*
¡Perdóname!	*Excuse me!*
papás	*parents*
Distrito Federal	*Mexico City*

Answers:
Miguel: 21, soltero, Madrid, 4, 2, España
Laura: 36, casada, México, 1, 2, Mexico

Miguel tiene _____ años y es _____ (soltero/casado). Ahora él vive en la ciudad de _____. Miguel tiene _____ hermano(s) y _____ hermana(s). Sus parientes viven en diferentes partes de _____.

Laura tiene _____ años y está _____ (soltera/casada). Ahora ella vive en la Ciudad de _____. Laura tiene _____ hermano(s) y _____ hermana(s). Sus parientes viven en diferentes partes de _____.

Visit

http://poco.heinle.com

¡A leer!

Lea el siguiente anuncio de un bautismo *(baptism)*.

SÍNTESIS

¿Comprendió Ud.?

1. ¿Cuándo es el cumpleaños de la bebé?
2. ¿En qué fecha es su bautismo? ¿Dónde es?
3. ¿Cuál es el nombre completo de la bebé?
4. ¿Cómo se llaman los padrinos de ella?
5. ¿Dónde viven Lucía y su familia?

¡A escribir!

En uno o dos párrafos describa a su familia, específicamente...

1. quiénes son (nombre y cuántos años tienen).
2. dónde viven (ciudad, casa o apartamento).
3. dónde trabajan o estudian.
4. sus pasatiempos y deportes favoritos.

¡A conversar!

Charle con otro(a) estudiante.

1. Bring to class some photographs of your family to share with a classmate. Describe your family as well as you can in Spanish.

2. Describe one of your favorite relatives in Spanish to a classmate. Use the vocabulary you have learned up to now; do not use a dictionary.

Lucia

Nací en la Ciudad de Mexico, D.F. el día 28 de julio de 1997 y me bautizaron el día 8 de diciembre del mismo año en la Parroquia del Verbo Encarnado (La Sagrada Familia)

Mis Padres:
Gonzalo Aguilar Abarca
Y
Norma M. de Aguilar

Mis Padrinos:
Marcelo Maldonado A.
Y
Josefina R. de Maldonado

Answers:
1. *Su cumpleaños es el 28 de julio.*
2. *Su bautismo es el 8 de diciembre. Es en la Parroquia del Verbo Encarnado (La Sagrada Familia).*
3. *Su nombre completo es Lucía Aguilar M.*
4. *Sus padrinos se llaman Marcelo y Josefina Maldonado.*
5. *Viven en México, D.F. (la Ciudad de México).*

This activity reinforces orally what students have done in writing in the *¡A escribir!* activity above.

Atajo

VOCABULARIO

Sustantivos

el hombre *man*
la mujer *woman*
el (la) niño(a) *child*
la telenovela *soap opera*

Los parientes

la abuela *grandmother*
el abuelo *grandfather*
la cuñada *sister-in-law*
el cuñado *brother-in-law*
la esposa *wife*
la hija *daughter*
el hijo *son*
el marido *husband*
la nieta *grandaughter*
el nieto *grandson*
la nuera *daughter-in-law*
el (la) primo(a) *cousin*
la sobrina *niece*
el sobrino *nephew*
la suegra *mother-in-law*
el suegro *father-in-law*
la tía *aunt*
el tío *uncle*
la yerna *daughter-in-law*
el yerno *son-in-law*

Adjetivos

cada *each*
cansado *tired*
casado *married*
contento *happy*
divorciado *divorced*
enfermo *sick*
enojado *angry*
esa (+ noun) *that*
mayor *older*
menor *younger*
ocupado *busy*
preocupado *worried*
soltero *single*
todo *all*
triste *sad*
viudo *widowed*

Verbos

adorar *to adore*
asistir a *to attend (e.g., a class)*
comenzar (e → ie) *to begin, to start*
estar *to be*
me gustaría *I would like*
pensar (e → ie) *to think, to plan on*
preferir (e → ie) *to prefer*
querer (e → ie) *to want, to love*
venir (e → ie) *to come*

Adverbios

siempre *always*

Expresiones idiomáticas

muchas veces *often*
para siempre *forever*
pues *well*
tener ganas de (+ infinitive)
    to feel like
tener celos *to be jealous*
tener miedo *to be afraid*
tener prisa *to be in a hurry*
tener razón *to be right*
tener sueño *to be sleepy*

5

¡Qué rica está la comida!

▶ COMMUNICATIVE GOALS

You will be able to talk and write about foods and some of your daily activities.

▶ LANGUAGE FUNCTIONS

Stating preferences
Expressing opinions
Expressing likes and dislikes
Ordering food in a restaurant
Making a luncheon invitation
Describing daily activities
Indicating specific things

http://poco.heinle.com

▶ VOCABULARY THEMES

Main dishes, beverages, desserts
Idioms: *tener hambre, sed*

Atajo

▶ GRAMMATICAL STRUCTURES

Present tense of stem-changing verbs (*o → ue, e → i*)
Demonstrative adjectives
Neuter demonstrative pronouns
The verb *gustar* + noun

VIDEO

If you wish to obtain free information on Venezuela, write: Venezuela Tourist Office, 20 North Wacker Drive, Room 750, Chicago, IL 60606; telephone: (312) 236-9655.

▶ CULTURAL INFORMATION

Table manners in Spanish-speaking countries
Mealtimes in Latin America and Spain

Play Lab Tape

EN CONTEXTO

Hoy es domingo, el 10 de junio. Es la una y media de la tarde, y la familia Velarde está almorzando en casa.(1) Hay sopa de pescado,° arroz con pollo,° ensalada y mucho más.°

fish soup / chicken and rice
more

MATILDE: Debes comer más arepas, Lorena.(2)

LORENA: Ay, no, abuelita. Estoy satisfecha.(3) No puedo comer más.

BETI: ¡Yo, sí! ¡Qué rica° está la comida, mamá! ¡Me gustan mucho estas arepas! Quiero dos más, por favor.

delicious

ROSA: ¡Cómo no, hija!(4) Tienes mucha hambre° hoy, ¿verdad?

You're very hungry

BETI: Pues, sí. Esta tarde voy a jugar vólibol con mis amigos y necesito mucha energía para jugar bien.

ROBERTO: Siempre tienes mucha energía, Beti. Oye, mamá, tengo sed.°

I'm thirsty

ROSA: Aquí hay agua° mineral y jugos naturales. ¿Qué prefieres, hijo?

water

ROBERTO: Agua mineral, por favor.

BETI: ¿Qué hay de postre,° mamá?

dessert

ROSA: Bueno, hija. De postre hay fruta, arroz con leche° o flan.° ¿Qué te apetece?(6)

rice pudding / caramel custard

BETI: Hmmm... Pues, prefiero fruta. Voy a comer una naranja.

LORENA: Oye, papá. Tengo una idea. Vamos a la Isla de Margarita en diciembre.(7) Podemos nadar, ir de compras, hacer un picnic y...

JUAN: ¿Cómo? ¿A la Isla de Margarita? ¡Por Dios, Lorena!(8) Trabajo en un banco, pero no soy el presidente allí.

Notas de texto

1. Many Latin Americans and Spaniards have lunch, their main meal of the day, between 1:00 and 3:00 in the afternoon. Since increasingly more people are working or attending school from 8:30 a.m. to 3:30 p.m., in some places supper (dinner) is now the main meal.

2. *Arepas* are flat pancakes made from white corn flour, water, and salt. They are deep fried or baked and are filled with butter, meat or cheese. *Arepas* are very popular in Venezuela and Colombia.

3. To decline second helpings of food, Spanish speakers say: "I am satisfied," (*Estoy satisfecho.*) rather than "I'm full," which would be considered rude in many Spanish-speaking countries.

4. In Spanish there are many idiomatic expressions with the word *cómo* such as *¡Cómo no!* (Sure! or Why not?) and *¿Cómo?* (Huh? or What?).

5. Notice that Rosa does not mention milk or wine to her oldest son. Usually, milk is served only to young children. In Spanish-speaking countries wine is often served at lunch or supper (dinner); of course, one does not quench one's thirst with wine. Usually at lunch or supper, people drink fresh fruit juices such as mango, papaya, orange, and melon. Another popular beverage is *batido* a shake made of milk and fruit juice such as *batido de papaya* and *batido de plátano*.

6. The question *¿Qué te apetece?* (What would you like?) is usually used when asking about what someone wants to eat.

7. *La Isla de Margarita* is a Venezuelan resort island in the Caribbean Sea, northeast of Caracas. Venezuelans go there year round, drawn to the island's many shops where goods from all over the world are sold in duty-free stores.

8. *¡Por Dios!* (For Heaven's sake!) is not considered to be a blasphemous phrase in Hispanic cultures. It is acceptable to use exclamations containing the word *Dios* (God) because they have lost their religious connotations. Other common expressions include *¡Gracias a Dios!* (Thank goodness!), *¡Dios mío!* (My gosh!), *¡Válgame Dios!* (Bless me!), and *¡Vaya con Dios!* (May you go with God!).

No. 8: Add other exclamations along with their meaning and use.

Follow-up activity: Students could write their impressions of the Velarde family based on this dialogue and the one on page 95 *(En contexto)* in *Lección 4*.

¿Comprendió Ud.?

Complete las siguientes oraciones.

1. Es evidente que la familia Velarde _____ .
   a. es antipática
   c. come rápidamente
   b. está contenta
   d. tiene poca hambre
2. Doña Matilde y su familia están comiendo _____ .
   a. a una hora típica
   c. comida mexicana
   b. en un restaurante
   d. con otra familia
3. A Beti Velarde le gusta _____ .
   a. tomar refrescos
   c. tocar la guitarra
   b. montar su bicicleta
   d. jugar al vólibol
4. Lorena no quiere comer más porque _____ .
   a. no tiene hambre
   c. tiene prisa esta tarde
   b. está un poco enferma
   d. el almuerzo no está bueno
5. Juan está un poco enojado con Lorena porque ella _____ .
   a. come mucho esta tarde
   b. siempre tiene mucha prisa
   c. quiere visitar la Isla de Margarita
   d. no va a sus clases al politécnico

NOTAS CULTURALES

Modales° hispanos en la mesa

En los países hispanos, las sillas° en las puntas° de la mesa están reservadas para el padre y la madre o para el abuelo y la abuela como signo de cortesía y respeto.

Mientras que muchos estadounidenses cortan° la comida,° colocan el cuchillo° a un lado° del plato,° comen y vuelven a cortar, los latinoamericanos y los españoles comen con el tenedor° en la mano° izquierda° y el cuchillo en la mano derecha.° Durante la comida, el cuchillo y el tenedor se colocan con las puntas en el plato. Las frutas se pelan° y se comen con cuchillo y tenedor.

Si Ud. quiere repetir° la comida, puede decir: ¿Me sirve más ensalada, por favor?, pero si ya no quiere comer más, ponga los cubiertos° a un lado del plato, y puede decir: Ya estoy satisfecho(a), muchas gracias.

Charla

1. ¿Hay en su casa una etiqueta especial a la hora de comer? ¿Sí? ¿Cómo es?
2. En su casa, ¿qué costumbres hay para comer?

VOCABULARIO ÚTIL

In this section you will learn to name and describe the kinds of food you like and dislike.

Cómo conversar sobre la comida

¿Qué come usted para...

el desayuno?	el almuerzo?	la cena?
(breakfast)	*(lunch)*	*(supper)*

1. Ask your students to bring from home color photographs of these food items found in magazines, pamphlets and newspapers. Use these materials to teach and review food vocabulary in Spanish.
2. Tell students that another way to say "lunch" in Spanish is *la comida*, which also means "food" in English.

Las carnes y el pescado

el bistec con papas fritas   **el pollo con ensalada**

el jamón con huevos fritos   **el pescado con arroz**

Las sopas

de tomate   **de verduras**

You may want to add *panecillo* (roll) or *bolillo;* (which is used mainly in Mexico).

Los panes

el pan y mantequilla

el pan tostado con mermelada

Las bebidas

If you wish, introduce the following words (which are formally presented in *Lección 12: la botella* = bottle (for water, beer, soft drinks, etc.), *la copa* = glass (for wine, champagne, ice cream), *el vaso* = glass (for water, soft drinks, beer), and *la taza* = cup (for coffee, tea).

el agua mineral

la leche

el café

el té caliente

el jugo de naranja

el refresco

el vino tinto

la cerveza

Los postres

1. If you wish, introduce *el flan* (caramel custard) and *la torta* (cake).
2. You could write on the board some flavors *(los sabores)* of ice cream that your students like such as: *de vainilla, de fresa, de cereza.*
3. The vocabulary for fruits and vegetables appears in *Lección 10.*

el pastel

el helado

el queso

la fruta

Expresiones de cortesía

¡Salud!	*Cheers!*
¡Buen provecho!	*Enjoy your meal!*
¿Qué te apetece?	*What would you like (to eat)?*

Practiquemos

A. ¿Qué prefieres? Pregúntele a otro(a) estudiante sus preferencias.

Ejemplo:　　A: *¿Prefieres té helado o té caliente?*
　　　　　　　B: *Prefiero té caliente.*
　　　　　　　O: *Prefiero té caliente por la mañana.*
　　　　　　　O: *No me gusta ni té caliente ni té helado.*

¿Prefieres...

1. té helado o té caliente?
2. vino tinto o vino blanco?
3. jugo de naranja o jugo de tomate?
4. sopa de verduras o sopa de tomate?
5. pan con mantequilla o pan con mermelada?
6. helado de chocolate o helado de vainilla?
7. pollo con ensalada o pollo con papas fritas?

B. ¿Qué bebidas le apetecen? Complete las siguientes oraciones para expresar sus preferencias.

1. Para el desayuno, prefiero tomar...	**té**
2. Cuando estudio en casa, tomo...	**leche**
3. Cuando tengo mucha sed, bebo...	**café**
4. Para el almuerzo, me gusta beber...	**chocolate**
5. En las fiestas siempre tomo...	**limonada**
6. Los fines de semana me gusta tomar...	**agua mineral**
7. Para la cena prefiero beber...	**jugo de tomate**
8. Cuando estoy en el cine, tomo...	**un refresco**
	una cerveza
	vino tinto/blanco

C. Mis opiniones personales. Primero, complete apropiadamente las siguientes oraciones con diferentes tipos de comida. Luego léale sus oraciones a otro(a) estudiante, quien debe responder, con su opinión.

Ejemplo:　　Estudiante A: *El queso contiene mucho colesterol.*
　　　　　　　Estudiante B: *Estoy de acuerdo.* (I agree.)
　　　　　　　　　　　　O: *No estoy de acuerdo.* (I disagree.)

1. Un sandwich de _____ con sopa es delicioso.
2. Es recomendable tomar vino _____ con pescado.
3. El arroz con _____ es una comida muy nutritiva.
4. Pan tostado con _____ y jugo es un buen desayuno.
5. El bistec con _____ y vino es un almuerzo perfecto.
6. Los mariscos con _____ y pan es una cena excelente.

D. ¡A comer! Pregúntele a otro(a) estudiante.

El desayuno: ¿A qué hora desayunas? ¿Desayunas solo(a) *(alone)* o con otras personas? ¿Qué prefieres tomar por la mañana: café, té, leche, chocolate o jugo? ¿Qué te gusta comer para el desayuno?

El almuerzo: Normalmente, ¿dónde almuerzas? ¿Con quién te gusta comer por la tarde? ¿A qué hora? ¿Qué comes para el almuerzo?

La cena: Normalmente, ¿a qué hora cenas? ¿Cenas con tu familia, con otras personas o solo(a)? ¿Comes mucho o poco para la cena? Por ejemplo, ¿qué comes?

E. Café Monterrey. ¿A usted le gusta el café? Lea el siguiente anuncio, luego conteste las preguntas.

1. ¿En qué país se produce el Café Monterrey?
2. ¿Qué palabras describen ese café?
3. ¿Cómo se dice "instantáneo en polvo" en inglés?

F. Una invitación. Converse con un(a) compañero(a) de clase.

Estudiante A	**Estudiante B**
1. Greet your friend.	2. Respond appropriately. Then invite your friend over for lunch on Saturday.
3. Decline the invitation, and say what you are going to do on that day.	4. React to what your friend said. Then invite him or her to lunch on another day.
5. Accept the invitation and thank your partner. Ask a few questions about the invitation.	6. Respond to the questions.
7. Ask if his or her family will be at the lunch.	8. Answer the questions about your family.
9. Express your feelings (gratitude for the invitation, impressions of his or her family, etc.)	10. Respond, then end the conversation.

G. ¡Buen provecho! Hable con un(a) compañero(a) de clase.

1. Comparen la información de la lectura de la siguiente página con las horas cuando ustedes desayunan, almuerzan y cenan.
2. ¿A qué hora toman ustedes la merienda? ¿Qué comen y beben?

NOTAS CULTURALES

A la hora de comer

En el mundo hispánico se desayuna entre las seis y las ocho de la mañana. Es una comida muy sencilla,° que los europeos llaman un desayuno continental. En general, el desayuno consiste en una taza de café, pan con mermelada o mantequilla y, a veces, fruta. En Latinoamérica, sin embargo,° el desayuno casi° siempre es con queso, jamón, huevos, pan, mermelada, café o chocolate.

La siguiente comida del día es el almuerzo, que se toma entre la una y las tres de la tarde. El almuerzo consiste en una sopa, pescado o carne, verduras, y papas o arroz, una ensalada, luego fruta u otro postre. Se sirven pasteles sólo° en ocasiones especiales. Después° del almuerzo, los adultos toman café o té y charlan por media hora o más, una costumbre que se llama *la sobremesa*. En algunos países, muchas oficinas cierran° por dos horas o más para permitirles a los empleados almorzar. En otros países los empleados tienen solamente una hora, o media hora para almorzar. En estos casos, el almuerzo consiste en algo ligero° como un sandwich y café o té caliente o un refresco.

En algunos países latinoamericanos se cena después de las siete de la noche y en otros países, como España y la Argentina, se sirve la cena entre las nueve y las diez. Esta comida es algo más ligera que el almuerzo. Puede consistir en un sandwich o una tortilla.° Puesto que° la cena se sirve tan tarde, algunos hispanos toman una merienda° entre las cinco y las seis de la tarde.[1] La merienda consiste en sándwiches o pasteles servidos con chocolate, té, café con leche o algún refresco.

Assign this reading for homework. Then have students take turns reading it aloud in class. Add relevant information based on your knowledge of Hispanic cultures and your experience in Spanish-speaking countries.

simple

nevertheless / almost

only
After
close

something light

hecha de huevos con papas
Since / snack

GRAMÁTICA FUNCIONAL

Expressing what people do

—Ahora voy a jugar vólibol.
—¿A qué horas vuelves, Beti?
—A las cinco. ¿Puedes venir conmigo?
—Mi mamá dice que no puedo salir hoy.

Point out that the stem of the *nosotros* and *vosotros* forms are identical to the infinitive stem; for example: *dormimos/dormís* ▸ *dormir*.

Present tense of verbs with stem-vowel change: o → ue, e → i

As you learned in *Lección 4*, some Spanish verbs have vowel changes in the stem of the present tense.

---

[1] En Chile, la merienda se llama **las once,** que se toma a las cinco de la tarde. Se dice que durante la época colonial cuando los hombres chilenos querían salir a tomar aguardiente *(brandy)*, palabra que contiene once letras, les decían a las mujeres "Vamos a tomar once", para no ofenderlas. En Colombia, "tomar las once" significa tomar un pequeño refrigerio o un aperitivo hacia las once.

1. The following verbs change their stem vowel from *o* to *ue*, except in the *nosotros(as)* and *vosotros(as)* forms.

jugar¹ (to play)	**almorzar** (to have lunch)	**poder** (to be able)	**volver** (to return)	**dormir** (to sleep)
ju**e**go	alm**ue**rzo	p**ue**do	v**ue**lvo	d**ue**rmo
ju**e**gas	alm**ue**rzas	p**ue**des	v**ue**lves	d**ue**rmes
ju**e**ga	alm**ue**rza	p**ue**de	v**ue**lve	d**ue**rme
jugamos	almorzamos	podemos	volvemos	dormimos
jugáis	*almorzáis*	*podéis*	*volvéis*	*dormís*
ju**e**gan	alm**ue**rzan	p**ue**den	v**ue**lven	d**ue**rmen

2. The three verbs below change their stem vowel from *e* to *i*, except in the *nosotros(as)* and *vosotros(as)* forms.

servir (to serve)	**pedir** (to ask for, to order)	**decir** (to say, to tell)
sirvo	pido	digo²
sirves	pides	dices
sirve	pide	dice
servimos	pedimos	decimos
servís	*pedís*	*decís*
sirven	piden	dicen

—Mi mamá **dice** que **sirven** buenas arepas en este restaurante.
—Pues, ¿por qué no **pedimos** arepas?
—¡Perfecto!

My Mom says that they serve good arepas in this restaurant.
Well, why don't we order arepas?
Great!

Practiquemos

A. Madre e hija. Beti Velarde está hablando con su mamá. Complete la conversación, usando las formas apropiadas de **conocer, poder** y **saber.**

BETI: ¿ _____ (tú) qué, mamá? (Yo) no _____ a mis tíos y primos de Caracas. ¿ _____ (tú) decirme cómo son?

ROSA: Cómo no, Beti. Tu tía Carlota es profesora de geografía. Ella _____ muchas partes del mundo y _____ hablar tres lenguas. (Yo) no _____ bien a tu tío Pablo, pero (yo) _____ que está enfermo ahora.

BETI: ¿Y mis primos? ¿Cómo son?

ROSA: Bueno, tu prima Alicia tiene doce años y _____ tocar bien el piano. Tu primo Omar tiene catorce años, es deportista y _____ esquiar muy bien en el agua.

BETI: Mamá, tengo ganas de _____ a mis tíos y primos. También quiero _____ Caracas. ¿Cuándo _____ (nosotras) ir allí?

ROSA: ¿Quién _____ , hija? Tú no _____ ir ahora porque tienes clases.

Ex. A.
1. In this exercise we are recycling the verbs *conocer* and *saber,* and integrating those two verbs with forms of *poder.* Before your students do the exercise, you may want to review the uses and forms of *conocer* and *saber* on page 81 in *Lección 3.*
2. Answers: *Sabes, conozco, Puedes; conoce, sabe (puede), conozco, sé; sabe (puede), sabe (puede); conocer, conocer, podemos; sabe, puedes*

---

¹The verb *jugar* has *u → ue* stem changes.
²The *yo* form of *decir* is irregular.

B. Planes para el sábado. Beti y su hermano Tomás están hablando de sus planes. Complete su conversación con la forma correcta de los siguientes verbos: **almorzar, dormir, jugar, poder** y **volver.**

BETI: ¿Por qué no _____ (nosotros) tenis esta tarde?

TOMÁS: Yo no _____ tenis bien, Beti. Y después de mi accidente, no _____ hacer mucho ejercicio por una semana.

BETI: Pues, _____ (nosotros) ir al cine. ¿Qué te parece?

TOMÁS: Bien. Luego, ¿ _____ (nosotros) en el Café Suizo?

BETI: ¡Perfecto! Y después _____ (nosotros) a casa para dormir la siesta.

TOMÁS: ¿Cómo? Tú _____ dormir temprano, si quieres, pero yo nunca _____ temprano.

Exs. A, B, C
After students have completed these three exercises, have them role-play the dialogues in pairs.

Ex. B. Answers: *jugamos, juego, puedo, podemos, almorzemos, volvemos, puedes, duermo*

C. En el restaurante. Tomás y su novia Ceci están hablando en un restaurante. Complete su conversación con formas correctas de los verbos **decir, servir** y **pedir,** apropiadamente.

TOMÁS: Mi abuelita _____ que (ellos) _____ buena comida aquí.

CECI: Sí, lo sé. ¿Qué piensas _____ , Tomás?

TOMÁS: Hmmm. Pescado con arroz. Y voy a _____ una ensalada también.

CECI: Siempre _____ pescado, Tomás. ¿Por qué?

TOMÁS: Pues, mi tía _____ que es nutritivo. Y tú, ¿qué vas a _____ ?

CECI: Pollo. Mis padres _____ que el pollo está rico aquí.

TOMÁS: Bueno, ¿por qué no _____ (nosotros) ahora? ¡Tengo mucha hambre!

Ex. C. Answers: *dice, sirven, pedir, pedir, pides, dice, pedir, dicen, pedimos*

¿Quién?	**¿Qué deporte?**	**¿Donde almuerza?**	**¿A qué hora?**

D. Los sábados. Diga qué hacen las personas de la página anterior los sábados por la tarde.

Ejemplo: *Tomás juega al fútbol, almuerza en una cafetería y vuelve a casa a las cuatro.*

Charlemos

Ex. E.
1. In this activity we recycle some e › ie stem-changing verbs introduced in *Lección 4*, and integrate them with several o › ue stem-changing verbs.
2. Students could ask you these questions, using *usted* verb forms.
3. After completing this activity, students could write their answers to the questions as a homework assignment.

E. Charla. Pregúntele a otro(a) compañero(a) de clase.

1. ¿Cuántas horas duermes cada noche? ¿Duermes bastante o prefieres dormir más? Normalmente, ¿duermes bien o mal? ¿Tienes sueño ahora? ¿Duermes la siesta por la tarde? ¿Por qué?
2. ¿Dónde trabajas ahora? ¿A qué hora comienzas tu trabajo? ¿Qué tipo de trabajo haces? ¿A qué hora comienza tu primera clase? ¿Qué tienes ganas de hacer después de clase hoy? ¿A qué hora vuelves a casa hoy?
3. ¿Dónde almuerzas los días de trabajo? ¿y los días de clase? ¿Te gusta comer en los restaurantes? ¿Cuál es tu restaurante preferido? ¿Qué tipo de comida sirven allí? ¿Qué pides frecuentemente?

F. Una invitación. Hable con un(a) compañero(a) de clase.

Estudiante A	Estudiante B
1. Salude a su compañero(a).	2. Responda apropiadamente.
3. Invite a su amigo(a) a almorzar con usted.	4. Dígale que usted no puede hoy y por qué.
5. Pregúntele cuándo él/ella quiere almorzar.	6. Conteste con una fecha y una hora apropiada.
7. Dígale que usted puede ir.	8. Termine la conversación.
9. Respóndale apropiadamente.	10. Dígale "Hasta luego" o "Adiós".

GRAMÁTICA FUNCIONAL

Specifying people, things, places, and ideas

—¿Qué te apetece, Memo? ¿Esta naranja o este melón?
—Quiero ese melón, mamá. Con helado, por favor.

Demonstrative adjectives

You can use demonstrative adjectives to point out a specific noun. These adjectives must agree in gender (masculine or feminine) and number (singular or plural) with the noun to which they refer.

este queso	*this cheese*	**estos** huevos	*these eggs*
esta fruta	*this fruit*	**estas** papas	*these potatoes*
ese bistec	*that steak*	**esos** tomates	*those tomatoes*[1]
esa leche	*that milk*	**esas** verduras	*those vegetables*

1. The demonstrative adjective *aquel* and its other three forms are introduced in a footnote here because of their relatively low frequency of communicative use compared to the other demonstrative adjectives that appear on this page.
2. Initially, expect students to make many errors of gender agreement with demonstrative adjectives, but reinforce by correction to help prevent fossilization.

[1] To point out people, things and places that are far from the speaker and from the person addressed, and to indicate a long time ago, Spanish speakers use forms of the demonstrative adjective *aquel* as follows: **aquel** niño *that boy* **aquellos** años *those years* **aquella** niña *that girl* **aquellas** casas *those houses*

Neuter demonstrative pronouns[1]

The words *esto* (this) and *eso* (that) can refer either to non-specific things that are not yet identified or to ideas that were already mentioned.

—¿Qué es **esto**, mamá?   *What's this, Mom?*
—Es una papaya.   *It's a papaya.*

—¿Comprendes **eso**, papá?   *Do you understand that, Dad?*
—Sí, pero es difícil.   *Yes, but it's difficult.*

Point out that the accent mark on the demonstrative pronouns is used to distinguish them from demonstrative adjectives. Also, caution students that when translating, for example, "this one," they should not use a separate Spanish word for "one."

Practiquemos

A. ¡Qué rica está la comida! ¿Qué comentarios tienen estas personas sobre la comida? Complete sus comentarios, usando apropiadamente **este, esta, estos** o **estas**.

Ex. A. Answers: *Éste, esta, estas, este, Este, estos, Este*

Ejemplo: BETI: *¡Esta comida está rica!*

MEMO: Mmmm! _____ queso es mi favorito.
MATILDE: Bueno, y qué rica está _____ sopa.
TOMAS: Mamá, _____ arepas están fabulosas.
ELENA: Y _____ pescado está rico también.
JUAN: Ay! _____ café está muy delicioso.
SILVIA: Están muy ricos _____ mariscos, ¿eh?
ELENA: _____ arroz es está bueno, ¿verdad?

B. De compras. Ahora Rosa, Juan y su hija Beti están mirando la comida de un supermercado. Complete sus comentarios, usando apropiadamente **ese, esa, esos** o **esas**.

Ex. B. Answers:
Conversation 1 *Ese, esa, Esa, Esos*
Conversation 2 *Esas, esos, Esos, ese*

ROSA: _____ vino tinto es excelente, querido.
JUAN: Bueno, y _____ cerveza alemana también.
ROSA: _____ mantequilla tiene muchas calorías, Beti.
BETI: _____ pasteles también, mamá. ¡Pero qué ricos!
BETI: ¡Mira, mamá! _____ papas son muy grandes.
ROSA: Sí, pero mira _____ tomates. Son pequeños.
BETI: ¡Mira, mira, papá! _____ pollos son muy feos.
JUAN: ¡Uf! Y _____ pescado también. ¡Vamos a casa!

C. Productos importados. Beti está en un supermercado con su mamá. ¿Qué pregunta Beti y cómo responde Rosa?

Ex. C. Answers:
1. ¿...este café...? / No. ...ese café...
2. ¿...esta cerveza...? / No. ...esa cerveza...
3. ¿...este bistec...? / No. ...ese bistec...
4. ¿...estos quesos...? / No. ...esos quesos...
5. ¿...estas naranjas...? / No. ...esas naranjas...

Ejemplo: vino francés → vino italiano
             BETI: *¿Quieres este vino francés?*
             ROSA: *No. Prefiero ese vino italiano.*

---

[1] Demonstrative pronouns are used in place of nouns, and must agree with them in gender (masculine or feminine) and number (singular or plural); for example: *éste/ésta* (this one), *ésos/ésas* (those over there).

Beti		**Rosa**
1. café colombiano	→	café brasileño
2. cerveza alemana	→	cerveza mexicana
3. bistec argentino	→	bistec chileno
4. quesos canadienses	→	quesos holandeses
5. naranjas españolas	→	naranjas chilenas

D. ¡Buen provecho! Escriba dos párrafos, usando los siguientes como modelos.

Pienso almorzar a la(s) _____ esta tarde. Voy a comer con _____ . (Voy a comer solo[a].) Tengo ganas de comer _____ y tomar _____ .

Esta noche voy a cenar a las _____ en _____ con _____ . Quiero comer_____ y _____ . Y pienso beber _____ . De postre me apetece _____ .

Charlemos

Ex. E. Students could ask you these questions, using *usted* verb forms.

E. Entre amigos. Pregúntele a otro(a) estudiante.

1. ¿Dónde almuerzas durante la semana?
2. ¿A qué hora almuerzas normalmente? ¿Con quién almuerzas? ¿Qué comes?
3. ¿Vas a comer después de nuestra clase? ¿Por qué?
4. ¿Con qué frecuencia comes en un restaurante?
5. ¿En qué tipo de restaurante te gusta comer con tus amigos?
6. ¿Tienes un restaurante favorito en esta ciudad? (¿Sí? ¿Cuál es? Descríbelo, por favor.)
7. ¿Piensas comer en un restaurante este fin de semana? (¿Sí? ¿Dónde?)

GRAMÁTICA FUNCIONAL

Expressing Likes and Preferences

—¿Qué te apetece, Silvia?
—Pues, me gusta el pescado que sirven aquí.
—Yo prefiero los mariscos. Me gustan mucho.

The verb *gustar* + noun

As you learned in *Lección 3*, you can express your likes and dislikes in Spanish with the verb *gustar* (to be pleasing to someone).

1. You already know how to use a pronoun with the verb form gusta plus an infinitive.

—¿Qué **te gusta tomar**?   *What do you like to drink?*
—**Me gusta tomar** café.   *I like to drink coffee.*

2. When you use *gustar* with a noun, you must change the verb form to match the noun (singular or plural). Use one of the following indirect object pronouns with the verb form *gusta* or *gustan* plus a definite article and a noun.

1. Up to this point, students have been producing the *me/te gusta* + infinitive construction in speech and writing. Nevertheless, you may wish to review this structure once again at this time.
2. Write several more examples on the chalkboard or on an overhead transparency, if you wish.
3. Have students ask you about your likes and dislikes, using the grammatical construction: *le gusta(n)* + noun.
4. If you wish, tell students that the verb *apetecer* functions like the verb *gustar*; for example: *¿Te apetecen los mariscos? / —No, pero me apetece el pescado.*

me	*to me*	
te	*to you (informal)*	
le	*to you (formal)*	
le	*to him*	+ **gusta** + **el/la** + *singular noun*
le	*to her*	+ **gustan** + **los/las** + *plural noun*
nos	*to us*	
os	*to you (informal)*	
les	*to you*	
les	*to them*	

—¿**Te gusta el arroz?**   *Do you like rice?*
—No, pero **me gustan las papas.**   *No, but I like potatoes.*

3. To clarify or emphasize **to whom** something is pleasing, specify the person or persons with *a* (to); for example: *a Beti* and *a tus amigos*, and remember to include the pronoun *le* or *les*.

—¿**A Beti le** gusta el café?   *Does Beti like coffee?*
—No, pero le gustan los jugos.   *No, but she likes juices.*
—¿**Les gusta** el café **a tus amigos?**   *Do your friends like coffee?*
—Sí, les gusta el café expreso.   *Yes, they like espresso coffee.*

Practiquemos

A. ¿Qué les gusta? Complete las conversaciones, usando **gusta** o **gustan,** apropiadamente.

SILVIA: ¿Te _____ las sopas, Rosa?
ROSA: Sí, en particular me _____ la sopa de verduras.

MEMO: ¿Te _____ los refrescos, Beti?
BETI: Pues, me _____ la Coca-Cola, pero me _____ más los jugos.

LORENA: Me _____ comer en los cafés. Me _____ mucho el Café Suizo.
MATILDE: Prefiero el Café Austral. Me _____ sus pasteles ricos.

B. Los gustos. Lea los gustos de los Velarde, usando **le** o **les.**

1. A Juan _____ gusta el café colombiano.
2. A Beti y a Tomás no _____ gusta desayunar mucho.
3. A Lorena _____ gusta ir de compras los sábados.
4. A la familia Velarde _____ gustan las papas fritas.
5. A Elena y a Silvia _____ gusta el pan con mermelada.
6. A Roberto _____ gustan las carnes, especialmente el pollo.
7. A Matilde y a su hermano _____ gusta hablar por teléfono.

C. Memo y Matilde. Complete la conversación, usando **me, te, le, nos** o **les** para expresar qué cosas o acciones les gustan a las personas.

MATILDE: ¿Por qué no _____ gustan las verduras, Memo?
MEMO: Porque no _____ gustan, abuelita.
MATILDE: Pero _____ gustan las verduras a Beti y a Tomás.
MEMO: A Beti no _____ gustan mucho, ¿verdad?

MATILDE: Pues, sí... pero las verduras son muy nutritivas, niño.
MEMO: A mí _____ gusta el helado. ¿Es nutritivo, abuelita?
MATILDE: Un poco, sí. A nosotros _____ gusta el helado, ¿verdad?
MEMO: Sí, sí. A toda la familia _____ gustan todos los helados.

D. En el supermercado.
Juan y su esposa Rosa están en un supermercado. ¿Qué le dice Rosa a su marido?

1. fruta (+) / papayas (-)
2. jamón (+) / otras carnes (-)
3. jugo (+) / leche (-)
4. pasteles (+) / pan (-)

E. Gustos y disgustos.
1. Escriba una lista de diez cosas y actividades que le gustan a usted, y diez cosas y actividades que no le gustan. Luego hable con otro(a) estudiante para comparar sus listas.
2. Describa a un miembro de su familia o a un amigo/una amiga. Incluya su nombre, sus gustos y lo que no le gusta.

Ejemplo: *Mi amigo se llama Perry Howell. A Perry le gustan los deportes. Le gusta jugar al básquetbol en la escuela con sus amigos. A Perry no le gusta estudiar mucho, pero es un estudiante bueno. A él le gusta comer; por ejemplo, le gustan mucho los nachos con queso y le gusta tomar refrescos, especialmente la Coca-Cola.*

Charlemos

F. Otras preferencias.
Converse con otro(a) compañero(a).

Me gusta...	tomar té helado cuando tengo sed.
No me gusta...	comer en los restaurantes mexicanos.
	almorzar con mis amigos en la escuela.
	cenar con mi familia los domingos.

G. Mi familia y mis amigos.
Pregúntele a otro(a) estudiante.

Ejemplo: a tu papá / tomar café

A: *¿A tu papá le gusta el café?*
B: *Sí, le gusta. (O: No, no le gusta.)*

1. a tus padres / la cerveza
2. a tu familia / los mariscos
3. a tu hermano(a) / el pescado
4. a tu mejor amigo(a) / el vino
5. a tus amigos / los pasteles

H. ¡Mucho gusto!
Hable con otro(a) estudiante.

Student A: Ask your friend what he or she feels like doing, then listen carefully to the answer. Talk about your likes and dislikes until you come to an agreement on what you will do together today.

Student B: Think about several things you would like to do today. Express your likes and dislikes when you talk with your friend. Try to come to an agreement on how you will spend the day together.

PARA LEER MEJOR

Reviewing Your Reading Strategies

In this section you will review and practice some of the reading strategies that you have learned in previous lessons.

Activities

Skimming

Read the text below, then complete the following two statements.

Lo positivo y lo negativo del café

El café es una de las bebidas más populares en todo el mundo, pero pocas personas saben realmente lo que una taza de café significa. Como contiene cafeína es un estimulante del sistema nervioso, cardiovascular y muscular. Es diurético y estimula la digestión. En cantidades normales, una o dos tazas al día estimula además la actividad intelectual y física, así como la lentitud cardíaca y digestiva, pero en cantidades elevadas provoca taquicardia y como descontrola al sistema nervioso, puede ocasionar temblores. Es preferible que se abstenga de tomarlo si tiene úlcera, hipertensión, insomnio o padece de los nervios. Si es así, prefiera el que viene descafeinado y no abuse, para que pueda saborearlo siempre.

Source: "El café, lo positivo y lo negativo de esta bebida", Buenhogar, Año 23, No. 11, Mayo 17, 1988, página 11.

1. This reading is about . . .
    a. the intricacies of the human nervous system.
    b. the complexities of the human digestive system.
    c. the advantages of drinking decaffeinated coffee.
    d. the benefits and disadvantages of drinking coffee.

Answers: *1. d   2. a*

Lo positivo del café: *estimulante del sistema nervioso, cardiovascular y muscular; estimula la digestión; estimula la actividad intelectual y física; estimula la lentitud cardíaca y la digestión*

Lo negativo del café: *en cantidades elevadas, provoca taquicardia; descontrola al sistema nervioso; puede ocasionar temblores*

2. This _____ is based on _____ .
   a. article / fact   c. story / fact
   b. story / opinion   d. article / opinion

Scanning

On a separate sheet of paper, draw and fill in a chart like the one below. This task will help you locate and categorize the main ideas in the reading.

Lo positivo del café: _____

_____

Lo negativo del café: _____

_____

Guessing from context

The following sentences were taken from the article and modified slightly. Read each sentence and write the English equivalent for the italicized words without consulting a bilingual dictionary. If you wish, refer to the entire reading passage.

Answers: 1. *drinks* 2. *cup* 3. *large quantities* 4. *suffer* 5. *enjoy it*

1. El café es una de las *bebidas* más populares.
2. Pocas personas saben realmente lo que una *taza* de café significa.
3. En *cantidades elevadas* el café provoca taquicardia.
4. Es preferible que usted abstenga de tomar café si *padece* de los nervios.
5. No abuse del café, para que usted pueda *saborearlo* siempre.

PARA ESCRIBIR MEJOR

Writing a Descriptive Paragraph

A descriptive paragraph contains sentences that describe people, places, and things. In this section you will learn to write a descriptive paragraph in Spanish about one of your family's activities and how often they do it.

To express how often you or others do something, you can use adverbs of frequency. Here are some common ones:

nunca	*never*	**a veces**	*sometimes*
siempre	*always*	**muchas veces**	*often*
cada año	*each year*	**una vez al mes**	*once a month*
todos los días	*every day*	**dos veces a la semana**	*twice a week*

Activities

A. As you read the paragraph below, circle the adverbs of frequency.

Todos los días a las siete de la mañana mi hermano menor David y yo desayunamos con nuestros padres. Siempre David y yo tomamos leche y yo como pan tostado con mermelada y, a veces, un huevo frito. Mi papá siempre toma café, y a mi mamá le gusta tomar chocolate caliente. Una vez al mes mi familia y yo desayunamos en un restaurante. Muchas veces vamos al Restaurante México Lindo porque nos gusta la comida allí.

B. Now write a paragraph describing one activity that you and your family do together, and how often you do it, using the adverbs of frequency above.

Atajo

Functions:

Expressing time relationships; linking ideas; talking about habitual actions

Vocabulary:

Food: drinks, meals, pastry, table setting; time expressions

Grammar:

Verbs: *tener;* Demonstrative adjectives: *este, ese, aquel;* Demonstrative neuter pronouns: *esto, eso, aquello*

SÍNTESIS

¡A ver!

You are going to listen to two Hispanic men speaking about *taquerías*. Then you will watch two Mexican women going out for lunch in a restaurant. First, study the words and phrases and their meaning in the *Vocabulario esencial*. Second, read the sentences in the two activities below. Third, watch the videotape, then complete the sentences by checking the appropriate words and phrases in the activities.

Vocabulario esencial

la farolada	*corn tortilla with meat and melted cheese*
doble ración	*double serving*
variedad muy grande	*a wide variety*
comida de paso	*fast food*
buen sabor	*good flavor*
huele riquísima	*it smells delicious*
¡Provecho!	*Enjoy your meal!*
sabroso	*delicious*

A. En la taquería.

1. Tres platos típicos que se sirven en la taquería son...
   _____ tacos   _____ bistec   _____ chuletas
   _____ huevos   _____ pescado   _____ ensaladas

2. Muchas personas comen en la taquería porque...
   _____ la comida está rica.
   _____ se sirve comida rápida.
   _____ los precios son económicos.

3. La taquería es...
   _____ formal
   _____ informal

B. En el restaurante.

1. Laura come...
   _____ sopa   _____ ensalada
   _____ tacos   _____ chuletas

2. La amiga de Laura come...
   _____ sopa   _____ pollo
   _____ queso   _____ mariscos

Answers:
A. 1. *tacos, bistec, chuletas* 2. *se sirve comida rápida* 3. *informal*
B. 1. *ensalada* 2. *sopa* 3. *buena* 4. *buenos* 5. *formal*

SÍNTESIS

3. La comida del restaurante está...
_____ buena _____ mala

4. Los precios del restaurante son...
_____ buenos _____ malos

5. El restaurante es...
_____ formal
_____ informal

¡A leer!

¿A usted le gusta la miel *(honey)*? Lea la siguiente información para saber un poco de un producto nuevo en Latinoamérica.

INFORMACIÓN NUTRICIONAL

Los nutrimentos se necesitan en diferente cantidad. Para asegurarnos de recibir todos, debemos incluir en nuestra dieta alimentos de los tres grupos básicos, a saber:

1. Grupo que aporta energía: cereales, raíces feculentas como papa y camote.
2. Grupo que aporta proteínas: leguminosas, carnes, huevos y lácteos.
3. Grupo que aporta vitaminas y minerales: frutas y verduras.

Y PARA DESAYUNAR...

HONEY SMACKS
NUEVO
TRIGO INFLADO CON MIEL DE ABEJA

HONEY SMACKS está elaborado con trigo entero de la mejor calidad y además con deliciosa miel de abeja.

HONEY SMACKS de KE-LLOGG'S, un delicioso desayuno que con leche, además de rico sabor, proporciona el 25% del requerimiento diario de 6 vitaminas y hierro.

*KELLOGG'S recomienda un buen desayuno incluyendo una porción de **HONEY SMACKS** de KELLOGG'S con leche, jugo, pan tostado y un vaso con leche.

Para tomar un buen desayuno* basta incluir nuevo **HONEY SMACKS** de KE-LLOGG'S con leche.

Contenido neto 430 g
Reg. S.S.A. No. 140046 "A" * Marcas Registradas.
Bajo licencia de Kellogg Company
Battle Creek, Michigan, E.U.A.
Elaborado por:
KELLOGG DE MEXICO, S.A. DE C.V.
Km 1 Camino Campo Militar sobre Km 3 Carretera
Querétaro - San Luis Potosí, Querétaro, Qro.
Hecho en México

Answers: 1. *Con leche, jugo, pan tostado u un vaso de leche.*
2. *Seis.* 3. *Grupo que aporta energía, grupo que aporta proteínas, grupo que aporta vitaminas y minerales.*
4. *[open]*

¡Comprendió Ud.?

1. ¿Cómo puede usted incorporar a Honey Smacks en un desayuno completo?
2. ¿Cuántas vitaminas importantes contiene este cereal?
3. ¿Cuáles son los tres grupos básicos mencionados?
4. ¿Quiere usted comer Honey Smacks para el desayuno? ¿Por qué?

SÍNTESIS

¡A conversar!

Imagínese que usted está en un restaurante en Venezuela. Su compañero(a) de clase es el (la) mesero(a).

CAFÉ SOL

SOPAS		POSTRES	
Consomé	300	Quesos variados	600
Sopa del día	350	Fruta	300
Sopa de pescado	400	Pastel de chocolate	750
PLATOS PRINCIPALES		**BEBIDAS**	
Pollo de la casa	900	Agua mineral	250
Pollo al limón	1200	Limonada	300
Bistec con papas fritas	1500	Café	200
Hamburguesa Sol	1100	Té	200

1. Greet the server.
2. Say that you're very thirsty. Order something to drink from the menu.
3. Change your mind and order something else to drink.
4. Say you're hungry. Order something to eat from the menu.
5. Order dessert and coffee, if you wish.

Visit

http://poco.heinle.com

¡A escribir!

Imagine that you are going to stay with the Velarde family for three weeks. Naturally, they want to make your stay as enjoyable as possible. In their letter to you, they expecially want to know about the kinds of foods you like and don't like. Answer them, beginning your letter with *Querida familia.* Be sure to . . .

1. greet the family.
2. thank them for their letter.
3. say how you are.
4. ask them a few questions about the family and San Felipe.
5. mention whether or not you eat meat or fish.
6. describe what other foods you like and dislike.
7. explain what time you usually have breakfast, lunch, and supper.
8. ask them when they eat these meals.
9. close your letter appropriately.

VOCABULARIO

Sustantivos

el banco bank
la comida food, meal, lunch

Las comidas

el almuerzo lunch
la cena dinner, supper
el desayuno breakfast
la merienda snack time

Las bebidas

el agua (mineral) (mineral) water
el café coffee
la cerveza beer
el chocolate chocolate
el jugo juice
la leche milk
la limonada lemonade
el refresco soft drink
el té tea
el té helado iced tea
el vino blanco white wine
el vino rosado pink wine
el vino tinto red wine

Los platos principales
(Main dishes)

el bistec steak
la carne meat
los huevos (fritos) (fried) eggs
el jamón ham
los mariscos shellfish
el pescado fish
el pollo chicken

Las frutas y los vegetales
(Fruits and vegetables)

el arroz rice
la naranja orange
las papas (fritas) (French fried)
   potatoes

el tomate tomato
las verduras vegetables

Otra comida

la ensalada salad
el pan bread
el pan tostado toast
la sopa soup

Los condimentos

la mermelada jam
la mantequilla butter

Los postres
(Desserts)

el flan caramel custard
la fruta fruit
el helado ice cream
el pastel pastry
el queso cheese

Adjetivos

caliente hot
rico delicious

Verbos

almorzar (o → ue) to have lunch
cenar to have supper (dinner)
decir (e → i) to say, to tell
desayunar to have breakfast
dormir (o → ue) to sleep
jugar (u → ue) to play
gustar to be pleasing, to like
necesitar to need
pedir (e → i) to ask for, to order
poder (o → ue) to be able, can
servir (e → i) to serve
volver (o → ue) to return, to go back

Adverbios

más more
solo(a) alone

Preposiciones

después de after

Pronombres indirectos

me to me
te to you (informal)
le to you (formal), to him, to her
nos to us
os to you (informal)
les to you (formal), to them

Expresiones idiomáticas

¡Buen provecho! Enjoy your meal!
¿cómo? what?, huh?
cómo no of course
estar de acuerdo to agree
¿Qué te apetece? What would you
   like (to eat)?
¡Salud! Cheers!
tener hambre to be hungry
tener sed to be thirsty

Adjetivos demostrativos

este, esta, esto this
estos, estas these
ese, esa, eso that
esos, esas those

6

¡Felicidades, Beti!

▶ COMMUNICATIVE GOALS

You will be able to comment on the weather and describe your daily routines.

▶ LANGUAGE FUNCTIONS

Describing people
Describing the weather
Specifying dates
Expressing opinions
Describing daily routines
Comparing and contrasting
Expressing preferences

▶ VOCABULARY THEMES

Weather expressions
Idioms: *tener frío, calor*
Seasons of the year
Numbers 100–1,000
Parts of the body

▶ GRAMMATICAL STRUCTURES

Reflexive verbs and pronouns
Comparatives and superlatives
The verbs *ser* versus *estar* (summary)

▶ CULTURAL INFORMATION

The *quince años* celebration
The centigrade system
Climate in Spanish-speaking countries

http://poco.heinle.com

Atajo

Play Lab Tape

1. Before assigning the *En contexto* reading, discuss with your students whether or not teenagers celebrate "sweet sixteen" in their country. If so, ask them what teenagers do to celebrate that day. If you have a "sweet sixteen" birthday card and a *"quince años"* birthday card, bring to class. Show and discuss these cards with your students.

2. Preview the reading by having students listen to it on tape. You could also break up the passage into three parts, the first one ending with Tomás saying *"Siempre dices eso."* and the second one ending with the description *"...hay un enorme pastel de cumpleaños."* Stop the tape at the end of the first and second parts, then ask students: *¿Qué creen ustedes que va a ocurrir ahora?*

3. Tell your students that one way to better understand the contents of a reading selection is to visualize the descriptions and actions as you read. Suggest to them that as they read this text, they should try to create a mental picture of what is happening, who says what to whom, and how the characters interact with one another. Ask them to imagine that they are watching a video of Beti's fifteenth birthday celebration.

EN CONTEXTO

Es el 24 de junio y son las cinco y media de la tarde. Hace mucho calor°; la temperatura está a 26 grados centígrados. (1) Es un día muy especial para Beti Velarde porque hoy cumple° quince años, edad° importante para una joven venezolana.

Ahora Beti está en Santa Catalina, la catedral católica de San Felipe. Ella está allí con sus padres, sus hermanos Roberto, Lorena y Tomás, su abuela Matilde, su tía Elena, su sobrino Memo, su mamá Silvia y otros parientes y amigos de la familia. La misa° acaba de terminar° y en este momento todos están saliendo de la catedral muy felices.°

MATILDE: ¡Qué misa tan° bonita! ¡Felicidades,° Beti!
BETI: Muchas gracias, abuela. ¡Ay, mamá, estoy tan contenta!
ROSA: También eres tan inteligente y estás muy bonita hoy, hija. ¡Felicidades!
BETI: Gracias. Oye, Tomás... ¿qué te pasa?°
TOMÁS: Pues, tengo calor y tengo mucha hambre también. Vamos a casa, ¿eh?
ROSA: Paciencia, hijo. Siempre tienes prisa cuando quieres comer.
TOMÁS: Ay, mamá. Siempre dices eso.

En media hora todos están en la casa de los Velarde, que está decorada para la fiesta de quince años de Beti. En una mesa° hay muchos regalos: unas cintas de música, una bonita blusa blanca, un álbum para fotos, una calculadora pequeña, un certificado de regalo de una boutique, chocolates

Hace mucho calor *It's very hot*   **cumple** *turns*   **edad** *age*   **misa** *Mass*   **acaba de terminar** *has just ended*   **felices** *contentos*   **tan** *so*   **Felicidades** *Congratulations*   **¿Qué te pasa?** *What's the matter with you?*   **mesa** *table*

y un maravilloso estéreo de disco compacto de sus tíos de Caracas. (2) En otras dos mesas hay platos de comida venezolana: mondongo, sancocho, pabellón criollo y un bien me sabe. (3) En otra mesa hay café, vinos, cerveza y refrescos fríos.° En el centro de una mesa bonita hay una enorme torta de cumpleaños.

cold

Ahora dos hombres con guitarra y una mujer con violín tocan un bonito vals venezolano. Beti y su papá comienzan a bailar. La reacción de los invitados es inmediata: ¡aplausos y más aplausos para la quinceañera! La música continúa y todos bailan con Beti y su papá. Están muy felices, excepto Tomás.

Después de bailar un poco más, todos hacen cola° y se sirven comida al esti-lo bufet. Claro que Tomás está muy feliz ahora.

get in line

TOMÁS: Ay, abuelita, no sabes qué hambre tengo.
MATILDE: Por Dios, niño. ¿Qué te pasa? Es el cumpleaños de tu hermana, no el tuyo. Paciencia, ¿eh?
BETI: ¿Qué quieres comer, Tomás?
TOMÁS: Bueno, quiero comer un poco de todo. ¿Qué quieres tú?
BETI: La torta. También me gusta el bien me sabe.
ROSA: ¡Beti! ¡Estás comiendo muchos dulces! ¿No quieres comer otra cosa, mi hija? Hay ensalada, pabellón criollo, sándwiches de pollo y...
BETI: Sí, sí, mamá. Lo sé, pero tú sabes que me gustan los dulces. Y mañana voy a hacer mucho ejercicio.
ROSA: ¡Está bien! ¡Te quiero mucho!

Notas de texto

1. San Felipe is located north of the equator and therefore is in the Northern Hemisphere where it is summer in June.
2. The girl who is turning 15 *(quinceañera)* receives many gifts *(regalos)* including clothes, jewelry *(joyas)*, sweets *(dulces)*, and sometimes high-tech appliances and accessories.
3. Some typical Venezuelan foods include: *mondongo* (tripe with vegeta-bles), *sancocho* (meat stew with squash, sweet potatoes, and bananas), *pabellón criollo* (shredded beef in spiced tomato sauce served with fried bananas, white rice, and black beans), and *bien me sabe* (coconut cus-tard on cake topped with meringue).

¿Comprendió Ud.?

Conteste las siguientes preguntas.

1. ¿Qué tiempo hace esta mañana?
2. ¿Cuántos años tiene Beti hoy?
3. ¿Cómo comienza el día de su cumpleaños?
4. ¿Por qué está muy impaciente Tomás?
5. ¿Cuál regalo de Beti le gusta más a usted?
6. ¿Qué le apetece más a usted de comida?

Answers: 1. *Hace mucho calor.* 2. *Cumple quince.* 3. *Comienza con una misa.* 4. *Tiene mucha hambre.* 5. [open] 6. [open] 7. [open] 8. [open]

7. ¿Qué impresión tiene usted de esta fiesta?

8. ¿Qué diferencias hay entre la fiesta de Beti y las fiestas de cumpleaños que usted conoce? ¿Qué cosas similares hay?

Escriba en español un resumen de la lectura en tres o cuatro oraciones.

NOTAS CULTURALES

Los quince años

En los países de Latinoamérica, la fiesta de los quince años es una celebración muy especial. En este día, la quinceañera° tiene una fiesta semiformal que representa el paso que la persona da° de niña a mujer.° Ahora, la quinceañera entra en la vida° social de su comunidad y puede maquillarse° y usar ropa de persona° adulta.

En las familias tradicionales y católicas, la celebración de quince años comienza° con la misa junto a la familia y a los amigos. Luego, comienza la fiesta de quince años que puede ser desde una fiesta familiar hasta una gran celebración con cientos° de personas.

La fiesta comienza cuando la quinceañera baila el primer baile con su padre, hermano o tío. Luego todas las personas bailan y después se reúnen para comer, beber y hablar. La fiesta de quince años es una muestra° más de la unión entre las familias hispanas.

la quinceañera the girl who is turning 15 years old **representa el paso que la persona da** represents the step that a person takes **mujer** woman **la vida** life **maquillarse** to put on makeup **persona** person **comienza** starts **cientos** hundred **muestra** indication

En tus 15 Años

Actividades

A. Una tarjeta *(A card)*. Lea la tarjeta, luego responda a las siguientes preguntas.

1. ¿Para quién es esta tarjeta?
2. ¿Cuántos años cumple esa persona?
3. ¿Cuál es la ocasión que se celebra?

B. Celebraciones importantes. Conteste las siguientes preguntas.

1. ¿Cuáles son las celebraciones importantes para una señorita de su país? ¿y para un joven de su país?
2. ¿Cómo se celebran estos eventos?

VOCABULARIO ÚTIL

In this section, you will learn how to comment on the weather and to use specific years in Spanish.

¿Qué tiempo hace?

Tell students that another way to say ¿Qué tiempo hace? is ¿Qué tal el tiempo? (How's the weather?).

Hace buen tiempo

| Hace sol. | Hace fresco. | Hace calor. | Está despejado. |

TRANSPARENCY No. 11: Seasons

Hace mal tiempo

Hace mucho frío.   Hace viento y está muy nublado.   Está lloviendo. (la lluvia)   Está nevando. (la nieve)

Las estaciones del año

Llueve mucho.   Hace sol.   Hace fresco.   Nieva mucho.

Cómo hablar del tiempo

—¿Tienes calor, abuelita?   *Are you hot, Grandma?*
—No, Lorena. Tengo frío.   *No, Lorena. I'm cold.*

—¿Cómo? ¿A cuánto está la temperatura?   *Huh? What's the temperature?*

—18°. Voy a ponerme un suéter.   *18°. I'm going to put on a sweater.*

Practiquemos

Ex. A. Before students begin this activity, review the names for the months of the year in Spanish.

A. Las estaciones y los meses. Hable con un(a) compañero(a) de clase, y complete las siguientes oraciones, según la ciudad en que viven ustedes.

1. Los meses de la primavera son...
2. Los meses del otoño son...
3. Los meses del invierno son...
4. Los meses del verano son...
5. De las cuatro estaciones, prefiero el/la _____ porque...

B. Mis preferencias. Hable con otro(a) estudiante.

1. Cuando hace buen tiempo en el verano, me gusta...
2. En el invierno cuando hace frío, prefiero...
3. Me gusta _____ cuando hace fresco en el otoño.
4. Cuando hace sol en la primavera, prefiero...

Ex. C. Have students ask you these questions, using *usted* verb forms and other formal forms (e.g., *sus, le gusta*).

C. Charla. Converse con un(a) compañero(a) de clase.

1. ¿Hace buen o mal tiempo hoy? ¿A cuánto está la temperatura? ¿Qué tienes ganas de hacer hoy?
2. ¿Qué haces los fines de semana cuando hace buen tiempo? Y cuando hace mal tiempo, ¿qué te gusta hacer los fines de semana?
3. ¿Qué clima te gusta mucho? ¿Por qué? ¿Cuál es tu estación del año preferida? ¿Por qué?
4. ¿Te gusta el verano? ¿Cómo es el verano aquí? ¿Qué hacen tú y tus amigos en verano? ¿Sabes nadar? ¿Sabes esquiar en el agua?
5. ¿Te gusta el invierno? ¿Cómo es el invierno aquí? ¿Te gusta la nieve? ¿Qué hacen tú y tus amigos en invierno? ¿Sabes esquiar o patinar?

Ex. D. Allow students to continue their conversation, if they wish. Some students will need more guidance than others, depending on their proficiency in Spanish and their willingness to express themselves.

D. A larga distancia. Hable con un(a) compañero(a) de clase. Imagínese que ustedes están hablando por teléfono: una persona está en los Estados Unidos y la otra persona está en Caracas, Venezuela.

Estudiante A (en los Estados Unidos)	Estudiante B (en Venezuela)
1. Oye, ¿qué tiempo hace hoy en Caracas?	2. _____.
3. Ah, ¿sí? ¿En qué estación están ustedes ahora?	4. Aquí _____. Ahora la temperatura está a _____ °C.
5. ¡Qué bien (horrible)! ¿Te gusta el clima de Caracas?	6. Bueno, pienso que _____ .

E. ¡A escribir! Escriba un mes, la estación y el tiempo para cada dibujo. Luego escriba sobre su mes favorito y por qué le gusta.

Ejemplo: *Es el mes de diciembre y es invierno. A veces, hace mal tiempo; por ejemplo, hace frío y nieva mucho.*
Mi mes favorito es diciembre porque me gusta esquiar y patinar.

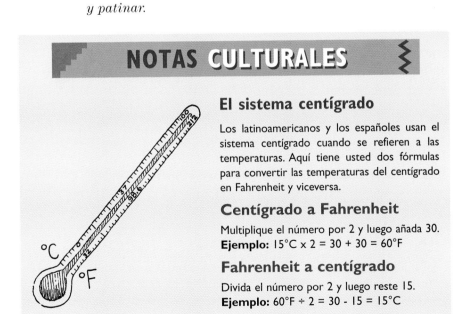

NOTAS CULTURALES

El sistema centígrado

Los latinoamericanos y los españoles usan el sistema centígrado cuando se refieren a las temperaturas. Aquí tiene usted dos fórmulas para convertir las temperaturas del centígrado en Fahrenheit y viceversa.

Centígrado a Fahrenheit

Multiplique el número por 2 y luego añada 30.
Ejemplo: 15°C x 2 = 30 + 30 = 60°F

Fahrenheit a centígrado

Divida el número por 2 y luego reste 15.
Ejemplo: 60°F ÷ 2 = 30 - 15 = 15°C

Two more accurate, but more complicated, formulas:

Centigrade to Fahrenheit: Multiply centigrade degrees by 1.8 and add 32.
Fahrenheit to centigrade: Subtract 32 from Fahrenheit degrees and divide by 1.8.

TRANSPARENCY No. 5: Time
and Weather

shoveling / outside (of)
beach

¿A cúanto está la temperatura? Calcule las siguientes temperaturas.

1. centígrado → Fahrenheit: -10° 16° 40°
2. Fahrenheit → centígrado: -10° 68° 104°

El clima alrededor del mundo

Las estaciones del año en el Hemisferio Norte son al contrario en el Hemisferio Sur.
Por ejemplo, cuando es invierno en Fairbanks, Toronto, Madrid, Moscú y Tokio, es verano en Buenos Aires, Johanesburgo y Sydney. Cuando los canadienses y los finlandeses
están limpiando° la nieve fuera de° sus casas, los chilenos y los neocelandeses están
tomando el sol en la playa.°

¿Qué tiempo hace hoy? Responda a las
siguientes preguntas.

1. ¿Qué sistema de temperaturas se usa
   aquí: centígrado o Fahrenheit?
2. ¿Cuál es la estación hoy en Nueva York?
   ¿Qué tiempo hace hoy en Nueva York?
3. ¿Qué tiempo hace en la capital de
   Venezuela?
4. ¿Por qué hay mucha diferencia entre
   las temperaturas de Montevideo,
   Uruguay y Pekín, China?
5. ¿En cuál ciudad prefiere usted estar
   hoy? ¿Por qué?

Temperaturas En el mundo

NUEVA YORK, 2 de julio (AP).— Temperaturas registradas en las principales ciudades, en las últimas 24 horas:

	Mínima	Máxima		Mínima	Máxima
Amsterdam ..	12	20			
Atenas	18	30	Montevideo ..	03	10
Barcelona ..	17	22	Montreal	13	20
Berlín	15	27	Moscú	12	27
Buenos Aires	05	14	Nueva Delhi .	26	36
Caracas	21	30	Nueva York ..	22	32
Chicago	15	33	Oslo	07	14
El Cairo	22	33	París	15	24
Ginebra	13	22	Pekín	19	33
Londres	13	18	Roma	16	26
Los Angeles ..	15	24	San Francisco	14	21
Madrid	17	31	Tokio	19	25
Miami	27	31	Toronto	09	24
			Viena	16	27

Los números 100–1,000

100	cien (ciento + número)	**600**	seiscientos(as)
200	doscientos(as)	**700**	setecientos(as)
300	trescientos(as)	**800**	ochocientos(as)
400	cuatrocientos(as)	**900**	novecientos(as)
500	quinientos(as)	**1000**	mil

1. Use numbers 1–2,000 to state a specific year in Spanish.

   1835 mil ochocientos treinta y cinco
   1998 mil novecientos noventa y ocho

2. Use the preposition *de* to connect a day, a month, and a year.

   Nací *(I was born)* el 24 de junio de 1979.

Cómo hablar de la edad

—¿Cuándo es tu cumpleaños?   *When is your birthday?*
—Es el veinticuatro de junio.   *It's on June 24th.*
—¿En qué año naciste?   *In what year were you born?*
—Nací en mil novecientos ochenta.   *I was born in 1980.*

Practiquemos

A. Eventos históricos. Lea cada oración con el año correcto.

Años históricos: 1492, 1519, 1607, 1776, 1860, 1957, 1976, 1992, 2001

1. Hernán Cortés llegó a México en _____ .
2. Los rusos lanzaron el "Sputnik" en _____ .
3. Abraham Lincoln fue elegido presidente en _____ .
4. Los peregrinos establecieron Jamestown en _____ .
5. Cristóbal Colón llegó al Nuevo Mundo el 12 de octubre de _____ . En el año _____ se celebró el quintocentenario de este descubrimiento.
6. Los Estados Unidos declararon su independencia de Inglaterra el 4 de julio de _____. Luego, doscientos años más tarde, en el año _____ , los norteamericanos celebraron el bicentenario de este evento importante.
7. En el año _____ vamos a comenzar otros 1.000 años de historia de nuestro mundo.
8. Mi papá nació en _____ , mi mamá nació en _____ y yo nací en _____ .

Ex. A.
Assign this activity for homework so that students have time to look up the historical events and their corresponding dates.
Answers: 1. *1519* 2. *1957*
3. *1860* 4. *1607* 5. *1492, 1992*
6. *1776, 1976* 7. *2001* 8. [open]
Follow-up: Discuss these historical events with your students, as well as other events and dates that interest the class.

B. Fechas importantes. Converse con un(a) compañero(a) de clase.

Ex. B. Before students begin this activity, review the names for the months of the year in Spanish.

Estudiante A

1. ¿Cuántos años tienes?
3. _____ . ¿Cuándo es tu cumpleaños?
5. Es el _____ . ¿En qué año naciste?
7. Nací en _____ . ¿Dónde naciste?
9. _____ .

Estudiante B

2. _____ . ¿Y tú?
4. Es el _____ . ¿Y el tuyo?
6. Nací en _____ . ¿Y tú?
8. _____ . ¿Y tú?
10. ¡Qué interesante!

GRAMÁTICA FUNCIONAL

Describing daily routines

—¿A qué hora te acuestas, abuelita?
—Hoy pienso acostarme a las nueve, Memo.
   Oye, ¿no tienes que lavarte los dientes ahora?
—Sí, abuelita. Siempre me lavo los dientes antes de acostarme.

Present tense of reflexive verbs

A reflexive construction consists of a reflexive pronoun and a verb. In English, reflexive pronouns end in **-self** or **-selves;** for example: myself, yourself, ourselves. In Spanish, reflexive pronouns are used with some verbs (called "reflexive verbs") that reflect the action back to the subject of a sentence.

Point out that subject pronouns are usually not used with reflexive verbs.

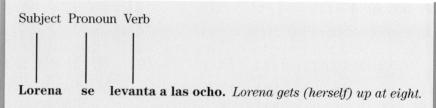

Subject Pronoun Verb

Lorena **se** **levanta a las ocho.** *Lorena gets (herself) up at eight.*

How to form reflexive constructions

1. Use a reflexive pronoun (e.g., *me*) with its corresponding verb form (e.g., *levanto*), according to the subject of the sentence (e.g., *yo*).

levantarse *(to get up)*

(yo)	**me levanto**	I get up
(tú)	**te levantas**	you get up
(usted, él/ella)	**se levanta**	you get up, he/she gets up
(nosotros/nosotras)	**nos levantamos**	we get up
(vosotros/vosotras)	***os levantáis***	you get up
(ustedes, ellos/ellas)	**se levantan**	you get up, they get up

2. Place reflexive pronouns as follows:

   a. Place the pronoun in front of the conjugated verb.

   Lorena **se levanta** a las ocho.   *Lorena gets up at eight.*

   b. When a reflexive verb is used as an infinitive or as a present participle, place the pronoun either before the conjugated verb or attach it to the infinitive or to the present participle.

Beti **se** va a levantar pronto.
            or   *Beti is going to get up soon.*
Beti va a levantar**se** pronto.

Beti **se** está levantando ahora.
            or   *Beti is getting up now.*
Beti está levantándo**se** ahora.[1]

Reflexive verbs for daily routines[2]

despertarse (e → ie)   *to wake up*
levantarse   *to get up*

TPR activity: Explain to your students that you are going to ask them to do various actions. They must listen to what you say, then act out the actions to show they have understood you. Note that although students have not yet studied formal commands in this textbook, they will be able to understand these commands because they have already learned the root meaning of the verbs. *Ustedes están durmiendo. ¡Brrrn! Es hora de despertarse. Despiértense. Levántense, por favor. Vayan al baño. Lávense los dientes. Ahora quítense el pijama y entren en la ducha. Comiencen a ducharse. Lávense la cara... las orejas... los ojos... los brazos... las manos... y los pies. Canten en la ducha. Ahora pongan un poco de champú en el pelo. Lávense bien el pelo. Bueno, salgan de la ducha. Séquense muy bien todo el cuerpo. Péinense. Ahora vístanse.*

---

[1] When a reflexive pronoun is attached to a present participle (e.g., *levantándose*), an accent mark is added to maintain the correct stress.

[2] When the action is performed on another person, a reflexive pronoun is **not** used with these verbs. Compare these two examples:
Me despierto a las ocho.   *I wake up at eight o'clock.*
Despierto a mi mamá a las ocho.   *I wake up my mom at eight.*

ducharse	to take a shower
bañarse	to take a bath
secarse (el cuerpo)	to dry off (one's body)
afeitarse	to shave
peinarse	to comb one's hair
pintarse (la cara)	to make up (one's face)
vestirse (e → i)	to get dressed
ponerse (la ropa)	to put on (one's clothes)
lavarse los dientes[1]	to brush one's teeth
quitarse (la ropa)	to take off (one's clothes)
lavarse	to wash up
acostarse (o → ue)	to go to bed
dormirse (o → ue)	to fall asleep

Las partes del cuerpo

el pelo	hair	las orejas	ears
la cara	face	los brazos	arms
los ojos	eyes	las piernas	legs
la nariz	nose	los pies	feet

Practiquemos

A. Los domingos por la mañana. Complete las siguientes oraciones, usando formas apropiadas de los verbos entre paréntesis y su información personal.

Ejemplo: (levantarse) Los domingos Beti *se levanta* a las ocho y yo *me levanto a las diez.*

1. **(levantarse)** Los domingos Beti y Lorena _____ a las ocho, y Tomás _____ a las nueve. Yo _____ .

2. **(lavarse)** Después, las dos hermanas siempre _____ los dientes, pero a veces Tomás no _____ los dientes. Y yo _____ .

3. **(bañarse)** Beti y Tomás se duchan, pero Lorena prefiere _____ . Yo prefiero _____ .

4. **(vestirse)** Beti y Lorena _____ elegantemente, y Tomás _____ de jeans. Yo _____ . A veces, mis amigos y yo _____ .

5. **(peinarse)** Después, Beti y Lorena _____ bien, pero Tomás no _____ porque es un poco perezoso. Y yo _____ .

Ex. A. Answers:
1. se levantan, se levanta, me levanto + [open]
2. se lavan, se lava, (no) me lavo los dientes
3. bañarse, bañarme
4. se visten, se viste, me visto + [open], nos vestimos + [open]
5. se peinan, se peina, (no) me peino + [open]

_____

[1] When reflexive verbs are used with parts of the body or with article of clothing, use the definite article *(el, la, los, las)*, as shown in the following examples.
Juan se lava *los* dientes. *Juan brushes his teeth.*
Beti está poniéndose *el* pijama. *Beti is putting on her pajamas.*
Tomás va a quitarse *los* jeans. *Tomás is going to take off his jeans.*

B. Asociaciones. Complete las siguientes oraciones con los nombres apropiados para diferentes partes del cuerpo de la lista. Es posible usar unas palabras más de una vez.

la cara	**los pies**	**las manos**	**los dientes**
el pelo	**la nariz**	**los brazos**	**las piernas**

1. Antes de comer, una buena idea es lavarse las _____ . Después de comer, es mejor lavarse los _____ . Comemos con los _____ y las _____ .
2. Muchos hombres se afeitan la _____ y muchas mujeres se pintan la _____ .
3. Cuando nos bañamos, nos lavamos la cara y también nos lavamos los _____ , la _____ y las _____ . También nos lavamos el _____ , las _____ y los _____ .

C. Conversaciones familiares. Complete las conversaciones con la forma correcta de los infinitivos.

dormirse	**acostarse**	**levantarse**

TOMÁS: ¿A qué hora _____ ustedes por la noche?

CECI: Pues, mi hermano de dos años _____ a las ocho, mis padres y yo _____ a las once. A veces, mi hermano _____ rápidamente, luego durante la noche _____ para tomar agua, y _____ otra vez.

TOMÁS: ¿A qué hora _____ (tú) por la mañana?

CECI: Los días de trabajo, _____ a las siete. Y mis padres _____ a las seis   y media.

lavarse	**secarse**	**ducharse**	**vestirse**	**afeitarse**

MEMO: Papá, ¿por qué _____ (tú) la cara?

ROBERTO: _____ la cara porque me gusta, hijo.

MEMO: Y luego, ¿qué haces, papá?

ROBERTO: _____ , _____ y _____ . Y tú, ¿por qué _____ los dientes?

MEMO: ¡Porque es importante y necesario!

D. ¡Qué mujer más ocupada! Para comprender la rutina que tiene Lorena durante la semana, lea la siguiente descripción con formas apropiadas de los verbos entre paréntesis.

Los días de trabajo Lorena _se despierta_ (despertarse) a las siete. Ella _____ (levantarse) a las siete y cuarto. Primero, ella _____ (ir) al baño donde _____ (ducharse) por diez minutos. Cuando ella _____ (tener) más tiempo, _____ (bañarse). Después, _____ (secarse) bien todo el cuerpo y _____ (peinarse). Entonces Lorena _____ (vestirse) elegantemente, _____ (pintarse) la cara y _____ (ponerse) un poco de perfume. Después, _____ (desayunar) y _____ (hablar) con su familia. Luego ella _____ (lavarse) los dientes y _____ (salir) de su casa. Ella _____ (caminar) a su oficina donde _____ (trabajar) como secretaria bilingüe. Lorena _____ (trabajar) por cinco horas hasta *[until]* la una de la tarde. Luego _____ (volver) a casa. Ella _____ (lavarse) las manos y _____ (almorzar) con su familia.

E. La rutina de Juan. Mire los dibujos y diga qué está haciendo Juan en este momento.

Ejemplo: *Juan está despertándose a las seis...*
O: *Juan se está despertando a las seis...*

TRANSPARENCY No. 12: Daily Routine

F. ¿Y usted? Escriba un párrafo sobre su rutina diaria. Luego léale su descripción a otro(a) estudiante. El ejercicio "¡Qué mujer más ocupada!" en la página 150 puede servirle como modelo.

Los días de escuela me despierto a las _____ . Me levanto a las _____ , luego...

Charlemos

G. ¿Qué hace usted? Dígale a otro(a) estudiante lo que usted hace antes de *(before)* acostarse y cuando se levanta por la mañana.

1. Antes de acostarme...   2. Cuando me levanto...

H. Los fines de semana. Pregúntele a otro(a) estudiante.

1. ¿A qué hora te levantas los fines de semana?
2. ¿Te levantas inmediatamente? ¿Por qué?
3. Cuando te levantas, ¿prefieres ducharte o bañarte?
4. Normalmente, ¿te afeitas o te pintas la cara?
5. ¿Te vistes elegantemente o te vistes de jeans?
6. Los fines de semana, ¿a qué hora te acuestas?

I. ¿A qué hora? Conozca mejor a otro(a) estudiante de su clase.

Find out . . .
1. what time your partner wakes up on school days.
2. what time he or she gets up.
3. how he or she feels in the morning.
4. if he or she takes a shower or a bath.
5. what your friend eats for breakfast.
6. what time your partner leaves for school.
7. what time he or she returns home.
8. what time your friend usually goes to bed.

GRAMÁTICA FUNCIONAL

Making comparisons

—¿Hace tanto frío aquí como en tu ciudad?
—Sí, pero no tenemos tanta nieve como aquí.

Comparatives

English speakers make comparisons either by adding the ending *-er* to an adjective (e.g., warmer) or they use the words **more** or **less** with an adjective (e.g., more interesting, less expensive). Spanish speakers make comparisons in the following manner.

How to express comparisons of inequality

1. Use *más* (more) or *menos* (less) before an adjective, an adverb, or a noun, and *que* (than) after it.

más		*adjective* (**tímido**)		
	+	*adverb* (**pronto**)	+	**que**[1]
menos		*noun* (**hambre**)		

[1] Use the preposition *de* (than) before a number; for example:
Beti tiene más de diez amigos.   *Beti has more than ten friends.*

—Tomás quiere comer **más** pronto **que** su hermana Beti.

Tomás wants to eat sooner than his sister Beti.

—Sí. Creo que es **menos** tímido **que** ella y es **más** impaciente.

Yes. I think he's less shy than she is and he's more impatient.

—Posiblemente, pero hoy también ella tiene **menos** hambre **que** él.

Possibly, but today she is also less hungry than he is.

2. Use *más que* or *menos que* after a verb form.

—Estudias mucho, Lorena.

You study a lot, Lorena.

—Tú estudias **más que** yo.

You study more than I do.

3. Irregular comparatives

mejor(es)	*better*	**peor(es)**	*worse*
menor(es)	*younger*	**mayor(es)**	*older*

—El tiempo en San Felipe es **mejor** que en Chicago.

The weather in San Felipe is better than in Chicago.

—Sí, pero la temperatura en Fairbanks está **peor.**

Yes, but the temperature in Fairbanks is worse.

—Lorena y Roberto son **mayores** que Beti y Tomás, ¿verdad?

Lorena and Roberto are older than Beti and Tomás, right?

—Sí. Lorena es **menor** que Roberto y Tomás es **mayor** que su hermana Beti.

Yes. Lorena is younger than Roberto, and Tomás is older than his sister Beti.

How to express comparisons of equality

1. Use *tan*[1] (as) before an adjective or an adverb and *como* (as) after it.[2]

	adjective (**nublado**)		
tan +		+	**como**[3]
	adverb (**frecuentemente**)		

—A veces está **tan** nublado en San Felipe **como** en Caracas.

Sometimes it is as cloudy in San Felipe as in Caracas.

—También llueve **tan** frecuentemente en Caracas **como** en San Felipe.

Also, it rains as frequently in Caracas as in San Felipe.

---

[1] Tan can also be used by itself to show a great degree of a given quality; for example: **¡Qué día tan perfecto!** *What a perfect day!*

[2] Note that one can make comparisons with verbs. For example: **Estudias tanto como yo.** *You study as much as me.*

[3] One can change a comparison of equality to one of inequality by using the word *no* before a verb. For example: **No llueve tanto en San Felipe como en Caracas.** *It doesn't rain as much in San Felipe as in Caracas.*

2. Use *tanto/tanta* (as much) or *tantos/tantas*[1] (as many) before a noun, and *como* (as) after it.

> **tanto** (calor)
> **tanta** (nieve)
>   + **como**
> **tantos** (días)
> **tantas** (fiestas)

—¿Hace **tanto** calor en Miami **como** en Caracas?

Is it as hot in Miami as in Caracas?

—Sí. Y hay **tantas** fiestas en Miami **como** en Caracas.

Yes. And there are as many parties in Miami as in Caracas.

—¿Tiene Colorado **tantos** días de sol **como** Venezuela?

Does Colorado have as many sunny days as Venezuela?

—¡No! Y Venezuela no tiene **tanta** nieve **como** Colorado.

No! And Venezuela does not have as much snow as Colorado.

Practiquemos

Ex. A. Answers: 1. *mayor* 2. *menor* 3. *más* 4. *más* 5. *más* 6. *más* 7. *menos*

A. Cuatro hermanos. Complete las siguientes oraciones según la información que usted sabe sobre Roberto, Lorena, Tomás y Beti Velarde. Use **más, menos, mayor** o **menor.**

Ejemplo: Lorena es *mayor* que Beti.

1. Roberto es _____ que Lorena.
2. Beti es _____ que sus hermanos.
3. Beti está _____ contenta que Tomás.
4. Tomás tiene _____ hambre que todos.
5. Lorena está _____ ocupada que Tomás.
6. Lorena juega a _____ deportes que Beti.
7. Roberto estudia _____ que sus hermanos.

Ex. B.
1. Answers: 1. *Lorena es mayor que Beti.* [open] 2. *Beti es más popular que Lorena.* [open] 3. *Lorena es más trabajadora que Beti.* [open] 4. *Lorena juega a menos deportes que Beti.* [open]
2. After students have completed this exercise, have them compare their answers with those of another classmate.

B. Dos hermanas y usted. Compare Lorena Velarde con su hermana Beti, contestando las preguntas.

Ejemplos: ¿Quién es más joven?
Beti es más joven que Lorena.

¿Es usted menor o mayor que Lorena?
Soy menor que Lorena; tengo veinte años.

---

[1] Tanto(s)/Tanta(s) can also be used on their own to show a great amount of something. For example: **¡Hace tanto calor!** *It's so hot!*

	Edad	Estudia/ Trabaja al día	Amigos	Intereses
Lorena	23	8 horas	12	libros, arte, conciertos
Beti	15	2 horas	26	vólibol, rap, fiestas
Usted	____	____	____	_____

1. ¿Quién es mayor? ¿Es usted menor o mayor que Lorena? ¿Cuántos años tiene usted?
2. ¿Quién es más popular? ¿Tiene usted más o menos amigos que Beti?
3. ¿Quién es más trabajador(a)? ¿Es usted más o menos trabajador(a) que Beti? ¿Cuántas horas estudia o trabaja usted al día?
4. ¿Quién juega a menos deportes? ¿A qué deportes juega usted? ¿Qué otros intereses tiene usted?

C. Juan y Rosa. Juan y Rosa Velarde tienen muchos intereses en común. Complete las siguientes oraciones apropiadamente, usando **tan, tanto, tanta, tantos** o **tantas.**

Ex. C. Answers: 1. *tanta* 2. *tanto* 3. *tantas* 4. *tanto* 5. *tan* 6. *tan* 7. *tantos* 8. *tanto*

Ejemplo: Rosa es *tan* inteligente como Juan.

1. Rosa tiene _____ energía como Juan.
2. Ella trabaja _____ como su marido.
3. Juan hace _____ actividades como Rosa.
4. Y él hace _____ ejercicio como ella.
5. Rosa juega al tenis _____ bien como Juan.
6. También ella está _____ contenta como él.
7. Juan tiene _____ amigos como su esposa.
8. A él le gusta ir al cine _____ como Rosa.

D. Comparaciones personales. Escriba diez oraciones en que usted compara a sí mismo(a) *(yourself)* con otras personas como, por ejemplo, sus amigos, sus parientes, sus profesores o personas famosas.

Ex. D. Assign this activity for homework. Have students exchange their sentences, read what each other wrote, then correct any grammatical errors they find in the sentences.

Ejemplos: *Soy más joven que mi novio.*
Tengo menos clases que mis amigos.
Estoy tan ocupada como mis profesores.
Me gusta ir al cine tanto como a mi novio.

Soy... guapo(a), joven, trabajador(a), simpático(a), inteligente,...
Tengo... amigos, hermanos, clases, talento, paciencia, buenas ideas,...
Estoy... ocupado(a), contento(a), preocupado(a), nervioso(a),...
Me gusta(n)... ir al cine, jugar a deportes, comer comida china,...

Charlemos

E. ¿Cómo es usted? Complete las siguientes oraciones con un(a) compañero(a) de clase.

Ejemplo: Soy tan inteligente como _____
                 Soy tan inteligente como Einstein.

1. Soy tan inteligente como _____ .
2. Soy tan guapo(a) como _____ .
3. Estoy tan ocupado(a) como _____ .
4. Hablo inglés tan bien como _____ .
5. Hago tanto ejercicio como _____ .
6. Tengo tantos problemas como _____ .

Ex. F. Follow-up activity: Assign this activity as a written homework task in which students write their reactions to these statements, then elaborate on them by including additional information about themselves.

F. Lo que hago yo. Lea cada oración y decida si describe su situación personal o no. Si usted está de acuerdo con la oración, dígale eso a un(a) compañero(a) de clase. Si usted no está de acuerdo, dígale la oración correctamente, usando **más... que** o **tan... como.**

Ejemplo: Nado más en el invierno que en el verano.
                 Sí, nado más en el invierno que en el verano.
        O: *¡No! Nado menos en el invierno que en el verano.*
        O: *¡No! Nado más en el verano que en el invierno.*

1. Camino más en el invierno que en el verano.
2. Duermo más horas cuando hace frío que cuando hace calor.
3. Me ducho más frecuentemente en el verano que en el invierno.
4. Tomo menos bebidas cuando hace calor que cuando hace fresco.
5. Me pongo un suéter tan frecuentemente en diciembre como en mayo.
6. Trabajo tan bien cuando hace mal tiempo como cuando hace buen tiempo.

GRAMÁTICA FUNCIONAL

Superlatives

English speakers single out someone or something from a group by adding the ending **-est** to an adjective (e.g., warmest), or they use expressions such as **the most, the least** with an adjective (e.g., the most elegant, the least expensive). Spanish speakers form superlatives in the following manner.

How to form superlatives

1. Use a definite article before the person or thing being compared, plus *más* (most) or *menos* (least), plus an adjective.

el (sobrino)		
la (familia)	**más**	
	+	+ *adjective*
los (amigos)	**menos**	
las (compañeras)		

—Estoy muy feliz.
—¿Por qué, Beti?
—Porque tengo **la** familia **más** inteligente, **el** sobrino **más** guapo, **los** amigos **más** generosos y **las** compañeras **más** simpáticas.

I'm very happy.
Why, Beti?
Because I have the most intelligent family, the handsomest nephew, the most generous friends, and the nicest girlfriends.

2. Irregular superlatives:

el la los las	**mejor(es)** *best* **peor(es)** *worst* **menor(es)** *youngest* **mayor(es)** *oldest*

—Hoy es **el mejor** día del año.
—¿Por qué, Beti?
—Porque es mi cumpleaños y soy **la menor** de mi familia.

Today is the best day of the year.
Why, Beti?
Because it is my birthday, and I am the youngest in my family.

¡CUIDADO! The preposition *de* can mean **of, in,** or **at** after superlatives, as shown in the two example sentences above.

Give students more examples, if necessary.

Practiquemos

G. La familia Velarde. Compare a las siguientes personas y lo que tienen.

Ejemplo: Beti tiene dos cintas de música rap, y Lorena tiene tres cintas de música Mozart. (moderno)
Beti tiene las cintas más modernas.

1. Lorena escucha música clásica, y Tomás escucha música rock. (moderno)
2. Beti tiene una caja de 50 chocolates, y Rosa tiene una caja de 30 chocolates. (grande)
3. Juan tiene una calculadora con cuarenta funciones, y Beti tiene una calculadora con veinticuatro funciones. (complicado)
4. Doña Matilde es una señora de setenta y ocho años, y su hija Rosa es una mujer de cuarenta y seis años. (anciano)
5. Rosa tiene un álbum de su colegio, y doña Matilde tiene un álbum de su colegio. (viejo)

H. ¡Vamos a votar! Escriba cuatro oraciones que describan a cuatro estudiantes diferentes de su clase de español, según las cuatro categorías de personalidad en la lista. Luego usted va a darle *(give)* las oraciones a su profesor(a), quien va a anunciar los resultados.

Ex. H. If you wish, award prizes to the four winners.

Ejemplos: *Janice es la estudiante más generosa de la clase.*
Greg es el estudiante menos tímido de la clase.

CATEGORÍAS DE PERSONALIDAD

más contento(a)	menos tímido(a)
más generoso(a)	menos perezoso(a)

Charlemos

I. Más opiniones personales. Exprese sus opiniones con un(a) compañero(a) de clase.

1. En mi opinión, el mejor restaurante de esta ciudad es _____ . Creo que una de las mejores comidas de ese restaurante es _____ . Al contrario, el peor restaurante de esta ciudad es _____ . ¿Qué crees tú?
2. La mejor música es _____ . Uno(a) de los (las) mejores cantantes (personas que cantan) se llama _____ ; me gusta mucho escuchar su música en la radio. Al contrario, uno(a) de los (las) peores cantantes se llama _____ ; su música es horrible.
3. Una de las mejores películas que conozco es _____ . Los artistas de esa película son _____ y _____ . Al contrario, una de las peores películas se llama _____ .

GRAMÁTICA FUNCIONAL

Describing people, things, places, and conditions

—¿Cómo está tu abuela, Lorena?
—Está mejor, gracias, Ceci. Ahora está durmiendo.
—Tu abuela es tan simpática. Este regalo es para ella.
—Muchas gracias. Eres muy generosa, Ceci.

Ser and estar (summary)

As you have learned, the verbs *ser* and *estar* both mean "to be," but they are used to express different kinds of information.

How to use ser

The verb *ser* often implies a fundamental quality that describes the essence of a person, thing, place, or idea. Use *ser* to express the following information:

1. These two summaries include all uses of *ser* and *estar* presented and practiced so far in this book.
2. Most of the examples here describe Lorena and her family to provide some context. The verb forms *soy* and *estoy* are used in the examples because Spanish speakers use these forms in everyday communicative situations.
3. Activity: Have students read aloud these examples to a classmate, changing the information to fit their own situations.
4. Explain to students the difference between *Es bonita* and *Está bonita.*
5. Emphasize the difference between using *ser* to express where an event takes place *(La fiesta es en nuestra casa)* and using *estar* to express where people, places, and things are located *(Papá está en nuestra casa).*
6. Ask your students these questions: 1. ¿Cómo está usted? ¿Cómo es usted? 2. ¿Cómo están sus padres? ¿Cómo son sus padres?

- Identification   **Soy** Lorena Velarde.
- Origin   **Soy** de Venezuela.
- Nationality   **Soy** venezolana.
- Profession   **Soy** secretaria.
- Marital status   **Soy** soltera.
- Physical features   **Soy** bonita.
- Personality traits   **Soy** inteligente.
- Ownership   El regalo **es** de Beti.
- Time of day   **Son** las dos de la tarde.
- Dates   **Es** sábado. **Es** el 24 de junio.
- Intentions   **Es** para ti, Beti. **Es** para tu cumpleaños.
- Impersonal statements   **Es** importante comer frutas y vegetales.
- Location of events   La fiesta de Beti **es** en mi casa.

¿Ser o estar? Ésa es la pregunta.

How to use estar

The verb *estar* often indicates a state or condition of a person, thing, place, or action, which may be the result of a change or a deviation from the norm. Use *estar* to express the following information:

- Location of people   **Estoy** en casa.
- Location of things   Mi casa **está** en San Felipe.
- Location of places   San Felipe **está** en Venezuela.
- Marital status   No **estoy** casada.[1]
- Physical condition   **Estoy** cansada.
- Emotional condition   **Estoy** ocupada.
- Action in progress   **Estoy** trabajando.

Practiquemos

A. ¿Ser o estar? Haga oraciones completas según la información que usted sabe de Lorena, Juan y doña Matilde. Use apropiadamente los verbos **es** y **está**.

Ejemplos: la madre de Rosa
Doña Matilde es la madre de Rosa.

nerviosa porque tiene un examen hoy
Lorena está nerviosa porque tiene un examen hoy.

       Lorena   **Juan**   **doña Matilde**

1. la abuela de nueve nietos
2. hablando con otra estudiante
3. una secretaria muy inteligente
4. delgado, un poco alto y guapo
5. viuda y tiene setenta y ocho años
6. una señora anciana y muy generosa
7. cansado porque trabaja mucho en el banco

Ex. A.
1. Students might wish to reread the passages in the three previous *En contexto* sections before beginning this exercise, which refers to the storyline in those sections.
2. Answers: 1. *Doña Matilde es...* 2. *Lorena está...* 3. *Lorena es...* 4. *Juan es...* 5. *Doña Matilde es...* 6. *Doña Matilde es...* 7. *Juan está...* 8. *Juan está...* 9. *Lorena es...* 10. *Doña Matilde está...*
3. Question 4: Tell students the difference between *es delgado* and *está delgado*.

---

[1] The verb *estar* is not usually followed by a noun. Because the words *soltero(a)* and *viudo(a)* are nouns, the verb *ser* is used with them to describe marital status; for example: **Soy soltera.**

8. casado con Rosa María, una mujer simpática
9. la persona más intelectual de su familia
10. en el sofá mirando la telenovela *Por este país*

B. En la fiesta de Beti. Complete la siguiente descripción y conversación con formas apropiadas de los verbos *ser* y *estar*.

Hoy _____ sábado, el 24 de junio. _____ las dos de la tarde. Hace calor y _____ lloviendo un poco. La temperatura _____ de veintiséis grados centígrados. Lorena Velarde, su familia y unos amigos _____ comiendo el pastel de cumpleaños de Beti. La fiesta _____ en su apartamento. Beti _____ hablando con su mamá.

—Mmm. Este pastel _____ rico, mamá.
—¿Te gusta? _____ tu pastel favorito.
—Pero _____ tan grande, mamá.
—Sí, cómo no. Nosotros _____ muchas personas hoy.
—Perdón, ¿dónde _____ mi abuelita?
—Ella _____ durmiendo ahora, Beti.
—¿ _____ enferma?
—No, mi hija. Ella _____ un poco cansada.
—Mi abuelita _____ muy anciana, ¿verdad?
—Pues sí. Tiene setenta y ocho años.

C. Querido(a)... Escríbale una carta de cuatro párrafos a la familia Velarde con quien usted va a vivir el próximo verano. Las siguientes frases contienen ideas útiles.

Querido(a) _____ ,

Párrafo 1: Su persona (de dónde es, su nacionalidad, su estado civil, su edad y cumpleaños, su personalidad)
Párrafo 2: Sus estudios (nombre de su escuela, cursos, profesores), su trabajo (dónde trabaja, qué hace) y su estado emocional
Párrafo 3: Su familia (nombre, edad, estado civil, características físicas y personalidad de las personas)
Párrafo 4: Sus amigos, sus pasatiempos (deportes y otras actividades) y sus otros gustos (posesiones materiales, comida)

Charlemos

D. Entrevista. Pregúntele a un(a) compañero(a) de clase.

1. ¡Hola! ¿Cómo estás hoy?
2. Yo soy (su nombre). ¿Quién eres tú?
3. ¡Mucho gusto! ¿De dónde eres?
4. ¿Eres estudiante? ¿Qué estudias?
5. ¿Eres soltero(a) o estás casado(a)? ¿Tienes niños? (¿Sí? ¿Cuántos?)
6. ¿Vives en una casa, en un apartamento o en una residencia *(dorm)*?
7. ¿Dónde está tu (casa/apartamento/residencia)?
8. ¿Cuál es tu dirección?
9. Y tu número de teléfono, ¿cuál es? Gracias.

Ahora su compañero(a) va a hacerle las preguntas a usted.

E. En la casa Velarde. Imagínese que usted está hablando con una persona de la familia Velarde (otro[a] estudiante).

1. Say where you are from, your age, and your marital status.
2. Tell the name of your town, where it is, and what it looks like.
3. Talk about your studies and/or what you do for a living.
4. Describe your family (names, ages, physical features, personalities).

PARA LEER MEJOR

Using Background Knowledge to Anticipate Content

In this lesson, you will learn about one of the most important days in the life of many girls who live in Spanish-speaking countries: their fifteenth birthday. For some background information on this happy event, please read the *Notas culturales* section on page 142 at this time.

Activities

A. The better you can anticipate what you will read, the easier you will be able to understand the main ideas in a reading passage. Before you read the invitation that follows, look at . . .

1. the style of print.
   a. Is it formal or informal?
   b. Is it simple or elegant?
   c. What information appears in the largest print? Why?
2. the overall layout.
   a. Is it formal or informal?
   b. What do you think is the purpose of the separate card?

B. Read the invitation once to get the gist of its content.

1. What is your impression of the invitation?
2. What is its main purpose?
3. What clues tell you that it is formal?
4. Why does the name "Patricia" seem so prominent?

C. Now scan the invitation for specific information.

1. Who is Patricia?
2. Who are her parents?
3. What day and time will the event take place?
4. What specifically is going to happen?

Dr. Gonzalo Aguilar Abarca

Norma Macedo de Aguilar

Tienen el honor de invitar a Usted y a su apreciable familia a la Celebración
Eucarística que con motivo del XV Aniversario del natalicio de su hija.

P a t r i c i a

Se dignará oficiar el Rv. Anselmo Loya, a las 19,30 hrs. del día 16 del
presente en el Templo de Santa Rosa de Viterbo

Apadrinarán el Acto:

Lic. Luis Rayas Díaz

Irma Macedo de Rayas

Después de la Ceremonia le
agradeceremos su presencia
en el Salón de las Estrellas
ubicado en Jacarandás 26
(Prolong. Zaragoza) Frace.
La Capilla.

PARA ESCRIBIR MEJOR

Adding Details to a Paragraph

In *Lección 4*, you learned how to write a topic sentence for a paragraph. The other sentences in the paragraph should contain details that develop the main idea stated in the topic sentence. The following procedure will help you develop a well-written paragraph in Spanish.

1. Write a topic sentence about a specific subject.
2. List some details that develop your topic sentence.
3. Cross out any details that are unrelated to the topic.
4. Number the remaining details in a clear, logical order.
5. Write the first draft of a paragraph based on your work.
6. Cross out any ideas that do not contribute to the topic.
7. Write the second draft of your paragraph as clearly as possible.

Activities

A. In the list below, cross out any detail that is not related to the topic sentence.

   Topic sentence: *Mi estación del año favorita es el verano.*

   Details: • *En el verano puedo nadar y jugar al tenis.*
   • *Me gusta el verano porque hace buen tiempo.*
   • *No me gusta mucho el invierno porque hace frío.*
   • *Mis amigos y yo damos muchas fiestas los sábados.*

B. In the following paragraph, some of the ideas are not important or do not provide information related to the topic. Cross out the unrelated details and any unimportant information, and combine some sentences to shorten the paragraph.

Mi estación del año favorita es el verano. Me gusta el verano porque no tengo clases en la universidad. Estudio español, historia, biología y química. No me gusta mucho el invierno porque hace frío. Me gusta el verano porque hace buen tiempo. También no tengo que despertarme a las seis y media de la mañana durante la semana. Mi primera clase comienza a las ocho de la mañana. En el verano puedo nadar. También puedo jugar al tenis y montar mi bicicleta. ¡Me gusta mucho el verano!

C. Following the seven-step procedure described above, write a paragraph in Spanish about your favorite season of the year and what you like to do then. Afterwards, exchange your paragraph with a classmate. He or she should . . .

   • cross out any details that are unrelated to the topic,
   • add any details that would develop the paragraph, and
   • correct any vocabulary, grammar, or spelling errors.

Atajo

Functions:
Expressing an opinion; describing the weather; linking ideas; talking about habitual actions

Vocabulary:
Calendar; seasons; body; sports

Grammar:
Verbs: reflexives, *ser & estar*; Comparisons: adjectives, equality, inequality

¿A qué nivel está Ud.?

¿Ser o estar? Ésa es la cuestión. Lorena __ estudiante. __ una mujer inteligente y no __ casada. Lorena __ secretaria ahora pero quiere __ directora. Review the chapter and then monitor your progress by completing the *Autoprueba* at the end of *Lección 6* in the **Workbook/Lab Manual.**

SÍNTESIS

¡A ver!

Claudia and Leo Manuel are going to talk about their daily routine. First, study the words and phrases and their meaning in the *Vocabulario esencial*. Second, read the two lists of activities below. Third, watch the videotape, then number the activities in each list according to the order in which Claudia and Leo Manuel say they do them.

Vocabulario esencial

arreglarse	*to get ready for the day*
dar una vuelta	*to take a walk*
instituto	*high school*
dormido	*asleep*
entrenando	*training, practicing*

Answers:
Claudia: *Me levanto. Desayuno. Me baño. Me arreglo. Salgo con mis amigas. Doy una vuelta.*
Leo Manuel: *Me levanto a las siete. Desayuno. Estoy en el instituto. Como en casa. Voy con mi hermano al colegio. Estoy entrenando. Estudio en casa. Ceno. Me acuesto.*

Claudia

___Me baño.
___Desayuno.
___Me levanto.
___Me arreglo.
___Doy una vuelta.
___Salgo con mis amigas.

Leo Manuel

___Ceno.
___Desayuno.
___Me acuesto.
___Como en casa.
___Estudio en casa.
___Estoy entrenando.
___Estoy en el instituto.
___Me levanto a las siete.
___Voy con mi hermano al colegio.

¡A leer!

You can find other weather forecasts in Spanish-language newspapers. This forecast is from a Puerto Rican newspaper, *El Nuevo Día*.

Lea el pronóstico *(forecast)* de tiempo de la página siguiente.

Answers: A. 1. *todo Puerto Rico* 2. *buen tiempo* 3. *mal tiempo* 4. *llover*
B. 1. *Lluvia = 20%, Temperatura = 70–85 grados Fahrenheit* 2. *Viento = 15 millas por hora, Temperatura = 70–87 grados Fahrenheit* 3. *Lluvia = 20%, Viento = 15 millas por hora*

¡Comprendió Ud.?

Complete las siguientes oraciones y la tabla según el pronóstico.

SÍNTESIS

A. Pronóstico general
1. Es para... (una parte de Puerto Rico/todo Puerto Rico).
2. Hoy hace... (buen tiempo/mal tiempo/frío/calor).
3. Mañana va a hacer... (buen tiempo/mal tiempo/calor).
4. El fin de semana va a... (llover/nevar/hacer sol).

B. Pronóstico local

	Lluvia	**Viento**	**Temperatura**
San Juan, la capital	__ %	15 millas por hora	__–__ grados
Oeste e interior	20 %	__ millas por hora	__–__ grados
Sur de Puerto Rico	__ %	__ millas por hora	84–87 grados

Pronóstico general

La alta presión atmosférica en los niveles altos se continúa intensificando. Se espera tiempo bueno tropical hasta mañana con vientos del Sureste y temperaturas diurnas cálidas. La perspectiva para el fin de semana luce algo lluviosa debido a que un frente frío se acerca a Puerto Rico desde el oeste.

Pronóstico local

SAN JUAN y VECINDAD: Mayormente despejado con 20 por ciento de probabilidad de aguaceros. Temperaturas altas de 85 grados y bajas de 70 grados. Vientos del Sureste de diez a 15 millas por hora.

PONCE y SECCIÓN SUR: Mayormente despejado con 20 por ciento de probabilidad de aguaceros. Temperaturas altas de 84 a 87 grados. Vientos del Sureste de 15 millas por hora.

MAYAGÜEZ, OESTE e INTERIOR: Parcialmente soleado con 20 por ciento de probabilidad de aguaceros vespertinos bien dispersos. Temperaturas altas de 70 grados en las montañas y 87 grados en el oeste. Vientos del Sureste de diez a 15 millas por hora, excepto por la brisa marina vespertina.

Visit

INTERNET

http://poco.heinle.com

¡A conversar!

Converse con un(a) compañero(a) sobre uno de sus lugares *(places)* favoritos.

Tell him or her . . .

Atajo

- where your favorite place is.
- why that place is so special.
- what time of the year you visit.
- how you get to that place.

- who goes there with you.
- what the weather is like.
- what you generally do there.
- when you plan to return there.

¡A escribir!

If you wish, tell your students to write a short composition to accompany their weather forecast. Topic: what they are going to do during that weekend.

Escriba un pronóstico del tiempo ideal para un fin de semana perfecto. Describa la temperatura en grados centígrados.

Párrafo 1: Pronóstico general de ___ (región/estado/país).

Párrafo 2: Pronóstico local de ___ (lugar específico).

VOCABULARIO

Sustantivos

el baño bathroom
el cumpleaños birthday
los dulces sweets
la edad age
el lugar place
la lluvia rain
la mesa table
la misa Mass
la nieve snow
el pijama pajamas
el pronóstico weather forecast
la quinceañera fifteen-year-old girl
el regalo gift
la residencia dormitory
la ropa clothing

Las partes del cuerpo (Parts of the body)

los brazos arms
la cara face
los dientes teeth
la nariz nose
los ojos eyes
las orejas ears
el pelo hair
las piernas legs
los pies feet

Las estaciones del año (Seasons of the year)

el invierno winter
el otoño fall, autumn
la primavera spring
el verano summer

Los números

cien one hundred
doscientos two hundred
trescientos three hundred
cuatrocientos four hundred
quinientos five hundred
seiscientos six hundred
setecientos seven hundred
ochocientos eight hundred
novecientos nine hundred
mil one thousand

Adjetivos

feliz happy
frío cold
generoso generous
mayor older
mejor better
menor younger
peor worse

Comparativos

más... que more ... than
el (la, los, las) más the most
menos... que less ...than
el (la, los, las) menos the least
tan... como as ... as
tanto(a)... como as much ...as
tantos(as)... como as many ...as

¿Qué tiempo hace?

Está despejado/nublado.
  It's clear/cloudy.
Está lloviendo/nevando.
  It's raining/snowing.
Llueve/Nieva. It rains/snows.
Hace buen tiempo. It's nice out.
Hace mal tiempo. It's bad out.
Hace calor/frío. It's hot/cold.
Hace fresco. It's cool.
Hace sol. It's sunny.
Hace viento. It's windy.

Verbos

acabar de + infinitive to have just
acostarse (o → ue) to go to bed
afeitarse to shave
bañarse to take a bath
continuar to continue
cumplir to be/turn (a certain age)
despertarse (e → ie) to wake up
dormirse (o → ue) to fall asleep
ducharse to take a shower
lavarse to wash up
lavarse los dientes to brush
  one's teeth
levantarse to get up
nacer to be born
peinarse to comb one's hair
pintarse to put on makeup
ponerse to put on
quitarse to take off
secarse to dry off
terminar to finish, to end
vestirse (e → i) to get dressed

Preposiciones

antes de + infinitive before (-ing)
después de + infinitive after (-ing)

Adverbios de tiempo

antes beforehand
después afterwards
hasta until
luego then
más tarde later
pronto soon

Expresiones idiomáticas

¡Felicidades! Congratulations!
hacer cola to get in line
¿Qué te pasa? What's the matter
  with you?
tener frío/calor to be cold/hot
todos everyone

Día tras día
Los Estados Unidos

Julio and Gloria Sepúlveda are a young Puerto Rican couple who now live in New York City. Shortly before Christmas, they go shopping for clothing with their two small children at Macy's department store. On December 24th, Julio's mother arrives in New York and has several unfortunate experiences on the way from the airport to her son's apartment.

¡Julio, es hora de levantarte!

▶ COMMUNICATIVE GOALS

You will be able to describe where you live, your household chores, and what activities you and others did recently.

▶ LANGUAGE FUNCTIONS

Describing one's personal residence
Expressing preferences
Describing one's household chores
Discussing past activities
Specifying how long ago
Communicating more smoothly

▶ VOCABULARY THEMES

Rooms of a house
Furniture and appliances
Household chores

▶ GRAMMATICAL STRUCTURES

Preterite of regular verbs
The verb form *hace* + time (ago)
Direct object pronouns

Write or call for free information on Puerto Rico: Puerto Rico Tourism Company, 757 Fifth Avenue, 23rd floor, New York, NY 10017; telephone: (800) 223-6530.

▶ CULTURAL INFORMATION

Housing in Latin America and Spain
Gender roles in Hispanic cultures

http://poco.heinle.com

EN CONTEXTO

 Play Lab Tape

Although this dialogue contains some verb forms in the preterite, a tense that is introduced only later in this lesson, students will be able to understand the conversation based on context and their knowledge of Spanish vocabulary.

Hace tres años° que Julio y Gloria Sepúlveda se mudaron° de San Juan, Puerto Rico a la ciudad de Nueva York. (1) Ahora viven en un apartamento pequeño con dos dormitorios en el centro de Manhattan. Julio tiene treinta y cinco años y es policía. Su esposa tiene treinta y tres años y es directora de una escuela primaria. Tienen dos niños: Juan Carlos, que tiene siete años, y Susana María, que tiene dos años.

Three years ago / moved

Ayer° a las ocho de la mañana Gloria se levantó, fue a la cocina° y se preparó el desayuno: café con leche y pan tostado con mermelada. Luego desayunó en la sala° y miró la televisión por media hora. A las ocho y media Gloria fue a despertar a su marido.

Yesterday / kitchen

living room

—¿Julio? ¿Julio? ... ¡Julio!
—¡¿Cómo?! ¿Qué... qué quieres?
—¡Es hora de levantarte! Ya son las ocho y media y todavía° estás en la cama,° hombre.

still
bed

—¡Por Dios! ¿Son las ocho y media ya, Gloria?
—Sí. Hoy es sábado y tenemos que hacer muchas cosas.
—Bueno, pero estoy muy cansado. Quiero dormir un poco más.
—Estás muy cansado porque te acostaste a las dos y media de la mañana.
—Claro que sí. Me acosté tarde porque trabajé hasta la una y media. Bueno, no importa°... ya me levanto. Uy, ¡pero qué sueño tengo!

no es importante

—Julio, tenemos muchos quehaceres° hoy.

chores

—¿Qué quehaceres, querida?
—Pues, limpiar° el apartamento y lavar la ropa... hay mucha ropa.

clean

—Bueno, tú lavas la ropa y yo limpio el apartamento, ¿eh?
—Bien. Y después del almuerzo tenemos que ir de compras. Juan Carlos necesita unos suéteres y Susan María necesita una cobija° nueva.

comforter

—Sí, sí... ya lo sé, querida. Estamos en diciembre y hace mucho frío aquí en Nueva York, mientras que en mi Isla hace calor y mucho sol.(2)

Notas de texto

1. Over one million Puerto Ricans live in New York City today. Since 1917 Puerto Rico has been an *Estado Libre Asociado* (Commonwealth) of the United States and, therefore, all Puerto Ricans are American citizens. Puerto Ricans pay taxes on some goods to the U.S. Government and may vote in national elections if they officially reside in the United States.
2. Julio and many other Puerto Ricans who have immigrated to the United States refer to their homeland affectionately as *mi Isla* or *mi Puerto Rico.*

¿Comprendió Ud.?

1. Complete el siguiente formulario.

Marido: _____   Esposa: _____
Edad: _____   Edad: _____
Profesión: _____   Profesión: _____

Hijos: _____ no _____ sí   ¿Cuántos? _____
Nombres: _____   → _____
Edades: _____   → _____

2. ¿De dónde es la familia Sepúlveda originalmente? ¿Dónde viven ahora?
3. ¿A qué hora se despertaron Julio y Gloria ayer? ¿A qué hora se acostó Julio?
4. ¿Qué quiere hacer Julio esta mañana? ¿Por qué?
5. ¿Qué tienen que hacer Julio y Gloria este sábado?
6. ¿Qué piensa usted de Gloria y de Julio? ¿Conoce usted a personas de Puerto Rico? (¿Sí? ¿En qué parte de la isla vive[n]?)

VOCABULARIO ÚTIL

In this section, you will learn to describe your home and your household chores.

Cómo conversar sobre la casa

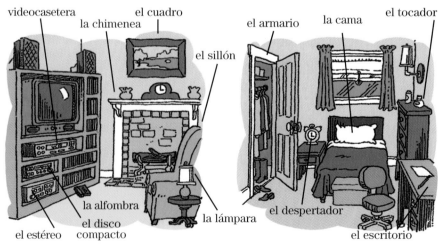

videocasetera   el cuadro   el armario   la cama   el tocador
la chimenea   el sillón
el despertador
la alfombra   la lámpara   el escritorio
el estéreo   el disco compacto
la sala   **el dormitorio**

el espejo   la ducha

la bañera

el baño

el horno de microondas   la ventana

la puerta   la estufa   el refrigerador

el reloj

la mesa   las sillas   el lavaplatos
                                el tostador

la cocina / el comedor

Practiquemos

A. Los muebles y aparatos eléctricos. Complete las oraciones con el nombre apropiado de un mueble o un aparato eléctrico.

Ejemplo: Para saber la hora necesito ver *un reloj.*

1. Escribo todas mis cartas en...   una cama.
2. Preparo la comida rápida en...   un sillón.
3. Preparo el pan tostado en...   un espejo.
4. Por la noche duermo bien en...   una estufa.
5. Preparo mi sopa favorita en...   una bañera.
6. Cuando me afeito necesito usar...   un tostador.
7. Mi televisor está conectado a...   un escritorio.
8. Pongo la leche y los huevos en...   un refrigerador.
9. Normalmente, prefiero lavarme en...   una videocasetera.
10. Me gusta mucho leer libros en...   un horno de microondas.

B. Así es donde vivo. Descríbale las cosas que usted tiene en su casa, apartamento o residencia.

1. En mi dormitorio tengo...   3. En mi sala hay...

2. Mi baño tiene...   4. En mi cocina hay...

C. Los domingos por la mañana. Complete la descripción con el nombre de los cuartos apropiados.

Gloria Sepúlveda y su marido Julio duermen en un _____ pequeño. Los domingos Gloria se levanta a las nueve y va al _____ para ducharse. Luego ella va a la _____ donde se prepara una taza de café. Después, Gloria va a la _____ donde toma su café y lee el periódico. Más tarde, ella desayuna en el _____ con Julio y sus niños.

D. Un dormitorio-estudio. Con otro(a) estudiante, describa esta foto.

Este es un dormitorio-estudio que puede lograr el deseo de privacidad de una joven estudiante y a la vez contar con un sitio agradable donde recibir a sus compañeras de clase...

E. Mi casa preferida. Dibuje *(Draw)* un plan simple de su casa o su apartamento ideal. Luego escriba una descripción de los cuartos, los muebles y los aparatos eléctricos que usted quiere tener en su casa o apartamento.

Ejemplos: Quiero una casa con tres dormitorios, una cocina y...
En mi dormitorio quiero una cama grande y bonita, y...
Mi cocina va a tener un lavaplatos, una estufa blanca y...

Ahora dígale a un(a) compañero(a) de clase...

1. dónde quiere usted vivir y por qué.
2. cuántos cuartos quiere usted, y cuáles son.
3. qué muebles y aparatos eléctricos va a tener.
4. quiénes van a vivir en su casa o apartamento.

TRANSPARENCY No. 16:
Household Chores

1. Act out these household chores and have your students say what you are doing. For example, pretend you are making a bed; your students could say: *Usted está haciendo la cama.*
2. If you wish, tell students the Spanish words for other household chores such as **to dust** *(sacudir)*, **to sweep** *(barrer)*, **to iron** *(planchar)*, and **to hang up clothes** *(colgar la ropa)*.
3. Distribute slips of paper containing descriptions of different household chores in Spanish. Have your students pantomime what they read on their papers, and ask other students to guess the action.

Cómo conversar sobre los quehaceres

hacer la cama

limpiar la casa

poner la mesa

sacar la basura/lavar los platos

pasar la aspiradora

**lavar la ropa
(la lavadora / la secadora)**

**cortar el césped (el jardín,
el patio, la terraza)**

Practiquemos

F. Día tras día. Su profesor(a) va a leer diez preguntas. Escuche cada pregunta dos veces, luego indique la respuesta más lógica con el número de la pregunta.

Ejemplo: *"Número uno. ¿En qué lavamos la ropa?"*

_____ en la secadora
__1__ en la lavadora
_____ después de levantarnos
_____ si no tenemos lavaplatos
_____ para limpiar las alfombras
_____ en primavera, verano y otoño
_____ en la sala y los dormitorios
_____ de todos los cuartos de la casa
_____ en la terraza, el patio o el garaje
_____ antes de desayunar, almorzar y cenar

G. Entrevista. Pregúntele a un(a) compañero(a) de clase.

1. ¿Vives en una casa, en un apartamento o en una residencia?
2. ¿Hay un lavaplatos donde vives? (¿Sí? ¿De qué color es?) ¿Quién lava los platos en tu casa? ¿Te gusta lavar los platos? ¿Por qué?

Ex. F.
1. Before reading the questions, have students read the list of alternative answers.
2. Read each question twice: 1. *¿En qué lavamos la ropa?* 2. *¿Cuándo ponemos la mesa?* 3. *¿En qué secamos la ropa?* 4. *¿Dónde pasamos la aspiradora?* 5. *¿Por qué pasamos la aspiradora?* 6. *¿De dónde sacamos la basura?* 7. *¿Cuándo debemos hacer las camas?* 8. *¿Dónde podemos lavar un perro?* 9. *¿En qué estaciones cortamos el césped?* 10. *¿Cuándo tenemos que lavar los platos a mano?*
3. Answers (from top to bottom): 3, 1, 7, 10, 5, 9, 4, 6, 8, 2

Ex. G.
1. Have students ask you these questions, using formal forms of the verbs and pronouns.
2. Follow-up activity: As a homework assignment, have students write their responses to these questions in a paragraph.

If you have slides of different kinds of housing in North America and in Spanish-speaking countries, show them to the class and discuss the similarities and differences between them.

NOTAS CULTURALES

Viviendas en Latinoamérica y España

En Latinoamérica y España, las viviendas° varían° de acuerdo al país, la región, el clima, la posición económica y el gusto° de las personas. La arquitectura varía desde pequeñas° casas coloniales° hasta edificios° de apartamentos muy altos ó desde condominios hasta casas de adobe o de cartón.°

*viviendas housing   varían vary
gusto taste   pequeñas small   casas coloniales
colonial homes   edificios buildings
cartón cardboard*

¿Cómo son estas casas de La Grita, Venezuela (arriba) y San José, Costa Rica (abajo) y el edificio de apartamentos de Murcia, España (a la izquierda)?

Charla

1. Descríbale a otro(a) estudiante cómo son las casas donde vive usted.
2. Ahora descríbale a su compañero(a) otras áreas de su ciudad donde vive gente de diferentes condiciones económicas. ¿Cómo son las casas allí? ¿Cómo vive la gente? ¿Qué tipo de trabajo hace?

3. ¿Quién lava la ropa donde vives? ¿Dónde lavas la ropa: en casa o en una lavandería?

4. ¿Es fácil o difícil limpiar tu casa (apartamento/residencia)? Normalmente, ¿tienes poca o mucha basura para sacar? ¿En qué cuarto hay más basura? ¿Quién saca la basura donde vives? ¿Prefieres sacar la basura o pasar la aspiradora? ¿Por qué?

5. ¿Te gusta cortar el césped? ¿Quién corta el césped en tu familia? ¿Cuándo cortas el césped más frecuentemente: en la primavera, en el verano o en el otoño? ¿Hay un jardín donde vives? ¿Tienes pocas o muchas plantas en tu jardín o casa?

H. ¿Con qué frecuencia? Vamos a ver si usted trabaja para vivir o si vive para trabajar. Primero, complete el siguiente formulario según la frecuencia que usted hace los quehaceres indicados. Luego compare sus resultados con los resultados de otro(a) estudiante. Use esta escala:

0 = nunca   1 = a veces   2 = frecuentemente   3 = todos los días

_____ lavo la ropa		_____ lavo los platos	
_____ hago la cama		_____ seco los platos	
_____ pongo la mesa		_____ corto el césped	
_____ limpio el baño		_____ paso la aspiradora	
_____ saco la basura		_____ trabajo en el patio	

Puntos	**Interpretación**
0–10	Aparentemente, ¡el trabajo no es una de sus virtudes!
11–20	Usted no es trabajador(a), pero su casa está en orden.
21–30	Usted trabaja mucho. Salga un poco más con sus amigos.

GRAMÁTICA FUNCIONAL

Describing past activities

—¿Ya desayunó Juan Carlos?
—Sí. Comió cereal y bebió jugo.
—¿No lavaste los platos todavía?
—No, Gloria. Bañé a Susana.
—¿A qué hora se despertó ella?
—A las nueve. Descansó bien.

Preterite of regular verbs

Spanish speakers use the preterite tense to describe what occurred in the past.

Ex. H. An alternate way of doing this activity is as follows: Students ask several of their classmates who in their family does these chores. Afterwards, compare students' results.

Point out that the *nosotros* forms of -*ar* and -*ir* verbs are identical to the present tense forms. Context clarifies meaning. Also, emphasize that the preterite endings of -*er* and -*ir* verbs are identical.

Tell students a story in the preterite about Carlos and Anita (*Lecciones 1–3*) and/or the Velarde family (*Lecciones 4–6*), using details you learned about the situation and characters. This technique reinforces listening skills and the use of the preterite within a familiar contextual framework.

How to form the preterite

1. To form the preterite for most Spanish verbs, add the following endings to the verb stem. Note the identical endings for -*er* and -*ir* verbs.

	habl**ar**	**com**er	**viv**ir
(yo)	habl**é**	com**í**	viv**í**
(tú)	habl**aste**	com**iste**	viv**iste**
(usted, él/ella)	habl**ó**	com**ió**	viv**ió**
(nosotros/as)	habl**amos**	com**imos**	viv**imos**
(vosotros/as)	*habl**asteis***	*com**isteis***	*viv**isteis***
(ustedes, ellos/ellas)	habl**aron**	com**ieron**	viv**ieron**

2. -*ar* and -*er* stem-changing verbs have **no** stem change in the preterite; use the same verb stem as you would for a regular verb.

   pensar: pensé, pensaste, pensó, pensamos, pensasteis, pensaron
   volver: volví, volviste, volvió, volvimos, volvisteis, volvieron

   —**Pensé** mucho en Julio.   *I thought a lot about Julio.*
   ¿Cómo está?   *How is he?*
   —Está bien. **Se acostó** a las dos   *He's fine. He went to bed at two*
   porque **volvió** tarde del trabajo.   *o'clock because he returned*
                                               late from work.

3. Verbs ending in -*car*, -*gar*, and -*zar* have a spelling change in the *yo* form of the preterite tense.

c changes to *qu*	*g* changes to *gu*	*z* changes to *c*
to**car** → to**qué**	lle**gar** → lle**gué**	comen**zar** → comen**cé**

   Ayer visité a mi novia María. Salí de casa con mi guitarra y mi cámara, y tomé el autobús a su apartamento. **Llegué** a las dos y **almorcé** con su familia. Después, **toqué** la guitarra y **saqué** unas fotos de María. Más tarde, **jugué** a las cartas con ella y sus hermanos.

4. -*ir* and -*er* verbs that have a vowel before the infinitive ending require the following change in the *usted/él/ella* and *ustedes/ellos/ellas* forms of the preterite tense: *i* between two vowels changes to *y*.

	creer	**leer**	**oír**
(usted, él/ella)	creyó	leyó	oyó
(ustedes, ellos/ellas)	creyeron	leyeron	oyeron

   Antes de acostarse, Julio y Gloria **leyeron** un poco, luego se durmieron. A las seis de la mañana, sonó el despertador y Gloria se despertó. Julio no **oyó** nada y se levantó una hora después. Cuándo llegó tarde al trabajo, su jefe no **creyó** su historia.

How to use the preterite

1. Spanish speakers use the preterite tense to express the beginning and completion of past actions, conditions, and events.

> Ayer Julio **se despertó** un poco tarde porque no **oyó** su despertador. Gloria **llamó** a su esposo dos veces y finalmente él **se levantó**. Luego Julio **se duchó** y **desayunó** con su familia.

2. To express how long ago an action or state occurred, Spanish speakers use the preterite tense with the verb form *hace* with an amount of time.

> —¿**Cuánto tiempo hace** que **se mudaron** ustedes de Puerto Rico?
> —**Hace un año** que **nos mudamos** aquí. (**Nos mudamos** aquí **hace un año**.)

> *How long ago did you move from Puerto Rico?*
> *We moved here a year ago.*

Some expressions referring to the past

anteayer	*the day before yesterday*	**la semana pasada**	*last week*
ayer	*yesterday*	**el mes pasado**	*last month*
anoche	*last night*	**el año pasado**	*last year*

Point out that reflexive verbs retain their pronouns in the preterite tense, as shown in these sentences; e.g., se *despertó*, se *levantó*, se *duchó*.

Practiquemos

A. Nieto y abuela. Juan Carlos está hablando por teléfono con su abuela Bienvenida, que vive en Puerto Rico. Ayer Bienvenida fue de compras con unas amigas, y ahora su nieto está haciéndole preguntas. ¿Qué preguntas le hace Juan Carlos y qué le contesta Bienvenida?

Ejemplo: ¿Cuándo (volver) a casa, abuelita? (Volver) un poco tarde.
¿Cuándo volviste a casa, abuelita? → *Volví un poco tarde.*

Juan Carlos
1. ¿A qué hora (llegar)? →
2. Luego, ¿(comer) un poco?
3. Después, ¿(descansar)?
4. ¿(Recibir) unas cartas?
5. ¿(Mirar) la televisión?
6. ¿A qué hora (acostarse)?
7. ¿No (lavarse) antes?
8. ¿(Dormirse) rápidamente?

Bienvenida
(Llegar) a las seis, Juan Carlos.
Sí, (comer) una pizza muy rica.
Pues, sí. (Descansar) un poco.
No, no (recibir) ninguna carta.
No. (Mirar) una película en vídeo.
(Acostarse) a las nueve y media.
Claro que (lavarse), Juan Carlos.
No sé si (dormirse) rápidamente.

Ex. A. Answers:
1. ¿...llegaste? / Llegué...
2. ...¿comiste...? / ...comí....
3. ...¿descansaste? / ...Descansé...
4. ¿Recibiste...? / ...recibí...
5. ¿Miraste...? / ...Miré...
6. ¿...te acostaste? / Me acosté...
7. ¿...te lavaste...? / ...me lavé...
8. ¿Te dormiste...? / ...me dormí...

Follow-up activity: Have your students individually ask you the questions using *usted* verb forms.

B. Una mujer ocupada. Ayer Gloria hizo *(did)* muchas cosas en casa.

1. Diga las actividades que ella hizo.
   Gloria (trabajar) mucho por la mañana. Primero, (lavar) la ropa. Luego (pasar) la aspiradora en la sala y (sacar) la basura. Después, (bañar) a Susana María, (limpiar) la bañera y más tarde (jugar) con Juan Carlos.

Ex. B.
1. Assign this exercise for homework. Then have students compare their answers in class with a classmate.

Por la tarde Gloria (preparar) el almuerzo y (comer) con sus niños. Después, (lavar) y (secar) los platos. Finalmente, (descansar) en un sillón de la sala, (leer) un periódico y (tomar) una taza de té.

2. Julio llegó a casa a las cinco, y Gloria le explicó qué hizo por la mañana y por la tarde.

—Por la mañana trabajé mucho. Primero,...

C. Dos novios. Complete los siguientes párrafos con las formas apropiadas del pretérito.

Ejemplo: (Yo) _____ a mi marido en la universidad.
Conocí[1] a mi marido en la universidad.

tomar	aprender	conocer	estudiar

Mi nombre es Gloria Sepúlveda. Yo _____ a mi marido en la Universidad de Puerto Rico donde él _____ para ser policía y yo _____ clases en educación. Julio y yo _____ mucho allí y _____ a mucha gente interesante.

comer	invitar	conocer
llegar	**caminar**	**comenzar**

Un día Julio y yo _____ a salir. Él me _____ al cine y después (nosotros) _____ en un restaurante italiano. En otra ocasión (nosotros) _____ por el parque. Un domingo Julio _____ a mi familia, y poco después él y yo _____ a ser novios.

oír	bañarse	continuar	llegar
salir	**pintarse**	**despertar**	**desayunar**
sonar	**vestirse**	**levantarse**	

Después de dos años como novios, _____ el día de nuestro matrimonio. Mi despertador _____ a las siete de la mañana, pero yo no lo _____ y (yo) _____ durmiendo. Quince minutos más tarde, mi mamá me _____. Luego (yo) _____ de mi cama, _____ en el baño, _____ elegantemente y _____ la cara en mi dormitorio. Mis padres y yo _____ en la cocina, entonces (nosotros) _____ para la catedral.

D. ¿Qué hicieron? Mire la ilustración de la rutina de Juan Velarde en la página 151 *(Lección 6)* de este libro, y descríbale a otro(a) estudiante qué hizo él ayer.

Ejemplo: *Juan se despertó a las seis de la mañana.*

---

[1]The preterite tense of *conocer* expresses the meaning of ***met*** (for the first time) in English.

E. La semana pasada. Escriba diez oraciones en español sobre algunas actividades que uno(a) de sus amigos(as) hizo la semana pasada. Los verbos y las frases en la lista son posibilidades.

Ex. E. Assign this exercise for homework. Then at the next class session, have students share their sentences with another classmate. You also might ask them to correct each other's written errors.

Ejemplo: *La semana pasada mi amiga Debbie trabajó en casa. Ella pasó la aspiradora en su dormitorio y...*

jugar	almorzar	montar a caballo
nadar	descansar	tocar la guitarra
lavar	sacar fotos	escribir una carta
cantar	trabajar en casa	mirar la televisión
correr	estudiar español	hablar por teléfono
visitar	leer una novela	ver una película en video
caminar	salir con amigos	escuchar música rock (clásica)
bailar	limpiar la casa	pasar la aspiradora en la sala

Charlemos

F. Lo que yo hice. *(What I did.)* Dígale a otro(a) estudiante lo que usted hizo la semana pasada.

1. En casa...
   a. me levanté tarde.
   b. me lavé el pelo.
   c. limpié mi dormitorio.
   d. cené con mi familia.

2. En el trabajo...
   a. no trabajé mucho.
   b. recibí un cheque.
   c. hablé con mi jefe(a).
   d. conocí a otro(a) empleado(a).

3. En la escuela...
   a. jugué a un deporte.
   b. comí en la cafetería.
   c. aprendí mucho español.
   d. tomé un examen difícil.

4. En la biblioteca...
   a. dormí la siesta.
   b. leí un periódico.
   c. estudié para un examen.
   d. escribí una composición.

G. ¿Cuánto tiempo? Hágale a otro(a) estudiante las siguientes preguntas.

1. ¿Cuánto tiempo hace que te graduaste de la escuela primaria? ¿y de la secundaria? ¿En qué año te graduaste? ¿Estudiaste mucho en la escuela secundaria? ¿Qué curso te gustó más? ¿Por qué te gustó tanto?

2. ¿Cuánto tiempo hace que comenzaste a estudiar español? ¿Quién fue tu profesor o profesora de español? ¿Aprendiste mucho en esa clase? ¿Te gustó la clase? ¿Por qué? ¿Qué cosa te gustó menos en esa clase?

H. ¿Qué hay de nuevo? Dígale a otro(a) estudiante algunas actividades que usted hizo ayer. Él (Ella) debe escribir lo que usted dice.

Ex. H. Assign this activity for written homework.

Ejemplo: *Ayer me levanté a las siete y jugué al tenis con mi amigo Paul. Después, desayunamos en un restaurante y...*

La rutina diaria: acostarse a las... / soñar con... / despertarse a las... / levantarse a las... / lavarse los dientes / ducharse (bañarse) / afeitarse / pintarse / peinarse / vestirse / desayunar con... / comer... / beber... / almorzar (en casa / en... / con mi novio / con...)

El trabajo: trabajar en... / leer... / escribir... / estudiar... / pasar la aspiradora / lavar los platos (la ropa) / limpiar la casa / sacar la basura / cortar el césped

Los pasatiempos: bailar / cantar / nadar / caminar / invitar a... / descansar / esquiar / patinar / salir con amigos a... / mirar la televisión / montar en bicicleta (a caballo) / hablar por teléfono con... / escuchar música / tocar la guitarra (el piano) / jugar a las cartas (al tenis / al béisbol) / comenzar a (leer una novela) / escribir una carta / sacar fotos de (mis amigos / mi familia)

Ahora su compañero(a) va a decirle a otro(a) estudiante algunas cosas que usted mencionó. Usted debe escuchar bien para determinar si su compañero(a) dice la verdad o no.

Ejemplo: *Ayer Linda se levantó a las siete y jugó al tenis con su amigo Paul. Después, desayunaron en un restaurante y...*

I. Lotería biográfica. First, draw a large bingo card like the one below. Then in each of the squares, write a different phrase in Spanish from the list below in any order. Now walk around the classroom with your card and ask your classmates the questions you wrote in the squares. For example: *"¿Hablaste por teléfono hoy?"* If your classmate answers *"Sí,"* write his or her initials in the appropriate box, then ask other students the remaining questions on your card and write their initials in the correct boxes. The first student to get a vertical, horizontal, or diagonal line of initialed boxes says *"¡Lotería!"* and wins the game.

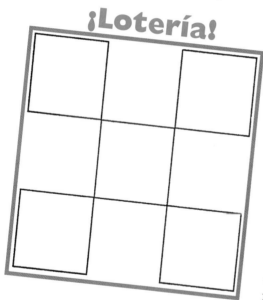

¡Lotería!

talked on the phone today
took a shower last night
ate pizza yesterday afternoon
watched television last night
played soccer last month
rode a bicycle last summer
drank coffee this morning
ran through a park last week
ate in the cafeteria yesterday

J. Situaciones. Converse con un(a) compañero(a) de clase.

ESTUDIANTE A: You meet a Spanish-speaking friend (your classmate) at school. Greet your friend, then ask about his or her day yesterday (e.g., what time he or she got up, what he or she ate, what your friend did at home and school, what sports he or she played, what time he or she went to bed, etc.)

ESTUDIANTE B: Answer your friend's questions, then ask about the activities she or he did yesterday. Try to keep your conversation going as long as possible, using only the Spanish words and phrases you know.

NOTAS CULTURALES

El papel de la mujer en Latinoamérica

Latinoamérica tiene los grupos de mujeres más activos en el mundo. Estos grupos han escrito° los documentos más importantes para la Conferencia de Mujeres de las Naciones Unidas en 1994. Estos documentos proponen° el derecho° a la salud° de la mujer, la defensa contra° la violencia doméstica, mejor° sueldo° en los trabajos y finalmente el derecho a la educación.

have written
propose / right / health
against / better / salary

Aunque° la educación es el elemento más relevante para obtener un balance en el desarrollo° socioeconómico de la mujer, no se le ha dado° la importancia necesaria. En algunos países como Argentina, Bolivia, Brasil, Costa Rica, Chile, México, Perú, Puerto Rico, Uruguay y Venezuela comienzan programas sobre Estudios de la Mujer a nivel universitario.° Los graduados de estos programas deben proponer cambios° sociales y económicos dentro de la sociedad para mejorar° la situación de la mujer.

Even though
development / it has not been given

university level
changes / to improve

Charla

Hable con otro(a) estudiante.

1. First, make a list in English of some male and female roles that exist in Hispanic and Anglo-Saxon cultures.

Hispanic Cultures		Anglo-Saxon Cultures	
Men	Women	Men	Women
———	———	———	———
———	———	———	———
———	———	———	———
———	———	———	———

2. Second, share your list with a classmate. Compare and contrast your ideas, using Spanish as much as possible.

GRAMÁTICA FUNCIONAL

Communicating smoothly in Spanish

—Los platos. ¿Ya los lavaste, Gloria?
—Pues, sí, Julio. Los lavé anoche.
—¿Y la ropa también?
—No, ¿pero puedes lavarla tú ahora, querido?
—Cómo no, Gloria. Voy a lavarla ahora.

1. At this early stage of language acquisition, expect students to understand the meaning of direct object pronouns when they hear or read them. Using the pronouns correctly in speech and writing, however, requires considerable communicative practice, effort, and time.

2. Remind students that the direct object pronoun *os* is used in some areas of Spain such as in Madrid and Barcelona.

Direct object pronouns

1. All sentences have a subject and a verb. Many sentences also have an object that receives the action of the verb. For example, in the sentence below, the direct object *(el apartamento)* receives the action of the verb *(limpió)* performed by the subject *(esposa)*.

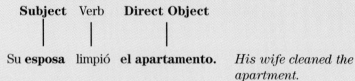

Subject	Verb	**Direct Object**	
Su **esposa**	limpió	**el apartamento.**	*His wife cleaned the apartment.*

2. Because the direct object of a sentence is usually a person or a thing, it answers the questions **whom?** or **what?** in relation to the sentence's subject and verb.

Julio llamó a **su mamá.**   →   *Whom did he call?*
Su esposa limpió **el apartamento.**   →   *What did she clean?*

Identify the direct objects in the following sentences:

Julio despertó a Juan Carlos a las ocho.
Su esposa miró la televisión en la sala.
Juan Carlos sacó la basura de la cocina.
Después, pasó la aspiradora en su dormitorio.

How to use direct object pronouns

A direct object pronoun may be used in place of a direct object noun.

Singular		**Plural**	
me	*me*	**nos**	*us*
te	*you (informal)*	**os**	*you (informal)*
lo	*him, you (formal), it (masculine)*	**los**	*you (formal), them (masculine)*
la	*her, you (formal), it (feminine)*	**las**	*you (formal), them (feminine)*

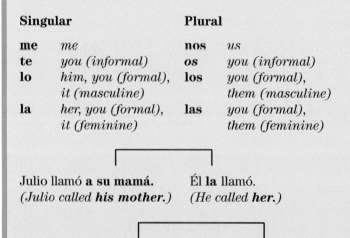

Julio llamó **a su mamá.**   Él **la** llamó.
*(Julio called **his mother.**)*   *(He called **her.**)*

Su esposa limpió **el apartamento.**   Ella **lo** limpió.
*(His wife cleaned **the apartment.**)*   *(She cleaned **it.**)*

In the preceding sentences, the direct object pronouns *la* and *lo* replace the direct object nouns *mamá* and *apartamento*, respectively.

Julio, ¿conoces **a los Reynosa?**
(*Julio, do you know **the Reynosas?***)

Sí, **los** conozco.
(*Yes, I know **them.***)

Gloria, ¿lavaste **mi suéter?**
(*Gloria, did you wash **my sweater?***)

No, no **lo** lavé.
(*No, I didn't wash **it.***)

Papá, ¿dónde están **mis cintas?**
(*Dad, where are **my tapes?***)

Las tengo aquí, hijo.
(*I have **them** here, son.*)

Where to place direct object pronouns

1. Place the pronoun in front of the conjugated verb.

—¿Lavaste los platos, Julio?   *Did you wash the dishes, Julio?*
—Sí, **los lavé** anoche.   *Yes, I washed them last night.*

2. In negative sentences, place the *no* in front of the pronoun.

—¿Me llamaste, Gloria?   *Did you call me, Gloria?*
—No, Julio. **No te** llamé.   *No, Julio. I didn't call you.*

3. When the direct object pronoun is used with an infinitive or a present participle, place it either before the conjugated verb or attach it to the infinitive or the present participle. (A written accent is needed to retain the stressed vowel of a present participle when a direct object pronoun is attached to it.)

Lo voy a llamar mañana.
   or   *I'm going to call him tomorrow.*
Voy a llamarlo mañana.

Lo estoy llamando ahora.
   or   *I'm calling him now.*
Estoy llamándolo ahora.

Practiquemos

A. A la hora del almuerzo.
Julio y Gloria están almorzando con su hijo Juan Carlos. Complete las conversaciones con los pronombres **lo, la, las** o **los.**

Ejemplo: —Mamá, no quiero comer mi pan.
                —Puedes comer*lo* más tarde, hijo.

1. —Mamá, no puedo tomar toda mi leche.
   —Puedes tomar_____ más tarde, mi hijo.

2. —Juan Carlos, ¿ya comiste tu pescado?
   —Pues... no, papá. El gato está comiéndo_____.

Ex. A.
1. Remind students that they can place the pronouns before the conjugated verb or attach them to the infinitive or to the present participle.
2. After students have completed this exercise, go over the answers to it. Then your students could role-play the dialogues in pairs or with several students.
3. Answers: *la, lo, los, las*

3. —Esta noche quiero comer dos huevos fritos, mamá.
   —No, Juan Carlos. Voy a preparar_____ para el desayuno.

4. —De postre quiero una de esas naranjas, papá.
   —Bien. Acabo de comprar_____ en el mercado.

B. Un marido simpático. Complete la conversación con los pronombres **lo, la, las** o **los**.

Ejemplo: ¿Sacaste la basura, Julio?
Sí, *la* saqué esta manaña.

GLORIA: ¿Lavaste los platos, Julio?
JULIO: Sí, _____ lavé por la tarde.
GLORIA: ¿Y la bañera y la ducha?
JULIO: Pues, ya _____ limpié ayer, querida.
GLORIA: Bien. Ah, la ropa. Debemos lavar _____ hoy.
JULIO: Tú _____ puedes lavar, si quieres.
GLORIA: Bien. Voy a lavar _____ esta noche.
JULIO: También limpié el horno de microondas y la estufa.
GLORIA: ¿_____ limpiaste? ¿Y las alfombras de la sala también?
JULIO: Sí, _____ limpié con la aspiradora.
GLORIA: Bueno, ahora voy a preparar el almuerzo.
JULIO: No necesitas preparar _____ , Gloria.
GLORIA: ¡Por Dios! ¿_____ preparaste tú?
JULIO: No, no _____ preparé. Vamos a un restaurante. Estamos muy cansados, querida.
GLORIA: Ay, Julio, ¡eres tan simpático y amable!

C. Una invitación. Complete las conversaciones con **me, te, nos, lo, la, los** o **las**.

En casa

GLORIA: ¿Conoces a Ramón Valenzuela, Julio?
JULIO: Pues... sí, _____ conozco un poco. ¿Por qué?
GLORIA: Porque Ramón y su esposa _____ invitaron a una fiesta.
JULIO: ¿_____ invitaron a nosotros? Hmm... _____ conocimos el año pasado, ¿no?
GLORIA: Sí, en una fiesta, pero nunca _____ visitamos. ¿Vamos a la fiesta?
JULIO: Sí, cómo no. Vamos.

En la fiesta

GLORIA: Gracias por tu invitación, Ramón. _____ recibimos la semana pasada.
RAMÓN: De nada, Gloria. ¿Conocen ustedes a mis hijas?
JULIO: Pues no... Creo que no _____ conozco.
RAMÓN: Bueno, ésta es Angelina y ésta es Berta.

BERTA: Mucho gusto.

GLORIA: Berta, ¿no _____ recuerdas *(don't you remember me)*? Soy la señora Sepúlveda. _____ conocí hace dos años.

BERTA: Ah, sí, señora Sepúlveda. Ahora _____ recuerdo.

D. En casa. Lea las siguientes situaciones, luego escriba las conversaciones en un papel separado.

Ejemplo: Julio está en la sala con su esposa.
—¿Por qué estás escuchando música clásica, Julio?
—*Estoy escuchándola porque quiero descansar un poco.*

1. Julio y Gloria están comiendo un pollo exquisito con papas, ensalada, sopa de tomate y vino blanco.
—¿Por qué preparaste una comida especial esta noche, Gloria?
—_____

2. Gloria está hablando con su hijo, que va a jugar con sus amigos.
—¿Por qué tengo que ponerme el suéter, mamá? No lo quiero.
—_____

3. Julio sacó la basura y ahora está en la cocina con su hijo.
—¿Por qué estás lavándote las manos, papá?
—_____

4. Son las nueve de la noche. Juan Carlos está hablando con su mamá en el baño.
—¿Por qué tengo que lavarme los dientes cada noche, mamá?
—_____

5. Hoy Gloria volvió a casa muy cansada de su trabajo. Luego ella miró la televisión. Diez minutos más tarde, su hijo entró en la sala.
—¿Por qué estás mirando la tele, mamá?
—_____

Charlemos

E. Entrevista. Pregúntele a otra persona en clase.

Ex. E. Have students ask you these questions, using formal forms.

1. ¿Cómo se llama tu mejor amigo? ¿Dónde lo conociste? ¿Cómo es? ¿Quién es tu mejor amiga? ¿Dónde la conociste? ¿Cómo es ella? ¿Con qué frecuencia la llamas por teléfono? ¿De qué hablan ustedes?

2. ¿Cuál es tu deporte favorito? ¿Cuándo y dónde lo juegas? Normalmente, ¿con quién lo juegas? ¿Lo juegan ustedes bien o mal? ¿Qué otro deporte te gusta mucho?

3. ¿Miras mucho o poco la televisión? ¿Por cuántas horas la miras cada semana? ¿Qué programas de televisión te gustan? ¿En qué días y a qué hora los miras?

PARA LEER MEJOR

Clustering Words

Reading one word at a time is inefficient because it slows down your reading speed. It is more efficient to read meaningful groups or clusters of words.

Activities

A. Read the following advertisement to get the gist of its content. Then complete the accompanying statements.

Gracias a la calidad del material, a la multiplicidad de sus usos, a la variedad de diseños y colores, la fórmica se ha convertido en la pieza fundamental para la decoración, no sólo de casas sino también de oficinas. La fórmica ofrece la posibilidad de poder transformar un lugar en cuestiones de horas con un acabado perfecto y expresión de buen gusto. Es, definitivamente, el material del Siglo XX; ya que no hay rincón que se escape sin decorar. Lo cubre todo, esquinas o bordes, curvas de hasta 180°, tabiques, fachadas, sofisticados modelos de bases y topes de escritorios, mesas, cocinas... en fin, toda clase de muebles. Las amas de casa la prefieren en su hogar, y los empresarios le han dado el sí en las oficinas.

Fórmica Cyanamid de Venezuela, láminas decorativas en fórmica.

B. Complete the following statements, based on what you read in the advertisement.

1. La fórmica es...
   a. un color
   b. un material
   c. una decoración
   d. un aparato eléctrico

2. Se puede usar la fórmica en...
   a. una casa
   b. una oficina
   c. un apartamento
   d. a, b y c

C. Concentrate on reading clusters of three or four words. Reread the following passage at your usual speed to understand information you missed on the first reading. Then complete the following checklist.

es fácil usar, es muy moderna, es muy útil para decorar, tiene colores diferentes, tiene muchas posibilidades

Según el anuncio, la fórmica...

_____ es fácil usar.
_____ es muy moderna.
_____ no cuesta mucho dinero.
_____ se usa en restaurantes.
_____ es muy útil para decorar.
_____ es para escuelas también.
_____ tiene colores diferentes.
_____ tiene muchas posibilidades.

Gracias a la calidad del material, a la multiplicidad de sus usos, a la variedad de diseños y colores, la fórmica se ha convertido en la pieza fundamental para la decoración, no sólo de casas sino también de oficinas. La fórmica ofrece la posibilidad de poder transformar un lugar en cuestiones de horas con un acabado perfecto y expresión de buen gusto. Es, definitivamente, el material del Siglo XX, ya que no hay rincón que se escape sin decorar. Lo cubre todo, esquinas o bordes, curvas de hasta 180°, tabiques, fachadas, sofisticados modelos de bases y topes de escritorios, mesas, cocinas... en fin, toda clase de muebles. Las amas de casa la prefieren en su hogar, y los empresarios le han dado el sí en las oficinas.

D. As you read the following paragraph, circle clusters of words in meaningful groups.

Un diseñador de los Estados Unidos, desconocido hasta hace pocos años, irrumpe con gran éxito en los círculos más selectos de la élite social norteamericana y de las estrellas de Hollywood, para decorar sus residencias con muebles cuyas líneas innovan por completo lo que hasta ahora había sido considerado como de "buen gusto". Impresiona la combinación de materiales y colores que realiza "Segil", y por otra parte, su similitud con el estilo de algunos artistas colombianos.

Source: *Cromos*, Edición 3663, 5 de abril de 1988, página 66.

E. Read the paragraph again, then answer the following questions.

1. ¿Cómo se llama el diseñador de estos muebles? ¿De dónde es?
2. ¿Quiénes son los clientes de este señor famoso?
3. ¿Qué estilo tiene el artista?

Answers:
1. Segil, los Estados Unidos
2. la gente de la élite social norteamericana y las estrellas de Hollywood 3. el estilo de algunos artistas colombianos

Atajo

Functions:
Describing people; describing objects, linking ideas; talking about habitual actions; talking about past events

Vocabulary:
House: bathroom, bedroom, furniture, kitchen, living room; personality; professions

Grammar:
Verbs: preterite; Personal pronoun: direct

¿A qué nivel está Ud.?

Utilice el pretérito de los verbos entre paréntesis: Sí __ (almorzar) con Juan Carlos. Nosotros __ (comer) un sandwich. Yo __ (tomar) __ un café y él __ (beber) chocolate con leche.
Review the chapter and then monitor your progress by completing the *Autoprueba* at the end of *Lección 6* in the **Workbook/Lab Manual.**

PARA ESCRIBIR MEJOR

Sequencing Paragraphs

One characteristic of a coherent composition is the careful sequencing of its paragraphs. The ideas should flow smoothly from one paragraph to the next one so the reader can easily follow your thoughts.

Activity

Describe a relative, a friend, or an acquaintance in a four-paragraph composition. Use the following outline and model composition to guide you.

I. Introduction
 1. What is the person's name you are writing about?
 2. What sort of person is he or she?
II. Residence
 1. Where does this person live?
 2. What does his or her home look like?
III. Activities
 1. What activities does this person do during the week?
 2. What activities does he or she do on weekends?
IV. Conclusion
 What can you say in general about this person?

Example:

Gloria Sepúlveda es una mujer puertorriqueña que tiene treinta y tres años. Ella está casada y tiene dos niños: Juan Carlos y Susana María. Gloria es directora de una escuela primaria en la ciudad de Nueva York. Ella es inteligente, trabajadora y le gustan los niños.

Gloria vive con su marido Julio y sus niños en un apartamento pequeño en el centro de Manhattan. Su apartamento tiene dos dormitorios, un baño, una cocina y una sala.

Cada semana Gloria trabaja por cuarenta horas en su escuela. Durante el día sus niños están en su apartamento con una buena amiga anciana de la familia. Después del trabajo, Gloria prepara la cena, luego come con su familia. Los fines de semana ella hace muchos quehaceres en casa con Julio. También ellos van de compras con sus niños y visitan a sus amigos.

Gloria es una mujer ocupada, pero está contenta con su trabajo y su familia. Para ella, su familia es la cosa más importante de su vida.

SÍNTESIS

VIDEO

¡A ver!

You are going to watch Miguel show his apartment to a potential roommate. First, study the words and their meaning in the *Vocabulario esencial*. Second, read the words and sentences in the two activities below. Third, watch the videotape, then do the activities according to the instructions indicated.

Vocabulario esencial

el frigorífico	*refrigerator*
el congelador	*freezer*
el fregadero	*kitchen sink*
el salón	*living room*
el alquiler	*rent*
el sótano	*basement*
el techo	*ceiling*
la vasija	*nightstand*

A. Number the rooms in the order that Miguel shows them or points them out.

_____ el patio   _____ el cuarto de baño
_____ la cocina   _____ la habitación de Miguel
_____ el salón   _____ el cuarto para alquilar

B. Indicate the person who says the following sentences. Miguel (M) or his potential roommate (RM).

1. _____ "Es un patio pequeño."
2. _____ "¿Cuánto será el alquiler?"
3. _____ "Está incluido el agua."
4. _____ "¿Hace mucho tiempo que vives aquí?"
5. _____ "Tenía un compañero que vivía conmigo."
6. _____ "Estudio música en el conservatorio."

Answers:
A. la cocina, el salón, el patio, el cuarto para alquilar, el cuarto de baño, la habitación de Miguel
B. 1. M 2. RM 3. M 4. RM 5. M 6. RM

Visit

INTERNET

http://poco.heinle.com

SÍNTESIS

¡A leer!

Busque *(Look for)* la mejor residencia para los siguientes clientes. Después, compare sus selecciones con las selecciones de otro(a) estudiante. Los precios *(prices)* son en dólares norteamericanos.

CONDOMINIOS

VENUS PLAZA I: Aprovéchese de los intereses bajos de este edificio aprobado por FHA con 3 dorms., 2 baños, en el corazón de Hato Rey. Sólo $75,000 con pronto bajo. 722-6363.

SAN MATEO PLAZA: En excelentes cond. y bien mantenido, apto. de 1 dorm. muy ventilado, hipoteca asumible de $32,400. elevador con llave, paga sólo $361.00. 722-6363.

CON. VISTA VERDE: ¡Pronto sólo $6,000 si cualifica! Lindo apto. 2 habs., 2 baños, piscina, guardi 24 horas y más! TIRI: 720-9331.

TORRIMAR: ¡Nueva en el mercado! Amplia y fresca res. 4 habs., 2 baños, family, cristalina piscina. ¡Pronto de $31,000 si cualifica! Llame 720-9331.

OASIS GDNS.: Bella res. remodelada 4 habs., 2½ baños, family. Bella piscina. ¡Pronto desde $20,000 si cualifica! 720-9331.

SANTA MARIA ESTATES: ¡Un paraíso! Espectacular res. 4 habs., 5 baños, family, estudio. Jacuzzi en el baño del master, piscina con cascada, todo lujo imaginable. Alarma sofisticada. Jardines preciosos. Piden $1,000,000. Llame TIRI, 720-9331.

VILLA CAPARRA: ¡Asuma hip. de $240,000! Espectacular res. 3 habs., 3½ baños, family, piscina, pisos de mármol. Calent. solar, alarma. Area exclusiva. Llame 720-9331 para cita.

CAPARRA HILLS: ¡Vecindario prestigioso! Magnífica res. 4 dorms., 3 baños, family, estudio. Pisos preciosos. Areas amplias. Véa para apreciar. Pronto desde $59,000 si cualifica. 720-9331.

Point out that some of these advertisements use the expression *si califica,* and that a more widely accepted expression is *si usted llena los requisitos.* If you have access to Spanish-language newspapers, bring some advertisements for apartments and housesto class. Having students read authentic realia makes learning Spanish a more realistic and exciting experience for them.

1. Andrés Aguirre es un estudiante soltero que tiene veinticuatro años. Busca un apartamento bueno, pero económico.
2. Mario Zamudio y su esposa Juanita tienen un hijo adolescente y una hija de cinco años. Quieren comprar *(to buy)* una casa, pero no pueden pagar más de $40.000.
3. La familia Ramírez es grande; son siete personas: Luis y Juana Ramírez, sus cuatro hijos: Víctor, Cristóbal, Angélica e Inés, y el papá de la Sra. Ramírez. El Sr. Ramírez es arquitecto y gana *(earns)* $3.000 al mes, su esposa es ingeniera nuclear y gana $3.250 al mes. Tienen ganas de vivir en una casa en condiciones excelentes.
4. Ahora busque una casa o un apartamento para usted y su familia, o para usted y un amigo o una amiga.

SÍNTESIS

¡A conversar!

1. *Estudiante A:* Imagínese que usted tiene un apartamento para alquilar *(to rent)*. En un papel separado, copie el siguiente formulario sobre el apartamento. Después, complete el formulario con la información apropiada.

> ## ESTUPENDO APARTAMENTO
> alfombrado, recién pintado, cocina amueblada, entrega inmediata.
> Ver hoy 10-13 y 16-19 horas.
> Tel: 251-2988.

2. *Estudiante B:* Imagínese que usted busca un apartamento para alquilar.
Copie el formulario en un papel separado. Luego llame por teléfono (a su compañero[a] de clase) para informarse del apartamento.

3. Después de terminar la actividad, ustedes pueden comenzarla otra vez con otros dos compañeros.

¡A escribir!

Escriba un párrafo sobre su casa, apartamento o residencia, y mencione...

1. la ciudad en que usted está viviendo ahora.
2. si vive en una casa, un apartamento o en una residencia.
3. el número de cuartos que tiene.
4. los muebles y aparatos eléctricos.
5. otras cosas interesantes de donde vive usted.

Atajo

Número de cuartos: _____	Dirección: _____
¿Amueblado? ___ no ___ sí	Muebles: _____
¿Incluye... ___ agua? ___ gas? ___ luz eléctrica?	
Extras: _____	
Precio al mes: $_____	Horas de visita: _____

VOCABULARIO

Los cuartos (Rooms)

la cocina *kitchen*
el comedor *dining room*
el cuarto de baño *bathroom*
el dormitorio *bedroom*
la sala *living room*

Otras partes de la casa (Other parts of the house)

la chimenea *fireplace*
el jardín *flower garden*
el patio *yard*
la puerta *door*
la terraza *terrace*
la ventana *window*

Los muebles (Furniture)

la alfombra *carpet, rug*
el armario *closet*
la bañera *bathtub*
la cama *bed*
el cuadro *painting*
la ducha *shower*
el escritorio *desk*
el espejo *mirror*
el lavabo *sink*
la mesa *table*
la silla *chair*
el sillón *easy chair*
el tocador *dresser*

Los aparatos eléctricos (Electric appliances)

la aspiradora *vacuum cleaner*
el despertador *alarm clock*
el disco compacto
   compact disk player (CD)

el estéreo *stereo*
la estufa *stove, range*
el horno (de microondas)
   (microwave) oven
la lámpara *lamp*
la lavadora *clothes washer*
el lavaplatos *dishwasher*
el reloj *clock, watch*
la secadora *clothes dryer*
el tostador *toaster*
la videocasetera *videocassette
   player (VCR)*

Los quehaceres (Chores)

cortar el césped *to mow the lawn*
hacer la cama *to make one's bed*
lavar los platos *to wash the dishes*
lavar la ropa *to wash clothes*
limpiar la casa *to clean the house*
pasar la aspiradora *to vacuum*
poner la mesa *to set the table*
sacar la basura *to take out the
   garbage*

Verbos

buscar (qu) *to look for*
fue *went*
hizo *did*
mudarse *to move (to a place)*
oír *to hear*
recordar (o → ue) *to remember*
sonar (o → ue) *to go off
   (e.g., an alarm)*

Adverbios

anoche *last night*
anteayer *the day before yesterday*
ayer *yesterday*
el año pasado *last year*
el mes pasado *last month*
la semana pasada *last week*

todavía *still, yet*
ya *already*

Pronombres directos

me *me*
te *you (informal)*
lo *him, you (formal), it (masculine)*
la *her, you (formal), it (feminine)*
nos *us*
os *you (informal)*
los *you (formal), them (masculine)*
las *you (formal), them (feminine)*

Expresiones idiomáticas

es hora de + infinitive *it's time to*
hace (dos) años *(two) years ago*
tener que + infinitive *to have to*

EN CONTEXTO

 Play Lab Tape

Although this dialogue contains some verb forms in the preterite, a tense that is introduced only later in this lesson, students will be able to understand the conversation based on context and their knowledge of Spanish vocabulary.

Hace tres años° que Julio y Gloria Sepúlveda se mudaron° de San Juan, Puerto Rico a la ciudad de Nueva York. (1) Ahora viven en un apartamento pequeño con dos dormitorios en el centro de Manhattan. Julio tiene treinta y cinco años y es policía. Su esposa tiene treinta y tres años y es directora de una escuela primaria. Tienen dos niños: Juan Carlos, que tiene siete años, y Susana María, que tiene dos años.

Three years ago / moved

Ayer° a las ocho de la mañana Gloria se levantó, fue a la cocina° y se preparó el desayuno: café con leche y pan tostado con mermelada. Luego desayunó en la sala° y miró la televisión por media hora. A las ocho y media Gloria fue a despertar a su marido.

Yesterday / kitchen

living room

—¿Julio? ¿Julio? ... ¡Julio!

—¡¿Cómo?! ¿Qué... qué quieres?

—¡Es hora de levantarte! Ya son las ocho y media y todavía° estás en la cama,° hombre.

still
bed

—¡Por Dios! ¿Son las ocho y media ya, Gloria?

—Sí. Hoy es sábado y tenemos que hacer muchas cosas.

—Bueno, pero estoy muy cansado. Quiero dormir un poco más.

—Estás muy cansado porque te acostaste a las dos y media de la mañana.

—Claro que sí. Me acosté tarde porque trabajé hasta la una y media. Bueno, no importa°... ya me levanto. Uy, ¡pero qué sueño tengo!

no es importante

—Julio, tenemos muchos quehaceres° hoy.

chores

—¿Qué quehaceres, querida?

—Pues, limpiar° el apartamento y lavar la ropa... hay mucha ropa.

clean

—Bueno, tú lavas la ropa y yo limpio el apartamento, ¿eh?

—Bien. Y después del almuerzo tenemos que ir de compras. Juan Carlos necesita unos suéteres y Susan María necesita una cobija° nueva.

comforter

—Sí, sí... ya lo sé, querida. Estamos en diciembre y hace mucho frío aquí en Nueva York, mientras que en mi Isla hace calor y mucho sol.(2)

Notas de texto

1. Over one million Puerto Ricans live in New York City today. Since 1917 Puerto Rico has been an *Estado Libre Asociado* (Commonwealth) of the United States and, therefore, all Puerto Ricans are American citizens. Puerto Ricans pay taxes on some goods to the U.S. Government and may vote in national elections if they officially reside in the United States.

2. Julio and many other Puerto Ricans who have immigrated to the United States refer to their homeland affectionately as *mi Isla* or *mi Puerto Rico*.

Answers: 1. Marido: Julio, 35 años, policía; Esposa: Gloria, 33 años, directora de una escuela primaria; sí, tienen dos hijos: Juan Carlos (7 años) y Susana María (2 años) 2. Puerto Rico; viven en Nueva York (en un apartamento en Manhattan) 3. Gloria: a las ocho, Julio: a las ocho y media; Julio se acostó a las dos y media de la mañana. 4. Julio quiere dormir más; está cansado. 5. Tienen que limpiar el apartamento, lavar la ropa e ir de compras. 6. [open]

¿Comprendió Ud.?

1. Complete el siguiente formulario.

Marido: _____	Esposa: _____
Edad: _____	Edad: _____
Profesión: _____	Profesión: _____
Hijos: _____ no _____ sí	¿Cuántos? _____
Nombres: _____	→ _____
Edades: _____	→ _____

2. ¿De dónde es la familia Sepúlveda originalmente? ¿Dónde viven ahora?
3. ¿A qué hora se despertaron Julio y Gloria ayer? ¿A qué hora se acostó Julio?
4. ¿Qué quiere hacer Julio esta mañana? ¿Por qué?
5. ¿Qué tienen que hacer Julio y Gloria este sábado?
6. ¿Qué piensa usted de Gloria y de Julio? ¿Conoce usted a personas de Puerto Rico? (¿Sí? ¿En qué parte de la isla vive[n]?)

VOCABULARIO ÚTIL

1. Collect and use color magazine photographs depicting the vocabulary presented here. Have your students contribute to the collection. Laminate the pictures for future use with other classes.
2. Have students bring prints, slides, or a short video of their house, apartment, or dormitory to show to the class with explanations in Spanish.

TRANSPARENCY No. 14:
Living Room and Bedroom

Tell students that other words for **bedroom** are *la alcoba* (Spain), *la recámara* (Mexico), and *el cuarto* (Puerto Rico and several other countries).

In this section, you will learn to describe your home and your household chores.

Cómo conversar sobre la casa

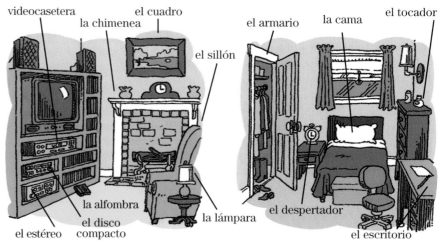

videocasetera / el cuadro / el tocador / la chimenea / el armario / la cama / el sillón / la alfombra / el disco compacto / la lámpara / el despertador / el escritorio / el estéreo

la sala

el dormitorio

¿Cómo me queda?

▶ COMMUNICATIVE GOALS

You will be able to describe the kinds of clothes you like and some activities you and others did.

▶ LANGUAGE FUNCTIONS

Describing clothing
Stating preferences
Stating clothing sizes
Speaking with store clerks
Communicating more smoothly
Describing past activities

▶ VOCABULARY THEMES

Clothing
Clothing accessories
Numbers over 2,000

▶ GRAMMATICAL STRUCTURES

Preterite of irregular verbs
Preterite of stem-vowel changing verbs
Indirect object pronouns

▶ CULTURAL INFORMATION

Clothing sizes
Dressing up appropriately

http://poco.heinle.com

 **Play Lab Tape**

EN CONTEXTO

Hoy es sábado, el dieciocho de diciembre. Julio y Gloria Sepúlveda y sus dos niños están en el famoso almacén Macy's. (1) En este momento Gloria está probándose° un vestido° blanco que quiere llevar° a la fiesta de los Reynosa. Julio está esperándola° con sus niños Juan Carlos y Susana María.

trying on / dress / to wear
to wait for

—¿Qué te parece este vestido, Julio? ¿Cómo me queda?°

to fit

—¡Me gusta mucho! Te queda muy bien, Gloria. Estás muy elegante.

—Gracias. Me gusta este color porque va bien con el collar° y los aretes° que me diste para mi cumpleaños. Creo que el vestido va a ser perfecto para la fiesta de los Reynosa el viernes, ¿verdad?

necklace / earings

—¡Claro que sí! ¿Recuerdas la fiesta estupenda que dieron Jorge y Hortensia el año pasado?

—Nunca voy a olvidarla.° Cómo nos divertimos,° ¿no? Bailamos merengue, cumbia, salsa, (2) comimos tantas cosas ricas y conocimos a mucha gente.

never forget / to have fun

—Sí, sí. La fiesta fue fabulosa. Bueno, ahora voy a pagar° este vestido con mi tarjeta de crédito.

pay for

—¿Cuánto cuesta,° Gloria?

does it cost

—Casi cien dólares. Es un buen precio, ¿no crees, Julio?

—Pues, creo que sí. Oye, Gloria, tenemos que volver a la zapatería° para cambiar° estos zapatos que le compramos a Juan Carlos la semana pasada. Le quedan un poco grandes.

shoe store
to change

—Bueno. Y después vamos a casa porque los niños tienen hambre y yo estoy muy cansada.

—Yo también, Gloria. Pues, tú compras el vestido y te esperamos aquí.

—De acuerdo, Julio.

Notas de texto

1. Macy's is one of the largest department stores in New York City. It has many branch stores throughout the metropolitan area and the United States.
2. *El merengue, la cumbia,* and *la salsa* are some popular dances that originated in Latin America. Others include *la bossa nova* and *el tango*.

Play records or tapes of Latin American music, including the kinds of dance music listed here.

1. Están en el almacén Macy's en Nueva York. 2. Gloria está probándose un vestido. 3. Van a una zapatería. 4. recibió 5. blanco 6. baile 7. tienda 8. Reynosa 9. nuevos 10. [open]

¿Comprendió Ud.?

1. ¿Dónde están los Sepúlveda en este momento?
2. ¿Qué están haciendo allí?
3. Y después, ¿qué van a hacer?
4. Gloria (compró / recibió / pagó) unos aretes.
5. Su vestido es (blanco / verde / rojo / negro).
6. La salsa es un tipo de (bebida / vestido / baile).
7. La zapatería es un tipo de (tienda / comida / ropa).
8. La fiesta va a ser en la casa de los (Reynosa / Sepúlveda).
9. Los zapatos de Juan Carlos son relativamente (viejos / nuevos).
10. Lea la lectura otra vez. Luego escriba un párrafo breve sobre lo que usted leyó.

VOCABULARIO ÚTIL

In this section you will talk and write about clothing and clothing accessories.

Cómo conversar de la ropa
La ropa y los accesorios

el traje de baño
la camiseta
la blusa
los anteojos para el sol
la mochila
los guantes
la falda
las sandalias
la gorra de béisbol
las botas

Tell students the Spanish word for **raincoat** (el impermeable).

If you wish, tell students other ways to say "sunglasses" are *las gafas de sol, los lentes de sol,* and *los espejuelos de sol;* some Spanish speakers say *los anteojos de sol.*

TRANSPARENCIES No. 11 and 17: Seasons and Clothing

Ask your students to bring from home large color photographs from magazines that illustrate the names of the clothing and accessories introduced here. Use these pictures to teach and review this new vocabulary.

Practiquemos

A. Mis preferencias. Pregúntele a un(a) compañero(a) de clase.

1. ¿Con qué frecuencia llevas un sombrero o una gorra de béisbol? ¿De qué color es tu sombrero o gorra de béisbol?
2. ¿Tienes pocas o muchas camisetas? Más o menos, ¿cuántas? ¿De qué colores son? ¿Cuál es tu color preferido?
3. ¿Te gusta llevar los jeans? ¿Cuántos pares de jeans tienes? ¿Dónde los compraste?
4. ¿Tienes muchos o pocos zapatos? ¿De qué colores son? ¿Cuántos pares de zapatos de tenis tienes? ¿Están viejos o nuevos? ¿Tienes un par de sandalias? (¿Sí? ¿Cuándo las llevas?) ¿Tienes botas? ¿Te gusta llevar botas?
5. ¿Cómo llevas tus libros a clase: en la mano, en una mochila o en una bolsa? ¿Cuántos libros llevas a nuestra clase? ¿Qué cosas llevaste a clase hoy?
6. Cuando llueve, ¿llevas un paraguas? (¿Sí? ¿De qué color es? ¿Cuántos paraguas tienes?) Cuando hace frío, ¿qué ropa te pones? ¿Qué tiempo va a hacer mañana? ¿Qué ropa piensas llevar mañana?

B. ¿Qué lleva usted? Complete las siguientes oraciones, según la situación.

1. A clase llevo...
2. Cuando voy a nadar llevo...
3. Cuando hace frío prefiero llevar...
4. En ocasiones formales llevo...

1. Before students begin the activities, walk around your classroom and point to students' clothing, asking *¿Qué es esto?* and *¿De qué color es?*
2. Have your students organize a fashion show in groups of 5–6 people. One student could describe what the others are wearing or each student could describe the clothes that he or she is modeling. The fashion show could be divided by seasons: Spring, Summer, Fall, Winter (review vocabulary from Lección 6). This show could be a rehearsal for the fashion show mentioned later in this lesson.

Ex. B.
1. Before students do this activity, you may want to review the names of colors in Spanish (see pages 48–49 in *Lección 2*).
2. Once students complete this activity, ask them to share information they obtained with another student.
3. Have students ask you some of these questions, using the usted forms.

C. Zapatos "Hush Puppies". Lea el siguiente anuncio, usando un diccionario bilingüe cuando sea necesario. Luego conteste las siguientes preguntas.

Linea
Body Shoes
by Hush Puppies

- El zapato más cómodo del mundo.
- Planta extraliviana con diseño que absorbe los impactos.
- Talón acolchado.
- Forro en cuero H.P. Pigskin de mayor suavidad y capacidad de respiración.

1. ¿Por qué son tan cómodos *(comfortable)* los zapatos Hush Puppies?
2. ¿De qué material son estos zapatos?
3. En su opinión, ¿por qué se usa un poco de inglés en el anuncio?

D. Situaciones. Hable con otro(a) estudiante. Primero, lean las siguientes situaciones. Luego respondan a las preguntas.

1. Estamos en octubre, hace sol y no hace viento. Ustedes y dos amigos quieren montar en bicicleta en un parque bonito. ¿Qué ropa van a ponerse y qué cosas van a llevar con ustedes?
2. El próximo domingo su amiga puertorriqueña va a cumplir quince años. Ustedes reciben una invitación a la fiesta de los quince años. ¿Qué ropa van a llevar? ¿Qué regalo van a darle a la quinceañera?
3. Ustedes piensan ir de vacaciones a Cancún, México, por dos semanas en diciembre cuando hace buen tiempo allí. ¿Qué ropa y accesorios van a llevar?
4. Una amiga los invitó a ustedes a esquiar en Vail, Colorado, por cinco días. Ustedes aceptan la invitación y ahora tienen que decidir qué ropa van a llevar.

Ex. E. Follow up this activity with a fashion show written and narrated by your students with your guidance. If possible, make a video of the fashion show and replay it at a later date.

E. ¡Soy rico(a)! Imagínese que uno de sus parientes ricos *(rich)* le dio a usted mil dólares para su cumpleaños. Ahora usted quiere comprar ropa con el dinero, pero ¿qué va a comprar? Escriba un párrafo con descripciones de: 1) las prendas *(articles)* de ropa, 2) los números o las tallas, 3) los colores y 4) los precios.

NOTAS CULTURALES

Las tallas de ropa

En España y en la mayoría de los países latinoamericanos, los números de las tallas de ropa difieren de las tallas de ropa de los Estados Unidos y del Canadá. Consulte la siguiente tabla para determinar las tallas correctas para usted.

DAMAS

Vestidos / Trajes

norteamericano	6	8	10	12	14	16	18	20
europeo	34	36	38	40	42	44	46	48

Calcetines / Pantimedias

norteamericano	8	$8\frac{1}{2}$	9	$9\frac{1}{2}$	10	$10\frac{1}{2}$
europeo	0	1	2	3	4	5

Zapatos

norteamericano	6	$6\frac{1}{2}$	7	8	$8\frac{1}{2}$	9
europeo	36	37	38	$38\frac{1}{2}$	39	40

CABALLEROS

Trajes / Abrigos

norteamericano	36	38	40	42	44	46
europeo	46	48	50	52	54	56

Camisas

norteamericano	14	$14\frac{1}{2}$	15	$15\frac{1}{2}$	16	$16\frac{1}{2}$	17	$17\frac{1}{2}$	18
europeo	36	37	38	39	41	42	43	44	45

Zapatos

norteamericano	5	6	7	8	$8\frac{1}{2}$	9	$9\frac{1}{2}$	10	11
europeo	$37\frac{1}{2}$	38	$39\frac{1}{2}$	40	41	42	43	44	46

TRANSPARENCIES No. 11 and 17: Seasons and Clothing

Actividad

1. Señora/Señorita: Indique su número o talla.

   Zapatos: _____
   Vestidos/Trajes: _____
   Calcetines/Pantimedias: _____

2. Señor: Indique su número o talla.

   Trajes/Abrigos: _____
   Camisas: _____
   Zapatos: _____

3. Ahora compare sus tallas de ropa con otro(a) estudiante.

1. Have students work in pairs to role-play this dialogue.
2. Have students form small groups of three or four members. Ask them to tell each other where they bought some of their clothes or clothing accessories, and how much they paid for them. Encourage the group members to ask and answer follow-up questions, using as much Spanish as possible.
3. Have groups of four students write a script and then role-play a situation in a store. One student in each group could be the salesperson, and the other three students could "buy" different articles of clothing, using the chart on page 199.

Say aloud the following numbers which students should write as they are written here: *1.515, 20.457, 100.300, 1.850.786, 2.678.902*

Cómo comprar la ropa

—¿En qué puedo servirle?   *May I help you?*
—Quiero comprar un suéter.   *I want to buy a sweater.*
—¿Qué talla usa usted, señor?   *What size do you wear, sir?*
—Cuarenta y dos.   *Forty-two.*
—Aquí hay dos de esa talla.   *Here are two in that size.*
—Prefiero este azul.   *I prefer this blue one.*
—¿Quiere usted probárselo?   *Do you want to try it on?*
—Sí, gracias. ... ¿Qué le parece?   *Yes. . . . What do you think?*
—Le queda muy bien, señor.   *It fits you very well, sir.*
—¿Cuánto cuesta?   *How much is it?*
—Veinte mil pesos, señor.   *Twenty thousand pesos, sir.*
—Bueno. Me lo llevo.   *Good. I'll take it.*

Los números más de 2,000

2,000	dos mil
200,000	doscientos(as) mil
1,000,000	un millón
2,000,000	dos millones

1. Use *mil* to express numbers over 1,000.

2,000	dos mil
20,000	veinte mil

2. Note that when writing numbers, Spanish uses a period where English uses a comma, and vice versa.

   English: $1,500.75
   Spanish: $1.500,75

Practiquemos

F. ¡Qué precios! El Corte Inglés, un almacén popular de España, tiene una liquidación hoy. Lea los precios normales y los precios especiales de las siguientes cosas.

Ejemplo: Suéter PIERRE CARDIN 17.250 ptas. → 14.000 ptas.
El precio normal de un suéter Pierre Cardin es diecisiete mil doscientos cincuenta pesetas. Hoy el precio es catorce mil pesetas.

Ex. F. Follow this exercise with an auction of unwanted used clothing brought in by your students. To make the auction more realistic, create and distribute even amounts of mock money to each student. If you wish, you could base the rate of exchange on a specific country.

	Precio Normal	Precio Especial
Bolsa **GUCCI**	40.250 ptas.	35.500 ptas.
Reloj **ROLEX**	575.000 ptas.	500.000 ptas.
Chaqueta **VACCA**	230.000 ptas.	160.450 ptas.
Zapatos **FERRAGAMO**	57.500 ptas.	40.000 ptas.
Vestido **CALVIN KLEIN**	1.150.000 ptas.	975.000 ptas.
Traje de baño **GOTTEX**	37.500 ptas.	32.350 ptas.
Traje **GIORGIO ARMANI**	172.500 ptas.	157.500 ptas.

G. En una tienda de ropa. Hable con otro(a) estudiante: una persona es el (la) dependiente *(salesclerk)* y la otra persona es su cliente.

Exs. G. and H.
Videotape your students' role plays, if you have the equipment.

Dependiente
1. Greet your customer.
3. Ask how you can help.
5. Inquire about size(s).
7. Find the correct size(s).
9. End the conversation.

Cliente
2. Answer appropriately.
4. Say what you want to try on.
6. Respond to the question(s).
8. Decide whether or not to buy.
10. Respond appropriately.

H. Situaciones. Converse con otro(a) estudiante.

1. A: You are a new employee in a shoe store. You want to impress your boss and make many commissions. Try to convince your customer to buy two pairs of shoes and several pairs of socks.

   B: You are a frugal customer. You want to buy an inexpensive pair of shoes. Once you find a pair you like, buy only the shoes.

2. A: You are going to a semi-formal party with one of your best friends. You want to really dress up for the occasion because you enjoy wearing beautiful well-made clothes and clothing accessories, and you want to create a good impression at the party. Telephone your friend to convince him or her to dress as well as you do.

   B: You are an easy-going person who takes life as it comes. You like to dress casually no matter what the occasion, and you don't like to spend a great deal of money, especially on the latest fashions in clothing and clothing accessories. Express these feelings when your friend speaks with you over the phone.

Ex. H. Before students do this activity, you could give them some useful expression such as: *Me encanta(n)..., ¡Son preciosos!, ¡Qué horrible(s)!,* and *Me queda(n) apretados(s).*

NOTAS CULTURALES

Cómo vestirse apropiadamente

it comes to

La gente de habla española da mucha importancia a la apariencia física, especialmente cuando se trata de° la ropa. En general, los jóvenes hispanos llevan ropa informal, aunque algunos prefieren ropa de estilos y colores conservadores. Los jeans y las camisetas son extremadamente populares entre los jóvenes hispanos.

shorts / beaches / beach resorts

towns / churches

Por lo general, es apropiado llevar pantalones cortos° en las playas° y los balnearios.° Normalmente, los hispanos no llevan pantalones cortos ni en las ciudades ni en los pueblos,° ni en las iglesias° ni en las sinagogas.

I. ¿Cómo se visitan? Describa cómo se visten las siguientes personas.

1. usted (en clase / en una fiesta / en una iglesia)
2. su profesor(a) de español en la sala de clase
3. el presidente de los Estados Unidos y su esposa

GRAMÁTICA FUNCIONAL

Describing past activities

—¿Qué **hicieron** ustedes anoche?
—**Dimos** una fiesta. ¿Qué **hiciste** tú?
—**Fui** de compras con una amiga.

Preterite tense of irregular verbs

As you know, Spanish speakers use the preterite tense to express the beginning of past actions, conditions and events, and the completion of past actions, conditions and events.

How to form irregular preterites

Some Spanish verbs have irregular verb stems in the preterite. Their endings have no accent marks.

Some verbs that describe actions

hacer:	hice	hiciste	hizo[1]	hicimos	*hicisteis*	hicieron
poner:	puse	pusiste	puso	pusimos	*pusisteis*	pusieron
venir:	vine	viniste	vino	vinimos	*vinisteis*	vinieron

Emphasize that the preterite forms of irregular verbs have no written accent marks.

Explain to students that not all action verbs are irregular in the preterite (in fact, most are not irregular). Provide some examples such as *comprar, correr,* and *escribir.*

Point out that the preterite forms of *ir* and *ser* are identical. Context clarifies meaning.

dar:	di	diste	dio	dimos	*disteis*	dieron
ver:	vi	viste	vio	vimos	visteis	vieron

decir:	dije	dijiste	dijo	dijimos	*dijisteis*	dijeron
traer:	traje	trajiste	trajo	trajimos	*trajisteis*	trajeron

ir:	fui	fuiste	fue	fuimos	*fuisteis*	fueron

Some verbs that describe states of being

estar:	estuve	estuviste	estuvo	estuvimos	*estuvisteis*	estuvieron
tener:	tuve	tuviste	tuvo	tuvimos	*tuvisteis*	tuvieron
poder:	pude	pudiste	pudo	pudimos	*pudisteis*	pudieron
saber:	supe	supiste	supo	supimos	*supisteis*	supieron
querer:	quise	quisiste	quiso	quisimos	*quisisteis*	quisieron
ser:	fui	fuiste	fue	fuimos	*fuisteis*	fueron[2]

Have students role-play the dialogues on these pages.

—¿Dónde **estuviste** ayer?	*Where were you yesterday?*
—**Estuve** en Macy's.	*I was at Macy's.*
—¿En Macy's? Trabajé allí por un día. **Fui** dependiente.	*At Macy's? I worked there for one day. I was a salesclerk.*
—¿Cómo? ¿Qué pasó?	*Huh? What happened?*
—No me gustó. ¿Qué compraste?	*I didn't like it. What did you buy?*
—**Tuve** que comprar unas medias.	*I had to buy some stockings.*

1. As you know, the preterite tense is used to express the beginning or the completion of past actions, conditions, and events. Sometimes— but not always—the preterite of *poder, saber,* and *querer* may be translated into English as follows:[3]

pude	*I could (and did)*	**no pude**	*I (tried and) could not*
supe	*I found out*	**no supe**	*I never knew*
quise	*I wanted (and tried)*	**no quise**	*I refused*

—**Quise** cambiar estos zapatos, pero **no pude.**	*I tried to exchange these shoes, but I couldn't.*

---

[1] Note the spelling change from *c* to *z* in the *usted/él/ella* form.
[2] Note that the preterite forms for *ir* and *ser* are identical; context clarifies their meaning in a sentence.
[3] Emphasize the underlying principle of the preterite tense; that is, to express the completion or the beginning of past actions, conditions and events. This principle governs the verbs *poder, saber, querer,* and *conocer* just as it governs all other Spanish verbs.

—¿Qué pasó, Gloria?

—El dependiente **no quiso** cambiarlos.

—Pero ¿por qué?

—Porque **supo** que los compré en liquidación.

What happened, Gloria?

The salesclerk refused to exchange them.

But why?

Because he found out I bought them on clearance.

2. The preterite of *hay* is *hubo.*

—**Hubo** un accidente hoy.

—¿Qué pasó?

—No sé, pero **hubo** policías investigando toda la mañana.

There was an accident today.

What happened?

I don't know, but there were police officers investigating all morning.

Practiquemos

A. Conversaciones cortas. Complete las siguientes conversaciones cortas (short), usando formas apropiadas de los verbos indicados.

Ejemplo: venir

> —¿Quién *vino* a la casa hoy, Gloria?
> —Dos amigas *vinieron* a visitarme.

1. **decir**

> —¿Qué _____ mi abuelita por teléfono, papá?
> —Pues, mi hijo, ella me _____ que hace sol en San Juan.
> —Luego, ¿qué le _____ tú a mi abueltia, papá?
> —Le _____: "Mamá, ¡hace mucho frío aquí"!

2. **ir**

> —¿Adónde _____ ayer, Gloria?
> —Una amiga y yo _____ de compras.
> —¿Adónde _____ ustedes?
> —_____ a Macy's. Más tarde, mi amiga _____ a una fiesta y yo _____ a casa.

3. **tener**

> —Ayer Julio y yo _____ que hacer muchas cosas.
> —¿Como qué cosas _____ ustedes que hacer, Gloria?
> —Pues, Julio y Juan Carlos _____ que comprar comida. Y yo _____ que ir a la tienda con Susana María. Más tarde nosotros _____ que ir a una fiesta de cumpleaños. Y tú, ¿qué _____ que hacer ayer?
> —Bueno, no _____ que hacer nada.

B. Un padre preocupado. Complete los siguientes párrafos con formas apropiadas del pretérito de los infinitivos indicados.

Ejemplo: Ayer por la tarde Julio / saber que...
> *Ayer por la tarde Julio supo que...*

Ayer por la tarde Julio / saber que su hijo Juan Carlos / tener un accidente en su bicicleta. Julio / ir al hospital, / ver a Juan Carlos y / hablar con el médico, quien le / decir que el niño / salir bien del accidente. Más tarde, / llegar Gloria, quien le / traer unos chocolates a su hijo. Después, Juan Carlos y sus padres / ir a casa.

Anoche Julio / querer descansar un poco, pero no / poder. Primero, / hacer ejercicios por veinte minutos, / ir al baño y / ducharse por quince minutos. Luego / ir a su dormitorio, / ponerse el pijama y / acostarse. Pero Julio no / poder dormir bien y / tener que levantarse dos veces. / Ser una noche terrible, pero afortunadamente él no / tener que trabajar al día siguiente.

C. La mamá de Julio. Complete la siguiente conversación, usando la forma apropiada del pretérito de los verbos **poder, querer** y **saber**.

—Anoche (yo) _____ que mi mamá tuvo un problema en una tienda.
—¿Qué pasó, Julio?
—Ella _____ cambiar un vestido por otro color, pero ella no _____ hacerlo.
—¡Por Dios! Pero ¿por qué el dependiente no _____ cambiarlo?
—¡Porque él _____ que mi mamá compró el vestido hace un mes!
—Pues, ¿qué hizo ella?
—Ella no _____ hacer nada *(nothing)*. Por eso, fue a otra tienda y compró un vestido del mismo estilo, pero de otro color.

D. De compras. En un papel separado, describa una experiencia que usted tuvo cuando fue a un centro comercial *(shopping mall)*.

Por ejemplo,

1. ¿Adónde fue usted?
2. ¿Con quién fue?
3. ¿Que compró usted?
4. ¿Por qué lo compró?
5. ¿Cuánto costó (costaron)?
6. ¿Qué más hizo usted allí?

Charlemos

E. Una fiesta estupenda. Pregúntele a un(a) compañero(a) de clase.

1. ¿Cuándo fuiste a una fiesta estupenda? 2. ¿Qué tipo de fiesta fue (por ejemplo, una fiesta de cumpleaños)? 3. ¿Dónde fue la fiesta? 4. ¿Con quién fuiste allí? 5. ¿A qué hora comenzó la fiesta? ¿A qué hora llegaste tú? 6. ¿Llevaste un regalo? (¿Sí? ¿Qué llevaste? ¿Dónde compraste el regalo? ¿Cuántos dólares costó? ¿Para quién fue el regalo?) 7. ¿Qué otras personas fueron a la fiesta? 8. ¿A quién conociste allí? 9. ¿Qué hicieron tú y tus amigos en la fiesta? 10. ¿A qué hora volviste a casa? 11. ¿Qué impresión tuviste de la fiesta?

F. Un buen fin de semana. Descríbale a un(a) compañero(a) de clase un fin de semana maravilloso que usted tuvo.

Por ejemplo:

1. ¿Adónde y cuándo fue usted?
2. ¿Quiénes fueron con usted?
3. ¿Qué deportes practicaron?
4. ¿Qué vieron ustedes allí?
5. ¿Qué otras cosas hicieron?
6. ¿Qué no pudieron hacer?

GRAMÁTICA FUNCIONAL

Describing more past experiences

—¿Qué hicieron Julio y su hijo?

—**Se divirtieron** en el restaurante.

—Bueno, ¿qué pasó después?

—Juan Carlos **pidió** un refresco y su papá le **sirvió** una Coca.

Preterite with stem-vowel changing verbs

Spanish -*ir* verbs that have a stem-change in the present tense also have a stem change in the *usted / él / ella* and *ustedes / ellos / ellas* forms of the preterite tense: *e* becomes *i* and *o* becomes *u*.

servir

Present (e → i)	Preterite (e → i)
sirvo	serví
sirves	serviste
sirve	sirvió
servimos	servimos
servís	*servisteis*
sirven	sirvieron

divertirse

Present (e → ie)	Preterite (e → i)
me divierto	me divertí
te diviertes	te divertiste
se divierte	se divirtió
nos divertimos	nos divertimos
os divertís	*os divertisteis*
se divierten	se divirtieron

dormir

Present (o → ue)	Preterite (o → u)
duermo	dormí
duermes	dormiste
duerme	durmió
dormimos	dormimos
dormís	*dormisteis*
duermen	durmieron

Practiquemos

A. Una llamada telefónica. Gloria está hablando con Bienvenida, su suegra que vive en San Juan, Puerto Rico. Complete la conversación entre Gloria y Bienvenida con formas apropiadas de los verbos indicados.

pedir

—¿Qué _____ ustedes en el restaurante anoche?

—Pues, yo _____ un bistec. Julio y Juan Carlos _____ pescado. Después, nosotros _____ queso y fruta como de postre.

dormir

—¿_____ ustedes bien?

—Yo _____ muy bien. Los niños _____ muy bien, pero Julio _____ mal. Ahora está mejor, gracias a Dios.

divertirse

—¿ _____ ustedes anoche, Gloria?

—Pues, yo _____ jugando con Juan Carlos, pero Julio no _____ porque estuvo enfermo. Y tú, Bienvenida, ¿cómo _____?

—Salí con un amigo. Fuimos al cine.

B. Una pequeña fiesta.
El sábado pasado Julio y Gloria dieron una fiesta en su apartamento. Diga qué pasó allí.

A las siete Julio y Gloria / ducharse (*se ducharon*), luego / vestirse. A las ocho y media / llegar los primeros invitados. Gloria / servir unos sándwiches, pero una amiga de ella / preferir no comer nada. Un señor / pedir una cerveza y su esposa / preferir tomar vino; Julio les / servir estas dos bebidas. Todos / divertirse mucho en la fiesta: ellos / bailar y / cantar hasta la una de la mañana. Cuando los invitados / salir, Julio y Gloria / acostarse y / dormir bien porque / trabajar mucho para dar una fiesta divertida.

Ex. B. Answers:
se vistieron, llegaron, sirvió, prefirió, pidió, prefirió, sirvió, se divirtieron, bailaron, cantaron, salieron, se acostaron, durmieron, trabajaron

C. En la casa de los Sepúlveda.
Diga cuánto tiempo hace que estas personas hicieron las siguientes actividades. Imagínese que ahora es la una de la tarde.

Ejemplo: *Julio pasó la aspiradora hace cuatro horas.*

Ex. C. Before your students begin this activity, remind them how Spanish speakers express how long ago an action or event occurred by using the construction: *hace* + time; for example: —¿*Cuánto tiempo hace que **llamaste** a tu mamá?* / —*La llamé **hace dos días**.* Or: ***Hace dos días** que la **llamé**.*

Ex. D. Follow-up activity: Have students ask each other these questions, using informal forms.

D. ¿Qué pasó? Escriba una composición de tres párrafos sobre una fiesta en la que usted se divirtió mucho. Use las siguientes preguntas como guía.

Párrafo 1: ¿Dónde fue la fiesta? ¿Con quién fue usted? ¿Cómo se vistió usted (vistieron ustedes)?

Párrafo 2: ¿A qué hora llegó usted (llegaron ustedes) a la fiesta? ¿Cómo se divirtieron usted y sus amigos? ¿Qué comieron y bebieron ustedes? ¿Quién sirvió la comida y las bebidas? ¿Qué quiso usted hacer, pero sus amigos no quisieron hacerlo?

Párrafo 3: ¿A qué hora salió usted de la fiesta? ¿Adónde fue? ¿A qué hora se acostó usted? ¿Se durmió usted inmediatamente o no? ¿Por qué?

Charlemos

E. ¿Cuánto tiempo? Pregúntele a otro(a) estudiante.

1. ¿Cuánto tiempo hace que compraste ropa nueva? ¿Qué compraste? ¿De qué color es (son)?
2. ¿Llevas anteojos para el sol? ¿Sí? ¿Cuándo los llevas? ¿Cuánto tiempo hace que los compraste? ¿Dónde los compraste? ¿Cuánto te costaron?
3. ¿Cuánto tiempo hace que compraste un paraguas? ¿Dónde lo compraste? ¿Todavía lo tienes? ¿Dónde está en este momento?
4. ¿Llevas tus libros en una mochila? ¿Sí? ¿Cuánto tiempo hace que la compraste o la recibiste? ¿De qué color es tu mochila?

1. At this early stage of language acquisition, expect students to recognize indirect object pronouns. Using them correctly will require a great deal of communicative practice over time. As usual, some practice is provided in this text.
2. Refer students to page 130 [*Lección 5:* The verb *gustar* + noun] to review how the verb *gustar* functions with indirect object pronouns. You may also wish to have student redo the exercises and activities in that section to build their confidence and language proficiency.

GRAMÁTICA FUNCIONAL

Communicating more smoothly in Spanish

¿Dónde está mi vaso de leche, Juan Carlos?

¡Lo tomé Papá!

¿Y mi sandwich de pescado?

Le di el sandwich a Beto.

Indirect object pronouns

What are indirect object pronouns?

1. All sentences have a subject and a verb. As you learned in *Lección 7,* many sentences also have a direct object or a pronoun that refers to it (direct object pronoun).

Subject	Verb	Direct Object		S.	D.O.P.	V.
|	|	|		|	|	|
Gloria	limpió	el apartamento.	→	Gloria	lo	limpió.
(Gloria cleaned the apartment.)			→	*(Gloria cleaned it.)*		

2. Some sentences also have an indirect object.

Subject	Verb	Direct Object	Indirect Object
|	|	|	|
Gloria le compró		una corbata	a su **marido.**
(Gloria bought a necktie for her husband.)			

Circle the indirect objects in the following sentences:

Julio le dio cinco dólares a Juan Carlos.
El niño les compró dulces a sus padres.
Ellos le dijeron a su hijo: —¡Gracias!

3. Indirect object pronouns refer to people already mentioned as indirect objects; that is, the pronoun tells **to whom** or **for whom** the action of the verb is performed.

Julio le dio dos dólares a su hijo.
*Él **le** dio el dinero anoche.*   **To whom** did he give
                                           the money?

El niño les compró dulces a sus amigos.
*Él **les** compró los dulces esta mañana.*   **For whom** did he buy
                                              the candy?

In the sentences above, the indirect object pronouns *le* and *les* replaced the indirect object nouns *hijo* and *amigos*, respectively.

How to form and where to place indirect object pronouns

Singular		**Plural**	
me	*to/for me*	**nos**	*to/for us*
te	*to/for you (informal)*	**os**	*to/for you (informal)*
le	*to/for you (formal), him, her*	**les**	*to/for you (formal), them*

Indirect object pronouns are placed in the same positions as direct object pronouns.

1. Place the pronoun in front of the conjugated verb.

—¿Gloria **te dio** esa camisa?   *Did Gloria give you that shirt?*
—Sí. También **me compró** estos   *Yes. She also bought me these*
   jeans.   *jeans.*

2. In negative sentences, place the *no* in front of the pronoun.

—Le di una fiesta a mi amiga.   *I gave a party for my friend.*
—¿Por qué **no nos diste** una?   *Why didn't you give us one?*

3. When the pronoun is used with an infinitive or a present participle, place it either before the conjugated verb or attach it to the infinitive or the present participle. (A written accent is needed to mark the stressed vowel of a present participle when a direct object pronoun is attached to it.)

Les voy a escribir a mis amigos.
            or   *I'm going to write to my friends.*
Voy a escribirles a mis amigos.

Les estoy escribiendo ahora.
            or   *I'm writing to them now.*
Estoy escribiéndoles ahora.

How to clarify or emphasize indirect object pronouns

Because *le* and *les* have different meanings, you may add the expressions *a él, a ella, a usted, a ellos, a ellas* or *a ustedes* to the sentence for clarification or emphasis.

1. For clarification:

   —¿Le dijiste **a él** o **a ella?**   *Did you tell **him** or **her?***
   —**Le** dije a **ella.**   *I told **her.***

2. For emphasis:

   —¿A quién le está hablando?   *To whom are you speaking?*
   —Estoy hablándole **a usted.**   *I'm speaking **to you.***

Practiquemos

A. Un regalo para la abuelita. En el siguiente párrafo, ponga un círculo alrededor de *(around)* los pronombres del objeto indirecto y dibuje una flecha *(arrow)* a los objectos a que correspondan.

Julio (le) dio diez dólares a su hijo Juan Carlos. Luego el niño le compró a su abuela Bienvenida una camiseta que dice: "Bienvenida a New York!" Después, Juan Carlos le mandó la camiseta a ella. También le escribió una carta en que le dijo: —Abuelita, con esta carta te mando un regalo pequeño. Durante la semana Bienvenida le respondió a su nieto: —¡Gracias por la camiseta, niño! Te mando un beso grande. También les mando besos a tus padres y a tu hermana Susana María.

B. Quiero mucho a mi familia. Julio quiere mucho a su familia. ¿Qué dice Julio que hace por su familia?

Ejemplo: comprar comida y ropa a mis niños y / dar mucho amor
               Les compro comida y ropa a mis niños y les doy mucho amor.

1. dar besos a Susana María y / comprar mucha ropa bonita
2. dar un abrazo a mi hijo por la mañana y / dar un beso a todos
3. comprar rosas a Gloria y / escribir poemas de amor, a veces
4. tocar la guitarra y cantar a mis dos niños, y / dar abrazos
5. contestar las preguntas a Juan Carlos y / leer libros de Disney
6. escribir frecuentemente a mis padres y / decir que estamos bien

C. Una conversación. Gloria volvió al almacén Macy's para comprar un regalo. En otro papel, escriba una conversación entre ella (G) y el (la) dependiente (D).

G: Buenos (Buenas) _____ .
D: _____ , señora. ¿En qué puedo servirle?
G: Quiero comprarle(s) un regalo a mi(s) _____ .
D: ¿A su(s) _____ ? Bien. ¿Qué tipo de regalo busca?
G: Pues, a _____ (le/les) gusta mucho la ropa.
D: ¿Ropa? ¿Qué tipo de ropa, por ejemplo?
G: _____ .
D: Comprendo. Bueno, ¿a usted le gusta (este/esta) _____ ?
G: Sí, pero no me gusta el color. Prefiero uno(a) de color _____ .
D: Aquí tiene usted uno(a) de ese color, señora.
G: ¿Cuánto cuesta?
D: _____ , señora.
G: Bien. Me (lo/la) llevo. Pago con mi tarjeta de crédito.

Charlemos

D. Entre amigos. Hable con otro(a) estudiante, usando las siguientes oraciones apropiadamente, según sus intereses personales.

1. Cuando visito a mis amigos...
2. Cuando una amiga está enferma...
3. Si tú vienes a mi fiesta...
4. Si salimos bien en este curso...

E. Perdón... Forme preguntas de las siguientes frases y hágaselas a diferentes compañeros de clase. Ellos deben escribir su nombre en la línea apropiada.

Ejemplo:　escribirles muchas cartas a tus amigos
　　　　A: *¿Les escribes muchas cartas a tus amigos?*
　　　　B: *Sí.*
　　　　A: *Escribe tu nombre aquí, por favor.*

Nombre

1. darles un poco de dinero a algunos de tus amigos　_____
2. comprarle cosas bonitas a tu mejor amigo(a)　_____
3. hacerle muchos favores a tu papá o a tu mamá　_____
4. pedirle perdón a gente cuando no tienes razón　_____
5. escribirles cartas a amigos en otros estados　_____

Ex. E.
1. Students should be able to understand these directions and the example, even though double object pronouns and informal commands have not been introduced yet. Students will understand from previous experience with this activity format, from context, and from the example.
2. Students could also do this activity in pairs, omitting the signature feature.

PARA LEER MEJOR

Guessing Meaning From Word Roots

You can guess the meaning of some Spanish words if you know the meaning of their root. For example, if you know the word *vestirse*, you could guess the meaning of the word *vestido*, especially if you saw it in context like this:

> *Después de ducharse, Gloria se vistió elegantemente. Se puso un **vestido** blanco que ella compró en Macy's esa mañana.*

Words like *vestirse* and *vestido* that have the same root (e.g., *vest-*) are called "word families" because they are related to each other.

Activities

A. Skim the following text to get the general gist of its content. Then complete these statements.

CON NUESTRO EXCLUSIVO SISTEMA REVOLVENTE.

DESCUBRA EL PLACER DE COMPRAR Y LA FACILIDAD DE PAGAR.

Galerías Preciados

GALERIAS

Con la Tarjeta Revolvente de Galerías usted y su familia dispone de una Cuenta de Compras, abierta permanentemente, en las 30 tiendas de Galerías.

Solicítela, indíquenos el límite de crédito que desea (superior a 75.000 ptas.) y se la entregamos inmediata y totalmente GRATIS.

ELIJA LA FORMA DE PAGO

- 10% mensualmente.*
- Una cantidad fija al mes.*
- Cada mes el total de sus compras a 60 días aproximadamente y sin recargo.

Sus compras importantes, con un pago aplazado de hasta 24 meses, se las gestionamos inmediatamente.

Cada mes recibe una factura con el detalle de sus compras y el importe del recibo que enviamos a su banco.

CAMBIO DE FORMA DE PAGO

Si desea cambiar la forma de pago que tenía establecida no tiene más que comunicárnoslo y su próxima factura la abonará según sus deseos.

Y ADEMAS...

- Participa en todas nuestras acciones promocionales con grandes ventajas para usted.
- La Tarjeta Revolvente puede utilizarla en todas las Secciones y Servicios de Galerías: Supermermercados, Cafeterías, Agencia de Viajes, etc.
- Dispone de DOS horas de aparcamiento GRATIS.

This ad contains a typographical error in the word *Supermercados*. All authentic materials in this book have not been altered.

1. This text is a(n) ...
   a. memo   b. recipe   c. ad   d. menu

2. Galerías Preciados is a...
   a. store   b. credit card   c. product   d. bank

3. The main purpose of this text is to...
   a. inform   b. persuade   c. announce   d. sell

B. Check whether or not Galerías Preciados offers the following benefits.

	Yes	No
1. payment by mail	___	___
2. unlimited credit	___	___
3. dining facilities	___	___
4. more than 30 stores	___	___
5. limited free parking	___	___
6. installment payments	___	___
7. bimonthly statements	___	___

C. Scan the text to find words that have the same root as the words below. Write the words on the appropriate lines.

1. fácil   *facilidad*
2. abrir   _____
3. total   _____
4. servir   _____
5. recibir   _____
6. limitación   _____
7. participación   _____

PARA ESCRIBIR MEJOR

Editing Your Writing

Editing your written work is an important skill to master. It is a good idea to edit it several times; for example, check your compositions for:

1. **Content**
   a. Is the title of your composition captivating?
   b. Is the information you wrote pertinent to the topic?
   c. Is the composition interesting to your readers?

2. **Organization**
   a. Is there one main idea in each paragraph of the composition?
   b. Do the details in each paragraph relate to a single idea?
   c. Is the order of the sentences correct in each paragraph?
   d. Is the order of the paragraphs correct in your composition?

3. **Cohesion and style**
   a. Does your composition communicate exactly what you mean?
   b. Does your composition "flow" easily from beginning to end?
   c. Have you chosen the precise vocabulary words you need?
   d. Are the grammar and spelling correct in your composition?

Activities

A. Edit the paragraph below three times and rewrite it correctly. The first time, check the content. The second time, correct its organization. The third time, check for cohesion and style. (Remember to use correct capitalization and punctuation.) Make any other changes you think are necessary.

En Nueva York

Ayer fue Sábado, el dieciocho de Diciembre. Julio y Gloria Sepúlveda y sus dos niños fueron a la almacén Macy's. En la ciudad de Nueva York. Hizo mucho frío en Puerto rico. Gloria se pusó un blanco vestido. Ella le pidó la opinión su esposo. A julio le gustó mucho. Gloria la compró con su tarjeta de crédit. La familia sepúlveda fueron a otra departamento. Julio compra una camisa bonito. Él compró una corbata.

When you finish, exchange paragraphs with a classmate and check each other's work for errors. Then write a second draft of your paragraph, and give it to your instructor for correction of any remaining errors.

B. Write a three-paragraph composition about a chore (e.g., shopping, household, favor) that you did recently. You may wish to include a short dialogue in your composition as well. Then edit your work carefully using the guidelines that you learned in this section.

Atajo

Functions:
Talking about past events; talking about the recent past; sequencing events

Vocabulary:
Clothing; fabrics; colors; stores & products; house: household chores

Grammar:
Verbs: irregular preterite; Personal pronouns; indirect *le, les*

¿A qué nivel está Ud.?

¿Qué talla de camisa usa Ud.? ¿Qué talla de zapato? Review the chapter and then monitor your progress by completing the *Autoprueba* at the end of *Lección 8* in the **Workbook/Lab Manual.**

SÍNTESIS

¡A ver!

Laura and her friend are going shopping for clothes today. First, study the words and their meaning in the *Vocabulario esencial*. Second, read the activity to know what information you need to listen for. Third, watch the videotape, then do the activity.

Vocabulario esencial

Discúlpame.	*Excuse me.*
traje sastre	*tailored suit*
chaleco	*vest*
mostrar	*to show*
la tela	*material, cloth*
el vestidor	*dressing room*
combina	*goes well, matches*

All the sentences below are false according to the information in the video. In each sentence, change the appropriate words to make it true.

Ejemplo: La dependiente vendía ropa para hombres.
*La dependiente vendía ropa para **mujeres.***

1. Antes de ir de compras, Laura y su amiga hablaron en la calle.
2. Laura y su amiga fueron a un almacén muy bonito en México, D.F.
3. Los colores que le gustaban a Laura eran el rojo y el blanco.
4. La dependiente de la tienda se vestía bastante mal.
5. La dependiente que atendió a Laura usó "usted" con ella.
6. Laura decidió comprar un vestido azul y una blusa blanca.
7. La amiga de Laura compró un traje azul y un top marrón.

Answers:
1. *Antes de ir de compras, Laura y su amiga hablaron en **un restaurante**.*
2. *Laura y su amiga fueron a **una tienda de ropa/una boutique** muy bonita en México, D.F.*
3. *Los colores que le gustaban a Laura eran **el azul y el marrón**.*
4. *La dependiente de la tienda se vestía bastante b**ien**.*
5. *La dependiente que atendió a Laura usó **"tú"** con ella.*
6. *Laura decidió comprar **un traje sastre azul y un top marrón**.*
7. *La amiga de Laura **no compró nada**.*

¡A leer!

Skim through the following reading selection to get the gist of it. Then scan the selection to locate specific information you need to participate in the activity that follows.

SÍNTESIS

El guardarropa básico

El hombre consciente de la elegancia no tiene que invertir una suma excesiva de dinero en ropa. Sólo necesita buen gusto, escoger cuidadosamente las piezas básicas que compondrán su guardarropa y combinarlas estratégicamente para siempre lucir bien vestido. He aquí una guía.

- Cinco trajes: azul marino, gris, a cuadros, negro y caqui
- 15 camisas: cuatro blancas, dos azules, una rosa, cinco de otros colores, tres de mangas cortas, sólidas y con estampados
- Cinco pares de zapatos: uno negro y uno marrón para vestimenta formal, botas, mocasines y *oxfords*
- 16 corbatas variadas: a rayas, puntos y con estampados
- Cuatro camisas de manga larga: sudaderas, polos de cuello alto y *turtlenecks*
- Cuatro chaquetas o *blazers*: azul marino, negra, *tweed* y una de color brillante
- Ocho pantalones: uno claro y otro oscuro en algodón, uno gris en franela, uno negro en lana, uno caqui, uno a cuadros, otro a rayas, una sudadera
- Accesorios: un par de pijamas, un traje de baño, dos pantalones bermudas, dos pares de tirantes, cinco correas
- 12 pares de ropa interior: casi todos blancos y el resto *boxers*
- 18 pares de medias: ocho oscuras para vestir; el resto blancas de algodón, colores brillantes y con patrones o estampados
- Dos chaquetas livianas: una de mahón y la otra de algodón o nilón
- 25 *T-shirts*: cinco negras, siete blancas, ocho en colores variados y cinco con logos
- Dos pares de tenis: uno para hacer deportes y otro para vestimenta casual

Source: *Imagen*, mayo 1992, página 226.

¿Comprendió Ud.?

1. En un papel separado, describa dos guardarropas más básicos que el guardarropa de esta lectura: uno para damas y otro para caballeros. Use la información y las palabras de la lectura con lo que usted sabe de la lengua española.

2. Después, compare sus guardarropas con los dos guardarropas que describió otro(a) estudiante.

SÍNTESIS

¡A conversar!

¡Felicitaciones! ¡Usted acaba de ganar *(to win)* un viaje *(trip)* para dos personas a Puerto Rico! Piense en su viaje por un momento, y dígale a un(a) compañero(a) de clase sus planes, usando las siguientes preguntas como guía para sus ideas.

1. ¿Con quién quiere usted ir a Puerto Rico? ¿Por qué prefiere ir con él (ella)?
2. ¿Qué tiempo hace en Puerto Rico? Por eso, ¿qué ropa van a llevar?
3. ¿Qué otras cosas va(n) usted(es) a llevar?
4. ¿Adónde van de compras en Puerto Rico? ¿Qué ropa piensan comprar?
5. ¿Qué otras cosas van a comprar allí?

¡A escribir!

Según el sicólogo Max Luschen, nuestro color favorito revela mucho sobre nuestra personalidad. Primero, lea "Interpretaciones del test sobre el color de Luschen". Segundo, piense en la ropa y los colores que les gusta llevar a estas personas. Luego escriba unas oraciones sobre la personalidad y otra información interesante.

1. yo
2. mi papá / hermano
3. mi mamá / hermana
4. mi mejor amigo(a)

Ejemplo: yo
Me gusta llevar ropa de color rojo. Soy competitiva y entusiasta. Me gustan mucho los deportes, especialmente el béisbol y el básquetbol. Soy una estudiante excelente en mis clases.

1. This article was originally written for women. For that reason, several feminine forms appear in the article such as *la rodea* and *la rodean.*

2. Preguntas: ¿Cuál es su color favorito? ¿Cómo es su personalidad? Para usted, ¿es correcta la información en este artículo? ¿Por qué?

Interpretaciones del test sobre el color de Luschen

Amarillo. Indica disposición alegre y positiva. Sugiere habilidad para apartarse de los problemas, da vitalidad y contrarresta la depresión. Se asocia con urgencia.

Verde. Alejado de la tensión, sabe enfrentar el estrés. Está en armonía con lo que la rodea, tiene apariencia equilibrada, un poco egoísta.

Rojo. Competitivo, entusiasta, sensual.

Atajo

SÍNTESIS

Visit

http://poco.heinle.com

Azul. Leal, tranquilo, feliz con su posición; lleva buenas relaciones con quienes la rodean, busca calma o liberarse de una crisis.

Indigo/Violeta. Calmante, mayor cualidad sensitiva e intuitiva que los que prefieren aquél (indigo), un poco inmaduro, mentalidad ansiosa o una tendencia a permanecer en la sombra.

Negro/Café/Gris. Revela una posición extrema y la determinación al sacrificio, reprime emociones y retrasa discusiones, inquietos e inseguros.

Source: "Lo que su color favorito dice de usted", *Buenhogar*, Año 23, No. 5, 23 de febrero, 1988, páginas 16–17.

VOCABULARIO

Sustantivos

el almacén *department store*
el centro comercial *shopping mall*
el (la) dependiente *salesclerk*
el dinero *money*
la iglesia *church*
el pueblo *town*
la sinagoga *synagogue*
la talla *size (clothing)*
la tarjeta *card*
la tienda *store*

La ropa
(Clothing)

el abrigo *overcoat*
la blusa *blouse*
las botas *boots*
los calcetines *socks*
la camisa *shirt*
la camiseta *T-shirt*
el cinturón *belt*
la corbata *necktie*
la chaqueta *jacket*
la falda *skirt*
la gorra de béisbol *baseball cap*
los guantes *gloves*
las medias *stockings*
los pantalones *pants*

los pantalones cortos *shorts*
las sandalias *sandals*
el sombrero *hat*
el suéter *sweater*
el traje *suit*
el traje de baño *swimsuit*
el vestido *dress*
los zapatos *shoes*

Los accesorios
(Accessories)

los anteojos para el sol *sunglasses*
los aretes *earrings*
la bolsa *purse, bag*
el collar *necklace*
la mochila *backpack*
el paraguas *umbrella*

Los números

dos mil *two thousand*
doscientos(as) mil *two hundred
  thousand*
un millón *one million*
dos millones *two million*

Adjetivos

aburrido *boring*

Verbos

cambiar *to change*
contestar *to answer*
costar (o → ue) *to cost*
divertirse (e → ie, e → i)
  to have fun
esperar *to wait for*
llevar *to wear, to carry*
olvidar *to forget*
pagar *to pay for*
probarse (o → ue) *to try on*
quedarle (a uno) *to fit (someone)*
vender *to sell*

Los pronombres
indirectos

me *to/for me*
te *to/for you (informal)*
le *to/for you (formal), him, her*
nos *to/for us*
os *to/for you (informal)*
les *to/for you (formal), them (ellos/ellas)*

Expresiones idiomáticas

¿En qué puedo servirle? *What can
  I do for you?*
por eso *therefore, so*

9

¡Feliz Navidad!

▶ COMMUNICATIVE GOALS

You will be able to describe your city, give advice, and ask for street directions.

▶ LANGUAGE FUNCTIONS

Describing locations in a city
Asking for street directions
Expressing negative ideas
Giving advice to others
Making polite requests

▶ VOCABULARY THEMES

Places in a city
Street directions

▶ GRAMMATICAL STRUCTURES

Affirmative and negative expressions
Formal commands

▶ CULTURAL INFORMATION

How to get around in cities
Hispanic Christmas customs

http://poco.heinle.com

EN CONTEXTO

 Play Lab Tape

Ayer fue domingo, veinticuatro de diciembre. Eran las once y cuarto de la mañana y la temperatura en Nueva York estaba a catorce grados centígrados bajo cero. Gloria estaba dándole de comer a su bebé, y Julio vestía a su hijo porque muy pronto toda la familia iba a ir a la iglesia. De repente,° sonó el teléfono y Julio fue a contestarlo.

Suddenly

—Hello?(1)
—¡Hola, hijo! Habla tu mamá.
—Mamá, ¿cómo estás?
—Bien, bien. Acabo de llegar de San Juan.(2) Estoy aquí en el aeropuerto Kennedy.
—¡Mamá! ¿Estás aquí en Nueva York?
—Sí, hijo. Decidí venir a última hora.° Hace dos años que no te veo, y quiero conocer a mi nieta Susana María.

last minute

—¡Qué bueno, mamá! Voy al aeropuerto a...
—No, mi hijo. Puedo ir a tu apartamento en taxi porque aquí hay mucho tráfico y vives muy lejos° del aeropuerto.

far

—Pero mamá, el taxi va a costarte una fortuna.
—No te preocupes,° hijo. Tengo el dinero.

Don't worry

—Bueno. Entonces te esperamos aquí en casa, ¿eh?
—Sí, sí. Nos vemos pronto. Hasta luego, hijo.
—Hasta luego, mamá.

Bienvenida salió de la terminal del aeropuerto con su maleta,° encontró un taxi y se subió.° Luego ella le dio al taxista la dirección del apartamento de Julio.

suitcase
got in

—Ah, sí. Este apartamento está en Manhattan, señora.
—¿Cómo? ¿Habla usted español?
—Sí, señora. Soy de la República Dominicana.

Mientras° Bienvenida y el taxista iban a Manhattan, conversaban sobre el mal tiempo de Nueva York, el buen tiempo en sus islas y un poco sobre sus familias. Pero el taxista estaba tan cansado que casi se durmió dos veces.

While

De repente, ¡pum! El taxi chocó con° un autobús que venía de otra calle° y los dos vehículos se pararon° inmediatamente. El taxista estaba tan cansado que no vio el autobús. Afortunadamente, nadie se lastimó,° pero Bienvenida estaba nerviosa.

crashed into / street
stopped
got hurt

—¡Ay! ¿No vio usted ese autobús? ¿Por qué no vuelve a casa a dormir? ¡Está muy cansado de trabajar!

Dos horas más tarde, el taxi llegó finalmente al apartamento de los Sepúlveda, quienes esperaban a Bienvenida en la puerta. Ella salió del taxi y todos se saludaron con abrazos y besos y le dijeron:

—¡Feliz Navidad!°

Merry Christmas

Some of the verbs in this reading are in the imperfect tense. Although students have not yet studied that tense, they should be able to understand the reading based on their knowledge of the infinitive forms of the verbs, and from context. The imperfect tense is introduced and practiced in *Lección 10*.

Answers: *1. Sí 2. Sí 3. a 4. c 5. b 6. Sí 7. Sí 8. No*

Notas de texto

1. Julio is bilingual as is much of the Spanish-speaking population of the United States.
2. San Juan is the capital of Puerto Rico, located about four hours by jet from New York City.

¿Comprendió Ud.?

Responda apropiadamente como está indicado.

1. Hacía frío el día en que llegó Bienvenida.   Sí _____ No _____
2. El taxista hablaba español muy bien.   Sí _____ No _____
3. _____ causó el accidente entre el taxi y el autobús.
   a. El taxista   b. Bienvenida   c. Julio   d. Otra persona
4. Bienvenida llegó _____ al apartamento de su hijo.
   a. en autobús   b. rápidamente   c. en taxi   d. por la noche
5. Ella llegó a Nueva York en...
   a. verano   b. invierno   c. primavera d. otoño
6. Los Sepúlveda son una familia religiosa.   Sí _____ No _____
7. La madre de Julio no tiene miedo de nada.   Sí _____ No _____
8. Julio estaba triste cuando su mamá lo llamó.   Sí _____ No _____

VOCABULARIO ÚTIL

1. If you wish, tell students another word for *la cuadra* (city block) is *la manzana*.
2. Tell students to use *Perdón* to get someone's attention or if they step on someone's toe by mistake, and to use *Con permiso* when excusing themselves from a place and/or to get past someone.
3. Point out that *Pase usted* is used when speaking to **one** person; *Pasen ustedes* is used when speaking to more than one person.
4. Use this paragraph for a dictation.
5. Rewrite this paragraph to depict a different city scene. Then read it slowly as students listen and draw each place according to your directions.

Cómo pedir y comprender instrucciones

In this section, you will learn the names of some places in a city, and how to ask for and understand street directions.

Los lugares en la ciudad

La plaza está en el centro de la ciudad. Allí hay un parque que está **detrás de** (behind) la biblioteca. Hay un museo **entre** (between) el banco y la oficina de correos. **Enfrente del** (Across from the) parque está la iglesia con la terminal de autobuses a la izquierda. **A la derecha** (On the right) hay una gasolinera **al lado del** (next to the) mercado central. **Cerca de** (Near) la terminal está la estación de trenes, **delante del** (in front of the) mercado. El aeropuerto está **lejos de** (far from) la ciudad.

En la calle

—Perdón, ¿dónde está el banco?   *Excuse me, where is the bank?*
—Está todo derecho en la próxima   *It's straight ahead in the*
   cuadra.   *next block.*
—¿Cerca de la iglesia?   *Near the church?*
—Sí. Está en la esquina.   *Yes. It's on the corner.*
—¿Está abierto el banco ahora?   *Is the bank open now?*
—No. Lo siento, está cerrado. Hoy   *No. I'm sorry, it's closed.*
   es un día festivo.   *Today is a holiday.*
—Muchas gracias. Con permiso.   *Thanks a lot. Excuse me.*
—Pase usted. Adiós.   *After you. Good-bye.*

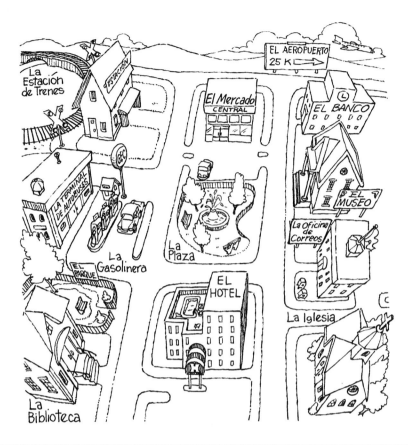

1. If possible, show photographs of these buildings and places located in Spanish-speaking countries.
2. Preguntas: a. ¿Dónde está la oficina de correos más cercana de aquí? b. ¿Como se llama una iglesia católica aquí? ¿Dónde está? c. ¿Dónde hay un museo interesante en nuestra ciudad? ¿Por qué es interesante? d. ¿Cómo se llama su banco? ¿Dónde está? e. ¿A qué gasolinera va usted frecuentemente? ¿Dónde está? f. ¿Cuál es su supermercado favorito? ¿En qué calle está? ¿Está lejos o cerca de aquí?

TRANSPARENCY No. 18: Civic Institutions

NOTAS CULTURALES

Cómo viajar° en las ciudades

to travel

En autobús: Los autobuses ofrecen el transporte más económico en las ciudades latinoamericanas y españolas. Los hay de todo tipo: hay autobuses modernos con asientos cómodos,° ventanillas° grandes y aire acondicionado, y hay otros que son viejos e incómodos, pero baratos.°

comfortable seats / windows
inexpensive

En metro: Algunas ciudades tienen sistemas modernos de metro que son eficientes y económicos. Estos sistemas de transporte público existen en México, D.F., Caracas, Buenos Aires, Santiago, Madrid, Barcelona y Sevilla.

En taxi: En la mayoría de las ciudades de Latinoamérica y de España, es posible encontrar un taxi en la calle o pedir uno por teléfono. En algunos países hay taxis especiales llamados "colectivos", que son microbuses que llevan entre seis y diez pasajeros. Los colectivos tienen una ruta fija,° y los pasajeros pagan según la distancia que viajan. Antes de subir a un taxi, es mejor preguntar cúanto cobra° para llegar a cierto destino. Si el/la taxista usa un contador,° esté usted seguro(a) que lo ponga bien. Muchas veces es necesario pagar al/a la taxista un poco más de noche, o si usted pide un taxi por teléfono o si lleva mucho equipaje.° A veces, los taxistas cobran más cuando salen de la estación de trenes o del aeropuerto.

fixed route
costs
meter

luggage

Preguntas. Pregúntele a otro(a) estudiante.

1. ¿Qué medio de transporte usas para venir a la universidad o a la escuela?
2. ¿Conoces algún metro en los Estados Unidos? (¿Sí? ¿Cuál? ¿Es limpio y ordenado?)
3. ¿Cómo viajas en esta ciudad (este pueblo)?

Practiquemos

Ex. A. Answers:
1. ...donde almorzó con dos amigas cubanas.
2. ...donde cambió unos cheques personales.
3. ...donde vio una exposición naval.
4. ...donde compró frutas y vegetales.
5. ...donde hubo una misa el domingo.

A. ¿Adónde fue Bienvenida? La semana pasada Bienvenida fue a diferentes lugares en San Juan, Puerto Rico donde vive. Dígale a otro(a) estudiante adónde fue ella y qué hizo en ese lugar.

Ejemplo: *Bienvenida fue al Museo Marítimo donde vio una exposición naval.*

Lugar	Actividad
1. Café Solymar	comprar frutas y vegetales
2. Banco de Ponce	haber una misa el domingo
3. Museo Marítimo	cambiar unos cheques personales
4. Mercado "León"	almorzar con dos amigas cubanas
5. Iglesia Santa Ana	ver una exposición naval

B. ¿Y usted? Hable con un(a) compañero(a) de clase.

1. Primero, dígale a su compañero(a) adónde fue usted la semana pasada, y qué hizo usted allí.

Ejemplos: *El lunes pasado fui a la biblioteca donde estudié inglés.*
El martes por la tarde fui al mercado y compré vegetales.

Lugares posibles:

el museo	la escuela	el mercado
el banco	la biblioteca	la gasolinera
el parque	la universidad	el restaurante
la iglesia	la casa de _____	el supermercado
la oficina de correos	la clase de _____	el centro comercial

2. Ahora dígale a su compañero(a) adónde va usted esta semana, en qué día va allí y qué va a hacer en ese lugar.

Ejemplo: *El miércoles voy a la casa de una amiga. Vamos a ver una película en video allí.*

Ex. C.
1. Have students ask you these questions, using formal forms.
2. This exercise could be assigned as written homework.

C. Entrevista. Pregúntele a otro(a) estudiante.

1. ¿Cómo se llama el supermercado en donde compras más frecuentemente? ¿Está cerca o lejos de donde vives? ¿Qué compraste allí recientemente? ¿Cómo son los precios de ese supermercado?

2. ¿Vives cerca o lejos de un banco? ¿Cómo se llama el banco? ¿Cuándo está abierto durante la semana? ¿Está abierto o cerrado el banco los fines de semana?

3. ¿Dónde está la oficina de correos más cercana de tu casa (apartamento / residencia)? ¿Con qué frecuencia vas allí? Normalmente, ¿qué cosas compras en la oficina de correos?

4. ¿Hay algún museo en tu ciudad? (¿Sí? Describe uno de los museos; por ejemplo: ¿Cómo se llama? ¿Dónde está exactamente? ¿Qué cosas interesantes hay en el museo?)

D. En el Viejo San Juan. Hable con otro(a) estudiante. Una persona es un(a) turista en San Juan, Puerto Rico, y la otra persona vive allí. Comiencen su conversación (ustedes están hablando donde hay una X) según el plano *(map).*

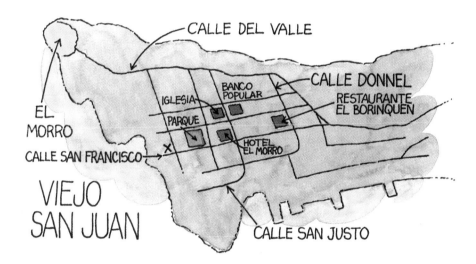

Turista

1. Perdón, (señor / señorita / señora). ¿Hay un banco por aquí?
3. Lo siento. No comprendí bien.
5. ¿Está cerca o lejos de aquí?
7. ¿Cómo se llama el banco?
9. ¿Está abierto o cerrado ahora?
11. _____ .

13. Bueno, muchas gracias, (señor / señorita / señora).

Residente

2. Sí, hay uno que está en _____ .
4. Hay un banco que está en _____ .
6. _____, (señor / señorita / señora).
8. _____ .
10. Pues... ¿qué hora es?
12. Creo que el banco está _____ en este momento.
14. _____ . Que le vaya bien.

E. Una ciudad que conozco. En un párrafo describa el centro de una ciudad que usted conoce personalmente, usando las palabras y expresiones que usted aprendió en esta lección.

Ex.E.
1. Have students exchange their written descriptions with a classmate, then ask them to find and correct the errors in them.
2. Use this example paragraph for a dictation.

GRAMÁTICA FUNCIONAL

Making affirmative and negative statements

—Recibimos algunas tarjetas de Navidad, hijo.
—¿Hay una para mí, mamá?
—Pues, lo siento. No recibiste ninguna hoy.
—Ay, nadie me escribe, mamá. Nadie me quiere.
—Pues no, Juan Carlos. Tú no le escribes a nadie tampoco.

Exercise: Say one word in each set; ask students to say the opposite of that word.

Affirmative and negative expressions

algo	*something, anything*	**nada**	*nothing, not anything*
alguien	*somebody, anybody*	**nadie**	*nobody, no one*
alguno(a/os/as)	*some, any*	**ninguno(a)**	*none, not any*
algún	*some, any*	**ningún**	*none, not any*
siempre	*always*	**nunca**	*never*
también	*also, too*	**tampoco**	*neither, not either*
o... o	*either... or*	**ni... ni**	*neither... nor*

How to use these expressions

1. In a negative Spanish sentence, at least one negative word comes before the verb. Sometimes there are several negative words in one sentence.

   —¿Tienes algo en la mano?   *Do you have something in your hand?*
   —**No, no** tengo **nada,** mamá.   *No, I don't have anything, Mom.*

   —¿Hay alguien a la puerta?   *Is there someone at the door?*
   —**No, no** hay **nadie,** Gloria.   *No, there's no one, Gloria.*

2. Omit the word *no* if a negative word precedes the verb.

   no + verb + negative word   Negative word + verb

   No viene **nadie** conmigo.   →   **Nadie** viene conmigo.
   No voy **nunca** al centro.   →   **Nunca** voy al centro.

3. The words *alguno, alguna, algunos, algunas* are adjectives; use *algún* before a masculine singular noun.

   —¿Hay **algún** postre, mamá?   *Is there any dessert, Mom?*
   —No, pero tengo **algunos**   *No, but I have some chocolates.*
   chocolates.

4. The plural forms *ningunos* and *ningunas* are not used; instead, use the singular form; use *ningún* before a masculine singular noun.

   —¿Cúantos dólares tienes?   *How many dollars do you have?*
   —No tengo **ningún** dinero.   *I don't have any money.*

—¿A qué hora viene mi abuela? *What time is my grandma coming?*
—No tengo **ninguna** idea, hijo. *I have no idea, son.*

—¿Cuántas amigas tiene Ana? *How many friends does Ana have?*
—Ella no tiene **ninguna.** *She doesn't have any.*

5. Express **neither** with a subject pronoun (*yo, tú, usted, él, ella, nosotros/as, ustedes*) + *tampoco.*

—Nunca voy al centro. *I never go downtown.*
—**Yo tampoco.** *Me neither.*

Tell students that *Yo también* means "Me too."

6. Place *ni* before a noun or a verb to express the idea of **neither** or **nor.**

—¿Quieres leche o jugo, hijo? *Do you want milk or juice, son?*
—No quiero **ni** leche **ni** jugo. *I want neither milk nor juice.*

Practiquemos

A. Entre amigos. Complete la siguiente conversación, usando **también, tampoco, siempre** y **nunca.**

—¿ _____ das una fiesta en casa durante la Navidad?
—No _____ , pero, a veces, sí. ¿Y tú?
—Pues, yo _____ doy fiestas porque es mucho trabajo. Casi _____ tengo tiempo porque estoy tan ocupado en mi oficina.
—Yo _____ tengo mucho trabajo, pero mi familia es muy importante para mí. En la Navidad _____ estamos juntos. ¿Quieres celebrarlo con nosotros este año?
—Pues, gracias, pero _____ voy a la iglesia y...
—Bueno, no importa. Nosotros _____ vamos a la iglesia.

Ex. A. Answers: *Siempre, siempre, nunca, nunca, también, siempre, nunca, tampoco*

B. Entre esposos. Complete las siguientes dos conversaciones, usando **algo, nada, alguien, nadie, o... o,** y **ni... ni.**

—Julio, voy al supermercado porque no hay casi _____ en el refrigerador. ¿Quieres comer _____ especial esta noche?
—No, gracias, Gloria. No quiero comer _____ porque comí mucho en el almuerzo.
—Pero, ¿qué te pasa, Julio?
—_____ , _____ . Es que no tengo hambre, Gloria.
—Bueno. Hasta luego.

Más tarde...
—¡Hola, Julio! Conocí a _____ en el supermercado que te conoce.
—Ah, ¿sí? Debe ser _____ un amigo _____ un compañero de trabajo. ¿Cuál es?
—Bueno, no es _____ un amigo _____ un compañero tuyo. Se llama Lucía Reynosa.
—¿Cómo? ¿Lucía Reynosa? No conozco a _____ con ese nombre.
—¿No? Pues, ella me dijo que fue tu novia.
—¿Mi novia? Gloria, _____ estás inventando _____ estás jugando conmigo.
—¿No recuerdas a Lucía? Era tu novia cuando tenía catorce años.
—Ah sí, ahora recuerdo, era muy amable conmigo y con mi mamá.

Ex. B. Answers:
Conversation 1: *nada, algo, nada, Nada, nada*
Conversation 2: *alguien, o, o, ni, ni, nadie, o, o,*

C. En la calle. Complete la siguiente conversación, usando **algún, alguna, algunos, algunas, ningún, ninguna, ninguno.**

—Perdón, estoy buscando la piscina.

—¿Cómo? No hay _____ por aquí, señor.

—_____ amigos me dijeron que hay una piscina pública cerca de un mercado.

—No. No hay _____ mercado por aquí. Hay una piscina, pero está lejos.

—¿Está abierta o cerrada?

—No tengo idea, señor.

—¿Hay un teléfono aquí en la tienda?

—Aquí no hay _____ . _____ día quiero tener un teléfono, pero ahora no tengo dinero.

—Muchas gracias.

—De nada.

D. De mal humor. Juan Carlos está de mal humor hoy y, por eso, siempre les contesta negativamente a sus amigos. ¿Qué les dice?

Ejemplo: AMALIA: —¿Quieres jugar conmigo? (nadie)
            MARTÍN: —*No quiero jugar con nadie.*

Amigos Juan Carlos

1. BENITO: ¿Quieres jugar conmigo?   (nunca)
2. SUSANA: ¿No quieres jugar conmigo?   (nadie)
3. SAMUEL: ¿Te gusta patinar o esquiar?   (ni... ni)
4. ANÍBAL: ¿Haces ejercicio?   (ningún)
5. LORENA: ¿Qué vas a hacer hoy?   (nada)
6. MAGÁLY: ¿Quieres nadar en mi piscina?   (ninguna)
7. NÁTALI: ¿Prefieres ir a mi casa?   (Tampoco)

E. Algunos problemas de mi ciudad. Escriba un párrafo sobre su ciudad, usando el siguiente párrafo como modelo.

En mi ciudad _____ (algunas veces / siempre) hay mucho tráfico por la _____ (mañana / tarde / noche). También hay algunos accidentes especialmente cuando _____ (nieva / llueve).

Tenemos otros problemas en mi ciudad; por ejemplo, cuando alguien... Creo que es posible hacer algo para resolver ese problema. Por ejemplo,...

Charlemos

F. Dos conversaciones. Practique el primer diálogo con otro(a) estudiante. Luego inventen ustedes otra conversación.

A: —¿Quieres visitar a Puerto Rico algún día?
B: —Sí, pero no tengo ni el tiempo ni el dinero ahora.
B: —¿Cuándo quieres ir allí?
A: —En diciembre porque hace buen tiempo.

G. ¿Es verdad o no? Converse con un(a) compañero(a) de clase. Una persona va a leer las siguientes oraciones. La otra persona cierra *(closes)* el libro y responde apropiadamente a cada situación.

Ejemplo: (Nada / Nunca) hace frío en la ciudad de Nueva York.
A: *Nunca hace frío en la ciudad de Nueva York.*
B: *No tienes razón. En Nueva York hace frío en el invierno.*

1. Julio y Gloria (nadie/nunca) desayunan juntos por la mañana.
2. Creo que ellos no tienen (ningún/ninguno) niño.
3. Julio tiene un trabajo, pero Gloria no tiene (ninguno/tampoco).
4. En Puerto Rico (algún/nunca) hace frío en el invierno.
5. (Nadie/Algunos) residentes de Nueva York son puertorriqueños.
6. Julio no trabaja en una primaria. Gloria (tampoco/también).
7. La familia Sepúlveda no es (o/ni) rica (o/ni) pobre.

H. Mis preferencias. Hable con otro(a) estudiante, usando las oraciones incompletas como guías.

Ejemplo: Siempre me gusta jugar al *tenis* con mi *novio*.

En el verano me gusta jugar al _____ con algunos(as) _____ . También me gusta _____ , pero casi nunca juego al _____ porque... Tampoco...

En el invierno me gusta _____ en _____ donde siempre hace _____ . En el invierno, normalmente no juego al _____ ni _____ porque... Algún día quiero aprender a _____ con alguien muy _____ .

NOTAS CULTURALES

La Navidad

La Navidad es una de las fiestas religiosas celebradas con más alegría en el mundo hispano. En España, la Navidad comienza el 8 de diciembre con la fiesta de la Virgen María, la Inmaculada Concepción.° Se celebra con una danza de seis niños enfrente de la Catedral Gótica en Sevilla.

El 24 de diciembre, o Nochebuena,° se celebra en familia junto al nacimiento° que hay en todas las casas. Un dulce tradicional para la Navidad es el turrón,° un tipo de caramelo de almendras. Los niños en España como en Puerto Rico reciben regalos en la fiesta de Epifanía° o la fiesta de los Reyes Magos,° el 6 de enero.

En México, la celebración de la Navidad comienza el 16 de diciembre con las posadas,° que cuentan la historia de María y José en busca de un lugar donde dormir en Belén.° La familia y los amigos visitan a otros amigos hasta que una familia abre la puerta e invita a pasar a todos a la casa donde hay puesto un nacimiento y donde se sirve de comer a los invitados, mientras que los niños rompen° la piñata.

En Venezuela, la celebración comienza el 16 de diciembre con misas muy temprano, a las cuatro de la mañana. Estas misas se llaman "Misa de Aguinaldo".° En Caracas, se acostumbra a patinar° después de la misa y muchas calles se cierran hasta las ocho de la mañana. Después de la misa, las personas comen arepas, y toman café y chocolate caliente.

Immaculate Conception

Christmas Eve / nativity scene
a kind of almond candy

Epiphany / Wise Men (Kings)

inns
Bethlehem

break

Early Morning Mass
roller skate

Actividad

1. Describa las fotos en esta página. ¿Qué están celebrando?
2. ¿Cómo se celebra la Nochebuena en España?
3. ¿Qué son las posadas? ¿Cuándo se rompen las piñatas?
4. ¿Cómo se celebra la Navidad en Venezuela?

GRAMÁTICA FUNCIONAL

Giving advice and making requests

—Perdón, ¿dónde está la plaza?
—Siga usted todo derecho, señor.
—¿Es posible tomar un autobús?
—Pues, sí. Tome el número 25.

Formal commands

When we give advice to others or ask them to do something, we often use commands such as *Take bus No. 25* and *Give me your address.* Spanish speakers use formal commands when they address people as **usted** or **ustedes**.

How to form formal commands

1. For most Spanish verbs, drop the *-o* ending from the present tense *yo* form and add the following endings to the verb stem: *-e/-en* for *-ar* verbs; *-a/-an* for *-er* and *-ir* verbs.

	Infinitive	yo form	usted	ustedes
-ar verbs	hablar	hablo	habl**e**	habl**en**
-er verbs	volver	vuelvo	vuelv**a**	vuelv**an**
-ir verbs	venir	vengo	veng**a**	veng**an**

Vengan a visitarme pronto. *Come to visit me soon.*
No **olvide** mi dirección. *Don't forget my address.*

2. Verbs ending in *-car*, *-gar*, and *-zar* have a spelling change: *c* changes to *qu*, *g* changes to *gu*, and *z* changes to *c*.

Infinitive	usted	ustedes
sacar	sa**que**	sa**quen**
llegar	lle**gue**	lle**guen**
comenzar	comien**ce**	comien**cen**

Saque una foto de nosotros. *Take a picture of us.*
Lleguen a tiempo, por favor. *Arrive on time, please.*
Comience a preparar la cena. *Start preparing supper.*

> **¡CUIDADO!** Stem-changing verbs retain their vowel change in formal commands, as in the example above (*comenzar: e → **ie** = com**ie**nce*)

Explain that the purpose of this spelling change is to retain the sound of *c, g,* and *z* in the infinitive form of these verbs.

Point out that the preposition **a** follows **comenzar** when this verb is used before an infinitive, as illustrated in this example.

3. Several irregular verbs vary from the pattern above.

Infinitive	usted	ustedes
dar	**dé**	**den**
estar	**esté**	**estén**
ir	**vaya**	**vayan**
saber	**sepa**	**sepan**
ser	**sea**	**sean**

Sean buenos estudiantes. *Be good students.*
Déme su número de teléfono. *Give me your phone number.*

4. In affirmative commands, attach reflexive and object pronouns to the end of the command, thus forming one word. If the command has three or more syllables, write an accent mark over the stressed vowel. In negative commands, place the pronouns separately in front of the verb.

Póngase el abrigo. *Put on your overcoat.*
No **se lo ponga.** *Don't put it on.*

Cómprelo ahora. *Buy it now.*
No lo compre mañana. *Don't buy it tomorrow.*

How to make polite requests

1. You can soften commands to make them sound more like requests than demands, by using *usted* or *ustedes* after the command form.

   Pasen ustedes por aquí.   *Come this way.*
   No hable usted tan rápido. *Don't speak so fast.*

2. When you want people to do something, but you wish to say so tactfully, ask a question or make a simple statement with reference to your wish rather than using a direct command. For example, suppose you are a dinner guest at a friend's house. The dining room is uncomfortably hot, and you want a window opened or the air conditioner turned on. You might say: *Hace un poco de calor, ¿no?*

Practiquemos

A. ¡Qué ricas! Bienvenida va a preparar un postre de una receta que ella leyó en un periódico. Complete la receta, usando mandatos formales de estos verbos en el siguiente orden: **cortar** *(to cut)*, **sacar** *(to take out)*, **remojar** *(to soak)*, **escurrir** *(to drain)*, **poner** *(to put in)*, **adornar** *(to adorn)*.

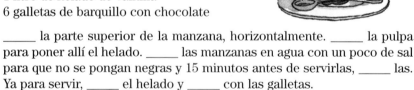

Manzanas rellenas de helado

6 manzanas rojas
1 litro de helado de vainilla
6 galletas de barquillo con chocolate

_____ la parte superior de la manzana, horizontalmente. _____ la pulpa para poner allí el helado. _____ las manzanas en agua con un poco de sal para que no se pongan negras y 15 minutos antes de servirlas, _____ las. Ya para servir, _____ el helado y _____ con las galletas.

B. Escuche a su jefe. Gloria está en el supermercado de su amigo Héctor Rodríguez. En este momento el Sr. Rodríguez está hablando con un nuevo empleado de diecisiete años. ¿Qué le dice al joven?

Ejemplo: llegar a tiempo todos los días
              Llegue a tiempo todos los días.

1. comenzar a trabajar a las nueve
2. tener paciencia con los clientes

Source: *Hogar Práctico*, No. 27, junio de 1992, página 84.

3. servirles a los clientes rápidamente
4. nunca comer mientras está trabajando
5. llamarme si no puede venir a trabajar
6. ser simpático con todos en el supermercado
7. lavarse las manos antes de cortar la carne

C. Cómo vivir bien.
Bienvenida está mirando un programa de televisión. En este programa, Marisa, una presentadora, entrevista a una sicóloga. Complete la entrevista con mandatos afirmativos y negativos de los verbos entre paréntesis.

Ex. C. Answers: *coma, ponga, sirva(les), beba, tome, Duerma, se acueste, se levante, escuche, piense, Haga, salga, Vaya, corra, invite(los), diviértase, se preocupe*

Ex. C. Follow-up: Have small groups of students recommend to their classmates other ways to live well; they should use plural formal commands to give this advice.

MARISA: Doctora, ¿qué consejos tiene usted para nuestro público sobre cómo vivir bien y por muchos años?

DOCTORA: Primero, (tomar) *tome* un buen desayuno todos los días, pero no (comer) _____ mucha comida muy dulce como los pasteles. Segundo, (poner) _____ en la mesa fruta fresca especialmente para los niños, y (servir) _____ les yogur porque es nutritivo.

MARISA: Mmm. ¡A mí me gusta el yogur! Y los refrescos de dieta, ¿está bien tomarlos, doctora?

DOCTORA: Pues, en moderación, sí, Marisa. Pero no los (beber) _____ con frecuencia porque pueden contener mucha cafeína. Por esta razón tampoco (tomar) _____ mucho café.

MARISA: Muy buenos consejos, doctora. ¿Cuántas horas cree usted que debemos dormir cada día, perdón... cada noche?

DOCTORA: Depende de la persona. (Dormir) _____ lo necesario y nada más. No (acostarse) _____ muy tarde ni (levantarse) _____ muy tarde por la mañana. Si duerme mal, (escuchar) _____ música clásica antes de acostarse y (pensar) _____ en algo tranquilo.

MARISA: Claro que sí. Doctora, es importante tener una vida social, ¿verdad?

DOCTORA: Sí, sí. (Hacer) _____ muchos amigos y (salir) _____ tan frecuentemente como pueda. (Ir) _____ con ellos al cine, (correr) _____ con ellos por algún parque o (invitar) _____ los a casa para comer. En un sola palabra: (divertirse) _____ con sus amigos, y no (preocuparse) _____ por nada.

MARISA: Doctora, muchas gracias por sus consejos tan valiosos.

DOCTORA: De nada, Marisa.

D. Entre amigos.
Julio está hablando por teléfono con Jorge, un amigo frugal que quiere visitarlo con su esposa. Julio está dándoles direcciones para llegar en autobús a su apartamento. Complete la siguiente conversación con formas correctas de los verbos entre paréntesis.

Ex. D.
Answers: *caminen, doblen, vayan, vayan, esperen, Tómen(lo), Bájense, Pregúnten(le), Digan(le), bájense, cambien, Súbanse, tómen(lo), sigan, salgan*

—Primero, (salir) *salgan* ustedes de su hotel. Luego (caminar) _____ dos cuadras a la derecha hasta la Calle Fonseca. Allí (doblar) _____ a la izquierda y (ir) _____ una cuadra más hasta la Calle Fayette.

—Hasta la Calle Fayette, ¿dices, Julio?

—Sí, Jorge. Luego (ir) _____ ustedes al otro lado de esa calle y (esperar) _____ en el autobús número 32.

—¿El autobús 32, Julio?

—Correcto, amigo. (Tomar) _____ lo hasta la Avenida Carlson. (Bajarse) _____ allí en esa avenida.

—¿Cómo sabemos dónde está la Avenida Carlson? No somos de aquí, Julio.

—Bueno, (preguntar) _____ le ustedes al chofer del autobús. (Decir) _____ le que quieren bajarse en la Avenida Carlson. Pues, (bajarse) _____ allí y (cambiar) _____ a otro autobús... el número 19. (Subirse) _____ a ese autobús y (tomar) _____ lo hasta la Calle Perry.

—¿Está lejos esa calle?

—No, Jorge. Está a como siete cuadras más o menos. Entonces (seguir) _____ ustedes en bus todo derecho hasta la Calle Perry. Luego (salir) _____ del autobús y en esa esquina les espero. ¿Qué te parece?

—Pues, es un poco complicado. Pero nos vemos pronto, ¿eh, Julio?

—Claro que sí. Hasta luego, Jorge.

Ex. E. Have students form small groups in which they read and discuss their responses to the letter.

E. Querida Amanda... Imagínese que usted escribe una columna sentimental para un periódico español. Primero, lea la siguiente carta que usted acaba de recibir. Luego contéstela en forma de carta, usando algunos mandatos afirmativos y negativos.

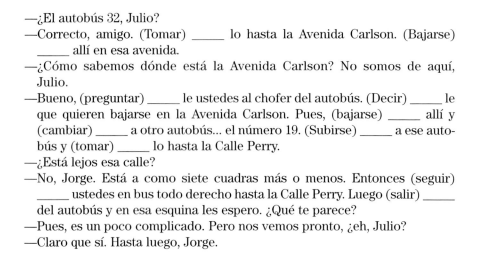

Querida Amanda,

Tengo muchos problemas en mi vida. Primero, el sábado pasado mi novia me dijo que ya no me quería y que ahora sale con mi mejor amigo. Segundo, el lunes murió mi abuelito a los 93 años de edad. Él vivió con mi familia por más de quince años y yo lo quería mucho. Finalmente, hoy en la tienda de ropa donde trabajo como dependiente, mi jefe me despidió porque dijo que yo no me concentraba bien cuando atendía a los clientes. Le expliqué lo de mi ex-novia y lo de la muerte de mi abuelito, pero mi jefe no tuvo ninguna compasión. En este momento estoy muy triste. Tengo veinticinco años. ¿Qué debo hacer?

Tomás G.

Ejemplo:

> *Querido Tomás G.,*
>
> *Muchas gracias por su carta. Comprendo muy bien su situación. Primero, hable con su jefe... También no le diga nada a su amigo porque...*

Charlemos

F. Turista en Puerto Rico. Converse con otro(a) estudiante, usando mandatos cuando sea posible.

Ex. F. Follow-up activity: Have students write this conversation for a homework assignment.

Turista

1. Perdón. ¿Hay un supermercado por aquí?
3. ¿Es posible ir en autobús?

5. ¿Dónde debo bajarme?
7. Luego, ¿adónde voy?
9. ¿Cómo? No comprendí. ¿Adónde?
11. [Exprese su gratitud.]

Residente

2. Sí. Para ir allí...
   [responda apropiadamente].
4. Sí, cómo no, señor (señorita / señora)... [responda].
6. _____.
8. Pues, _____ .
10. _____ .
12. _____ .

G. ¡Bienvenidos! Imagínese que usted trabaja como guía estudiantil en su universidad. Usted es responsable de acompañar a un grupo de profesores españoles (dos o tres de sus compañeros de clase), quienes le hacen preguntas sobre varios lugares que quieren visitar. Conteste según el plano.

Ex. G.
1. Before students do this activity, review the prepositions of place that were introduced in *Lección 9* on page 122 *[Vocabulario útil]*.
2. Follow-up activity: Have students form small groups in which one person plays the role of the tour guide and other persons ask directions to walk to various places at school.

Ejemplo: Profesor Martínez: Busco una librería. ¿Hay una por aquí?
              Ud. puede decirle: *Cómo no, profesor. Está cerca de Sever Hall. Camine usted... Luego vaya...*

1. Señor Lozano:
   —Perdón, ¿dónde está la cafetería de la universidad?
2. Señorita Guzmán y Señora Ortiz:
   —Estamos buscando la biblioteca central.
3. Profesor Corral:
   —Perdón, ¿dónde dijo usted que puedo comprar una camiseta de la universidad?
4. Profesores García y Gutiérrez:
   —Perdón, ¿hay un centro de computación por aquí?
5. Doctora Letrán:
   —¿Me puede decir dónde están los baños, por favor?

PARA LEER MEJOR

Analyzing Your Reading Strategies

In this section you will analyze what reading strategies are most helpful to you.

Activities

A. Read the lyrics to the song below, then complete the following sentences.

1. This song is...
   a. sad   b. cheerful   c. violent   d. humorous
2. I think the title of this song in English is " _____ ."
   I came to that conclusion because...

CASCABEL

Andando por la nieve, en un lindo trineo,

con la bella Susanita, salimos de paseo.

Brillaba la alegría, en nuestros corazones

en aquella tarde fría tan llena de ilusiones.

Cascabel, cascabel, música de amor,

dulces horas, gratas horas,

Juventud en flor.

Cascabel, cascabel, tan sentimental,

no dejes, cascabel, de repiquetear.

B. Read the lyrics again, then respond to the following items.

1. List the words and phrases in the song that convey the feeling of winter.
2. List the words and phrases in the song that connote **happiness.**

C. Read the lyrics once again and guess the meaning of the following words.

1. **trineo**   *barn / sleigh / path / tree*
2. **paseo**   *ride / home / together / out*
3. **brillaba**   *was glowing / brilliant / dancing*
4. **cascabel**   *candy / trumpet / welcome / bell*
5. **gratas**   *free / thankful / pleasant / many*
6. **repiquetear**   *to jingle / to sing / to repeat*

D. Check the strategies that helped you **most** in answering the statements above.

_____ word families	_____ clustering words
_____ my skimming skills	_____ guessing from context
_____ my scanning skills	_____ my knowledge of Spanish
_____ using a dictionary	_____ my knowledge of the song
_____ recognizing cognates	_____ visual presentation of text

PARA ESCRIBIR MEJOR

Giving Directions to a Place

The most important element of explaining to someone how to get from one place to another is accuracy. If you explain your directions clearly and concisely, people will be able to follow them easily.

Here are six basic requirements for giving directions to a place:

1. Choose the easiest route.
2. Be very clear in your directions.
3. Give the directions in chronological order.
4. Use linking expressions such as: *Primero... Luego... Después de eso... Entonces... Usted debe... Después... Finalmente...*
5. Identify clearly visible landmarks such as:

la calle	*street*	**el letrero**	*sign*
la colina	*hill*	**el bulevar**	*boulevard*
el camino	*road*	**el edificio**	*building*
el puente	*bridge*	**el semáforo**	*traffic light*
la avenida	*avenue*	**el cruce de caminos**	*intersection*

6. Include a sketch of the route such as the example on page 235.

Atajo

Functions:
Asking for and giving
directions; linking ideas;
expressing distance;
expressing location

Vocabulary:
City; directions & distance;
means of transportation;
metric systems &
measurements

Grammar:
Verbs: imperative *usted(es)*,
ser & estar, tener & haber;
Negation *no, nadie, nada*;
Interrogative adverbs
¿dónde?, ¿adónde?

¿A qué nivel está Ud.?

Adivina, adivinanza: ¿En
qué ciudad se celebra la
Navidad con piñatas:
México, Madrid o Caracas?
Review the chapter and then
monitor your progress by
completing the *Autoprueba*
at the end of *Lección 9* in the
Workbook/Lab Manual.

Example:

Para llegar a mi casa desde el aeropuerto, siga estas direcciones. Primero, siga la calle del aeropuerto hasta la salida. Allí está un letrero que dice "STOP". Luego doble a la derecha y siga por el Bulevar Man O' War dos kilómetros hasta el primer semáforo donde hay un cruce de caminos. Entonces, doble a la izquierda y siga por el Camino Parkers Mill dos kilómetros (pasando debajo de un puente) hasta la Calle Lane Allen. En esa calle, doble a la derecha y siga otros dos kilómetros (pasando un semáforo) hasta el segundo semáforo. Después, doble a la izquierda en el Camino Beacon Hill y siga derecho medio kilómetro hasta el Camino Normandy. Doble a la izquierda y vaya a la cuarta casa a la derecha. Allí vivo yo, y ¡allí tiene su casa!

Activity

1. Write a composition in which you explain to a Spanish-speaking visitor how to get by car, bus, or subway from your town's airport or bus station to where you live. Before you begin, reread the six basic requirements and refer to the example paragraph above.

2. Edit your composition carefully. Use the checklist below to guide you.

   _____ easiest route   _____ chronological order
   _____ main landmarks   _____ correct punctuation
   _____ clear directions   _____ correct grammar
   _____ linking expressions   _____ correct spelling

3. Exchange your composition and sketch (if any) with a classmate. Correct each other's paragraph, then discuss your corrections together.

SÍNTESIS

¡A ver!

Miguel is asking directions to Paseo Linares near Madrid. First, study the phrases and sentences with their meaning in the *Vocabulario esencial*. Second, read the sentences in the two activities that follow. Third, watch the videotape, then complete both activities according to the directions.

Vocabulario esencial

Cójete un taxi.	*Take a taxi.*
Te bajas y coges...	*You get off and take . . .*
Te lleva hasta...	*It will take you to . . .*
dar tantas vueltas	*to go back and forth a lot*

A. Complete las siguientes oraciones apropiadamente.

1. En este momento Miguel está en...
   a. una estación de metro.
   b. una terminal de autobuses.
   c. una universidad madrileña.

2. El señor le dijo a Miguel que es posible ir a Paseo Linares en...
   a. taxi o metro.
   b. metro o autobús.
   c. taxi, metro o autobús.

3. El señor prefiere ir a Paseo Linares en...
   a. taxi.
   b. metro.
   c. autobús.

4. Miguel prefiere ir al Paseo Linares en...
   a. taxi.
   b. metro.
   c. autobús.

Answers:
A. 1. a 2. c 3. a 4. c
B. 1. *Sí* 2. *No* 3. *Sí* 4. *No* 5. *Sí*

SÍNTESIS

Situation No. 2: Tell students that sometimes taxi drivers in Latin America and Spain include a surcharge if it is raining, or if their customer has a great deal of luggage.

B.   Conteste **sí** o **no,** según lo que usted vio en el video.

1. El señor usa "tú" con Miguel.   sí _____ no _____
2. Miguel usa "tú" con el señor.   sí _____ no _____
3. Paseo Linares está un poco lejos.   sí _____ no _____
4. Miguel necesita tomar el autobús 40.   sí _____ no _____
5. Es posible comprar el boleto en bus.   sí _____ no _____

¡A leer!

little boat   **Mi botecito°**

toy el único juguete° que tuve	todavía bebo tu sonido
fue un barquito	(de flor sedienta)
usado	de restricciones
first-class cabin de metal	en el camarote de primera°
traveled / poop deck viajó° conmigo	mal pintado en su popa° de metal.
silencioso	
en su música	juguete único
rust (de flor sedienta	te marchitaste en un olvido de óxido°
de vino encantado	estoy seguro
de llovizna de plata)	quizás te vendiste por un beso
el único juguete que tuve	o eres hoy juguete de otro niño
fue un barquito	que no toca el sueño
chiquito y tan bonito	¡Ay mi botecito!

_____

Source: "En el ala del mosquito", por Emilio Mozo. *El Editor Interameriano*, Buenos Aires, 1988, página 23.

SÍNTESIS

¿Comprendió Ud.?

A. Primero, lea rápidamente poema para tener una impresión general.

    1. Generalmente, el tono de este poema es...
       a. triste
       b. curioso
       c. alegre

    2. Para el poeta, el botecito simboliza...
       a. sus amigos
       b. su familia
       c. su niñez

B. Ahora lea el poema otra vez y conteste las preguntas que siguen.

    1. ¿Cómo sabe usted que Emilio Mozo se refiere al pasado?
    2. ¿Qué adjetivos usa para describir el juguete?
    3. ¿Qué palabras y frases se repiten en el poema y por qué?
    4. ¿Qué pasó finalmente con el juguete?

¡A conversar!

Converse con un(a) compañero(a) de clase.

1. Estudiante A: Usted está en una ciudad hispana donde va a visitar a una familia que lo (la) invitó a comer para una ocación especial. Usted no sabe dónde está el apartamento de la familia y, por eso, le hace algunas preguntas al padre (a la madre). Usted necesita saber cómo llegar allí en autobús (dónde debe subirse y bajarse).

    Estudiante B: Usted es el padre (la madre) de su hijo(a) que invitó a un(a) amigo(a) a comer con su familia. Ahora usted le da la información que le pide. Escuche bien lo que quiere y sea cortés.

SÍNTESIS

2. Estudiante A: Usted decidió tomar un taxi para llegar al apartamento de sus amigos hispanos. Ahora antes de subir al taxi, hable con el (la) taxista para confirmar la distancia y negociar el costo.

Estudiante B: Usted tiene diez años de experiencia como taxista. Está lloviendo y es de noche, por eso, la tarifa (el costo) es diferente a la del día cuando hace buen tiempo. Hable ahora con su cliente.

¡A escribir!

En dos o tres párrafos, describa cómo celebró usted la última Navidad, Hanukkah u otro día festivo. Por ejemplo, describa...

Atajo

1. cuándo fue la celebración (día y mes).
2. dónde celebró usted ese día festivo.
3. por qué lo celebró en ese lugar.
4. con quiénes celebró usted ese día.
5. qué comieron y qué tomaron ustedes.
6. qué otras cosas hicieron ustedes.

VOCABULARIO

Sustantivos

la calle *street*
el centro *center, downtown*
la cuadra *city block*
el día festivo *holiday*
la esquina *street corner*
la maleta *suitcase*
la Navidad *Christmas*
el plano *map (of a city)*

Los lugares en la ciudad
(Places in the city)

el aeropuerto *airport*
el banco *bank*
la estación de trenes *railway station*
la gasolinera *gas station*
la iglesia *church*
el mercado *market*
el museo *museum*
la oficina de correos *post office*
la plaza *town square*
el supermercado *supermarket*
la terminal de autobuses *bus station*

Adjetivos

abierto *open*
cerrado *closed*
cercano *near*
último *last*

Verbos

bajar(se) (de) *to get off*
chocar con *to crash into*
decidir *to decide*
doblar *to turn*
lastimarse *to get hurt*
parar(se) *to stop*
pasar *to spend (time)*
preocuparse (por) *to worry (about)*
seguir (e → i) *to continue*
subir(se) (a) *to get on/in*

Adverbios

cerca *nearby*
hasta *up to, until*
lejos *far (away)*
mientras *while*

Preposiciones

sin *without*

Direcciones
(Directions)

a la izquierda *to the left*
a la derecha *to the right*
al lado de *next to*
cerca de *near*
delante de *in front of*
detrás de *behind*
enfrente de *across from*
entre *between*
lejos de *far from*
todo derecho *straight ahead*

Expresiones negativas

nada *nothing, not anything, at all*
nadie *nobody, no one*
ningún *none, not any*
ninguno(a) *none, not any*
ni... ni *neither . . . nor*
nunca *never*
tampoco *neither, not either*

Expresiones afirmativas

alguien *somebody, someone, anybody, anyone*
algún *some, any*
alguno(a/os/as) *some, any*
o... o *either . . . or*
algo *something, anything*

Expresiones idiomáticas

así *thus, so*
con permiso *excuse me*
dar las gracias *to thank*
de repente *suddenly*
Feliz Navidad *Merry Christmas*
hacia *toward*
lo siento (mucho) *I'm (very) sorry*
pase(n) usted(es) *after you*
perdón *excuse me*
por aquí *around here*
¡Qué le vaya bien! *I wish you well.*
última hora *last minute*
un momento *just a minute*

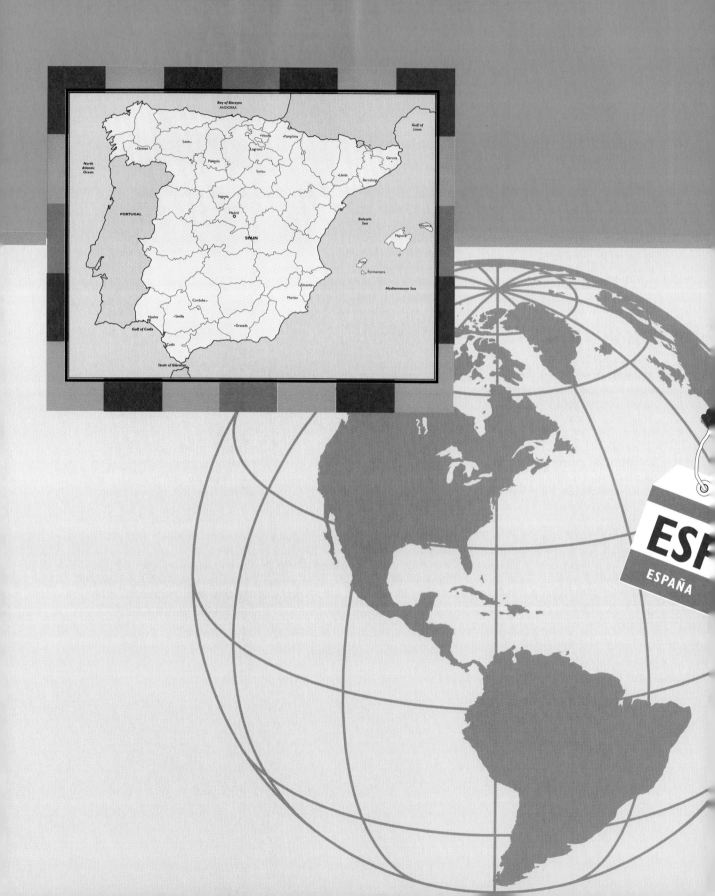

Bay of Biscayne
ANDORRA

North Atlantic Ocean

PORTUGAL

Orense

Leon

Palencia

Vitoria

Pamplona

Logrono

Soria

Segovia

Madrid

SPAIN

Lleida

Gerona

Barcelona

Balearic Sea

Majorca

Minorca

Ivisa

Formentera

Mediterranean Sea

Alicante

Cordoba

Murcia

Huelva

Sevilla

Granada

Gulf of Cadiz

Cadiz

Strait of Gibraltar

Gulf of Lions

ESP

ESPAÑA

¡A pasarlo lo máxima!
▶ *España*

Elena Navarro is a single parent who lives in Barcelona with her six-year old daughter, Rita. They go grocery shopping in speciality stores, look for bargains in a department store, and visit the island of Mallorca with several relatives.

LECCIÓN

¿En qué puedo servirle?

▶ COMMUNICATIVE GOALS

You will be able to talk and write about common foods and describe how life was when you were younger.

▶ LANGUAGE FUNCTIONS

Expressing opinions
Specifying preferences
Stating grocery needs
Expressing likes and dislikes
Communicating more smoothly
Describing past experiences

▶ VOCABULARY THEMES

Specialized food stores
Fruits and vegetables

▶ GRAMMATICAL STRUCTURES

Double object pronouns
Imperfect tense

For free information on Spain, write to Spanish National Tourist Office, 665 Fifth Avenue, New York, NY 10022; or telephone: (212) 759-8822.

▶ CULTURAL INFORMATION

Shopping for groceries
Hispanic markets

http://poco.heinle.com

Atajo

VIDEO

EN CONTEXTO

 **Play Lab Tape**

Elena Navarro es una mujer divorciada de treinta años. Tiene una hija de seis años que se llama Rita. Ellas viven en Barcelona, una de las ciudades más grandes de España. (1) El sábado pasado a las nueve y media de la mañana, Elena y Rita salieron de su pequeño apartamento y fueron a comprar comestibles. (2)

Después de caminar diez minutos, entraron en la carnicería del señor Romero, quien conocía bien a Elena. Ellos se saludaron y hablaron del tiempo y de sus familias. Luego el señor Romero preguntó:

—¿En qué puedo servirle, doña Elena?
—¿Cómo está la carne de vaca° hoy?
—Está muy buena. Aquí tenemos la carne más fresca° de toda Barcelona.
—Bueno, déme un kilo, por favor.

Elena le pagó al señor Romero, (3) se despidió° de él, tomó la mano de su hija y las dos salieron de la carnicería.

—Ahora vamos a la heladería, mamá. Quiero un helado de chocolate.
—No, Rita, porque acabas de desayunar. Te compro un yogur por la tarde.
—¡Mmmm! Me gusta el yogur.

Cinco minutos más tarde, Elena y Rita entraron en la panadería *Ideal* donde vendían panes de diferentes tipos, galletas saladas,° galletas dulces° y una buena selección de tortas y otros pasteles. (4) Allí trabaja Magdalena Ramírez, quien tiene dieciséis años.

—Buenos días, señora. ¿Cómo está?
—Bien, bien. ¿Qué tal, Magda?
—Bien, gracias. ¡Hola, Rita! ¿Cómo estás?
—Muy bien, Magda.
—Oye, hace mucho tiempo que no te vemos.
—Ah sí, señora. Mi familia y yo fuimos de vacaciones a Mallorca. (5)
   Mis tíos tienen una casa grande allí y pasamos dos semanas con ellos.
—¿Dos semanas en Mallorca? ¡Pero qué maravilloso, Magda! ¿Qué te pareció la isla? Muy bonita, ¿eh?
—Ay, sí. Nos divertimos mucho allí, y todos los días hizo buen tiempo.
—Mejor que aquí, ¿verdad, Magda?
—Pues, claro que sí. Bueno, ¿en qué puedo servirle, señora?

Elena compró pan y medio kilo de galletas saladas y medio kilo de galletas dulces para la merienda. Ella continuó hablando con Magdalena sobre sus vacaciones mientras Rita miraba todos los pasteles que se vendían allí. Luego madre e hija salieron de la panadería y fueron al mercado para comprar vegetales y frutas. Más tarde, Elena llevó a Rita a comer yogur y Rita estaba muy contenta.

beef
fresh

said good-bye

crackers / cookies

Students could rewrite this reading passage into a short play, which they could perform in class.

Notas de texto

1. Barcelona, located on the northeastern coast of Spain, is the country's largest port. The summer Olympic Games were held there in 1992.
2. There are several ways to say *grocery store* in Spanish. Spaniards commonly use *tienda de ultramarinos*. In different areas of Latin America, people use *tienda de comestibles*, *tienda de víveres*, and *tienda de abarrotes*. *Colmado* is used in Puerto Rico and in some areas of South America.
3. Elena pays the bill in the monetary unit of Spain, the *peseta*. The current dollar value of the *peseta* is published in the business section of many American and Canadian newspapers; currently, one U.S. dollar equals approximately between 155–170 *pesetas*.
4. In Spanish-speaking countries, bakeries often sell both bread products and pastries; therefore, these stores are sometimes called *panadería-pastelería*.
5. Many Spanish and foreign tourists visit Mallorca, the largest of the *Islas Baleares* located off the east coast of Spain. The beautiful beaches and chic boutiques of the island attract thousands of visitors from many countries.

¿Comprendió Ud.?

1. Los eventos de esta lectura ocurrieron en... (Barcelona / Madrid / Mallorca).
2. Elena y Rita fueron... (a casa / al cine / de compras).
3. El Sr. Romero es... (programador / dependiente / profesor).
4. Magdalena es... (la hermana de Rita / dependiente de una panadería / la hija del Sr. Romero).
5. ¿Adónde fue Elena con Rita, y qué compró la señora allí?
6. ¿Adónde quería ir Rita, y por qué?
7. ¿Qué sabe usted de Magdalena Ramírez? Diga un mínimo de tres cosas.
8. ¿Adónde fueron Elena y Rita después de salir de la panadería, y por qué?

VOCABULARIO ÚTIL

Cómo comprar la comida

In this section you will learn how and where to buy food in Spanish-speaking countries.

En las tiendas especializadas se venden muchos productos

pan   panecillos   tortas

galletas saladas

galletas dulces   pasteles

la panadería   **la pastelería**

Margin notes (left column):

Tell students that another word for *comestibles* is *víveres* from the verb *vivir*.

Spanish bills come in denominations of one thousand, two thousand, five thousand, and ten thousand *pesetas*. Spanish coins come in one, five, ten, twenty-five, fifty, one hundred, two hundred, and five hundred *pesetas*. If you have some *pesetas* or if you can obtain some at a local bank or money exchange office, show them to your students. Bring the financial section of a newspaper to tell your students the current value of the *peseta*.

Point out that there are two other well-known islands in the Baleares group: Menorca and Ibiza. Tourism is one of Spain's main industries and sources of revenue.

Answers: 1. Barcelona 2. de compras 3. dependiente 4. dependiente de una panadería 5. Elena fue a la carnicería donde compró un kilo de carne de vaca, y fue a la panadería donde compró pan y medio kilo de galletas saladas. 6. Rita quería ir a la heladería para comprar helado. 7. Magdalena tiene dieciséis años, trabaja en una panadería, está bien hoy, es una amiga de Elena y Rita, fue de vacaciones a Mallorca con su familia donde se divirtió por dos semanas. 8. Fueron al mercado para comprar frutas y vegetales.

These lists integrate new food vocabulary with words introduced in previous lessons. Encourage students to use a bilingual dictionary to learn vocabulary for other foods whose names they would like to learn in Spanish.

la lechería[1]

la pescadería

la carnicería

A. ¿Tienda o supermercado? Indique la tienda con la cual usted asocia más las siguientes frases.

S = Supermercado / T = Tienda especializada

___Precios altos
___Mejor servicio
___Muchos anuncios
___Uso de computadoras

___Productos importados
___Variedad de productos
___Los productos más frescos
___Buena cantidad de productos

B. Charla. Hable con otro(a) estudiante.

1. ¿Dónde compras comestibles? ¿Qué comestibles compraste esta semana?
2. A veces, ¿compras comestibles en una tienda especializada? (¿Sí? ¿Qué productos prefieres comprar allí y no en un supermercado? ¿Por qué?)
3. En tu opinión, ¿qué ventajas hay en comprar comestibles en tiendas especializadas? En comparación, ¿qué beneficios hay en comprar en un supermercado? De los dos sistemas, ¿cúal prefieres tú, y por qué?

---

[1] In some Spanish-speaking countries, such as Colombia and Venezuela, the word **lechería** is not used.

[2] The word **gambas** is used in Spain, and **camarones** is more comonly used in Latin America. The word **mariscos** means seafood in general; in some countries it means shellfish.

[3] The expressions **carne de vaca** and **carne de cerdo** are used in Spain, Argentina, and the Andean countries (**carne de chancho** in Chile). The expressions **carne de res** and **carne de puerco** are commonly used in Mexico, Central America, and in other areas of Latin America.

Most American and Canadian cities have food specialty stores similar to those in the Hispanic world. Have students work in pairs to tell each other in Spanish about such stores. Each should say where the store is located, describe what it sells there, comment on the prices and merchandise, and give an opinion of the store. Suggestions: *una carnicería, una panadería, una pescadería, una pastelería, una dulcería.*

NOTAS CULTURALES

A comprar comestibles

Aunque cada año los supermercados en Latinoamérica y España son más populares, muchas personas prefieren comprar comestibles en tiendas pequeñas donde se venden productos de primera necesidad. Por ejemplo, se puede ir a una panadería para comprar pan, y a una carnicería para todo tipo de carnes. Muchas veces se encuentran dos tiendas combinadas en un solo lugar como, por ejemplo, la panadería-pastelería o la carnicería-pescadería.

open air

touching

cash register

En estas tiendas especializadas tanto como en los mercados al aire libre,° los clientes le indican al empleado lo que quieren, algunas veces sin tocar° las cosas. Cuando quieren comprar alguna cosa, el empleado la lleva a la caja° donde los clientes le pagan al cajero o a la cajera. Luego esta persona les da a los clientes la compra en una bolsa.

1. Bring to class magazine photographs of these fruits and vegetables. As you show each picture, your students should say the Spanish name for the food.
2. Tell students that *los plátanos* is used in Spain, Mexico, the Caribbean, and Central America. Puerto Ricans use *los guineos,* Venezuelans say *los cambures,* and in many areas of South America people use *las bananas.* Another word for *los duraznos* is *los melocotones.*

We do not want to overwhelm beginning students of Spanish by introducing too many new words. However, if you wish to tell your students the Spanish names of additional fruits and vegetables, here are some words. *LAS FRUTAS: las uvas* (grapes), *la sandía* (watermelon), *las frambuesas* (raspberries), *las moras* (blackberries), *las ciruelas* (plums), *los dátiles* (dates), *la toronja* (grapefruit), *LOS VEGETALES: el apio* (celery), *el pepino* (cucumber), *los rábanos* (radishes), *las espinacas* (spinach), *las alcachofas* (artichokes), *los espárragos* (asparagus).

En el mercado se venden frutas y vegetales

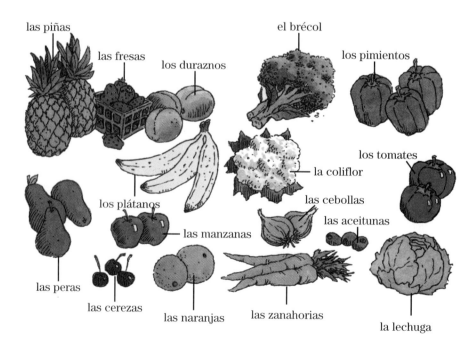

las piñas

las fresas

los duraznos

el brécol

los pimientos

la coliflor

los tomates

los plátanos

las cebollas

las aceitunas

las manzanas

las peras

las cerezas

las naranjas

las zanahorias

la lechuga

Cómo indicar la cantidad de comida

—¿En qué puedo servirle, señor?	*May I help you, sir?*
—Déme una docena de huevos y un litro¹ de leche, por favor.	*Give me a dozen eggs and a liter of milk, please.*
—Bien. ¿Algo más, señor?	*Okay. Anything else, sir?*
—Sí. Déme un kilo² de carne de vaca y medio kilo de salchichas.	*Yes. Give me a kilo of beef and a half kilo of sausages.*
—Bien. ¿Qué más, señor?	*Okay. ¿What else, sir?*
—Quiero 200 gramos³ de estas galletas dulces. Y un kilo de azúcar, por favor. Eso es todo.	*I want 200 grams of these cookies. And one kilo of sugar, please. That's all.*
—Aquí tiene usted.	*Here you are.*
—Muchas gracias.	*Thank you very much.*
—De nada, señor.	*You're welcome, sir.*

Practiquemos

A. En categorías. En cada grupo diga qué palabra pertenece (*belongs*) a otra categoría, y por qué.

Ejemplo: el pollo, la carne de res, la cebolla, el jamón
La cebolla pertenece a otra categoría porque no es carne.

1. la fresa, el litro, el kilo, la docena
2. el queso, el yogur, la mantequilla, el pastel
3. el pollo, los huevos, el jamón, las salchichas
4. las peras, los duraznos, los pimientos, las cerezas
5. la panadería, la cantidad, la pastelería, la carnicería
6. las tortas, las piñas, las galletas dulces, los pasteles
7. las cebollas, las aceitunas, las zanahorias, los camarones

B. ¿Qué es? Su profesor(a) va a leer descripciones de diez comidas y tiendas diferentes. Escuche cada descripción, luego busque el nombre de la comida o la tienda de la lista. Número uno sirve de ejemplo.

la torta	**el plátano**	**la aceituna**	**la panadería**	**la pastelería**
el helado	**la naranja**	**la zanahoria**	**la pescadería**	**la carnicería**

1. *la panadería*   6. _____
2. _____   7. _____
3. _____   8. _____
4. _____   9. _____
5. _____   10. _____

¹ 1 litro = 1.05 quarts
² 1 kilo = 2.2 pounds
³ 1,000 gramos = 1 kilo

C. Mis preferencias de niño(a) y ahora. Dígale a otro(a) estudiante sus preferencias.

1. De niño(a) prefería comer _____ para el almuerzo. Ahora prefiero comer _____ para el almuerzo.
   a. un sandwich de pollo
   b. salchichas con panecillos
   c. un sandwich de jamón y queso
   d. sopa de vegetales con galletas saladas
   e. otra combinación: _____

2. Cuando era niño(a), me gustaba la ensalada de _____. Ahora me gusta la ensalada de _____.
   a. aceitunas y zanahorias
   b. brécol, coliflor y lechuga
   c. lechuga, cebollas y tomates
   d. lechuga con tomates orgánicos
   e. otra combinación: _____

3. De niño(a) prefería beber _____ con el almuerzo. Ahora prefiero tomar _____ con el almuerzo.
   a. un refresco frío
   b. leche fría (leche con chocolate)
   c. café con leche (con / sin) azúcar
   d. jugo de manzana (piña / naranja)
   e. otra bebida: _____

4. Prefería _____ de postre cuando era niño(a). Ahora prefiero _____.
   a. yogur con cerezas
   b. un pastel pequeño
   c. helado con duraznos
   d. un plátano o una manzana
   e. otra combinación: _____

D. ¿En qué puedo servirle? Imagínese que usted está en la sección de un supermercado hispano donde se venden carnes y quesos. Hable con otro(a) estudiante; una persona es el/la dependiente y la otra persona es su cliente.

Dependiente
1. Buenos _____. (Buenas _____.)
3. ¿En qué puedo...?
5. ¿Algo más, señor (señorita / señora)?
7. Aquí tiene usted. ¿Qué más?

Cliente
2. _____.
4. Pues, déme _____, por favor.
6. Sí, quiero _____ (litro / kilo / gramos) de _____.
8. ¿Tiene usted _____?

9. _____, señor (señorita/señora).   10. _____.
11. ¿Otra cosa?   12. No, eso es todo, gracias.
13. Gracias a usted.   14. _____.

TRANSPARENCY No. 10:
Picnic

Ahora imagínense que ustedes están en un mercado hispano en que se venden frutas y vegetales. Comiencen otra conversación, usando el mismo modelo.

E. ¡Vamos a acampar!

1. Imagínese que usted está viviendo con una familia española en Barcelona. Este fin de semana ustedes van a acampar *(camping)* y, por eso, tienen que comprar comestibles. Con un "hermano" o una "hermana" (otro/a estudiante) haga una lista de comestibles que necesitan.

2. Ahora vaya con su "hermano(a)" a diferentes tiendas especializadas para comprar sus necesidades; otro(a) compañero(a) puede ser el/la dependiente. Antes de comenzar, repase *(review)* las palabras y frases que va a usar en cada tienda. Aquí tiene usted otras expresiones útiles:

Dependiente	Cliente	Cantidades
¿En qué puedo servirle?	Déme...	# litro(s) de _____
¿Algo más?	Tambien quiero...	# kilo(s) de _____
¿Qué más?	¿Hay...?	# docena(s) de _____
¿Otra cosa?	No. Eso es todo.	# gramos de _____
Aquí tiene usted.	Muchas gracias.	otros(as) # _____

F. Planeando una fiesta.
Trabaje con un(a) compañero(a) de clase. Imagínense que Ud. y su amigo(a) se comunican por correo electrónico. Uds. planean una fiesta y tienen que decidir quién va a traer qué. Escriban juntos una conversación.

Ejemplo: A: *¿Y Lidia? Ella viene a la fiesta ¿no? ¿Nos va a traer unas bebidas?*
          B: *Sí, nos las va a traer./Sí va a traérnoslas.*

Ex. F.
1. Be sure that students thoroughly review their food vocabulary before they begin this game.
2. This game can also be played in the reverse; students could make cards of all the food items, and then name the food category of the card of top.

G. ¡Vamos a jugar!
Write the following categories on index cards: *frutas, vegetales, carnes, bebidas, dulces, postres, panadería, pescadería.* Shuffle the cards and place them face down. Your partner takes the top card and reads it, then names items in Spanish that belong to that category. Set a specific time limit per round (e.g., one minute), and take turns. Add one point for each item categorized correctly, and subtract one point for each item categorized incorrectly. The person who has the highest score at the end of three rounds wins the game. Use only Spanish during this activity!

An excellent way to check students' comprehension of this cultural note is to have them summarize it in English in a few sentences.

NOTAS **CULTURALES**

Los mercados hispanos

enclosed

En casi todas las ciudades hispanas hay un mercado cerrado° o al aire libre. Mucha gente compra en el mercado porque sabe que allí puede encontrar mejores precios que en los supermercados o en las tiendas especializadas. Frecuentemente los productos agrícolas de los mercados están más frescos que en otros lugares porque la gente compra directamente de los agricultores, quienes los cultivan en sus granjas.°

farms

Generalmente, los mercados están divididos en varias secciones. En una sección se venden frutas y vegetales frescos a precios razonables. En otra sección hay una selección de carnes y pescados; también se puede comprar allí mantequilla, huevos, arroz y pan. Otra sección de los mercados está dedicada a la venta de ropa. En algunos mercados de las ciudades grandes se pueden comprar cosas de interés turístico como, por ejemplo, artesanías° típicas de la región.

crafts

to bargain / fixed

high

En general, se puede regatear° en los mercados porque los precios no son fijos.° Se comienza a regatear preguntándole al vendedor por el precio del artículo, pero sin demostrar mucho interés para que no le pida un precio muy alto.° Luego se ofrece aproximadamente 30% menos del precio indicado hasta llegar a un acuerdo.

Preguntas

1. En su opinión, ¿cuál es un aspecto interesante de los mercados hispanos? ¿Quiere usted visitar uno? ¿Por qué?
2. ¿Dónde y cuándo se puede regatear en su país? ¿Cómo se regatea allí? ¿Qué cosas compró usted regateando? ¿Qué precio quería el vendedor y cuánto pagó usted finalmente?

Practiquemos

Practique con un(a) compañero(a) de clase. Una persona es el vendedor o la vendedora y la otra persona es su cliente.

Vendedor(a)	Cliente
1. Pregúntele qué va a llevar.	2. Pregúntele el precio de una cosa, pero no exprese mucho interés.
3. Responda apropiadamente.	4. Exprese sorpresa. Comience a regatear, diciendo un precio más bajo *(lower)*.
5. Conteste apropiadamente.	6. Pregúntele si es su mejor precio.
7. Responda a la pregunta.	8. Decida comprar o no comprar la cosa, luego dígale su decisión.
9. Conteste apropiadamente.	10. Despídase con cortesía.

GRAMÁTICA FUNCIONAL

Communicating smoothly in Spanish

—¿Compraste el helado, mamá?
—Sí, te lo compré esta mañana.
—Y la torta; ¿me la compraste?
—Sí. También te la compré, hija.
—¡Mmm! ¡Los quiero ahora, mamá!
—El helado te lo doy ahora y la
  torta te la doy mañana en tu fiesta.
  ¿Está bien?
—Sí, mamá.

Have students role play this short dialogue between mother and daughter. Male students could assume the role of either a father or a son, substituting the words *papá* and *hijo* for *mamá* and *hija*.

Double object pronouns

In *Lecciones 7* and *8*, you learned how to use direct and indirect object pronouns, respectively. Sometimes you may want to use both kinds of pronouns in the same sentence. Double object pronouns consist of direct and indirect object pronouns used together.

How to use double object pronouns

1. Indirect object pronouns always **precede** direct object pronouns.

Indirect before Direct

me	
te	**lo**
le (→ **se**)	**la**
nos	**los**
os	**las**
les (→ **se**)	

Tell students the following mnemonic device for remembering that indirect object pronouns always precede direct object pronouns: ID as in their student ID.

2. The indirect object pronouns *le* and *les* always change to *se* when they are used together with the direct object pronouns *lo*, *la*, *los*, and *las*.

Elena **le** compró **un regalo** a su hija.

Elena **se lo** compró ayer en el centro.

También **le** compró **una torta** a Rita.

Elena **se la** compró en una pastelería.

3. To contrast, emphasize or clarify the meaning of the indirect object pronoun *se*, use *a usted*, *a él*, *a ella*, *a ustedes*, *a ellos*, or *a ellas*, as shown below.

La torta está rica. Elena **se** la compró **a su hija.**

Elena **se** la compró **a ella** para su cumpleaños.

Emphasize the identical meanings in the first two sets of sentences here.

4. In verb phrases, pronouns may be placed before conjugated verbs or attached to infinitives or present participles, but they always come before negative commands. Pronouns must be attached to affirmative commands; when two pronouns are attached, an accent mark is written over the stressed vowel.

Elena quiere comprarle zapatos a Rita.

Se los va a comprar hoy.	↔	Va a **comprárselos** hoy.
Se los está comprando ahora.	↔	Está **comprándoselos** ahora.
No **se los** compre allí.	↔	**Cómpreselos** en esa tienda.

Practiquemos

Ex. A. Have students complete this exercise in class, then go over the answers, preferably using an overhead projector or a chalkboard.
Then assign the second part of the exercise for homework, and check students' answers at the next class meeting.

A. En el mercado. Elena está hablando con un vendedor en un mercado. Busque los pronombres en su conversación, y dibuje una flecha a los sustantivos a que se refieren.

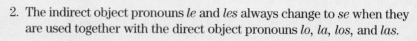

VENDEDOR: ¿En qué puedo servirle, doña Elena?

ELENA: Déme doscientos gramos de aceitunas, pero las quiero con pimientos.

VENDEDOR: Bueno, aquí las tiene, señora. ¿Algo más?

ELENA: Sí. Quiero cuatro cebollas, pero métamelas en una pequeña bolsa plástica, por favor. Hoy no traje mi bolso.

VENDEDOR: Bueno, cuatro cebollas en una bolsa plástica. Aquí las tiene. ¿Y tomates? ¿No los quiere? Están muy frescos, señora.

ELENA: No. Ya los compré ayer. Perdón, estas fresas... ¿puedo probar una?

VENDEDOR: Cómo no, señora. Sírvase. ... ¿Qué le parece? ¿Le gusta?

ELENA: Mmmm. ¡Qué rica! Déme medio kilo de las fresas. ¿Me las puede meter en otra bolsa plástica, por favor?

VENDEDOR: Sí, señora. Con mucho gusto.

Ahora lea otra vez la lectura en la página 247 e identifique con flechas los sustantivos que correspondan a sus pronombres directos e indirectos.

B. ¡Qué tía tan generosa! Isabel, una tía de Rita, acaba de volver de Mallorca donde les compró varios regalos a sus parientes. Rita quiere saber a quiénes se los dio su tía. ¿Cómo respondió Isabel a cada pregunta de su sobrina?

Ejemplo: RITA: ¿A quién le compraste ese reloj? → a mi hijo
   ISABEL: *Se lo compré a mi hijo.*

Rita	**Isabel**
1. ¿A quién le compraste esas botas?	a mi hijo
2. ¿A quién le compraste ese vino?	a una amiga
3. ¿Y esos anteojos para el sol?	a mi esposo
4. ¿Y esa camiseta tan bonita, tía?	a ti, Rita
5. ¿A quién le compraste esos quesos?	a tu mamá
6. ¿Y ese paraguas rojo y blanco?	a mi abuelita

Ex. B. Answers:
1. Se las compré a mi hijo. 2. Se lo compré a una amiga. 3. Se los compré a mi marido. 4. Te la compré a ti, Rita. 5. Se los compré a tu mamá. 6. Se lo compré a mi abuelita.

Ex. B. After students have completed this exercise, have them role-play it with a conversation partner.

C. En un restaurante. Complete las siguientes conversaciones, usando pronombres apropiados.

Ejemplo: —*Me trae la ensalada, por favor?*
   —*Sí, señorita.* **Se la** *traigo ahora.*

—Quiero sopa de tomate, por favor.
—Cómo no (señor / señorita / señora). _____ traigo pronto.

—Tráigame pescado con un poco de limón, por favor.
—¿Pescado con limón? Sí, _____ sirvo en seguida.

—Déme otros dos refrescos, por favor. Tengo mucha sed.
—Sí, (señor / señorita / señora). _____ traigo ahora mismo.

—De postre, déme manzanas rellenas, por favor.
—Bien. _____ sirvo muy pronto, (señor / señorita / señora).

Ex. C.
1. Answers: Se la, se lo, Se los, Se las
2. After students have completed this exercise, have them role play the dialogues with a classmate.

D. Entre parientes y conocidos. Termine las siguientes conversaciones, usando formas de verbos apropiadas con pronombres apropiados, según el ejemplo.

Ejemplo: —*Voy a comprarle una blusa a mi hija.*
   —*¿Dónde quiere comprársela?*
   —*Pienso que se la compro en un almacén.*
   —*No se la compre allí, señora.*
   —*¿Por qué no?*
   —*Hay mejores precios en la tienda "Fantasía". Comprésela allí.*

Ex. D. Answers:
1. hacérselo, hacérselo, se lo haga, se lo hago, Hágaselo
2. escribírsela, se la escribimos, se la escriban, Escríbansela

1. —Pienso hacerle un vestido a mi sobrina, Rita.
   —¿Por qué quiere _____ , doña Isabel?
   —Quiero _____ porque soy la tía.
   —No _____ por esa razón , señora.
   —¿Por qué _____ , entonces?
   —_____ porque usted quiere a su sobrina.

2. —Queremos escribirles una carta a nuestros abuelos.
   —¿Cuándo piensan ustedes _____ ?
   —Creo que _____ ahora. ¿Qué le parece?
   —No _____ ahora, niños.
   —¿Cuándo debemos escribir la carta a los abuelos?
   —_____ mañana porque van a tener mucho más tiempo.

E. Y ¿qué más te trajo? Trabaje con un(a) compañero(a) de clase. Imagínense que, Ud. y su amigo(a), se comunican por correo electrónico. La tía de su amiga acaba de regresar de unas vacaciones y le trajo muchos regalos. Escriban juntos una conversación.

Ejemplo: —¿Te trajo tu tía unos regalos de sus vacaciones?
—Sí, me los trajo.

Charlemos

F. Entrevista. Pregúntele a otro(a) estudiante.

1. Cuando necesitas dinero para ir de compras, ¿a quiénes se lo pides? (¿Y te lo dan?) Cuando eras niño(a), ¿a quienes les pedías dinero? ¿Te lo daban?

2. Y tus padres, ¿te dan mucho o poco dinero? ¿Se lo pides con mucha o con poca frecuencia? Cuando eras niño(a), ¿te daban mucho o poco dinero tus padres? ¿Con qué frecuencia se lo pedías? ¿Qué comprabas con tu dinero?

3. Cuando vas de compras, ¿a quiénes les compras regalos? ¿Qué cosas les compras? ¿A quiénes les comprabas regalos de niño(a)? ¿Qué les comprabas a ellos?

4. ¿Cuándo fue la última vez que fuiste de compras? ¿Con quién fuiste? ¿Qué compraste allí? ¿A quién les compraste esa(s) cosa(s)?

5. ¿Te gusta escribir cartas? ¿Escribes cartas frecuentemente o solamente a veces? ¿A quiénes les escribes cartas? ¿Quiénes te escriben a ti? ¿Cuándo fue la última vez que escribiste una carta? ¿A quién le escribiste, y por qué?

6. ¿Quién te mandó una carta recientemente? ¿De dónde te la mandó?

G. Unos favores. Converse con un(a) compañero(a) de clase.

Ejemplo: A: *¿Me das diez dólares hasta la próxima semana?*
B: *¿Por qué los necesitas?*
A: *Los necesito para comprar comestibles.*
B: *Bueno, te los doy porque eres mi amigo(a).*
O: B: *Lo siento. No te los doy porque no tengo dinero.*

Estudiante A

1. ¿Me das (10 dólares / tu cámara) hasta la próxima semana?
3. ____ necesito para...

5. ¿Me das tu ____ hasta mañana?
7. ____ necesito para...

Estudiante B

2. ¿Para qué ____ necesitas?

4. Bueno, ____ doy porque... (Lo siento, pero...)

6. ¿Para qué ____ necesitas?
8. Bueno, ____ porque... (Lo siento, pero...)

GRAMÁTICA FUNCIONAL

Describing past experiences

—¿Cómo te divertías cuando eras niña, mamá?
—Pues, salía con mis padres e íbamos al cine.
—Nunca fueron ustedes a Mallorca, mamá?
—Claro, Rita. Visitábamos la isla cada verano.

Imperfect tense

Spanish speakers use the imperfect tense to describe past actions, conditions, and events that were in progress or that occurred habitually or repetitiously.

How to form the imperfect

1. To form the imperfect, add the following endings to the verb stem. Note the identical endings for -er and -ir verbs.

infinitive	jugar	hacer	divertirse
(yo)	jug**aba**	hac**ía**	me divert**ía**
(tú)	jug**abas**	hac**ías**	te divert**ías**
(usted, él/ella)	jug**aba**	hac**ía**	se divert**ía**
(nosotros/as)	jug**ábamos**	hac**íamos**	nos divert**íamos**
(vosotros/as)	*jugabais*	*hacíais*	*os divertíais*
(ustedes, ellos/ellas)	jug**aban**	hac**ían**	se divert**ían**

Emphasize that the yo forms of the imperfect are identical to the usted, él, and ella forms. Context clarifies the meaning.

2. Three Spanish verbs are irregular in the imperfect.

ir	ser	ver
iba	era	veía
ibas	eras	veías
iba	era	veía
íbamos	éramos	veíamos
ibais	*erais*	*veíais*
iban	eran	veían

—¿Qué **ibas** a preguntarme?   *What were you going to ask me?*

—¿**Veías** muchos videos cuando   *Did you watch a lot of videos*
  eras niño?   *when you were a child?*

—Sí. Mi familia y yo veíamos   *Yes. My family and I watch lots*
  muchos.   *of them.*

3. The imperfect tense of *hay* is *había.*

—¿**Había** muchas personas en   *Were there a lot of people at*
  el mercado?   *the market?*

—Sí, Rita. **Había** mucha gente.   *Yes, Rita. There were many people.*

How to use the preterite (review)

You have learned that Spanish speakers use the preterite tense to describe past actions, conditions, and events that began in the past or were completed at some point in the past. For example, notice how Elena uses the preterite to tell what happened at her home this morning.

> Esta mañana mi despertador **sonó** a las seis como siempre. **Me levanté, fui** al baño, **me duché** y **me vestí.** Luego **desperté** a mi hija Rita y **preparé** el desayuno. **Comimos** fruta, pan tostado y **tomamos** chocolate. Después, **nos lavamos** los dientes y **salimos** de casa. **Fuimos** en autobús al centro de Barcelona.

How to use the imperfect

Spanish speakers use the imperfect tense to express actions, conditions, and events that were in progress at some focused point in the past. For example, notice how Elena uses the imperfect tense to tell what was going on when she got off the bus with her daughter.

> Cuando nos bajamos del autobús, **hacía** un poco de frío y **llovía.** Rita no **quería** ir conmigo porque todavía **estaba** cansada.

Spanish speakers also use the imperfect to describe actions, conditions, and events that occurred habitually or repetitiously in the past. Notice how Elena uses the imperfect to describe how her life was when she was a girl.

> De niña, todo **era** diferente de lo que es ahora. Yo **tenía** menos responsabilidades y creo que **estaba** más contenta. Todos los sábados **me levantaba** tarde porque no **había** mucho que hacer en casa. Luego iba a la cocina, **me servía** un vaso de leche y **miraba** la tele. Por la tarde mis amigas y yo **jugábamos** juntas.

Spanish speakers also use the imperfect to past actions, conditions, and events that were anticipated or planned. For example, read what Elena planned to do yesterday.

> Yo **quería** ir de compras ayer. Pero yo no **podía** salir de casa porque **tenía** que lavar la ropa y limpiar el apartamento.

Use the example paragraphs on this page for dictation practice.

Have your students circle all the preterite verb forms and underline all the imperfect verb forms in the *En contexto* reading of this lesson. Afterwards, they should analyze how and why these verb forms were used.

> The imperfect tense can be translated in different ways, depending on the context. For example, read the following paragraph and notice the English meaning of the forms in parenthesis.
>
> De niña yo **vivía** *(lived)* en un pueblo cerca de Barcelona. Los sábados mi mamá y yo **íbamos** *(used to go)* de compras al centro donde **mirábamos** *(we would look at)* muchas cosas en las tiendas. Un sábado, cuando **caminábamos** *(we were walking)* en la plaza, vimos un festival de música cerca de la plaza.

Practiquemos

A. Querido abuelo. Use los verbos de la siguiente lista para completar el primer párrafo de una carta que Elena le escribió a su abuelo.

Ex. A. Answers: *quería, podía, tenía, estaba, iba, escribía, hablaba, trabajaba*

| iba | tenía | estaba | escribía |
| podía | quería | hablaba | trabajaba |

¿Cómo estás, abuelito? Yo _____ escribirte antes pero no lo _____ hacer porque _____ tantos quehaceres aquí en casa. Rita y mi trabajo ocupan casi todo mi tiempo. Ayer ella _____ preguntándome sobre ti y le dije que _____ a escribirte muy pronto. Recuerdo que te _____ cartas y que te _____ por teléfono más frecuentemente cuando no _____ tanto como ahora.

B. Elena de niña. Elena está contándole *(telling)* a Rita algunas cosas que ella hacía de niña. ¿Qué le dice a su hija?

Ex. B. Answers:
1. *vivíamos* 2. *teníamos, teníamos*
3. *era, compraba, vendía* 4. *trabajaba*
5. *nos divertíamos, montábamos, íbamos* 6. *estábamos, había* 7. *leía, contaba, era* 8. *tocaba, cantaba*
9. *quería, decía, podía*

Ejemplo: Yo / jugar al vólibol.   → *Yo jugaba al vólibol.*

1. Mi familia y yo / vivir en un rancho veinte kilómetros al norte de Barcelona.
2. (nosotros) no / tener auto, pero / tener muchos caballos.
3. Tu abuelo / ser agricultor; también, / comprar y / vender caballos.
4. Mi mamá / trabajar en casa.
5. Mis dos hermanos y yo / divertirse mucho: / montar en bicicleta, / montar a caballo e / ir a jugar a diferentes lugares.
6. (Nosotros) Nunca / estar aburridos porque / haber muchas cosas que hacer.
7. Antes de acostarnos por la noche, mi mamá nos / leer o nos / contar historias sobre cuando ella / ser niña.
8. A veces, mi papá / tocar la guitarra y nos / cantar viejas canciones catalanas.
9. Yo / querer mucho a mis padres y muchas veces les / decir que (yo) no / poder vivir sin ellos.

C. Hace mucho tiempo. Elena está conversando con Rita en la sala sobre los primeros años de su matrimonio con su ex-marido. Complete su conversación, indicando los verbos correctos entre paréntesis.

Ex. C. Answers: *vivisteis, Vivimos, teníamos, hacía, Trabajaba, Vendía, ganaba, era, vinisteis, naciste, os divorciasteis, pasó, quería, volvió, recibí, escribió, quería, iba*

RITA: Mamá, ¿dónde (vivísteis / vivíais) tú y papá después de casados?
ELENA: (Vivimos / Vivíamos) por un año y medio con mis padres cerca de Barcelona porque no (tuvimos / teníamos) mucho dinero.
RITA: ¿Qué tipo de trabajo (hizo / hacía) mi papá?

ELENA: (Trabajó / Trabajaba) como dependiente en un almacén. (Vendió / Vendía) zapatos allí. Tu papá (ganó / ganaba) poco dinero, pero (fue / era) suficiente para vivir.

RITA: ¿Cuándo (vinisteis / veníais) vosotros a vivir aquí en Barcelona?

ELENA: Dos meses después de que (naciste / nacías), mi hija.

RITA: ¿Y por qué tú y papá (os divorciasteis / os divorciáis), mamá?

ELENA: Pues, no sé lo que (pasó / pasaba), Rita. Yo (quise / quería) mucho a tu papá, pero un día él no (volvió / volvía) de su trabajo. Una semana más tarde (recibí / recibía) una carta de tu papá. Me (escribió / escribía) que ya no me (quiso / quería) y que no (fue / iba) a volver a casa.

D. ¿Y usted? Escriba un párrafo sobre algunas actividades que usted, su familia y sus amigos hacían cuando usted tenía diez años.

Ejemplo: *Cuando yo tenía diez años, mi familia y yo vivíamos en... Nuestra casa (Nuestro apartamento)... Mi papá trabajaba en... y mi mamá... En general, mis padres... Mis hermanos y yo nos divertíamos mucho. Por ejemplo... Yo tenía un(a) amigo(a), que se llamaba _____. A veces, él (ella)... y yo... También nosotros...*

Charlemos

Ex. E. Follow-up activity: Ask students bring photographs of themselves when they were younger. Have them share these pictures and talk about what they used to do back then.

E. Recuerdos. Pregúntele a un(a) compañero(a) de clase.

1. **La familia:** ¿Dónde y con quién vivías cuando tenías seis años? ¿Cuántos hermanos tenías? ¿Quién era el menor? ¿y el mayor? ¿Qué tipo de trabajo hacía tu papá? ¿Trabajaba tu mamá también? (¿Sí? ¿Dónde? ¿Qué hacía ella?) ¿Cuándo visitabas a tus tíos y a tus abuelos? ¿Qué otras cosas hacías con tu familia?

2. **Las posesiones:** De niño(a), ¿tenías una bicicleta? (¿Sí? ¿Era grande o pequeña? ¿De qué color era?) ¿Tenías un perro o un caballo? (¿Sí? ¿Cómo se llamaba?) ¿Qué otras cosas tenías? ¿Cuál era la cosa más importante que tenías?

3. **Los amigos:** ¿Tenías muchos o pocos amigos en la escuela primaria? ¿Cómo te divertías con ellos? ¿Cómo se llamaba tu mejor amigo o amiga en la escuela secundaria? ¿Dónde vivía? ¿Qué hacían ustedes juntos(as)? ¿Tenías novio(a)? (¿Sí? ¿Cómo se llamaba? ¿Cómo era él/ella? ¿Dónde vive ahora?)

4. **Los pasatiempos:** De adolescente, ¿cómo pasabas el tiempo cuando no estudiabas o trabajabas? ¿Practicabas algún deporte? (¿Cuál?) ¿Con qué frecuencia ibas al cine? ¿Qué tipo de películas veías? ¿Qué programas de televisión mirabas? ¿Con quién los mirabas? ¿Qué otras cosas hacías para divertirte?

F. ¿Qué hacías? Estudie las siguientes actividades. Luego dígale a otro(a) estudiante las actividades que usted hacía a las horas indicadas.

Ejemplo: Anoche a las once... → *Anoche a las once yo dormía.*

comer...	volver a...	leer un libro (...)
dormir...	trabajar en...	lavar los platos (...)
estudiar...	comenzar a...	salir con amigos (...)

descansar...   divertirse con...   escuchar música (...)
bañarse...   hacer ejercicio en...   tomar una cerveza (...)

1. Ayer a las diez de la mañana...
2. Ayer a las cuatro de la tarde...
3. Anoche a las once...
4. Esta mañana a las siete y media...
5. Hoy antes de venir a clase...

G. Nuestra adolescencia. Imagínese que usted y su amigo(a) ya tienen cincuenta años. Ahora conversen ustedes sobre su adolescencia.

1. ¿Cómo / ser cuando / tener 15 o 16 años?

2. Bueno, recuerdo que yo / ser un poco... Y tú, ¿cómo / ser de adolescente?

3. Pues, mis padres / creer que / yo / ser muy..., pero creo que / ser...

4. ¡Qué interesante! ¿Cómo se llamar / tu primer(a) novio(a)?

5. Él (Ella) se / llamar y / tener años.

6. ¿Cómo se / divertir ustedes?

7. (Nosotros) / ir a muchos lugares; por ejemplo... ¿Tener / novio(a)?

8. Claro que sí... (Pues, realmente no porque...)

9. ¡Qué bueno (triste)! ¿Qué tipo de ropa / llevar de adolescente?

10. Pues, me / gustar llevar... ¿Y a ti?

11. Cuando / ir a clase / llevar..., pero, a veces, me poner un(a)...

12. ¡Qué interesante! ¿Y qué tipo de comida / comer?

13. Bueno, me / gustar comer... ¿Qué te / gustar comer a ti?

14. Pues, por la mañana... Para el almuerzo... Y en la noche mi familia y yo...

15. Creo que tú y yo..., ¿no?

16. Creo que sí (no) porque...

PARA LEER MEJOR

Improving Your Reading Efficiency

Reading efficiently involves a great deal of guessing. By considering several organizational features of a passage, you can often guess its theme even before you begin reading it.

Activities

A. Prereading strategies

1. Read the **title** of the poem on page 264.
   • What do you suppose is its main topic?

2. Look at the **photograph.**
   • How does this picture complement the title of the poem?
   • Now guess what the poem is about.

A. [Open] B. *1. c* 2. *d* 3. *d*
C. *1. Chile, diciembre* 2. *La cebolla*
3. *Cuchillo* 4. *Aceite* 5. *fogoso, frescura* D. [open]

Oda al Tomate

La calle
se llenó° de tomates,
mediodía,
verano,
la luz
se parte
en dos mitades°
de tomate,
corre
por las calles
el jugo.
En diciembre
se desata°
el tomate,
invade
las cocinas,
entra por los almuerzos,
se sienta
reposado°
en los aparadores,°
entre los vasos,
las mantequilleras,
los saleros azules.
Tiene
luz propia,
majestad benigna.
Debemos, por desgracia,
asesinarlo:
se hunde°
el cuchillo
en su pulpa viviente,
es una roja
vícera,
un sol
fresco,
profundo,
inagotable,
llena las ensaladas
de Chile,
se casa alegremente
con la clara cebolla...
y para celebrarlo
se deja

caer
aceite,
hijo
esencial del olivo,
sobre sus hemisferios
   entreabiertos,
agrega°
la pimienta
su fragancia,
la sal su magnetismo:
son las bodas
del día
el perejil°
levanta
banderines,°
las papas
hierven° vigorosamente,
el asado
golpea
con su aroma
en la puerta,
es hora!
vamos!
y sobre
la mesa, en la cintura
del verano,
el tomate,
astro de tierra,
estrella
repetida
y fecunda°,
nos muestra
sus circunvoluciones,
sus canales,
la insigne plentitud
y la abundancia
sin hueso°,
sin coraza,
sin escamas ni espinas,
nos entrega
el regalo
du su color fogoso
y la totalidad de su frescura.

Pablo Neruda (*Odas Elementales*, 1954)

was filled
halves / adds
is untied / parsley
small flags
boil
quiet
shop windows
sinks into
fruitful
bone

B. Skimming

Skim the poem to get the gist of it. Then complete the following sentences.

1. El tema principal del poema es...
   a. la cebolla
   b. las frutas
   c. el tomate
   d. la comida

2. El tomate es...
   a. un vegetal sin importancia
   b. una fruta poco conocida
   c. una fruta muy conocida
   d. un vegetal con importancia

3. El tomate y las cebollas se unen con...
   a. la sal y las papas
   b. la pimienta y el asado
   c. las papas y el asado
   d. la pimienta, la sal y el perejil

C. Scanning

Scan the poem to locate specific information asked for in the comprehension exercise below.

1. El tomate aparece por las calles de _____ en el mes de _____.
2. En las ensaladas, el tomate se casa alegremente con _____.
3. El _____ se usa para poder ver la pulpa roja del tomate.
4. El _____ es el hijo esencial del olivo.
5. El tomate nos entrega su color _____ y su _____.

D. Personal impressions

¿Qué impresión tiene usted de este poema?

Creo que el poema es (interesante / aburrido / descriptivo) porque...

PARA ESCRIBIR MEJOR

Writing a Summary

A good summary tells the reader the problem and the events that lead to the solution in a narrative. Here is a list of important information to include in a summary:

1. An interesting title
2. Where and when the action takes place
3. The main characters (if any)
4. The problem or conflict
5. The solution to the problem or conflict

Activity

1. Summarize the reading passage in the *En contexto* section of this lesson. Write the following information in Spanish on a separate piece of paper.

   - Write a new title for the passage.
   - Where did the action take place?
   - When did the action occur?
   - Who were the main characters in the story?

Atajo

Functions:
Writing about characters; writing about theme, plot, or scene; expressing a need

Vocabulary:
Food: fruits, legumes & vegetables, meat; stores; metric system & measurements; prose; punctuation marks

Grammar:
Verbs: imperfect; personal pronouns: indirect/direct

¿A qué nivel está Ud.?

A ver si puede encontrar los pronombres dobles de objeto adecuados. ¿Compraste mi torta de cumpleaños, mamá? ___ ___ compré esta mañana. Y el helado. ¿También ___ ___ compraste?
Review the chapter and then monitor your progress by completing the *Autoprueba* at the end of *Lección 10* in the **Workbook/Lab Manual.**

- List the events that led up to the action.
- What was the central problem in the story?
- How was the problem solved at the end?

2. Using the information that you listed on your paper, write a summary of the reading passage.

3. Edit your summary; check it for:
   - Content
     a. Is the title of your summary captivating?
     b. Is the information concise and to the point?
     c. Is the information interesting to the reader?
   - Organization
     a. Does each paragraph begin with a topic sentence?
     b. Do the details in each paragraph relate to the topic sentence?
     c. Are the sentences and paragraphs ordered logically?
   - Cohesion and style
     a. Is your summary clearly and concisely written?
     b. Does your summary "flow" easily from beginning to end?
     c. Have you used correct grammar, spelling, and punctuation?

4. Exchange your summary with a classmate's, and check each other's work for errors. Then write a second draft of your summary and give it to your instructor for correction of any remaining errors.

SÍNTESIS

VIDEO

¡A ver!

Laura and her friend Juanita are planning something special, as you will see. First, study the phrases and sentences with their meaning in the *Vocabulario esencial.* Second, read the sentences in the activity below. Third, watch the videotape, then complete the activity according to the directions.

Vocabulario esencial

se me olvidó	*I forgot*
invitados	*guests*
¿Qué hacemos de cenar?	*What should we make for dinner?*
bien rico	*really delicious*
de postre	*for dessert*
déjame apuntar	*let me jot down*
carne molida	*ground meat*
nueces	*nuts*

Complete las siguientes oraciones apropiadamente.

1. Laura y Juanita están planeando...
   a. una cena.
   b. un picnic.
   c. una fiesta.

2. El evento es...
   a. el viernes.
   b. el sábado.
   c. el domingo.

3. Laura va a tener...
   a. cuatro invitados.
   b. seis invitados.
   c. ocho invitados.

4. Juanita y Laura fueron al...
   a. cine.
   b. parque.
   c. mercado.

Answers: 1. *a* 2. *b* 3. *b* 4. *c* 5. *c* 6. *b*

Visit

INTERNET

http://poco.heinle.com

SÍNTESIS

5. Estas dos mujeres compraron principalmente...
   a. frutas.
   b. dulces.
   c. vegetales.

6. Ellas compraron en cantidades de...
   a. kilos.
   b. gramos.
   c. kilos y gramos.

¡A leer!

frost   La cebolla es escarcha°
           cerrada y pobre.
           Escarcha de tus días
           y de mis noches.
           Hambre y cebolla,
           hielo negro y escarcha
round   grande y redonda.°

Source: Fragment de "Namas de la cebolla" by Miguel Hernández in *Obra poética completa, Colección Guérnica*, 1976, pages 138–141.

¿Comprendió Ud.?

1. ¿Cómo es el tono *(tone)* de este poema?
2. ¿Qué palabras negativas hay en el poema?
3. ¿De qué color es el hambre para Hernández?

VOCABULARIO

Sustantivos

el azúcar *sugar*
los comestibles *groceries*

Las tiendas
(Stores)

la carnicería *butcher shop*
la lechería *dairy store*
la panadería *bakery*
la pastelería *pastry shop*
la pescadería *fish shop*

En la lechería

el yogur *yogurt*

En la carnicería-pescadería

la carne de cerdo (puerco) *pork*
la carne de vaca (res) *beef*
las gambas (los camarones) *shrimp*
los mariscos *shellfish*
las salchichas *sausages*

En la panadería-pastelería

la galleta dulce *cookie*
la galleta salada *cracker*
el panecillo *roll*
la torta *cake, torte*

Las frutas

la cereza *cherry*
el durazno *peach*
la fresa *strawberry*

la manzana *apple*
la naranja *orange*
la pera *pear*
la piña *pineapple*
el plátano *banana*

Los vegetales

la aceituna *olive*
el brécol *broccoli*
la cebolla *onion*
la coliflor *cauliflower*
la lechuga *lettuce*
el pimiento *pepper*
el tomate *tomato*
la zanahoria *carrot*

Las cantidades
(Quantities)

la docena *dozen*
el gramo *gram*
el kilo *kilo*
el litro *liter*
medio *one-half*

Adjetivos

alto *high*
bajo *low*
fresco *fresh*

Verbos

acampar *to camp*
ayudar *to help*
contar (o→ue) *to tell (a story)*
despedir (e→i, i) *to fire (dismiss)*
    someone
despedirse de (e→i, i) *to say good-bye*

jubilarse *to retire*
meter *to put (in)*
repasar *to review*

Expresiones idiomáticas

¿Algo más? *Anything else?*
Eso es todo. *That's all.*
Nada más. *Nothing else.*
¿Qué más? *What else?*

11

Aquí vendemos de todo

▶ COMMUNICATIVE GOALS

You will be able to ask questions and express your opinions in department stores and non-food specialty shops.

▶ LANGUAGE FUNCTIONS

Giving advice
Making requests
Stating reasons
Asking for information
Naming non-food items
Expressing preferences

http://poco.heinle.com

▶ VOCABULARY THEMES

Jewelry, writing materials
Electronic gadgets, photo supplies
Shopping expressions

Atajo

▶ GRAMMATICAL STRUCTURES

The prepositions *por* and *para*
Adverbs

VIDEO

▶ CULTURAL INFORMATION

Department stores
Specialized non-food stores

EN CONTEXTO

Play Lab Tape

El miércoles pasado a las cuatro y media de la tarde, Elena Navarro lavaba los platos del almuerzo y escuchaba la radio en la cocina mientras su hija Rita jugaba con su muñeca° y miraba la televisión en la sala. De repente, la niña oyó el siguiente anuncio:

doll

El Corte Inglés anuncia su sensacional Rebaja° del Año este viernes y sábado.(1) El Corte Inglés va a rebajar° los precios de muchas cosas de un 20 hasta un 60 por ciento. Aquí vendemos de todo. Venga a ver nuestra enorme selección de elegantes chaquetas sport. Hay de todos los colores y estilos, y la calidad es superior. Venga a ver nuestros tostadores, televisores, radios estéreos, videocámaras, grabadoras,° ordenadores,° impresoras,° máquinas de escribir° y mucho, mucho más. Tenemos una buena selección de bicicletas, juguetes y juegos de video para toda la familia. Tenemos la mejor calidad y los mejores precios de Barcelona. Prácticamente todo está rebajado al costo o por debajo del costo. ¡En esta Rebaja del Año usted va a encontrar miles de gangas!° Aproveche° estas fantásticas rebajas. Esta rebaja es solamente una vez al año. ¡Vaya a El Corte Inglés este viernes y sábado —y ahorre más que nunca!°

sale
to reduce

tape recorders / computers
printers / typewriters

bargains
Take advantage of
save more than ever

Después de ver este anuncio, Rita estaba tan contenta que corrió rápidamente a la cocina con su muñeca en la mano.

—¡Mamá! Vamos a El Corte Inglés. Quiero otra muñeca.
—Elena se rió,° luego le contestó a su hija.
—¿Cómo? ¿El Corte Inglés? Ah sí, Rita. El Corte Inglés va a tener una rebaja grande. Lo oí en la radio. ¿Por qué no vamos el sábado? Necesitamos otro televisor porque el nuestro ya no funciona bien.
—¡Qué bueno, mamá! Y yo quiero comprar otra muñeca. ¿Ves mi muñeca? Está muy vieja. ¿Me compras otra nueva, mamá?
—Pues, vamos a ver, hija. Paciencia, ¿eh?

laughed

El próximo sábado a las once de la mañana, Elena y Rita fueron a El Corte Inglés para aprovecharse de la fabulosa Rebaja del Año. Ellas subieron al tercer piso (2) donde se venden muebles° y artículos eléctricos. Allí una dependiente le saludó a Elena.

—Buenos días. ¿En qué puedo servirle, señora?
—Quiero ver el televisor Sony que está rebajado.
—Cómo no, señora. Aquí está. Es una ganga por 29.500 pesetas.
—¡Por Dios! Pero es tan pequeño.
—Sí, señora. Tenemos otros televisores más grandes, pero no están rebajados en este momento.
—Bueno, muchas gracias.
—De nada, señora. Hasta luego.

Elena y Rita subieron al cuarto piso donde se venden juguetes, muñecas, bicicletas y juegos. Allí Elena habló con otra dependiente.

Tell students that reading passages usually contain cues that can help them make predictions about what actions and events are most likely to occur in the reading. For example, as they read the *En contexto,* tell them to notice the following cues: certain words and phrases that signal the beginning of a sentence or a paragraph, dashes indicate the beginning of conversation, and exclamation marks suggest surprise, hesitation, anger, and other emotions.

Read the announcement aloud with the emphasis used in actual TV commercials.

—Dígame, señora.

—Mi hija quiere ver la muñeca Gimnasta que está rebajada.

cries

—Lo siento, señora, pero ya las vendimos todas ayer. Pero hay otras muñcas y todas están rebajadas hoy. Por ejemplo, ésta llora° y también dice cosas en español y catalán. (3) Cuesta solamente 3.240 pesetas.

—Ah, ¿sí?— dijo Elena. ¿Te gusta la muñeca, Rita?

—Sí, mamá. ¡Me gusta mucho!

—Pues, te la compro. Aquí tiene usted mi tarjeta de crédito, señorita.

—Gracias.

Notas de texto

1. The sale takes place on Friday and Saturday because most stores in Spain are closed on Sundays.

2. In Hispanic countries, the *tercer piso* of a department store is what Americans call the fourth floor, not the third floor. The reason for this is that the street-level or entrance floor is called *la planta baja* (abbreviated *PB* in elevators). Therefore, the second floor is called *el primer piso*, the third floor is *el segundo piso*, etc. The floor below the *planta baja* is called *el sótano*, and there may be several of them (e.g., *Sótano 1*, *Sótano 2*).

3. Catalán is the co-official language (with Spanish) spoken in the autonomy *(comunidad autónoma)* of *Cataluña*, or Catalonia of which Barcelona is the capital. Closely akin to Provençal, Catalán is also spoken in the autonomy of Valencia, the Balearic Islands, in parts of southwestern France, and in western Sardinia. The total population of Catalán speakers is about 10,540,000 people.

¿Comprendió Ud.?

Lea la lectura rápidamente. Luego conteste las siguientes preguntas.

1.*a* 2.*b* 3.*a* 4.*d* 5.*b* 6.*c*
7. [open] 8. [open]

1. La idea más importante del anuncio comercial es:
   a. ¡Ahorre en El Corte Inglés!
   b. ¡Traiga su tarjeta de crédito!
   c. ¡Compre un artículo eléctrico!

2. En El Corte Inglés...
   a. todo estaba rebajado.   c. siempre hay gangas.
   b. hubo una buena rebaja.   d. los precios eran altos.

3. Ese almacén tiene una rebaja...
   a. una vez cada año.   c. cada dos fines de semana.
   b. los fines de semana.   d. los viernes y los sábados.

4. Rita supo de la rebaja...
   - a. de una amiga.
   - b. del periódico.
   - c. de la radio.
   - d. de la televisión.

5. Elena y Rita fueron de compras...
   - a. por la tarde.
   - b. antes de almorzar.
   - c. después de cenar.
   - d. el viernes pasado.

6. Elena...
   - a. compró una muñeca gimnasta.
   - b. compró un televisor pequeño.
   - c. le compró una muñeca a Rita.
   - d. no compró nada en el almacén.

Ahora hágale las siguientes preguntas a otro(a) estudiante.

7. De todas las cosas rebajadas en El Corte Inglés, ¿cuál te gustaría comprar? ¿Qué cosas no te interesan nada de allí, y por qué? ¿Cuáles son algunas características de un buen almacén?

8. ¿Cómo son las dos dependientes de El Corte Inglés? ¿Cómo son los dependientes que trabajan en tu almacén favorito? ¿Cuáles son algunas características de un(a) dependiente ideal?

NOTAS CULTURALES

Los almacenes hispanos

Hay almacenes muy grandes en todas las ciudades grandes de España y de Latinoamérica. La mayoría de los almacenes se abren° a las diez y no se cierran° hasta las ocho y, a veces, más tarde. Aquí se venden cosas para el hogar° como, por ejemplo, electrodomésticos, muebles y plantas. También hay ropa para niños, jóvenes, damas y caballeros, y cosméticos, artículos eléctricos y equipo fotográfico. En algunos almacenes hay un supermercado y una cafetería, y muchos tienen un aparcamiento para los autos de sus clientes.

En los almacenes se paga en efectivo,° con tarjeta de crédito o con un cheque personal. Algunos almacenes tienen su propia tarjeta de crédito como El Corte Inglés y Galerías Preciados en España. Además, muchos almacenes aceptan tarjetas de crédito internacionales como Visa, MasterCard y American Express.

se abren open   **se cierran** close   **hogar** home   **en efectivo** cash

Use this cultural note as a point of departure for a discussion on what items and services North American department stores offer customers compared with, for example, *El Corte Inglés* (where one may obtain a hunter's license, exchange money, and hire an interpreter).

TPR activity: Tell students you are going to review formal commands in Spanish. Explain that you will read aloud a series of commands that the students should pantomime to verify that they have understood you. *Bueno, imagínense que ahora ustedes van de compras a El Corte Inglés. 1. Busquen su chaqueta. 2. Póngansela. 3. Salgan de la casa. 4. Caminen hasta el almacén. 5. Entren y vayan al Departamento de Ropa. 6. Miren la ropa que se vende allí. 7. Seleccionen algo que les interese. 8. Vayan ustedes a la caja con la ropa. 9. Saluden al dependiente. 10. Saquen su dinero o tarjeta de crédito. 11. Paguen la ropa. 12. Denle las gracias al dependiente. 13. Vuelvan a casa.*

Charla.

Converse con un(a) compañero(a) de clase.

Imagínate que ahora tú y yo estamos en el almacén de la foto.

1. ¿A qué planta te gustaría ir primero? ¿Por qué?
2. Y después, ¿a qué planta quieres ir y qué vas a hacer allí?
3. ¿Dónde podemos comer algo en el almacén?
4. ¿En qué planta puedo comprar un regalo para un(a) amigo(a)? ¿Qué debo comprarle?

VOCABULARIO ÚTIL

TRANSPARENCY No. 21:
Personal Possessions

Cómo comprar en un almacén o en una tienda

In this section you will learn to identify and buy merchandise in department stores and non-food specialty shops.

Los artículos eléctricos

Have your students bring from home large color photographs of the merchandise illustrated here from magazines, brochures, leaflets, and newspapers. Mount the photos on paperboard, and use them to teach and review this vocabulary.

la máquina de escribir

el secador de pelo

la computadora

el juego de video

la grabadora

el disco compacto

la impresora

la calculadora

la maquina de afeitar

If you wish, you could add more words to this category, such as *los lentes (telefoto/de ángulo ancho), el estuche de cámara (videocámara), la pila, el proyector.*

Equipo fotográfico

la cámara

los rollos para fotos

las casetas de video

las diapositivas

la videocámara

En la joyería

los relojes

los collares

los aretes

los anillos

los brazaletes

En la papelería

los sobres

el papel
para cartas

el álbum
de fotos

los lápices

los bolígrafos

las tarjetas postales

Tell students that another word for *anillos* is *sortijas,* another word for *brazaletes* is *pulseras,* and another word for *aretes* is *(los) pendientes.* You could also add *las cadenas* as well as *la plata* and *el oro.*

You could give students a list of other speciality stores such as: *camisería, cristalería, florería, juguetería, librería, mueblería, perfumería, relojería, sombrerería, tabaquería, zapatería.* Then have students use a bilingual dictionary to look up words for items sold in those stores. Afterwards, the students could share their vocabulary lists in small groups.

Cómo hablar con los dependientes

—¿Hay una rebaja de juguetes hoy?
—Sí, aproveche y ahorre.
—¿Qué gangas tiene usted?
—Pues, esta muñeca que se ríe y llora está muy barata.
—Está bonita. ¿Cuánto cuesta?
—Solamente dos mil pesetas.
—No está cara. Me la llevo.
—¿Quiere usted pagarla a crédito?
—No. Pago en efectivo.

Is there a toy sale today?
Yes, take advantage and save.
What bargains do you have?
Well, this doll that laughs and cries is very inexpensive.
It's pretty. How much is it?
Only two thousand pesetas.
It's not expensive. I'll take it.
Do you want to charge it?
No. I'll pay in cash.

Have pairs of students role-play this short dialogue, then switch roles and act it out again.

Practiquemos

A. En categorías.

1. En un papel separado organice todas las palabras en estas seis categorías:

| **Ropa** | **Juguetes** | **Equipo fotográfico** |
| **Muebles** | **Accesorios** | **Artículos eléctricos** |

anillos, anteojos para el sol, aretes, armarios, aspiradoras, bicicletas, blusas, bolsas, botas, brazaletes, calcetines, calculadoras, cámaras, camas, camisas, camisetas, cintas de video, collares, computadoras, corbatas, chaquetas, despertadores, discos compactos, escritorios, estufas, faldas, grabadoras, hornos de microondas, impresoras, joyas, juegos de video, juegos electrónicos, lámparas, lavadoras, lavaplatos, máquinas de afeitar, máquinas de escribir, medias, mesas, mochilas, muñecas, pantalones, paraguas,

Ex. A.
1. This exercise recycles many vocabulary items introduced in previous lessons and, at the same time, integrates new words introduced in this lesson.
2. Before beginning this activity, use illustrations from your picture file to review the Spanish names for the articles listed here.

películas en video, pijamas, relojes, rollos para diapositivas, rollos para fotos, secadoras, secadores de pelo, sillas, sillones, sombreros, suéteres, teléfonos, televisores, tocadores, tostadores, trajes de baño, trajes, vestidos, videocámaras, videocaseteras, zapatos

2. Compare sus listas con las listas de otro(a) estudiante.

3. Hágale las siguientes preguntas a su compañero(a) de clase.
   a. ¿Qué cosas ya **tienes** de cada categoría?
   b. ¿Qué cosas **necesitas** de tus listas?
   c. ¿Qué cosas **quieres** comprar? ¿Por qué?

Ex. B. Follow-up activities:
1. Have students ask you some of these questions, using appropriate formal language.
2. Have students write their answers to these questions at home.

B. Entrevista. Hable con un(a) compañero(a) de clase.

De compras

1. ¿Con qué frecuencia compras en un almacén? ¿Cómo se llama tu almacén favorito? ¿Por qué te gusta tanto? ¿Cuándo fue la última vez que fuiste allí? ¿Qué compraste? ¿Pagaste con cheque, a crédito o en efectivo?

2. ¿Tienes pocas o muchas joyas? ¿Por ejemplo? ¿Cuándo fué la última vez que fuiste a una joyería? ¿Qué compraste allí? ¿Te costó (costaron) mucho o poco?

3. ¿Escribes pocas o muchas cartas? ¿y tarjetas postales? ¿A quiénes les escribes? ¿Prefieres escribir en una máquina de escribir, en una computadora, con bolígrafo o con lápiz? Normalmente, ¿dónde compras los artículos que necesitas para escribir y mandar cartas y tarjetas postales?

Diversiones

4. ¿Con qué frecuencia sacas fotos? ¿De quiénes y de qué sacas fotos? ¿Qué tipo de cámara o videocámara tienes? ¿Dónde la compraste? ¿Cuántos rollos para fotos o para diapositivas (¿Cuántas casetas de video...) compras al año? ¿Cuántos álbumes de fotos tienes? ¿Quién sacó las fotos? ¿Contiene tu álbum fotos de cuando eras niño(a)? (¿Sí? Háblame de esas fotos, por favor.)

5. ¿Con qué frecuencia juegas a los juegos de video? ¿Cuál es tu juego de video favorito? ¿Dónde y con quién lo juegas? ¿Con qué frecuencia lo juegas? ¿Lo jugabas también cuando eras niño(a)? ¿Con quién?

6. ¿Con qué frecuencia escuchas cintas en una grabadora? ¿Qué tipo de cintas escuchas? ¿Tienes un disco compacto? ¿Qué tipo de música prefieres escuchar en tu grabadora o disco compacto?

C. ¡Felicidades! Dos amigos de Elena Navarro, Daniel y Cecilia, van a casarse pronto. Lea cada situación. Luego escriba a qué tienda cada persona va y qué cosas va a comprar allí.

Ejemplo: Daniel y Cecilia necesitan comprar sus anillos de matrimonio.
Van a una joyería para comprarlos.

Situaciones

1. Ellos tienen que comprar algunas tarjetas de invitación.
2. Los jóvenes necesitan pedir la comida para la recepción.
3. También ellos tienen que pedir una torta de matrimonio.
4. Daniel quiere comprar una camisa blanca para la ocasión.
5. Cecilia y su madre van a llevar rosas rojas a la iglesia.
6. Daniel y Cecilia van a vivir en un apartamento, pero tienen solamente un refrigerador, una estufa y un lavaplatos.
7. Daniel quiere comprarle algo muy especial a su novia Cecilia.
8. Cecilia también tiene ganas de comprarle algo a Daniel.
9. Daniel y Cecilia quieren recordar su día especial para siempre.
10. Los dos novios quieren darles las gracias a todos por sus regalos.

Tiendas

joyería	**mueblería**	**papelería**
florería	**zapatería**	**carnicería**
librería	**relojería**	**pastelería**
panadería	**camisería**	**perfumería**

Compare lo que usted escribió con las decisiones de un(a) compañero(a) de clase.

D. En El Corte Inglés. Converse con un(a) compañero(a) de clase, usando vocabulario de esta sección.

Ex. D. Allow students time to role-play these personalized dialogues several times with different conversation partners.

Dependiente	Cliente
1. Buenos(as) _____ . ¿En qué...?	2. Estoy buscando un(a) _____ .
3. Pues, tenemos... ¿Le gusta?	4. No mucho porque... Quiero...
5. Cómo no. Aquí tiene usted...	6. ¿Cuánto cuesta?
7. _____ .	8. ¿Está rebajado(a)?
9. _____ .	10. Bueno, me (lo/la) llevo.
11. Muy bien. ¿Quiere otra cosa?	12. _____ , gracias.
13. [Termine la conversación.]	14. _____ .

GRAMÁTICA FUNCIONAL

Expressing different kinds of information

—Hoy por la tarde voy a una joyería.
—¿Por qué vas allí, Elena?
—Quiero comprar un brazalete para mi sobrina.

Uses of *por*

You may have noticed that the prepositions *por* and *para* have different uses and meanings. The preposition *por* has a wider range of uses than *para*.

Do not expect students to always use *por* and *para* correctly in speaking and writing Spanish; accuracy takes time and practice. For now, concentrate on the most common uses of these two prepositions: *por* (duration of time and idiomatic expressions); *para* (recipient and purpose).

Have students role-play these short dialogues in pairs.

In general, *por* conveys the underlying idea of a cause, reason, or source behind an action.

1. Duration of time (for, in, during)
   —¿**Por cuánto tiempo** viviste en España?
   —Viví allí **por más de tres años.**
   —¿Trabajas en el almacén todo el día?
   —Sí, **por la mañana** y **por la tarde.**

2. Gratitude (for)
   —Gracias **por** todo, señora Navarro.
   —De nada. ¡Hasta luego, Magda!

3. On behalf of (for)
   —Gracias **por** llevar a tu mamá al centro.
   —De nada, papá. Lo hice **por ti.**

4. In place of (for)
   —Yo no sabía que trabajas aquí, Tomás.
   —Trabajo **por** Juan, que está muy enfermo.

5. Motion (through, along)
   —¿Quieres caminar conmigo **por el parque**?
   —No. Prefiero caminar **por la Calle Sexta.**

6. Mistaken identity (for)
   —En España me tomaron **por canadiense.**
   —¿Sabes qué? ¡Me tomaron **por mexicana**!

7. Value or cost (for)
   —¿Cuánto pagaste **por esos zapatos,** Elena?
   —Pagué 9.600 pesetas **por los dos pares.**

8. In exchange (for)
   —¿Desea cambiar esta blusa, dijo usted?
   —Sí, señorita... **por** una de color rosado.

9. Unit of measurement (by, per)
   —En el mercado venden pescado **por kilo.**
   —Sí, también venden huevos **por docena.**

10. General area (around)
    —Perdón, ¿hay una juguetería **por aquí**?
    —Sí, señorita. Hay una **por allí,** ¿ve?

11. Reason (because of)
    —¿**Por qué** llegaste tan tarde al centro?
    —Llegué tarde **por el tráfico** tan tremendo.

12. Purpose (for, after)
    —¿Vas a la oficina **por tu cheque,** Magda?
    —Sí, y después voy a la tienda **por leche.**

13. Idiomatic expressions
    —Quiero probarme estos aretes, **por favor.**
    —¡**Por Dios!** Le quedan bien con esa blusa.

Uses of *para*

In general, *para* conveys the underlying idea of purpose, use, and destination.

1. Recipient (for)
   —Estos regalos son **para ti,** mi hija.
   —¿**Para mí**? ¡Qué bonitos! Muchas gracias.

2. Employment (for)
   —¿**Para quién** trabajas ahora, Magda?
   —Trabajo **para mi papá** en su tienda.

3. Specific time (by, for)
   —¿**Para cuándo** necesita el traje, señora?
   —Lo necesito **para el próximo sábado.**

4. Destination (to)
   —¿**Para dónde** sales mañana por la tarde?
   —Salgo **para Madrid.** ¿Quieres ir conmigo?

5. Purpose (in order to) [followed by infinitive]
   —¿Por qué estudias inglés, Magdalena?
   —Lo estudio **para hablar** con los turistas.

Practiquemos

A. ¿Es usted una persona generosa? Primero, indique con números con qué frecuencia hace usted las siguientes actividades. Luego calcule el promedio *(average)* para determinar su generosidad.

Pocas veces = 1   Algunas veces = 2   Muchas veces = 3

_____ Hago cosas para servir a mi comunidad.
_____ Invito a mis amigos a mi casa para comer.
_____ Trabajo como voluntario(a) para servir a otros.
_____ Para mí, es mejor dar asistencia que recibirla.
_____ Compro muchos regalos para mis parientes y amigos.
_____ Escucho a mis amigos para comprender sus problemas.
_____ Le doy a la gente pobre comida y ropa para vivir mejor.
_____ No espero recibir las gracias por los favores que hago.
_____ Escribo o leo cartas para gente mayor que está enferma.
_____ Hago favores por otras personas para ponerlas contentas.
_____ TOTAL

Interpretaciones

24–30   ¡Usted es una de las personas más generosas del mundo!

17–23   Usted es bueno(a). ¡Probablemente tiene muchos amigos!

10–16   Usted es un poco egoísta. ¡Debe tener más compasión!

B. Queridos padres... Elena les escribió la siguiente carta a sus padres. Complétela apropiadamente con las preposiciones **por** y **para.**

Gracias _____ vuestra carta. Todo va bien _____ aquí, pero no contesté la carta _____ dos semanas porque estoy bien ocupada. _____ la mañana trabajo _____ una amiga en su pastelería y _____ la tarde trabajo en una panadería.

Esta mañana fui a una zapatería _____ comprar botas _____ Rita. Las quería comprar _____ su cumpleaños. Pagué 4.000 pesetas _____ las botas pero están muy buenas.

Cuando volvía a casa _____ la Avenida Ramblas un turista me paró _____ hacerme una pregunta. ¿Sabéis qué? No comprendí la pregunta porque me la hizo en inglés. ¡_____ Dios! ¡Tengo que estudiar inglés!

Bueno, eso es todo _____ ahora. Ahora tengo que ir a la farmacia _____ comprar medicina _____ una amiga que está enferma. Les escribo pronto.

Abrazos de vuestra Elena

C. Una encuesta *(survey).* Una empleada de El Corte Inglés está haciéndole a Elena algunas preguntas. Complete su conversación, usando las preposiciones **para** o **por** en sus respuestas.

Ex. A.
1. After students have completed this exercise, have them compare their results with a classmate.
2. Calculate the average score of your class, then discuss the results.

Ex. B. Answers:
Paragraph 1: *por, por, por, Por, para, por*
Paragraph 2: *para, para, para, por*
Paragraph 3: *por, para, Por*
Paragraph 4: *por, para, por*

Ex. C. Follow-up activity: Have students role play the dialogue twice with a classmate, changing roles once.

Empleada

1. ¿ _____ qué compra usted aquí, señora?

3. ¿ _____ qué decidió usted venir aquí esta mañana?

5. ¿Cuándo le gusta venir aquí _____ comprar, señora?

7. Veo que usted compró algunos lápices. ¿Cuánto pagó?

9. ¿ _____ quién los compró?

11. ¿Le pasó a usted una cosa interesante aquí hoy?

13. Permítame otra pregunta, _____ favor: ¿Qué impresión tiene usted de El Corte Inglés?

15. Gracias _____ su cooperación, señora.

Elena

2. _____ los buenos precios. Hay muchas gangas todos los días.

4. _____ aprovecharme de las rebajas.

6. Los sábados _____ la mañana.

8. 450 pesetas _____ docena.

10. _____ mi hija de seis años.

12. Sí, alguien me tomó _____ una de las dependientes. ¡Ja, ja!

14. _____ mí, es un almacén fabuloso.

16. De nada.

Charlemos

D. En la tienda de ropa. Imagínese que usted y otro(a) estudiante están en una tienda de ropa en Barcelona. Conversen ustedes, usando las preposiciones **por** y **para** donde hay líneas (_____) y otras palabras donde hay tres puntos (...).

Cliente

1. ¿Perdón, ¿se venden trajes _____ aquí?

3. Es un regalo _____ mi ...

5. Usa una (camisa/blusa) talla...

7. Pues, ..., creo yo. Prefiero el color ...

9. _____ el próximo sábado _____ la tarde. ¿Cuánto cuesta?

11. Muy bien. Lo llevo. Gracias _____ todo.

Dependiente

2. Sí, (señor/señorita/señora). ¿ _____ caballero o _____ dama?

4. ¿Qué talla usa (él/ella), _____ favor?

6. ¿Y la talla de los pantalones, (señor / señorita/señora)?

8. Es bonito, ¿no? ¿ _____ cuándo necesita usted el traje?

10. _____ usted, puedo vendérselo _____ ... pesetas.

12. De nada, (señor/señorita/señora). Adiós.

E. De compras. Hágale las siguientes preguntas a otro(a) estudiante. Él /Ella debe contestar usando las preposiciones **por** o **para,** como en el ejemplo.

Ejemplo: ¿Por qué compras ropa rebajada?
Para ahorrar un poco de dinero.

1. ¿Por qué te gusta ir a los centros comerciales?
2. ¿Para qué centros comerciales te gusta ir?
3. ¿Cuándo prefieres ir de compras allí?
4. ¿Por qué vas de tienda en tienda cuando vas de compras?
5. ¿Para quién compras la ropa en los centros comerciales?
6. ¿Cómo pagas tus compras: en efectivo, con cheque personal o con tarjeta de crédito? ¿Por qué?

NOTAS CULTURALES

Las tiendas especializadas

Las pequeñas tiendas que se especializan en ciertas mercancías° son más comunes en los países de habla española que en los Estados Unidos o en el Canadá. En general, estas tiendas se abren a las nueve y se cierran entre la una y las tres de la tarde durante la hora del almuerzo, luego se cierran otra vez a las siete. Muy pocas tiendas están abiertas los domingos y los días festivos.

merchandise

En la *Lección 10* usted aprendió los nombres de algunas tiendas especializadas como, por ejemplo: la panadería, la carnicería y la pastelería. A veces, se encuentran dos tiendas combinadas en una sola tienda, por ejemplo: una joyería-relojería o una lavandería-tintorería.° Otras tiendas especializadas tienen dos nombres para el mismo tipo de tienda, por ejemplo: en México se compran aspirinas en una farmacia, en una botica o en una droguería. En otros países se pueden comprar flores en una florería o en una floristería. Los hombres y las mujeres van a una peluquería° para un corte de pelo, pero solamente los hombres van a una barbería. En la mayoría de las tiendas especializadas, los precios son fijos, y los clientes casi siempre pagan en efectivo, con cheque o a crédito también.

dry cleaner's

hair salon

Charla

1. Dígale a otro(a) estudiante qué se vende en las siguientes tiendas especializadas.

TRANSPARENCY No. 22: Shopping Mall

Ejemplo: joyería → *Se venden joyas.*

florería	mueblería	juguetería
librería	zapatería	tabaquería
relojería	papelería	cristalería
camisería	perfumería	sombrerería

2. Imagínese que en este momento usted está en una de estas tiendas especializadas ya mencionadas. Converse con un(a) compañero(a) de clase; una persona es el/la dependiente y la otra persona es su cliente. Hagan preguntas sobre los productos y los precios. Discutan apropiadamente. No olvide *(don't forget)* saludarse y despedirse.

1. Point out that adverbs ending in -mente are not used as frequently in Spanish as their English equivalent adverbs ending in **-ly.** (Therefore, they are introduced at this point in the textbook.)
2. As an oral exercise, say each of the following adjectives and have students give the adverbial form (e.g., exacto → exactamente): natural, especial, perfecto, fácil, rápido, regular, completo, inmediato, paciente, puntual, franco, frecuente, básico.
3. Have students role-play the short dialogues on this page.
4. If you wish, explain and illustrate how adverbs can modify adjectives and other adverbs (e.g., Mi profesor[a] habla bien rápido; Usted habla demasiado rápidamente, profesor[a]).

If you wish, explain: sólo = only; solo = alone, lonely → solamente = only.

GRAMÁTICA FUNCIONAL

Describing how and how often

—Voy a la tienda frecuentemente.
—¿Compras muchas cosas?
—Naturalmente. Mi familia es grande.

Use of adverbs (summary)

An adverb is a word that modifies a verb, an adjective, or another adverb. It may describe how, when, where, why, or how much. You already know many adverbs such as *muy, ayer, siempre, después,* and *mucho.*

How to form adverbs

1. For most Spanish adverbs, add *-mente* (English -ly) to an adjective.

natural → natural**mente** *naturally*
frecuente → frecuent**emente** *frequently*

2. If an adjective ends in *-o,* change the *-o* to *-a,* then add *-mente.*

perfect**o** → perfect**a** → **perfectamente** *perfectly*

3. If an adjective has an accent mark, the adverb retains it.

fácil → **fácilmente** *easily*
rápido → **rápidamente** *rapidly*

> **¡CUIDADO!** Because Spanish adverbs do not modify nouns, they do not change for agreement of gender and number; therefore, they have only one form.

Other adverbs and adverbial expressions

In previous lessons, you learned many adverbs and adverbial expressions that are listed below with their English equivalents.

1. Use the following adverbs to express how often something is done.

una vez	*once*	**nunca**	*never*
otra vez	*again*	**siempre**	*always*
dos veces	*twice*	**casi siempre**	*almost always*
a veces	*sometimes*	**cada día**	*each (every) day*
muchas veces	*very often*	**todos los años**	*every year*

—Voy al mercado **cada día.**   *I go to the market every day.*
—**Siempre** voy allí los martes.   *I always go there on Tuesdays.*

2. Use the following adverbs to express the order of events.

primero	*first*	**después**	*afterwards*
luego	*then*	**finalmente**	*finally*
entonces	*then, so*	**por fin**	*at last, finally*

—¿Adónde vamos **primero,** mamá? *Where are we going first, Mom?*
—Al cine. **Luego** al mercado.   *To the movies. Then to the market.*
—¿Y **después**?   *And afterwards?*
—Volvemos a casa.   *We're going back home.*

Practiquemos

A. Algunos parientes de Elena. Complete lógicamente las conversaciones entre Elena y su amiga Sara.

Ejemplo: ELENA: Tienes un examen mañana, ¿verdad?
       SARA: Sí, pero no tengo ganas de estudiar.
       ELENA: Debes comenzar a estudiar *inmediatamente.*
           (inmediato/natural)

1. SARA: Mi tía Mariana no tiene trabajo ahora.
  ELENA: ¿Qué hace todos los días?
  SARA: Busca trabajo _____ . (intensivo/triste)
2. ELENA: Mi hermano Pepe está ocupado por la tarde.
  SARA: Pero siempre almuerza, ¿verdad?
  ELENA: Sí, pero almuerza _____. (fácil/rápido)
3. SARA: Mi prima Lucía es pianista.
  ELENA: ¿Cómo toca el piano, Sara?
  SARA: Lo toca _____. (perfecto/incorrecto)
4. ELENA: Mi papá siempre está nervioso.
  SARA: Pues, ¿qué puedo hacer yo, Rita?
  ELENA: Puedes hablarle _____ . (paciente/frecuente)
5. ELENA: Mi mamá estuvo un poco enferma ayer.
  SARA: ¿Tomó ella alguna medicina, Rita?
  ELENA: No, pero descansó en la cama _____ . (puntual/tranquilo)

B. Rebaja del Año. Complete los siguientes párrafos con las apropiadas frases adverbiales de las listas.

allí	**una vez**	**el próximo día**
cuando	**primero**	**la semana pasada**

_____ hubo una rebaja en El Corte Inglés. Esa rebaja ocurre _____ al año. _____ abrieron las puertas del almacén el viernes a las nueve de la mañana, muchas personas entraron para aprovecharse de las rebajas.

_____ a las once y media Elena y Rita fueron al almacén. _____ subieron al tercer piso donde se venden aparatos eléctricos. _____ Elena miró un televisor pequeño, pero no le gustó.

ya	luego	mientras
ayer	un poco	solamente

_____ Elena y Rita subieron al cuarto piso donde se venden los juguetes. Elena habló con la dependiente _____ su hija jugaba con las muñecas.

—Lo siento, señora, pero _____ vendimos todas las muñecas Gimnasta _____.

Rita estaba _____ triste cuando oyó eso, pero se puso contenta cuando su mamá le compró una muñeca que toma, llora y habla español y catalán. La muñeca costó _____ 3.240 pesetas.

C. Los fines de semana. En un papel separado escriba cuatro párrafos sobre cómo pasaba usted típicamente los fines de semana cuando era niño(a), y cómo los pasa usted ahora. Use las siguientes frases como guía.

Cuando era niño(a), me gustaban los fines de semana porque... A veces los sábados por la mañana mis amigos y yo íbamos a... Allí hacíamos varias cosas; por ejemplo,... Luego, por la tarde íbamos a... donde... Por la noche nos gustaba...

Casi todos los domingos por la mañana me levantaba a las... Primero,...Luego,... Después,... Por la tarde me gustaba..., pero muchas veces prefería... Los domingos por la noche...

Todavía me gustan los fines de semana porque... A veces los sábados por la mañana mis amigos y yo vamos a... Allí hacemos varias cosas; por ejemplo,... Luego, por la tarde vamos a... donde... Por la noche nos gusta...

Casi todos los domingos por la mañana me levanto a las... Primero,... Luego,... Después,... Por la tarde me gusta..., pero muchas veces prefiero... Los domingos por la noche...

Charlemos

D. Actividades familiares. Cuéntele a otro(a) estudiante algunas actividades que hacen sus parientes.

Ejemplo: _Mi papá me llama por teléfono frecuentemente._

¿Quién(es)?	¿Qué hace(n)?	¿Con qué frecuencia?
Mi papá (mamá)	venir a visitarme	a veces
Mi tío(a)	escribirme una carta	casi cada mes
Mis primos	llamarme por teléfono	una vez al día
Mi abuelo(a)	darme un regalo bonito	frecuentemente
Mi hermano(a)	jugar al béisbol (golf)	todos los años
Mi(s) _____	ir de compras (al cine)	cada fin de semana

E. Los quehaceres. Forme preguntas según el ejemplo. Luego hágale las preguntas a otro(a) estudiante. Él/Ella debe responder apropiadamente con **"Sí, casi siempre"**, **"Sí, a veces"**, **"No, casi nunca"** o **"Tampoco"**.

Ejemplo: lavar los platos después de cenar
A: *¿Lavas los platos después de cenar?*
B: *Sí, a veces. ¿Y tú?*
A: *Sí, casi siempre. Y de niña, ¿lavabas los platos después de cenar?*
B: *No, casi nunca. ¿Y tú?*
A: *Tampoco.*

1. lavar los platos después de desayunar
2. sacar la basura de la cocina de tu casa
3. hacer la cama todos los días antes de salir
4. poner la mesa para el almuerzo los domingos
5. limpiar la casa, especialmente tu dormitorio
6. pasar la aspiradora en la alfombra de la sala

F. ¿Cómo o cuánto lo hacen? Converse con un(a) compañero(a) de clase, usando adverbios apropiados.

Ejemplo: Voy al supermercado *frecuentemente.*

1. _____ compro leche y pan en el supermercado.
2. Voy al centro comercial _____ porque me gusta.
3. Allí busco gangas _____ para ahorrar dinero.
4. Cuando encuentro una ganga, la compro _____ .
5. Voy de compras _____ cuando hay una rebaja.
6. Puedo encontrar _____ la ropa rebajada.
7. _____ llego a casa con ninguna compra.

PARA LEER MEJOR

Using Format Clues

Printed material often contains different kinds of cues that can help you skim, scan, and guess meaning. For example, some words and phrases appear in large, boldface, or italic print to attract the reader's attention. Some words are repeated several times to persuade the reader. And other words appear together with a graphic design to help the reader remember a particular concept.

Activities

A. Skim the following printed materials, then respond to these three items.
   1. What do you think El Corte Inglés is?

2. What do you think is the main purpose of this advertisement?
3. Check the cues that most helped you to reach those conclusions.

_____ type of print used in ad   _____ my knowledge of the subject

_____ certain words and phrases   _____ my experience in reading ads

_____ the layout of the ad itself   _____ the graphic designs in the ad

B. Scan the printed materials to find the information that answers the following items.

1. According to the headline in the ad, the main feature that El Corte Inglés has to offer is . . .

    a. its own credit card   c. superb, efficient service

    b. many customer services   d. friendly, helpful employees

2. El Corte Inglés does **not** have . . .

    a. a laundromat   c. household products

    b. a travel agency   d. childcare services

3. Which words, phrases, and symbols are readers most likely to remember after reading this ad, and why?

EL CORTE INGLÉS CUENTA CON 16 GRANDES CENTROS COMERCIALES REPARTIDOS POR TODA ESPAÑA, DEDICADOS A LA MODA Y SUS COMPLEMENTOS, EL HOGAR, LA DECORACIÓN, LOS DEPORTES... PERO, ADEMÁS CADA CENTRO DE **EL CORTE INGLÉS** ES TODO UN MUNDO DE ATENCIONES Y SERVICIOS: AGENCIA DE VIAJES, CAMBIO DE MONEDA EXTRANJERA, CARTA DE COMPRAS, RESTAURANTES-CAFETERÍA, BOUTIQUES INTERNACIONALES, SOUVENIRS Y ARTÍCULOS TURÍSTICOS, ADMISIÓN DE TARJETAS DE CRÉDITO... TODO PARA HACER MÁS FÁCILES SUS COMPRAS.

PARA ESCRIBIR MEJOR

Atajo

Functions:
Talking about daily
routines; talking about
past events; linking ideas

Vocabulary:
House: bathroom; toilet;
office; studies; time
expressions

Grammar:
Verbs: reflexives, irregular
preterite, imperfect;
Personal pronouns:
reciprocal *se, nos;* Adverbs;
Prepositions: *por, para*

Writing a Past Narrative

A past narrative tells a story of conditions, actions and events that occurred in a chronological order. The writer must help the reader to follow this order easily by showing the time relationship between sentences.

To show the sequence of time in a past narrative, link sentences together using the following expressions, as shown in the example.

a las siete	*at 7 o'clock*	**en ese momento**	*at that moment*
anoche	*last night*	**entonces**	*then*
anteayer	*the day before yesterday*	**hasta las ocho**	*until 8 o'clock*
antes de + infinitive	*before (-ing)*	**la semana pasada**	*last week*
ayer	*yesterday*	**luego**	*then*
cuando	*when*	**más tarde**	*later*
de repente	*suddenly*	**mientras tanto**	*meanwhile*
después	*afterwards*	**por fin**	*finally*
después de + infinitive	*after (-ing)*	**por media hora**	*for a half-hour*
el mes pasado	*last month*	**primero**	*first*
el próximo día	*the next day*	**un poco después**	*a bit afterwards*

Example:

> *La semana pasada* estuve muy ocupada con mis clases y mi trabajo. Todos los días me levantaba *a las siete de la mañana. Después de* bañarme y vestirme, desayunaba con mi familia. Salía para la escuela *a las ocho* y llegaba allí *un poco después.* En la escuela hablaba con mis amigos *por media hora, luego* iba a mi primera clase, biología, que me gustaba mucho. Pasaba *toda la mañana* en mis clases.

> *Por la tarde* almorzaba en la cafetería, *entonces* iba a la biblioteca donde estudiaba *por dos horas. Después,* volvía a casa y descansaba un poco. *A las tres y media* iba a mi trabajo en un restaurante. Siempre ceno allí porque la comida está rica.

> *Ayer* trabajé *hasta las ocho, luego* regresé a casa y estudié *por dos o tres horas. Más tarde* miré la televisión o hablé con mis amigos por teléfono. *Por fin,* me acosté *a las once* porque estaba muy cansada.

Activities

A. Write a past narrative summarizing what Elena and Rita did last week. Use the time expressions above to link together your sentences as you have just seen in the example composition.

B. Write a past narrative summarizing what you did last week. Again, use the time expressions above to link your sentences and paragraphs together.

SÍNTESIS

¡A ver!

You are going to watch Carmen buying a train ticket and Miguel buying different items in a pharmacy. First, study the questions and their meaning in the *Vocabulario esencial*. Second, read the four questions in the activity below. Third, watch the videotape, then answer the questions in the activity.

Vocabulario esencial

¿Me dice el precio?	*Would you tell me the price?*
¿Qué hay?	*How's everything?*
¿Algo más?	*Anything else?*
¿Eso es todo?	*Is that all?*
¿Cuánto es?	*How much is it?*

En la agencia de viajes

Answers: *1. Clase turista = 9.100 pesetas, Clase preferente = 12.800 pesetas, Clase club = 16.500 pesetas 2. con tarjeta de crédito 3. 840 pesetas 4. en efectivo*

1. ¿Cuánto cuestan los billetes para cada clase de servicio en el tren?
   Clase turista _____ pesetas
   Clase preferente _____ pesetas
   Clase club _____ pesetas

2. ¿Cómo quiere pagar Carmen los billetes?
   _____ en efectivo
   _____ con cheque personal
   _____ con tarjeta de crédito

En la farmacia

3. ¿Cuánto cuestan las cosas que Miguel compró?
   _____ pesetas

4. ¿Cómo pagó Miguel por esas cosas?
   _____ en efectivo
   _____ con cheque personal
   _____ con tarjeta de crédito

SÍNTESIS

¡A leer!

LLEGARON...¡LOS ESPECIALES!

En su tienda favorita... ¡todo en rebaja! ¿Qué hacer? Le damos algunas sugerencias que le pueden ser muy útiles.

✔ Antes de salir, revise su guardarropa, los enseres de cocina, sus muebles, etc., y prepare una lista detallada de las cosas que necesita por orden de prioridades.

✔ Luego determine la cantidad de dinero que puede gastarse. Si tiene una calculadora de bolsillo, llévela con usted para que no se pase del dinero indicado. Si no la tiene, puede llevar un lápiz y un papel.

✔ Trate de ir los primeros días de la rebaja ya que es cuando más variedad de artículos, tallas y colores va a encontrar. Es importante que vaya sin prisa para que pueda hacer una buena compra.

✔ Una vez en la tienda, vaya directamente al departamento donde vendan lo que usted busca. Si encuentra algo muy barato y bonito pero que realmente usted no lo necesita, es mejor que no lo compre a que desperdicie el dinero.

✔ Revise cuidadosamente cada prenda o artículo, ya que en muchas tiendas no aceptan devoluciones cuando se ha tratado de una venta especial. Si encuentra lo que necesita y resulta que está maltratado, asegúrese de que la reparación sea sencilla y que valga la pena con respecto al precio. Si se trata de prendas de vestir, revise los botones, los ojales, las cremalleras y los dobladillos.

✔ Si va a comprar algún equipo eléctrico para su casa, asegúrese de que incluyan las instrucciones y el papel de garantía.

✔ Si va a comprar muebles, revise cuidadosamente el barniz, el tapiz y las patas, no vaya a ser que luego tenga que pagar una reparación costosa.

✔ No compre productos enlatados que estén maltratados o que no especifiquen la fecha de vencimiento aunque tengan un precio muy tentador.

Recuerde que la mejor compra no está determinada por la cantidad, sino por la calidad y el uso que se le vaya a dar al artículo, además del precio que pagó por él.

IDEAS 141

¿Comprendió Ud.?

Primero, lea la lectura rápidamente para comprender las ideas principales. Luego complete las siguientes oraciones apropiadamente.

1. Esta lectura es... (una carta/un anuncio/una invitación).
2. Un buen título para esta lectura es _____ .
3. Me gusta (muy poco/un poco/mucho) esta lectura porque...

Answers: 1. *un anuncio* 2. [open] 3. [open] Statements refer to the following paragraphs: 2, 4, 6, 3, 7, 1, 9, 5, 8

SÍNTESIS

Ahora lea la lectura por segunda vez. Luego identifique las siguientes oraciones con los números 1 hasta el 9, según los párrafos correspondientes de la lectura.

_____ No gaste más de lo que usted pueda.
_____ Compre solamente lo que usted necesite.
_____ Compre equipo eléctrico que tenga garantía.
_____ Vaya usted los primeros días a la rebaja.
_____ Cuando compre muebles, busque los defectos.
_____ Haga una lista en orden de sus prioridades.
_____ La gente inteligente compra por la calidad y no por cantidad.
_____ Siempre revise todos los objetos en rebaja.
_____ No compre productos enlatados que no tengan fecha de vencimiento.

Las cosas

Las cosas, nuestras cosas,
les gusta que las quieran;
a mi mesa le gusta que yo apoye los codos,° *that I rest my elbows*
a la silla le gusta que me siente en la silla,
a la puerta le gusta que la abra y la cierre
como al vino le gusta que lo compre y lo beba,
mi lápiz se deshace° si lo cojo° y escribo *loves it / I take*
mi armario° se estremece° si lo abro y me asomo,° *closet / is thrilled / I look at it*
las sábanas,° son sábanas cuando me echo° sobre ellas *bed sheets / I lay down*
y la cama se queja° cuando yo me levanto. *gets upset*

Source: *Salvo el crepúsculo* por Julio Cortázar. México: Editorial Nueva Imagen, 1984, página 215.

¿Comprendió Ud.?

Primero, lea el poema dos veces. Luego complete las siguientes oraciones apropiadamente.

Answers: 1. *feliz* 2. *como personas* 3. *casa* 4. [open] 5. [open]

1. Este poema tiene un tono bastante... (triste/feliz).
2. Para el poeta nuestras cosas son... (como personas/inútiles).
3. Se refiere a las cosas que hay en (casa/la escuela/el jardín).
4. Otro título para este poema puede ser _____.
5. Me gusta (muy poco/un poco/mucho) este poema porque...

SÍNTESIS

¡A conversar!

Imagínese que usted está visitando Madrid, la capital de España. Usted entra en una tienda especializada porque le interesa mirar lo que tienen y posiblemente va a comprar algo allí. Hable con otro(a) estudiante: una persona es el/la dependiente (quien debe cerrar su libro en este momento) y la otra es su cliente.

Students will need time at home or in class to prepare adequately for this activity.

1. Salude al (a la) dependiente y dígale exactamente lo que usted quiere comprar (artículo, color, talla).
2. Pídale que le muestre los artículos que le interesan.
3. Pregúntele los precios de los artículos que realmente le gustan. Sea indiferente o reaccione con sorpresa o felicidad.
4. Dígale lo que usted quiere comprar y cómo va a pagarlo.
5. Pregúntele dónde está la otra tienda que busca.
6. Termine la conversación apropiadamente.

¡A escribir!

1. Con otro(a) estudiante escriba un anuncio comercial para un periódico. Ustedes pueden anunciar un producto verdadero o ficticio, una tienda especializada o un almacén que conocen. Usen lenguaje descriptivo y persuasivo (adjetivos, adverbios, comparaciones, superlativos y mandatos apropiados) para atraer *(attract)* a muchos clientes hispanos. Su anuncio debe incluir una fotografía o un dibujo atractivo. Refiéranse a varios anuncios comerciales de periódico para sacar otras ideas realistas. Luego presenten sus anuncios en la clase oralmente.

2. Opcional: Sus compañeros de clase pueden votar por los mejores anuncios en diferentes categorías, por ejemplo: el anuncio más atractivo, el anuncio más persuasivo, el anuncio más original.

Atajo

Visit

http://poco.heinle.com

VOCABULARIO

Sustantivos

el anuncio *advertisement, announcement*
la calidad *quality*
el costo *cost*
el estilo *style*
la ganga *bargain*
el juego *game*
el juguete *toy*
la muñeca *doll*
la rebaja *sale (Spain), reduction (in price)*

En la joyería

el anillo *ring*
los aretes *earrings*
el brazalete *bracelet*
el collar *necklace*
las joyas *jewelry*
el reloj *watch*

En la papelería

el álbum de fotos *photo album*
el bolígrafo *pen*
el lapiz *pencil*
el papel para cartas *stationery*
el sobre *envelope*
la tarjeta postal *postcard*

Los artículos eléctricos

la calculadora *calculator*
la caseta de video *videotape*
la computadora (el ordenador) *computer*
el disco compacto *compact disk (CD)*
la grabadora *tape recorder*
la impresora *printer*
la máquina de afeitar *shaver*
la máquina de escribir *typewriter*
el secador de pelo *hair dryer*

Los artículos fotográficos

la cámara *camera*
el rollo para fotos *print film*
el rollo para diapositivas *slide film*
el tripié *tripod*
la videocámara *video camera*

Adjetivos

barato *inexpensive, cheap*
caro *expensive*
rebajado *reduced (in price)*

Verbos

ahorrar *to save (money)*
anunciar *to announce*
aprovechar(se) *to take advantage*
encontrar (o→ue) *to find*
funcionar *to work (function)*
gastar *to spend (money)*
llorar *to cry*
mostrar (o→ue) *to show*
preocuparse (por) *to worry (about)*
rebajar *to reduce (in price)*
reírse (e→i, e→i) *to laugh*

Adverbios

a veces *sometimes*
casi *almost*
después *afterwards*
dos veces *twice*
entonces *then, so*
muchas veces *very often*
otra vez *again*
por fin *at last, finally*
solamente *only, just*
una vez *once*

Expresiones idiomáticas

a crédito *on credit*
con cheque *by check*
en efectivo *in cash*
Vamos a ver. *Let's see.*
ya no *no longer*

¿Qué van a comer?

▶ COMMUNICATIVE GOALS

You will be able to order a meal in a restaurant and describe some of your past experiences.

▶ LANGUAGE FUNCTIONS

Naming tableware items
Ordering a meal
Making requests
Stating preferences
Expressing opinions
Describing recent activities
Narrating childhood experiences

▶ VOCABULARY THEMES

Table setting
Restaurant expressions

▶ GRAMMATICAL STRUCTURES

Present perfect indicative
Preterite and imperfect (summary)

▶ CULTURAL INFORMATION

Restaurant customs
Tapas **bars**

http://poco.heinle.com

Play Lab Tape

sit down

parrot

followed / place

soda / ice

shouted

loud

pitcher

to jot down

EN CONTEXTO

Recientemente Elena Navarro, su hija Rita, los tíos Simón y Rosa Álvarez y sus dos hijos, Amalia (11 años) y Toño (20 años), fueron de vacaciones a la isla de Mallorca. Un domingo a las dos y quince de la tarde todos tenían mucha hambre. Decidieron ir al "Torremolinos", un restaurante de tres tenedores que conocieron el año pasado. (1) Un camarero (2) los saludó:

—Buenas tardes. ¿Cuántos son?

—Somos seis —dijo Simón.

—¿Seis personas? Muy bien. Síganme, por favor.

Luego Rita le preguntó a su mamá si ellos podían sentarse° en la terraza como lo hicieron el año pasado cuando almorzaron allí. Elena le explicó al camarero que su hija quería sentarse en la terraza porque a ella le gustaba el papagayo° que tenían allí.

—¿El papagayo? —preguntó el camarero.   —Ah, sí, señora. Por favor, pasen ustedes por aquí.

> 1. ¿Qué pasó?
> 2. ¿Dónde pasó la acción?
> 3. ¿Qué quería Rita Navarro?

Los seis turistas siguieron° al camarero a un lugar° tranquilo en la terraza donde se sentaron a una mesa grande. Luego el camarero les dio el menú y preguntó si querían tomar algo antes de pedir la comida. Amalia respondió inmediatamente:

—Una gaseosa° para mí, por favor. ¡Con mucho hielo!°

—Para mí también, ¡pero bien grande! —gritó° Rita con entusiasmo.

—Rita, no hables tan fuerte,° por favor.

—Lo siento, mamá —dijo la niña.

—¿Qué os parece pedir una jarra° de sangría? (3) —les preguntó Rosa a los mayores.

—Buena idea —contestó su marido.

El camarero salió con el pedido y nuestros turistas hablaron sobre lo que iban a comer. Después de diez minutos el camarero volvió con las bebidas, las sirvió y sacó un lápiz para apuntar° el resto del pedido.

—Ahora, ¿qué van a comer?

—Hemos decidido comer paella valenciana (4) porque es la especialidad de la casa y a todos nos gusta mucho —dijo Simón.

---

[1] The *En contexto* section for this lesson is an example of a past narrative. It is divided into three parts. After each part, you will be asked to respond to three questions. Keep these questions in mind as you read each part.

1. **Entremeses:** Hay muchos entremeses en el menú, por ejemplo: _____.
   ¿Quieres un entremés? (¿Sí? ¿Cuál prefieres?) Y yo voy a pedir _____.
2. **Sopas:** Vamos a tomar una sopa. Dice aquí que tienen _____. ¿Qué sopa
   quieres? Y yo quiero _____. (Creo que no como sopa hoy.)
3. **Huevos:** ¿Te gustan los huevos? (¿Sí? Pues, tienen _____.) Creo que
   voy a pedir _____. (No voy a comer huevos hoy porque...)
4. **Legumbres:** Tienen legumbres, que es otra palabra para vegetales. ¿Te
   gustan las legumbres? (¿Sí? Bueno, hay una buena selección. Por
   ejemplo, hay _____. ¿Qué te apetece?) Y yo quiero _____.
5. **Pescados / Asados y parrillas:** ¿Prefieres comer pescado o carne?
   (¿Pescado? Pues, hay _____. ¿Qué quieres pedir?)
   (¿Carne? Bueno, hay _____. ¿Qué te apetece?)
   A mí me gusta (el pescado / la carne); voy a comer _____.
6. **Postres:** ¡Y ahora los postres! Ay, ¡qué ricos! Hay _____. ¿Cuál te
   gustaría pedir? Y yo voy a pedir _____. (Creo que no pido ningún
   postre hoy.)
7. **Bebidas:** El menú no dice qué bebidas se sirven aquí. Me imagino que
   hay vino tinto, vino blanco, cerveza, agua mineral y gaseosas. ¿Qué
   quieres tomar? Y yo voy a tomar _____.

D. La hora de cenar. Haga esta actividad con otros tres o cuatro estudiantes. Una persona es el (la) camarero(a) y las otras son sus clientes. Los
clientes miran el menú en la página 298. Pida un entremés, una sopa, algún
plato, postre y bebida.

Ex. D.
1. Follow-up activities: You could
   have students prepare their own
   Spanish-language menus; then ask
   them to repeat this activity using
   their menus.
2. If you wish, you could use this as
   a whole class activity in a TPR
   format.

NOTAS CULTURALES

Las costumbres en los restaurantes hispanos

En Latinoamérica y en España, la mayoría de los restaurantes tienen un menú a la
entrada. El menú indica los precios de la comida a la carta, de los platos combinados,
del plato del día o del cubierto o la comida corriente.

Cuando uno entra en un restaurante, el camarero o la camarera lo saluda y le indica
dónde sentarse. Por lo general, no hay ninguna sección de no fumar° como en los
restaurantes estadounidenses o canadienses.

Al terminar la comida, el camarero o la camarera le ofrece café y postre.
Generalmente no le trae la cuenta hasta que usted se la pide. Para atraer su atención,
usted tiene que decirle: "Camarero" o "Señorita" o "Mozo", según el país en que se
encuentre. Con frecuencia la cuenta incluye la propina; si no, es normal dejar una
propina apropiada. Si usted no está seguro(a) de si la cuenta incluye la propina, es
necesario preguntar.

non-smoking

E. ¿Qué dice usted? Pregúntele a otro(a) estudiante.

1. ¿Por qué hay un menú a la entrada de muchos restaurantes en Latinoamérica y España? ¿A usted le gusta esta costumbre? ¿Por qué?
2. ¿Cómo se atrae la atención del camarero o de la camarera en nuestra ciudad?
3. ¿Cuándo traen la cuenta en casi todos los restaurantes norteamericanos? ¿Por qué? ¿A usted le gusta esta costumbre? ¿Por qué?
4. Generalmente, ¿qué por ciento de la cuenta deja usted de propina en un restaurante? En su opinión, ¿es una buena idea incluir la propina en la cuenta? ¿Por qué?

GRAMÁTICA FUNCIONAL

Describing recent actions, conditions, and events

—¿Qué han pedido ustedes?
—Nada. Te hemos esperado.
—¿Han comido aquí antes?
—No. Nunca hemos estado aquí.

Present perfect indicative

Spanish speakers use the present perfect indicative tense to describe what has and has not happened recently.

How to form the present perfect

Use the present tense forms of the auxiliary verb *haber* (to have) with the past participle of a verb.

Present of *haber* + past participle

(yo)	**he**		*I have*	
(tú)	**has**		*you have*	
(usted, él/ella)	**ha**	} **comido**	*you have, he/she has*	} *eaten*
(nosotros/as)	**hemos**		*we have*	
(vosotros/as)	***habéis***		*you have*	
(ustedes, ellos/ellas)	**han**		*you, they have*	

Be sure that students differentiate between the endings for present participles (*-ando/-iendo*) and the endings for past participles (*-ado/-ido*). Compare: *Estoy comiendo* (I am eating) versus *He comido* (I have eaten).

How to form past participles

1. Add *-ado* to the stem of *-ar* verbs, and *-ido* to the stem of *-er* and *-ir* verbs.

-*ar* verb	stem + -*ado*		-*er*/-*ir* verb	stem + -*ido*	
hablar	**hablado**	*spoken*	comer	**comido**	*eaten*
pensar	**pensado**	*thought*	vivir	**vivido**	*lived*
llegar	**llegado**	*arrived*	dormir	**dormido**	*slept*

2. Several *-er* and *-ir* verbs have an accent mark on the *i* of their past participles.

leer	leído	*read*	traer	traído	*brought*
creer	creído	*believed*	reír	reído	*laughed*

—Te **he traído** un regalo, Rita.   *I've brought a gift for you, Rita.*
—¿Qué me **has traído**, mamá?   *What have you brought me, Mom?*
—Un libro que no **has leído.**   *A book that you have not read.*

3. Other verbs have irregular past participles.

abrir	**abierto**	*opened*	morir	**muerto**	*died*
decir	**dicho**	*said, told*	poner	**puesto**	*put*
escribir	**escrito**	*written*	ver	**visto**	*seen*
hacer	**hecho**	*done, made*	volver	**vuelto**	*returned*

—¿Qué han hecho ustedes hoy?   *What have you done today?*
—Hemos visto una película.   *We have seen a movie.*
—He escrito algunas cartas.   *I have written some letters.*

Emphasize that when the past participle is used to form the present perfect tense, it always ends in *-o*. (When the past participle is used as an adjective, it agrees with the gender and number of the noun to which it refers. For example: *Las tortillas españolas están hech**as** de patatas, huevos y cebollas.*)

Practiquemos

A. En la terraza del Torremolinos. Complete la siguiente conversación con la forma correcta de **haber: he, has, ha, hemos, han.**

CAMARERO: ¿ _____ estado ustedes en Mallorca antes?
RITA: Sí, señor. _____ venido aquí el año pasado.
CAMARERO: Oye, niña. ¿ _____ visto nuestro papagayo?
RITA: Sí, sí. Yo le _____ dado una galleta salada.
CAMARERO: Y luego, ¿qué _____ hecho el papagayo?
RITA: Pues, el papagayo _____ comenzado a hablar.
CAMARERO: Creo que te _____ divertido mucho aquí, niña.
RITA: Sí, señor. También nosotros _____ comido bien aquí.

Ex. A. Answers: *Han, Hemos, Has, he, ha, ha, has, hemos*

Exs. A and B.
After students have completed each of these exercises, have them practice the dialogues with a classmate.

B. Mis queridos padres... Elena está escribiéndoles a sus padres sobre algunas actividades que ella y sus parientes han hecho en Mallorca. ¿Qué les dice en su carta?

Ejemplo: (yo) hacer mucho ejercicio aquí.
         He hecho mucho ejercicio aquí.

Yo... / nadar en la piscina de nuestro hotel y / jugar al tenis con Simón. También / montar en bicicleta dos veces esta semana. Claro que / sacar muchas fotos de Mallorca. Pero no / comprar muchas cosas aquí porque no / ir a ninguna tienda. (Yo) / estar muy ocupada.

Rita... / estar bien. Ella / aprovecharse mucho de estas vacaciones. Por ejemplo, ella / jugar con su prima Amalia, / leer todos sus libros de Disney y / desayunar con dos amigas que ella / conocer aquí. Rita / tener ganas de escribirles a ustedes, pero todavía no lo / hacer.

Ex. B. Spaniards often use the present perfect to describe simple past events: *He visitado a Elena.* Latin Americans usually use the preterite for this purpose: *Visité a Elena.*

Ex. B. Answers:
Paragraph 1:
He nadado..., he jugado..., he montado..., he sacado, he comprado, he ido, he estado
Paragraph 2:
ha estado, se ha aprovechado, ha jugado, ha leído, ha desayunado, ha conocido, ha tenido, ha hecho
Paragraph 3:
nos hemos divertido, hemos almorzado, hemos comido, hemos tomado, hemos visto, hemos pasado

Rita, la familia de Simón y yo... / divertirse mucho. Esta tarde / almorzar en un buen restaurante donde / comer una rica paella valenciana. Simón, Rosa y yo / tomar una jarra de sangría. En la terraza / ver un papagayo fabuloso que hablaba sin parar. En total, lo / pasar muy bien aquí en esta isla maravillosa.

C. Otras conversaciones. Complete las siguientes conversaciones, usando los participios de los verbos indicados.

Ex. C. Answers:
1. *hecho, escrito, visto*
2. *muerto, dado, jugado, enamorado*
3. *comido, dicho, venido*

1. ver / escribir / hacer
RITA: ¿Qué has _____ hoy, Amalia?
AMALIA: He _____ algunas tarjetas postales. ¿Y tú?
RITA: Mi mamá y yo hemos _____ una película de Disney.

2. morir / jugar / dar / enamorar
AMALIA: Papá, creo que el papagayo ha _____ .
SIMÓN: No, está durmiendo. Rita le ha _____ muchas galletas.
AMALIA: Ella ha _____ mucho hoy con el papagayo, ¿verdad?
SIMÓN: Sí, porque se ha _____ de él.

3. decir / venir / comer
ELENA: ¿Qué tienes en la mano, hija?
RITA: Más galletas. El papagayo ya ha _____ las otras.
ELENA: ¿Qué te he _____ , Rita? El papagayo no quiere más.
SIMÓN: Sí, Rita. Hemos _____ aquí para almorzar, ¿comprendes?
RITA: Sí, tío... comprendo.

D. ¿Y usted? Escríbale una carta a un amigo o a una amiga que lee español y descríbale lo que usted, su familia y sus amigos han hecho recientemente. También hágale algunas preguntas para saber de sus actividades recientes. Trate de usar el vocabulario que usted ha aprendido en otras lecciones.

Ex. D. After students have completed this activity, they could exchange letters with a classmate, then answer each other's letters.

Párrafo 1: información sobre sí mismo(a) (su salud, sus estudios, su trabajo, sus pasatiempos y sus problemas)

Párrafo 2: actividades de su familia y sus amigos (sus clases, su trabajo, sus quehaceres, sus fiestas, sus vacaciones)

Párrafo 3: preguntas para su amigo(a) (sobre su familia, sus actividades)

Charlemos

E. Recientemente... Hable con otro(a) estudiante, usando las siguientes oraciones.

Ex. E. Be sure students change the infinitives to past participles in each item when they do this activity.

1. En mis clases (no) he...
   a. aprender mucho.
   b. estar muy aburrido(a).
   c. tomar exámenes difíciles.

2. En casa (no) he...
   a. dar una fiesta.
   b. lavar los platos.
   c. mirar mucho la tele.

3. En mi trabajo (no) he...
   a. hacer mucho.
   b. tener problemas.
   c. ahorrar mucho dinero.

4. El último fin de semana, he...
   a. dormir mucho en casa.
   b. ver una buena película.
   c. comer en un restaurante.

F. Charla. Pregúntele a un(a) compañero(a) de clase. También usted puede hacerle otras preguntas, según sus respuestas.

Ex. F. Follow-up activity: Have students ask you these questions, using formal forms.

1. ¿Has visitado a tu/tus _____ (amiga / novio / abuelos / padres / ...) recientemente? (¿Sí? ¿Qué hicieron ustedes?)
2. ¿Has ido a un centro comercial _____ esta semana? (¿Sí? ¿En qué día fuiste allí? ¿A qué hora? ¿Con quién fuiste allí? ¿Qué hiciste / hicieron ustedes en el centro comercial?)
3. ¿Has visto la película " _____ "? (¿Sí? ¿Dónde la viste? ¿Te gustó o no? ¿Por qué?)
4. ¿Has jugado al _____ esta semana? (¿Sí? ¿Dónde y con quién lo jugaste? ¿Qué otro deporte has jugado recientemente? ¿Te gusta mucho ese deporte? ¿Por qué?)
5. ¿Has leído el periódico hoy? (¿Sí? ¿Qué aprendiste leyendo el periódico?)

G. ¡Adivinen ustedes! Cada estudiante de su clase de español va a escribir en un papel pequeño una acción que él o ella ha hecho recientemente. Luego van a formar grupos de cinco o seis personas. Mientras cada persona dice con gestos (pantomima) lo que escribió, sus compañeros de grupo tratan de *(try to)* adivinarlo; luego esa persona dice si lo adivinaron o no.

Ejemplo: Usted escribe: *He leído un periódico.* → (pantomima...)
Se adivina así: *¿Has leído un periódico?*
Usted responde: *¡Sí! ¡Bravo!*

1. Tell students that the word *tapas* originates from the old tavern custom of covering a wine or shot glass with a slice of ham or hard sausage called *una tapa* (from *tapar* = to cover), which people would eat with their accompanying drink.
2. Remind students that Spaniards eat supper (dinner) rather late (about 10:00 pm) compared to North American mealtimes, so many people stop at one or more *tapa* bars for a snack after school or work. Also, the *tapa* bar is an important social institution in Spain; it is a meeting place for old friends.
3. *Tapas* party: Bring several *tapas* recipes to class, and have students prepare some *tapas* for a party at one of your class sessions.
4. An informative book on *tapas* is: *Tapas: The Little Dishes of Spain* by Penélope Casas, Borozoi Book, published by Alfred A. Knopf, Inc.

NOTAS CULTURALES

Los bares de tapas

Los bares de tapas son casi una institución social en España. Entre las cinco y las siete de la tarde, muchos españoles van a los bares de tapas para charlar con sus amigos y para hacer nuevos amigos.

Las tapas son aperitivos° como, por ejemplo, pedazos° de jamón o queso, salchichas pequeñas, calamares,° sardinas, y gambas al ajillo.° Otra tapa popular es la tortilla española, que es una tortilla de patatas, huevos y cebolla frita en aceite° de oliva. En los bares de tapas también se sirven bebidas alcohólicas como vino y cerveza, gaseosas y café.

appetizers (hors d'oeuvres) / pieces squid / fried shrimp flavored with garlic / oil

H. Pregúntele a un(a) compañero(a) de clase.

1. ¿Qué piensas de los bares de tapas?
2. ¿Te gustaría ir a algún bar de tapas? ¿Por qué?
3. ¿Qué tapas te gustarían probar algún día?
4. ¿Qué te gusta comer entre comidas? ¿Y qué bebes?
5. ¿Qué comiste entre comidas ayer? ¿Qué bebiste?

GRAMÁTICA FUNCIONAL

Narrating past experiences

—Anoche mientras leía, Marcos me llamó.
—¿Marcos? ¿Qué quería él, Elena?
—Pues, me invitó a comer el sábado.
—¡Qué bueno! ¿Y qué le dijiste?
—Le dije que no podía el sábado.
—Luego, ¿qué te dijo Marcos?
—Me invitó a comer el domingo y acepté.

Preterite and imperfect tenses (summary)

The choice of using the preterite tense or the imperfect tense is not arbitrary. The choice depends on how a speaker or writer views the past actions, conditions, and events that he or she describes.

How to use the preterite

Spanish speakers use the preterite tense to describe past actions, conditions and events that began in the past or were completed at some point in the past.

1. Actions that began and/or were completed in the past

    En Mallorca Elena y Rita **conocieron** a la familia Pérez, que las **invitó** a una fiesta de cumpleaños de su hija Ángela. El día de la fiesta Elena **bañó** a Rita y la **vistió.** Luego **se duchó, se puso** un vestido y **se pintó** la cara. Después, las dos **salieron** de su hotel y **tomaron** un taxi a la casa de los Pérez.

2. Events that began and/or were completed in the past

   Allí Ángela Pérez **celebró** sus nueve años. Muchas personas **estuvieron** en la fiesta: todos los parientes y amigos de Ángela. La fiesta **fue** maravillosa; a Elena y a Rita les **gustó** mucho.

3. Conditions that began and/or were completed in the past

   Después de llegar a su hotel, Rita **se sintió** cansada y un poco enferma, pero al día siguiente ella **estuvo** mucho mejor.

How to use the imperfect

1. The imperfect is used for describing past actions, conditions and events that occurred habitually or repetitiously.

   Cada verano mi esposa y yo **íbamos** de vacaciones a Francia. **Comíamos** en diferentes restaurantes, **montábamos** en bicicleta y **jugábamos** al tenis cerca de nuestro hotel. Ay, ¡cómo nos **divertíamos!**

2. The imperfect is also used for describing actions, conditions and events that were in progress at some focused point in the past. The person describing them tells what was happening, often when something else was going on at the same time.

   El verano pasado fuimos en autobús a Cannes en Francia. El día que salimos **hacía** buen tiempo. Mientras **esperábamos** en la estación de autobuses, mi esposa **leía** el periódico y yo **miraba** a la gente despidiéndose de sus parientes. **Estábamos** un poco cansados.

   Spanish speakers also use the imperfect to describe past actions, conditions, and events that were anticipated or planned.

   Queríamos quedarnos un día más en Cannes pero no **teníamos** dinero.

How to use the preterite and imperfect together

Spanish speakers often use these two tenses together to describe past experiences within the framework of the time they occurred.

   Eran las dos y cuarto de la tarde y todos **tenían** mucha hambre. Por eso, **fueron** al Restaurante Torremolinos. Rita le **preguntó** a su mamá si ellos **podían** sentarse en la terraza como lo **hicieron** el año pasado cuando almorzaron allí. Elena le **dijo** al camarero que su hija **quería** sentarse en la terraza porque a ella le **gustaba** el papagayo que **tenían** allí.

Teach how the preterite and imperfect are used together by telling a simple story in Spanish using one or more situation photographs or drawings. Try to personalize the storyline or make it as humorous as possible to motivate students to listen to you. Afterwards, give them a short oral or written true-false quiz.

Practiquemos

A. ¿Recuerda usted? Complete los siguientes párrafos, usando correctamente el pretérito o el imperfecto de los verbos dados.

1. *¿En qué puedo servirle?* (Lección 10)

ir	hablar	conocer
salir	entrar	saludar
tener	llegar	trabajar

Ex. A. Answers:
Paragraph 1:
fueron, llegaron, conocía, saludó, hablaron, entraron, trabajaba, tenía
Paragraph 2:
lavaba, escuchaba, jugaba, miraba, oyó, estaba, corrió, fueron, Subieron

Ex. A. After students complete this exercise, have them analyze why they used the preterite and the imperfect of each verb.

El sábado pasado a las nueve y media, Elena y Rita *salieron* de su pequeño apartamento y _____ a comprar comestibles. Después de caminar diez minutos, _____ a la carnicería del señor Romero, quien _____ bien a Elena. Ella lo _____ , luego ellos _____ del tiempo y de sus familias.

Más tarde, Elena y Rita _____ en la panadería Ideal donde se venden panes de diferentes tipos, galletas saladas y una buena selección de tortas y otros pasteles. Allí _____ a Magdalena Ramírez, quien _____ dieciséis años.

2. *Aquí vendemos de todo* (Lección 11)

oír	**mirar**	**correr**
ir	**jugar**	**subir**
lavar	**estar**	**escuchar**

El miércoles pasado a las cuatro y media de la tarde, Elena Navarro _____los platos del almuerzo en la cocina y _____ la radio mientras su hija Rita _____ con su muñeca y _____ la televisión en la sala. De repente, la niña _____ un anuncio. Después de verlo, Rita _____ tan contenta que _____ rápidamente a la cocina con su muñeca en la mano.

El próximo sábado a las once de la mañana, Elena y Rita _____ a El Corte Inglés para aprovecharse de la fabulosa rebaja. _____ al tercer piso donde se venden muebles y artículos eléctricos.

B. Queridos abuelitos...
Imagínese que usted es un(a) niño(a) español(a), quien acaba de volver de su primera visita a Mallorca. Escríbales una tarjeta a sus abuelos, describiéndoles sus impresiones allí.

¿Cómo era? (Hacer) muy buen tiempo en Mallorca y el aeropuerto (ser) muy grande. Mientras mamá, papá y yo (esperar) nuestras maletas, muchas otras personas (llegar) de diferentes partes del mundo. Ay, qué contento(a) (estar).

¿Qué pasó? [Nosotros] (dormir) en un hotel muy bonito. La próxima mañana (ir) en una excursión. [Yo] (ver) la plaza, un museo grande y papá (sacar) algunas fotos de mamá y mí delante de la catedral. En la tarde, [nosotros] (almorzar) en un café mexicano; papá y mamá (pedir) enchiladas con arroz y yo (comer) dos tacos. Luego [nosotros] (visitar) el Parque Bellver donde (divertirnos) en grande. [Yo] (comprar) un libro interesante sobre Mallorca y lo (leer) más tarde en el hotel donde [nosotros] (pasar) tres noches. ¡Cómo (divertirme) allí!

C. Personas y cosas nuevas.
Durante su visita a Mallorca, Elena y sus parientes conocieron a varias personas y algunos lugares bonitos. ¿Qué conocieron y qué hicieron allí?

Ejemplo: (Elena y Rita) *caminar* por un parque donde un hombre *vender* helados.
   *Ellas **caminaron** por un parque donde un hombre **vendía** helados.*

1. (Toño) *ir* a una fiesta que *ser* fabulosa porque *haber* mucha gente allí. *Conocer* a una joven venezolana, que *ser* estudiante en Mallorca y la *invitar* a salir al cine.

2. (Rita y Amalia) *querer* ir con sus padres a nadar en el Mar Mediterráneo. Primero, *ponerse* el traje de baño, luego *ir* en autobús a un lugar bonito donde *nadar* por tres horas. La temperatura *estar* a veinte grados centígrados. *Volver* a su hotel a las dos para almorzar.

Ex. B. Answers:
¿Cómo era? *Hacía..., era..., esperábamos..., llegaron..., estaba*
¿Qué pasó? *Dormimos..., fuimos..., Vi..., sacó..., almorzamos..., pidieron..., comí..., visitamos..., nos divertimos..., Compré..., leí..., pasamos..., me divertí*
2. After students complete this exercise, have them analyze why they used the preterite and the imperfect of each verb.
3. Finally, ask students to write a postcard to one of their friends, telling him or her about an imaginary trip to Mallorca.

Ex. C. Answers:
1. *fue, era, había, Conoció, era, invitó*
2. *querían, se pusieron, fueron, nadaron, estaba, Volvieron*
3. *fueron, conocieron, Se divirtieron, querían, volvieron, comenzó, Eran, estaban*
4. *tuvo, montaba, llevaron, estaba, Estuvo, dijo, estaba, tenía, podía*

Ex. C. After students complete this exercise, have them analyze why they used the preterite and the imperfect of each verb.

3. (Elena, Simón y Rosa) *ir* a una fiesta donde *conocer* a mucha gente por primera vez. *Divertirse* tanto que no *querer* irse. Finalmente, *volver* a su hotel cuando *comenzar* a llover. *Ser* las dos de la mañana, pero *estar* contentos.

4. (Amalia) *tener* un accidente cuando *montar* en bicicleta. Sus padres la *llevar* a un hospital porque ella no *estar* bien. *Estar* allí por una hora, luego el doctor les *decir* a sus padres que ella *estar* bien y que solamente *tener* un poco de miedo, pero que *poder* salir del hospital.

D. ¡Qué vacaciones! Escríbale una tarjeta postal a un(a) amigo(a) de habla española sobre sus últimas vacaciones. Por ejemplo, dígale adónde fue usted y con quién, en qué día salieron ustedes, qué cosas pasaban cuando llegaron, cómo se divirtieron cada día y qué tiempo hacía durante las vacaciones.

Charlemos

E. Entrevista. Pregúntele a otro(a) estudiante.

Ex. E. Follow-up actitivies: 1. Have students ask you these questions, using *usted* verb forms. 2. Have students write their answers to these questions as a homework assignment.

1. **Su niñez:** ¿De dónde eres originalmente? ¿Por cuánto tiempo viviste allí? ¿Te gustaba vivir allí? ¿Por qué? ¿Qué cosas no te gustaban allí? ¿Vivías en una casa o en un apartamento? ¿Cómo era? ¿Tenías pocos o muchos amigos? ¿Cómo eran? ¿Cuántos años tenías cuando fuiste a la escuela por primera vez? ¿Tenías miedo? ¿Cómo se llamaba la escuela? ¿Cómo celebrabas tus cumpleaños cuando eras niño(a)? Durante tu niñez, ¿qué actividades hacías?

2. **Su adolescencia:** ¿Cuántos años tenías cuando comenzaste clases en la secundaria? ¿Cómo se llamaba la escuela y dónde estaba? ¿Dónde vivías? ¿Tenías novio(a) cuando eras adolescente? (¿Sí? Háblame de él/ella, por favor.) Cuando eras adolescente, ¿qué hacías los fines de semana? ¿Adónde iban de vacaciones tú y tu familia? ¿Qué hacían allí? ¿Dónde y cómo era el lugar más bonito que visitaban durante tu adolescencia?

F. Había una vez... *(Once upon a time...)* Forme un grupo con otros dos o tres compañeros de clase. Luego una persona comienza con la siguiente oración: "Había una vez una persona invisible...". Luego las otras personas en su grupo toman turnos para continuar el cuento lógicamente hasta su terminación. Use su imaginación para crear un cuento interesante.

For extra practice, have students redo the exercises for practicing the preterite (page 179 in *Lección 7* and *page 206 in Lección 8*) and the imperfect (page 261 in *Lección 10*).

PARA LEER MEJOR

Following a Chronology

Diaries, anecdotes, and short stories usually contain a series of interrelated actions and events, including the writer's opinions. These kinds of narrative descriptions require the reader to follow a chronology. The central questions implicit in most narrations are:

• What happened?
• Where, when, and how did it happen?
• To whom did it occur, why, and for how long?
• What else was going on at the same time?

Activities

A. Read the following article, then answer these questions.

1. What is the main topic of this article?
2. What is the author's most important point?
3. What is the author's tone of voice in her article?

A. 1. The socialization of eating.
2. Eating should be a private activity. 3. sarcastic or cynical
B. 1. Eating as a heroic activity, Eating as a social activity, Eating as a private activity. 2. 19th Century
3. People had to dress in a certain way. 4. To the present
C. 1. No 2. Sí 3. Sí 4. Sí 5. No 6. No

La cocina

Pocas cosas poseen tanta atracción en esta civilización como cocinar° y comer.

Cuando la evolución produjo al hombre la cosa era muy simple: o comerse al enemigo o el enemigo se lo comía a uno. Poder comer era una demostración de habilidad, de triunfo.

Con el tiempo el comer dejó de ser una actividad heroica y precedida de peligros° mortales, que estimulaban el apetito, para convertirse en una actividad social.

Como actividad social la cosa se complicó, llegando a la cúspide de la complicación en el siglo° XIX. En ese siglo había que vestirse especialmente, usar los utensilios adecuados en el momento preciso y observar un protocolo de conversación.

Yo creo que si la cultura logra° sobrevivir al siglo XIX las horas de comida se van a transformar en ceremonias privadas.

El comer es una necesidad imprescindible° del cuerpo y como tal es una actividad predominantemente física. No es cultural, artística, bella ni moralizadora. Es la mera satisfacción de un apetito.

Invitar gente a comer es tan absurdo como invitar gente a cortarse las uñas° o sonarse.° Comprendo invitar a conversar, a oír música, a mirar las estrellas° o simplemente a ver televisión, pero no a comer.

Ver una persona comiendo es como ver un auto tomando gasolina. Es algo antiestético, prosaico, humillante. Es una necesidad ante la cual hay que inclinarse cuatro veces al día.

Hoy día el "comer afuera"° o "invitar a comer" se ha simplificado mucho, y si la humanidad sigue un camino avanzante, en uno de estos siglos se abolirá° completamente.

Glosses (left margin):
esencial
preparar la comida

fingernails / blow one's nose

dangers / stars

century

comer en un restaurante

va a

va a desaparecer

Source: *Carola*, No. 144, 2 de mayo de 1988, página 65, por Eliana Simón.

B. Read the article again to answer the following questions.

1. In which order did these activities appear in the article?
___ Eating as a social activity.
___ Eating as a heroic activity.
___ Eating as a private activity.
2. When did eating reach its climax as a social activity?
3. What else was going on at that time?
4. For how long did eating endure as a social activity?

C. Read the article once more to answer the following true-false statements.

	Sí	No
Información explícita		
1. Los caníbales eran personas muy complicadas.	___	___
2. En el siglo XIX la gente comía con mucho decoro.	___	___
3. Según la autora, el comer debe ser privado.	___	___
Información implícita		
4. La autora admira un poco a los caníbales.	___	___
5. Ella prefiere vivir en el siglo XIX.	___	___
6. Es probable que ella acepte invitaciones a comer.	___	___

PARA ESCRIBIR MEJOR

Writing an Anecdote

An anecdote is a short, entertaining account of an incident that really took place. An anecdote should answer the following seven questions:

1. When did the story take place?
2. Where did it occur?
3. Who was involved?
4. What was their relationship?
5. What actually happened?
6. Why did it take place?
7. What was the outcome?

Activities

A. Read the following anecdote and write the number of each of the seven questions above beside the sentence that answers it.

El verano pasado Elena Navarro, su hija Rita y la familia de su hermano Simón fueron a Mallorca para pasar una semana de vacaciones. Un día ellos decidieron almorzar en Torremolinos, un buen restaurante. Cuando entraron en el restaurante, Rita le dijo a su mamá que ella quería sentarse en la terraza porque había un papagayo allí. Después del almuerzo, la niña le dio al papagayo algunas galletas saladas. ¡Resultó que el animal no paró de hablar durante toda la tarde!

B. Write your own anecdote about an incident that happened to you. Use the seven questions and the example anecdote above to guide you. After you have finished, edit your composition carefully. Use the checklist below to help you.

____ When did the story occur?	____ Why did it take place?
____ Where did it happen?	____ What was the outcome?
____ Who was involved in it?	____ Did you check your grammar?
____ How did they interact?	____ Did you check your spelling?
____ What actually happened?	____ Did you check your punctuation?

Exchange your composition with a classmate. Correct each other's paragraphs, then discuss your corrections together.

Atajo

Functions:
Talking about past events; talking about the recent past; writing an essay

Vocabulary:
Time expressions; time of day; food: restaurant, place setting

Grammar:
Verbs: preterite, imperfect

¿A qué nivel está Ud.?

¿SÍ o NO? Por lo general, no hay ninguna sección de no fumar en los restaurantes de los países de habla español. Review the chapter and then monitor your progress by completing the *Autoprueba* at the end of *Lección 12* in the *Workbook/Lab Manual.*

SÍNTESIS

¡A ver!

You will see Miguel talking with some people at a *tapas* bar in Madrid. First, study the words with their meanings in the *Vocabulario esencial*. Second, read the questions and their possible answers in the activity below. Third, watch the videotape, then answer the questions.

Vocabulario esencial

la ensaladilla rusa	*potato salad*
un pincho de tortilla	*a slice of Spanish omelette*
calamares	*squid*
Vale.	*Okay.*
guisantes	*peas*
mayonesa	*mayonnaise*

Indique las respuestas correctas a cada pregunta.

1. ¿Qué bebida y comida pidió Miguel en el bar de tapas?
   ____ café   ____ refresco
   ____ gambas   ____ tortilla

2. ¿Qué comida pidió su amiga?
   ____ sardinas   ____ salchichas
   ____ calamares   ____ ensalada

3. Y su amigo, ¿qué comida pidió?
   ____ huevos   ____ jamón y queso
   ____ mariscos   ____ ensaladilla rusa

4. ¿Quién entró más tarde en el bar de tapas?
   ____ un amigo de Miguel   ____ el papá de Miguel
   ____ una amiga de Miguel   ____ un profesor de Miguel

5. ¿Qué bebida pidió esa persona?
   ____ té   ____ refresco
   ____ café   ____ chocolate

6. Por fin, ¿quién pagó la cuenta?
   ____ No se ha decidido.   ____ la amiga de Miguel
   ____ Miguel y un amigo   ____ dos amigos de Miguel

SÍNTESIS

¡A leer!

Lea el siguiente artículo, luego conteste las preguntas.

¿Son buenos los "bocatas"?

Como hemos comentado repetidamente en esta sección, un alimento no es bueno ni malo por sí mismo, pues depende del resto de la dieta de la que forma parte.

Pero, en principio, un bocadillo puede ser un alimento bastante aceptable, en el que se asocian proteínas de origen vegetal, como son las del pan, con las de origen animal, como son las de los embutidos, quesos... los productos más corrientemente utilizados para los bocadillos. Esto es positivo, ya que ambas proteínas se suplementan.

En relación con los embutidos, conviene que éstos sean de garantía, para que su contenido en grasas y proteínas sea el adecuado.

Si no abusamos de la práctica de comer bocadillos y éstos forman parte de una dieta variada, no hay ningún problema en su consumo. El problem surgiría si se tomaran exclusivamente o con enorme frecuencia bocadillos, o si utilizáramos embutidos de mala calidad.

Source: FEN (Fundación Española de la Nutrición), General Yagüe, 20. 28020, Madrid, Spain.

¿Comprendió Ud.?

En un papel separado, haga dos columnas como está indicado abajo. Luego escriba las ventajas y las desventajas de los bocadillos, según el artículo que usted acaba de leer.

Visit

http://poco.heinle.com

Las ventajas

_____

_____

_____

Las desventajas

_____

_____

_____

SÍNTESIS

¡A conversar!

Converse con un(a) compañero(a) de clase. Una persona es el (la) camarero(a) y la otra es su cliente.

Customer:

1. Find out what kinds of drinks they have, then order one.
2. Ask about the house specialty. What other entrées are there?
3. Find out what kinds of soups and salads they have.
4. Now order what you would like to eat.
5. Your food arrives, but something is wrong. Tell your server.
6. Find out what kinds of desserts they have, then order something.
7. If you would like an after-dinner tea or coffee, indulge.
8. Finish eating, then ask for the bill. Don't forget to leave a tip!

Atajo

¡A escribir!

Imagínese que usted es reportero(a) de un periódico hispano en su comunidad. Su próximo artículo va a ser una descripción de la comida y del servicio de un restaurante popular entre la gente de su edad. Vaya a ese restaurante, pida una comida completa y tome apuntes para escribir su artículo. Después, escriba el artículo e incluya la siguiente información:

- el nombre del restaurante y dónde está
- el día y la hora que usted comió allí
- una descripción de la comida que usted pidió
- el precio de cada cosa que usted comió y bebió
- sus impresiones de la comida y del servicio
- sus recomendaciones sinceras para el público

VOCABULARIO

Sustantivos

los anteojos *eyeglasses*
el (la) camarero(a) *server (Spain)*
la cuenta *bill*
el cuento *story*
la especialidad *specialty*
el hielo *ice*
la niñez *childhood*
el papagayo *parrot*
el pedido *order*
la propina *tip (gratuity)*

En la mesa

la botella *bottle*
la copa *glass (for wine)*
la cuchara *spoon*
el cuchillo *knife*
la jarra *pitcher (for liquids)*
el pimentero *pepper shaker*
el plato *plate*
el salero *salt shaker*
la servilleta *napkin*
la taza *cup*
el tenedor *fork*
el vaso *glass (for water)*

La comida

la entrada *main course; entrance*
el entremés *appetizer*
la gaseosa *soft drink (Spain)*
la pimienta *pepper (spice)*
las patatas fritas *French fries (Spain)*
la sal *salt*
las tapas *hors d'oeuvres*
la tortilla *omelette (Spain)*

Adjetivos

frito *fried*
fuerte *loud, strong*

Verbos

apuntar *to jot down*
ayudar *to help*
comentar *to comment*
enamorarse (de) *to fall in love (with)*
gritar *to shout*
morir (o→ue, o→u) *to die*
sacar *to take out*
seguir (e→i) *to follow*
sentarse (e→ie) *to sit down*

Expresiones idiomáticas

¡Buen provecho! *Enjoy your meal!*
dar las gracias *to thank*
estar de vacaciones *to be on vacation*

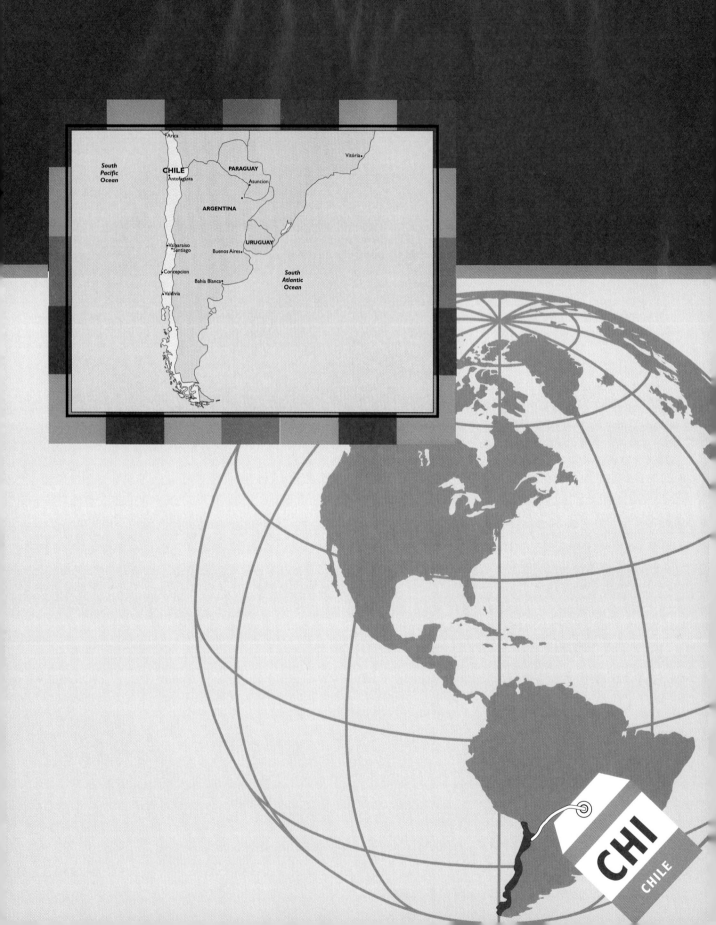

South
Pacific
Ocean

Arica

CHILE

Antofagasta

PARAGUAY

Asuncion

VitÓria

ARGENTINA

Valparaiso
Santiago

URUGUAY

Buenos Aires

Concepcion

Bahía Blanca

South
Atlantic
Ocean

Valdivia

CHI
CHILE

¡Que se diviertan Uds!

►*Chile*◄

We first meet Luis and Jorge as they vacation in the resort community of Viña del Mar. Back home in Santiago, the two university students learn that a young woman they saw at the beach has been selected as queen of an international song festival. Later, Jorge and his girl friend attend the festival queen's wedding, where they have a good time.

13

¡Que les vaya bien!

▶ COMMUNICATIVE GOALS

You will be able to describe your outdoor activities and a short vacation trip.

▶ LANGUAGE FUNCTIONS

**Giving advice
Expressing wants
Persuading others
Making invitations
Expressing intentions
Making recommendations
Describing weekend activities**

http://poco.heinle.com

▶ VOCABULARY THEMES

**Beach resort
Country outing**

▶ GRAMMATICAL STRUCTURES

Present subjunctive following *querer*
Present subjunctive following other verbs of volition

▶ CULTURAL INFORMATION

**Viña del Mar
The history of Viña del Mar**

Write for free information on
Chile: Chilean Embassy: 1732
Massachusetts Avenue, N.W.,
Washington, DC 20036.

EN CONTEXTO

 Play Lab Tape

Era un día de enero muy bonito en Viña del Mar, un balneario° popular en la *costa* chilena. (1) Hacía mucho sol y la temperatura subió a 30 grados centígrados. (2) Luis Weissman y su amigo Jorge Grandinetti, (3) estudiantes de la Universidad Católica de Chile, estaban de vacaciones en Viña durante todo el mes de enero. (4) Ese día mientras ellos tomaban el sol en la playa de Reñaca, (5) pasó cerca de ellos una *chica guapa* de 18 años. Ella caminó hacia el mar y entró en el agua a nadar.

beach resort

Some of the new words in this reading passage appear in italics to provide students with practice in contextual guessing.

—Mira a esa chica, Jorge. Muy bonita, ¿verdad?
—Sí, tienes razón. Hay tantas chicas bonitas por aquí.
—¡Uy! Hace mucho calor hoy. Oye, Jorge... vamos a nadar.
—¿Cómo que nadar? Recuerda que no nadas bien, Luis. ¿Por qué no tomas unas clases de *natación*?
—¿Dónde y con quién?
—¡Aquí en Reñaca, hombre! Esa chica que vimos te puede enseñar° a nadar.

teach

—¿Cómo sabes eso, Jorge?
—La vi ayer dándoles una lección a dos *chicos* adolescentes.
—Bueno, voy a preguntarle si tiene tiempo para darme una lección ahora mismo.° Chao, Jorge.
—Chao.

right now

Luis corrió por la playa donde charlaban la profesora de natación y un hombre alto y musculoso.

—Perdón, señorita. ¡Buenos días! ¿Cuándo puedo tomar mi primera clase de natación?
—¡Ahora mismo, señor! ¡Buenos días y mucho gusto! Me llamo María Cristina. ¿Y usted?
—Me llamo Luis. Encantado.
—Y este chico es mi novio (6) Gregorio. Él enseña a esquiar. Pero le sugiero que usted aprenda a nadar bien primero y luego aprenda a esquiar.

Luis y María Cristina caminaban al mar y Luis comenzó a nadar pero con un poco de dificultad. *Al poco tiempo*, él estaba nadando mejor. Cuando su amigo Jorge se despertó de la siesta que dormía en la playa, no podía creer que el chico que nadaba en el mar era su amigo Luis.

—Gracias, por la clase de natación. ¡Es usted una buena *nadadora* y profesora! ¿Nos vemos otra vez mañana?
—Claro que sí. Mi novio (6) Gregorio y yo estamos aquí entre las nueve de la mañana hasta la una de la tarde.
—Bien. Pues, ahora me voy. Mi amigo Jorge me está esperando. ¡Que les vaya bien!
—Gracias. ¡Que les vaya bien a ustedes también!

Notas de texto

1. The resort city of Viña del Mar (known locally as Viña) is located 85 miles (130 kilometers) west of Santiago, the capital of Chile. There are a half dozen beaches near Viña, but the water there can be quite frigid, even in summer.

2. Remember that the seasons in the Northern and Southern Hemispheres are reversed. Therefore, in Chile the summer months are December, January, and February.

3. Luis Weissman and Jorge Grandinetti are names that represent many Chileans who are of Jewish and Italian descent, respectively. Large numbers of immigrants from Great Britain, Germany, Croatia, Bosnia-Hertzogovina, and other countries have also contributed to the population of Chile.

4. Chilean students are on their summer vacation during January and February.

5. *Playa de Reñaca*, located about four miles (six kilometers) north of Viña del Mar, is a favorite beach for teenagers and young adults because of its white sand, huge waves, soda fountains, discos, and bowling alleys.

6. The words *novio* and *novia* mean "fiancé(e)" as well as "groom" and "bride," respectively. In most Spanish-speaking countries, *novio* also means boyfriend, and *novia* means girlfriend. In Chile, however, the words *pololo* and *polola* are the equivalent of boyfriend and girlfriend, respectively. In all Spanish-speaking countries, a man or woman who is a friend but is not going steady or engaged is called *amigo(a)*.

¿Comprendió Ud.?

Lea la lectura rápidamente para comprender las ideas más importantes. Luego complete las siguientes oraciones.

Answers: 1. [open] 2. *Viña del Mar (Playa de Reñaca / Chile)* 3. *nadar* 4. *tomar el sol*

Answers: 1. IP 2. IS 3. IS 4. IP 5. IP 6. IS 7. IS 8. IP 9. IP 10. IS
Answer: [open]

1. Otro título apropiado para esta lectura es _____.
2. La acción de esta lectura ocurrió en _____.
3. Luis quería (nadar / dormir / correr / pescar).
4. Jorge prefirió (hacer ejercicio / esquiar / tomar el sol).

Lea la lectura otra vez. Luego indique si las siguientes oraciones representan una idea principal (IP) o una idea secundaria (IS).

1. _____ Jorge y Luis son amigos.
2. _____ Hacía muy buen tiempo ese día.
3. _____ Luis no sabía nadar muy bien.
4. _____ Jorge y Luis fueron a una playa.
5. _____ Luis tomó una clase de natación.
6. _____ Los dos amigos estaban de vacaciones.
7. _____ Ellos son estudiantes universitarios.
8. _____ Mientras Luis nadaba, Jorge dormía la siesta.
9. _____ María Cristina era una buena nadadora.
10. _____ El novio de la joven se llamaba Gregorio.

Con un(a) compañero(a) de clase, lean otra vez y escriban un resumen de la lectura, en cinco minutos. Tengan cuidado con el vocabulario, la gramática y la puntuación. Luego compartan su resumen con la clase.

NOTAS **CULTURALES**

Viña del Mar

Viña del Mar es la ciudad balnearia más famosa de Chile. Cuenta con diversas playas rodeadas de amplias veredas peatonales° y hermosas plazas y jardines floridos. Sus calles principales están adornadas de grandes palmeras; por ejemplo, en la Avenida Libertad hay un bonito túnel de follaje° formado por enormes plátanos orientales. En los barrios residenciales de Viña se ven bellos "chalets" rodeados de jardines y en el borde del mar hay una larga avenida de altos edificios con balcones abiertos al océano, que se van alternando con una sucesión de plazas y jardines.

pedestrian sidewalks

foliage

La actividad de Viña es intensa y continuada: existe una infinidad de restaurantes, bares, fuentes de soda, cafés, confiterías, heladerías y salones de té. También hay sitios de esparcimiento° como lugares de baile, juego y de prácticas deportivas. La vida cívica de la ciudad se concentra en la calle Valparaíso, centro comercial y lugar de reunión a mediodía en sus cafés y confiterías; el esparcimiento se concentra en sus playas y, en las noches, en los miles de entretenimientos que ofrecen los distintos centros del litoral.°

recreation

costa

Source: *Turistel: Guía Turística de todo Chile*, páginas 238 y 244–245.

¿Qué dice usted?

1. ¿Conoce usted una ciudad balnearia como Viña del Mar? (¿Sí? ¿La conoce personalmente o solamente por un artículo que usted leyó?)
2. En comparación con Viña, ¿cómo es la ciudad balnearia que usted conoce? ¿En qué se diferencian estos dos balnearios?
3. ¿Qué debe tener un balneario ideal? (Por ejemplo: actividades deportivas, restaurantes, tiendas.)

Have students write their answers to these questions as a homework assignment.

VOCABULARIO ÚTIL

In this section you will learn to describe activities that take place at a beach and in the country.

TRANSPARENCY No. 24: At the Beach

En un balneario

—¿Qué quieres hacer hoy?
—Pues, no sé. Podemos...

la pelota

jugar al vólibol

bucear

correr las olas

hacer el esnórquel

pasear en velero

esquiar sobre el agua

Use illustrations from your picture file to review the following words related to this new vocabulary: *hacer sol, hacer buen tiempo, anteojos para el sol, traje de baño, nadar, piscina, paraguas, mariscos, pescado, pescar.*

En el campo *(country)*

—¿Qué piensas hacer mañana?
—Bueno, no sé. Podemos...

pasear en canoa	**caminar por las montañas**	**pescar en un lago**
acampar al lado de un río	**hacer un picnic**	**hacer una parrillada**

Practiquemos

A. ¿Con qué frecuencia? Indique con un número la frecuencia con la que usted hace las siguientes actividades cuando va a la playa o al campo.

0 = Nunca   1 = A veces   2 = Muchas veces

_____ Duermo la siesta.
_____ Esquío en el agua.
_____ Practico algún deporte.
_____ Tomo el sol y me bronceo.
_____ Paseo en velero o en canoa.
_____ Tomo jugo o algún refresco frío.
_____ Hago una parrillada o un picnic.
_____ Nado en un lago, un río o en el mar.

Ahora compare sus respuestas con las respuestas de un(a) compañero(a) de clase.

Ex. A. Follow-up activity: Have students compare their reactions to these statements with the reactions of a classmate.

B. En el campo. Descríbale a otro(a) estudiante lo que está pasando en este dibujo.

TRANSPARENCY No. 25: By the Lake

C. Problemas y soluciones. Converse con otra persona. Estudiante A debe leer el problema indicado y Estudiante B debe ofrecer una solución lógica.

Ejemplo: A: No me gusta nadar en el mar.
   B: *Puedes nadar en una piscina.*

1. Me gustaría ir a un balneario, pero no tengo auto.
2. No me gusta comer pescado porque soy vegetariano(a).
3. No sé bucear, pero quiero ver cómo es debajo del mar.
4. Algún día me gustaría aprender a bucear, pero no sé adónde ir.
5. Siempre tengo miedo de broncearme mucho cuando voy a la playa.
6. Me gusta pasear en canoa, pero no tengo dinero para comprar una.

Ahora cambien papeles y hagan otra conversación.

D. ¡A pasarlo bien! Hable con otro(a) estudiante. Imagínense que ustedes van a pasar un fin de semana en un balneario o en el campo. Primero, hagan una lista de las actividades que ustedes van a hacer en ese lugar el sábado y el domingo. Luego hagan una lista de todo lo que usted van a llevar allí. Traten de *(Try to)* usar el vocabulario de esta lección y de otras lecciones también. Mientras ustedes participan en esta actividad, hablen solamente en español.

Ejemplo:

Día	Lugar	Actividades	Cosas para llevar
sábado	Lago Mendota	sacar fotos	una cámara
	Café "Internet"	tomar el sol	un traje de baño
		comer mariscos	doscientos dólares

For extra conversation practice on a sports-related theme, have students redo Activities F, G, and H on page 77 [Lección 3].

E. Situaciones. Hable con otro(a) estudiante.

Estudiante A: Imagínese que ahora su amigo(a) chileno(a) ya conoce la ciudad y quiere comenzar a hacer ejercicio porque en Chile era un(a) gran deportista. Pregúntele cuál es su deporte favorito, si le gusta esquiar en el agua o en la nieve, si le gusta patinar, montar a caballo, jugar al fútbol, correr, caminar y en qué equipo o qué deporte le gusta practicar.

Estudiante B: Imagínese que usted ya visitó la ciudad y le pareció muy bonita. Ahora quiere comenzar a hacer más ejercicio ya que en Chile usted practicaba deportes todos los días. Converse con su compañero(a) y pregúntele sobre los deportes que puede practicar en la escuela o en la comunidad. Conteste las preguntas que él (ella) le va a hacer con respecto a sus gustos en los deportes.

GRAMÁTICA FUNCIONAL

Expressing wants and intentions

—Quiero que leas este libro, Luis.
—¿Un libro sobre cómo nadar, Jorge?
—Sí, hombre. Quiero que nades mejor.

Present subjunctive following the verb *querer*

You have used the present indicative to state facts, to describe conditions, to express actions, and to ask questions.

Luis **es** el amigo de Jorge.	*Luis is Jorge's friend.*
En enero **hace** calor en Viña.	*In January it's hot in Viña.*
Jorge **está bronceándose.**	*Jorge is getting a tan.*
¿Te **gusta** tomar el sol?	*Do you like to sunbathe?*

The present subjunctive has many uses. One purpose for which Spanish speakers use the subjunctive is to express what they want others to do.

Jorge quiere que Luis **nade** mejor.	*Jorge wants Luis to swim better.*
Él quiere que **tome** lecciones.	*He wants him to take lessons.*

This section introduces students to the forms of the present subjunctive and how to use them after the verb *querer*, one of its most common uses in Spanish. Since the subjunctive is acquired fairly late in the process of second language acquisition, do not expect students to master this mood in their first-year course. Instead, expect them to understand its meaning when they hear and read Spanish.

Point out the following rationale for using the *yo* form of the present indicative: it is a point of departure to construct present subjunctive forms for verbs having spelling changes; most of the information students need is contained in the stem of the *yo* form.

Point out that the personal endings for *-er* and *-ir* verbs are identical.

Tell students to use these charts as a source of reference, rather than to memorize them. At first, your students will make many errors in verb endings, but assure them that their spoken and written language will be understood in spite of these common initial errors.

Emphasize that the *usted* and *ustedes* forms of the present subjunctive are the same as the *usted* and *ustedes* command forms.

Point out that the stem changes *u* and *i* in the *nosotros* and *vosotros* forms also occur in the present participles: e.g., *durmiendo, divirtiéndose.* Write several more examples on the chalkboard or on an overhead transparency, if you wish.

How to form the present subjunctive

1. To form the present subjunctive of most verbs, drop the *-o* from the present indicative *yo* form, then add the endings shown.

	-ar verbs	**-er verbs**	**-ir verbs**
	lavarse	*hacer*	*escribir*
(yo)	me lave	haga	escriba
(tú)	te laves	hagas	escribas
(usted, él/ella)	se lave	haga	escriba
(nosotros/nosotras)	nos lavemos	hagamos	escribamos
(vosotros/vosotras)	*os lavéis*	*hagáis*	*escribáis*
(ustedes, ellos/ellas)	se laven	hagan	escriban

2. The stem of verbs that end in *-car*, *-gar*, and *-zar* have a spelling change to maintain pronunciation. Note the similarity to their formal command forms.

sacar (c→qu)	llegar (g→gu)	comenzar (z→c)
saque	llegue	comience
saques	llegues	comiences
saque	llegues	comience
saquemos	lleguemos	comencemos
saquéis	*lleguéis*	*comencéis*
saquen	lleguen	comiencen

—¿Quieres que yo **saque** fotos?   *Do you want me to take photos?*
—Sí, quiero que **comiences** ahora.   *Yes, I want you to start now.*

3. Stem-changing verbs that end in *-ar* and *-er* have the same stem changes *(e→ie, o→ue)* in the present indicative and in the present subjunctive.

pensar (e→ie)		poder (o→ue)	
Present Indicative	Present Subjunctive	Present Indicative	Present Subjunctive
pienso	piense	puedo	pueda
piensas	pienses	puedes	puedas
piensa	piense	puede	pueda
pensamos	pensemos	podemos	podamos
pensáis	*penséis*	*podéis*	*podáis*
piensan	piensen	pueden	puedan

—¿Qué te dijo tu mamá?   *What did your Mom tell you?*
—Quiere que yo **vuelva** a casa.   *She wants me to return home.*

4. Stem-changing verbs that end in *-ir* have the same stem changes
   (e→ie, o→ue) in the present indicative and in the present subjunctive. The *nosotros* and *vosotros* forms have a stem change *(e→i,
   o→u)* in the present subjunctive.

divertirse (e→ie)   dormir (o→ue)

Present Indicative	Present Subjunctive	Present Indicative	Present Subjunctive
me div**ie**rto	me div**ie**rta	d**ue**rmo	d**ue**rma
te div**ie**rtes	te div**ie**rtas	d**ue**rmes	d**ue**rmas
se div**ie**rte	se div**ie**rta	d**ue**rme	d**ue**rma
nos divertimos	nos div**i**rtamos	dormimos	d**u**rmamos
os divertís	*os div**i**rtáis*	*dormís*	*d**u**rmáis*
se div**ie**rten	se div**ie**rtan	d**ue**rmen	d**ue**rman

—Quiero que t**e** **diviertas** en Viña.   *I want you to have fun in Viña.*
—Gracias. Y quiero que **recuerdes**   *Thank you. And I want you to re-*
  mandarme una tarjeta postal.   *member to send me a postcard.*

5. The verbs *pedir* and *servir* have the same stem change *(e→i)* in
   the present indicative and in the present subjunctive. The *nosotros*
   and *vosotros* forms have a stem change *(e→i)* in the present
   subjunctive.

pedir (e→i)   servir (e→i)

Present Indicative	Present Subjunctive	Present Indicative	Present Subjunctive
pido	pida	sirvo	sirva
pides	pidas	sirves	sirvas
pide	pida	sirve	sirva
pedimos	pidamos	servimos	sirvamos
pedís	*pidáis*	*servís*	*sirváis*
piden	pidan	sirven	sirvan

—Quiero que nos **sirvan** pronto.   *I want them to serve us soon.*
—¿Quieres que yo **pida** por ti?   *Do you want me to order for you?*
—No, gracias. Yo puedo hacerlo.   *No, thanks. I can do it.*

6. Some verbs have irregular forms in the present subjunctive because
   their stems are not based on the *yo* form of the present indicative.

dar	estar	ir	saber	ser
dé	esté	vaya	sepa	sea
des	estés	vayas	sepas	seas
dé	esté	vaya	sepa	sea
demos	estemos	vayamos	sepamos	seamos
deis	*estéis*	*vayáis*	*sepáis*	*seáis*
den	estén	vayan	sepan	sean

—¿Quieres que te **dé** mi
dirección en Viña?

—Sí. Y quiero que **sepas** mi
número de teléfono de casa.

*Do you want me to give you my
Address in Viña?*

*Yes. And I want you to know my
home telephone number.*

How to use the present subjunctive with querer

1. A form of the verb *querer* (to want) is followed by a verb in the subjunctive when the subject of the dependent clause is **different** from the subject of the independent clause. The two clauses are linked together by the word *que* (that).

Change of subject

(*Luis*) quiere que   (*Jorge*) **nade** ahora.
Independent clause   Dependent clause

¡CUIDADO! Often it is incorrect to translate word for word from Spanish into English and vice versa. For example, note both the literal translation and the correct translation of the Spanish sentence in the example above.

Spanish sentence: **Luis quiere que Jorge nade ahora.**
Literal translation: Luis wants **that Jorge** swim now.
Correct translation: Luis wants **Jorge to swim** now.

2. In sentences that have **no change of subject**, an **infinitive** follows a form of the verb *querer.* Compare the following sentences.

No change of subject   **Change of subject**

Luis quiere **nadar** ahora. → *Luis* quiere que *Jorge* **nade** ahora.
Luis wants to swim now.   *Luis wants Jorge to swim now.*

3. Place pronouns before conjugated verbs in the present subjunctive.

—Queremos que **te diviertas.** *We want you to have fun.*
—Y yo quiero que **me escribas.** *And I want you to write me.*
—¿Quieres mi dirección? *Do you want my address?*
—Sí, quiero que **me la des.** *Yes, I want you to give it to me.*

Practiquemos

A. ¿Qué quieren mis padres? ¿Qué dice Jorge sobre lo que quieren sus padres para él? Termine cada oración con un verbo apropiado de la lista.

esté	saque	termine	encuentre
tenga	visite	me case	me divierta

Mis padres quieren que yo...

1. _____ buena salud toda mi vida.
2. _____ mucho cada día de mi vida.
3. _____ buenas notas en todos mis cursos.
4. _____ mis estudios de la universidad.
5. _____ un trabajo bien pagado en Santiago.
6. _____ feliz con mis ambiciones y decisiones.
7. _____ en cuatro años con mi novia Leticia.
8. los _____ frecuentemente después de casarme.

B. Consejos de mamá. La mamá de Jorge Grandinetti les dio algunos consejos a su hijo y a Luis en el día que salieron para Viña del Mar. En Viña Jorge recuerda a Luis lo que dijo la señora Grandinetti. ¿Qué dice Jorge?

Ejemplos: SEÑORA: Aprendan a nadar bien.
JORGE: *Mi mamá quiere que **aprendamos** a nadar bien.*

1. Escríbanles a los abuelos.
2. Saquen muchas fotos de Viña.
3. Corran mucho para hacer ejercicio.
4. No olviden de llamar por teléfono.
5. Regresen a Santiago en buena salud.
6. No coman en los restaurantes caros.
7. Paguen todo con dinero en efectivo.
8. No naden en las partes profundas del mar.

C. ¡Ay, los parientes! Cuando Jorge y Luis estaban en la playa de Reñaca, conocieron a Isabel, una chica de diez y siete años. ¿Qué les dice ella sobre algunos consejos que le dieron sus parientes?

Ejemplo: (hacer) *Hago* un poco de ejercicio ahora, pero mis padres quieren que *haga* mucho más.

1. (salir) _____ con mi pololo frecuentemente durante la semana, pero mi papá quiere que _____ con él solamente los fines de semana.
2. (venir) _____ a Viña para divertirme mucho, pero mi mamá quiere que _____ para descansar un poco de mis estudios del colegio.
3. (saber) _____ un poco de inglés, pero mi abuelito quiere que _____ hablar bien esa lengua.

4. (poner) _____ la mesa los fines de semana, pero mis padres quieren que la _____ todos los días.

5. (decir) Les _____ a mis amigos algunos secretos de mi hermano, pero él no quiere que les _____ ninguno.

6. (ser) _____ una buena estudiante en el colegio, pero mi tío quiere que _____ la mejor estudiante de la escuela

7. (ver) _____ muchas películas en vídeo, pero mi abuelita quiere que las _____ menos.

D. ¿Qué dice usted?

Imagínese que usted es el papá o la mamá de Gregorio, el hombre que enseña a esquiar y el novio de María Cristina. Gregorio y su novia van a casarse pronto. Escríbales una carta en la que usted les dice lo que ellos deben hacer antes del matrimonio. Primero, haga una lista de sus recomendaciones. Luego escriba la carta.

Ejemplos (lista): *Ahorren mucho dinero antes de casarse.*
Hablen tranquilamente sobre sus problemas.

Ejemplo (carta): *Quiero que ustedes ahorren mucho dinero antes de casarse porque van a necesitarlo. Quiero que hablen tranquilamente sobre sus problemas porque...*

Charlemos

E. Aspiraciones.

Primero, dígale a otro(a) estudiante lo que usted quiere. Luego dígale lo que quieren sus padres o su esposo/esposa.

Ejemplos: *Quiero hacer más ejercicio.*
Mis padres quieren que yo descanse mucho más.
Mi esposa quiere que yo haga más ejercicio.

Yo quiero...

Mis padres quieren que yo...

Mi marido/esposa quiere que yo...

1. ahorrar más dinero
2. hacer más ejercicio
3. descansar mucho más
4. dormir más horas cada noche
5. estudiar mucho en la escuela
6. llegar a mis clases a tiempo
7. pagar todas mis cuentas pronto
8. aprender a hablar bien el español
9. vivir en un país de habla española
10. visitar a mis abuelos frecuentemente

F. Otras conversaciones.

Hable con un(a) compañero(a) de clase, según las siguientes situaciones.

1. **Una invitación**
   a. Invítelo(la) a ir al campo con usted.
   b. Dígale cuándo y a qué hora usted quiere ir.
   c. Explíquele qué quiere hacer usted allí.

2. **Un favor**
    a. Pídale un pequeño favor.
    b. Explíquele por qué lo quiere.
    c. Dígale cuándo usted necesita el favor.

3. **Un plan**
    a. Dígale los planes de usted para este fin de semana.
    b. Explíquele qué quiere usted hacer allí.
    c. Dígale otra información apropiada.

NOTAS CULTURALES

La historia de Viña del Mar

La historia de Viña es corta, recién centenaria. El lugar fue una hacienda desde la época de la colonia y su nombre proviene de una viña° que existió donde hoy está la Quinta Rioja. En 1855 quedó unida a Valparaíso por el ferrocarril° y desde entonces los porteños° comienzan a visitar el valle de Viña, donde hacían paseos campestres, carreras° de caballos y asistían a los baños de mar instalados en la playa Miramar, hoy desaparecida. Hacia 1872, unos porteños, principalmente extranjeros,° obtuvieron sitios en arriendo° próximos a la línea del tren, donde edificaron sus casas rodeadas de grandes terrenos con jardín, que la estrechez de Valparaíso no permitía. La propietaria de la hacienda de Viña, doña Dolores P. de Álvarez, tenía su casa y un bellísimo y exótico parque en los terrenos de la actual Quinta Vergara.

vineyard
railroad
residents of Valparaíso, Chile
races
foreigners
rented

En 1874 se funda Viña del Mar; el Sporting Club se funda en 1882. Entretanto se había edificado el elegante Gran Hotel —hoy desaparecido— que inició las visitas, hasta hoy ininterrumpidas, de santiaguinos° a esta costa. En 1892 se comienza la construcción de grandes mansiones de veraneo y las de los nuevos residentes venidos de Valparaíso. El crecimiento° de la ciudad balnearia ha sido desde entonces constante.

residents of Santiago, Chile

growth

Source: *Turistel: Guía Turística de todo Chile*, página 244.

¿Comprendió Ud.?

Lea la lectura otra vez, luego ponga los números 1–6 al lado de cada frase, según el orden cronológico de la historia de Viña del Mar.

Answers:
Chronological order: 1, 3, 6, 5, 4, 2

_____ Se ve una sola hacienda rodeada de viñas.
_____ Se construyen casas grandes en el siglo XIX.
_____ Se construyen casas grandes y modernas en Viña.
_____ Se establece el Sporting Club de Viña del Mar.
_____ Se establece oficialmente la ciudad de Viña del Mar.
_____ Valparaíso y Viña del Mar se conectan por ferrocarril.

¡Conteste! ¿Qué piensa?

1. ¿En qué año se fundó la ciudad de Viña del Mar?
2. ¿De dónde originó el nombre "Viña del Mar"?

1. 1874 2. De una viña que estaba cerca del mar 3. Iban al mar, a carreras de caballos, asistían a los baños, iban a los hoteles grandes. 4. Grandes y elegantes 5. Grandes mansiones de veraneo

3. ¿Cómo se divertía la gente que vivía en aquella ciudad?
4. ¿Cómo eran algunas de sus casas?
5. ¿Cómo son algunas casas de Viña hoy día?

1. Point out that this dialogue contains examples of how the indicative and subjunctive are used together in a natural conversation.
2. Have students role-play this dialogue in pairs.

GRAMÁTICA FUNCIONAL

Expressing wishes, preferences, advice, suggestions, and recommendations

—Sugiero que volvamos al hotel.
—Prefiero ir al Bar Coyote.
—Mi papá me prohibe que vaya allí.
—¿No te permite que tomes?
—No. Insiste en que yo no tome alcohol.

Present subjunctive following other verbs of volition

In the previous section, you learned how to use the verb *querer* to express wants and intentions. Spanish speakers use other verbs of volition to persuade people to do something.

aconsejar	*to advise*	**permitir**	*to permit*
desear	*to desire, wish*	**preferir (e→ie)**	*to prefer*
decir (e→i)	*to order*	**prohibir**	*to forbid*
insistir (en)	*to insist (on)*	**recomendar (e→ie)**	*to recommend*
pedir (e→i)	*to request*	**sugerir (e→ie)**	*to suggest*

How to use verbs of volition

1. Use these verbs exactly as you did with the verb *querer*.

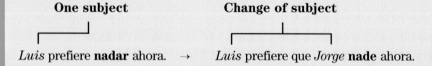

One subject	**Change of subject**
Luis prefiere **nadar** ahora. →	*Luis* prefiere que *Jorge* **nade** ahora.

2. An indirect object often precedes some verbs of volition in the independent clause (e.g., **aconsejar, decir, pedir, permitir, prohibir, recomendar, sugerir**). In this case, it is not necessary to include a subject pronoun before the subjunctive verb form in the dependent clause; the indirect object indicates the subject of the dependent clause.

—¿**Te permiten** tus padres que **salgas** ahora? (**te → salgas**)
—Sí, pero **me prohiben** que **vaya** al Bar Coyote. (**me → vaya**)

Practiquemos

A. Deseos y consejos. Luis está repitiéndole a Jorge lo que algunas personas quieren que haga. ¿Qué dice Luis?

Ejemplo: mi mamá / insistir en / lavar el auto
Mi mamá insiste en que yo lave el auto.

1. mi hermana Rona no / querer / le asustar *(to frighten, scare)*
2. mis profesores / insistir en / estudiar más
3. mis padres / desear / hacer más ejercicio
4. tú me / aconsejar no / nadar en agua profunda
5. mis amigos / sugerir / aprender a nadar mejor
6. mi amiga Ana / preferir / le dar rosas, no chocolates
7. María Cristina / me pedir / aprender a nadar primero

B. Preferencias. Jorge está haciéndole algunas sugerencias a Luis. ¿Qué quiere Jorge?

Ejemplo: Ya (tener) *tenemos* algunos amigos aquí. Deseo que *tengamos* muchos otros.

1. (jugar) _____ al tenis frecuentemente. Deseo que _____ a otro deporte mañana.
2. (hacer) _____ muy poco ejercicio, Luis. Mi mamá recomienda que _____ algo más, por ejemplo, podemos correr o montar en bicicleta.
3. (levantarse) _____ a las ocho de la mañana. Quiero que _____ más tarde porque estamos de vacaciones.
4. (dormir) _____ solamente cinco horas al día. Sugiero que _____ siete u ocho horas porque siempre estoy cansado.
5. Siempre (almorzar) _____ en el Restaurante Solymar. Insisto en que _____ en otros restaurantes.
6. A veces (ir) _____ a los restaurantes caros. Prefiero que no _____ a ningún otro restaurante caro porque no tenemos mucho dinero.

C. Necesito consejos. Imagínese que usted trabaja para un periódico y que contesta cartas de muchas personas que le piden sus consejos. Lea las siguientes cartas, y luego contéstelas con diplomacia.

1. *Vivo en una ciudad pequeña. Los fines de semana no hay nada que hacer. Tenemos un cine, pero las películas son viejas; también las cambian solamente una vez a la semana. Tengo muchos amigos de mi edad (20 años), pero ellos dicen que están tan aburridos como yo. ¿Qué recomiendas que hagamos?*

Humberto

Comprendo muy bien tu problema, Humberto. Recomiendo que tú y tus amigos...

2. *Tengo dos hermanas mayores que yo. Julia tiene veinticinco años, Lucía tiene veintidós y yo tengo catorce. Mis padres les dan a mis hermanas mucha libertad. Por ejemplo, ellas pueden pasar la noche en la casa de sus amigas, pueden salir con ellas a la playa o al cine y pueden volver a casa a la una de la mañana. En cambio, yo no tengo tanta libertad como ellas y, por eso, protesto mucho en casa. Ahora mis padres están furiosos conmigo. ¿Qué puedo hacer?*

Josefina

Primero, Josefina, quiero pedirte que no... Segundo, sugiero que...

Charlemos

D. Recomendaciones. Imagínese que usted trabaja de camarero(a) en el restaurante Solymar, donde algunos de sus clientes le piden que les recomiende algo del menú. ¿Qué le contesta usted a cada persona? (Los verbos entre paréntesis son sugerencias; usted puede usar otros verbos.)

Ejemplo: CLIENTE: Tengo mucha sed. (tomar)
              CAMARERO(A):   *Le recomiendo que tome agua mineral.*

1. Tengo mucha hambre, pero estoy a dieta esta semana. (pedir)
2. A mi niño le gustan los pasteles, pero es diabético. (comer)
3. Mi novio y yo somos vegetarianos y no sabemos qué pedir. (servir)
4. A mí me gusta mucho la carne. ¿Qué me recomienda usted? (traer)
5. Mis amigos y yo estamos aquí para celebrar mi cumpleaños. (comenzar)

Ex. E Follow-up: Students could write a composition based on the cues provided here.

E. ¡A viajar! Imagínese que usted y un(a) amigo(a) sólo se comunican por correo electrónico. Están planeado unas vacaciones en Viña del Mar. Una persona va a escribir sobre a qué lugar quieren ir juntos, cuándo desean salir, dónde van a alojarse, y qué quieren hacer allí. Y la otra persona va a recomendarle a su tío lo que debe ver, hacer, comer y comprar.

PARA LEER MEJOR

Reading Complex Sentences

Determining what is essential and what is non-essential in complex sentences will help you read Spanish efficiently. The core of a complex sentence consists of its subject and its main verb.

Activities

A. Identify the subject and the main verb in each of the following sentences.

Chile está dividido en varias regiones geográficas. La Quinta Región es la zona turística del país. Viña del Mar ofrece sus playas, balnearios, casino y su aire de gran ciudad. También Valparaíso, el puerto principal y la capital de la Quinta Región de Chile, merece° ser recorrido con atención: sus cerros° y casas colgantes° lo señalan como una ciudad "colgada para arriba".

deserves

hills / hanging

Por su cercanía a Santiago, capital de Chile, la Quinta Región concentra cada año la mayor cantidad de veraneantes y turistas en el país. Gran actividad social se desarrolla° aquí en los meses de enero y febrero con atractivos eventos deportivos y artísticos.

happens

Source: Adapted from Ladeco Airlines brochure

B. Read the article again to answer the following questions.

1. ¿En qué región están Viña del Mar y Valparaíso?
2. ¿Qué cosa de la ciudad de Valparaíso es interesante?
3. ¿En qué estación del año de Chile llegan muchos turistas a la Quinta Región?
4. De las actividades que les ofrece Viña del Mar a los turistas, ¿cuál le interesa a usted más? ¿Por qué?

Answers:
A. *Chile / está, La Quinta Región / es, Viña del Mar / ofrece, Valparaíso / merece, sus cerros y casas colgantes / señalan, la Quinta Región / concentra, Gran actividad social / se desarrolla*
B. 1. *la Quinta Región* 2. [open] 3. *el verano* 4. [open]

Atajo

Functions:
Writing a letter (informal); asking and giving advice; describing weather; weighing alternatives

Vocabulary:
Camping; beach; seasons; weather; sports; leisure

Grammar:
Verbs: imperative, subjunctive agreement; Conjunction *que*

PARA ESCRIBIR MEJOR

Giving Advice

When giving advice to people, we usually suggest some things they should and should not do. When doing so, we sometimes use affirmative commands (e.g., *Vaya*) and negative commands (e.g., *No compre*), which you learned to form and use in *Lección 9*. Use the following guidelines to help you give advice in writing.

I. Introductory paragraph: state the purpose of your letter.

II. Second paragraph: indicate specific things to do.
    A. Give three suggestions, using affirmative commands.
    B. Provide at least one detail to support each suggestion.

III. Third paragraph: indicate specific things not to do.
    A. Give two suggestions, using negative commands.
    B. Provide at least one detail to support each suggestion.

IV. Concluding paragraph: write some words of encouragement.

Example:

Queridos amigos,

Me pidieron algunos consejos sobre las actividades que pueden hacer durante sus vacaciones de verano aquí en el estado de Washington.

Primero, caminen por las montañas Cascades y hagan un picnic allí. Hay muchos lugares bonitos no lejos de Seattle y otras ciudades más pequeñas. Vayan a la costa y contemplen el Océano Pacífico. Allí corran las olas o paseen en velero. Es posible alquilar el equipo necesario si no lo tienen. También tomen el sol en la playa, pero recuerden llevar crema bronceadora porque aquí hay mucho sol en el verano, ¿eh?

Claro que hay tantas cosas de hacer aquí, pero no traten de hacerlas todas. Con esta carta les mando información que me dieron en la oficina de turismo. Ahora pueden informarse mejor. Una cosa importante: Nunca tiren basura en las montañas ni en el mar ni en las playas. Queremos mantener limpia nuestra región. Ya sé que ustedes son personas muy comprensivas.

Pues, sé que ustedes van a divertirse mucho en mi estado, amigos. Traigan su cámara y los espero en el aeropuerto. ¡Vamos a pasarlo muy bien aquí!

Su amigo, Diego

Activity

Write a letter to two Spanish-speaking friends, giving them advice on a topic of your choice. Refer to the outline and example composition in which the author gives a friend advice on some outdoor activities in Washington State.

SÍNTESIS

¡A ver!

Several Hispanics are going to talk about what and how they spend their free time outdoors. First, study the sentence and words with their meaning in the *Vocabulario esencial*. Second, read the direction line in the activity below. Third, watch the videotape, then complete the activity according to the directions.

Vocabulario esencial

Nos relajamos un rato.	*We relax for a while.*
riendo	*laughing*
los bosques	*the woods*

Escriba un mínimo de cuatro actividades que hacen Joel León, Luis Guillermo y Juan Carlos para pasar su tiempo libre los fines de semana. Ellos mencionan un total de siete actividades.

Answers: jugar fútbol, jugar fútbol americano, practicar karate, ir al bosque, ver los animales, correr

ir al parque _____   _____

_____   _____

_____   _____

_____

¡A leer!

Lea el anuncio en la siguiente página, luego conteste estas preguntas.

1. El Motel Amancay está en (Chile / España / México / Venezuela).
2. Este motel está (cerca / lejos) de la playa de Reñaca.
3. ¿Cuándo está abierto el motel durante el año?
4. ¿Por qué dice el anuncio que el motel es de "estilo americano"?
5. Para usted, ¿cuál es la cosa más atractiva de las cabañas del motel?
6. De todas las otras instalaciones *(facilities)* del motel, ¿cuál te parece más atractiva?
7. ¿A usted le gustaría ir al Motel Amancay por una semana? ¿Por qué?

Answers:
1. Chile 2. cerca 3. Está abierto todo el año. 4. Porque tiene kitchenette, snack bar con T.V. 5. [open] 6. [open] 7. [open]

Visit

http://poco.heinle.com

MOTEL ESTILO AMERICANO

BALMACEDA 455 - FONO 902643 - REÑACA
VIÑA DEL MAR - CHILE

A 300 mts. de la playa de Reñaca, se
encuentra MOTELES AMANCAY, un hermoso
conjunto de 24 cabañas de uno, dos y tres
ambientes.

Todas ellas cuentan con baño privado,
citófono, música ambiental, kitchenette con
refrigerador, estacionamiento y terraza
privada.

Además: piscina, snack bar con T.V., música
ambiental, rincón criollo para sus asados,
comedores y caja de seguridad.

MOTELES AMANCAY, un hermoso lugar para
su descanso en cualquier época del año.

CONSULTE NUESTROS PLANES ESPECIALES DE DESCUENTOS
FUERA DE TEMPORADA.

SÍNTESIS

¡A conversar!

Converse con otro(a) estudiante.

Estudiante A: Imagínese que usted está de visita en cierta región de los Estados Unidos o del Canadá. Usted va a una agencia de viajes *(travel agency)* para informarse de lo que usted y su familia pueden hacer durante un fin de semana.

Estudiante B: Imagínese que usted trabaja en una agencia de viajes que se especializa en viajes de la región del país donde usted vive. Prepárese a hacerles recomendaciones a su cliente de habla española sobre los lugares más interesantes que ofrece su región, según sus necesidades e intereses.

¡A escribir!

Prepare un reportaje oral sobre un balneario o un lugar en el campo que ya conoce usted o sobre uno que le gustaría conocer algún día, por ejemplo: Fort Lauderdale o la Playa de Daytona (Florida), la Playa de Waikikí (Hawaii), el Parque Nacional de Yellowstone (Wyoming), Cancún o Acapulco (México), Mallorca (España), Machu Picchu (Perú), Viña del Mar (Chile), la Península Gaspé (Canadá), Isla de Margarita (Venezuela). Preséntele el reportaje a su clase, usando fotos y otros materiales visuales.

Atajo

VOCABULARIO

Sustantivos

la chica *girl*
el chico *boy*
la natación *swimming*
el (la) nadador(a) *swimmer*
la salud *health*
la sorpresa *surprise*

En la playa / el campo (beach/country)

el balneario *beach resort*
la canoa *canoe*
la costa *coast*
la crema bronceadora *suntan lotion*
el lago *lake*
la montaña *mountain*
la ola *wave*
la parrillada *cookout*
la pelota *ball*
el río *river*
la toalla *towel*
el velero *sailboat*

Adjetivos

profundo *deep*

Pasatiempos

acampar al lado de un río *to camp beside a river*
broncearse *to get a suntan*
bucear *to scuba dive*
caminar por las montañas *to hike in the mountains*
correr las olas *to surf*
esquiar en el agua *to water-ski*
hacer una parrillada *to have a cookout*
hacer el esnórquel *to snorkel*
hacer un picnic *to have a picnic*
pasear en canoa *to go canoeing*
pasear en velero *to sail*
pescar en un lago *to fish in a lake*
tomar el sol *to sunbathe*

Verbos

aconsejar *to advise*
alquilar *to rent*
aplicarse *to put on (e.g., lotion)*
asustar *to scare, frighten, astonish*
desear *to desire, wish*
decir (e → i) *to order*
enseñar *to teach*
insistir (en) *to insist (on)*
pedir (e → i) *to request*
permitir *to permit*
prohibir *to forbid*
recomendar (e → ie) *to recommend*
sentirse (e → ie, e → i) *to feel*
sugerir (e → ie, e → i) *to suggest*
tocar *to touch*

Adverbios

hacia *toward*

Expresiones idiomáticas

ahora mismo *right now*
al poco tiempo *in a little while*

14

Veamos el Festival de la Canción

▶ COMMUNICATIVE GOALS

You will be able to express your preferences and opinions about watching television, movies, and theatrical presentations.

▶ LANGUAGE FUNCTIONS

Stating facts
Expressing opinions
Expressing confidence
Expressing desires and hope
Expressing likes and dislikes
Expressing doubt and indecision
Expressing agreement and disagreement

▶ VOCABULARY THEMES

Television, movies, theater

▶ GRAMMATICAL STRUCTURES

Present subjunctive following verbs of emotion and
impersonal expressions
Present subjunctive following verbs and expressions
of uncertainty

▶ CULTURAL INFORMATION

The *Festival de la Canción*
Music and folkloric dances

http://poco.heinle.com

MISTERIO

EN CONTEXTO

 Play Lab Tape

Santiago, Chile. Eran las nueve y media de una noche de febrero. Ya hace un mes que Luis Wiessman y su amigo Jorge Grandinetti están de vacaciones en Viña del Mar. Anoche cenaron en casa de Luis y después fueron a la sala para mirar la televisión. Luis puso el canal° veinte.

channel

Comenzaron a mirar el Festival de la Canción. (1) En la televisión vieron a un hombre guapo y bien vestido que anunciaba algo ceremoniosamente:

—*Señoras y señores, ahora hemos llegado al momento culminante de este magnífico Festival de la Canción aquí en Viña del Mar. Este es el momento que hemos esperado toda la semana. En este sobre que tengo en la mano está el nombre del ganador° o la ganadora de este Festival. Señoras y señores... este año la ganadora es una cantante° chilena. Se llama... ¡María Cristina Cabral Tártari!*

winner
singer

Aplausos por todas partes. De repente, Luis se levantó y gritó:

—¡Oye, Jorge! ¡Mira! ¡Mira! ¡Es ella! Es la chica que me enseñó a nadar en la playa de Reñaca el mes pasado. La conocí, a ella y a su novio Gregorio, mientras estuvimos allí de vacaciones. ¿Recuerdas? No puedo creerlo.

—Cálmate, hombre. No puedo oír nada. Escucha lo que está diciendo el señor.

—*Señorita Cabral, esta noche maravillosa es muy especial para toda Viña del Mar y para todo Chile. ¡Felicitaciones, señorita Cabral... Ganadora del Festival de la Canción!*

—*Muchas gracias. Quiero darles las gracias a todos los organizadores del Festival, al público, a mis amigos y especialmente a mi familia. Este es un gran honor para mí. Muchas gracias a todos.*

—¿Oíste, Jorge? María Cristina es la mejor cantante del Festival.

—A mí no me sorprende° que sea la ganadora. Pues, creo que la chica tiene mucho talento y es bien simpática.

surprise

—Sí, ¡es verdad! Tienes razón, Jorge. Y también es una excelente profesora de natación.

Have several groups of students role-play the action and dialogue in this reading to make it "come alive." This procedure allows students to become more involved in the reading process in an interactive way, and it makes learning an interesting experience.

Nota de texto

The *Festival Internacional de la Canción de Viña del Mar* is held for one week every February. Some of the best singers in the world compete in this important song festival.

¿Comprendió Ud.?

Lea la lectura rápidamente, luego responda a los siguientes ejercicios.

1. Escriba un título apropiado para esta lectura: _____ .

**FESTIVAL
INTERNACIONAL
DE LA CANCIÓN
DE VIÑA DEL MAR**

2. Con los números 1 a 5, indique el orden cronológico de las siguientes acciones principales de la lectura.

_____ Luis se entusiasmó cuando vio a María Cristina.
_____ Jorge y Luis miraron la continuación del Festival.
_____ Jorge y Luis comenzaron a mirar la televisión.
_____ La Srta. Cabral ganó el concurso como mejor cantante.
_____ Luis y Jorge discutieron sobre el programa que querían ver.

Lea la lectura otra vez, luego complete las siguientes oraciones lógicamente.

1. El Festival de la Canción ocurre en _____ de Chile.
   a. el otoño   c. el invierno
   b. el verano   d. la primavera

2. María Cristina es _____.
   a. casada   c. anciana
   b. talentosa   d. española

3. Después de oír el anuncio de la ganadora del Festival, _____.
   a. Luis quería jugar al fútbol   c. María Cristina estaba triste
   b. Jorge estaba un poco aburrido   d. Luis miró su programa favorito

NOTAS CULTURALES

El Festival de la Canción

charm / periódicos
put aside / turning aside
event

El Festival de la Canción de Viña del Mar es el triunfo del amor, la música y la ilusión. Su embrujo,° su atractivo, lo cambia todo. Las primeras páginas de los diarios,° por una semana, soslayan° u olvidan las noticias adversas, volcando° sus preferencias al acontecimiento° artístico-musical. El país cambia. Adquiere el aire festivalero que escapa a toda edad o condición social. Es Chile que se une a un ritmo que marca el embrujo del Festival.

spend the night / screen
competition

¿Qué decir de la TV, medio de difusión masivo que "se mete en nuestros hogares"? En esos días la televisión dirige las emociones de los chilenos al llevar a todo el país la fiesta viñamarina "en vivo y en directo". Y todos trasnochamos° frente a la pantalla° chica. Es que el Festival atrapa con la incertidumbre de la competencia° y el espectacular show renovado año tras año. Sólo se habla del Festival. Nadie se acuerda de la política, la economía u otros temas contingentes.

Source: "La semana del amor, de la música y la ilusión...", por Hernán Gálvez, *La gaviota de la ilusión*, por Hernán Gálvez G., Editado por Mompracem

Preguntas: 1. ¿Dónde ocurre el Festival de la Canción? 2. ¿Qué importancia tiene el Festival en Chile? 3. Si los chilenos no pueden ver el Festival en persona, ¿qué pueden hacer? 4. ¿A usted le gustaría ver el Festival de la Canción? ¿Por qué?

Follow-up activity: Discuss with your students the following question: ¿Qué tipo de celebraciones y festivales mira usted en la televisión o en persona? Por ejemplo: los desfiles (parades) en los días festivos (Año Nuevo, Día Memorial, Cuatro de julio, Día de Acción de Gracias; los premios (awards) Oscar y Tony.

¿Qué dice usted?

1. ¿Qué acontecimiento artístico de los Estados Unidos o del Canadá atrae tanta atención pública como el Festival de la Canción?
2. ¿Qué otros acontecimientos (políticos, educacionales, comerciales, etcétera) atraen tanta atención pública en los Estados Unidos o en el Canadá como el Festival de la Canción?

VOCABULARIO ÚTIL

In this section you will learn to describe television programs, movies, and theatrical presentations you like and dislike.

¿Qué hay en la tele?

las noticias

el pronóstico del tiempo

un documental

un programa deportivo

un programa de concursos

un programa de entrevistas

Practiquemos

A. Entrevista. Pregúntele a otro(a) estudiante.

1. ¿Cuántos televisores tienes en casa?[1]
2. ¿Con qué frecuencia miras la televisión?
3. ¿Cuál es tu programa favorito? ¿Por qué te gusta tanto?
4. Para ti, ¿qué programa de televisión es ridículo? ¿Por qué crees eso?

[1] Spanish speakers use *el televisor* for "television set," and *la televisión* to mean "television programming."

TRANSPARENCY No. 26: TV
Programs

B. Vamos a ver. Primero, complete esta actividad por escrito. Luego dígale a un(a) compañero(a) de clase los tipos de programas de televisión que usted mira y no mira, y por qué.

Ejemplo: *Casi siempre me gustan las noticias internacionales porque quiero saber lo que pasa en el mundo.*

Casi nunca = 1   **A veces = 2**   **Casi siempre = 3**

Tipo de programas:

____ noticias locales   ____ programas de concursos
____ noticias internacionales   ____ pronósticos del tiempo
____ programas deportivos   ____ programas de entrevistas
____ programas en español   ____ documentales interesantes

Ahora sea usted más específico(a).

Uno de mis programas de televisión preferidos es "_____" porque... Un programa que quiero ver otra vez se llama "_____". Creo que es un programa muy _____ porque... Un programa de televisión que no te recomiendo ver se llama "_____". No te recomiendo verlo porque...

Ex. C. This is the most creative activity in this sequence —and the most time-consuming; however, most students enjoy it very much. Remember: it is not necessary to do all the activities in this book. Do the activities that you feel are most beneficial for your students according to their personal interests and their level of proficiency.

Ex. C. Follow-up activity: Assign groups of students to watch one type of television program such as news, editorial, weather, or sports. The following day, students who watched a particular TV program discuss the program together. Then one spokesperson in each group tells the class about that program.

C. ¡Luz, cámara, acción! Con otros dos o tres estudiantes, escriba un programa breve de "Las noticias del día" o "El pronóstico del tiempo para mañana". Sigan ustedes el orden de los siguientes pasos para que salga bien su programa de televisión.

a. Recojan *(Collect)* la información necesaria para su programa.
b. Organicen esta información en una forma lógica.
c. Escriban las ideas más importantes sobre esta información en algunos párrafos breves.
d. Cambien estos párrafos con los párrafos de otro grupo; luego corrijan *(correct)* los errores en ellos.
e. Revisen los párrafos de ustedes; luego dénselos a su profesor(a) para que él (ella) los corrija.
f. Escriban la versión final del programa.

Después, preséntenle su programa a la clase. Si es posible, filmen el programa con una videocámara para verlo después y para divertirse un poco más.

¿Qué película van a poner en el cine?

un drama

una comedia

un documental

una película del oeste

una película de ciencia ficción

una película de intriga/misterio

Practiquemos

D. Películas clásicas. La siguiente lista contiene títulos de películas clásicas producidas en los Estados Unidos. Indique el tipo de cada película, como en el ejemplo.

Ejemplo: *Close Encounters of the Third Kind*
Es una película de ciencia ficción.

Título de película	Tipo de película
1. *Sherlock Holmes*	drama
2. *Beauty and the Beast*	comedia
3. *Laurel and Hardy*	dibujo animado
4. *Gone With the Wind*	película del oeste
5. *How the West Was Won*	película de intriga
6. *ET: Extraterrestrial*	película de ciencia ficción

Game: Write names of different types of programs and movies on separate pieces of paper and put the papers in a container. Divide your class into two teams, and appoint one reader for each team. Flip a coin to determine which team goes first. The reader for the first team takes one paper from the container and reads it aloud to his or her team whose members name an actual program or movie that corresponds with the paper. Allow five seconds for a response. Afterwards, the reader for the second team repeats this procedure for his or her team. Tally the scores for each team to determine the winner.

Have students form pairs and role-play this short dialogue. Tell them that they may change the names, if they wish.

E. Entre compañeros. Hable con un(a) compañero(a) de clase.

Estudiante A

1. ¡Hola, ———! ¿Qué tal?
3. ———. Oye, ¿qué hay de nuevo?

5. ¿Cómo se llama la película?
7. Sí, y (no) me gustó.
   (No, no la vi.)
9. Pues, ———. ¿Y a ti?

Estudiante B

2. ———. Y tú, ¿cómo estás?
4. Pues, vi una buena (mala) película en el Cine ———.
6. "———". ¿La viste tú?
8. ¿Que tipo de películas te gusta?

10. Me gusta(n) ———.

F. Entrevista. Pregúntele a otro(a) estudiante.

1. ¿Con qué frecuencia vas al cine?
2. Si tienes un cine favorito, ¿cuál es?
3. Normalmente, ¿con quién vas al cine?
4. ¿Quién es tu actor favorito y por qué?
5. ¿Quién es tu actriz favorita y por qué?
6. ¿Has visto una película buena recientemente? ¿Cuál fue?

¿Qué función van a presentar en el teatro?

un concierto   una función musical   un drama

Una conversación entre amigos

—Hola, Jorge. ¿Qué hay de nuevo?
—Hola, Luis. Leticia y yo lo pasamos bien anoche en el teatro.
—¿En serio? ¿Qué función vieron?
—Vimos una función musical. Fue estupenda.

Hi, Jorge. What's new?
Hi, Luis. Leticia and I had a good time last night at the theater.
Really? What show did you see?
We saw a musical. It was great.

Practiquemos

G. Mis gustos. Dígale a otro(a) estudiante sus gustos de presentaciones en el teatro.

Ejemplos:　*Me gustan las funciones musicales.*
No me gustan nada los conciertos de jazz.

Me gustan (mucho)...
No me gustan (nada)...

los ballets
las funciones musicales
los dramas de Shakespeare
los conciertos de jazz
los conciertos de rock
los conciertos de música clásica

K. Una experiencia dramática. Converse con un(a) compañero(a) de clase.

Estudiante A	Estudiante B
1. Una vez lo pasé bien en el teatro.	2. ¿En serio? ¿Cuándo fue eso?
3. Pues, _____.	4. ¿Qué función viste?
5. _____. La función fue estupenda porque...	6. Una vez vi una función en el teatro. Vi _____.
7. ¿Cuándo fue eso?	8. _____.
9. ¿Te gustó?	10. Bueno, _____.

NOTAS CULTURALES

Música y danzas folklóricas

Los latinoamericanos han contribuido al mundo con una gran variedad de música y danzas folklóricas. La música latinoamericana ha tenido tres influencias principales: la española, la indígena y la africana. Los instrumentos de cuerda° tales como la guitarra, la mandolina y el arpa son de origen español. Los instrumentos de viento, especialmente la flauta, demuestran la influencia indígena. Los instrumentos de percusión, como el tambor, son de influencia africana. Cada región o país en Latinoamérica tiene sus características distintas en la música y las danzas, las cuales son determinadas por la influencia dominante.

Aparte de la música y las danzas folklóricas, muchos bailes populares como el tango, la conga, la rumba, la salsa, la samba, el mambo, la cumbia, el bossa nova, el merengue y el chachachá tienen su origen en Latinoamérica.

string

1. If possible, play one or more of the kinds of music mentioned in the cultural note. Teach students one or more of the kinds of dances listed here, if you have this knowledge and skill.
2. You might talk to your students about current influences on Latin American music such as the *nueva trova cubana* and the *nueva canción chilena, el ballenato colombiano.*

¿Qué dice usted?

1. ¿Qué tipo de música regional es popular en su país?
2. ¿Qué tipo de danzas folklóricas hay en su país?
3. ¿Qué tipo de música le gusta a usted?

GRAMÁTICA FUNCIONAL

Expressing feelings, attitudes, and opinions

—¿Te gustan ver los dibujos animados, Jorge?
—Sí, Luis, pero me molesta que algunos sean violentos.
—Ojalá los cambien pronto, especialmente por los niños.
—De acuerdo. Es ridículo ver tantos violentos dibujos animados.

Present subjunctive following verbs of emotion and impersonal expressions

In the previous lesson, you learned how to use the present subjunctive to express wishes, intentions, preferences, advice, suggestions and recommendations. Spanish speakers also use verbs of emotion with the subjunctive to express their emotions and opinions.

How to use the present subjunctive

1. The list below contains verbs of emotion for expressing feelings, and impersonal expressions for expressing opinions.

Verbs of emotion		Impersonal expressions	
alegrarse (de)	*to be glad*	**es mejor**	*it's better*
esperar	*to hope*	**es lógico**	*it's logical*
gustar	*to like*	**es ridículo**	*it's ridiculous*
molestar	*to bother*	**es bueno/malo**	*it's good/bad*
preocuparse (de/por)	*to worry (about)*	**es necesario**	*it's necessary*
quejarse (de)	*to complain*	**es importante**	*it's important*
sentir (e → ie)	*to be sorry*	**es (im)posible**	*it's (im)possible*
sorprender	*to surprise*	**es una lástima**	*it's a shame*

2. Use these verbs and impersonal expressions exactly as you did with the verb *querer.*

One subject	Change of subject
Luis espera **mirar** el Festival.	**Luis** espera que **Jorge** lo **mire.**
Luis hopes to watch the Festival.	*Luis hopes Jorge watches it.*

Impersonal Expression

Es bueno tener un televisor.
It's good to have a TV set.

Es bueno que **Luis tenga** un televisor.
It's good that Luis has a TV set.

3. You have learned that one way to express your desires and hopes is to use verbs like *querer*, *desear*, and *esperar*. Another way to express those feelings is to use the expression o*jalá (que)* with the subjunctive. This expression has several English equivalents including: "Let's hope that...," "I hope that...," and "If only...." *Ojalá (que)* is **always** followed by the subjunctive whether there is a change of subject or just one subject. The word *que* is often used after *ojalá* in writing, but it is usually omitted in conversation.

ojalá (que) + subjunctive

Ojalá lo **pases** bien en Viña.   *I hope you have a good time in Viña.*
Ojalá haga buen tiempo allá.   *Let's hope the weather is good there.*
Ojalá que recibas esta carta.   *I hope you will receive this letter.*

Practiquemos

A. ¿Está usted de acuerdo? Lea cada oración, luego decida si usted está acuerdo, indicando su decisión con **sí** o **no**.

Ex. A. Follow-up activity: Have students form pairs and compare their reactions to these statements.

En la televisión

1. sí _____ no _____ Me molesta que las noticias casi siempre sean malas.
2. sí _____ no _____ Es ridículo poner tantos programas deportivos los sábados.

En el cine

1. sí _____ no _____ Es una lástima que no se produzcan más películas del oeste.
2. sí _____ no _____ Es posible que yo sea actor o actriz de cine algún día.

En el teatro

1. sí _____ no _____ Me quejo que no haya suficientes conciertos en mi escuela.
2. sí _____ no _____ Es lógico que los dramas de Shakespeare sean muy populares.

B. Entre hermanos. Complete la siguiente conversación entre Rona y Luis Weissmann, usando los verbos apropiados entre paréntesis.

Ex. B. Answers: gusten, mirar, criticarme, ver, mires, guste

RONA: Es una lástima que no te (gustar / gusten) los programas de concursos. Es bueno (mirar / mires) ese tipo de programas para aprender algo.

LUIS: Es ridículo (criticarme / me critiques) por los programas que veo. Es importante (ver / vea) el Festival cada año. Siento que no lo (mirar / mires), Rona.

RONA: Lo miré muchas veces. Es lógico que no me (gustar / guste) ahora, ¿comprendes?

C. Dos hermanos. Complete las siguientes oraciones para conocer un poco mejor a Luis y a Rona.

Ejemplos: Rona tiene quince años. Es normal que ella _____ (ir a fiestas / expresar sus opiniones).
Es normal que ella vaya a fiestas.
Es normal que ella exprese sus opiniones.

1. A Rona no le gusta ver los programas deportivos. Es posible que ella _____ (no ser deportista / no practicar ningún deporte / preferir escuchar cintas o discos compactos / pasar mucho tiempo hablando por teléfono)
2. Rona es una estudiante excelente en el colegio donde tiene muchos amigos. Es bueno que ella _____ (estudiar todos los días / tocar el piano / tener muchos amigos / ser una chica popular).
3. A veces, Luis y su hermana Rona tienen conflictos. Es normal que ellos _____ (no siempre estar de acuerdo / discutir mucho en casa / expresar sus opiniones / darse consejos el uno al otro con cariño.

D. ¡Ojalá! Usando la expresión **ojalá,** escriba diez deseos que a usted le gustaría realizar dentro de tres años.

Ejemplos: *Ojalá que yo encuentre trabajo.*
Ojalá que yo viva en Hawaii.

Charlemos

E. ¿Qué opina usted? Pregúntele a otro(a) estudiante sus opiniones sobre los concursos que se ven en la televisión.

1. ¿Qué piensas de la entrega del Óscar? ¿y del Tony? ¿Qué piensas de consursos como Miss América?
2. ¿Qué te gusta o qué te molesta de esos concursos? ¿Qué es lo bueno de ese tipo de concursos?
3. Ahora piensa por un momento en un actor o una actriz, director(a) o productor(a) que acaba de ganar el Óscar por su última película. ¿De qué se alegra él o ella? ¿De qué tiene miedo? ¿Qué esperan del futuro? ¿De qué pueden quejarse a veces?

F. ¿Qué le parece? Primero, escriba sus opiniones positivas y negativas sobre la importancia de la televisión y las películas en nuestra sociedad. Luego léale sus opiniones a otro(a) estudiante, quien debe reaccionar positiva o negativamente.

Ejemplos: A: *Es normal mirar la televisión dos horas al día porque hay muchos programas interesantes.*

B: *Tienes razón. Miro la tele tres horas cada día.*
A: *Es una lástima que muchas personas vayan al cine tan frecuentemente. Deben hacer otros pasatiempos como jugar a un deporte o visitar a sus amigos.*
B: *No estoy de acuerdo. Me gusta ir al cine; hay tantas películas interesantes y quiero verlas todas.*

1. **Opiniones positivas**

Es bueno (que)...	Es mejor (que)...
No es malo (que)...	Es importante (que)...
Es natural (que)...	Es interesante (que)...

2. **Opiniones negativas**

Es malo (que)...	Es ridículo (que)...
Es terrible (que)...	Es una lástima (que)...

G. Un debate. Escriba sus reacciones a dos de los siguientes temas. Luego forme un grupo con otros dos o tres estudiantes y discutan sus opiniones sobre estos temas.

Ejemplos: los concursos de Miss Universo

A: *Me alegro que haya esos concursos. Les dan muchas oportunidades profesionales a las chicas que ganan.*

B: *No estoy de acuerdo. Es malo que pongan esos concursos en la tele. Las chicas son personas, no cosas.*

La televisión

1. la violencia en los dibujos animados
2. el sexo explícito en la televisión norteamericana

El cine

1. el sistema de evaluar las películas nuevas
2. los precios altos de ver una película nueva

Ex. G. Follow-up activity: Have your students conduct an opinion survey of their reactions to each of these themes. They could report the results in another class session.

GRAMÁTICA FUNCIONAL

Expressing doubt and indefiniteness

—¿Crees que Rona esté enojada, Jorge?
—No dudo que está enojada contigo, Luis.
—No creo que ella me comprenda mucho.
—Pues, yo creo que ella te comprende bien.

Present subjunctive following verbs and expressions of uncertainty

Spanish speakers also use the subjunctive mood to express doubt, uncertainty, disbelief, unreality, nonexistence, and indefiniteness.

How to use the present subjunctive

1. You can use the following verbs and expressions to communicate uncertainty; they are used like those shown in the previous grammar section.

dudar	*to doubt*	**Dudo** que Rona **esté** muy enojada.
es dudoso	*it's doubtful*	**Es dudoso** que la niña **tenga** novio.
no creer	*not to believe*	**No creo** que la chica **llore** mucho.
no estar seguro	*to be uncertain*	**No estoy seguro** que ella **sea** mala.

Review how Spanish speakers use the present subjunctive with verbs of volition (see *Lección 13*).

If necessary, provide additional examples to show your students how Spanish speakers use the indicative and the subjunctive after *que*.

2. Spanish speakers use the **indicative mood** after *que* to refer to people and things they are certain about and believe to be true.

Me llamo Jorge Grandinetti. Vivo en Santiago que **es** *una ciudad grande. Sé que el aire* **está** *contaminado aquí. Creo que* **hay** *demasiados autos que contaminan el aire. No dudo que* **necesitamos** *más transporte público.*

Jorge tells us that he lives in Santiago, a large city. He also knows that the air is polluted there, caused by so many cars in the city. He has no doubt that Santiago needs more public transportation. Since Jorge knows these facts or feels certain about them, he uses verbs in the indicative after *que.*

Spanish speakers use the **subjunctive mood** after *que* when they describe hypothetical people, places, things, or conditions, or when they do not believe that they exist at all.

Quiero vivir en una ciudad que **sea** *tan bonita como Viña del Mar. Busco una ciudad que no* **tenga** *mucha violencia y que* **esté** *cerca del mar.*

Now Jorge tells us about an idealized city that he is searching for. The city must have certain qualifications such as being in a beautiful location, having a low crime rate, and being near the sea. Since it is indefinite or uncertain that Jorge will find such a city, he uses the subjunctive after *que.* Note that the use of the indicative or the subjunctive does **not** depend on the concept conveyed by the verb in the independent clause.[1]

Practiquemos

Ex. A. Answers: *vayan, quiere, quiera, quieras, debo, es, cases, case*

A. Entre Luis y Jorge. Complete la siguiente conversación entre Luis y Jorge, usando los verbos apropiados entre paréntesis.

LUIS: ¿Crees que tú y Leticia (van / vayan) a casarse algún día?

JORGE: Pues, sé que Leticia me (quiere / quiera), pero no estoy seguro que ella me (quiere / quiera) tanto para casarse conmigo.

LUIS: ¿Dudas que la (quieres / quieras) tú?

JORGE: No, quiero mucho a Leticia, pero necesitamos pasar más tiempo juntos. Mi papá me dijo que (debo / deba) pensarlo bien. Él piensa que el matrimonio (es / sea) una cosa seria. Y tú, ¿crees que te (casas / cases) algún día?

LUIS: Pues, claro que sí. Pero es dudoso que me (caso / case) antes de terminar mis estudios.

---

[1] **¡CUIDADO!** Use the personal *a* before a direct object that refers to a specific person (in the indicative). If the person referred to is not specified, however, omit the personal *a*, except before *alguien, nadie, alguno,* and *ninguno.*

    ¿Conoces **a** alguien que vaya al Festival?   (*a + alguien*)
    Conozco **a** María Cristina que es cantante.   (*a + specific person*)
But: Necesito un amigo que vaya conmigo.   (omit *a* = non-specific person)

B. Dos amigos. Con otro(a) estudiante, complete las siguientes conversaciones entre Luis (L) y Jorge (J), como en el ejemplo.

Ejemplo: L: mis padres creen / (yo) estudiar mucho

J: ¿Cómo? no creo / (tú) estudiar mucho porque...

L: *Mis padres creen que estudio mucho.*

J: *¿Cómo? No creo que estudies mucho porque eres perezoso.*

1. J: Creo / ir a comprarme un radio Walkman
   L: Dudo / (tú) comprar uno porque...
   J: No creo / (tú) tienes razón porque...

2. J: Quiero / tú y yo volver a Viña en mayo
   L: Es dudoso / (nosotros) volver porque...

3. J: Mis padres creen / (yo) ser perezoso
   L: No dudo / (tú) ser trabajador porque...

4. L: Rona no está segura / yo la querer
   J: No hay duda / (tú) la querer porque...

**eres perezoso
hablas bien de ella
estudias día y noche
hay clases en ese mes
no tienes mucho dinero
mi tío me dio el dinero**

C. ¡Qué molestias! Cuando Luis y Jorge fueron a Viña del Mar, vivieron en un hotel donde ellos se quejaron un poco. ¿Qué le dijeron al recepcionista?

Ejemplo: ¿Hay un cuarto / tener dos camas?
   ¿Hay un cuarto que tenga dos camas?

Antes de ver el cuarto:

1. ¿No tiene usted otros cuartos / costar un poco menos?
2. ¿Puede usted darnos un cuarto / estar en el tercer piso?
3. ¿Es posible darnos un cuarto / tener una vista del mar?
4. ¿Hay alguien / poder ayudarnos con nuestras maletas?

Después de ver el cuarto:

5. Deseamos un cuarto / no ser tan feo como ése.
6. Buscamos un empleado / poder darnos más toallas.
7. Queremos otro cuarto con una ducha / funcionar mejor.

D. ¿Qué cree usted? Escriba una lista de cinco ideas en las cuales usted cree, y otra lista de cinco ideas en las cuales usted no cree.

Ejemplos: La familia:
   Creo que la familia es muy importante.
   No creo que los niños deban mirar programas de terror.

Temas posibles:

1. La familia
2. La educación
3. La buena salud
4. La vida social
5. La sociedad
6. El universo

Ex. E. Follow-up: This activity could also serve as a written homework assignment.

Charlemos

E. El futuro incierto. No hay otra cosa más incierta que el futuro, pero es importante hacer planes. Converse con un(a) compañero(a) de clase sobre sus ambiciones.

Ejemplo: *Algún día quiero vivir en un lugar que esté cerca del mar...*

• Algún día quiero vivir en un lugar que...

• Para vivir allí sé que..., pero dudo que...

• No estoy seguro(a) que... en ese lugar, pero creo que... allí.

• En ese lugar, hay...

• Por eso, estoy seguro(a) que...

PARA LEER MEJOR

Guessing Unfamiliar Words and Phrases

When you read a passage in English and come to an unfamiliar word or phrase, you probably try to guess its meaning from context or skip over it and continue reading. If you use this strategy when you read in Spanish, your reading comprehension and reading speed will increase significantly over time.

Activities

A. The following reading passage contains a number of boldfaced words and phrases that you may not understand. As you read it, try to guess their meaning from context.

> *El Festival Internacional de la Canción es el principal evento artístico de Chile que **se realiza** desde el año 1959 en el Teatro al Aire Libre de la Quinta Vergara durante el mes de febrero. Participan artistas y **compositores** en los géneros internacional y folklórico en un show de extraordinaria calidad. La difusión del Festival **en el extranjero** se hace a través de transmisión televisiva a más de veinte países.*
>
> *La Quinta Vergara está **ubicada** en pleno centro de Viña del Mar. **Antiguamente** formaba parte de la propiedad de la familia Vergara-Alvarez, fundadora de Viña del Mar y de la cual se conserva su casa palaciega, hoy ocupada por el Museo de Bellas Artes. En este **recinto** se encuentra el Teatro al Aire Libre, donde se realiza todos los años el Festival Internacional de la Canción, principal evento turístico del país (febrero).*

Source: Passages adapted from booklet entitled V*iña del Mar: Inventario turístico,* Municipalidad de Viña del Mar.

I. MUNICIPALIDAD DE VIÑA DEL MAR

RUT 69.031.000-0

MUSEO DE BELLAS ARTES

INTERIOR QUINTA VERGARA

ENTRADA ADULTOS $50

SERIE A   Nº 13151

This ticket stub is from the art gallery located in a beautiful palace within the Quinta Vergara gardens. The entrance fee is fifty Chilean pesos (about 20 American cents). An RUT number is required on all receipts in Chile for purposes of fiscal control by the federal government.

B. Answer the following questions, based on the reading.

1. ¿En qué ciudad y en qué mes es el Festival de la Canción?
2. ¿En qué lugar específico ocurre este festival?
3. ¿Cómo sabe usted que el Festival es internacional?
4. ¿Qué es la Quinta Vergara?
5. ¿A usted le gustaría ver el Festival de la Canción? ¿Por qué?

Answers:

B. *1. Viña del Mar, febrero 2. el Teatro al Aire Libre 3. Porque se ve el Festival en la televisión en más de veinte países 4. Es una propiedad vieja. 5. [open]*

C. Complete the following sentences appropriately.

1. El verbo **realizarse** significa (pasar / servir / invitar).
2. El sustantivo **compositor** significa (un tipo de computadora / una tienda especializada / una persona que compone música).
3. La expresión idiomática **en el extranjero** significa (internacional / en otras naciones / en algunas regiones).
4. El adjetivo **ubicada** significa (situada / celebrada / centralizada).
5. El adverbio **antiguamente** significa (ayer / el año pasado / hace mucho tiempo).
6. El sustantivo **recinto** significa (balneario / plataforma / lugar encerrado).

Answers:

C. *1. pasar 2. una persona que compone música 3. en otras naciones 4. situada 5. hace mucho tiempo 6. lugar encerrado*

PARA ESCRIBIR MEJOR

Writing a Critical Essay

Every day we evaluate many conditions, situations, and people. Occasionally, we write down our comments and opinions about them. In this section you will write a critical essay about a subject of your choice. To do so, use the following guidelines to help you:

1. Choose a subject that interests you.
2. Write a brief introduction about the subject you chose.
3. List three or four things that you like about your subject.

Atajo

Functions:
Writing an essay; writing an introduction; writing a conclusion; expressing an opinion

Vocabulary:
Arts; poetry; prose; musical instruments

Grammar:
Verbs: subjunctive

¿A qué nivel está Ud.?

¿Ciencia ficción, drama, horror?
Son los películas de Spielberg películas del oeste? Review the chapter and then monitor your progress by completing the *Autoprueba* at the end of *Lección 14* in the ***Workbook/Lab Manual.***

4. List one or two things that could be done realistically to improve your subject.
5. Come to a conclusion about your subject.

Example:

  El Museo de Historia y Arte de mi ciudad es muy interesante. Me gustan las exhibiciones de arte por artistas locales. Cada martes a las doce y quince de la tarde, hay un evento especial en el museo. Por ejemplo, la semana pasada un señor presentó una charla interesante sobre el arte de Egipto. En verano el museo tiene conciertos de música clásica. Me gusta comer un sandwich y escuchar la música. No cuesta nada entrar en el museo. ¡Eso me gusta mucho! Hay algo que no me gusta mucho: Quiero que cambien más frecuentemente las exhibiciones, que están allí por tres o cuatro meses.

  En general, me gusta mucho el Museo de Historia y Arte. Aprendo mucho allí y me divierto al mismo tiempo.

Activity

Write a critical essay in Spanish, following the five guidelines above.

Some possible subjects for your essay are: a painting, a newspaper article, a literary piece such as a poem or a short story, a restaurant, a new product, a movie, a television program, a planned development, an event such as a performance or a vacation trip, a sports hero, and a person in a leadership position.

SÍNTESIS

¡A ver!

Miguel and his friends are going to the movies. First, study the sentences with their meaning in the *Vocabulario esencial*. Second, read the seven statements in the activity below. Third, watch the videotape, then decide whether the statements are true or false.

Vocabulario esencial

Siento llegar tarde.	*Sorry I'm late.*
He cogido yo este papelito.	*I picked up this paper.*
¡No tienes ni idea!	*You have no idea!*

Lea cada oración, luego indique si es cierto o no, según el segmento de vídeo que usted acaba de ver.

Answers: *1. Sí 2. No 3. No 4. No
5. Sí 6. Sí 7. Sí*

1. Sí _____ No _____ Miguel llegó al cine un poco tarde.
2. Sí _____ No _____ Miguel prefirió ver la película "Salto al vacío".
3. Sí _____ No _____ Sylvia quería ver la misma película que Miguel.
4. Sí _____ No _____ Teresa y Juan ya conocían a Sylvia.
5. Sí _____ No _____ Miguel, Juan y Teresa prefirieron ver la misma película.
6. Sí _____ No _____ Miguel habló bastante sobre el director de una película.
7. Sí _____ No _____ Miguel y sus amigos decidieron ver "Salto al vacío".

¡A leer!

La televisión forma parte esencial de la vida moderna, y es importante mirarla correctamente para preservar la salud de la vista. ¿Está seguro(a) de que sabe lo suficiente al respecto? Complete esta prueba *(test)*, y usted va a saber la verdad.

¿Verdadero(v) o falso(f)?

	V	F	
1. Es mejor observar la televisión en la oscuridad o en la penumbra que con la pieza° iluminada de modo regular.	[ ]	[ ]	cuarto
2. Los televisores deben colocarse al nivel° de la vista.	[ ]	[ ]	*level*
3. Es un mito° que resulte perjudicial sentarse muy cerca del televisor. En realidad, cualquier sitio es bueno.	[ ]	[ ]	*myth*
4. El mejor asiento para ver televisión debe ser amplio y suave, del tipo que invita a "derrumbarse"° cómodamente haciendo un ovillo° con las piernas.	[ ]	[ ]	*to curl up* / *knot*
5. No es conveniente ejecutar otra labor (hacer ejercicios, tejer,° planchar° la ropa, etc.) mientras se mira televisión.	[ ]	[ ]	*knit / iron*

SÍNTESIS

Respuestas

1. Falso. Los especialistas de la visión recomiendan que se ilumine la pieza en la forma normal.
2. Verdadero. Es lo mejor para la vista, y por otra parte evita tensiones y contracciones en el cuello,° la espalda,° etc.
3. Falso. Sí, su mamá tenía razón cuando lo (la) aconsejaba de niño(a) no acercarse mucho al televisor.
4. Falso. El asiento perfecto es una butaca cómoda, con dos brazos y un respaldo recto, que proporcione un buen soporte a la espalda.
5. Falso. En realidad, lo más indicado es dar un descanso a los ojos mirando ocasionalmente hacia otro sitio.

neck / back

Source: "Mirando la televisión: Un 'test' útil", *De todo un poco*, Año 1, No. 9, 27 de septiembre de 1988, página 21.

¿Comprendió Ud.?

Mire este dibujo y dígale a otro(a) estudiante lo que es correcto o incorrecto, según la lectura.

¡A conversar!

Lea la página de una teleguía mexicana y piense en las películas que a usted le gustaría ver y en las que no le gustaría ver. Luego compare sus gustos con un(a) compañero(a) de clase, usando las siguientes frases.

• Me gustaría ver la película _____ porque...
• También quiero ver _____ porque...
• Una película que no me interesa es _____ porque...
• Tampoco quiero ver _____ porque...

¡A escribir!

Con un compañero(a) de clase, escriba otra prueba útil con respuestas sobre uno de los siguientes temas. Luego intercambien su prueba con otros dos estudiantes y completen las dos pruebas juntos.

SÍNTESIS

GUIA DE PELICULAS

★★★★★ ....EXCELENTE
★★★★ ....MUY BUENA
★★★ ....BUENA
★★ ....REGULAR
★ ....POBRE

SABADO 19 DICIEMBRE

9:30 ⑪ El Hijo de Montecristo (Aventuras) ** Louis Hayward, Joan Bennett.— Continuación de "El Conde de Montecristo", en donde el hijo del legendario personaje trata de seguir los pasos del padre.

11:00 ② El Padre Trampitas (Comedia) * Adalberto Martínez "Resortes", Patricia Rivera.

1:00 ② Los Caifanes (Melodrama) **** Enrique Alvarez Félix, Julissa.— Una pareja de jóvenes burgueses medio intelectuales se ve enredada en una noche de juerga popular y una relación insólita con cuatro mecánicos.

⑨ La Horripilante Bestia Humana (Horror) * José Elías Moreno, Norma Lazareno.

2:00 ⑤ Los Cuentos de Pepito (Dibujos Animados) **

3:30 ⑪ Gestapo (Thriller) ***** Rex Harrison, Margaret Lockwood.— Un agente británico trata de rescatar a un científico que ha escapado de las garras de la Gestapo.

6:00 ⑤ La Estrella de Navidad (Melodrama) ** Ed Asner, Rene Auberjonos.— Historia de unos niños que verdaderamente creen que un hombre que se ha vestido de Santa Claus a disgusto, es el verdadero que llega a hacerles feliz navidad.

7:00 ④ Anita la Huerfanita (Melodrama Musical) *** Albert Finney, Carol Burnett.— En un orfanatorio, varias niñas sufren lo indecible, y una logra escapar

9:00 ⑨ Angel del Barrio (Melodrama) * Gonzalo Vega, Leticia Perdigón.— Melodrama populachero con personajes barriobajeros castigados inmisericorde-

mente por la vida, que se ensaña mucho más con algunos de ellos.

9:30 ⑤ Coctel (Drama) ** Tom Cruise, Brain Brown.— Un joven que aprende los secretos para ser un buen barman, llega a comprender que el verdadero amor es más importante que el dinero.

10:30 ⑪ Breve Película sobre el Amor (Melodrama) **** Grazyna Szapolowska, Olaf Lubaszenko.— Un adolescente se enamora de una mujer de cierta edad, a la que espía con un teleobjetivo.

11:30 ⑤ Poder (Drama) ** Richard Gere, Julie Christie.— Trepidante drama acerca de un consultor político, que no está muy de acuerdo con el proceder de sus clientes, así que decide manipularlos.

DOMINGO 20 DICIEMBRE

1:30 ⑤ La Enemiga Encantadora (Melodrama) *** Merle Oberon, David Niven.— Durante la rebelión irlandesa de 1921, la prometida de un oficial británico se enamora del líder de los revolucionarios.

9:30 ⑪ El Jardinero Español (Drama) *** Dirk Bogarde, Jon Whitley.— El hijo de un diplomático hace amistad con un jardinero, que le cambia el punto de vista de muchas de sus apreciaciones.

10:30 ⑤ Callejón sin Salida. (Aventuras) ** Greg Henry, Bruce Groenwood.

12:00 ⑤ Un Cuento de Navidad (Melodrama) *** George C. Scott, Nigel Davemport.— Versión televisiva del celebérrimo cuento de Dickens, en el que un amargado recibe una suprema lección de amor en Navidad.

1:00 ⑨ Santo contra las Bestias del Terror (Aventuras) * Santo, Blue Demon.—

---

1. Have students converse in pairs about their reactions to the results of this test.
2. Have students role-play a father/mother and a son/daughter discussing what television programming is appropriate for general viewing.

Temas:

1. Cómo estudiar
2. Cómo broncearse
3. Cómo ir de compras
4. Cómo comer bien
5. Cómo escribir mejor
6. Cómo hacer ejercicio

Atajo

VOCABULARIO

Sustantivos

el canal *channel (TV)*
el (la) cantante *singer*
el concurso *contest*
la duda *doubt*
el (la) ganador(a) *winner*
el partido *game, match*
el teatro *theater*

Programas y películas

la comedia *comedy*
el concierto *concert*
el dibujo animado *cartoon*
el documental *documentary*
el drama *drama, play*
la función *show (theatrical)*
la función musical *musical (play)*
las noticias *news*
la película de ciencia ficción
 science fiction film
la película de intriga/misterio
 mystery film
la película del oeste *western film*
el programa de concursos *game show*
el programa de entrevistas *talk show*

el programa deportivo *sports program*
el pronóstico del tiempo *weather report (forecast)*

Adjetivos

aburrido *boring*
dudoso *doubtful*
estupendo *wonderful, great*
lógico *logical*
mismo *same*
ridículo *ridiculous*
seguro *sure, certain*

Verbos

alegrarse de *to be glad*
calmarse *to calm down*
creer *to believe*
dejar *to leave, let, allow*
dudar *to doubt*
esperar *to hope*
ganar *to win*
molestar *to bother*
poner *to turn on, to show (a movie)*
quejarse (de) *to complain*
sentir (e → ie, e → i) *to be sorry*
sorprender *to surprise*

Expresiones impersonales

es mejor *it's better*
es lógico *it's logical*
es ridículo *it's ridiculous*
es bueno / malo *it's good / bad*
es necesario *it's necessary*
es importante *it's important*
es (im)posible *it's (im)possible*
es una lástima *it's a shame*

Expresiones idiomáticas

¿En serio? *Really?*
¡Ojalá! *Hope so!*
pasarlo bien *to have a good time*
¿Qué hay de nuevo? *What's new?*
¡Qué lástima! *What a shame!*

15

¿Quieres ir al matrimonio conmigo?

▶ COMMUNICATIVE GOALS

The students will be able to discuss and write about their thoughts and feelings toward love, marriage, and family.

▶ LANGUAGE FUNCTIONS

Giving advice
Describing a courtship
Describing a wedding
Expressing emotions
Expressing opinions
Narrating in the past
Describing habitual actions
Expressing cause-and-effect relationships

▶ VOCABULARY THEMES

Courtship
Wedding

▶ GRAMMATICAL STRUCTURES

Present subjunctive in purpose and time clauses
Past (imperfect) subjunctive

▶ CULTURAL INFORMATION

Courtship customs
Marriage customs

http://poco.heinle.com

Atajo

VIDEO

MISTERIO

 **Play Lab Tape**

EN CONTEXTO

El 14 de marzo Leticia Landeros, la polola de Jorge Grandinetti, recibió la siguiente invitación de su amigo Gregorio Vega.

The note in the left margin

1. Point out how the indicative and subjunctive verb forms are used in this reading passage.
2. Have students summarize this reading selection in about fifty words in English. Then discuss with students what they included and excluded in their summaries, and why.

Augusto Cabral Aguirre   José Vega Scherer
Brenda Tártari de Cabral   Rosa Bardehle de Vega

Participan a Ud. (s) el matrimonio de sus hijos
María Christina y Gregorio Miguel
y le (s) invitan a la ceremonia religiosa que se efectuará el día 16 de
abril a las 20,00 horas, en la Catedral de Rancagua, Rancagua.

. . . .

Habrá una recepción en "Calabrano" camino Sta. Juana.
Se ruega confirmar asistencia a los teléfonos
238714-225015 antes del 3 de abril.

Luego Leticia llamó por teléfono a Jorge.

—Aló.
—Hola, Jorge. ¿Cómo estás?
love —Bien, mi amor.° ¿Qué tal?
—Muy bien. Oye, Jorge, ¿sabes qué? Acabo de recibir muy buenas noticias de
next mi amigo Gregorio Vega. Se va a casar el próximo° mes con María Cristina
Cabral Tártari.
You're kidding! —¡No me digas!° ¿Con la Ganadora del Festival?
—Sí, en serio. Dice la invitación que van a casarse el 16 de abril en
Rancagua. (1) ¿Quieres ir al matrimonio conmigo?
—Pues, claro que sí, Leticia. ¡Muchas gracias!
—De nada... vamos a pasarlo bien. Bueno, ahora voy a llamar a Gregorio para
to congratulate him felicitarlo.° Chao, Jorge.
—Chao, Leticia.

wedding Después de un mes, llegó el 16 de abril, el día de la boda.° A las siete y media
de la tarde más de cien parientes y amigos de María Cristina y Gregorio

asistieron° a la ceremonia religiosa en la Catedral de Rancagua. Pronto llegó Gregorio, que llevaba un elegante traje negro. Estaba muy contento, pero un poco nervioso. A las ocho menos quince llegó el Sr. Cabral con su bonita hija vestida de blanco. A Gregorio le pareció un ángel. *attended*

Por fin, comenzó la marcha nupcial.° Los novios caminaron lentamente° hacia el altar donde el padre Contreras celebró la misa y casó a Gregorio y María Cristina. Cuando el padre les dijo que ya eran "esposos", los dos jóvenes se besaron.° Luego ellos salieron de la catedral y los invitados les tiraron° arroz, los abrazaron y besaron. Entonces todos fueron al restaurante Calabrano donde tuvo lugar° la recepción. *wedding march / slowly* *kissed each other* *threw* *was held*

Cuando Gregorio y su esposa entraron en el restaurante, los invitados los aplaudieron y sacaron fotos. Después de un brindis° a los recién casados, esta pareja° y sus invitados entraron en un salón comedor donde tuvieron un banquete maravilloso: palta Reina, consomé de ave, filete Rossini con ensalada surtida, vino tinto y blanco y café con torta mil hojas. (2) *toast* *couple*

Después de esta rica cena, la orquesta comenzó a tocar música moderna y todos los invitados bailaron, hasta el abuelo de María Cristina, un señor simpático de ochenta y tres años. Claro que bailaron la cueca (3) en la que Jorge y Leticia salieron expertos. Más tarde, María Cristina les tiró su ramo de flores° a las solteras y Leticia lo agarró.° Gregorio le quitó la liga° a su esposa y se la tiró a los solteros. Un primo de María Cristina la agarró. (4) Luego Leticia y el primo bailaron juntos y todos los aplaudieron. *bouquet of flowers* *caught / garter*

Más tarde, Gregorio y María Cristina cortaron la torta nupcial, que a los invitados les gustó mucho. Entonces, el papá de Gregorio hizo un brindis por la felicidad° de los jóvenes: *happiness*

—María Cristina y Gregorio: espero que ustedes estén muy contentos en su nueva vida°, que pasen muchos años juntos en buena salud y que siempre estén tan enamorados como lo están en este momento. ¡Muchas felicidades! *life*

Todos aplaudieron y dijeron "¡Felicidades!". Entonces, tomaron una copa de champán en honor de los recién casados. Después, bailaron y tomaron hasta las cinco de la mañana.

Notas de texto

1. Rancagua is a city of about 150,000 inhabitants located about 200 miles (325 kilometers) south of Santiago, the capital of Chile.
2. This menu typifies Chilean cuisine: *palta Reina* (a half avocado stuffed with chicken and topped with mayonnaise); *consomé de ave* (chicken broth); *filete Rossini* (steak served with onions and small potatoes); *ensalada surtida* (mixed salad of lettuce, tomatoes, avocado, and beets); and *torta mil hojas* (cake with thin, crusty layers).
3. *La cueca* is the national dance of Chile. The instruments that are played to accompany this dance are the guitar, accordion, harmonica, harp, and *caja* (a kind of drum).

Note #2: If you have access to easy-to-prepare recipes of Chilean cuisine, bring them to class. Perhaps several of your students could prepare one or more of the dishes for the class. If so, collect sufficient money from each student to pay for the necessary ingredients.

Note #3: Bring to class a record or tape recording of *cueca* music and play it in class. Try to locate a film or a video recording of people dancing the *cueca*, and show it to your class.

4. The woman who catches the bouquet of flowers and the man who catches the garter will be next to marry, not necessarily to each other.

¡Comprendió Ud.?

Lea la lectura rápidamente, luego haga los siguientes ejercicios.

1. ¿Cuál es el tema principal de esta lectura?

2. Indique el título más apropiado que describe la lectura.
   a. Una invitación fabulosa
   b. Cuando se casa muy joven
   c. ¿Quieres casarte conmigo?
   d. El matrimonio de mis amigos

Lea la lectura otra vez. Luego complete las siguientes oraciones lógicamente.

1. Indique el orden cronológico (1→ 5) de las acciones de la lectura.
   _____ Los invitados tuvieron un banquete.
   _____ Los recién casados bailaron juntos.
   _____ Gregorio se casó con María Cristina.
   _____ El padre de Gregorio hizo un brindis.
   _____ Leticia recibió una invitación bonita.

2. ¿Cuál es el primer nombre de los padres del novio? ¿y de la novia?

3. Leticia recibió su invitación _____ antes de la boda.
   a. un mes
   b. dos días
   c. tres semanas

4. Gregorio y María Cristina se casaron _____.
   a. por la mañana
   b. por la tarde
   c. por la noche

5. Los recién casados y sus invitados cenaron en _____.
   a. un hotel
   b. un restaurante
   c. la casa de Gregorio

6. La cueca es un tipo de _____.
   a. canción chilena
   b. baile folklórico
   c. instrumento musical

7. _____ participaron en agarrar el ramo de flores y la liga.
   a. Todos los solteros
   b. Todos los invitados
   c. Gregorio y María Cristina

VOCABULARIO ÚTIL

In this section you will learn some words and phrases for describing a courtship and a wedding.

Cómo describir un noviazgo

la amistad	*friendship*
el amor (a primera vista)	*love (at first sight)*
el cariño	*affection*
la (primera) cita	*(first) date*
enamorarse (de)	*to fall in love (with)*
llevarse bien	*to get along well*
el noviazgo	*courtship*
el compromiso (corto/largo)	*(long/short) engagement*

Una conversación entre novios

—¿Recuerdas cuándo comenzó nuestra amistad, Gregorio?
—Claro, María Cristina. Nos conocimos en la playa de Reñaca.
—Para mí, fue el amor a primera vista.
—Para mí también. Me enamoré de ti en un instante.
—Ay, tenía mucho cariño por ti, mi amor.
—Oye, ¿recuerdas nuestra primera cita?
—Claro, Gregorio. Me invitaste al cine, luego a comer.
—Cómo nos llevamos bien, ¿verdad?
—Sí. Y al poco tiempo me pediste casarme contigo.
—Nuestro noviazgo fue tan corto, ¿no crees?
—Claro que sí, Gregorio. Pero fue tan romántico.

Have several "couples" (males and females) practice this conversation, then role-play it in class. Tell them to add extra appropriate words and sentences, if they wish.

Cómo describir una boda[1]

En la iglesia

Possible narration for this picture sequence: *1. Los novios llegan a la iglesia. Ellos parecen un poco nerviosos. 2. Ahora los novios caminan lentamente hacia el altar. 3. Durante la ceremonia nupcial el novio le pone el anillo a su novia. 4. Luego los dos se besan; ahora están casados. 5. Cuando salen de la iglesia, los parientes y amigos de los novios les tiran arroz y les dicen: —¡Felicidades! 6. Entonces los invitados abrazan y besan a los recién casados.*

el novio / la novia

el ramo de flores

Se casan.

Se besan.

Les tiran arroz.

Ellas se abrazan y
ellos se dan la mano.

los invitados,
los recién casados

En la recepción

Possible narration for this picture sequence: *1. Ahora comienza la recepción. Cuando llegan los recién casados, todos los invitados los aplauden. 2. Los novios y sus parientes y amigos comen bien en un gran banquete. Luego un invitado les hace un brindis: —¡Felicidades! ¡Que pasen ustedes muchos años juntos! 3. Después, los recién casados cortan la torta nupcial. 4. Entonces ellos y sus invitados bailan con la música de la orquesta. 5. Más tarde, la novia tira su ramo de flores y una chica soltera lo agarra. 6. Final- mente, los dos novios salen para su luna de miel.*

Aplauden.

el brindis

la torta nupcial

la orquesta

Tira el ramo de flores.
/ Lo toma.

la luna de miel

---

[1] Chileans use the word *matrimonio* rather than the more common word *boda*, meaning wedding. In all other Spanish-speaking countries, *matrimonio* refers to a married couple or matrimony.

Practiquemos

A. Preparaciones para una boda. Complete los dos párrafos con palabras y frases apropiadas de la lista.

flores	**orquesta**	**la recepción**
la novia	**invitados**	**recién casados**
una boda	**la iglesia**	**ramo de flores**
el novio	**luna de miel**	**la torta nupcial**

Normalmente, las preparaciones para _____ consumen mucho tiempo y mucha energía. Primero _____ tiene que comprar su vestido. También ella pide _____ de una florería, así como el _____ que ella va a llevar al altar de _____. _____ compra un traje nuevo o puede alquilar un smoking *(tuxedo)*. También pide la comida y las bebidas para _____ .

Los dos novios deciden qué _____ quieren emplear, según el tipo de música que les gusta. También necesitan pedir _____, según el número de _____ que van a asistir a la recepción. Finalmente, los novios planean su _____, según el dinero que han ahorrado. A veces, los _____ van a otro país, pero frecuentemente lo pasan bien cerca de su casa.

B. Recomendaciones. Complete las siguientes oraciones según sus opiniones.

1. Creo que un lugar ideal para casarse es _____ porque...
   a. una iglesia muy famosa en Europa
   b. un velero elegante en el Mar Caribe
   c. una casa grande con un jardín bonito
   d. una isla exótica en el Océano Pacífico
   e. otro lugar: _____ .

2. Un brindis apropiado para los recién casados es _____ porque...
   a. ¡Que tengan buena salud!
   b. ¡Que se diviertan mucho!
   c. ¡Que estén muy contentos!
   d. ¡Que ahorren mucho dinero!
   e. otro brindis: _____ .

3. Un buen regalo para los novios que tienen poco es _____ porque...
   a. una videocámara
   b. un horno de microondas
   c. cien dólares en efectivo
   d. media docena de toallas elegantes
   e. otro regalo: _____ .

4. Un lugar ideal para pasar una luna de miel es _____ porque...
   a. Maui, Hawaii
   b. Cancún, México
   c. Mallorca, España
   d. Viña del Mar, Chile
   e. otro lugar: _____ .

Ex. C. Have your students ask you some of these questions, using formal forms.

TRANSPARENCY No. 27: Wedding

Ex. D. Follow-up activity: Ask your students to bring to class photographs of a wedding they have attended. If they have not attended one, they could bring wedding photos of a relative or a close friend. Have them share these pictures with their classmates in small groups. Their discussion of the photos could be based upon the information described in this activity.

C. Entrevista. Pregúntele a otro(a) estudiante.

1. ¿Eres soltero(a) o estás casado(a)?
2. Si eres soltero(a), ¿tienes novio o novia ahora? / Si estás casado(a), ¿cuándo y dónde te casaste?
3. Para ti, ¿es importante casarse en nuestra sociedad? ¿Por qué?
4. Para ti, ¿qué es una familia? En tu opinión, ¿qué futuro tiene la familia en nuestra sociedad?
5. ¿Por qué hay tanto divorcio en nuestro país?
6. ¿Qué se puede hacer para tener éxito *(success)* en el matrimonio?

D. Descripciones.

1. Mire las dos series de dibujos en la página 364. Luego descríbale en español a otro(a) estudiante la acción en una de las series. Después, su compañero(a) de clase va a describirle a usted la acción en la otra serie.
2. Escriba una descripción de una boda verdadera o ficticia. Su descripción debe incluir la siguiente información:
   • cómo se llaman los novios
   • cuándo y dónde fue la boda
   • qué tiempo hizo ese día
   • quiénes estuvieron allí
   • con quién fue usted a la boda
   • a qué hora comenzó la ceremonia
   • qué pasó después de esa ceremonia
   • qué comieron los novios y sus invitados
   • qué cosa interesante pasó en la recepción
   • dónde pasaron los novios su luna de miel

NOTAS CULTURALES

Los novios hispanos

Las costumbres tradicionales de salir en pareja están cambiando rápidamente en Latinoamérica y en España pero, por lo general, todavía son distintas de las costumbres norteamericanas. Por ejemplo, los jóvenes hispanos comienzan a participar en actividades coeducacionales en grupos alrededor de los catorce años. Ellos salen juntos al cine, a fiestas, a la playa y a eventos deportivos. Generalmente, los jóvenes hispanos comienzan a salir en pareja a una edad mayor que la de la mayoría de los jóvenes norteamericanos, y aún así están más restringidos que éstos. A veces, ya a los dieciocho o diecinueve años, salen en pareja. Al contrario de lo que creen muchas personas, la costumbre de salir en pareja acompañados con un chaperón o una chaperona ya no existe en los países de habla española.

Preguntas extras: 1. ¿A qué edad salen en pareja los novios norteamericanos? 2. ¿Adónde les gusta salir juntos? 3. ¿Quién paga cuando van al cine o a un café? 4. ¿De qué manera están limitados?

¿Qué dice usted?

1. Por lo general, ¿a qué edad salen en pareja los jóvenes de su país?
2. ¿Qué beneficios hay en salir en grupo? ¿Cuáles son algunas limitaciones de salir en grupo? ¿y de salir en pareja?

GRAMÁTICA FUNCIONAL

Expressing cause-and-effect relationships

—Jorge, antes de que vayamos a la catedral, quiero visitar a mi tía en Rancagua.

—Está bien, Leticia. Entonces debemos salir por la mañana para que lleguemos a tiempo a la misa que comienza a las ocho.

Present subjunctive in purpose and time clauses

A conjunction is a word that links together words or groups of words such as an independent clause and a dependent clause. Conjunctions of purpose and of time are listed below along with explanations and examples of how to use them.

Conjunctions of purpose

sin que	*without*	**con tal (de) que**	*provided (that)*
para que	*so (that)*	**en caso (de) que**	*in case (of)*
a menos que	*unless*		

1. **Always** use the subjunctive after the five conjunctions listed above.

Independent clause	**Conjunction**	**Dependent clause**
|	|	|
Voy a la boda	con tal (de) que	**vayas** conmigo.

I'm going to the wedding provided you go with me.

2. When expressing an idea with the conjunction *aunque* (although, even though), use the indicative to state certainty, and use the subjunctive to imply uncertainty.

certainty (indicative)

Aunque la boda **es** en abril, no puedo ir.
*Although the wedding **is** in April, I can't go.*

uncertainty (subjunctive)

Aunque la boda **sea** en abril, no puedo ir.
*Although the wedding **may be** in April, I can't go.*

Conjunctions of time

antes (de) que	*before*	**cuando**	*when*
después (de) que	*after*	**hasta que**	*until*
tan pronto como	*as soon as*		

1. The conjunctions listed above may be followed by a verb in either the subjunctive or the indicative mood (see the one exception that follows). When referring to habitual or completed actions, use the

Point out: 1. The de *is optional in* con tal de que, en caso de que, antes de que, *and* después de que. *2. Use* antes de/después de + *infinitive when there is no change of subject; e.g.,* Después de llegar a casa, me acosté.

indicative in the dependent clause. When an action, condition, or event has not yet taken place, use the subjunctive in the dependent clause.

pending action (subjunctive)

Los invitados van a aplaudir **cuando lleguen** los recién casados.

The guests are going to applaud when the newlyweds arrive.

habitual action (indicative)

Los invitados siempre aplauden **cuando llegan** los recién casados.

The guests always applaud when the newlyweds arrive.

completed action (indicative)

Los invitados aplaudieron **cuando llegaron** los recién casados.

The guests applauded when the newlyweds arrived.

2. One exception: **always** use the subjunctive after *antes (de) que.*

Los invitados van a la recepción **antes de que lleguen** los recién casados.

The guests go to the reception before the newlyweds arrive.

Practiquemos

Ex. A . This exercise emphasizes the meaning of conjunctions in complex sentences.

Ex. A.

1. This conversation contains much recycled vocabulary as well as some important uses of the present tense in the indicative and subjunctive moods.

2. Answers: *aunque, Antes de que, después (de) que, con tal (de) que, Cuando, a menos que*

A. Malas noticias para Luis. Después de hablar por teléfono con Leticia, Jorge llamó a su amigo Luis. Para saber lo que dijeron, complete su conversación, usando conjunciones apropiadas de la lista.

aunque	a menos que	después de que
cuando	antes de que	con tal de que

—Oye, Luis. Tengo malas noticias _____ no vas a creerme.

—¿Malas noticias? Por Dios, ¿qué pasó, Jorge?

—_____ te lo diga, espero que no vayas a estar enojado conmigo.

—No, hombre. Dime, ¿qué pasó?

—¿Recuerdas a María Cristina, la cantante ganadora del Festival?

—Claro. La conocí en Viña _____ llegamos a la playa de Reñaca.

—Sí, sí. Pues, ella se va a casar el próximo mes.

—¡No me digas! Pero... ¿cón quién?

—Te lo digo _____ te calmes, Luis.

—Estoy calmado, hombre. Dime más.

—Bueno, María Cristina va a casarse con Gregorio Vega, su novio el que viste en Reñaca. Le dije a Leticia: _____ le diga a Luis que María Cristina se casa en abril, va a estar triste.

—Pues, sí, pero no puedo hacer nada _____ los novios decidan no casarse.

—Es verdad, no puedes hacer nada.

B. La ceremonia civil. Complete la siguiente descripción, usando las formas correctas.

Normalmente, la ceremonia civil de una boda chilena (tiene / tenga) lugar en la casa de la novia a menos que su casa (es / sea) muy pequeña. En ese caso, la ceremonia (es / sea) en la casa del novio. El día antes de que (comienza / comience) la ceremonia civil, los parientes de los novios (decoran / decoren) la casa con flores para que (está / esté) muy bonita.

Al día siguiente (llegan / lleguen) los novios, sus padres y sus hermanos y otros invitados, que (charlan / charlen) hasta que (viene / venga) el juez o la juez *(judge)*. Tan pronto como (llega / llegue) él o ella, (comienza / comience) la ceremonia civil. Después de que (termina / termine) la ceremonia, los invitados (aplauden / aplaudan) a los recién casados, y alguien les (hace / haga) un brindis. Luego todos (toman / tomen) una copa de champán o, en caso de que a alguien no le (gustan / gusten) bebidas alcohólicas, (puede / puedan) tomar jugo. Finalmente, los invitados (abrazan / abracen) y (besan / besen) a la novia y al novio.

C. Entre amigos. ¿Qué sugerencias le dio Leticia a su amigo Gregorio antes de la boda?

Ejemplo: Compra una casa tan pronto como *ser* posible.
Compra una casa tan pronto como sea posible.

1. Antes de que tú y María Cristina se *casar*, piénsalo bien.
2. No compres nada muy caro sin que tu esposa lo *saber*.
3. Cuando ella *estar* enferma, haz todo lo posible para ayudarla.
4. No le des consejos a tu esposa a menos que ella te los *pedir*.
5. Habla frecuentemente con tu esposa para que Uds. *se comprender*.
6. En caso de que tú *tener* algún problema serio, llámame, por favor.
7. Vengan a visitarme después de que Uds. *volver* de su luna de miel.

D. Solamente un sueño. Imagínese que usted va a casarse y que sus padres van a pagar hasta cinco mil dólares por la luna de miel. Escriba un párrafo sobre sus planes.

Describa...

1. el lugar que les gustaría visitar y por qué. *(porque)*
2. cuándo usted y su esposo(a) quieren ir de luna de miel. *(cuando)*
3. lo que ustedes van a hacer tan pronto como lleguen al lugar. *(tan pronto como)*
4. lo que ustedes necesitan antes de hacer el viaje. *(antes de / antes de que)*
5. lo que ustedes van a hacer en caso de que llueva o nieve. *(en caso de que)*
6. lo que ustedes van a hacer después de regresar a casa. *(después de / después de que)*

Charlemos

E. Entrevista. Pregúntele a otro(a) estudiante.

Preguntas para los solteros

1. ¿Qué vas a hacer cuando termines tus estudios?
2. ¿Qué tienes que hacer antes de terminarlos?
3. ¿Piensas casarte algún día?
   (¿Sí? ¿Cuándo piensas casarte? ¿Con quién?)
   (¿No? ¿Prefieres vivir solo[a] o con otra persona?)
4. ¿Qué importancia tiene el matrimonio para ti?

Preguntas para los casados

1. ¿Cuándo te casaste? ¿Con quién te casaste? ¿Dónde se casaron ustedes? Dime cómo es ese lugar.
2. ¿Qué hiciste tan pronto como te casaste?
3. ¿Dónde viviste con tu marido (esposa) después de casarte? Dime algo de ese apartamento (esa casa).
4. ¿Tienes niños? (¿Sí? ¿Cómo se llaman y cuántos años tienen?) (¿No? ¿Quieres tener niños algún día?)

NOTAS CULTURALES

Las bodas hispánicas

engaged

Cuando dos novios piensan casarse, es posible que estén comprometidos° por varios años mientras trabajan y ahorran dinero para alquilar un apartamento y comprar muebles. Muchas veces, posponen la boda hasta que el novio y la novia terminan sus estudios. Normalmente, los hombres hispanos se casan alrededor de los veintisiete años y las mujeres, entre los veinte y veinticuatro años.

Es común que el novio le pida la mano de su novia al padre de ella. Si éste está de acuerdo, las dos familias comienzan a planear juntas la boda.

Muchas bodas en Latinoamérica y en España consisten en dos ceremonias oficiales: una civil y otra religiosa. Si los novios desean una ceremonia religiosa, se casan dos veces. Tradicionalmente, la ceremonia más importante para los novios y sus familias es la religiosa. A veces, la ceremonia civil tiene lugar en la casa de la novia o del novio, y participan en ella algunos familiares y amigos íntimos de las dos familias. Un(a) juez casa a los novios, leyendo palabras de un texto oficial. Después de que se prometen cumplir con todas las responsabilidades del matrimonio, los novios están casados oficialmente. Luego ellos y sus testigos° firman° los documentos correspondientes.

witnesses / sign

Your students could write a summary (in Spanish or English) of this reading to practice that skill.

¿Qué dice usted?

1. ¿Qué impresiones tiene usted de las bodas hispánicas?
2. ¿Cómo son las bodas norteamericanas en comparación con las hispánicas?
3. ¿A usted le gustaría tener una boda norteamericana o una boda hispana?

GRAMÁTICA FUNCIONAL

Expressing past actions, conditions, and situations

—Los padres de María Cristina se alegraban que por fin tuvieran un "hijo": su yerno Gregorio.

—Claro. Ellos le dijeron a Gregorio que les trataran de "tú" y que les dijera "papá" y "mamá".

Past (imperfect) subjunctive

Spanish speakers use the past subjunctive to express wishes, emotions, opinions, uncertainty, and indefiniteness about the past.

How to form the past subjunctive

For **all** Spanish verbs, drop the *-on* ending from the *ustedes* form of the preterite tense, then add the personal endings shown in boldface below. The *nosotros* form always has an accent mark.[1]

	hablar	**venir**	**irse**
ustedes...	hablar**on**	vinier**on**	se fuer**on**
	hablar**a**	vinier**a**	me fuer**a**
	hablar**as**	vinier**as**	te fuer**as**
	hablar**a**	vinier**a**	se fuer**a**
	hablár**amos**	viniér**amos**	nos fuér**amos**
	*hablar**ais***	*vinier**ais***	*os fuer**ais***
	hablar**an**	vinier**an**	se fuer**an**

How to use the past subjunctive

1. You have learned to use the present subjunctive to express actions, conditions and situations that take place in the present or the future. Spanish speakers use the past subjunctive to communicate the same information about the past.

• To express wishes, preferences, suggestions, requests, and recommendations.

Gregorio **esperaba** que Leticia **viniera** a su matrimonio. Claro que él **quería** que ella **invitara** a su pololo Jorge.

Gregorio hoped that Leticia would come to his wedding. Of course, he wanted her to invite her boyfriend, Jorge.

• To express happiness, hope, likes, complaints, worries, regret, sorrow, surprise, fear, and other emotions.

---

[1] The past subjunctive has alternate forms that use *-se* instead of *-ra* endings. For example: *hablase, hablases, hablase, hablésemos, hablaseis, hablasen / fuese, fueses, fuese, fuésemos, fueseis, fuesen.* These forms are often used in Spain and in literaryworks.

Gregorio y María Cristina **se alegraron** que todo **saliera** bien en su matrimonio.

Gregorio and María Cristina were glad that everything turned out okay at their wedding.

Gregorio esperaba que **hiciera** buen tiempo, pero su novia **tenía** miedo que **lloviera.**

Gregorio hoped the weather would be nice, but his bride was afraid that it might rain.

• To express opinions and attitudes.

Era bueno que **hubiera** suficiente comida para todos los invitados.

It was good that there was enough food for all the guests.

• To express uncertainty and indefiniteness.

Leticia **dudó** que Gregorio y María Cristina **pudieran** bailar la cueca, pero la bailaron bien.

*Leticia doubted that Gregorio and María Cristina could dance the **cueca,** but they danced it well.*

Los recién casados **querían** vivir en un apartamento que **estuviera** cerca del mar.

The newlyweds wanted to live in an apartment that was close to the sea.

2. Spanish speakers also use the past subjunctive of the verbs *querer*, *saber*, and *poder* to soften requests, to make polite suggestions, and to persuade gently.

—¿**Quisieran** ustedes acompañarnos? — *Would you like to accompany us?*
—Gracias, pero **debiéramos** volver. — *Thank you, but we should return.*
—Quizás **pudiéramos** ir otra noche. — *Maybe we could go another night.*

Practiquemos

Ex. A. Answers:
Paragraph 1: *tomaban, decía, nadaran, broncearse, fuera, nadaba, tomara*
Paragraph 2: *visitaba, vieran, miraran, pudiera, se fuera*

A. ¿Recuerda usted? Indique las formas correctas.

Un día cuando Luis y Jorge (tomaban / tomaran) el sol en la playa de Reñaca, vieron un quiosco que (decía / dijera): "Se enseña a nadar". Luis le sugirió a Jorge que (nadaron / nadaran), pero éste insistió en (broncearse / se bronceara). Jorge le aconsejó a Luis que no (fue / fuera) a la parte profunda del agua porque sabía que su amigo no (nadaba / nadara) bien. También Jorge le aconsejó a Luis que (tome / tomara) una clase de natación.

Una noche cuando Jorge (visitaba / visitara) a su amigo Luis, había un conflicto entre éste y su hermana Rona. Luis quería que todos (vieron / vieran) el Festival de la Canción, pero Rona insistió en que (miraron / miraran) un programa de concursos. Ella quería ver un programa en que (podía / pudiera) aprender algo y, por eso, fue a su dormitorio para mirar la tele. Luis se alegró de que ella (se fue / se fuera).

B. Deseos y preferencias. Gregorio y María Cristina estuvieron en su luna de miel en Viña del Mar. Mientras que estaban allí, ¿qué dijeron ellos sobre sus deseos?

Ejemplo: Gregorio quería que su esposa...
jugar al vólibol
Gregorio quería que su esposa jugara al vólibol.

1. Gregorio quería que su esposa...
   a. correr las olas
   b. pasear en velero
   c. divertirse mucho
   d. ir al cine con él
   e. aprender a jugar al póker
   f. decirle que lo quería mucho
   g. sacar muchas fotos de ellos
   h. bañarse con él en el jacuzzi

2. María Cristina deseaba que su marido...
   a. quererla para siempre
   b. abrazarlo un poco más
   c. no cantar en la ducha
   d. afeitarse todos los días
   e. hacer el esnorquel con ella
   f. no nadar en el agua profunda
   g. caminar con ella por la playa
   h. dormir la siesta por la tarde

C. Páginas de mi diario. Escriba dos párrafos sobre su niñez y su adolescencia.

Mi niñez:

Cuando era niño(a), era importante que yo... Mi(s) (papá / mamá / padres) prohibía(n) que...   No me gustaba que mi(s) (papá / mamá / padres)..., pero sí me gustaba que (él / ella / ellos)....

Mi adolescencia:

De adolescente, no estaba seguro(a) que... Por ejemplo, dudaba que... A veces, sentía que...; en otras ocasiones me alegraba de que...

Charlemos

D. Recuerdos de mi niñez. Hágale las siguientes preguntas a un(a) compañero(a) de clase para saber un poco sobre su niñez.

1. **La familia:** ¿Qué te gustaba que hicieran tus padres cuando eras niño(a)?
2. **La escuela:** ¿Qué te prohibían tus profesores en la escuela primaria? ¿y en la secundaria?
3. **Los pasatiempos:** ¿Qué deportes practicabas cuando eras niño(a)? ¿En qué deportes te prohibían tus padres que participaras? ¿Por qué?

E. Es mejor ser cortés. Imagínese que usted y un(a) compañero(a) de clase están de vacaciones en Chile. Ustedes desean ser corteses con los chilenos y, por eso, usan el subjuntivo del pasado de los verbos querer, deber y poder. ¿Qué les dirían a las siguientes personas?

Ejemplo: You ask someone to help you with your suitcase.
   A: *¿Pudiera ayudarme con esta maleta?*
   B: *Sí, con mucho gusto.*

1. You want a friend to show you how to surf.
2. One of your Chilean friends uses the word *pololo*, which you don't understand. Ask for an explanation.
3. A maid knocks at your hotel door and asks if she may clean your room. Since you just got up, you ask her to come back in an hour.

4. You telephone a friend to persuade him or her to go shopping with you tomorrow.
5. You can't understand a police officer because he's speaking too fast.
6. While sightseeing in Viña del Mar, you and a friend meet a young couple whom you invite to dinner.

PARA LEER MEJOR

Summarizing a Reading Passage

Summarizing in English a reading passage that you have read in Spanish can help you synthesize the most important ideas in it. Some guidelines for writing this type of summary are as follows:

• Underline the main ideas in the reading passage.
• Circle the key words and phrases in the passage.
• Write the summary of the passage in your own words.
• Do not include your personal reactions in the summary.
• Avoid the following common errors in writing a summary:

| too long | wrong key ideas | main ideas not expressed |
| too short | too many details | key ideas do not stand out |

Correo de amor

Querido Dick:

No estoy segura de que me pueda ayudar. Hace seis meses cumplí veinte años y tengo una vida social saludable. Disfruto el ser soltera y nunca pensé que me gustaría cambiar. Eso fue hasta hace poco. Hay un joven llamado Pedro, guapo, muy bueno y con gran sentido del humor. Cada vez que nos vemos el cielo se me abre. Sé que él me desea y yo a él, tanto que deseo gritar. Pero hay un problema, él se ve con mi amiga Lisa. Están saliendo desde hace un tiempo y no les ha ido mal. Lo que quiero decir es que a ella le gusta, pero no lo quiere; se ve con él por no estar sola. Pero mientras tanto, yo estoy loca por Pedro.

Dick, Lisa es una vieja amiga y me moriría si ella se enfada por robarle su novio, pero temo que se aleje y que pierda la oportunidad de vivir la vida con un hombre que me atrae tanto. ¿Debo decirle a Lisa cómo me siento, debo decírselo a Pedro y dejar que él sea el que confronte la situación? Por favor, Dick, apúrese. Me estoy volviendo loca, especialmente cuando los veo juntos y me digo que Pedro podría ser más feliz conmigo.

Firmado: "Enamorada del novio de una Amiga"

Estimada "Enamorada...".

Estás corriendo el riesgo de perder una buena amiga. Desde aquí, no estoy seguro si esa amistad con Lisa puede pasar esta prueba. Si crees que puedes hacerlo, pregúntale. Esto te dá dos alternativas: Dejar que Pedro hable con Lisa acerca de la situación de sus relaciones y su deseo de entablar una relación contigo, o esperar pacientemente que ellos rompan su amistad amorosa, de la forma que sea. Quizás Lisa te sorprenda y deje a Pedro, pero esto es una línea muy fina. Por favor, déjame saber qué ha pasado. Me gustaría también saber de otros lectores que se encuentren en la misma situación.

Activities

A. Read the two letters on the preceding page, and underline the main ideas in them to understand the gist of their content.

B. Read both letters again, then circle the key words and phrases in them to understand the letters more thoroughly.

C. Write a brief summary in English of the first letter, stating the specific problem expressed by its writer.

D. Write a brief summary in English of the advice given by Dick in his response to the writer of the letter.

E. Scan both letters for information to complete the following statements correctly.

Primera carta

1. (Un chico / Una chica) escribió esta carta.
2. Esa persona (es soltera / está casada).
3. Él / Ella) tiene (miedo / hambre / razón).
4. Esta persona le pide (dinero / amor / consejos) a Dick.
5. Pedro y Lisa son (amigos / novios / esposos).

Segunda carta

6. Dick es (optimista / pesimista / neutral) en su respuesta.
7. Es probable que Dick sea (menor / mayor) que sus lectores.
8. De las dos alternativas que ofrece Dick, la (primera / segunda) es mejor.

Reacciones personales

9. ¿Qué piensa usted del problema de la persona que escribió la primera carta? ¿Ha tenido usted este problema también? (¿Sí? ¿Cómo lo resolvió?)
10. ¿Qué piensa usted de los consejos de Dick? ¿Qué consejos tiene usted?

PARA ESCRIBIR MEJOR

Writing a Persuasive Essay

In this section you will learn to write an essay in which you try to convince your reader of your point of view. Writers often use the following words and phrases to connect ideas in this type of composition.

To express opinions:

creo que	*I believe*
pienso que	*I think*
en mi opinión	*in my opinion*

To show contrast:

pero	*but*
aunque	*although*
por otro lado	*on the other hand*

To support opinions:

primero	*first*
una razón	*one reason*
por ejemplo	*for example*

To summarize:

por eso	*therefore*
finalmente	*finally*
en conclusión	*in conclusion*

Atajo

Functions:
Persuading; expressing an opinion; agreeing & disagreeing; comparing & contrasting

Vocabulary:
Dreams & aspirations; media; family members; upbringing

Grammar:
Verbs: irregular preterite, subjunctive; But; *pero, sino (que), nada más que*

Activity

1. Formulate your opinion on **one** of the following topics:
   - La luna de miel ideal
   - La mejor edad para casarse
   - Los beneficios de no casarse nunca
   - La adopción de niños por una pareja
   - El matrimonio de una pareja homosexual
   - El mejor tiempo de tener el primer niño

2. Write an essay in which you state your point of view; list two reasons plus relevant facts and examples to support your opinion; and then write a conclusion that restates your viewpoint. Your essay will have four paragraphs, as shown in the following outline and model on the topic: La mejor edad para casarse.

   I. Introduction — state your point of view.
   No hay una mejor edad para casarse.

   II. First reason for your opinion and an example.
   Una persona no sabe cuándo va a terminar sus estudios.
   Algunos terminan a los 18 años, otros a los 30 años.

   III. Second reason for your opinion and an example.
   La gente vive más años ahora.
   En el pasado vivían no más de 50 años.

   IV. Conclusion — summarize your point of view.
   Una persona debe casarse cuando quiera.

   Example:

   Creo que no hay una mejor edad para casarse en nuestra sociedad. Es mejor que cada persona decida por sí misma cuándo quiere casarse.

   Una razón es que una persona no sabe cuándo va a terminar sus estudios. Por ejemplo, algunos estudiantes los terminan después de pasar cuatro años en la escuela secundaria. Por otro lado, otros siguen estudiando en la universidad hasta los treinta años o más.

   Otra razón es que la gente vive más años en nuestra sociedad, en comparación con el pasado cuando vivían normalmente no más de cincuenta años, por ejemplo.

   En conclusión, pienso que en nuestra sociedad no es necesario sentirse obligado a casarse a cierta edad. Debemos casarnos cuando queramos. Somos individuos y, por eso, somos independientes.

SÍNTESIS

¡A ver!

You are going to listen to several people talk about different kinds of foods that Hispanics enjoy. First, study the words with their meaning in the *Vocabulario esencial*. Second, read the questions and their possible answers in the activity below. Third, watch the videotape, then complete the activity according to the directions.

Vocabulario esencial

jubilados	*retired people*
bocadillos	*sandwiches*
frijoles	*beans*
salsa especial	*special sauce*
tortilla de maíz	*corn tortilla*

Conteste cada pregunta con la mejor respuesta.

1. Más o menos, ¿cuántas personas piden comida rápida por teléfono los fines de semana de la tienda en que trabaja el joven madrileño?
   a. 200
   b. 300
   c. 400

2. ¿Quién come comida rápida en el mundo hispano, según ese joven?
   a. personas jubiladas
   b. todo tipo de personas
   c. principalmente jóvenes

3. ¿Qué dijo el joven sobre en que consiste la comida rápida?
   a. salchichas, mariscos, café
   b. pizza, hamburguesas, refrescos
   c. bocadillos, ensalada, Coca-Cola

4. El joven mencionó dos ingredientes de la comida rápida. ¿Cuáles son?
   a. pescado y gambas
   b. jamón y champiñones
   c. lechuga y aceitunas

5. ¿Cuáles son algunos ingredientes del plato típico mexicano?
   a. carne asada, salsa, frijoles, cebollas
   b. camarones al horno, huevos fritos, papas
   c. jamón, lechuga, aceitunas, frutas frescas

Answers:
1. c 2. b 3. c 4. b 5. a

SÍNTESIS

¡A leer!

Eduardo Barrios (1884–1963) fue un escritor chileno que se interesaba mucho por la sicología de sus personajes. Escribío muchas novelas: El niño que enloquecío de amor *(1915), que trata de un niño locamente enamorado de una mujer que finalmente se vuelve loco;* El hermano asno *(1922), que nos presenta a Fray Rufino, quien se destruye; y* Un perdido *(1917), en que Lucho, el protagonista, se pierde en una vida llena de vicio y sufrimiento. En este cuento, también vamos a apreciar sus observaciones de la vida chilena y de la sicología de los personajes.*

SÍNTESIS

Papá y mamá

Eduardo Barrios

Es de noche en la paz de una calle de humildes hogares.° Un farol,° detrás de un árbol, alumbra el muro.° Cerca se abre la ventana de la salita modesta, en cuya sombra° se ve a la joven esposa sentada en el balcón, con los ojos como fijos en pensamientos. ¿Qué piensa todas las noches sentada en el balcón, mientras la criada lava dentro los platos y los niños juegan un rato° en la acera?° . . .¿Añora?° ¿Sueña? . . .¿O simplemente escucha el péndulo que en el misterio de la sombra marca el paso al silencioso ejército de las horas?°

modest homes / light
wall
shadow

a while
sidewalk / Does she yearn?
marks the step of the silent army of hours

Es plácida, la noche. El cielo, claro, las nubes, transparentes, y muy blanca y muy redonda,° la luna que recuerda viejas estampas° de romanticismo y de amor.

round / moments

Dos niños juegan en la acera: Ramón y Juanita. Un tercero, nene° que aún no anda, sentado en el umbral° de la puerta de calle, escucha sin comprender y mira con ojos maravillados. Ramoncito ha mudado ya los dientes;° es vivo, habla mucho, y sus pernecillas° nerviosas están en constante movimiento. Juanita es menor. Sentada como el nene sobre la piedra del umbral, acomoda en un rincón de la puerta paquetitos de tierra, y botones, y cajas de fósforos, y palitos°. . .

bebé
threshold
has lost his baby teeth
his little legs

little packages of dirt, and buttons, and matchboxes, and little twigs

Juegan a la gente grande, porque ellos, como todos los niños, tienen, sobre todo en las noches, una inconsciente necesidad de imaginar y preparar la edad mayor.

Activities

A. Mire el dibujo y el nombre de la selección:

1. El nombre de la selección es "Mamá y Papá". Cuál es el tema principal de esta lectura?
2. ¿Que esta haciendo la mujer en el dibujo?
3. ¿Quienes son esos niños y qué estan haciendo?
4. ¿Esta el papa en el dibujo?

B. Lea la selecion rapidamente y localice la siguiente informacion:

1. ¿Que palabras asocia con la casa y la familia?
2. ¿Qué palabras asocia con el tiempo?

SÍNTESIS

C. Opiniones Personales
1. ¿Le recuerda la lecura a su familia?
2. ¿Cree Ud. que el padre debe cuidar a los niños tambien?
3. ¿Como son sus padres y sus hermanos? ¿Sus hermanos son mayores o menores que Ud.? ¿Que hacen ahora? ¿Se reune su familia frecuentemente?

¡A conversar!

Converse con otro(a) estudiante.

Estudiante A:

Imagínese que usted se casó hace seis meses, y que ahora tiene algunos problemas. Por ejemplo, usted...

- se preocupa mucho por su futuro
- dice que necesita más dinero que nunca
- trabaja más de sesenta horas a la semana
- quiere mudarse a otro apartamento más grande

Estos problemas han causado conflictos entre usted y su esposo(a). Otra cosa más: usted y él (ella) van a tener un niño en cinco meses. Usted está muy preocupado(a) y, por eso, habla con un(a) amigo(a), que es Estudiante B.

Estudiante B:

Usted va a hablar con su amigo(a), Estudiante A, que tiene algunos problemas. Primero, escúchele muy bien. Luego hágale algunas preguntas para saber más de cada problema. Finalmente, trate de ayudarle a encontrar algunas soluciones para que se sienta mejor. Sea positivo(a) y paciente con su amigo(a).

¡A escribir!

Lea otra vez "Papá y mamá". Luego escriba una conversación entre la maná y sus hijos, según la información que usted ha leído. Invente otros detalles apropiados, si usted quiere.

Be sure to give students adequate time —either in class and/or out of class to prepare this activity.

Option: Have students write a letter to Dr. Cardenal from the daughter's point of view.

Visit

http://poco.heinle.com

Atajo

VOCABULARIO

Sustantivos

la amistad *friendship*
el amor *love*
la asistencia *attendance*
el banquete *banquet*
la boda *wedding*
el brindis *toast*
el cariño *affection*
la cita *date (social)*
el compromiso *engagement*
la flor *flower*
el invitado *guest*
la liga *garter*
la luna de miel *honeymoon*
la marcha nupcial *wedding march*
el matrimonio *wedding (Chile)*
el noviazgo *courtship*
la novia *bride*
el novio *groom*
la orquesta *band*
la pareja *couple*
el ramo *bouquet*
los recién casados *newlyweds*
la torta nupcial *wedding cake*
la vida *life*

Adjetivos

corto *short*
largo *long*
próximo *next*

Verbos

abrazar(se) *to hug (each other)*
acompañar *to accompany*
agarrar *to catch*
aplaudir *to applaud*
asistir (a) *to attend (a function)*
besar(se) *to kiss (each other)*
casarse *to get married, to marry*
decorar *to decorate*
efectuarse *to take place*
enamorarse (de) *to fall in love (with)*
felicitar *to congratulate*
llamar *to call*
sonreír (e→i) *to smile*
terminar *to end*
tirar *to throw*

Adverbios

hasta *even*
lentamente *slowly*

Conjunciones

a menos que *unless*
antes (de) que *before*
aunque *although*
con tal (de) que *provided (that)*
cuando *when*
después (de) que *after*
en caso (de) que *in case (of)*
hasta que *until*
para que *so (that)*
sin que *without*
tan pronto como *as soon as*

Expresiones idiomáticas

amor *love; honey (term of affection)*
a primera vista *at first sight*
conmigo *with me*
contigo *with you*
darse la mano *to shake hands*
llevarse bien *to get along well*
¡No me digas! *You're kidding!*
tener lugar *to take place*
tener éxito *to be successful*
vestido(a) de *dressed in*

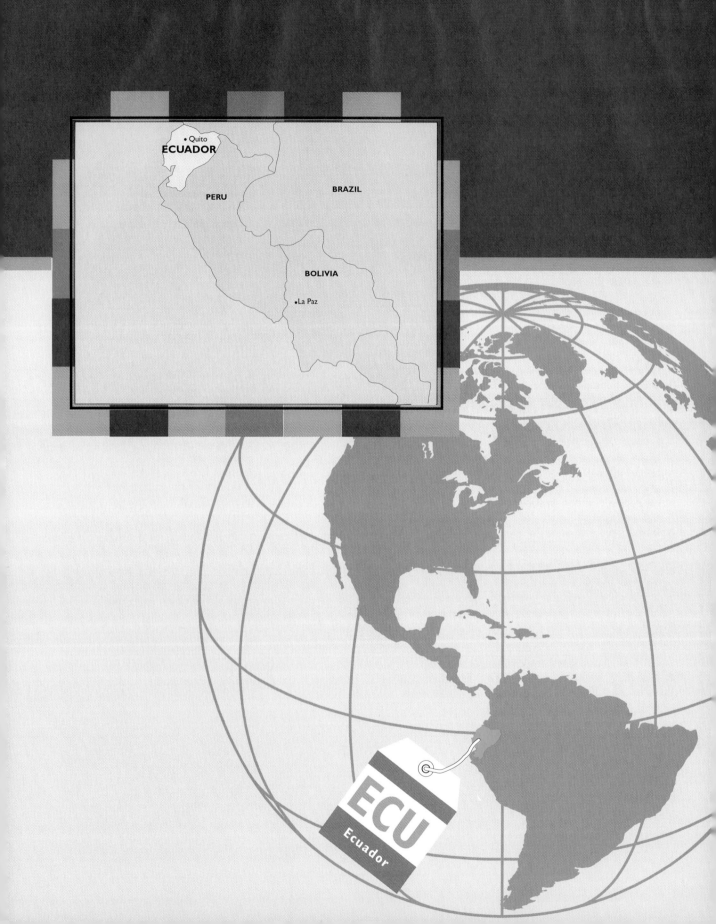

Quito
ECUADOR

PERU

BRAZIL

BOLIVIA

La Paz

ECU
Ecuador

En busca de aventura
Ecuador ◄

Keri Cranson and her Japanese friend, Makiko Akaishi, are students at Florida International University, where they have studied Spanish for three years. During their summer vacation, they travel together around Ecuador for one month. In Keri's diary we read about their marvelous adventures in Quito, the Amazon jungle, and the Galápagos Islands.

LECCIÓN

16

Quito: La Florencia de las Américas

▶ COMMUNICATIVE GOALS

You will be able to communicate in travel agencies and airports in Spanish-speaking countries and describe a vacation trip you have taken.

▶ LANGUAGE FUNCTIONS

Giving advice
Making requests
Expressing opinions
Expressing preferences
Discussing travel plans
Describing a vacation trip

http://poco.heinle.com

▶ VOCABULARY THEMES

Air travel

▶ GRAMMATICAL STRUCTURES

Informal commands
Adjectives used as nouns

▶ CULTURAL INFORMATION

Getting around Latin America
Getting around Spain

Write for free information about Ecuador: FEPROTUR (Fundación Ecuatoriana de Promoción Turística): 1390 Brickell Avenue, Miami, FL 33131-3324, or 510 5th Street S.W., Suite 1422, Calgary, Alberta T2P 3S2.

EN CONTEXTO

Play Lab Tape

Keri Cranson y su amiga japonesa Makiko Akaishi son estudiantes de la Universidad Internacional de la Florida en Miami donde han estudiado español por tres años. Ahora ellas están de vacaciones en el Ecuador. Lo que sigue es una parte del diario de Keri.

Querido Diario,

27 de junio. *Ahora Makiko y yo estamos en el Hotel Inca Imperial en Quito. (1) Cuando llegamos aquí anoche, estábamos tan cansadas que nos acostamos inmediatamente. Esta mañana caminamos por la ciudad vieja y vimos algunas plazas e iglesias coloniales. En una librería compramos tarjetas postales que les mandamos a nuestros padres y amigos. Luego tomamos un autobús al Cerro Panecillo (2) desde donde contemplamos la capital, los Andes y el volcán Cotopaxi en vista panorámica. (3) En el Cerro comimos en un restaurante donde conocimos a una familia muy simpática de la ciudad de Cuenca. (4) Eran Eduardo Pérez, su esposa Gabriela y sus dos hijas, Lucía de diez años y Elena de seis. Ellos nos invitaron a su casa. Ojalá que podamos visitarlos algún día.*

Each diary entry is followed by comprehension questions to encourage students to think about what they have just read.

1. Keri y Makiko visitaron la capital del Ecuador. ¿Qué hicieron allí? Sea usted específico(a).
2. Ellas conocieron a una familia ecuatoriana. ¿Dónde? ¿Quiénes son ellos? ¿De dónde son?

28 de junio. *Se dice que Quito es "la Florencia de las Américas" por su arquitectura magnífica como en Florencia, Italia. Hoy visitamos La Compañía, que es una iglesia conocida por sus maravillosas esculturas y pinturas. (5) Por la tarde, fuimos al mercado para comprar algunos recuerdos.° Yo compré un anillo y unos aretes, y Makiko compró un sombrero y una camiseta muy bonita. Allí conocimos a Juan Ochoa Valderrama y José Hernández Lillo, que son estudiantes de la Universidad Católica de Quito. Juan tiene veintitrés años y José tiene veinte. Ellos nos invitaron a tomar café en un pequeño restaurante donde charlamos por dos horas. Antes de salir, Juan nos invitó a una fiesta en su casa mañana. Hemos estado en Quito solamente dos días y ya tenemos seis amigos. ¡Qué simpáticos son los ecuatorianos!*

souvenirs

3. Keri y Makiko hicieron otras cosas en Quito. ¿Qué hizo Keri? ¿y Makiko? ¿Qué hicieron juntas?
4. Ellas conocieron a otros dos ecuatorianos. ¿Dónde? ¿Quiénes son ellos? ¿De dónde son?

29 de junio. *Anoche fuimos a la fiesta en la casa de Juan. Allí conocimos a algunos de sus parientes y amigos, aprendimos a bailar salsa y tomamos pisco, que es el licor más fuerte que hemos bebido hasta ahora. (6) Pudimos comunicarnos en español con todos los invitados,* *aunque algunas personas hablaban bien el inglés. Mañana José, Juan, Makiko y yo vamos a hacer una excursión en auto. Espero que lo pasemos bien.*

---

5. Keri y Makiko fueron a una fiesta. ¿Dónde fue? ¿Quién las invitó? ¿Qué hicieron allí?

Ask students why this site is called *la "Mitad del Mundo."*

30 de junio. *Hoy a las nueve de la mañana, Juan y José nos recogieron y fuimos en auto a la "Mitad del Mundo" que está aproximadamente a veinticinco kilómetros al norte de Quito. (7) Visitamos un museo, un planetario y un monumento. Allí Makiko y yo pusimos el pie izquierdo en el Hemisferio Norte y el pie derecho en el Hemisferio Sur. José se rió de eso y nos sacó unas fotos con nuestras cámaras. Esa noche volvimos a Quito muy cansados, pero contentos. Makiko y yo intercambiamos direcciones con José y Juan. Tal vez° ellos puedan visitarnos algún día. Me gustan tres cosas de Quito: su gente simpática, su clima agradable° y su arquitectura maravillosa.*

maybe

pleasant

Obtain a map of Ecuador (mailed free of charge from FEPROTUR), and have students locate the places that Keri and Makiko visit in this last *Paso.*

6. Keri y Makiko salieron con sus amigos ecuatorianos. ¿Con quiénes y a qué hora salieron? ¿Adónde fueron ellos?
7. Los cuatro amigos se divirtieron mucho. ¿Qué hicieron juntos? ¿Qué impresiones tuvieron Keri y Makiko?

Add as much information as you can to these cultural notes. Use your experience, knowledge, and any appropriate printed or audiovisual materials you may have.

Notas de texto

1. Quito lies nestled in a valley at 9,400 feet (2,800 meters), surrounded on all sides by the northern Andes mountains. This city of over one million people has reigned as the colonial capital of Ecuador since the eighteenth century. Quito still has many charming colonial buildings and beautiful Spanish architecture in the old part of the city.
2. The *Cerro Panecillo* ("Little Breadloaf Hill") offers a sweeping view of the old section of Quito and the rugged Andes mountains that surround the city. According to legend, the Inca Indians reshaped the *Cerro* as a monument to the sun god.
3. *Cotopaxi*, located only 30 miles (45 kilometers) south of Quito, is the world's highest active volcano, at an altitude of 19,347 feet (5,825 meters).
4. Cuenca, located in southern Ecuador, is a city of over 100,000 people. The city was built on an Inca site and is famous for its colonial homes with overhanging balconies.
5. *La Compañía* is a large Catholic church with extraordinary Moorish architecture, gold altars, as well as sculptures and paintings dating from the 16th, 17th, and 18th centuries.
6. *Pisco* is a strong brandy that takes its name from the port city of Pisco, Peru.
7. The *Mitad del Mundo* ("Middle of the World") is a popular tourist attraction located 15 miles (25 kilometers) north of Quito at an altitude of 7,700

feet (2,320 meters). Many visitors enjoy having their picture taken there with one foot in the Northern Hemisphere and the other in the Southern Hemisphere. This popular site has a monument with a line indicating where both hemispheres meet.

¿Comprendió Ud.?

1. Según lo que usted ha leído en esta lectura, ¿por qué se dice que Quito es "la Florencia de las Américas"?
2. Haga una lista de los lugares que Keri y Makiko visitaron durante sus primeros días en el Ecuador y las actividades que ellas hicieron allí.
   Por ejemplo:

Lugares	Actividades
Hotel Inca Imperial	Durmieron en ese hotel.
una librería	Compraron tarjetas postales allí.

3. Escriba uno o dos párrafos con un resumen de lo que hicieron Keri y Makiko, usando la información de la lista que usted hizo en la Actividad 2.
4. Imagínese que usted está en Quito ahora. De las cosas que Keri y Makiko vieron e hicieron en Quito, ¿cuáles le gustaría ver y hacer a usted?
5. ¿Qué impresiones tiene usted de Makiko y Keri hasta ahora?

VOCABULARIO ÚTIL

De viaje en avión

In this section you will learn words and phrases for traveling by airplane.

En la agencia de viajes

by plane	KERI:	Queremos ir en avión° a Quito el 26 de junio.
round-trip	AGENTE:	¿Quieren ustedes un boleto de ida o de ida y vuelta?°[1]
	KERI:	De ida y vuelta, por favor.
flight	AGENTE:	Hay un vuelo° que sale para Quito el domingo a las cuatro menos cuarto de la tarde con Ecuatoriana. ¿Está bien?
stops	MAKIKO:	Pues, ¿cuántas escalas° hace el avión, señor?
	AGENTE:	Ninguna, señorita. Es un vuelo directo, sin escala.
	MAKIKO:	Perfecto. ¿Cuánto es el boleto?
taxes	AGENTE:	Setecientos dólares por el boleto, más cincuenta dólares por los impuestos° de aeropuerto, señorita.
schedule	KERI:	Está bien. ¿Me puede dar el horario° de los vuelos, por favor?
	AGENTE:	Cómo no, señorita. Aquí tiene usted.
	KERI:	Muchas gracias.
You're welcome	AGENTE:	Por nada.°

1. Ask students the following questions: *¿Por qué van al Ecuador Keri y Makiko? ¿Cómo van allí? ¿Adónde van para comprar sus boletos?*
2. If possible, invite a Spanish-speaking travel agent or airline representative to speak with your class about his or her profession and services.

Have students role-play these two dialogues in groups of three persons.

En el aeropuerto

passports	REP:	Sus pasaportes,° por favor.
	MAKIKO:	Sí, señorita. Aquí los tiene.
baggage	REP:	Gracias. ¿Tienen equipaje?°
backpacks	KERI:	Sí, tenemos solamente estas dos mochilas.°
smoking	REP:	Bien. ¿Prefieren sentarse en la sección de fumar° o de no fumar?
seat	KERI:	En la sección de no fumar, por favor. Prefiero un asiento° de
aisle		pasillo.°
window	MAKIKO:	Y yo un asiento de ventanilla.°
security / Have a nice trip!	REP:	Bueno, pasen ustedes por el control de seguridad.° ¡Buen viaje!°
	MAKIKO:	Gracias.

---

[1] Spaniards use *el billete* instead of *el boleto*, which is commonly used in Latin America.

En la sala de espera

Su atención, por favor. Ecuatoriana de Aviación anuncia una demora° de media hora del vuelo número 71 con destino a° Quito. Muchas gracias.

Su atención, por favor. Ecuatoriana de Aviación anuncia la salida de su vuelo número 71 con destino a Quito. Los pasajeros° pueden abordar° el avión por la puerta° H-6. Muchas gracias por su paciencia.

delay

departing for

passengers / to board
gate

En el avión

Abróchense° el cinturón de seguridad, por favor.

Fasten

Tell students that the words for "flight attendant" are *el (la) asistente de vuelo; la azafata* and *el (la) aeromozo(a)* are also used, depending on the country.

La llegada

Su atención, por favor. Ecuatoriana de Aviación anuncia la llegada de su vuelo número 71 procedente de° Miami. Todos los pasajeros deben pasar por la inmigración° y la aduana.° Favor de recoger° su equipaje en el área "B". Gracias por su atención y bienvenidos a Quito.

Point out the construction *favor de + (no)* verb as another way to make requests; for example: *Favor de recoger su equipaje. Favor de no pasar por esta área.*

arriving from

passport control
customs / claim

Practiquemos

A. Definiciones. Lea cada frase, luego identifique su definición.

1. la gente que paga para viajar en avión
2. el lugar adonde ir para abordar un avión
3. la lista de los días y las horas de vuelos
4. el documento para poder entrar en otro país
5. el asiento desde el cual se ven los aviones
6. el equipaje que no se lleva a bordo del avión
7. el lugar donde se ve lo que hay en las maletas
8. la tienda donde se compran los boletos de avión
9. el boleto que se compra cuando uno no quiere volver
10. lo que uno les dice a los amigos antes que viajen

de ida
la aduana
la puerta
el horario
las maletas
¡Buen viaje!
el pasaporte
los pasajeros
la ventanilla
la agencia de viajes

B. ¡De vacaciones! Lea el siguiente anuncio y conteste las preguntas correspondientes.

*Sólo IBERIA une 19 ciudades de América
con 27 destinos europeos, vía Madrid.*

IBERIA es la línea aérea europea líder en todo Iberoamérica.
Por eso, sea cual sea la ciudad europea que elija,
IBERIA le lleva volando. Porque IBERIA une 19 ciudades de América
con 27 destinos europeos, vía Madrid. Y todo, disfrutando,
si lo desea, de nuestro exclusivo programa "Amigo".
Elija una ciudad de Europa y decídase por la mejor compañía:
IBERIA, la línea aérea del '92.

**Asunción. Bogotá. Buenos Aires. Cancún. Caracas. Guatemala. La Habana.
Lima. Managua. México. Montevideo. Panamá. Quito. Río de Janeiro. San José.
San Juan. Santiago de Chile. Santo Domingo. Sao Paulo.**

1. ¿Cómo se llama la línea aérea principal de España?
2. ¿Cuántos destinos sirve esta línea aérea en Europa?
3. ¿Cuántas ciudades latinoamericanas sirve la línea aérea? ¿En qué países están estas ciudades? De estas ciudades, ¿cuál le gustaría visitar a usted, y por qué?

C. De viajes. Hágale a otro(a) estudiante las siguientes preguntas.

1. ¿Tienes pasaporte?
   (¿Sí? ¿De qué país es? ¿Cuándo conseguiste tu pasaporte?)
   (¿No? ¿Piensas conseguir un pasaporte algún día? ¿Por qué?)
2. ¿A qué países has viajado? ¿Cuál es tu país favorito? ¿Qué otros países te gustaría visitar algún día? ¿Por qué?
3. Normalmente, ¿llevas mucho o poco equipaje cuando viajas?
4. ¿Cuándo fue la última vez que viajaste en avión? ¿Adónde fuiste? ¿Por qué fuiste a ese lugar?

5. ¿Prefieres sentarte en el pasillo o al lado de la ventanilla cuando viajas en avión?
6. En un vuelo internacional, ¿te gustaría sentarte en la sección de fumar o en la sección de no fumar?

D. Mis preferencias. Indique sus preferencias personales.

1. Normalmente, cuando compro un boleto de avión, pago...
   a. en efectivo porque...
   b. con un cheque personal porque...
   c. con una tarjeta de crédito porque...

2. Generalmente, cuando viajo en avión prefiero un asiento...
   a. de pasillo porque...
   b. de ventanilla porque...
   c. en la sección de fumar/no fumar porque...

3. Cuando hay una demora de vuelo por más de una hora,...
   a. no hago nada.　　 d. tomo un café (té).
   b. leo un periódico.　 e. descanso y espero.
   c. miro los aviones.　 f. hago otra cosa: _____ .

4. Por lo general, cuando hago un viaje de dos semanas o más, llevo...
   a. poco equipaje; por ejemplo: _____ .
   b. mucho equipaje; por ejemplo: _____ .

E. ¿Qué opina usted? Léale las siguientes oraciones a otro(a) estudiante, quien debe decirle a usted si está de acuerdo o no, y por qué.

Ejemplo:　　A: *Es mejor pedir un vuelo sin escalas que con escalas.*
　　　　　　　B: *Estoy de acuerdo.*
　　　　　　　A: *¿Por qué?*
　　　　　　　B: *Porque los pasajeros llegan más rápidamente.*

1. Es mejor sentarse a la ventanilla que al pasillo de un avión.
2. Es difícil viajar en avión con un bebé o con un niño pequeño.
3. Es una buena idea llevar poco equipaje cuando se viaja en avión.
4. Es preferible pagar un boleto de avión antes de viajar que después de viajar.
5. Es importante sentarse cerca de una puerta de emergencia en el avión.
6. Es más interesante sentarse en la sección de clase turista que en la primera clase.

F. En el aeropuerto. Haga esta actividad con otros dos estudiantes. Dos personas son pasajeros en el aeropuerto de Quito, y la otra persona es el (la) agente de Ecuatoriana.

Agente

1. Greet your passengers.
3. Find out where they are going.
5. Ask for their tickets and passport.

Pasajeros

2. Respond appropriately.
4. Answer the question.
6. Do what the agent asks and say something appropriate.

Ex. D.
1. You could use this activity in several ways: a. students could work in pairs or in groups of 3-4 persons, b. you could call on individual students to respond in class, c. you could have students write their sentences at home or in class.
2. If some of your students have no air travel experience, they could talk about another mode of public transportation such as *autobús* or *tren.*
3. Encourage your students to express their preferences freely in this semi-structured activity. Most of the items will then be open-ended.

Ex. E.
1. Tell students to decide which partner will read these statements first (the other partner should close his or her book). After the partners have completed this activity, they should switch roles and do it again.
2. Follow-up: Assign this activity for written homework.

Ex. F.
1. These instructions appear in English to guide the content of the students' conversation. The students should feel free, however, to use appropriate vocabulary items and grammatical structures to express their thoughts. This procedure is similar to that used in the Oral Proficiency Interview (OPI) technique developed by the American Council on the Teaching of Foreign Languages (ACTFL).

7. Ask their seating preference (smoking/nonsmoking; window/aisle).
9. Answer the question, then check in their luggage.
11. Respond, then say where they should board the airplane.
13. Explain, then return their travel documents. Express appreciation.
15. Answer the question.
17. Respond, then wish them a good trip.
19. Say good-bye.

8. Answer, then ask if your plane will leave on time.
10. Ask how the weather is at your destination.
12. Ask for directions to your departure gate.
14. Find out where you can change dollars into *sucres*.
16. Ask what time it is.
18. Express your appreciation.
20. Answer appropriately.

G. Un viaje interesante. En uno o dos párrafos, describa un viaje interesante que usted haya hecho recientemente. En su descripción, mencione...

1. adónde fue usted en su viaje.
2. cuándo lo hizo usted.
3. con quién fue usted.
4. por qué hizo el viaje.
5. qué hizo usted en ese lugar.
6. cuándo volvió usted a casa.

NOTAS CULTURALES

Cómo viajar en Latinoamérica

En avión y tren. Muchos latinoamericanos usan el transporte público porque los autos, las piezas de recambio,° la gasolina y el petróleo son caros. Además, el aparcamiento es limitado y costoso, y muchas áreas no son accesibles por auto. Si usted piensa viajar a regiones de selva° o de desierto, en las montañas o durante la temporada lluviosa, es mejor ir en avión o en tren. Varias aerolíneas sirven a los países latinoamericanos, y hay un servicio excelente de tren entre muchas ciudades.

En autobús. Existe un sistema extenso de autobuses para el público, que ofrece transporte bastante barato entre las ciudades latinoamericanas. Algunos autobuses son modernos con aire acondicionado, películas en video y servicio de bebidas. Otros autobuses son más viejos y paran frecuentemente a lo largo de° su ruta para que los pasajeros puedan subir o bajar, aunque normalmente esto sucede en las terminales centrales de la ciudad.

piezas de recambio parts *selva* jungle *a lo largo de* along

Preguntas

1. ¿Cómo es el transporte público en su ciudad y en su país?
2. ¿Con qué frecuencia viaja usted en transporte público? Explique.
3. ¿Cuáles son algunas ventajas y desventajas del transporte público?

GRAMÁTICA FUNCIONAL

Giving advice and making requests

—José, sácame una foto.
—Bien. Ahora sonríe, Makiko.
—Saca otra, pero más cerca.

Informal commands

Spanish speakers use informal commands mainly to tell children, close friends, relatives, and pets to do or not to do something.

How to form affirmative informal commands

1. For most Spanish verbs, use the *él/ella* verb forms of the present indicative.

Infinitive	él/ella		tú command
hablar	habla	→	**habla**
comer	come	→	**come**
escribir	escribe	→	**escribe**
cerrar	cierra	→	**cierra**
dormir	duerme	→	**duerme**

2. Eight verbs have irregular affirmative *tú* commands.

decir	**di**	salir	**sal**
ir	**ve**	poner	**pon**
ser	**sé**	tener	**ten**
hacer	**haz**	venir	**ven**

—**Ven** conmigo al mercado.   *Come with me to the market.*
—Sí, pero **ten** paciencia, Makiko.   *Yes, but be patient, Makiko.*

3. Attach pronouns to affirmative *tú* commands. If the command form has two or more syllables, it carries an accent mark over the stressed vowel to retain the stress of the verb.

—**Dame** tu dirección, Keri.   *Give me your address, Keri.*
—Aquí la tienes. **Escríbeme.**   *Here it is. Write to me.*

How to form negative informal commands

1. For **all** Spanish verbs, use *no* before the *tú* verb forms of the present subjunctive.

Infinitive	tú pres. subj.		tú command
hablar	hables	→	**no hables**
comer	comas	→	**no comas**
escribir	escribas	→	**no escribas**

1. Emphasize that the present indicative *él/ella* verb forms and 99% of the affirmative *tú* commands are identical.
2. The *vosotros* commands have not been introduced here because of their relatively limited use in the Spanish-speaking world (i.e., exclusive to certain areas of Spain).

Point out that the irregular affirmative *tú* commands form their negative commands like all Spanish verbs; for example: *¡Dime algo! ¡No me digas nada!*

Emphasize that pronouns are **attached** to affirmative commands, but they are placed **before** negative commands.

cerrar	cierres	→	**no cierres**
dormir	duermas	→	**no duermas**
decir	digas	→	**no digas**

—**No compres** esa camiseta, Keri. *Don't buy that T-shirt, Keri.*
—**No digas** eso. ¡Me gusta! *Don't say that. I like it!*

2. Place pronouns before negative command verbs.

—**No te olvides** de escribirme. *Don't forget to write me.*
—Sí, Makiko. **No te preocupes.** *Yes, Makiko. Don't worry.*

Practiquemos

A. Conflictos entre amigas. Complete la siguiente conversación entre Makiko y su amiga Keri, usando los mandatos de la lista, según el contexto.

| ten | espera | descansa | no fumes |
| dime | cálmate | olvídate | no escribas |

MAKIKO: Ay, Keri. _____ en tu diario ahora. Vamos a cenar. Tengo mucha hambre.

KERI: _____ diez minutos más, Makiko. Quiero terminar este párrafo.

MAKIKO: Pues, ya escribiste mucho. _____ un poco ahora. Vamos ya.

KERI: ¿No me oíste, Makiko? _____ paciencia. ¿No puedes esperar diez minutos?

MAKIKO: ¡_____ , amiga! Te espero, te espero. Voy a fumar un cigarrillo.

KERI: Makiko, _____ aquí. Sabes que eso me molesta bastante.

MAKIKO: Bueno, ¿qué puedo hacer? _____ , ¿qué puedo hacer?

KERI: Mejor _____ , Makiko. Vamos al restaurante.

B. Consejos para Makiko. Antes de salir para el Ecuador, una amiga ecuatoriana de Makiko le dio algunos consejos sobre su viaje. ¿Qué le dijo su amiga? Conteste esta pregunta, usando mandatos afirmativos.

Ejemplos: hablar / solamente en español
Habla solamente en español.

1. sacar / muchas fotos
2. ser / cortés con todos
3. ver / películas en español
4. comer / en los cafés locales
5. tratar / de pensar en español
6. escribir / tu diario en español
7. escuchar / anuncios de la radio
8. ir / a una presentación folklórica
9. hacer / muchos amigos ecuatorianos
10. leer / los periódicos de cada ciudad
11. mirar / la televisión frecuentemente
12. tener / mucha paciencia con la gente

Ex. A.

1. This initial exercise allows students to focus on the meaning of the informal commands without concentrating on their formation. Subsequent exercises in this section focus on form.

2. Answers: *No escribas, Espera, Descansa, Ten, Cálmate, no fumes, Dime, olvídate*

Ex. B.

1. Answers:
1. *Saca...* 2. *Sé...* 3. *Ve...* 4. *Come...*
5. *Trata...* 6. *Escribe...* 7. *Escucha...*
8. *Ve...* 9. *Haz...* 10. *Lee...* 11. *Mira...*
12. *Ten...*
2. Follow-up: Change the context by having students imagine that Makiko's Spanish instructor gave her this advice. Now have your students redo this exercise, using *usted* commands (caution: item No. 6 will require a change from *tu* to *su*).

C. Una invitación. Mientras Makiko y Keri estaban en Quito, conocieron a la familia Guzmán. La señora Guzmán las ha invitado a almorzar en su casa, y ahora está diciéndole a Makiko por teléfono cómo llegar a su apartamento. ¿Qué dice la señora?

Ejemplo: *Salir* de tu hotel. → *Sal de tu hotel.*

Doblar a la derecha y *caminar* dos cuadras por la Calle Bogotá. *Esperar* el autobús número 4 en la esquina de Bogotá con Carchi. *Subir* al autobús y *sentarse* cerca de la puerta. *Leer* los nombres de las calles. Después de pasar el Restaurante "La Choza", *bajarse* en la Calle Cevallos. Luego *seguir* por la Cevallos hasta llegar al número 1072, que es nuestro edificio de apartamentos. *Subir* al apartamento número 42.

Ex. C.
1. Answers: *Dobla... camina...; Espera...; Sube... siéntate...; Lee...; bájate...; sigue...; Sube...*
2. Follow-up activity: Have students redo this exercise, using *usted* commands.

D. Consejos de un amigo. José Hernández le dio a Keri algunos consejos sobre lo que ella debe y no debe hacer mientras está en el Ecuador. ¿Qué le dijo José?

Ejemplo: Beber / un poco de pisco, pero no _____ mucho.
Bebe un poco de pisco, pero no bebas mucho.

1. Alquilar / un auto barato, pero no _____ ninguno viejo.
2. Cambiar / tu dinero en un banco; no lo _____ en tu hotel.
3. Caminar / en todas partes de Quito, pero no _____ sola de noche.
4. Ir / a las Islas Galápagos, pero no _____ con un grupo grande.
5. Pasar / más tiempo en Quito; no _____ mucho tiempo en Guayaquil.
6. Tomar / agua mineral o un refresco; no _____ el agua de tu cuarto.
7. Comer / en los restaurantes; no _____ la comida de los mercados.
8. Llevar / ropa conservadora en Quito; no _____ pantalones cortos.
9. Sacar / fotos de los indios, pero no las _____ sin pedirles permiso.
10. Salir / frecuentemente de tu hotel, pero no _____ sin tu cámara.

Ex. D.
1. Answers:
1. *Alquila... alquiles...* 2. *Cambia... cambies...* 3. *Camina... camines...* 4. *Ve... vayas...* 5. *Pasa... pases...* 6. *Toma... tomes...* 7. *Come... comas...* 8. *Lleva... lleves...* 9. *Saca... saques...* 10. *Sal... salgas...*
2. Follow-up activity: Have students redo this exercise, using *usted* commands.

E. Querido(a) amigo(a)... Imagínese que uno(a) de sus amigos(as) va a vivir con una familia ecuatoriana por un mes. Haga una lista de consejos sobre lo que él (ella) debe y no debe hacer en el Ecuador, usando mandatos informales.

Ejemplo: *Sé educado(a) y **haz** la cama todos los días.*
*No **hables** inglés; **habla** solamente en español.*

Charlemos

F. ¡Qué lástima! Imagínese que usted está comiendo con un(a) amigo(a) en un restaurante de Quito. Responda a sus quejas, usando los mandatos informales (afirmativos o negativos) que corresponden a los verbos indicados o a otros verbos apropiados.

Ejemplo: A: No me gusta esta sopa.   dar, decir, comer
B: *Bueno, dámela, por favor.*
o: *Dile algo al camarero.*
o: *Entonces, no la comas.*

Quejas

1. Pero esta salsa está muy picante.
2. Ay, el camarero no me escucha.
3. ¿Cómo? Esta cuenta no está correcta.
4. No sé si la propina está incluida.
5. No llevo mucho dinero en efectivo.

Verbos posibles

comer, tomar, beber
llamar, preocuparse
mostrar, dar, preguntar
preguntar, dejar, olvidar
pagar, olvidar, preocuparse

G. Problemas y consejos. Imagínese que algunos de sus amigos de habla española tienen los siguientes problemas. ¿Qué consejos puede darles? Dé por lo menos un mandato positivo y un mandato negativo. Trate de ser diplomático(a) con ellos.

Ejemplo: Ana dice que le gusta ir a fiestas, pero no baila bien.
Ana, escúchame bien. Baila solamente con tus amigos y no te preocupes tanto.

1. Teresa es tímida. No le gusta hablar con otras personas.
2. Miguel tiene poco dinero. Dice que le gustaría visitar a sus abuelos en Puerto Rico porque ya están muy mayores.
3. Mercedes está triste porque su novio se fue con otra chica. Ahora ella no sabe qué hacer.
4. Esta mañana Roberto llegó tarde a clase por tercera vez. Dice que su despertador no funciona bien.

H. En la estación de ferrocarril. Hable con otro(a) estudiante: una persona es agente de billetes y la otra persona es su cliente.

Cliente

1. Greet the ticket agent.
3. Say where you want to go.
5. Ask about the train fare.
7. Reply appropriately.
9. Buy the ticket; say thank-you.

Agente

2. Return the greeting.
4. Say when the train leaves.
6. Ask: one-way or round-trip?
8. Say how much it costs.
10. Express your appreciation.

NOTAS CULTURALES

Cómo viajar en España

En avión. Generalmente en España es más caro viajar en avión de una ciudad española a otra en comparación con los precios en los Estados Unidos o el Canadá. Sin embargo,° es recomendable informarse sobre descuentos de estudiante y otras tarifas especiales en los vuelos de noche. Iberia es la línea aérea nacional que sirve a todas las ciudades principales de España.

Nevertheless

En tren. La mayoría de los españoles viaja de una ciudad a otra en tren. España tiene un sistema excelente de ferrocarriles que se llama RENFE, Red° Nacional de Ferrocarriles Españoles. Casi todos los trenes tienen secciones de primera y de segunda clase, y la mayoría de los trenes nocturnos tiene coches-cama para dormir.

Network

En autobús. El excelente sistema de autobuses en España sirve a los pueblos° pequeños que no tienen servicio de tren, además de los otros pueblos y ciudades del país. La mayoría de los autobuses son cómodos, son más económicos que los trenes, y pueden llevarlo a uno a su destino más rápidamente que un tren, especialmente si las distancias son cortas. Si uno quiere viajar por las rutas principales de los autobuses, es recomendable hacer reserva.

towns

En auto. Viajar en auto es la manera más conveniente y cómoda para visitar los lugares remotos de España. Aunque las carreteras° de España son relativamente buenas, muchos españoles no viajan largas distancias en auto porque la gasolina es cara —más de tres veces el precio de la gasolina en los Estados Unidos y en el Canadá. Sin embargo, muchos turistas extranjeros° prefieren viajar por España en auto a pesar del alto costo de la gasolina porque esto les permite visitar muchos lugares interesantes.

highways

foreign

Invite a Spanish-speaking guest who is from Spain or has recently visited that country. Before he or she visits the class, your students could write one or two questions to ask the guest speaker about his or her country or trip abroad.

GRAMÁTICA FUNCIONAL

Referring to specific things and places and expressing abstract ideas

—Makiko, ¿compro estas tarjetas grandes o las pequeñas?
—Compra las pequeñas porque están más baratas, Keri.
—Ay, lo bueno de viajar contigo es que aprendo a ahorrar dinero.

Adjectives used as nouns

1. In Spanish, you can avoid repeating a noun by replacing it with a definite or indefinite article plus an adjective. The adjective must match the gender (masculine or feminine) and the number (singular or plural) of the noun to which it refers.

—Quiero comprar un **anillo.**	*I want to buy a ring.*
—Ya tienes **uno nuevo,** Keri.	*You already have a new one, Keri.*
—¿Te gusta éste blanco?	*Do you like this white one?*
—No. Compra **el amarillo.**	*No. Buy the yellow one.*
—¿Vas a comprar una **bolsa**?	*Are you going to buy a purse?*
—Ya compré **una pequeña.**	*I already bought a small one.*
—A mí me gustaron **las grandes.**	*I liked the big ones.*

2. To express abstract ideas such as "thing" or "part," use *lo* with a masculine singular adjective.

—**Lo bueno** de viajar es que conocemos a mucha gente.	*The good thing about travel is that we meet a lot of people.*
—Sí, Keri. ¡Pero **lo malo** es que cuesta mucho dinero!	*Yes, Keri. But the bad part is that it costs a lot of money!*

Practiquemos

A. En el departamento de ropa. Keri y Makiko están expresando sus preferencias en un almacén de Quito. ¿Qué dicen ellas?

Ejemplo: KERI: —¿Te gusta esta camiseta azul o ésa roja?
MAKIKO: —Prefiero *la roja* porque me gusta el color rojo.

1. KERI: —¿Compro esta blusa amarilla o ésa azul clara?
   MAKIKO: —Compra _____ porque el color amarillo es feo.

2. KERI: —¿Debo comprar estos pantalones baratos o ésos caros?
   MAKIKO: —Compra _____ porque no tienes mucho dinero, Keri.

3. MAKIKO: —¿Prefieres este suéter gris o ése blanco?
   KERI: —Prefiero _____ porque el gris me parece un color triste.

4. KERI: —¿Te gustaría probarte esta falda grande o ésa pequeña?

    MAKIKO: —Quiero probarme _____ porque estoy más delgada ahora.

5. MAKIKO: —¿Compro estas botas negras o ésas de color café?

    KERI: —Debes comprar _____ porque ya tienes unas de color café.

6. MAKIKO: —¿Vas a comprar este vestido verde o este rosado?

    KERI: —No voy a comprar ni _____ ni _____ porque no tengo dinero.

B. Decisiones.
Ayer Makiko y Keri visitaron la Mitad del Mundo con sus amigos Juan y José. ¿Qué dijeron ellos durante el viaje?

Ejemplo: JUAN: ¿Quieres ir a un café grande o pequeño?

          KERI: Prefiero *uno pequeño*. No me gustan los grandes.

1. JUAN: ¿Quieren ustedes ir a un restaurante barato o caro?

    KERI: Vamos a _____ . Somos estudiantes como tú y José.

    MAKIKO: El otro día fuimos a _____ y nos costó una fortuna.

2. JUAN: ¿Prefieren ir a un restaurante pequeño o grande?

    MAKIKO: Vamos a _____ . A veces, los grandes son impersonales.

    KERI: Tienes razón. A mí me gusta ir a _____ también, Juan.

3. JUAN: ¿Les gustaría ir a un restaurante chino o italiano?

    KERI: Quiero ir a _____ porque me gusta la pizza.

    MAKIKO: Prefiero ir a _____ ; no me gusta la comida italiana.

    JOSÉ: A mí no me importa si vamos a _____ o a _____ .

4. JUAN: Este café mexicano tiene tacos picantes o no picantes.

    KERI: Voy a pedir _____ porque me gustan los chiles.

    MAKIKO: A mí no. Voy a pedir _____ . ¿Y tú, José?

    JOSÉ: Como Keri, quiero comer _____ . Juan, ¿qué dices tú?

    JUAN: Prefiero ir a un restaurante japonés.

Ex. B. Answers:
1. *uno barato, uno caro*
2. *uno pequeño, uno pequeño*
3. *uno italiano, uno chino, uno chino, uno italiano*
4. *unos picantes, unos no picantes, unos picantes*

C. Querido(a)...
Escríbale una carta a un(a) compañero(a) de clase, completando las siguientes frases.

Ex. C. After students complete this activity, have them exchange letters with classmates, then answer each other's letters.

Mi vida académica

Ahora estudio en... Lo bueno de mi escuela es (son)..., y lo triste es (son)... Al momento, estudio... Lo interesante de mis estudios es (son)... Lo aburrido de la vida académica es (son)...

Mi vida social

Al momento, mi vida social es (fantástica/inexistente/...) porque... Lo agradable (desagradable/ridículo) de esto es... Creo que lo importante de tener amigos es... Mi mejor amigo(a) se llama _____ . Lo mejor de él (ella) es...

Charlemos

D. ¡Bienvenido a Quito!
Imagínese que su amigo(a) ecuatoriano(a) (otro[a] estudiante) acaba de recibirlo(la) a usted en el aeropuerto de Quito. Ahora él (ella) le hace algunas preguntas. Contéstelas según sus preferencias, como en el ejemplo.

Ejemplo: AMIGO(A): En Quito hay hoteles de todos precios. Hay algunos hoteles baratos, otros que son económicos y otros que están caros. ¿Qué tipo de hotel prefieres, y por qué?

USTED: *Prefiero uno económico porque no me gustan los muy baratos y no tengo mucho dinero para ir a uno caro.*

1. En Quito hay algunas partes que son viejas y otras que son modernas. ¿Qué partes de la ciudad te gustaría visitar primero: las viejas o las modernas, y por qué?
2. Hay restaurantes excelentes en Quito. ¿En cuál te gustaría cenar esta noche: en un restaurante cubano, o en uno chino o en uno alemán? ¿Por qué?
3. En Quito hay muchas tiendas diferentes. ¿Adónde te gustaría ir de compras mañana, a las tiendas grandes o a las pequeñas? ¿Por qué?

E. Lo mejor y lo peor. Dígale a otro(a) estudiante sus opiniones sobre lo mejor y lo peor de las siguientes ideas.

Ejemplo: llevar poco equipaje en un viaje de avión
Lo mejor es que los pasajeros viajan más fácilmente.
Lo peor es que los pasajeros no tienen mucha ropa.

1. ir en un vuelo que hace dos escalas
2. sentarse en la sección turista en un avión
3. viajar en avión con un grupo de estudiantes
4. sentarse en primera clase de un avión grande
5. llegar al aeropuerto dos horas antes de un vuelo

PARA LEER MEJOR

Reading Critically

This section will help you develop your ability to read critically in Spanish. One way to read critically is to distinguish factual information from an author's point of view and possible bias. The better you can separate fact from opinion, the better you will understand the writer's intentions.

Activities

A. 1. Opinion 2. Fact 3. Fact
4. Fact 5. Opinion 6. Opinion
B. & C. Answers will vary among
students.

A. Read the following statements and check whether they are **facts** or **opinions.** Then compare your decisions with those of a classmate.

	Fact	Opinion
1. Traveling to foreign countries is educational.	____	____
2. Most Americans travel to South America by plane.	____	____
3. Ecuador is a small country compared with the U.S.	____	____
4. Quito, Guayaquil, and Cuenca are Ecuadorian cities.	____	____
5. It's hard to imagine why few tourists visit Ecuador.	____	____
6. Ecuador is the most fascinating country in the world.	____	____

B. Read the following advertisement. Look at the underlined statements and decide whether they are facts or opinions. If you think they are opinions, write down the words that influenced your decision.

CUENCA

Cuenca es tan bonita

... ¡Visítela!

Cuenca, <u>tal vez la capital de la artesanía ecuatoriana</u>, se encuentra en una amplia hoya de la provincia del Azuay al sur del Ecuador. <u>Regada por cuatro ríos</u> que hacen de la llanura "grande como el cielo" o Guapdondeleg, <u>una de las áreas más bellas y plácidas del país</u>. <u>En este ambiente de flores</u>, de gente de riqueza intelectual y espiritual surge <u>una de las escuelas más finas</u> de la artesanía ecuatoriana.

C. Read the following narrative. As you read it, decide whether each sentence is based mainly on factual information **(F)** or on personal opinion **(O),** then mark it accordingly (F or O) in the right margin. Afterwards, compare your decisions with those of a classmate.

Su visita al Ecuador puede convertirse en las vacaciones más completas que jamás haya tenido. Nuestro país no es grande, pero cuenta con una gran variedad de ecosistemas y culturas tradicionales.

La variedad es el sabor de la vida para los visitantes que desean conocer el Ecuador. Les ofrecemos muchos mundos para descubrir:

- La Costa
- Las Sierras
- El Amazonas
- Las Islas Galápagos

Al regresar del Ecuador, los viajeros relatan increíbles historias. Cuentan haber visto pingüinos de la Antártida nadando en medio del ecuador o que estuvieron en la "mitad del mundo" con un pie en cada hemisferio... Que en un solo día viajaron desde las altas cordilleras andinas hasta las planicies tropicales con sus bananales... Que se maravillaron viendo catedrales adornadas con oro y caminaron por ruinas incas

You could assign this as a one-time activity or an ongoing project. If the latter, collect student's diaries periodically, then read what they have written since the last time you collected them. Comment on the diary entries, responding primarily to students' messages rather than the form (e.g., grammatical usage, vocabulary choice, spelling, punctuation). This writing activity and reaction strategy build students' self-confidence in expressing themselves in a natural, non-threatening way.

Atajo

Functions:
Expressing an opinion; expressing irritation; describing people; talking about daily routines

Vocabulary:
People; personality; senses; dreams & aspirations; gestures

Grammar:
Adjective agreement; verbs: imperative *tú*

cuyas edificaciones, construidas sin argamasa alguna, han resistido el paso de los siglos... Que recorrieron pintorescos mercados indígenas y compraron las mejores artesanías directamente a sus productores... Y, sobre todo, que lo pasaron estupendamente.

Source: Adapted from the brochure *Ecuador*.

PARA ESCRIBIR MEJOR

Writing a Diary

Writing is a skill that improves with practice. A personalized way to develop your writing skills as well as your ability to think in Spanish is to keep a diary of your daily activities and thoughts. Here are some tips to get you started.

Activity

1. Buy a bound composition book or a notebook with lines.

2. Write your first diary entry with today's date. Write in your diary on a regular basis about topics that interest you. You might begin by describing your Spanish class, as in the example below. What do you like about your class? What do you dislike about it? What do you find difficult? What is easy for you?

   Example:

   17 de marzo de 19__

   Normalmente, me gusta mi clase de español. Aprendo mucho de mi profesora, quien es inteligente y simpática. Me gusta escuchar la música que ella trae a la clase, pero no me gusta cantar. No canto muy bien. Tampoco me gustan los exámenes de español porque son difíciles, especialmente la gramática. Para mí, el vocabulario es fácil, pero la gramática es más difícil.

3. As you write in your diary every day, concentrate most on expressing your ideas and feelings, rather than on writing grammatically perfect sentences.

SÍNTESIS

¡A ver!

Carmen is at a travel agency in Spain where she is buying tickets to travel on one of Spain's high-speed trains called *Alta Velocidad Española* (AVE). First, study the words and expressions with their meaning in the *Vocabulario esencial*. Second, read the reservation form and the statement in the activity below. Third, watch the videotape, then complete the activity.

Vocabulario esencial

quisiera	*I would like*
no fumadores	*non-smoking section*
ida y vuelta	*round-trip*
clase turista	*tourist class*

1. Complete la siguiente reserva para Carmen, según su conversación entre ella y la agente de viajes.

reserva: tren "ave"

	ida		**vuelta**
Destino	_____	Destino	_____
Día de salida	_____	Día de salida	_____
Hora de salida	_____	Hora de salida	_____
Hora de llegada	_____	Hora de llegada	_____

2. Carmen prefiere viajar en...
   ____ clase club.
   ____ clase turista.
   ____ clase preferente.

Answers:

1. IDA: Destino = Madrid, Día de salida = 24 / jueves, Hora de salida = 8:00 de la mañana, Hora de llegada = 10:15 de la mañana VUELTA: Destino = Sevilla, Día de salida = 26 / sábado, Hora de llegada = 9:00 de la noche
2. clase turista

¡A leer!

¿A usted le gustaría visitar el Ecuador? Lea el anuncio que sigue para saber lo atractivo de ese país.

Visit

http://poco.heinle.com

SÍNTESIS

VISITE
ECUADOR
sin costo alguno

ECUATORIANA
¡Excelente Elección!

En su viaje al norte o sur del Continente, sea nuestro invitado en Quito o Guayaquil, ECUATORIANA le ofrece la oportunidad de conocer una de estas atractivas ciudades sin costo adicional.

Con el pasaporte "mitad del mundo" usted podrá disfrutar de los siguientes servicios:

- Transporte aeropuerto-hotel-aeropuerto.
- Cocktail de bienvenida.
- Alojamiento en hotel cinco estrellas.
- Alimentación. • Tour por la ciudad.

El pasaporte "mitad del mundo" es otro gran detalle que hace de ECUATORIANA una excelente elección!

Informes sobre este servicio en su agencia de viajes preferida o en las oficinas de ECUATORIANA de AVIACIÓN.

¿Comprendió Ud.?

Conteste las siguientes preguntas.

1. ¿A qué "Continente" se refiere?
2. Busque las ciudades de Quito y Guayaquil en un mapa del Ecuador. ¿Qué ciudad le gustaría visitar, y por qué?
3. ¿Qué es "La Mitad del Mundo"?
4. Para usted, ¿qué es lo más atractivo de este anuncio? ¿Por qué?

¡A conversar!

Hable con otro(a) estudiante; una persona es agente de viajes y la otra es su cliente.

SÍNTESIS

Cliente

1. Salude al (a la) agente de viajes.

2. Conteste: usted acaba de llegar a Quito y quiere conocer la ciudad y sus alrededores.

5. Dígale qué excursión le interesa más y pregúntele sobre el costo, la duración y las fechas del viaje.

7. Mire el papel y reaccione positivamente a lo que lee.

9. Responda apropiadamente y pague el viaje (en efectivo, con cheque o con tarjeta de crédito).

11. Conteste apropiadamente y despídase del (de la) agente.

Agente

2. Responda apropiadamente. Luego dígale a su cliente que se siente, "¿En qué puedo servirle?"

4. Descríbale una excursión de la capital en autobús, y otra a la "Mitad del Mundo" en auto.

6. Conteste a todas las preguntas y escriba esta información en un papel. Luego déselo a su cliente.

8. Muéstreselo. Pregúntele cómo le gustaría pagar por la excursión.

10. Dele las gracias. Escriba un recibo y déselo con el boleto de viaje.

12. Responda apropiadamente.

¡A escribir!

Imagínese que usted es agente de viajes. Escriba un anuncio atractivo para atraer a clientes latinoamericanos y españoles a visitar los Estados Unidos o el Canadá. El anuncio debe incluir la siguiente información:

1. todo lo que se incluye en la excursión
2. las fechas del viaje o la duración de éste
3. el precio total de la excursión en dólares
4. la agencia de viajes (nombre, dirección, teléfono)
5. los nombres de algunos lugares de interés turístico

Atajo

VOCABULARIO

Sustantivos

el cigarrillo *cigarette*
el diario *diary*
la escultura *sculpture*
Florencia *Florence*
el hemisferio *hemisphere*
el impuesto *tax*
el monumento *monument*
el pie *foot*
la pintura *painting*
el planetario *planetarium*
el recuerdo *souvenir*
la vista *view*

Viajar en avión

abrocharse *to buckle up*
el cinturón de seguridad *safety belt*
el control de seguridad *security control*
hacer escala (en) *to make a stop (on a flight)*
ir en avión *to go by plane*
la puerta *gate*
sin escala *nonstop (flight)*
el vuelo *flight*

Viajar en general

abordar *to board*
la aduana *customs area*
la agencia de viajes *travel agency*

el asiento *seat*
el boleto (billete) de ida *one-way ticket*
el boleto (billete) de ida y vuelta *round-trip ticket*
¡Buen viaje! *Have a nice trip!*
con destino a *departing for*
el cheque de viajero *traveler's check*
la demora *delay*
el equipaje (de mano) *(carry-on) baggage, luggage*
el horario *schedule*
la inmigración *passport control*
la llegada *arrival*
el (la) pasajero(a) *passenger*
el pasaporte *passport*
el pasillo *aisle*
procedente de *arriving from*
recoger (recojo) *to pick up, claim*
la sala de espera *waiting area*
la salida *departure*
la sección de (no) fumar *(non) smoking section*
la ventanilla *window*
viajar *to travel*
el viaje *trip*

Adjetivos

agradable *pleasant*
famoso *famous*
situado *situated*

Adverbios

tal vez *maybe, perhaps*

Verbos

fumar *to smoke*
intercambiar *to exchange*

Expresiones idiomáticas

por nada *you're welcome*

Aventuras en el Amazonas

▶ COMMUNICATIVE GOALS

You will be able to obtain lodging in Spanish-speaking countries, discuss your travel plans, and speculate on future events.

▶ LANGUAGE FUNCTIONS

Specifying lodging needs
Complaining about a hotel room
Discussing future plans
Agreeing and disagreeing
Making predictions
Speculating
Expressing preferences

http://poco.heinle.com

▶ VOCABULARY THEMES

Lodging (hotel)

▶ GRAMMATICAL STRUCTURES

Future tense
Conditional tense

▶ CULTURAL INFORMATION

Where to stay in Latin America
Where to stay in Spain

EN CONTEXTO

Makiko y Keri leen el siguiente anuncio en su guía sobre el Ecuador, y se deciden a hacer el viaje.

ECUADOR: UNA AVENTURA EN EL AMAZONAS

jungla
town

Cuando vengan al Ecuador no dejen de experimentar una aventura en la selva.° Visiten Coca, un pequeño pueblo° situado en el Río Napo en la selva amazónica. ¡Pero recuerden en el verano hace mucho calor y mucha humedad! En autobús pueden llegar hasta un barco extraordinario llamado el Flotel Orellana.(1) Sus guías serán los señores Óscar Montoya y Luis Vargas, unos indígenas de la región, quienes les explicarán detalladamente con un mapa los lugares que visitarán en su viaje.

dugout canoe / trees

butterflies

Una de las excursiones que se hacen desde el Flotel Orellana es pasear en piragua° para ver árboles° grandes que parecen paraguas abiertos, flores de muchos colores y grandes mariposas.° Luego se llegará hasta el Lago Tarocoa para comer un rico almuerzo de bistec, papas fritas y plátanos. En el lago se puede pescar pirañas —si desea. Al segundo día, se irá en piragua del Flotel hasta Limoncocha donde trabajan algunos misioneros norteamericanos. (2) Por la noche, se visitará la Hacienda Primavera donde se les servirá una rica cena de jabalí, plátanos y chica. (3)

Al tercer día, se visitará la Isla de los Monos° donde viven algunos monos Wooly. De este lugar, seguiremos por el río hasta llegar a un pueblo pequeño donde viven los indios aucas. (4) Ellos les demostrarán cómo usar una cerbatana° para cazar° animales en la selva.

Estamos seguros de que les gustará mucho esta aventura y nunca podrán olvidarse de la selva amazónica del Ecuador.

monkeys

blowgun
to hunt

Después de pasar tres días llenos de las actividades que se describen en el anuncio, Makiko le escribe una carta a su amiga Ana Álvarez, qué conoció en Quito.

Querida Ana:

¡Hola! ¿Cómo estás? ¿Cómo están todos los amigos? Mándales saludos a todos de mi parte y de Keri.

Ana, ¡imagínate que fuimos a visitar la selva amazónica! Llegamos en avión a un pueblo llamado Coca. De aquí nos fuimos en el Flotel Orellana, un hotel flotante por el río hacia la selva. Nuestros guías, Óscar y Luis, fueron muy simpáticos y pacientes con nosotras y nos enseñaron mucho de este mundo diferente. Viajamos en piraguas, y vimos miles de pájaros° en los árboles y muchas tortugas° en rocas tomando el sol, y también pescamos pirañas. ¡Qué increíble!

Fuimos a la Isla de los Monos donde saqué muchas fotos de monos Wooly. Te mando una de las fotos. ¿Qué te parece? En este viaje hemos comido jabalí, plátanos y hemos tomado chicha que es una bebida fermentada de maíz.° ¡Muy sabrosa!°

La última noche del viaje tuvimos una fiesta en la terraza del Flotel. Keri y yo cantamos canciones de nuestros países y yo toqué la guitarra. Los guías, Óscar y Luis, y los demás° turistas cantaron canciones ecuatorianas. También bailamos música latinoamericana y conversamos hasta la una de la mañana. ¡Qué viaje tan maravilloso!

Ask students what they feel is Makiko's intention and tone in writing her letter. They should also provide some evidence for their feelings.

birds / turtles

corn / rica

rest

Muchos cariños,
Keri y Makiko

Notas de texto

1. *El Flotel Orellana*, named after the Spaniard Francisco Orellana, who explored the Ecuadorian jungle in 1541, is a luxurious floating hotel (hence "Flotel"). This 124-foot, three-deck, flat-bottom riverboat was built to navigate the wide rivers of the Amazon jungle. Several of the vessel's crew members are Napo Indians who take Flotel passengers ashore in wooden dugout canoes equipped with outboard motors. Once ashore, the passengers accompany experienced guides on side trips.

2. Since 1953, missionaries at the *Instituto Lingüístico de Verano* have been studying the many languages spoken by different Indian tribes in the Amazon region. The missionaries teach these native peoples how to read and write in their tribal language as well as in Spanish. The missionaries also translate the Bible, and they educate young people to be bilingual-bicultural instructors.

3. *Jabalí* is wild boar; *chicha* is a strong liquor made from fermented corn.

4. Many Indian tribes, such as the Aucas, the Napos, and the Jívaros, live in the Amazon jungle where they preserve their languages and traditions, in spite of increasing contact with outside civilizations.

¿Comprendió Ud.?

El anuncio

1. ¿Qué parte del Ecuador se describe en esta guía turística?
2. ¿Qué tiempo hace en aquella región?
3. ¿Qué tipo de plantas y animales se pueden observar allí?
4. ¿Qué le parece a usted más interesante de las actividades que se describen en la guía turística?

La carta

5. ¿Qué le gustó a usted más de las actividades que describe Makiko en su carta?
6. Compare y contraste tres elementos que Keri describió en su carta con los mismos elementos donde vive usted. Hable con un(a) compañero(a) de clase.

- la vida
- la música
- la gente
- la comida
- la región
- los animales

Answers:
1. *la selva amazónica*
2. *Hace mucho calor y mucha humedad.*
3. *Plantas: árboles, flores, plátanos Animales: mariposas, pirañas, jabalí, monos*
4. [open]
5. [open]
6. [open]

VOCABULARIO ÚTIL

Cómo comunicarse en un hotel

In this section you will learn to express your needs for lodging in a Spanish-speaking country or area.

These new words and phrases are commonly used when dealing with accommodations in Spanish-speaking countries. Do not hesitate to add other useful vocabulary for students traveling abroad.

En la recepción

TRANSPARENCY No. 30: Hotel

KERI:	Necesitamos un cuarto para dos personas.[1]	
MAKIKO:	Sí, con dos camas sencillas,° por favor.	*single*
RECEP:	¿Desean ustedes un baño privado?°	*private (not shared)*
MAKIKO:	Sí, y con ducha.	
KERI:	Por favor, queremos un cuarto que no dé° a la calle. Hay mucho ruido° por aquí.	*face* / *noise*
RECEP:	Sí, señorita... por el tránsito.°	*traffic*
MAKIKO:	¿Tiene aire acondicionado° el cuarto?	*air conditioning*
RECEP:	No, señorita, porque aquí en Quito no es necesario.	

Point out the idiomatic expression *dar a la calle*, meaning "to face the street" (literally "to give to the street").

Have students act out these dialogues in groups of three persons.

MAKIKO:	¿Cuánto es el cuarto?	
RECEP:	80.000 sucres por día, señorita.	
KERI:	¡Uy! Eso es demasiado,° señor.	*too much*
RECEP:	Pues, hay un cuarto más barato por 45.000 sucres. Tiene una cama doble,° pero el cuarto es cómodo.° Está en el tercer piso, número 304.	*double / comfortable*
KERI:	¿Hay ascensor?°	*elevator*
RECEP:	Cómo no,° señorita. Está aquí a la izquierda.	*of course*
MAKIKO:	Bueno, denos ese cuarto. Estamos cansadas.	
RECEP:	Muy bien. Aquí tienen su llave,° señoritas.	*key*
KERI:	Muchas gracias, señor.	

---

[1] Spaniards use the word *(la) habitación* for room.

Cómo quejarse del cuarto

made up / dirty

towels / soap / toilet paper

clean

KERI: Señor, el cuarto 304 no está arreglado° y está muy sucio.°

MAKIKO: Sí, y no hay toallas° ni jabón° ni papel higiénico.°

RECEP: Ay, perdón. Olvidé que estamos renovando el cuarto 304. Aquí está la llave del cuarto 321. Está limpio° y bien completo. Lo siento mucho, señoritas.

Practiquemos

A. ¡Adivínelo! Lea cada descripción, luego indique su definición.

Ejemplo: Se duerme en esta cosa.
  la cama

1. Es una cama para una persona.   el ruido
2. Se usa para lavarse las manos.   sencilla
3. Es otra palabra para "cuarto".   habitación
4. En este lugar uno se registra.   el ascensor
5. Se usa esto para subir o bajar.   el jabón
6. El tránsito causa esta molestia.   la recepción

B. Hotel La Pacífica. Lea el anuncio y conteste las preguntas.

1. ¿Dónde está el Hotel La Pacífica?
2. ¿Qué servicios le ofrece al público?
3. ¿Por qué usa el hotel el símbolo de un tucán?

Ahora escriba un anuncio atractivo que tenga un plan especial de un hotel que usted conoce personalmente. En la próxima clase preséntelo a su compañero(a), discútalo y luego preséntelo a toda la clase.

Teléfono: (506) 69 00 50

Guanacaste, Costa Rica

La Pacífica
LA PACÍFICA

Hotel - Restaurant

ubicado en una hacienda de 1500 hectáreas, rodeado de la más bella naturaleza

- **Hotel-Bar-Restaurant**
- **Sala de reunión – TV**
- **Piscina, gymnasio, ping-pong**

- **Paseo a caballo**
- **Sendero regulado**
- **Rafting por el Río Corobicí**

Venga a relajarse con la naturaleza. Disfrute viendo hermosos y exóticos pájaros, mamíferos y plantas del bosque seco. La Pacífica es el lugar ideal para programar sus visitas a importantes parques y reservas.

Carretera Interamericana, 4 kms. después de Cañas.

C. ¡Bienvenido a Quito! Converse con un(a) compañero(a) de clase.

Ex. C. Record some or all of these role plays on videotape, then replay them in class.

Cliente

1. Greet the receptionist.
3. Ask for a single room with a private bath.
5. Find out how much the room costs.
7. Ask about the hotel facilities.
9. Describe the kind of room you want.
11. Express your appreciation.

Recepcionista

2. Return the greeting.
4. Ask how many days he or she is going to stay.
6. Inform your guest about your various room rates.
8. Answer your guest's questions.
10. Respond, then say the number and floor of the room.
12. Respond, then say something to make your guest feel welcome.

D. Situaciones. Lea cada problema. Luego hable con un(a) compañero(a) de clase de la mejor solución para resolverlo.

Ex. D. Follow-up activity: Have students role-play these situations.

1. Usted y su amigo(a) acaban de llegar al aeropuerto de una ciudad latinoamericana. Ustedes hablan con una empleada en la oficina de turismo para que ella les encuentre un cuarto barato en la ciudad. La empleada les informa que el cuarto más barato cuesta cuarenta dólares, pero ustedes no quieren pagar más de veinticinco. Son las diez de la noche y ustedes están muy cansados.

2. Después de entrar en su cuarto de hotel, ustedes se duchan, miran las noticias de la televisión, luego se acuestan. A las tres de la mañana un ruido tremendo les despierta. Una pareja en otro cuarto comienza a hablar muy alto y ustedes no pueden dormirse.

NOTAS CULTURALES

Dónde alojarse en Latinoamérica

stars
facilities
prices

simple

Los hoteles de Latinoamérica van de cinco estrellas° hasta pequeñas hosterías en lugares remotos. Para informarse sobre los diferentes hoteles y de sus instalaciones° tanto como de sus tarifas,° consulte con un(a) agente de viajes o con varias guías de viaje.

En casi todas las ciudades latinoamericanas hay pequeños hoteles sencillos° pero limpios cuyas tarifas son menos de veinte dólares al día por un cuarto doble. Por supuesto, hay hoteles de lujo cuyos clientes pagan más de cien dólares por día. Estos hoteles ofrecen una abundancia de instalaciones tales como piscina, aire acondicionado, sauna, restaurante, bar y diversiones nocturnas.

Como alternativa al hotel hay pensiones que se pueden encontrar en cualquier ciudad latinoamericana. Puesto que la mayoría de las pensiones son parte de la casa de una familia, éstas son pequeñas e informales, pero cómodas. Por lo general, se puede pedir media pensión (cama y desayuno) o pensión completa (cama y tres comidas). Las pensiones son ideales tanto para la familia como para personas que buscan un lugar económico para alojarse.

Add your own comments about the types, facilities, and prices of lodging in Latin America, if you know this information. Two excellent resources are guidebooks from the library and free brochures from travel agencies. An excellent guidebook is the *South American Handbook* from Passport Books.

Preguntas

1. ¿Cuáles son los beneficios de una pensión en comparación con un hotel de cinco estrellas? ¿Cuáles son las desventajas?
2. ¿Dónde preferiría usted alojarse: en un hotel de lujo, en un hotel sencillo o en una pensión? ¿Por qué?

GRAMÁTICA FUNCIONAL

Expressing future plans

—¿Cuándo llegaremos a Coca?
—En media hora, Makiko.
—Luego, ¿qué pasará, Keri?
—Nos llevarán al Flotel.

Future tense

In *Lección 3*, you learned to use the present indicative forms of *ir a* + infinitive to express actions, conditions, and events that are going to take place (e.g., *Voy a viajar al Ecuador este verano.* **I'm going to travel to Ecuador this summer.**). Spanish speakers use this construction frequently in everyday conversation. Another way to express these ideas in Spanish is to use the future tense.

How to form the future tense

1. Add these personal endings to the infinitive of most verbs:
   é, ás, á, emos, éis, án.

viajar	**volver**	**vivir**	**irse**
viajar**é**	volver**é**	vivir**é**	me ir**é**
viajar**ás**	volver**ás**	vivir**ás**	te ir**ás**
viajar**á**	volver**á**	vivir**á**	se ir**á**
viajar**emos**	volver**emos**	vivir**emos**	nos ir**emos**
*viajar**éis***	*volver**éis***	*vivir**éis***	*os ir**éis***
viajar**án**	volver**án**	vivir**án**	se ir**án**

2. Several verbs have a different future stem than the infinitive form.

Verb	**Stem**	**Ending**	**Example**
decir	**dir**		
hacer	**har**	é	**diré**
poder	**podr**	ás	**dirás**
saber	**sabr**	á	**dirá**
salir	**saldr**	emos	**diremos**
tener	**tendr**	*éis*	***diréis***
poner	**pondr**	án	**dirán**
venir	**vendr**		
querer	**querr**		

Note: The future tense of *hay* is *habrá* (there will be).

—¿**Habrá** tiempo para nadar?	*Will there be time to swim?*
—Sí, Keri. **Tendrás** una hora.	*Yes, Keri. You'll have an hour.*
—¿Qué otras cosas **haremos**?	*What else will we do?*
—Te lo **diré** en Limoncocha.	*I'll tell you in Limoncocha.*
—¿**Podremos** pescar pirañas?	*Will we be able to fish for piranhas?*
—Cómo no. **Tendremos** tiempo.	*Of course. We'll have time.*

How to use the future tense

1. Spanish speakers use the future tense to express actions, conditions, and events that will take place, particularly at a distant future time.

   Su excursión a bordo de nuestro maravilloso Flotel Orellana **comenzará** en Coca, un pueblo pintoresco situado en el Río Napo. Usted **llegará** al aeropuerto de Coca a las once de la mañana, luego **abordará** el Flotel donde **tendrá** una orientación completa por uno de nuestros guías. Después de un rico almuerzo, el barco **saldrá** en la excursión más fascinante de su vida. ¡Buen viaje!

Emphasize: 1. The stem for these future tense forms is the infinitive. 2. The future tense endings are identical for all regular and irregular verbs.

Point out that except for the nosotros form, the future tense endings have accent marks on the stressed syllable.

Have students act out these short dialogues in pairs.

Point out that in Spanish, the future tense is commonly used in the media, especially in newspapers and magazines as well as on television. The future tense, however, is not used in conversation as much as the ir a + infinitive construction.

2. Spanish speakers also use the future tense to speculate about actions, conditions, and events that are probably taking place at the moment or will most likely occur sometime in the future. If the future of probability is expressed in a **question,** it carries the meaning of "I wonder" in English; if it is expressed in a **statement,** it means "probably."

—¿Qué tiempo **hará** en Coca?	*I wonder how the weather is in Coca.*
—**Estará** a 35 grados.	*It's probably 35° (centigrade).*
—Siempre hace calor allí.	*It's always hot there.*
—**Será** por la humedad.	*It's probably due to the humidity.*

Practiquemos

Ex. A. Answers:
1. *aprenderá, encontrará, se casará, irá, vivirá, estará, mirará, recordará, les escribirá, les mandará*
2. *cumplirá, comenzará, aprenderá, leerá, trabajará, saldrá, hará, les dará, les dirá*
3. *se casarán, vivirán, tendrán, darán, harán, ahorrarán, comprarán, visitarán, pescarán*

A. En un año. ¿Qué harán las siguientes personas el próximo año?

Ejemplo: Makiko: volver al Japón / tomar una clase de español
Volverá al Japón. Tomará una clase de español.

1. **Makiko:** aprender más español / encontrar un buen trabajo / casarse con su novio / ir a Hawai para su luna de miel / vivir en un apartamento de Tokio / estar muy contenta / mirar sus fotos del Ecuador / recordar su viaje con Keri / escribirles a sus amigos ecuatorianos / mandarles unas tarjetas postales

2. **Keri:** cumplir veintiún años / comenzar a estudiar japonés / aprender a hablarlo un poco / leer sobre la cultura japonesa / trabajar para una compañía de negocios / salir frecuentemente con sus amigos / hacer un viaje al Japón para visitar a Makiko y a su esposo / darles un regalo de boda / decirles —¡Felicidades!

3. **Óscar y su novia:** casarse en Limoncocha / vivir en Coca / tener un niño guapo / dar una fiesta grande / hacer muchos amigos / ahorrar su dinero / comprar una piragua motorizada / visitar a los misioneros / pescar en el Lago Taracoa

Ex. B. 1. The purpose of this exercise is to have students recognize the meaning of future tense forms in contexts.
2. Answers:
1. *Irán, pagarán, llamarán, esperarán, saldrán*
2. *limpiará, pasará, hará, sacará, lavará, pondrá*
3. *iremos, Nos bajaremos, tomaremos, abordaremos, conoceremos, viajaremos*

B. ¿Qué pasará? Complete las siguientes oraciones, usando los verbos indicados en las listas.

1. ¿Qué harán Makiko y Keri después de hacer la mochila en su cuarto de hotel en Quito?

ir	bajar	llamar
salir	pagar	esperar

Las chicas *bajarán* en el ascensor desde el tercer piso hasta la planta baja del hotel. _____ a la recepción donde _____ la cuenta de su cuarto. Después, _____ un taxi por teléfono, _____ hasta que llegue, luego _____ para el aeropuerto.

2. ¿Qué hará una empleada del hotel después de que Makiko y Keri salgan para el aeropuerto?

hacer	**sacar**	**poner**
pasar	**lavar**	**limpiar**

La empleada _____ el cuarto de Keri y Makiko. Por ejemplo, ella _____ la aspiradora, _____ las camas y _____ la basura. Después, _____ la ducha y _____ jabón y toallas limpias en el baño.

3. ¿Qué dice Keri sobre lo que ella y Makiko harán después de hacer su viaje en el Flotel?

ir	**viajar**	**abordar**
tomar	**conocer**	**bajarse**

Nosotros _____ en avión a las Islas Galápagos. _____ del avión en la Isla Baltra, luego _____ un taxi hasta el lugar donde _____ nuestro barco pequeño, que se llama "Tortuga". Entonces, _____ a los otros pasajeros con quienes _____ a varias islas.

C. ¿Qué serán? Mire el foto y el dibujo, luego conteste las preguntas.

¿Qué será este hombre? ¿Qué tipo de trabajo hará? ¿Será simpático o antipático, y por qué? ¿Quiénes serán las otras personas en la foto?

¿Qué serán estas personas? ¿De dónde serán? ¿Dónde vivirán ahora? ¿Qué harán allí? ¿Qué lenguas hablarán? ¿Cómo se divertirán? ¿Qué problemas tendrán? ¿Cuándo saldrán de la selva?

D. ¿Qué haremos? Forme un grupo pequeño con otros 3–4 estudiantes. Una persona comienza, diciendo una actividad que hará en el futuro. Entonces, otro(a) estudiante repite lo que dijo la primera persona, luego dice lo que él o ella hará en el futuro. Así sigue este juego.

Ejemplo: PETE: *Buscaré otro trabajo.*
              BETH: *Pete buscará otro trabajo y yo daré una fiesta.*
              JUDY: *Pete buscará otro trabajo, Beth dará una fiesta y yo haré un viaje.*

Ex. E. At your next class session, have students compare their predictions with those of classmates.

E. Cinco predicciones. Escriba cinco acciones, condiciones o eventos interesantes que pasarán en su vida dentro de los próximos cinco años.

Ejemplos: *Compraré un auto nuevo.*
               Me casaré y viviré en Colorado.
               Viajaré a Europa con una amiga.

Charlemos

F. ¡Bienvenido(a)! Imagínese que uno(a) de sus compañeros(as) de clase acaba de llegar a un hotel de un país de habla española. Hágale las siguientes preguntas y escuche bien sus respuestas.

1. ¿Qué tipo de hotel será? ¿Con quién hablarás primero? ¿Qué le dirás? ¿Qué tipo de cuarto pedirás? ¿Qué otras preguntas harás? ¿Quién te ayudará con las maletas? ¿A quién le darás una propina en el hotel?

2. ¿Qué harás en tu cuarto? ¿Dónde y qué comerás? ¿Cómo te divertirás? ¿Qué problemas tendrás en el hotel? ¿Qué comprarás y para quién?

`3. ¿Cuándo saldrás del hotel? ¿Cómo pagarás la cuenta? ¿Adónde irás después? ¿Cómo llegarás allí?

Ahora cambien papeles y hagan esta actividad otra vez.

G. Plan de vacaciones. Piense en un plan para sus próximas vacaciones. Luego hable con un(a) compañero(a) de clase sobre ese plan.

Ex. G. Follow-up activity: Assign this activity for written homework.

Say . . .

1. where you will go.
2. why you plan to go there.
3. how long you will be gone.
4. who will go with you.
5. what day you plan to leave.
6. what time you will depart.
7. where you will stay.
8. what you plan to do there.
9. how much the trip will cost.
10. what you will buy on the trip.
11. how you will pay for it.
12. when you will return.

NOTAS CULTURALES

Dónde alojarse en España

En España, los hoteles están divididos en diferentes categorías, según sus cualidades e instalaciones. Un hotel (H) puede tener de una a cinco estrellas; un hotel de cinco estrellas representa lo mejor y lo más caro. Un hostal (Hs) tiene las mismas instalaciones que un hotel, pero normalmente ocupa sólo una parte de un edificio y tiene un ascensor común. Un hostal residencia (HsR) ofrece habitaciones y desayuno. Una pensión (P) tiene menos de doce habitaciones, y el dueño° o gerente° tiene el derecho de cobrar por tres comidas diarias. Una fonda (F) ofrece las instalaciones más económicas.

owner / manager

Hay algunos hoteles muy buenos que se llaman paradores. Muchas veces estos hoteles son castillos° históricos con magníficas vistas, y contienen muebles antiguos y excelentes instalaciones, incluso restaurantes. Por lo general, los paradores son caros. También hay albergues° pequeños pero cómodos, que son principalmente para los viajeros que llegan en auto.

castles

inns

Para los viajeros que tienen poco dinero hay más de cuarenta albergues para la juventud.° Desgraciadamente, muchos están situados lejos de los lugares de mayor interés turístico y, por eso, es difícil alcanzarlos con medios de transporte público. Durante los meses de verano es posible alquilar una habitación económica en las residencias de muchas universidades, que se llaman colegios mayores. Para alojarse allí, hay que tener una tarjeta de estudiante internacional.

youth

El medio más barato de alojarse en España es acampar. Hay más de quinientos campamentos en el país. Por supuesto, hay que traer todo el equipo necesario para acampar, pero es posible comprar comida en esos lugares.

El gobierno español establece las tarifas para todo tipo de alojamiento en España. Si el viajero tiene una queja legítima sobre alguna tarifa, servicio o empleado, debe registrarla en el libro de reclamaciones. Los empleados del hotel están obligados a informarle al gobierno sobre cualquier queja en un plazo° de veinticuatro horas.

within

Write to the Spanish National
Tourist Bureau for lodging
information in Spain: 665 Fifth
Avenue, New York, NY 10022.

Charla

¿Dónde preferíran ustedes alojarse si fueran a España algún día? Discutan sus preferencias y razones. Converse con un(a) compañero(a) de clase.

- Fonda
- Hostal
- Parador

- Pensión
- Albergue
- Campamento

- Hostal residencia
- Hotel de _#_ estrellas
- Albergue para la juventud

GRAMÁTICA FUNCIONAL

Expressing conditional situations

—¿Harías un viaje en el Flotel?
—Cómo no. ¡Me gustaría salir hoy!

Conditional tense

In English, we express hypothetical ideas using the word **would** with a verb (e.g., *I would travel if I had the time and money*). Spanish speakers also express these ideas by using the conditional tense, which you have already used in the expression *me gustaría: Me gustaría viajar a Latinoamérica* (I would like to travel to Latin America.).

Emphasize: 1. The stem for these
conditional tense forms is the
infinitive. 2. The conditional tense
endings are identical for all regular
and irregular verbs.

How to form the conditional tense

1. Add these personal endings to the infinitive of most verbs: *ía, ías, ía, íamos, íais, ían.*

viajar	**volver**	**vivir**	**irse**
viajar**ía**	volver**ía**	vivir**ía**	me ir**ía**
viajar**ías**	volver**ías**	vivir**ías**	te ir**ías**
viajar**ía**	volver**ía**	vivir**ía**	se ir**ía**
viajar**íamos**	volver**íamos**	vivir**íamos**	nos ir**íamos**
*viajar**íais***	*volver**íais***	*vivir**íais***	*os ir**íais***
viajar**ían**	volver**ían**	vivir**ían**	se ir**ían**

Point out that the irregular stems
for the conditional tense and the
future tense are identical.

2. Add the conditional endings to the irregular stems of these verbs (these are the identical stems you used to form the future tense):

Verb	Stem	Ending	Example
decir	**dir**		
hacer	**har**	ía	**diría**
poder	**podr**	ías	**dirías**
saber	**sabr**	ía	**diría**
salir	**saldr**	íamos	**diríamos**
tener	**tendr**	íais	*diríais*
poner	**pondr**	ían	**dirían**
venir	**vendr**		
querer	**querr**		

Note: The conditional tense of *hay* is *habría* (there would be).

—¿A qué hora dijo Óscar que **saldríamos** para Limoncocha?

What time did Óscar say we would leave for Limoncocha?

—Dijo que lo **sabría** después de hablar con el capitán.

He said that he would know after speaking with the captain.

How to use the conditional tense

1. Spanish speakers use the conditional tense to express what would happen in a particular situation, given a particular set of circumstances.

—¿Qué **harías** con mil dólares?

What would you do with $1,000?

—Yo **viajaría** a Latinoamérica.

I would travel to Latin America.

¡CUIDADO! When **would** implies **used to** in English, Spanish speakers use the **imperfect tense,** not the conditional tense. For example, compare the meaning in these two sentences:

Imperfect: Cuando era niña, **viajaba** mucho con mi familia. *When I was a girl, I would (used to) travel a lot with my family.*

Conditional: Ahora **viajaría** más con mi familia si tuviera tiempo. *Now I would travel more with my family if I had time.*

---

2. Spanish speakers use the conditional tense with the past subjunctive to express hypothetical or contrary-to-fact statements about what **would** happen in a particular circumstance or under certain conditions.

Si **tuviéramos** el dinero, **iríamos** al Ecuador.

If we had the money, we would go to Ecuador.

In the example above, the "if" clause *(Si tuviéramos el dinero)* states a hypothesis, and the conditional clause *(iríamos al Ecuador)* states the probable result if that hypothesis were true.

Explain that the future tense refers to an action or an event that is more likely to occur than one expressed in the conditional tense; for example, have students compare these two sentences: *Makiko dice que volverá al Japón* and *Makiko dice que volvería al Japón.*

Exercise: Read aloud each of the sentences below, and have your students tell you whether they would use the imperfect tense or the conditional tense to translate them into Spanish.
1. Which countries would you visit in Latin America if you have the time? (conditional)
2. Would you like to visit Ecuador some day? (Conditional)
3. Where would you and your family vacation when you were younger? (imperfect)
4. Where would you stay if you went to Latin America? (conditional)
5. Where would you stay when you vacationed with your family? (imperfect)

Practiquemos

A. ¿Qué haría usted? ¿Qué haría usted si pudiera visitar el Ecuador por un mes? Lea las siguientes ideas y responda según sus gustos.

Ejemplo: ¿Iría usted a un hotel o a una pensión?
Iría a un hotel.
O: *Iría a una pensión.*

1. ¿Iría usted a un hotel o a una pensión?
2. ¿Preferiría usted dos camas sencillas o una doble?
3. ¿Pediría usted un baño con ducha o un baño privado?
4. ¿Querría usted un cuarto grande o uno pequeño?
5. ¿Pagaría usted más de veinte dólares o menos de veinte dólares?

B. Situaciones. ¿Qué harían las siguientes personas si les pasaran las circunstancias indicadas?

Ejemplo: Si Makiko viera un mono, ella le / sacar una foto
Si Makiko viera un mono, ella le sacaría una foto.

1. Si Óscar fumara durante el viaje, Keri / enojarse mucho
2. Si comenzara a llover por la tarde, Makiko / abrir su paraguas
3. Si hiciera mucho sol, Keri y Makiko / ponerse el sombrero
4. Si los pasajeros quisieran nadar, Óscar / poder decirles dónde
5. Si Makiko deseara aprender a pescar pirañas, Luis / le enseñar
6. Si los indios vendieran sus cerbatanas, Keri / comprar una
7. Si yo tuviera el dinero y el tiempo, / hacer un viaje al Ecuador
8. Si un(a) amigo(a) y yo fuéramos al Ecuador, / visitar la selva

C. ¡Ojalá! ¿Qué harían las siguientes personas si tuvieran más dinero?

Ejemplo: visitar a su familia en Cuenca.
Óscar visitaría a su familia en Cuenca.

Óscar **Makiko** **Keri y Makiko**	casarse con su novia este año hacer otro viaje a Latinoamérica les mandar regalos a Juan y José no ser guía en el Flotel Orellana llamar a sus padres en Osaka, Japón quedarse en la selva por más tiempo

D. ¡Bienvenidos al Flotel! Imagínese que usted va a hacer un viaje a bordo del Flotel Orellana. Escriba dos párrafos para describir las actividades que usted haría antes de y durante su viaje. Las preguntas pueden ayudarlo(la) a pensar un poco.

Párrafo 1: Las preparaciones

- ¿Con quién iría usted en el viaje?
- ¿Cuántos dólares llevaría usted?
- ¿Qué tipo de ropa le gustaría llevar?

- ¿Preferiría llevar una cámara o una videocámara?
- ¿Qué otras cosas pondría en su mochila o maleta?
- ¿Qué otras preparaciones haría usted antes de salir?

Párrafo 2: La salida y la llegada

- ¿En qué estación del año le gustaría salir?
- ¿Cómo llegaría usted al Ecuador? ¿y al Flotel?
- ¿Dónde dormiría a bordo de ese barco?
- ¿Qué haría usted primero en su cabina?
- ¿Qué comería a bordo del Flotel? ¿Y qué bebería?
- ¿Qué lugares visitaría usted en la selva?

Charlemos

E. Un viaje fantástico. Imagínese que usted hará un viaje a Acapulco con un grupo de estudiantes de su clase de español. Diga lo que usted, su profesor(a) y sus compañeros harían allí.

1. En el hotel nosotros...
2. En el café mi profe...
3. En el mar mi amigo(a)...
4. En la playa yo...

Ex. E. Encourage students to use verbs and verb phrases from previous lessons if they wish.

F. Problemas de hotel. Dígale a un(a) compañero(a) de clase lo que usted haría en las siguientes situaciones, y por qué. La letra **d** sugiere otras posibilidades.

Ejemplo: Usted vuelve por la tarde y su cuarto está desarreglado.
hacer la cama   no hacer ni decir nada
hablar con un empleado   d. ...
No haría ni diría nada porque mi cuarto en casa siempre está desarreglado.
O: *Yo arreglaría el cuarto porque no querría molestar a ningún empleado.*

1. Usted vuelve a su hotel por la tarde y ve que su cuarto no está arreglado.
   a. hacer la cama
   b. hablar con un empleado
   c. no hacer ni decir nada
   d. ...

2. A la una de la mañana, dos personas en otro cuarto comienzan a hablar tan fuertemente que usted se despierta.
   a. leer un libro
   b. tratar de dormir
   c. no hacerles caso
   d. ...

3. Usted está duchándose en su cuarto cuando suena el teléfono.
   a. (no) contestarlo
   b. continuar duchándome
   c. enojarme un poco
   d. ...

4. Usted está nadando en la piscina del hotel cuando un niño le echa agua.
   a. no hacer nada
   b. echarle agua al niño
   c. buscar a sus padres
   d. ...

5. Usted mira la cuenta de su cuarto y ve que no es correcta.
   a. salir sin pagarla
   b. gritarle al recepcionista
   c. pagar la cuenta incorrecta
   d. ...

Ex. G. Use this activity as a model to discuss other environmental issues in pairs, in small groups, or with your entire class.

G. Especulaciones. ¿Cómo serían la selva y sus residentes si los turistas estuvieran prohibidos allí? Dígale a otro(a) estudiante su opinión, y por qué.

Ejemplo: La humedad (ser/no ser) más baja.
             La humedad sería más baja.
         O: *La humedad no sería más baja.*

1. La región (ser/no ser) mucho más progresiva.
2. Los misioneros (traducir/no traducir) la Biblia.
3. Los indios (ser/no ser) más pobres que ahora.
4. Ellos (saber/no saber) leer ni escribir su lengua.
5. (Haber/No haber) más animales y plantas en la selva.
6. Los animales (tener/no tener) menos miedo de la gente.
7. El aire y el agua (estar/no estar) menos contaminados.
8. Los residentes (estar/no estar) más contentos que ahora.
9. Mis amigos y yo (poder/no poder) conocer esa región.
10. Yo (saber/no saber) mucho sobre la selva y su gente.

PARA LEER MEJOR

Understanding a Writer's Perspective

People write for many different reasons. Some write to entertain their readers, others write to reassure, to inform, to persuade or to shock. Often you can sense a writer's attitude toward his or her subject matter in a reading passage. For example, the tone may be humorous, angry, persuasive, ironic, or matter-of-fact. If you are aware of the writer's intention and tone, you will more easily understand what you read.

Activity

Read the following three descriptions. Then respond to these statements; there may be more than one answer.

Answers will vary among students.

1. What do you suppose the writers' intention was when they wrote these descriptions?
   ___ to shock   ___ to persuade   ___ to criticize
   ___ to inform   ___ to reassure   ___ to entertain

2. What do you feel is the writers' tone in these passages?
   ___ ironic   ___ favorable   ___ sympathetic
   ___ humorous   ___ skeptical   ___ indifferent
   ___ eloquent   ___ persuasive   ___ matter-of-fact

3. In each of the descriptions, circle the words and phrases that reveal the writer's tone. What patterns do these words and phrases form (e.g., adjectives, comparatives)?

4. Which of the three descriptions is most attractive, and why? Which is the least attractive one, and why do you think so?

HOTEL DE TURISMO

Montecarlo

El Hotel Montecarlo está ubicado en pleno centro de la ciudad, a un costado del Cerro Santa Lucía, lo que le permitirá disfrutar de un inolvidable panorama al despertar.

Las Hamacas

Es un hotel que le encantará por su ambiente único. El hotel se encuentra localizado en la bahía de Acapulco, dentro de una plantación de coco con bellísima y exhuberante vegetación. Todas las habitaciones tienen aire acondicionado y están alfombradas y decoradas con buen gusto. Se cuenta con todas las facilidades de un hotel moderno como son: amplia piscina, bar, grill, restaurant con un servicio de primer orden, agencia de viajes (Wagons Lits Cook) oficinas de American Airlines y Night Club El Fuerte con estupenda variedad Flamenca.

motel nilahue
Reñaca
Chile

El Motel Nilahue es un lugar diferente, ubicado en el mismo borde costero en la recta de Reñaca, avenida preferida por los miles de turistas que año a año llegan a la V Región para disfrutar de unas excitantes e inolvidables vacaciones.

PARA ESCRIBIR MEJOR

Writing From an Idea Map

An idea map is a tool for organizing your ideas before you begin developing them in a composition. In this section you are going to write about the trip of your dreams with the aid of an idea map.

Activity

1. Write the words *Mi viaje futuro* in the center of a piece of paper. This will be the title of your composition.

2. Write a key phrase under the title. Later you will incorporate this phrase into the topic sentence of your paragraph.

3. Write down your ideas related to this topic. These ideas are the details that support your topic sentence.

4. Connect the ideas that seem to fit together well, as in the example that follows.

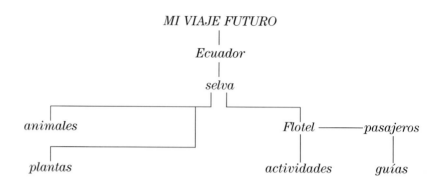

5. Look at your idea map and make a list of sentences you think would make a good paragraph about your topic. To help you decide, answer the following questions and refer to the example paragraph below.

   - Will the information interest your reader?
   - Do you have enough information for a paragraph?
   - Can you limit the information to one paragraph?

6. Follow steps 2–5 to develop ideas for several more paragraphs.

7. Now write your composition about your dream trip, using your idea map to guide you.

Example:

Mi viaje futuro

En mi viaje futuro, pienso hacer un viaje al Ecuador. Quiero visitar la selva amazónica para ver los animales y las plantas allí. También me gustaría viajar por dos o tres días a bordo del Flotel con pasajeros ecuatorianos y extranjeros. Haríamos muchas actividades con nuestros guías.

SÍNTESIS

¡A ver!

You will see Carmen making a hotel reservation, then checking into her hotel. First, study the words and phrases with their meaning in the *Vocabulario esencial*. Second, read the questions and their possible answers in the activity below. Third, watch the videotape, then answer the questions.

Vocabulario esencial

hotel de tres estrellas	*three-star hotel*
reserva	*reservation*
sexta planta	*sixth floor*

En la agencia de viajes

1. ¿En qué clase de hotel prefiere alojarse Carmen?
   _____ Ella no ha decidido.   _____ mínimo de tres estrellas
   _____ dos o tres estrellas   _____ cuatro o cinco estrellas

2. Por fin, ¿en qué clase de hotel decidió ella?
   _____ dos estrellas   _____ cuatro estrellas
   _____ tres estrellas   _____ cinco estrellas

3. ¿Cuál es el número de teléfono de Carmen?
   Escríbalo aquí: _____

En el hotel

4. ¿Qué le pidió el recepcionista a Carmen?
   _____ su pasaporte   _____ su número de confirmación
   _____ su carta de identidad   _____ su licencia de manejar un auto

5. ¿Qué número de habitación tiene Carmen?
   Escríbalo aquí: _____

6. ¿Qué información le dijo el recepcionista a Carmen al fin del segmento?
   _____ dónde está la piscina   _____ dónde están los ascensores
   _____ cómo llegar a la cafetería   _____ cómo llegar a la cafetería

Answers: 1. *dos o tres estrellas* 2. *tres estrellas* 3. *20 - 30 - 62* 4. *su carta de identidad* 5. *610* 6. *dónde están los ascensores*

SÍNTESIS

¡A leer!

Lea el siguiente poema, luego conteste las preguntas.

El viaje definitivo

will stay	y yo me iré. Y se quedarán° los pájaros cantando;
orchard	Y se quedará mi huerto,° con su verde árbol,
well	y con su pozo° blanco.
sky	Todas las tardes, el cielo° será azul y plácido;
will ring	y tocarán,° como esta tarde están tocando,
bell tower	las campanas del campanario.°
	Se morirán aquéllos que me amaron;
	y el pueblo se hará nuevo cada año;
corner / whitewashed	y en el rincón° aquel de mi huerto florido y encalado,°
will wander	mi espíritu errará° nostálgico...
	Y yo me iré; y estaré solo, sin hogar, sin árbol
	verde, sin pozo blanco,
	sin cielo azul y plácido...
	Y se quedarán los pájaros cantando.

Source: *Antología poética* por Juan Ramón Jiménez, Editorial Losada, S.A., Buenos Aires, 1966, páginas 106–107.

Visit

http://poco.heinle.com

¿Comprendió Ud.?

1. ¿Qué significa "el viaje definitivo" para Jiménez?
2. ¿Por qué dice el poeta que "el cielo será azul y plácido"?
3. ¿Qué simbolizan los pájaros, el huerto y el pozo para el poeta? ¿Con qué contrastan estas cosas?
4. Al final del poema, dice Jiménez que "se quedarán los pájaros cantando". ¿Qué quiere decir el poeta?

SÍNTESIS

¡A escribir!

Atajo

Escríbale una carta al gerente de reservaciones del Hotel Inca Imperial. En su carta, indique...

1. que usted quiere reservar un cuarto.
2. el número de días y las fechas de la reservación.
3. cuántos adultos y niños estarán en su grupo.
4. que le mande a usted más información sobre el hotel.
5. que quiere que le mande una lista de todas las tarifas.
6. su nombre completo, su dirección y número de teléfono.

¡A conversar!

Imagínese que usted es el (la) gerente de reservaciones del Hotel Inca Imperial. Léale a su asistente (otro[a] estudiante) la información de la carta (de la Actividad *¡A escribir!*) mientras él (ella) completa la siguiente tarjeta de reservación.

HOTEL INCA IMPERIAL

Apellidos Nombre	No. personas
Domicilio No.	Ciudad
País	Teléfono
Fecha de entrada	Fecha de salida

VOCABULARIO

Sustantivos

la Biblia *Bible*
la cabina *cabin*
la chicha *corn liquor*
el maíz *corn*
el parque zoológico *zoo*
el pueblo *town*
el ruido *noise*
el tránsito *traffic*

En la selva
(In the jungle)

el árbol *tree*
el barco *boat*
la cerbatana *blowgun*
el (la) guía *guide*
la hacienda *ranch*
la humedad *humidity*
el (la) indio(a) *Indian*
el jabalí *wild boar*
la mariposa *butterfly*
el (la) misionero(a) *missionary*
el mono *monkey*
el pájaro *bird*
la piragua *dugout canoe*
la piraña *piranha*
la roca *rock*
la tortuga *turtle*

En el hotel

el aire acondicionado
  air-conditioning
el ascensor *elevator*
la cama sencilla (doble) *single
  (double) bed*
el cuarto sencillo (doble) *single
  (double) room*
la habitación *room (Spain)*
el jabón *soap*
la llave *key*
el papel higiénico *toilet paper*
la recepción *front desk*

Adjetivos

amazónico *Amazon*
cómodo *comfortable*
demás *rest*
limpio *clean*
motorizado *motorized*
privado *private*
sabroso *delicious*
sucio *dirty*

Verbos

arreglar *to make up (a room)*
cazar *to hunt*

cruzar *to cross*
registrarse *to register*
traducir *to translate*

Adverbios

demasiado *too much*
temprano *early*

Expresiones idiomáticas

a bordo de *aboard*
cómo no *of course*
dar a la calle *to face the street*

Viaje a las islas encantadas

▶ COMMUNICATIVE GOALS

You will be able to discuss health-related matters and describe hypothetical situations.

▶ LANGUAGE FUNCTIONS

Expressing opinions
Giving recommendations
Giving advice on health
Making speculations
Describing impressions
Explaining medical problems
Stating factual information

http://poco.heinle.com

▶ VOCABULARY THEMES

Common illnesses and treatments
The human body (review)

Atajo

▶ GRAMMATICAL STRUCTURES

"If" clauses
Infinitive and subjunctive uses (summary)
Indicative and subjunctive uses (summary)

VIDEO

▶ CULTURAL INFORMATION

Medical advice for travellers
Medical assistance abroad

MISTERIO

Play Lab Tape

Bring to class one or more books or articles with photographs on the Galápagos Islands. Share these materials with your students before assigning this section.

EN CONTEXTO

enchanted

were located

Después de la excursión a bordo del Flotel, Makiko y Keri volvieron a Quito donde pasaron unos días. Allí se encontraron con sus amigos Juan y José, y ellos les comentaron sobre un viaje a las islas encantadas.° Cuando Makiko le preguntó a Juan en qué lugar quedaban° estas islas, Juan le dio la siguiente guía.

VIAJE A LAS ISLAS ENCANTADAS

tortoise

bay

En avión pueden llegar fácilmente a las Islas Galápagos.° En el aeropuerto se toma un autobús que los llevará a una bahía° bonita. Aquí los esperará el capitán del barco "Tortuga", Alfredo Ochoa con quien visitarán las Islas Galápagos. En esta aventura, su guía será el Sr. Tomás Portero. La primera isla que visitarán será la Isla Bartolomé en donde subirán un volcán inactivo para ver el panorama maravilloso de la Bahía Sullivan, y luego pasarán el resto del día nadando en el mar y tomando el sol en la playa.

seals / crabs

flamingos

La segunda isla que visitarán será la Isla Santiago donde podrán ver focas,° iguanas marinas, cangrejos° grandes, algunos pelícanos y un grupo de flamencos° de color rosado.

sailors / put

El tercer día visitarán la Bahía Correo donde hace doscientos años los marineros° metían° cartas en un barril para intercambiar información con otros marineros. Luego irán al Punto Conmorán donde

observerán más flamencos y pájaros diferentes. **Continuarán su excursión hasta la Isla Española donde verán leones marinos, iguanas marinas de color verde y rojo y diferentes tipos de pájaros.**

La próxima parada° será en la Isla Santa Cruz, para visitar la Estación Charles Darwin. Aquí tendrán la oportunidad de hablar con científicos de la estación y observarán Galápagos de diferentes tamaños.°

stop

sizes

¡Les gustarán estas islas maravillosas!

Keri y Makiko decidieron hacer este magnífico viaje. Primero, ellas fueron desde Quito hasta Guayaquil en autoferro.(1) Luego fueron en avión a la

to tell her (about)

Isla Baltra en las Islas Galápagos. Después de su excursión allí, Keri le escribió a su amiga Ana para contarle° las aventuras de ella y Makiko en las Islas Galápagos.

Querida Ana:

¡Hola! ¿A qué no te imaginas el lugar que hemos visitado?

Bueno, fuimos a visitar las Islas Galápagos en un barco pequeño de nombre "Tortuga". El capitán del barco fue muy simpático con nosotras. El viaje fue muy interesante ya que iban personas de Alemania como Katrin Schärer, de Italia como Carla Risecchi, de Holanda como Peter y Tineke

Switzerland

Bouman y de Suiza° como Jürgen y Ulrike Rütti.

Todo el tiempo vimos cientos de focas, iguanas marinas, cangrejos, pelí- canos y flamingos. Algunas veces los suizos se quejaban porque siempre comíamos lo mismo: pescado fresco con arroz. A la señora Sandy Cherry de California, la llamábamos "Abuelita" porque tenía setenta y cinco años y se quejaba porque el capitán fumaba cigarrillos. ¡Así, que verás que estos

even

turistas hacían el viaje aún° más interesante!

fatigue

La pobre Makiko estuvo enferma unos días por el cansancio° que tenía y por eso no pudo visitar la Estación Darwin en la Isla de Santa Cruz. Aquí, una científica nos explicó cómo se conservaban los animales y las plantas en las islas. Lo increíble de este lugar es que los animales no tienen miedo de la gente. El 16 de julio, Makiko se sintió bien, ya que era su cumpleaños.

Ahora regresamos a Guayaquil, y después a Cuenca para visitar a la familia Pérez que conocimos en Quito. Te escribimos pronto.

Cariños,
Keri y Makiko

Nota de texto

The *autoferro* is a trolley-like bus that holds up to 40 passengers and runs on railroad tracks between Quito and Guayaquil, a bustling, prosperous port on the west coast of Ecuador. The inexpensive trip is a spectacular twelve-hour marathon through the Andes Mountains. The *autoferro* passes small Indian villages, fertile farmland, towering snow-capped volcanoes, desert areas, tropical forests, and flat lowlands lush with banana trees, sugarcane and pineapple. Trains make the same run in fourteen hours; buses, in eight hours; and airplanes, in only forty-five minutes!

1. [open] 2. [open] 3. [open] 4. a. = Keri; b. = Capitán Ochoa, a todos los pasajeros; c. = "Abuelita", al Capitán Ochoa, porque ella no quiere que él fume; d. = Keri, Tomás o Makiko, por la "Abuelita"; e. = Tomás, a todos los pasajeros; f. = todos los pasajeros, el cumpleaños de Makiko

¿Comprendió Ud.?

1. ¿Cuál será el día más interesante de esta excursión?

2. ¿Qué diferencias o similitudes hay entre las Islas Galápagos y la Selva Amazónica?

3. Si usted tuviera que decidir visitar uno de los dos lugares, ¿cuál escogería *(would you choose)*? ¿Por qué?

4. Conteste las siguientes preguntas, pensando en estas personas:

Keri	Makiko	Capitán Ochoa
Tomás	"Abuelita"	todos los pasajeros

a. —*Espero que no regresemos a Quito en autoferro, Makiko, porque vamos directamenta a Cuenca.*
   ¿Quién diría eso?

b. —*Bienvenidos a bordo del "Tortuga". Espero que les guste la excursión por estas islas.*
   ¿Quién diría esto y a quiénes se lo diría?

c. —*¡No! ¡Cigarrillos no!*
   ¿Quién diría esto, a quién se lo diría, y por qué?

d. —*Capitán, ella dice que usted debe fumar en otra parte del barco.*
   ¿Quién diría esto y por quién lo diría?

e. —*En esta isla vamos a ver más iguanas terrestres. Por favor, no las toquen ni les den comida.*
   ¿Quién diría esto y a quién(es)?

f. —*¡Feliz cumpleaños, Makiko!*
   ¿Quién(es) haría(n) estas exclamaciones y en qué ocasión?

VOCABULARIO ÚTIL

Cómo hablar de la salud

In this section you will learn words and phrases for discussing health-related matters.

First, model the two dialogues (En la clínica; Los problemas médicos) for your students. Then have them role-play the dialogues in pairs.

En la clínica°

clinic

MAKIKO: Ay, no me siento bien. Me enfermé° anoche.

I got sick

DOCTOR: ¿Qué tiene usted,° señorita?

What's the problem?

MAKIKO: Me duele° el estómago, doctor.[1] Creo que fue por la comida del barco.

hurts

DOCTOR: Voy a examinarla. Abra la boca,° por favor.

mouth

---

[1] When speaking **about** a physician, use *el (la) médico*. When speaking directly **to** a physician, use *doctor(a)*.

to die
serious
pill

MAKIKO: ¿Voy a morirme,° doctor?

DOCTOR: No, señorita. No es nada grave.° Usted está muy cansada. Tome esta pastilla° y trate de descansar más.

Los problemas médicos

Add other words, phrases, and expressions to this medical vocabulary, if you wish.

cold / headache
fever / (inner) ears

DOCTOR: ¿Qué tiene usted, capitán?

CAPITÁN: Tengo catarro° y dolor de cabeza.°

DOCTOR: También tiene fiebre.° ¿Le duelen los oídos?°

CAPITÁN: No... nada, doctora.

DOCTOR: Voy a examinarlo. Siéntese aquí, por favor. (Más tarde...)

take care of myself

DOCTOR: Tome dos aspirinas y esta medicina, capitán.

CAPITÁN: Gracias, doctora. Trataré de cuidarme° mejor.

El cuerpo humano

¿Le duele(n)...?[1]

TRANSPARENCY No. 31:
Medical Exam

1. This drawing includes the following words that have been introduced in previous lessons: *el brazo, la cara, los dientes, la nariz, el ojo, la oreja, el pelo, el pie, las piernas.*
2. Point out that *la oreja* is the outer ear and *el oído* is the inner ear.

Game: Play *Simón dice* to help teach the parts of the body; e.g., *Tóquense la cabeza* (students touch their head).

Game: Say an appropriate infinitive or infinitive phrase. Your students should react by saying aloud or writing down a part of the body associated with carrying out the action. Examples: *abrazar, afeitarse, bailar, beber, besar, caminar, cantar, charlar, comer, comprender, correr, correr las olas, cortar el césped, despedirse, escribir, discutir, esquiar en el agua, fumar, gritar, hablar, jugar a las cartas, leer, meter, mirar, montar en bicicleta, nadar, oír, olvidar, patinar, pensar, poner la mesa, preocuparse, recordar, reírse, soñar, sonreír, tirar, tocar la guitarra, tomar, ver películas en vídeo.*

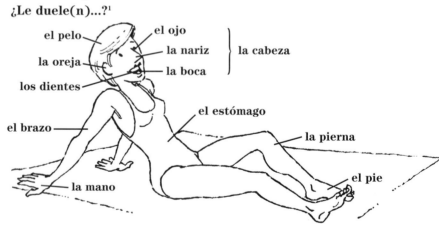

la boca	*mouth*	**la nariz**	*nose*
el brazo	*arm*	**el ojo**	*eye*
la cabeza	*head*	**la oreja**	*ear*
los dientes	*teeth*	**el pelo**	*hair*
el estómago	*stomach*	**el pie**	*foot*
la mano	*hand*	**la pierna**	*leg*

[1] Use only a definite article (*el, la, los, las*) when referring to a part of the body. For example: *Me duele la cabeza.* = My head hurts. *A ella le duelen los oídos.* = Her ears hurt. *Nos duele mucho el estómago.* = Our stomach hurts a lot.

Practiquemos

A. Renato Rivera, M.D. Lea el siguiente anuncio, luego conteste las preguntas.

RENATO RIVERA, M.D.
Neumólogo Pediátrico
Especialista en asma y
enfermedades pulmonares
en niños.
AVE. DEGETAU D-3 - CAGUAS
TEL. 746-3534
SE ACEPTAN PLANES
HORARIO:
Lunes a Jueves 1:00 P.M. a 6:00 P.M.
Sábados 9:00 A.M. a 1:00 P.M.

BLS

1. ¿En qué se especializa el Dr. Rivera?
2. ¿Cuál es la dirección de su clínica?
3. ¿Cuándo y a qué hora está abierta la clínica?

B. ¿Qué dice usted? Lea cada problema médico, luego decida lo que se debe hacer.

Ejemplo: *Una persona que tiene fiebre debe descansar un poco.*

Una persona que tiene... debe...

1. fiebre	ir a un hospital
2. catarro	dormir la siesta
3. diarrea	descansar un poco
4. insomnio	tomar Pepto Bismol
5. tensión nerviosa	tomar antibióticos
6. un problema grave	ir a una clínica dental
7. dolor de estómago	hablar con un(a) médico
8. un problema con los dientes	tomar una o dos aspirinas

C. ¿Qué haría usted? Dígale a un(a) compañero(a) de clase lo que usted haría en las siguientes situaciones.

1. Si me doliera el estómago,…
2. Si yo tomara demasiado sol,…
3. Si yo tuviera catarro,…
4. Si me sintiera mal en clase,…

Ex. D. Be sure students cover their partner's cues while participating in these role plays.

D. En la clínica. Hable con otro(a) estudiante: una persona es el (la) médico y la otra persona es su paciente.

Médico

1. Buenos (Buenas) ____ , (señor / señorita / señora).
3. ____ ¿Qué tiene usted? doctor(a).
5. ¿Dónde le duele(n) exactamente?
7. ¿Por cuánto tiempo tiene ese dolor?
9. ¿Tiene usted fiebre o náusea?
11. Siéntese aquí, (señor / señorita / señora). Voy a examinarlo(la).
13. ____ , (señor / señorita / señora). ____ .

Paciente

2. ____ , doctor(a). ¿Cómo está / usted?
4. Pues, me duele(n) ____ ,
6. Aquí... Ay, ¡me duele(n) mucho!
8. Más o menos por ____ .
10. Pues, ____ .
12. ¿Es algo grave? Estoy muy preocupado(a).
14. Gracias, doctor(a). Ya me siento mejor.

Ex. E. Follow-up activities: 1) Have two pairs of students meet together to compare their reactions to these situations. 2) Your students could continue this activity by discussing other health-related situations and their reactions to them.

TRANSPARENCY No. 32: Doctor's Advice

E. Situaciones. Lea cada situación, luego discuta con un(a) compañero(a) de clase las recomendaciones que ustedes tienen para las siguientes personas.

Ejemplo: (Situación) Rubén fuma un paquete de cigarrillos al día. Dice que está nervioso, y fumar cigarrillos lo ayuda a calmarse. (Recomendaciones) *Rubén necesita fumar menos. También debe caminar o hacer otro ejercicio para calmarse.*

1. Cada día Linda corre diez kilómetros, nada en la piscina por dos horas y monta en bicicleta por una hora. Ella es soltera, vive sola y tiene pocos amigos.
2. Rafael es hipocondríaco. Él va a una clínica una o dos veces al mes y toma cinco pastillas diferentes diariamente. Varios médicos le han dicho a Rafael que está bien físicamente, pero él insiste que está enfermo.
3. Emilia tiene mucha tensión en su vida. Está muy ocupada con su trabajo como directora de un hospital. Toma entre 7–10 tazas de café al día y duerme solamente cinco horas.

Ex. F. Follow-up: Assign this activity for written homework.

F. ¡Viva la salud! Dígale a un(a) compañero(a) de clase sus consejos para que él o ella se sienta bien. Luego escuche sus reacciones y discútalas con su compañero(a).

Ejemplo: Para sentirte bien emocionalmente sugiero que...
A: *Para sentirte bien emocionalmente sugiero que tengas buenos amigos.*
B: *Estoy de acuerdo. ¿Cuántos buenos amigos tienes?*
A: *Tengo dos: mi novio y mi hermana mayor. ¿Y tú?*

1. Para sentirte bien emocionalmente sugiero que... (+ subjuntivo)
2. Para sentirte bien físicamente recomiendo que... (+ subjuntivo)
3. Para sentirte bien espiritualmente te aconsejo... (+ subjuntivo)

NOTAS CULTURALES

Consejos médicos para viajeros

El miedo a contraer la enfermedad de los viajeros, la diarrea, es bien conocido en Latinoamérica. El problema es que la gente de otros países no ha desarrollado° suficientemente las inmunidades necesarias para prevenir esta enfermedad en los países que visita. Tomar precauciones como, por ejemplo, tomar agua mineral en botella, hervir° el agua del grifo,° pelar° o cocinar° los vegetales y las frutas frescas, y mantener las manos limpias contribuirán a un viaje saludable en el extranjero.

developed

to boil / tap (faucet) / to peel / to cook

1. Give students additional medical advice for traveling abroad, depending on your knowledge and experience.
2. Other related cultural topics of discussion are: services offered by pharmacies in Latin America and Spain, faith healing *(curanderismo)*, witchcraft *(brujeria)*, and home remedies *(remedios caseros)* for illnesses.

¿Qué dice usted?

1. ¿Cuál es una buena medicina para la diarrea, en su opinión?
2. ¿Sabe usted eso por experiencia personal o según lo que usted ha leído?
3. ¿Qué otras precauciones pueden tomar los viajeros para no enfermarse?

GRAMÁTICA FUNCIONAL

Making speculative statements

—Si quieres viajar, tienes que ahorrar dinero.
—Claro. Y si tienes el tiempo, puedes viajar conmigo.
—Si yo tuviera el dinero, viajaría contigo.

"If" clauses

You have seen the conditional tense used with the past subjunctive to speculate about what **would** happen under certain conditions (for example: *Si tuviéramos el dinero, iríamos al Ecuador*). Now you will learn how to form and use these speculative statements that are often called "if" clauses.

How to form and use "if" clauses

1. To imply that a situation is **contrary to fact or is unlikely to occur,** use *si* (if) with a past subjunctive verb in the "if" (dependent) clause, and a conditional verb in the conclusion (independent clause).

Contrary to fact:

—Si **tuvieras** el dinero, *If you had the money, would you go*
¿irías a las Islas Galápagos? *to the Galápagos Islands?*
—¡Claro que sí! *Of course!*

1. Tell students that the present subjunctive is never used in an "if" clause.
2. Emphasize: Likely to occur = *si* + present indicative or future tense; unlikely to occur or contrary-to-fact = *si* + past subjunctive and conditional tense.
3. If you wish, introduce the use of *como si* (as if, as though) followed always by the past subjunctive to express contrary-to-fact statements; for example: *Keri habla español como si fuera de Latino américa.*

Unlikely to occur:

—Si yo **pagara** tu boleto, *If I pay for your ticket, would*
  ¿irías conmigo a las Islas? *you go with me to the Islands?*
—Sí, pero dudo que lo pagues. *Yes, but I doubt you'll pay for it.*

2. To imply that a situation is **a fact or is likely to occur**, however, use *si* with an indicative verb form in both the "if" clause and the conclusion.

Factual situation:

—Ya he ahorrado más de dos mil *I've already saved more than two*
  dólares para mis vacaciones. *thousand dollars for my vacation.*
—Si **tienes** tanto dinero, *If you have so much money, you*
  puedes visitar el Ecuador. *can visit Ecuador.*

Likely to occur:

—Si **ahorro** doscientos dólares *If I save two hundred dollars*
  más, **visitaré** ese país. *more, I will visit that country.*
—Creo que no tendrás ningún *I think that you will have no*
  problema. *problem.*

Practiquemos

A. A bordo del "Tortuga". Complete las siguientes oraciones con verbos apropiados de la lista.

viera	fuera	comieran	se sintiera
fumara	comenzara	cantaran	comprendiera

1. Si Makiko _____ mejor, podría visitar la Estación Darwin.
2. Si Peter y Tineke _____ en holandés, todos los aplaudirían.
3. Si Carla _____ a tomar sol en el barco, se aplicaría loción.
4. Si Katrin _____ una iguana marina, sacaría una foto del animal.
5. Si alguien no _____ al capitán Ochoa, Keri podría traducir.
6. Si Tomás _____ a explicar algo importante, todos le escucharían.
7. Si el capitán Ochoa _____ , Sandy le gritaría: —¡No cigarrillos!
8. Si Jürgen y Ulrike _____ pescado otra vez, se sentirían mal.

B. Conversaciones. Complete las siguientes conversaciones, usando el presente del indicativo o el pasado del subjuntivo, apropiadamente.

1. KERI: ¿Qué haríamos si _____ algunos días en Cuenca? (pasar)
   MAKIKO: Si _____ posible, quiero visitar a la familia Pérez. (ser)
   KERI: Creo que será posible, si ellos _____ en casa. (estar)

2. CARLA: Si yo _____ más rollos de película, sacaría más fotos aquí. (tener)
   KERI: Mañana estaremos en la Isla Santa Cruz todo el día. Si tú _____ conmigo, podemos comprar unos rollos en una tienda. (ir)
   CARLA: Buena idea, Keri. Y si _____ tiempo, vamos a comer juntas. (haber)

3. KERI: Sandy dice: —Si usted _____ fumar, fume por favor en otra parte del barco, capitán. (querer) Perdónele, capitán. A Sandy le molestan mucho los cigarrillos.

CAPITÁN: Dígale: --Lo siento, señora. Si usted _____ , nunca fumaré en su presencia. (desear)

MAKIKO: Keri, si el capitán no _____ tan simpático, no diría eso, ¿no? (ser)

KERI: Sí. Voy a decírselo a Sandy en inglés cuando la vea.

C Si viajara al Ecuador... ¿A usted le gustaría viajar al Ecuador algún día? Haga oraciones completas para expresar sus ideas como en el ejemplo.

Ejemplo: si / viajar / Ecuador, / ir / con _____
Si viajara al Ecuador, iría con mi amiga Heather.

1. si / viajar / Ecuador / día, ir / con
2. si / necesitar / maleta, / comprarla / en
3. si / tener / dinero, / alojarme / en
4. si / tener / problema / hotel, / hablar / con
5. si / estar / mercado, / comprar / un(a)

Ex. C. Students could do this exercise at home, then compare their answers in class with those of another student.

D. Filosofía de viajar. Complete por escrito las siguientes oraciones.

1. Cuando viajo, si tengo algún problema, yo...
2. Si necesito más dinero en mi viaje, yo...
3. Si olvido algo importante en el hotel, yo...
4. A veces, si tengo tiempo en mis viajes, yo...
5. Después de mi viaje, si tengo más de cincuenta dólares, yo...

Ex. D. Have students exchange their completed sentences, read them, then make some oral and/or written comments on them.

Charlemos

E. Entrevista. Pregúntele a otro(a) estudiante.

1. Si tuvieras el dinero y el tiempo, ¿te gustaría visitar las Islas Galápagos? ¿Cuándo saldrías?
2. Si pudieras ir allí con solamente una persona, ¿con quién irías? ¿Por qué?
3. ¿Con quiénes irías si pudieras ir allí con otras dos personas?
4. ¿Visitarías las Islas Galápagos con personas de otros países o solamente con gente de tu país? ¿Por qué?
5. Si estuvieras en las Islas en este momento, ¿cómo viajarías de isla a isla?
6. ¿Te gustaría viajar en un barco pequeño o grande? ¿Por qué?

Ex. E. Have students ask you these questions, using formal forms.

F. ¿Qué pasaría? Primero, lea la pregunta y la respuesta del anuncio. Luego hágale a otro(a) estudiante las preguntas especulativas y discuta sus respuestas con él (ella).

¿Qué pasaría si...

1. todos se cuidaran bien?
2. no hubiera antibióticos?
3. nadie tuviera problemas emocionales?
4. fuera posible vivir doscientos años?
5. no existiera una pastilla anticonceptiva?

¿Qué pasaría si la Cruz Roja no existiera?

No habría ayuda en caso de accidentes de tránsito, caseros, aéreos, en búsqueda de personas, en terremotos e inundaciones, a refugiados, enfermos y heridos ni a usted cuando la necesita.

"Téngalo siempre presente y ayude a la Cruz Roja"

BENEMÉRITA CRUZ ROJA COSTARRICENSE

NOTAS CULTURALES

Asistencia médica en el extranjero

A veces, los norteamericanos que visitan Latinoamérica o España no saben encontrar asistencia médica durante su viaje. Hay muchos tipos de médicos y especialistas en medicina cuyas tarifas son comparables o más bajas que las de los Estados Unidos y del Canadá. Aunque hay muchos médicos en el mundo hispánico, ellos tienen que servir un número mayor de personas que los médicos norteamericanos. La mayoría de los médicos hispanos trabajan en las ciudades grandes donde pueden atender a más pacientes y donde pueden aprovecharse de las instalaciones más modernas. Es importante que los visitantes extranjeros tengan seguro° médico o que lleven suficiente dinero para pagar su cuenta médica. Aquí tiene usted el nombre y la dirección de una organización que publica una lista de médicos de habla inglesa en muchos países del mundo: *International Association for Medical Assistance to Travelers, 417 Center Street, Lewistown, NY 14092; teléfono: (716) 754-4883.* Además, la siguiente organización vende brazaletes que contienen información médica para viajeros: *Medic Alert Foundation International, Turlock, CA 95381-1009; teléfono: (800) 344-3226.*

insurance

Actividades

1. ¿Qué pueden hacer los turistas cuando necesitan asistencia médica, pero no hablan el idioma del país que están visitando?
2. Escriba 4–5 oraciones o preguntas esenciales para comunicarse con un(a) médico en un país de habla española.

GRAMÁTICA FUNCIONAL

Expressing your thoughts and feelings

—Ay, estoy enferma, Keri. Creo que me enfermé por el pescado.
—Dudo que te enfermaras por la comida, Makiko. Acuéstate ahora.
—Quiero ir a una clínica tan pronto como lleguemos a Santa Cruz.
—Bien. Si te sientes peor mañana, te acompaño a la clínica allí.

Uses of infinitives and subjunctive forms (summary)

The following explanations and examples summarize how Spanish speakers use infinitives and the subjunctive to express wants, preferences, intentions, advice, suggestions, and opinions.

Use an infinitive...	Use a subjunctive verb form...
1. after verbs of volition when there is only one subject in a sentence.	1. after verbs of volition when there is a change of subject in a sentence.
Makiko quiere **nadar.** *(Makiko wants to swim.)*	**Makiko** quiere que **Carla nade.** *(Makiko wants Carla to swim.)*
2. after verbs of emotion when there is only one subject in a sentence.	2. after verbs of emotion when there is a change of subject in a sentence.
Keri espera **visitar** a Tomás. *(Keri hopes to visit Tomás.)*	**Keri** espera que **él** la **visite.** *(Keri hopes he will visit her.)*
3. after impersonal expressions when there is no personal subject in a sentence.	3. after impersonal expressions when there is a personal subject in a sentence.
Es bueno **viajar.** *(It's good to travel.)*	Es bueno que **usted viaje**. *(It's good that you travel.)*

Uses of the indicative and subjunctive moods (summary)

The following explanations and examples summarize how Spanish speakers use the indicative to describe factual information as well as habitual and completed actions, and the subjunctive to express doubt and indefiniteness.

Use an indicative verb form...	Use a subjunctive verb form...
1. to refer to habitual actions and completed actions.	1. to refer to a future action dependent on another action.
Llevo mi mochila cuando **viajo** al extranjero. *(I take my backpack when I travel abroad.)* Llevé mi mochila cuando **fui** a Chile. *(I took my backpack when I went to Chile.)*	Llevaré mi mochila cuando **vaya** al Ecuador. *(I will take my backpack when I go to Ecuador.)*
2. to refer to a specific person, place, or thing.	2. to refer to an unknown or non-existent person, place, or thing.
Tengo una maleta que **es** vieja. *(I have a suitcase that is old.)*	Quiero una que **sea** más grande. *(I want one that is larger.)*

3. to express certainty.

   Estoy seguro que **puedo** ir.
   (I am sure that I can go.)

4. in an "if" clause to imply
   that a situation is factual
   or will likely occur.

   Si tienes mil dólares, puedes
   ir al Ecuador.
   *(If you have a thousand dollars,
   you can go to Ecuador.)*

   Si ahorro cien dólares más,
   iré allí.
   *(If I save one hundred dollars
   more, I will go there.)*

3. to express uncertainty.

   No estoy seguro que **pueda** ir.
   (I am not sure that I can go.)

4. in an "if" clause to imply that
   a situation is contrary to fact
   or will not likely occur.

   Si tuvieras mil dólares, ¿irías
   al Ecuador?
   *(If you had a thousand dollars,
   would you go to Ecuador?)*

   Si ahorrara el dinero esta
   semana, iría contigo.
   *(If I saved the money this
   week, I would go with you.)*

Practiquemos

Ex. A. Have students explain why they used an infinitive, indicative, or subjunctive verb form in this exercise.

Ex. A. Answers:
Paragraph 1: *llevo, conocer, aprendo, sorprenden, molestan, preguntó, gano, gano, quiero*
Paragraph 2: *traigan, necesitan, sé, es, comprar, sea, puedo, tuviera, podría, estoy*

A. Para servirles. ¿Quiere usted aprender un poco más sobre el capitán Ochoa y su trabajo? Complete los siguientes párrafos, dando las formas correctas de los verbos entre paréntesis.

—En mi barco el "Tortuga" (llevo / lleve) a mis pasajeros a visitar difeentes islas. Prefiero (conozco / conozca / conocer) a mis pasajeros individualmente porque (aprendo / aprenda) mucho de ellos. A veces, sus preguntas me (sorprenden / sorprendan), pero nunca me (molestan / molesten). Por ejemplo, un día un pasajero me (preguntó / preguntara) cuánto dinero (gano / gane) con el "Tortuga". Le dije que (gano / gane) losuficiente para vivir más o menos cómodamente, pero que nunca (quiero / quiera) ser un hombre rico.

—Es normal que algunas personas (traen / traigan) más equipaje del que (necesitan / necesiten) aunque a veces no (sé / sepa) dónde ponerlo porque el "Tortuga" (es / sea) pequeño. Algún día voy a (compro / compre / comprar) un barco que (es / sea) un poco más grande, pero por el momento no (puedo / pueda) ahorrar el dinero. Si (tengo / tenga / tuviera) ese barco, (puedo / podré / podría) llevar a más pasajeros y ganar más sucres. Por el momento, (estoy / este) contento con mi vida aquí.

Ex. B. Answers: *es, fuera, te sientas, traiga, descansar, te sientes, vayas, sentirme*

Ex. B. Have students explain why they used an infinitive, indicative, or subjunctive verb forms in this exercise.

B. Pobrecita Makiko. Complete esta conversación entre Makiko y su amiga Keri, usando los verbos de la lista.

es	**vayas**	**sentirme**	**te sientas**
fuera	**traiga**	**descansar**	**te sientes**

MAKIKO: Ay, me duele el estómago. Creo que _____ por el desayuno que
comí esta mañana.

KERI: Es posible que _____ la comida, pero francamente lo dudo. Pero
espero que _____ mejor, Makiko. ¿Quieres que te _____ algo para
tomar... algún jugo?

MAKIKO: No, gracias, Keri. Ahora prefiero _____ un poco.

KERI: Si _____ peor, sugiero que _____ a la clínica cuando lleguemos
a la isla Santa Cruz.

MAKIKO: Sí, pero espero _____ mejor esta tarde.

C. En la clínica.
Cuando Makiko fue a la clínica, oyó la siguiente conversación entre un médico (M) y su paciente (P). Complete la conversación.

Ejemplo: M: –¿Cómo *está* (estar) usted hoy?

M: —¿Cómo _____ (sentirse) usted, (señor / señorita / señora)?

P: —No _____ (sentirse) bien, doctor(a). Creo que _____ (estar) muriéndome.

M: —¿Por qué _____ (creer) usted eso?

P: —Porque esta mañana cuando _____ (levantarse), _____ (tener) un dolor
de cabeza muy fuerte y _____ (sentirse) mal. No _____ (dormir) bien
anoche.

M: —¿Todavía le _____ (doler) la cabeza?

P: —Sí, mucho. Recientemente he _____ (sufrir) mucha tensión en mi
trabajo. Mi supervisora me _____ (decir) que yo _____ (tener) que
trabajar más horas al día.

M: —¿—(poder) usted encontrar otro trabajo que no le _____ (dar)
tantos problemas?

P: —No sé, doctor(a). Me _____ (gustar) encontrar un trabajo que me _____
(pagar) más porque _____ (necesitar) el dinero. Ojalá _____ (poder)
encontrar uno muy pronto.

M: —Ojalá, (señor / señorita / señora). Ahora yo _____ (ir) a darle
unas pastillas. Yo _____ (querer) que usted _____ (tomar) una antes
de acostarse.

P: —Sí, doctor(a). Muchas gracias.

D. ¡A escribir!
Escriba uno o dos párrafos sobre **uno** de los siguientes temas:

1. Sus planes futuros después de este semestre o trimestre.
2. Sus consejos y recomendaciones para los visitantes a su país.
3. Sus opiniones sobre viajar al extranjero en general.
4. Una descripción de algún viaje que le gustó a usted.
5. Una descripción de un viaje que a usted le gustaría hacer algún día.

Charlemos

E. ¡Buen viaje!
Converse con otro(a) estudiante.

Estudiante A: Imagínese que a usted le gustaría hacer un viaje al Ecuador.
Pregúntele a un(a) agente de viajes (otro[a] estudiante) sobre la siguiente
información de aquel país: actividades de interés turístico, clima, ropa

necesaria, alojamiento, recuerdos típicos, etcétera. Trate de conseguir la mayor información que sea posible. Aquí tiene usted algunas frases para ayudarlo(la):

Quiero visitar...	**Me gustaría comprar...**
¿Pudiera usted decirme...?	**Es importante que...**
Quiero un hotel que...	**Creo que... No creo que...**

Estudiante B: Imagínese que usted es un(a) agente de viajes en Los Angeles, California. Lea otra vez las lecturas de *En contexto* de las Lecciones 16, 17 y 18. Prepárese a contestar preguntas de uno(a) de sus clientes de habla española (otro[a] estudiante) sobre: 1) qué hacer en Quito, en la región amazónica y en las Islas Galápagos; 2) el clima en esos lugares y 3) lo que usted debe llevar en el viaje. Aquí tiene usted algunas frases para ayudarlo(la):

¿Cuánto tiempo...?	**Espero que usted...**
Es mejor que usted...	**Pues, recomiendo (que)...**
Es una lástima que usted...	**Creo que... No creo que...**

Ejemplo parcial:

CLIENTE: Prefiero un hotel que sea barato.
AGENTE: Pues, recomiendo el Hotel Imperial. ¿Cuánto tiempo quiere usted estar en Quito?
CLIENTE: Cuatro días, luego me gustaría visitar la selva.
AGENTE: Hay una excursión interesante en el Flotel Orellana.
CLIENTE: ¿Podría usted decirme algo sobre esa excursión?
AGENTE: Sí, cómo no, señorita...

PARA LEER MEJOR

Integrating Your Reading Strategies

In previous lessons, you have learned many strategies for becoming a more proficient reader of Spanish. In this section you will practice integrating several of these reading strategies and will also acquire some background knowledge for understanding the content of the reading passage in the *En contexto* section.

Activities

A. Pre-reading: to understand the theme of the reading

1. Look at the photograph and the map on this page. What do you suppose you are going to read about?
2. Read the title of the paragraph below. What does it reveal about the theme of the reading?
3. What background knowledge do you have about the theme of the paragraph?

Las Islas Galápagos

Las Islas Galápagos consisten en trece islas principales, seis menores y más de cuarenta islas pequeñas situadas en el Océano Pacífico aproximadamente a 995 kilómetros (600 millas) al oeste del Ecuador continental. Las Galápagos son un laboratorio viviente que inspiraron a Charles Darwin a escribir *El origen de las especies* luego de visitar las islas en 1835, dando origen a su Teoría de la Evolución. Las islas, que fueron formadas por erupciones volcánicas, tienen más de tres millones de años. El grupo entero de islas ha sido designado un parque nacional del Ecuador para conservar los animales salvajes, muchos de los cuales no se encuentran en ninguna otra parte del mundo. Las iguanas terrestres y marinas de las Islas Galápagos parecen dinosaurios en miniatura. Además, hay una gran variedad de pájaros en estas islas.

B. First reading: to understand the gist of the reading

1. Skim the paragraph above to get the gist of its content. Use cognates, word stems, prefixes, and suffixes to help you guess the meaning of words you do not know.

2. Underline the main ideas in the paragraph to help you concentrate on understanding the gist of its content as well as the writer's intention and tone.

C. Second reading: to locate specific information in the reading

Scan the paragraph and circle the details that elaborate upon the main ideas you underlined.

D. Third reading: to check for total comprehension of the reading

1. Respond to the following statements.
   a. Las Islas Galápagos están en Sudamérica.   ___ Sí ___ No
   b. Darwin escribió un libro sobre estas islas.   ___ Sí ___ No
   c. Hay pocos animales en las Islas Galápagos.   ___ Sí ___ No
   d. Algunos de los animales son únicos y raros.   ___ Sí ___ No
   e. Las Islas Galápagos son de origen volcánico.   ___ Sí ___ No
   f. Las iguanas son tan grandes como dinosaurios.   ___ Sí ___ No

2. Answer the following questions about the paragraph.
   a. ¿En qué país están las Islas Galápagos?
   b. ¿Dónde están las Galápagos exactamente?
   c. ¿Cuántas islas hay en total y cómo se formaron?
   d. ¿Qué científico trabajó allí y por qué es famoso?
   e. ¿Por qué son interesantes las Islas Galápagos?

3. Use the following scale to rate the reading strategies that helped you understand the paragraph on the Galápagos Islands.

0 = Not helpful   **1 = Somewhat helpful**   **2 = Very helpful**

____ Map of the islands	____ Guessing from context
____ My skimming skills	____ Title of the paragraph
____ My scanning skills	____ My knowledge of Spanish
____ Recognizing affixes	____ Photograph of the islands
____ Recognizing cognates	____ My knowledge of the topic

PARA ESCRIBIR MEJOR

Writing From Diagrams

In this section you will write several recommendations based on information in diagrams. Diagrams present charts, tables, and graphs of specific information that can be readily understood and remembered.

Activity

1. Read the following biographical sketch.

   MAKIKO: 21 años / fuma cigarrillos / no come muchos dulces / toma café por la mañana / toma tres botellas de cerveza al día / le gustan mucho los deportes / está en buenas condiciones físicas

2. Study the following charts.

   La siguiente tabla contiene datos sobre el número de calorías que contienen varios alimentos.

Alimento	Calorías
1 huevo frito	115
1 tortilla de queso (6 onzas)	340
1 panecillo con mantequilla	260
2 salchicas	120
1 hamburguesa (¹⁄₄ libra)	418
1 hamburguesa con queso (¹⁄₄ libra)	518
1 sandwich de jamón	350
1 sandwich de rosbif	429
1 biftec (3 onzas)	330
1 burrito (6¹⁄₂ libras)	466
1 cerveza regular	150
1 taza de café con crema y azúcar	70
1 taza de leche (2%)	120
1 taza de jugo de naranja	120
1 taza de helado	300
4 galletas dulces	200

La siguiente tabla contiene datos sobre el número de calorías que son consumidas por una persona que pesa 150 libras (pounds), que hace ejercicio por una hora.

Atajo

Actividad física	Calorías/Hora
Bailar	240–420
Caminar	210
Correr	540
Jugar al básquetbol	360–660
Montar en bicicleta	240–420
Nadar	540–660
Patinar	350–400
Jugar al tenis	420

3. Based on the information in each sketch and in the charts, write your recommendations for Jürgen, Sandy, and yourself. Concentrate on:

- what the person should do to be heathier,
- what he or she should eat or not eat, and
- what type of exercise would be most suitable for him or her.

Ejemplos:

Makiko no debe fumar. También recomiendo que ella no tome tanta cerveza; contiene muchas calorías. Es mejor que tome una botella al día. Es bueno que Makiko no coma muchos dulces y que no tome demasiado café. Ella puede participar en muchas actividades aeróbicas. Recomiendo que juegue al tenis, si tiene tiempo.

JÜRGEN: 22 años / un poco gordo / tiene buena salud / come mucho queso / toma mucha leche / nunca bebe café ni fuma / le gusta la comida mexicana / no le gustan mucho los deportes, pero le gusta caminar

SANDY: 75 años / fuma mucho / no come mucho / es vegetariana / le gustan los sándwiches / monta en bici y le gusta nadar / le gusta bailar el tango

YO: años / ...

¿A qué nivel está Ud.?

¿Y Ud., quiere saber más sobre las Islas Galápagos? Casi todas las personas que (viajar) __ a las Islas Galápagos quieren (conocer) __ los animales en su estado natural…

Review the chapter and then monitor your progress by completing the *Autoprueba* at the end of *Lección 18* in the **Workbook/Lab Manual.**

SÍNTESIS

¡A ver!

Laura's daughter Pati is not feeling well today, and she needs medical attention. First, study the words and sentences with their meanings in the *Vocabulario esencial*. Second, read the sentences in the activity below. Third, watch the videotape, then complete the activity according to the directions.

Vocabulario esencial

recoger	*to go and get someone*
39 grados de temperatura	*a temperature of 102.2°*
el pediatra	*the pediatrician*
el consultorio	*the doctor's office*
Abre grande.	*Open wide.*
Respira hondo.	*Take a deep breath.*

Indique todas las posibles respuestas correctas a las siguientes preguntas.

1. ¿Qué problemas tiene Pati?
   ____ Tiene fiebre.   ____ Le duele la garganta.
   ____ Le duele la cabeza.   ____ Le duele el estómago.

2. ¿Qué hace Laura para ayudar a Pati?
   ____ Llama a un médico.   ____ Toma su temperatura.
   ____ Le da alguna medicina.   ____ La acuesta en su cama.

3. ¿Qué hace el médico para ayudar a Pati?
   ____ Escribe una receta.   ____ Le da alguna medicina.
   ____ Le examina muy bien.   ____ Le pone una inyección.

4. Según el pediatra, ¿cómo es la situación de Pati?
   ____ No es grave.   ____ Va a estar mejor.
   ____ Es un poco grave.   ____ Debe ir al hospital.

¡A leer!

Algunas personas toman la vida como viene, sin preocuparse de lo que pueda suceder mañana. Dicho en otras palabras, parecen reírse de las peores dificultades. Otras, por el contrario, viven constantemente nerviosas y presas de la más absoluta ansiedad. ¿A qué categoría pertenece usted? Responda **Sí** o **No** a las siguientes preguntas y lo sabrá.

Visit

http://poco.heinle.com

SÍNTESIS

1. ¿Lo (La) sobresalta el sonido del teléfono?   Sí   No
2. ¿Consulta regularmente a adivinas o quirománticas?   Sí   No
3. ¿Le gusta pasear largo rato, sin pensar que está perdiendo
   el tiempo?   Sí   No
4. ¿Se siente al borde de la catástrofe cuando se da cuenta
   de que le falta dinero?   Sí   No
5. ¿Aprueba usted la máxima de que: "A cada día le basta su
   propia pena"?   Sí   No
6. ¿Sus preocupaciones y problemas le impiden dormir?   Sí   No
7. ¿Es capaz de adaptarse rápidamente a una situación nueva?   Sí   No
8. Cuando usted deja su trabajo, ¿ya no vuelve a pensar en él
   durante el resto del día?   Sí   No
9. ¿Siente a /veces necesidad de estar solo(a)?   Sí   No
10. La lectura, ¿es uno de sus pasatiempos favoritos?   Sí   No

Anótese un punto por cada respuesta apropiada.

Respuestas

Preguntas: 3 - 5 - 7 - 8 - 9 - 10:   Sí
Preguntas: 1 - 2 - 4 - 6:   No

Puntos

8 a 10 puntos: Usted es absolutamente optimista y sus amigos son los primeros en envidiarlo(la). Pero, tenga cuidado, su falta de preocupación por las cosas de la vida diaria puede llevarlo(la) a caer en un defecto muy desagradable: la irresponsabilidad.

5 a 7 puntos: De naturaleza bastante tranquila, usted es optimista, pero a veces también un poco fatalista. En la vida hay muchas cosas que están en su mano a solucionar. No se deje llevar por las depresiones.

2 a 4: Usted no da gran importancia a las situaciones que tiene que enfrentar a diario, pero cuando se enfrenta a una circunstancia absolutamente nueva, se siente algo atemorizado(a). Es necesario que aprenda a reaccionar positivamente ante imprevistos.

0 a 1 puntos: Usted es tan nervioso(a) que vive eternamente preocupado(a) por esto o por lo otro. Éste es el momento preciso para que empiece a considerar la posibilidad de practicar el yoga, y aprenda a tomar la vida más ligeramente, con sus altos y bajos.

Source: ¿Es extrovertida?", por Martha Lepz, *Claudia*, Año XVIII, No. 221, Febrero 1984.

SÍNTESIS

¿Comprendió Ud.?

Escriba una descripción breve de cuatro turistas que están viajando juntos por las Islas Galápagos. Cada persona debe representar una de las cuatro categorías de la sección "Punteo" en cuanto a su personalidad y sus acciones.

¡A conversar!

1. Imagínese que usted y un(a) compañero(a) de clase han decidido visitar las Islas Galápagos. Conversen sobre sus preparaciones para el viaje, diciendo...
   - cuándo piensan salir para las Galápagos
   - cuánto tiempo pasarán allí
   - si llevarán una maleta o una mochila
   - qué ropa y accesorios llevarán
   - qué otras preparaciones harán

2. Vaya a la biblioteca y aprenda sobre un aspecto de uno de los tres lugares principales que visitaron Keri y Makiko: Quito, la selva amazónica, las Islas Galápagos. Luego haga un informe oral en clase sobre lo que usted aprendió. Trate de concentrarse en un tema muy específico en su informe oral.

Ejemplos: *La arquitectura colonial de Quito*
Los indios jívaros de la selva amazónica
La Estación Darwin de las Islas Galápagos

¡A escribir!

Atajo

Escriba una prueba sobre una de las siguientes cuatro categorías, usando la prueba de la actividad anterior como modelo. No se olvide de incluir una lista separada de respuestas correctas y una interpretación en forma de punteo. Luego pídale a otro(a) estudiante que responda a las preguntas de la encuesta (survey); después, déle las respuestas y discuta los resultados con él (ella).

1. una persona simpática   3. una persona aventurera
2. una persona interesante   4. una persona inteligente

VOCABULARIO

Sustantivos

la bahía *bay*
el barril *barrel*
el cansancio *fatigue*
el (la) científico(a) *scientist*
el (la) marinero(a) *sailor*
la parada *stop*
Suiza *Switzerland*
el tamaño *size*

En la clínica (clinic)

la aspirina *asprin*
la medicina *medicine*
el (la) médico *physician, doctor*
el (la) paciente *patient*
la pastilla *pill*

Los problemas médicos

el catarro *cold*
el dolor *pain, ache*
el dolor de oídos *earache*
la fiebre *fever*

El cuerpo humano

la boca *mouth*
la cabeza *head*
el estómago *stomach*

Los animales

el cangrejo *crab*
la foca *seal*
el flamenco *flamingo*
el galápago *tortoise*
el pelícano *pelican*

Adjetivos

encantado *enchanted*
grave *serious (medical)*
increíble *incredible*
marino *marine*
terrestre *land*

Verbos

acercarse a *to get near, to approach*
contar *to tell (about)*

cuidar(se) **t***o take care (of oneself)*
doler (a alguien) (o→ue) *to hurt (someone)*
enfermarse *to get sick*
examinar *to examine*
explorar *to explore*
meter *to put (in)*
morirse (o→ue) *to die*
quedar *to be located*

Adverbios

aún *even*

Expresiones idiomáticas

¿Qué tiene usted? *What's the problem?*

El alfabeto español

The Spanish alphabet contains twenty-eight letters. The *rr* represents a single sound and is considered a single letter. The letters *k* and *w* occur only in words of foreign origin.

Letter	Name	Examples: People and Places		
a	a	Alonso	María	Panamá
b	be	Roberto	Bárbara	Bolivia
c	ce	Carlos	Carmen	Cuba
d	de	Diego	Amanda	El Salvador
e	e	Enrique	Angela	Ecuador
f	efe	Francisco	Alfreda	Francia
g	ge	Gilberto	Guillermina	Argentina
h	hache	Humberto	Hortensia	Honduras
i	i	Panchito	Alicia	Italia
j	jota	Alejandro	Juanita	Japón
k	ka	Kris	Kati	Kenya
l	ele	Luis	Claudia	Guatemala
m	eme	Mario	Marta	Colombia
n	ene	Nicolás	Anita	Santo Domingo
ñ	eñe	Ñato	Begoña	España
o	o	Pedro	Carlota	Puerto Rico
p	pe	Pepe	Pepita	Paraguay
q	cu	Joaquín	Raquel	Quito
r	ere	Fernando	Gloria	Nicaragua
rr	erre	Ramón	Rosa	Monterrey
s	ese	José	Susana	Costa Rica
t	te	Tomás	Catalina	Toledo
u	u	Lucho	Luisa	Uruguay
v	ve	Vicente	Victoria	Venezuela
w	doble ve doble u	Walter	Wendy	Washington
x	equis	Xavier	Máxima	México
y	y griega	Rey	Yolanda	Guayana
z	zeta	Fernández	Zelda	Zaragoza

Spelling Hints

1. The letters *b* and *v* are pronounced exactly alike in Spanish. To distinguish one letter from the other in spelling, one says "*b grande*" (big b) for *b*, and "*v chica*" (little v) for *v*. Also, some Spanish speakers say "*b de burro*" (b in *burro)* and "*v de vaca*" (v in *vaca*, meaning "cow").

2. When spelling a Spanish word containing an accent mark, one says the letter first, then the word *acento*. Example: *Perú: Pe - e - ere -u, acento.*

APÉNDICE B: Regular Verbs

Simple Tenses

Infinitive	Present Indicative	Imperfect	Preterite	Future	Conditional	Present Subjunctive	Past Subjunctive	Commands
hablar	hablo	hablaba	hablé	hablaré	hablaría	hable	hablara	habla
to speak	hablas	hablabas	hablaste	hablarás	hablarías	hables	hablaras	(no hables)
	habla	hablaba	habló	hablará	hablaría	hable	hablara	hable
	hablamos	hablábamos	hablamos	hablaremos	hablaríamos	hablemos	habláramos	hablad
	habláis	hablabais	hablasteis	hablaréis	hablaríais	habléis	hablarais	(no habléis)
	hablan	hablaban	hablaron	hablarán	hablarían	hablen	hablaran	hablen
aprender	aprendo	aprendía	aprendí	aprenderé	aprendería	aprenda	aprendiera	aprende
to learn	aprendes	aprendías	aprendiste	aprenderás	aprenderías	aprendas	aprendieras	(no aprendas)
	aprende	aprendía	aprendió	aprenderá	aprendería	aprenda	aprendiera	aprenda
	aprendemos	aprendíamos	aprendimos	aprenderemos	aprenderíamos	aprendamos	aprendiéramos	aprended
	aprendéis	aprendíais	aprendisteis	aprenderéis	aprenderíais	aprendáis	aprendierais	(no aprendáis)
	aprenden	aprendían	aprendieron	aprenderán	aprenderían	aprendan	aprendieran	aprendan
vivir	vivo	vivía	viví	viviré	viviría	viva	viviera	vive
to live	vives	vivías	viviste	vivirás	vivirías	vivas	vivieras	(no vivas)
	vive	vivía	vivió	vivirá	viviría	viva	viviera	viva
	vivimos	vivíamos	vivimos	viviremos	viviríamos	vivamos	viviéramos	vivid
	vivís	vivíais	vivisteis	viviréis	viviríais	viváis	vivierais	(no viváis)
	viven	vivían	vivieron	vivirán	vivirían	vivan	vivieran	vivan

Compound tenses

Present Progressive	estoy estás está estamos estáis están	hablando aprendiendo viviendo
Present Perfect Indicative	he has ha hemos habéis han	hablado aprendido vivido
Present Perfect Subjunctive	haya hayas haya hayamos hayáis hayan	hablado aprendido vivido
Past Perfect Indicative	había habías había habíamos habíais habían	hablado aprendido vivido

APÉNDICE C: Stem-changing Verbs

Infinitive / Present Participle / Past Participle	Present Indicative	Imperfect	Preterite	Future	Conditional	Present Subjunctive	Past Subjunctive	Commands
pensar *to think* **e→ie** pensando pensado	**pienso** **piensas** **piensa** pensamos pensáis **piensan**	pensaba pensabas pensaba pensábamos pensabais pensaban	pensé pensaste pensó pensamos pensasteis pensaron	pensaré pensarás pensará pensaremos pensaréis pensarán	pensaría pensarías pensaría pensaríamos pensaríais pensarían	**piense** **pienses** **piense** pensemos penséis **piensen**	pensara pensaras pensara pensáramos pensarais pensaran	**piensa** no **pienses** **piense** pensad (**no penséis**) **piensen**
acostarse *to go to bed* **o→ue** acostándose acostado	me **acuesto** te **acuestas** se **acuesta** nos acostamos os acostáis se **acuestan**	me acostaba te acostabas se acostaba nos acostábamos os acostabais se acostaban	me acosté te acostaste se acostó nos acostamos os acostasteis se acostaron	me acostaré te acostarás se acostará nos acostaremos os acostaréis se acostarán	me acostaría te acostarías se acostaría nos acostaríamos os acostaríais se acostarían	me **acueste** te **acuestes** se **acueste** nos acostemos os acostéis se **acuesten**	me acostara te acostaras se acostara nos acostáramos os acostarais se acostaran	**acuéstate** no te **acuestes** **acuéstese** **acostaos** (**no os acostéis**) **acuéstense**
sentir *to be sorry* **e→ie, i** **sintiendo** sentido	**siento** **sientes** **siente** sentimos sentís **sienten**	sentía sentías sentía sentíamos sentíais sentían	sentí sentiste **sintió** sentimos sentisteis **sintieron**	sentiré sentirás sentirá sentiremos sentiréis sentirán	sentiría sentirías sentiría sentiríamos sentiríais sentirían	**sienta** **sientas** **sienta** **sintamos** **sintáis** **sientan**	**sintiera** **sintieras** **sintiera** **sintiéramos** **sintierais** **sintieran**	**siente** no **sientas** **sienta** sentaos (**no sintáis**) **sientan**
pedir *to ask for* **e→i, i** **pidiendo** pedido	**pido** **pides** **pide** pedimos pedís **piden**	pedía pedías pedía pedíamos pedías pedían	pedí pediste **pidió** pedimos pedisteis **pidieron**	pediré pedirás pedirá pediremos pediréis pedirán	pediría pedirías pediría pediríamos pediríais pedirían	**pida** **pidas** **pida** **pidamos** **pidáis** **pidan**	**pidiera** **pidieras** **pidiera** **pidiéramos** **pidierais** **pidieran**	**pide** no **pidas** **pida** pedid (**no pidáis**) **pidan**
dormir *to sleep* **o→ue, u** **durmiendo** dormido	**duermo** **duermes** **duerme** dormimos dormís **duermen**	dormía dormías dormía dormíamos dormíais dormían	dormí dormiste **durmió** dormimos dormisteis **durmieron**	dormiré dormirás dormirá dormiremos dormiréis dormirán	dormiría dormirías dormiría dormiríamos dormiríais dormirían	**duerma** **duermas** **duerma** **durmamos** **durmáis** **duerman**	**durmiera** **durmieras** **durmiera** **durmiéramos** **durmierais** **durmieran**	**duerme** no **duermas** **duerma** dormid (**no durmáis**) **duerman**

APÉNDICE D: Change of Spelling Verbs

Infinitive / Present Participle / Past Participle	Present Indicative	Imperfect	Preterite	Future	Conditional	Present Subjunctive	Past Subjunctive	Commands
comenzar (e→ie) *to begin* **z→c before e** comenzando comenzado	comienzo comienzas comienza comenzamos comenzáis comienzan	comenzaba comenzabas comenzaba comenzábamos comenzabais comenzaban	**comencé** comenzaste comenzó comenzamos comenzasteis comenzaron	comenzaré comenzarás comenzará comenzaremos comenzaréis comenzarán	comenzaría comenzarías comenzaría comenzaríamos comenzaríais comenzarían	**comience** **comiences** **comience** **comencemos** **comencéis** **comiencen**	comenzara comenzaras comenzara comenzáramos comenzarais comenzaran	comienza (**no comiences**) **comience** comenzad (**no comencéis**) **comiencen**
conocer *to know* **c→zc before a, o** conociendo conocido	**conozco** conoces conoce conocemos conocéis conocen	conocía conocías conocía conocíamos conocíais conocían	conocí conociste conoció conocimos conocisteis conocieron	conoceré conocerás conocerá conoceremos conoceréis conocerán	conocería conocerías conocería conoceríamos conoceríais conocerían	**conozca** **conozcas** **conozca** **conozcamos** **conozcáis** **conozcan**	conociera conocieras conociera conociéramos conocierais conocieran	conoce (**no conozcas**) **conozca** conoced (**no conozcáis**) **conozcan**
construir *to build* **i→y** **y inserted before a, e, o** construyendo construido	**construyo** **construyes** **construye** construimos construís **construyen**	construía construías construía construíamos construíais construían	construí construiste **construyó** construimos construisteis **construyeron**	construiré construirás construirá construiremos construiréis construirán	construiría construirías construiría construiríamos construiríais construirían	**construya** **construyas** **construya** **construyamos** **construyáis** **construyan**	**construyera** **construyeras** **construyera** **construyéramos** **construyerais** **construyeran**	**construye** (**no construyas**) **construya** **construid** (**no construyáis**) **construyan**
leer *to read* **i→y; stressed i→í** **leyendo** **leído**	leo lees lee leemos leéis leen	leía leías leía leíamos leíais leían	leí leíste **leyó** leímos leísteis **leyeron**	leeré leerás leerá leeremos leeréis leerán	leería leerías leería leeríamos leeríais leerían	lea leas lea leamos leáis lean	**leyera** **leyeras** **leyera** **leyéramos** **leyerais** **leyeran**	lee (no leas) lea leed (no leáis) lean

APÉNDICE D: Change of Spelling Verbs *(continued)*

Infinitive
Present Participle
Past Participle

Infinitive / Present Participle / Past Participle	Present Indicative	Imperfect	Preterite	Future	Conditional	Present Subjunctive	Past Subjunctive	Commands
pagar *to pay* **g→gu before e** pagando pagado	pago	pagaba	**pagué**	pagaré	pagaría	**pague**	pagara	paga (no **pagues**)
	pagas	pagabas	pagaste	pagarás	pagarías	**pagues**	pagaras	**pague**
	paga	pagaba	pagó	pagará	pagaría	**pague**	pagara	pagad (no **paguéis**)
	pagamos	pagábamos	pagamos	pagaremos	pagaríamos	**paguemos**	pagáramos	**paguen**
	pagáis	pagabais	pagasteis	pagaréis	pagaríais	**paguéis**	pagarais	
	pagan	pagaban	pagaron	pagarán	pagarían	**paguen**	pagaran	
seguir *to follow* **(e→i, i)** **gu→g before a, o** siguiendo seguido	**sigo**	seguía	seguí	seguiría	seguiría	**siga**	**siguiera**	**sigue (no sigas)**
	sigues	seguías	seguiste	seguirías	seguirías	**sigas**	**siguieras**	**siga**
	sigue	seguía	**siguió**	seguiría	seguiría	**siga**	**siguiera**	seguid (no **sigáis**)
	seguimos	seguíamos	seguimos	seguiremos	seguiríamos	**sigamos**	**siguiéramos**	**sigan**
	seguís	seguíais	seguisteis	seguiréis	seguiríais	**sigáis**	**siguierais**	
	siguen	seguían	**siguieron**	seguirán	seguirían	**sigan**	**siguieran**	
tocar *to play, to touch* **c→qu before e** tocando tocado	toco	tocaba	**toqué**	tocaré	tocaría	**toque**	tocara	toca (no **toques**)
	tocas	tocabas	tocaste	tocarás	tocarías	**toques**	tocaras	**toque**
	toca	tocaba	tocó	tocará	tocaría	**toque**	tocara	tocad (no **toquéis**)
	tocamos	tocábamos	tocamos	tocaremos	tocaríamos	**toquemos**	tocáramos	**toquen**
	tocáis	tocabais	tocasteis	tocaréis	tocaríais	**toquéis**	tocarais	
	tocan	tocaban	tocaron	tocarán	tocarían	**toquen**	tocaran	

APÉNDICE E: Irregular Verbs

*Verbs with irregular *yo*-forms in the present indicative

Infinitive / Present Participle / Past Participle	Present Indicative	Imperfect	Preterite	Future	Conditional	Present Subjunctive	Past Subjunctive	Commands
andar *to walk* andando andado	ando andas anda andamos andáis andan	andaba andabas andaba andábamos andabais andaban	**anduve anduviste anduvo anduvimos anduvisteis anduvieron**	andaré andarás andará andaremos andaréis andarán	andaría andarías andaría andaríamos andaríais andarían	ande andes ande andemos andéis anden	**anduviera anduvieras anduviera anduviéramos anduvierais anduvieran**	anda (no andes) ande andad (no andéis) anden
*caer *to fall* **cayendo** caído	**caigo** caes cae caemos caéis caen	caía caías caía caíamos caíais caían	caí caíste **cayó** caímos caísteis **cayeron**	caeré caerás caerá caeremos caeréis caerán	caería caerías caería caeríamos caeríais caerían	**caiga caigas caiga caigamos caigáis caigan**	**cayera cayeras cayera cayéramos cayerais cayeran**	cae (**no caigas**) **caiga caed (no caigáis) caigan**
*dar *to give* dando dado	**doy** das da damos dais dan	daba dabas daba dábamos dabais daban	**di diste dio dimos disteis dieron**	daré darás dará daremos daréis darán	daría darías daría daríamos daríais darían	**dé des dé demos deis den**	**diera dieras diera diéramos dierais dieran**	da (no des) **dé** dad (**no deis**) den
*decir *to say, tell* **diciendo dicho**	**digo dices dice** decimos decís **dicen**	decía decías decía decíamos decíais decían	**dije dijiste dijo dijimos dijisteis dijeron**	**diré dirás dirá diremos diréis dirán**	**diría dirías diría diríamos diríais dirían**	**diga digas diga digamos digáis digan**	**dijera dijeras dijera dijéramos dijerais dijeran**	**di (no digas) diga** decid (**no digáis) digan**
*estar *to be* estando estado	**estoy estás está** estamos estáis **están**	estaba estabas estaba estábamos estabais estaban	**estuve estuviste estuvo estuvimos estuvisteis estuvieron**	estaré estarás estará estaremos estaréis estarán	estaría estarías estaría estaríamos estaríais estarían	**esté estés esté estemos estéis estén**	**estuviera estuvieras estuviera estuviéramos estuvierais estuvieran**	**está (no estés) esté** estad (**no estéis) estén**

APÉNDICE E: Irregular Verbs *(continued)*

Infinitive / Present Participle / Past Participle	Present Indicative	Imperfect	Preterite	Future	Conditional	Present Subjunctive	Past Subjunctive	Commands
haber *to have* habiendo habido	he has ha [hay] hemos habéis han	había habías había habíamos habíais habían	hube hubiste hubo hubimos hubisteis hubieron	habré habrás habrá habremos habréis habrán	habría habrías habría habríamos habríais habrían	haya hayas haya hayamos hayáis hayan	hubiera hubieras hubiera hubiéramos hubierais hubieran	
*hacer *to make, do* haciendo hecho	hago haces hace hacemos hacéis hacen	hacía hacías hacía hacíamos hacíais hacían	hice hiciste hizo hicimos hicisteis hicieron	haré harás hará haremos haréis harán	haría harías haría haríamos haríais harían	haga hagas haga hagamos hagáis hagan	hiciera hicieras hiciera hiciéramos hicierais hicieran	haz (no hagas) haga haced (no hagáis) hagan
ir *to go* yendo ido	voy vas va vamos vais van	iba ibas iba íbamos ibais iban	fui fuiste fue fuimos fuisteis fueron	iré irás irá iremos iréis irán	iría irías iría iríamos iríais irían	vaya vayas vaya vayamos vayáis vayan	fuera fueras fuera fuéramos fuerais fueran	ve (no vayas) vaya id (no vayáis) vayan
*oír *to hear* oyendo oído	oigo oyes oye oímos oís oyen	oía oías oía oíamos oíais oían	oí oíste oyó oímos oísteis oyeron	oiré oirás oirá oiremos oiréis oirán	oiría oirías oiría oiríamos oiríais oirían	oiga oigas oiga oigamos oigáis oigan	oyera oyeras oyera oyéramos oyerais oyeran	oye (no oigas) oiga oíd (no oigáis) oigan

APÉNDICE E: Irregular Verbs

*Verbs with irregular *yo*-forms in the present indicative

Infinitive
Present Participle
Present Indicative

Infinitive / Present Participle / Present Indicative	Present Indicative	Imperfect	Preterite	Future	Conditional	Present Subjunctive	Past Subjunctive	Commands
poder (o→ue) *can, to be able* **pudiendo** podido	**puedo** **puedes** **puede** podemos podéis **pueden**	podía podías podía podíamos podíais podían	**pude** **pudiste** **pudo** **pudimos** **pudisteis** **pudieron**	**podré** **podrás** **podrá** **podremos** **podréis** **podrán**	**podría** **podrías** **podría** **podríamos** **podríais** **podrían**	**pueda** **puedas** **pueda** podamos podáis **puedan**	**pudiera** **pudieras** **pudiera** **pudiéramos** **pudierais** **pudieran**	
*poner *to place, put* poniendo **puesto**	**pongo** pones pone ponemos ponéis ponen	ponía ponías ponía poníamos poníais ponían	**puse** **pusiste** **puso** **pusimos** **pusisteis** **pusieron**	**pondré** **pondrás** **pondrá** **pondremos** **pondréis** **pondrán**	**pondría** **pondrías** **pondría** **pondríamos** **pondríais** **pondrían**	**ponga** **pongas** **ponga** **pongamos** **pongáis** **pongan**	**pusiera** **pusieras** **pusiera** **pusiéramos** **pusierais** **pusieran**	**pon (no pongas)** **ponga** poned (**no pongáis**) **pongan**
*querer (e→ie) *to want, wish* queriendo querido	**quiero** **quieres** **quiere** queremos queréis **quieren**	quería querías quería queríamos queríais querían	**quise** **quisiste** **quiso** **quisimos** **quisisteis** **quisieron**	**querré** **querrás** **querrá** **querremos** **querréis** **querrán**	**querría** **querrías** **querría** **querríamos** **querríais** **querrían**	**quiera** **quieras** **quiera** queramos queráis **quieran**	**quisiera** **quisieras** **quisiera** **quisiéramos** **quisierais** **quisieran**	**quiere (no quieras)** **quiera** quered (no queráis) **quieran**
reír *to laugh* **riendo** **reído**	**río** **ríes** **ríe** **reímos** reís **ríen**	reía reías reía reíamos reíais reían	**reí** **reíste** **rió** **reímos** **reísteis** **rieron**	reiré reirás reirá reiremos reiréis reirán	reiría reirías reiría reiríamos reiríais reirían	**ría** **rías** **ría** **riamos** **riáis** **rían**	**riera** **rieras** **riera** **riéramos** **rierais** **rieran**	**ríe (no rías)** **ría** **reíd (no riáis)** **rían**
*saber *to know* sabiendo sabido	**sé** sabes sabe sabemos sabéis saben	sabía sabías sabía sabíamos sabíais sabían	**supe** **supiste** **supo** **supimos** **supisteis** **supieron**	**sabré** **sabrás** **sabrá** **sabremos** **sabréis** **sabrán**	**sabría** **sabrías** **sabría** **sabríamos** **sabríais** **sabrían**	**sepa** **sepas** **sepa** **sepamos** **sepáis** **sepan**	**supiera** **supieras** **supiera** **supiéramos** **supierais** **supieran**	**sabe (no sepas)** **sepa** **sabed (no sepáis)** **sepan**
*salir *to go out* saliendo salido	**salgo** sales sale salimos salís salen	salía salías salía salíamos salíais salían	salí saliste salió salimos salisteis salieron	**saldré** **saldrás** **saldrá** **saldremos** **saldréis** **saldrán**	**saldría** **saldrías** **saldría** **saldríamos** **saldríais** **saldrían**	**salga** **salgas** **salga** **salgamos** **salgáis** **salgan**	saliera salieras saliera saliéramos salierais salieran	**sal (no salgas)** **salga** salid (**no salgáis**) **salgan**

APÉNDICE E: Irregular Verbs *(continued)*

Infinitive / Present Participle / Past Participle	Present Indicative	Imperfect	Preterite	Future	Conditional	Present Subjunctive	Past Subjunctive	Commands
ser *to be* siendo sido	soy eres es somos sois son	era eras era éramos erais eran	fui fuiste fue fuimos fuisteis fueron	seré serás será seremos seréis serán	sería serías sería seríamos seríais serían	sea seas sea seamos seáis sean	fuera fueras fuera fuéramos fuerais fueran	sé (no seas) sea sed (no seáis) sean
*tener *to have* teniendo tenido	tengo tienes tiene tenemos tenéis tienen	tenía tenías tenía teníamos teníais tenían	tuve tuviste tuvo tuvimos tuvisteis tuvieron	tendré tendrás tendrá tendremos tendréis tendrán	tendría tendrías tendría tendríamos tendríais tendrían	tenga tengas tenga tengamos tengáis tengan	tuviera tuvieras tuviera tuviéramos tuvierais tuvieran	ten (no tengas) tenga tened (no tengáis) tengan
traer *to bring* trayendo traído	traigo traes trae traemos traéis traen	traía traías traía traíamos traíais traían	traje trajiste trajo trajimos trajisteis trajeron	traeré traerás traerá traeremos traeréis traerán	traería traerías traería traeríamos traeríais traerían	traiga traigas traiga traigamos traigáis traigan	trajera trajeras trajera trajéramos trajerais trajeran	trae (no traigas) traiga traed (no traigáis) traigan
*venir *to come* viniendo venido	vengo vienes viene venimos venís vienen	venía venías venía veníamos veníais venían	vine viniste vino vinimos vinisteis vinieron	vendré vendrás vendrá vendremos vendréis vendrán	vendría vendrías vendría vendríamos vendríais vendrían	venga vengas venga vengamos vengáis vengan	viniera vinieras viniera viniéramos vinierais vinieran	ven (no vengas) venga venid (no vengáis) vengan
ver *to see* viendo visto	veo ves ve vemos veis ven	veía veías veía veíamos veíais veían	vi viste vio vimos visteis vieron	veré verás verá veremos veréis verán	vería verías vería veríamos veríais verían	vea veas vea veamos veáis vean	viera vieras viera viéramos vierais vieran	ve (no veas) vea ved (no veáis) vean

SPANISH-ENGLISH GLOSSARY

This Spanish-English Glossary includes all the words and expressions that appear in the text except verb forms, regular superlatives and diminutives, and most adverbs ending in *-mente*. Only meanings used in the text are given. Gender of nouns is indicated except for masculine nouns ending in *-o* and feminine nouns ending in *-a*. Feminine forms of adjectives are shown except for regular adjectives with masculine forms ending in *-o*. Verbs appear in the infinitive form. Stem changes and spelling changes are indicated in parentheses: e.g., *divertirse (ie, i); buscar (qu)*. The number following each entry indicates the lesson in which the word with that particular meaning first appears. The following abbreviations are used:

adj.	adjective		*m.*	masculine
adv.	adverb		*pl.*	plural
conj.	conjunction		*prep.*	preposition
f.	feminine		*pron.*	pronoun
LP.	Lección preliminar		*s.*	singular

A

a *prep.* at, to LP.
   a bordo de aboard 17
   a crédito on credit 11
   a la derecha *prep.* to the right 9
   a la izquierda *prep.* to the left 9
   a menos que *conj.* unless 15
   a pie on foot 1
   a primera vista at first sight 15
   ¿A qué hora? At what time? 1
   a veces *adv.* sometimes 11
abierto *adj.* open 9
abolirse to disappear 12
abordar to board 16
abrazar(se) to hug (each other) 15
abrazo embrace, hug LP.
abrigo overcoat 8
abril April 3
abrir to open 8
abrocharse to buckle up, to fasten 16
abuela grandmother 4
abuelita grandma 4
abuelito grandpa 4
abuelo grandfather 4
abuelos grandparents 3
aburrido *adj.* boring 8
acabar de + infinitive to have just 6
acampar to camp 10
accesorio accessory 8
aceite *m.* oil 12

aceituna olive 10
acercarse (a) to get near, to approach 18
acompañar to accompany 15
aconsejar to advise 13
acontecimiento evento 14
acostarse(o→ue) to go to bed 6
actor *m.* actor LP.
actriz *f.* actress LP.
adaptable *adj.* adaptable 2
¡Adiós! Good-bye! LP.
adjetivo demostrativo demonstrative adjective 5
   adjetivo posesivo possessive adjective 2
adorar to adore 4
aduana customs, customs area 16
adverbio adverb LP.
   adverbio de tiempo adverb of time 6
aeropuerto airport 9
afeitarse to shave 6
agarrar to catch 15
agencia de viajes travel agency 16
agosto August 3
agradable *adj.* pleasant 16
agregar to add 10
agua *m.* water 5
ahora *adv.* now LP.
   ahora mismo *adv.* right now 13
ahorrar to save (money) 11

aire acondicionado air conditioning 17
ajillo fried shrimp flavored with garlic 12
al aire libre open air 10
   al lado de *prep.* next to 9; beside 13
   al poco tiempo in a little while 13
albergue *m.* inn 17
álbum de fotos *m.* photo album 11
alegrarse de to be glad 14
alegría joy 9
alemán *m.* German (language) 1
alfombra carpet, rug 7
álgebra *m.* algebra 1
algo something, anything, a bit 9
   ¿Algo más? Anything else? 10
algodón *m.* cotton 8
alguien someone, somebody 9
algún some, any 9
alguno(a/os/as) some, any 9
allí *adv.* there LP.
almacén *m.* department store 8
almorzar(o→ue) to have lunch 5
alquilar to rent 13
alto *adj.* tall 2; high 10
amarillo *adj.* yellow 2
amazónico *adj.* Amazon 17
ambicioso *adj.* ambicious 2
amigo(a) friend 1
amistad *f.* friendship 15

amor *m.* love 15; honey (term of endearment) 15
anaranjado *adj.* orange 2
anciano *adj.* elderly 2
anillo ring 11
animal *m.* animal 18
anoche *adv.* last night 7
anteayer *adv.* the day before yesterday 7
anteojos eyeglasses 12
   anteojos para el sol sunglasses 8
antes *adv.* beforehand 6
   antes (de) que *conj.* before 15
   antes de + *infinitive* before (-ing) 6
antipático *adj.* nasty, disagreeable 2
anunciar to announce 11
anuncio advertisement, announcement 11
año year 3
   año pasado *adv.* last year 7
aparador *m.* shop window 10
aparato eléctrico electric appliance 7
apartamento apartment 1
aperitivo appetizer (hors d'oeuvre) 12
aplaudir to applaud 15
aplicarse to put on (e.g., lotion) 13
aprender to learn 2
aprovechar(se) to take advantage 11
apuntar to jot down 12
aquel *adj.* that (way over there) 5
aquél *pron.* that one (way over there) 5
aquella *adj.* that (way over there) 5
aquélla *pron.* that one (way over there) 5
aquellas *adj.* those (way over there) 5
aquéllas *pron.* those (way over there) 5
aquellos *adj.* those (way over there) 5
aquéllos *pron.* those (way over there) 5
aquí *adv.* here LP.
árbol *m.* tree 17
aretes *m. pl.* earrings 8
armario closet 7
arreglado *adj.* made up 17
arreglar to make up (a room) 17
arroz *m.* rice 5
artesanías crafts 10
artículo article 1
   artículo eléctrico electric article 11
   artículo fotográfico photographic article 11

artístico *adj.* artistic 2
ascensor *m.* elevator 17
así thus, so 9
asiento seat 16
asistencia attendance 15
asistir(a) to attend (e.g., a function) 4
aspiradora vacuum cleaner 7
aspirina asprin 18
asustar to scare, frighten, astonish 13
atlético *adj.* athletic 2
aún *adv.* even 18
aunque *conj.* although 15
auto car 1
autobús *m.* bus 2
autor(a) author LP.
avergonzado *adj.* embarrassed LP.
avión *m.* airplane 16
ayer *adv.* yesterday 7
ayudar to help 10
azúcar *m.* sugar 10
azul *adj.* blue 2

B

bahía bay 18
bailar to dance 3
baile *m.* dance 1
bajar(se) (de) to get off 9
bajo *adj.* short (in height) 2; low 10
balneario beach resort 13
banco bank 5
bandarín small flag 10
banquete *m.* banquet 15
bañarse to take a bath 6
bañera bathtub 7
baño bathroom 6
barato *adj.* inexpensive, cheap 11
barco boat 17
barril barrel 18
Bastante bien. Rather well. LP.
bautismo baptism 4
bebé *m./f.* baby 2
beber to drink 2
bebida drink, beverage 5
bellas artes fine arts 1
besar(se) to kiss (each other) 15
Biblia Bible 17
biblioteca library 1
bicicleta bicycle 1

bien *adv.* well, fine LP.; okay 1
Bien, gracias. Fine, thank you. LP.
bilingüe *adj.* bilingual 2
billete *m.* ticket 16
biología biology 1
bisabuela great-grandmother 4
bisabuelo great-grandfather 4
bistec *m.* steak 5
blanco *adj.* white 2
blusa blouse 8
boca mouth 18
boda wedding 15
boleto ticket 16
   boleto de ida one-way ticket 16
   boleto de ida y vuelta roundtrip ticket 16
bolígrafo ballpoint pen 1
bolsa purse, bag 8
bonito *adj.* pretty 2
botas boots 8
botecito little boat 9
botella bottle 12
brazalete *m.* bracelet 11
brazos arms 6
brécol *m.* broccoli 10
brindis *m.* toast 15
broncearse to get a suntan 13
bucear to scuba dive 13
¡Buen provecho! Enjoy your meal! 5
   ¡Buen viaje! Have a nice trip! 16
¡Buenas noches! Good evening!, Good night! LP.
   ¡Buenas tardes! Good afternoon! LP.
bueno *adj.* good 2
   ¡Bueno! Great!, Okay!, well 1
   ¡Buenos días! Good morning! LP.
buscar (qu) to look for 7

C

cabeza head 18
cabina cabin 17
cabina telefónica telephone booth 3
cada *adv.* each, every 4
   cada año *adv.* each year 4
café *m.* coffee 5
caja cash register 10
calamar *m.* squid 12
calcetines *m. pl.* socks 8

calculadora calculator 11

cálculo calculus 1

calidad *f.* quality 11

caliente *adj.* hot 5

calmarse to calm down 14

cama bed 7

    cama doble double bed 17

    cama sencilla single bed 17

cámara camera 11

camarero(a) server (Spain) 12

camarones *m. pl.* shrimp 10

camarote de primera first-class cabin 9

cambiar to change 8

caminar to walk 3

    caminar por las montañas to hike in the mountains 13

camisa shirt 8

camiseta T-shirt 8

campo country(side) 13

canal *m.* channel (TV) 14

cangrejo crab 18

canoa canoe 13

cansado *adj.* tired 4

cansancio fatigue 18

cantante *m./f.* singer 14

cantar to sing 3

cantidad *f.* quantity 10

capintería carpentry 4

cara face 6

característica física physical characteristic 2

cariño affection 15

carne *f.* meat 5

    carne de cerdo (puerco) *f.* pork 10

    carne de vaca (res) *f.* beef 10

carnicería butcher shop 10

caro *adj.* expensive 11

carrera race (competition) 3

carretera highway 16

carta letter 2

casa house 7

casado *adj.* married 4

casarse to get married, to marry 15

caseta de vídeo videotape 11

casi *adv.* almost 11

castillo castle 17

catarro cold 18

catorce fourteen LP.

cazar to hunt 17

cebolla onion 10

cena dinner, supper 5

cenar to have supper (dinner) 5

centro center 1; downtown 9; comercial shopping mall 8

cerbatana blowgun 17

cerca *adv.* nearby 9

    cerca de *prep.* near 9

cercano *adj.* near 9

cereza cherry 10

cero zero LP.

cerrado *adj.* closed 9; enclosed 10

cerro hill 13

cerveza beer 5

¡Chao! Bye! (informal) LP.

chaqueta jacket 8

cheque de viajero *m.* traveler's check 16

chica girl 13

chicha corn liquor 17

chico boy 13

chimenea fireplace 7

chocar con to crash into 9

cien one hundred 6

ciencia science 1

ciencias políticas political science 1

científico(a) scientist 18

cigarrillo cigarette 16

cinco five LP.

cincuenta fifty 2

cine *m.* movie theater 3

cinta tape, tape recording 1

cinturón *m.* belt 8

    cinturón de seguridad *m.* safety belt 16

cita date (social) 15

ciudad *f.* city LP.

¡Claro que sí! Of course! 2

clase *f.* class LP.

clínica clinic 18

cocina kitchen 7

cocinar to cook 12

colgante *adj.* hanging 13

coliflor *f.* cauliflower 10

collar *m.* necklace 8

color *m.* color 2

comadre (the mother and godmother refer to each other as *comadre*) 4

comedia comedy 14

comedor *m.* dining room 7

comentar to comment 12

comenzar (e→ie) to begin, to start 4

comer to eat 2

    comer afuera to eat out (in a restaurant) 12

comestibles *m. pl.* groceries 10

comida food, meal, lunch 5

como *adv.* like 3

cómo *adv.* how LP.

    cómo no of course 5

¿Cómo? How? LP.; What?, Huh? 5

    ¿Cómo estás? How are you? (informal) LP.

    ¿Cómo está usted? How are you? (formal) LP.

    ¿Cómo te llamas? What's your name? (informal) LP.

    ¿Cómo se llama usted? What's your name? (formal) LP.

cómodo *adj.* comfortable 17

compadre (the father & the godfather refer to each other as *compadre*) 4

compañero(a) de clase classmate 1

    compañero(a) de cuarto roommate 1

compañía company 1

competencia competition 14

comprender to understand 2

comprometido *adj.* engaged 15

compromiso engagement 15

computación *f.* computer science 1

computadora computer (Latin America) 11

con *prep.* with LP.

    con cheque by check 11

    con destino a departing for 16

    con permiso excuse me 9

con tal (de) que *conj.* provided (that) 15

concierto concert 3

concurso contest 14

condimento condiment 5

conferencia lecture LP.

conjunción *f.* conjunction 15

conmigo with me 3

conocer to meet (someone) 3

    conocer (a) to know (a person or a place) LP.

contabilidad *f.* bookkeeping 4

contar to tell (about) 18

contar (o→ue) to tell (a story) 10

contento *adj.* happy 4

contestar to answer LP.

contigo with you 15

continuar to continue 6

control de seguridad *m.* security control 16

copa glass (for wine) 12

Copa Mundial World Cup 3

corbata necktie 8

correr to run, to jog 3

correr las olas to surf 13

cortar el césped to mow the lawn 7

costa coast 13

costar (o→ue) to cost 8

costo cost 11

crecimiento growth 13

creer to believe 14

crema bronceadora suntan lotion 13

cruzar to cross 17

cuadra city block 9

cuadro painting 7

¿Cuál(es)? What?, Which one(s)? 2

¿Cuál es tu dirección? What's your address? LP.

¿Cuál es tu nombre? What's your name? (informal) LP.

¿Cuál es tu número de teléfono? What's your telephone number? LP.

cuando *conj.* when 15

¿Cuándo? When? 1

¿Cuántos años tienes? How old are you? (informal) LP.

¿Cuántos(as)? How many? LP.

cuarenta forty 2

cuadro painting 7

cuarto room 7

cuarto de baño bathroom 7

cuarto doble double room 17

cuarto sencillo single room 17

cuatro four LP.

cuatrocientos four hundred 6

cuchara spoon 12

cuchillo knife 12

cuenta bill 12

cuento story 12

cuerpo body 6

¡Cuidado! Be careful! 1

cuidar(se) to take care (of oneself) 18

cumpleaños *m.* birthday 6

cumplir to be/turn (a certain age) 6

cuñada sister-in-law 4

cuñado brother-in-law 4

curso course 1

D

dar to give 3

dar a la calle to face the street 17

dar las gracias to thank 9

darse la mano to shake hands 15

de from, of LP.

¿De dónde? Where from? LP.

¿De dónde eres? Where are you from? (informal) LP.

¿De dónde es usted? Where are you from? (formal) LP.

de ida one-way 16

de ida y vuelta roundtrip 16

de la mañana in the morning 1

de la noche in the evening 1

de la tarde in the afternoon 1

De nada You're welcome 3

¿De quién(es)? Whose? 2

de repente suddenly 9

deber (+ infinitive) ought to, should 2

decidir to decide 9

decir (e→i) to say, to tell 5 ; to order 13

decorar to decorate 15

dejar to leave, let, allow 14

delante de *prep.* in front 9

delgado *adj.* thin 2

demás *adj.* rest, remainder 17

demasiado *adv.* too much 17

demora delay 16

dentista *m./f.* dentist LP.

dependiente *m./f.* salesclerk 8

deporte *m.* sport 3

derecho Law 1

derrumbarse to curl up 14

desarrollado developed 18

desarrollar to occur 13

desatar to untie 10

desayunar to have breakfast 5

desayuno breakfast 5

descansar to rest 1

desear to desire, wish 13

despedir (de) (e→i, e→i) to fire (dismiss) 10

despedirse (de) (e→i, e→i) to say good-bye LP.

despejado *adj.* clear 6

despertador *m.* alarm clock 7

despertarse (e→ie) to wake up 6

después *adv.* afterwards 6

después (de) que *conj.* after 15

después de + infinitive *prep.* after (-ing) 5

detrás de *prep.* behind 9

día *m.* day 1

día festivo *m.* holiday 9

diario newspaper 14

diario diary 16

dibujo animado cartoon 14

diciembre December 3

diecinueve nineteen LP.

dieciocho eighteen LP.

dieciséis sixteen LP.

diecisiete seventeen LP.

dientes *m./pl.* teeth 6

diez ten LP.

difícil *adj.* difficult 1

dinero money 8

dirección *f.* direction 9

disco compacto compact disk (CD) 3; compact disk player (CD) 7

divertirse (e→ie, e→i) to have fun 8

divorciado *adj.* divorced 4

doblar to turn (on a street) 9

doble *adj.* double 17

doce twelve LP.

docena dozen 10

documental *m.* documentary 14

doler (a alguien) (o→ue) to hurt (someone) 18

dolor pain, ache 18

dolor de cabeza headache 18

dolor de oídos earache 18

domingo Sunday 1

don title used as a man's first name LP.

¿Dónde? Where? 1

doña title used with a woman's first name LP.

dormir (o→ue) to sleep 5

dormirse (o→ue) to fall asleep 6

dormitorio bedroom 7

dos two LP.

dos mil two thousand 8

dos millones two million 8

dos veces *adv.* twice 11

doscientos two hundred 6

doscientos(as) mil two hundred

thousand 8

drama *m.* drama 14

dramático *adj.* dramatic 2

ducha shower 7

ducharse to take a shower, to shower 6

duda doubt 14

dudar to doubt 14

dudoso *adj.* doubtful 14

dueño owner 17

dulces sweets *m./pl.* 6

durante *prep.* during 3

durazno peach 10

E

economía economics 1

edad *f.* age 2

educación *f.* education 1

efectuarse to take place 15

ejemplo example LP.

él *pron.* he LP.

el the 1

    El gusto es mío. My pleasure. LP.

    el más the most 6

    el menos the least 6

ella *pron.* she LP.

ellas *pron.* they LP.

ellos *pron.* they LP.

embarazada *adj.* pregnant LP.

embrujo charm 14

en in LP.

    en arriendo rented 13

    en avión by plane 16

    en casa at home 1

    en caso (de) que *conj.* in case (of) 15

    en efectivo in cash 11

    en punto on the dot 1

    ¿En qué puedo servirle? What can I do for you? 8

    ¿En serio? Really? 14

enamorarse (de) to fall in love (with) 12

encantado *adj.* enchanted 18

    Encantado(a). Nice to meet you. LP.

encontrar (o→ue) to find 11

enero January 3

enfermarse to get sick, to become ill 18

enfermo *adj.* sick 4

enfrente de *prep.* across 9

enojado *adj.* angry 4

ensalada salad 5

enseñar to teach 13

entonces *adv.* then 6

entrada main course; entrance 12

entre *prep.* between 9

entremés *m.* appetizer 12

equipaje (de mano) (carry-on) baggage, luggage 16

equipo team 3

es it is LP.

    Es (im)posible. It's (im)possible. 14

    Es bueno. It's good. 14

    Es malo. It's bad. 14

    es hora de + infinitive it's time to 7

    Es importante. It's important. 14

    Es lógico. It's logical. 14

    Es mejor. It's better. 14

    Es necesario. It's necessary. 14

    Es ridículo. It's ridiculous. 14

    Es una lástima. It's a shame. 14

esa *adj.* that 5

    esa (+ *f.* noun) that 4

ésa *pron.* that one 5

ésas *pron.* those (there) 5

esas *adj.* those 5

escala stop, stopover 16

escribir to write 2

escritorio desk 7

escuchar to listen 1

escuela school 1

escultura sculpture 16

ese *adj.* that 5

ése *pron.* that one 5

eso *adj.* that 5

    Eso es todo. That's all. 10

esos *adj.* those 5

ésos *pron.* those (there) 5

español *m.* Spanish (language) LP.

    español(a) *noun* Spaniard 2

esparcimiento recreation 13

especialidad *f.* specialty 12

espejo mirror 7

esperar to wait for 8; to hope 14

esposa wife 4

esquiar to ski 3

    esquiar en el agua to waterski 13

esquina street corner 9

esta *adj.* this 5

    esta noche tonight 3

ésta *pron.* this one 5

Está despejado. It's clear. 6

    Está lloviendo. It's raining. 6

    Está nevando. It's snowing. 6

    Está nublado. It's cloudy. 6

estación *f.* season 6

    estación de trenes *f.* railway station 9

estado state 1

Estados Unidos *m. pl.* United States LP.

estar to be 4

    estar de acuerdo to agree 5

    estar de vacaciones to be on vacation 12

estas *adj.* these 5

éstas *pron.* these (here) 5

este *adj.* this 5

éste *pron.* this one 5

estéreo stereo 7

estilo style 11

esto *adj.* this 5

estómago stomach 18

estos *adj.* these 5

éstos *pron.* these (here) 5

estrellas stars 12

estudiante *m./f.* student LP.

estudiar to study 1

estudio *noun* study 1

estufa stove, range 7

estupendo *adj.* wonderful, great 14

examen *m.* test 1

examinar to examine 18

explorar to explore 18

expresión afirmativa affirmative expression 9

    expresión idiomática idiomatic expression LP.

    expresión negativa negative expression 9

extranjero *adj.* foreign 16

F

fácil *adj.* easy 1

falda skirt 8

familia family 2

famoso *adj.* famous 16

febrero February 3
fecha date 3
fecundo *adj.* fruitful 10
felicidad *f.* happiness 15
¡Felicidades! Congratulations! 6
felicitar to congratulate 15
feliz *adj.* happy 6
    Feliz Navidad Merry Christmas 9
feo *adj.* ugly 2
ferrocarril *m.* railroad 13
fiebre fever 18
fiesta party 1
fijo *adj.* fixed 11
fin de semana *m.* weekend 3
firmar to sign 15
flamenco flamingo 18
flan carmel custard 5
flor *f.* flower 15
Florencia Florence 16
foca seal 18
follaje vegetation 13
formulario form 17
foto *f.* photo, picture 3
francés *m.* French (language) 1
fresa strawberry 10
fresco *adj.* fresh 10
frío cold 6
frito *adj.* fried 12
fruta fruit 5
fuerte *adj.* loud; strong 12
fumar to smoke 12
función *f.* show (theatrical) 14
    función musical *f.* musical (play) 14
funcionar to work (function) 11
fútbol *m.* soccer 3

G

galápago tortoise 18
galleta dulce cookie 10
    galleta salada cracker 10
gambas shrimp 10
ganador(a) winner 14
ganar to win 14
ganga bargain 11
gaseosa soft drink (Spain) 12
gasolinera gas station 1
gastar to spend (money) 11
gato cat 2

gemelo(a) twin 2
generoso *adj.* generous 2
gente *f.* people LP.
geografía geography 1
geología geology 1
geometría geometry 1
gerente manager 17
gesto gesture 2
gimnasio gymasium 3
gordo *adj.* fat 2
gorra de béisbol baseball cap 8
grabadora tape recorder 11
gramo gram 10
grande *adj.* big, large 2
granja farm 10
grave *adj.* serious (medical) 18
grifo tap (faucet) 18
gris *adj.* gray 2
gritar to shout 12
guantes *m. pl.* gloves 8
guapo *adj.* good-looking 2
guía *f.* guidebook 17
    guía *m./f.* guide 17
guitarra guitar 1
gustar to be pleasing 3; to like 5

H

habitación room (Spain) 17
hablar to speak, to talk 1
hace (dos) años (two) years ago 7
    Hace buen tiempo. It's nice out. 6
    Hace calor. It's hot. 6
    Hace fresco. It's cool. 6
    Hace frío. It's cold. 6
    Hace mal tiempo. It's bad out. 6
    Hace sol. It's sunny. 6
    hace un año one year ago 7
    Hace viento. It's windy. 6
hacer to do, to make 2
    hacer cola to get in line 6
    hacer ejercicio to exercise 3
    hacer el esnórquel to snorkel 13
    hacer escala (en) to make a stop (on a flight) (at) 16
    hacer la cama to make one's bed 7
    hacer un picnic to have a picnic 13
    hacer una parrillada to have a cookout 13

hacia *adv.* toward 9
hacienda ranch 17
hasta *adv.* until 6
    hasta *adv.* up to 9
    ¡Hasta luego! See you later! LP.
    ¡Hasta mañana! See you tomorrow! LP.
    hasta que *conj.* until 15
hay there is, there are LP.
helado ice cream 5
hemisferio hemisphere 16
hermana sister 2
hermanastra stepsister 2
hermanastro stepbrother 2
hermano brother 2
hervir (ie, i) to boil 18
hielo ice 12
hierro iron 10
hija daughter 4
hijo son 4
historia history 1
hizo did 7
hogar *m.* home 11
¡Hola! Hi! (informal) LP.
hombre *m.* man 4
honesto *adj.* honest 2
hora hour, time 1
horario schedule 16
horno (de microondas) (microwave) oven 7
hotelería hotel management 4
hoy today 3
    hoy día nowadays 2
hueso bone 10
huevos (fritos) (fried) eggs 5
humano *adj.* human 18
humedad *f.* humidity 17
hundirse to sink into 10

I

idioma *m.* language LP.
iglesia church 8
importunar to bother LP.
imprescindible *adj.* essential 12
impresora printer 11
impuesto tax 16
increíble *adj.* incredible 18
indio(a) Indian 17
información *f.* information LP.

ingeniería engineering 1
ingeniero(a) engineer 1
inglés *m.* English (language) 1
inmigración *f.* passport control 16
insistir (en) to insist (on) 13
intelectual *adj.* intellectual 2
inteligente *adj.* intelligent 2
intercambiar to exchange 16
intérprete *m./f.* interpreter 1
intuitivo *adj.* intuitive 2
invierno winter 6
invitado guest 15
invitar to invite 3
ir to go 3
    ir al cine to go to the movies 3
    ir de compras to go shopping 3
    ir en avión to go by plane 16

J

jabalí *m.* wild boar 17
jabón soap 17
jamón *m.* ham 5
jardín *m.* flower garden 7
jarra pitcher (for liquids) 12
joven *adj.* young 2
joyas jewelry 11
joyería jewelry store 11
jubliarse to retire 10
juego game 3
jueves *m.* Thursday 1
jugar (o → ue) to play 5
    jugar (a las) cartas to play cards 3
    jugar (al) tenis to play tennis 3
jugo juice 5
juguete *m.* toy 9
julio July 3
junio June 3
juventud *f.* youth 17

K

kilo kilo 10

L

la the 1
    la *pron.* her, you (formal), it (feminine) 7

    la más the most 6
    la menos the least 6
lago lake 13
lámpara lamp 7
lápiz *m.* pencil 1
largo *adj.* long 15
las the 1
    las *pron.* you (formal), them (fe*m.*) 7
    las más the most 6
    las menos the least 6
lástima shame, pity 14
lastimarse to get hurt 9
lavabo sink 7
lavadora clothes washer 7
lavaplatos *m.* dishwasher 7
lavar to wash 7
    lavar la ropa to wash clothes 7
    lavar los platos to wash the dishes 7
lavarse to wash up 6
    lavarse los dientes to brush one's teeth 6
le *pron.* to you (formal), to him, to her 5; 8
lección *f.* lesson LP.
leche *f.* milk 5
lechería dairy store (Spain) 10
lettuce 10
lectura reading LP.
leer to read 2
lejos *adv.* far (away) 9
    lejos de *prep.* far from 9
llenar to fill 10
lenguas languages 1
lentamente *adv.* slowly 15
les *pron.* to you, to them 5; to/for you (formal), them 8
letras humanities, letters 1
levantarse to get up 6
libro book 1
    libro de texto textbook 1
líder *m./f.* leader LP.
liga garter 15
limón *m.* lemon 2
limonada lemonade 5
limpiar la casa to clean the house 7
limpio *adj.* clean 17
literatura Literature 1
litoral coast 13
litro liter 10

llamar to call 15
llave *f.* key 17
llegada arrival 16
llegar to arrive 1
llevar to wear, to carry 8
    llevarse bien to get along well 15
llorar to cry 11
Llueve. It rains. 6
lluvia rain 6
lo *pron.* him, you (formal), it (masculine) 7
    lo sé I know (it) LP.
    lo siento (mucho) I'm (very) sorry 9
lógico *adj.* logical 14
lograr to go, to reach 12
los the 1
    los *pron.* you (formal), them (masc.) 7
    los más the most 6
    los menos the least 6
luego *adv.* then 6
lugar *m.* place 6
luna de miel honeymoon 15
lunes *m.* Monday 1

M

madrastra step mother 2
madre *f.* mother 2
madrina godmother 4
maíz *m.* corn 17
maleta suitcase 9
malo *adj.* bad 2
mamá mother (Mom) LP.
mano *f.* hand 1
mantequilla butter 5
manzana apple 10
mapa map 1
máquina de afeitar shaver 11
    máquina de escribir typewriter 11
marcha nupcial wedding march 15
marido husband 4
marinero(a) sailor 18
marino *adj.* marine 18
mariposa butterfly 17
mariscos shellfish 5
marrón *adj.* brown 2
martes *m.* Tuesday 1
marzo March 3

más plus LP.

    más *adv.* more 5

    Más o menos. So-so. LP.

    más tarde *adv.* later 6

    más ... como more . . . que 6

matrimonio wedding (Chile) 15

mayo May 3

mayor *adj.* older 4; 6

me *pron.* to me 5; me 7; to/for me 8

    me gustaría I would like 4

    Me llamo ... My name is . . . LP.

medias stockings 8

medicina medicine 1

médico *m./f.* physician, doctor 18

    médico *adj.* medical 18

medio one-half 10

mejor *adj.* best 2; better 6

menor *adj.* younger 4

menos minus LP.

    menos ... que less . . . than 6

mercado market 9

mercancías merchandise 11

merecer to deserve 13

merienda snack 5

mermelada jam 5

mes *m.* month 3

    mes pasado *m.* last month 7

mesa table 6

meter to put (in) 10

metro subway 3

mexicano *adj.* Mexican 2

mi *pron.* my LP.

    mi(s) *adj.* my 2

mientras *adv.* while 9

miércoles *m.* Wednesday 1

mil one thousand 6

millón million 8

mirar (la) televisión to watch television 3

misa mass 6

misionero(a) missionary 17

mismo *adj.* same 14

mitad *f.* half 10

mito myth 14

mochila backpack 8

modismo *m.* idiom LP.

molestar to bother LP.

mono monkey 17

montaña mountain 13

montar a caballo to go horseback riding 3

montar en bicicleta to go bike riding 3

monumento monument 16

morir (o→ue) to die 12

morirse (o→ue) to die 18

mostrar (o→ue) to show 11

motocicleta motorcycle 1

motorizado *adj.* motorized 17

muchas veces *adv.* often 4

    ¡(Muchas) gracias! Thank you (very much)! LP.

Mucho gusto! Nice to meet you. LP.

mudarse to move (to a place) 7

muebles *m. pl.* furniture 7

mujer *f.* woman 4

mundo world 2

muñeca doll 11

museo museum 3

música music 1

¡(Muy) bien! (Very) well! LP.

N

nacer to be born 6

nada nothing, not . . . at all 9

    Nada más. Nothing else. 10

nadar to swim 3

nadie nobody, no one 9

nadador(a) swimmer 13

naranja orange 5

nariz *f.* nose 6

natación *f.* swimming 13

Navidad *f.* Christmas 9

necesitar to need 5

negocios business 1

negro *adj.* black 2

ni ... ni neither . . . nor 9

nieta grandaughter 4

nieto grandson 4

Nieva. It snows. 6

nieve *f.* snow 6

ningún none, not any 9

ninguno(a) none, not any 9

niñez *f.* childhood 12

niño(a) child 4

nivel *m.* level 10

¡No me digas! You're kidding! 15

    (no) me gusta + infinitive I (don't) like 1

nombre *m.* name LP.

nos *pron.* to us 5; us 7; to/for us 8

nosotros(as) *pron.* we LP.

noticias news 14

novecientos nine hundred 6

noventa ninety 2

novia girlfriend 1; bride 15

noviazgo courtship 15

noviembre November 3

novio boyfriend 1; groom 15

nublado *adj.* cloudy 6

nuera daughter-in-law 4

nuestro *adj.* our 2

nueve nine LP.

nuevo *adj.* new 2

número number LP.

nunca never 9

O

o ... o either . . . or 9

océano ocean 1

ochenta eighty 2

ocho eight LP.

ochocientos eight hundred 6

octubre October 3

ocupado *adj.* busy 4

oficina de correos post office 9

oído (inner) ear 18

oír to hear 7

¡Ojalá! Hope so! 14

ojos eyes 6

ola wave 13

olvidar to forget 8

once eleven LP.

ordenador *m.* computer (Spain) 11

orejas ears (outer) 6

orquesta band 15

os *pron.* to you (informal) 5; to/for you (informal) 8; you (informal) 7

otoño fall, autumn 6

otra vez *adv.* again 11

otro *adj.* other LP.

ovillo knot 14

óxido rust 9

P

paciente *adj.* patient 2; *m./f.* patient 18

padrastro stepfather 2

padre *m.* father 2

padres *m.pl.* parents 2
padrino godfather 4
pagar to pay for 8
país country 1
pájaro bird 17
palabra word LP.
pan *m.* bread 5
   pan tostado *m.* toast 5
panadería bakery 10
panecillo roll 10
pantalla screen 14
pantalones *m. pl.* pants 8
   pantalones cortos *m. pl.* shorts 8
pañuelo handkerchief 14
papá *m.* father (Dad) LP.
papagayo parrot 12
papas (fritas) (French fried) potatoes 5
papel *m.* paper 1
   papel higiénico *m.* toilet paper 17
   papel para cartas *m.* stationery 11
papelería stationery store 11
para *prep.* for 1
   para que *conj.* so (that) 15
   para siempre forever 4
parada stop 18
paraguas *m.* umbrella 8
parar(se) to stop 9
pareja couple 14
pariente *m.* relative 4
parque *m.* park 2
   parque zoológico *m.* zoo 17
parrillada cookout 13
parte *f.* part 6
partido game, match 14
pasajero(a) passenger 16
pasaporte *m.* passport 16
pasar to spend (time) 9
   pasar (por) to pick up (someone) 3
   pasar la aspiradora to vacuum 7
   pasarlo bien to have a good time 14
pasatiempo pastime, leisure-time activity 3
Pase(n) Ud(s). After you 9
pasear en canoa to go canoeing 13
   pasear en velero to sail 13
pasillo aisle 16
pastel *m.* pastry 5
pastelería pastry shop 10

pastilla pill 18
patatas fritas French fries (Spain) 12
patinar to skate 3
patio yard 7
pedazo piece 12
pedido order 12
pedir (e→i, e→i) to ask for LP.; to order 5; to request 13
peinarse to comb one's hair 6
pelar to peel 18
pelícano pelican 18
película movie, film 14
   película de ciencia ficción science fiction film 14
   película del intriga/misterio mystery film 14
   película del oeste western film 14
   película en video movie video 3
peligro danger 12
pelo hair 6
pelota ball 13
peluquería hair salon 11
península peninsula 1
pensar (e→ie) to think, to plan (on) 4
peor *adj.* worse 6
pequeño *adj.* small 2
pera pear 10
Perdón Excuse me 9
perejil *m.* parsley 10
perezoso *adj.* lazy 2
periódico newspaper 2
periodismo journalism 1
permitir to permit 13
pero *conj.* but 1
perro dog 2
personalidad *f.* personality 2
pescadería fish market 10
pescado fish 5
pescar to fish 3
piernas legs 6
pies *m.* feet 6
pieza cuarto 14
pijama *m.* pajamas 6
pimentero pepper shaker 12
pimienta pepper (spice) 12
pimiento pepper 10
pintarse to put on makeup 6
pintura painting 1
piña pineapple 10
piragua dugout canoe 17

piraña piranha 17
piscina swimming pool 3
planchar iron 14
planetario planetarium 16
plano map (of a city) 9
plátano banana 10
plato plate 12
   plato principal main dish 5
playa beach 13
plaza town square 9
poder (o→ue) to be able, can 5
pollo chicken 5
poner to put, put on (music) 3; to turn on, to show (movie) 14
   poner la mesa to set the table 7
ponerse to put on (clothing) 6
popa poop deck 9
por *prep.* for (duration of time) 1
   por aquí around here 9
   por eso therefore, so 8
   por favor please 1
   por fin *adv.* at last, finally 11
   por la noche at night 1
   ¿Por qué? why? 1
porteños person from Valparaíso, Chile 13
postre *m.* dessert 5
preferir (e→ie) to prefer 4
preocupado *adj.* worried 4
preocuparse (por) to worry (about) 9
presentaciones introductions (to someone) LP.
presentarse to introduce yourself LP.
presidente *m./f.* president LP.
primavera spring 6
primero first 3
primo(a) cousin 4
privado *adj.* private 17
probarse (o→ue) to try on 8
problema *m.* problem LP.
procedente de arriving from 16
profesión *f.* profession LP.
profesor(a) instructor, professor, teacher LP.
profundo *adj.* deep 13
programa de concursos *m.* game show 14
   programa de entrevistas *m.* talk show 14
   programa deportivo *m.* sports program 14

prohibir to forbid 13

pronombre *m.* pronoun LP.

   pronombre indirecto indirect pronoun 5

pronóstico weather forecast 6

   pronóstico del tiempo weather report 14

pronto soon 6

propina tip (gratuity) 12

próspero *adj.* prosperous 2

próximo *adj.* next 15

pueblo town 8

puerta door 7; gate 16

pues well 4

Q

que *pron.* which, that, than L.P.

¿Qué? What? LP.

   ¿Qué hay de nuevo? What's new? 3

   ¿Qué hora es? What time is it? 1

   ¡Qué interesante! How interesting! LP.

   ¡Qué lástima! What a shame! 14

   ¡Qué le vaya bien! I wish you well. 9

   ¿Qué más? What else? 10

   ¿Qué tal? How's everything? (informal) LP.

   ¿Qué te apetece? What would you like (to eat)? 5

   ¿Qué te parece? What do you think? 3

   ¿Qué te pasa? What's the matter with you? 6

   ¿Qué tiempo hace? What's the weather like? 6

   ¿Qué tiene usted? What's the problem? 18

quedar to be located 18

quedarle (a uno) to fit (someone) 8

quehacer *m.* chore 7

quejarse (de) to complain 14

querer (e →ie) to want, to love 4

queso cheese 5

quien *pron.* who L.P.

¿Quién(es)? Who? LP.

Quiero presentarte a . . . I want to introduce you to . . . (informal)

química chemistry 1

quince fifteen LP.

quinceañera fifteen-year-old girl 6

quinientos five hundred 6

quitarse to take off 6

R

radio radio 1

ramo bouquet 15

rebaja sale (Spain), reduction (in price) 11

rebajado *adj.* reduced (in price) 11

rebajar to reduce (in price) 11

recepción *f.* front desk 17

recibir to receive 2

recién casados newlyweds 15

recoger (recojo) to pick up, claim 16

recomendar (e →ie) to recommend 13

recordar (o →ue) to remember 7

recuerdo souvenir 16

refresco soft drink 5

regalo gift 6

regatear to bargain 10

registrarse to register 17

regresar to return 1

reírse (e →i, e →i) to laugh 11

rellenar to fill 10

reloj clock, watch 7

repasar to review 10

reportero(a) reporter LP.

reposado *adj.* quiet 10

reservado *adj.* reserved 2

residencia dormitory 6

rico *adj.* delicious 5

ridículo *adj.* ridiculous 14

río river 13

roca rock 17

rogar (o →ue) to request 15

rojo *adj.* red 2

rollo para diapositivas slide film 11

   rollo para fotos print film 11

ropa clothing 6; clothes 8

rosado *adj.* pink 2

ruido noise 17

S

sábado Saturday 1

saber to know 3

sabroso *adj.* delicious 17

sacar to take out 12

   sacar (fotos) to take (photographs) 3

   sacar la basura to take out the garbage 7

sal *f.* salt 12

sala living room 7

   sala de clase classroom LP.

   sala de espera waiting area 16

salchicha sausage 10

salero salt shaker 12

salida departure 16

salir to go out, leave 3

salud *f.* health 10

   Salud! Cheers! 5

saludar to greet LP.

saludo greeting 1

sandalias sandals 8

sangre *f.* blood 10

santiaguino residente of Santiago, Chile 13

secador de pelo *m.* hair dryer 11

secadora clothes dryer 7

secarse to dry off 6

sección de (no) fumar *f.* (non) smoking section 16

seguir (e →i) to continue 9

según according to 3

seguridad *f.* security 16

seguro *adj.* certain 14

seis six LP.

seiscientos six hundred 6

selva jungle 16

semana week 1

   semana pasada *adv.* last week 7

sencillo *adj.* single 17

sentarse (e →ie) to sit down 12

sentir (e →ie, e →i) to be sorry 14

sentirse (e →ie, e →i) to feel 13

señor (Sr.) Mr., sir LP.

señora (Sra.) Mrs., ma'am LP.

señorita (Srta.) Miss LP.

septiembre September 3

ser to be LP.

servilleta napkin 12

servir (e →i, e →i) to serve 5

sesenta sixty 2

setecientos seven hundred 6

setenta seventy 2

sí yes LP.

sicología pyschology 1

siempre *adv.* always 4

siete seven LP.

siglo century 12

silla chair 7

sillón *m.* easy chair 7

simpático *adj.* nice, agreeable 2

sin *prep.* without 9

   sin escala nonstop (flight) 16

   sin que *conj.* without 15

sinagoga synagogue 8

situado *adj.* situated 16

sobre *m.* envelope 11

sobrina niece 4

sobrino nephew 4

solamente *adv.* only 1; just 11

solo(a) *adv.* alone 5

soltero *adj.* single 4

sombrero hat 8

sonar (o→ue) to go off (e.g., an alarm) 7

sonarse blow one's nose 12

sonreír (e→i, e→i) to smile 15

sopa soup 5

sorprender to surprise 14

sorpresa surprise 13

soslayar put aside 14

su *adj.* her LP.

su(s) *adj.* his, her, your (formal), its 2

subir(se) (a) to get on/in 9

sucio *adj.* dirty 17

suegra mother-in-law 4

suegro father-in-law 4

suéter *m.* sweater 8

sugerir (e→ie, e→i) to suggest 13

Suiza Switzerland 18

supermercado supermarket 9

sustantivo noun LP.

T

tacaño *adj.* stingy 2

tal vez maybe, perhaps 16

talla size (clothing) 8

tamaño size 18

también *adv.* also, too LP.

tampoco neither, not . . . either 9

tan pronto como *conj.* as soon as 15

   tan ... como as . . . as 6

tanto(a) ... como as much . . . as 6

tantos(as) ... como as many . . . as 6

tapas hors d'oeuvres 12

tarjeta card 8

   tarjeta postal postcard 11

taza cup 12

té *m.* tea 5

   té helado *m.* iced tea 5

te *pron.* to you (informal) 5; to/for you (informal) 8; you (informal) 7

teatro theater **14**

tejer knit 14

teléfono telephone 1

telenovela soap opera 4

televisor TV set 1

temporada season 3

temprano *adv.* early 17

tenedor *m.* fork 12

tener (ie) to have 2

   tener (19 años) to be (19 years old) LP.

   tener calor to be hot 6

   tener celos to be jealous 4

   tener cuidado to be careful 2

   tener éxito to be successful 15

   tener frío to be cold 6

   tener ganas de (+ infintive) to feel like 4

   tener hambre to be hungry 5

   tener lugar to take place 15

   tener miedo to be afraid 4

   tener prisa to be in a hurry 4

   tener que + infinitive to have to 7

   tener razón to be right 4

   tener sed to be thirsty 5

   tener sueño to be sleepy 4

terminal de autobuses *f.* bus station 9

terminar to finish, to end 6

terraza terrace 7

terrestre *adj.* land 18

testigo witness 15

tía aunt 4

tiempo time 3

tienda store 8; shop 10

tintorería dry cleaner's 11

tío uncle 4

tipo kind, type 3

tirar to throw 15

título title LP.

toalla towel 13

tocador *m.* dresser 7

tocar to play (an instrument) 3; to touch 13

todavía *adv.* still, yet 7

todo all 4

   todo derecho *prep.* straight ahead 9

todos all 2; everyone 6

tolerante *adj.* tolerant 2

tomar to take 1; to drink 5; to catch 15

   tomar el sol to sunbathe 13

tomate *m.* tomato 5

torta cake, torte 10

   torta nupcial wedding cake 15

tortilla omelette (Spain) 12

tortuga turtle 17

tostador *m.* toaster 7

trabajador *adj.* hardworking 2

trabajar to work 1

traducir to translate 17

traer to bring 3

traje *m.* suit 8

   traje de baño *m.* swimsuit 8

tránsito traffic 17

trasnochar to stay overnight 14

trece thirteen LP.

treinta thirty LP.

tres three LP.

trescientos three hundred 6

tripié *m.* tripod 11

triste *adj.* sad 4

tú *pron.* you LP.

tu(s) *adj.* your (informal) 2

turismo tourism 1

U

última hora last minute 9

último *adj.* last 9

un(a) a, an 1

   un millón one million 8

   un momento just a minute 9

una vez *adv.* once 11

universidad *f.* university 1

uno one LP.

unos(as) some 1

uñas fingernails 12

usted(es) *pron.* you LP.

V

Vamos a ver. Let's see. 11

vaso glass (for water) 12

vegetal *m.* vegetable 5

veinte twenty LP.

velero sailboat 13

vender to sell 8

venir (e →ie, e → i) to come 4

ventana window 7

ventanilla window 16

ver to see 3

verano summer 6

verbo verb LP.

¿verdad? isn't that right? LP.

verde *adj.* green 2

verdura vegetable 5

veredas peatonales pedestrian sidewalks 13

vestido dress 8

   vestido(a) de dressed in 15

vestirse (e→i) to get dressed 6

viajar to travel 9

viaje *m.* trip 16

vida life 15

videocámara video camera 11

videocasetera videocassette player
(VCR) 7

viejo *adj.* old 2

viernes *m.* Friday 1

vino wine 5

   vino rosado rosé wine 5

   vino tinto red wine 5

viña vineyard 13

visitar to visit 3

vista view 16

viudo *adj.* widowed 4

vivir to live 2

volcando turning aside 14

volver (o→ue) to return, to go back 5

vosotros(as) *pron.* you (informal,
plural) LP.

vuelo flight 16

Y

y *conj.* and LP.

   ¿Y tú? And you? (informal) LP.

   ¿Y usted? And you? (formal) LP.

ya *adv.* already 7

   ya no no longer 11

yerna daughter-in-law 4

yerno son-in-law 4

yo *pron.* I LP.

yogur *m.* yogurt 10

Z

zanahoria carrot 10

zapatos shoes 8

ENGLISH-SPANISH GLOSSARY

A

a un(a) 1
a bit algo 9
aboard a bordo de 17
acccording to según 3
accessory accesorio 8
accompany acompañar 15
ache dolor 18
across enfrente de *prep.* 9
actor actor *m.* LP.
actress actriz *f.* LP.
adaptable adaptable adj. 2
add agregar 10
adore adorar 4
adverb adverbio LP.
    adverb of time adverbio de tiempo 6
advertisement anuncio 11
advise aconsejar 13
affection cariño 15
affirmative expression expresión afirmativa 9
after (-ing) después de + infinitive *prep.* 5
    after después (de) que *conj.* 15
    After you. Pase(n) usted(es). 9
afterwards después *adv.* 6
again otra vez *adv.* 11
age edad *f.* 2
agree estar de acuerdo 5
agreeable simpático *adj.* 2
air conditioning aire acondicionado 17
airplane avión *m.* 16
airport aeropuerto 9
aisle pasillo 16
alarm clock despertador *m.* 7
all todo 4; todos 2
allow dejar 14
almost casi *adv.* 11
alone solo(a) *adv.* 5
already ya *adv.* 7
also también *adv.* LP.
although aunque *conj.* 15

always siempre *adv.* 4
Amazon amazónico *adj.* 17
ambicious ambicioso adj. 2
an un(a) 1
and y *conj.* LP.
And you? (informal) ¿Y tú? LP.
And you? (formal) ¿Y usted? LP.
angry enojado *adj.* 4
animal animal *m.* 18
announce anunciar 11
announcement anuncio 11
answer contestar LP.
any algún; alguno(a/os/as) 9
anything algo 9
    Anything else? ¿Algo más? 10
apartamento apartment 1
appetizers (hors d'oeuvres) aperitivos, tapas 12
applaud aplaudir 15
apple manzana 10
approach acercarse (a) 18
April abril 3
arms brazos 6
around here por aquí 9
arrival llegada 16
arrive llegar 1
arriving from procedente de 16
article artículo 1
artistic artístico *adj.* 2
as many . . . as tantos(as)... como 6
as much . . . as tanto(a)... como 6
as . . . as tan... como 6
as soon as tan pronto como *conj.* 15
ask for pedir (e→i, e→i) LP.
asprin aspirina 18
astonish asustar 13
at a *prep.* LP.
    at first sight a primera vista 15
    at home en casa 1
    at last por fin *adv.* 11
    at night por la noche 1
    At what time? ¿A qué hora? 1
athletic atlético *adj.* 2
attend (a function) asistir (a) 4
attendance asistencia 15
August agosto 3
aunt tía 4
author autor(a) LP.
auto car 1
autumn otoño 6

B

baby bebé *m./f.* 2
backpack mochila 8
bad malo *adj.* 2
bag bolsa 8
baggage equipaje 16
bakery panadería 10
ball pelota 13
ballpoint pen bolígrafo 1
banana plátano 10
band orquesta 15
bank banco 5
banquet banquete *m.* 15
baptism bautismo 4
bargain regatear 10; ganga 11
barrel barril 18
baseball cap gorra de béisbol 8
bathroom baño 6; cuarto de baño 7
bathtub bañera 7
bay bahía 18
be ser LP.; estar 4
    be (a certain age) cumplir 6
    be able poder (o→ue) 5
    be afraid tener miedo 4
    be born nacer 6
    be careful tener cuidado 2
    be cold tener frío 6
    be glad alegrarse de 14
    be hot tener calor 6
    be hungry tener hambre 5
    be in a hurry tener prisa 4
    be jealous tener celos 4
    be located quedar 18
    be on vacation estar de vacaciones 12
    be pleasing gustar 3
    be pleasing gustar 5
    be right tener razón 4
    be sleepy tener sueño 4
    be sorry sentir (e→ie, e→i) 14
    be successful tener éxito 15
    be thirsty tener sed 5
beach playa 13
    beach resort balneario 13
bed cama 7
bedroom dormitorio 7
beef carne de vaca (res) *f.* 10
beer cerveza 5
before antes (de) que *conj.* 15

beforehand antes *adv.* 6
begin comenzar (e →ie) 4
behind detrás de *prep.* 9
believe creer 5
belt cinturón *m.* 8
beside al lado de 13
best mejor *adj.* 2
better mejor *adj.* 6
between entre *prep.* 9
beverage bebida 5
Bible Biblia 17
bicycle bicicleta 1
big grande *adj.* 2
bilingual bilingüe *adj.* 2
bill cuenta 12
biology biología 1
bird pájaro 17
birthday cumpleaños *m.* 6
black negro *adj.* 2
blood sangre *f.* 10
blouse blusa 8
blow one's nose sonarse 12
blowgun cerbatana 17
blue azul *adj.* 2
board abordar 16
boat barco 17
body cuerpo 6
boil hervir (ie, i)18
bone hueso 10
book libro 1
bookkeeping contabilidad *f.* 4
boot bota 8
boring aburrido *adj.* 8
bother molestar LP.
bottle botella 12
bouquet ramo 15
boy chico 13
boyfriend novio 1
bracelet brazalete *m.* 11
bread pan *m.* 5
breakfast desayuno 5
bride novia 15
bring traer 3
broccoli brécol *m.* 10
brother hermano 2
brother-in-law cuñado 4
brown marrón *adj.* 2
brush one's teeth lavarse los dientes 6
buckle up abrocharse 16

bus autobús *m.* 2
   bus station terminal de autobuses *f.* 9
business negocios 1
busy ocupado *adj.* 4
but pero *conj.* 1
butcher shop carnicería 10
butter mantequilla 5
butterfly mariposa 17
by por *prep.* 11
   by check con cheque 11
   by plane en avión 16
Bye! (informal) ¡Chao! LP.

C

cabin cabina 17
cake torta 10
calculator calculadora 11
Calculus cálculo 1
call llamar 15
calm down calmarse 14
camera cámara 11
camp acampar 10
can poder (o→ue) 5
canoe canoa 13
card tarjeta 8
carmel custard flan *m.* 5
carpentry capintería 4
carpet alfombra 7
carrot zanahoria 10
carry llevar 8
carry-on baggage equipaje (de mano) 16
cartoon dibujo animado 14
cash register caja 10
castle castillo 17
cat gato 2
catch agarrar 15
   catch tomar 15
cauliflower coliflor *f.* 10
CD disco compacto 7
center centro 1
century siglo 12
certain seguro *adj.* 14
chair silla 7
change cambiar 8
channel (TV) canal *m.* 14
charm embrujo 14
cheap barato *adj.* 11

Cheers! ¡Salud! 5
cheese queso 5
chemistry química 1
cherry cereza 10
chicken pollo 5
child niño(a) 4
childhood niñez *f.* 12
chore quehacer *m.* 7
Christmas Navidad *f.* 9
church iglesia 8
cigarette cigarrillo 16
city ciudad *f.* LP.
   city block cuadra 9
claim recoger (recojo) 16
class clase *f.* LP.
classmate compañero(a) de clase 1
classroom sala de clase LP.
clean limpio *adj.* 17
   clean the house limpiar la casa 7
clinic clínica 18
clock reloj *m.* 7
closed cerrado *adj.* 9
closet armario 7
clothes ropa 8
   clothes dryer secadora 7
   clothes washer lavadora 7
clothing ropa 6
cloudy nublado *adj.* 6
coast costa ; litoral *m.* 13
coffee café *m.* 5
cold *adj.*, noun frío 6
   cold catarro n. 18
color color *m.* 2
comb one's hair peinarse 6
come venir (e→ie) 4
comedy comedia 14
comfortable cómodo *adj.* 17
comment comentar 12
compact disk (CD) disco compacto 3
   compact disk player disco compacto 7
compañera couple 14
compañía company 1
competition competencia 14
complain quejarse (de) 14
computer computadora (Latin America) 11; ordenador (Spain) *m.* 11
computer science computación *f.* 1
concert concierto 3
condiment condimento 5

congratulate felicitar 15
Congratulations! ¡Felicidades! 6
conjunction conjunción *f.* 15
contest concurso 14
continue continuar 6; seguir (e→i) 9
cook cocinar 18
cookie galleta dulce 10
cookout parrillada 13
cool fresco *adj.* 6
corn maíz *m.* 17
   corn liquor chicha 17
cost costar (o→ue) 8; costo 11
cotton algodón *m.* 8
country(side) campo 13
couple pareja 15
course curso 1
courtship noviazgo 15
cousin primo(a) 4
crab cangrejo 18
cracker galleta salada 10
crafts artesanías 10
crash (into) chocar (con) 9
cross cruzar 17
cry llorar 11
cup taza 12
curl up derrumbarse 14
customs, customs area aduana 16

D

dance bailar 3
Dance baile *m.* 1
danger peligro 12
date fecha 3
   date (social) cita 15
daughter hija 4
   daughter-in-law nuera 4
day día *m.* 1
   day before yesterday anteayer
     adv. 7
December diciembre 3
decide decidir 9
decorate decorar 15
deep profundo *adj.* 13
delay demora 16
delicious rico *adj.* 5; sabroso 17
demonstrative adjective adjetivo
   demostrativo 5
dentist dentista *m./f.* LP.
departing for con destino a 16

department store almacén *m.* 8
departure salida 16
deserve merecer 13
desire desear 13
desk escritorio 7
dessert postre *m.* 5
developed desarrollado 18
diary diario 16
die morir (o→ue) 12; morirse (o→ue)
   18
difficult difícil *adj.* 1
dining room comedor 7
dinner cena 5
direction dirección *f.* 9
dirty sucio *adj.* 17
disagreeable antipático *adj.* 2
disappear abolirse 12
dishwasher lavaplatos *m.* 7
dismiss despedir (de) (e→i, e→i) 10
divorced divorciado *adj.* 4
do hacer 2
doctor médico 18
documentary documental *m.* 14
dog perro 2
doll muñeca 11
door puerta 7
dormitory residencia 6
double doble 17
   double bed cama doble 17
   double room cuarto doble 17
dormitory residencia 6
doubt duda 14
doubtful dudoso *adj.* 14
downtown centro 9
dozen docena 10
dramatic dramático *adj.* 2
dream (about) soñar (o→ue) (con) 7
dress vestido 8
dressed in vestido(a) de 15
dresser tocador *m.* 7
drink beber 2; tomar; bebida 5
dry cleaner's tintorería 11
dry off secarse 6
dugout canoe piragua 17
during durante *prep.* 3

E

each year cada año *adv.* 4
ear (inner) oído 18

ear (outer) oreja 18
earache dolor de oídos 18
early temprano *adv.* 17
earrings aretes *m. pl.* 8
ears (outer) orejas 6
ears (inner) orejas 18
easy fácil *adj.* 1
   easy chair sillón *m.* 7
eat comer 2
   eat out (in a restaurant) comer
     afuera 12
economics economía 1
education educación *f.* 1
egg huevo 5
eight ocho LP.
eight hundred ochocientos 6
eighteen dieciocho LP.
eighty ochenta 2
either . . . or o... o 9
elderly anciano *adj.* 2
electric appliance aparato eléctrico 7
   electric article artículo eléctrico
     11
elevator ascensor *m.* 17
eleven once LP.
embarrassed avergonzado *adj.* LP.
embrace, hug abrazo LP.
enchanted encantado *adj.* 18
enclosed cerrado *adj.* 10
end terminar 6
engaged comprometido *adj.* 15
engagement compromiso 15
engineer ingeniero (o) 1
engineering ingeniería 1
English (language) inglés *m.* 1
Enjoy your meal! ¡Buen provecho! 5
envelope sobre *m.* 11
essential imprescindible *adj.* 12
estado state 1
estudio study *noun* 1
even hasta *adv.* 15; aún *adv.* 18
event acontecimiento 14
everyone todos 6
examine examinar 18
example ejemplo LP.
exchange intercambiar 16
Excuse me Perdón 9; Con permiso 9
exercise hacer ejercicio 3
expensive caro *adj.* 11
explore explorar 18

eyeglasses anteojos 12

eyes ojos 6

F

face cara 6

   face (the street) dar (a la calle) 17

fall otoño 6

   fall asleep dormirse (o→ue) 6

   fall in love (with) enamorarse (de) 12

family familia 2

famous famoso *adj.* 16

far (away) lejos *adv.* 9

   far from lejos de *prep.* 9

farm granja 10

fasten (belt) abrocharse 16

fat gordo *adj.* 2

father padre *m.* 2

   Father (Dad) papá *m.* LP.

   father-in-law suegro 4

   father & the godfather refer to each other as *compadre* compadre 4

fatigue cansancio 18

February febrero 3

feel sentirse (e→ie, e→i) 13

   feel like tener ganas de (+ infinitive) 4

feet pies *m.* 6

fever *f.* fiebre 18

fiesta party 1

fifteen quince LP.

   fifteen-year-old girl quinceañera 6

fifty cincuenta 2

fill rellenar 10

film película 14

finally por fin *adv.* 11

find encontrar (o→ue) 11

fine bien *adv.* 1

Fine Arts bellas artes 1

Fine, thank you. Bien, gracias. LP.

fingernail uña 12

finish terminar 6

fire (dismiss) despedir (de) (e→i, e→i) 10

fireplace chimenea 7

first-class cabin camarote de primera 9

first primero 3

fish pescar 3; pescado 5

   fish market pescadería 10

fit (someone) quedarle (a uno) 8

five cinco LP.

five hundred quinientos 6

fixed fijo *adj.* 11

flamingo flamenco 18

flight vuelo 16

Florence Florencia 16

flower flor *f.* 15

   flower garden jardín *m.* 7

food comida 5

foot pie *m.* 16

for para *prep.* 1

   for (duration of time) por *prep.* 1

forbid prohibir 13

foreign extranjero *adj.* 16

forever para siempre 4

forget olvidar 8

fork tenedor *m.* 12

form formulario 17

forty cuarenta 2

four cuatro LP.

   four hundred cuatrocientos 6

fourteen catorce LP.

French (language) francés *m.* 1

   French fries (Latin America) papas fritas 5

   French fries (Spain) patatas fritas 12

fresh fresco *adj.* 10

Friday viernes *m.* 1

fried frito *adj.* 12

   fried shrimp flavored with garlic ajillo 12

   fried eggs huevos fritos 5

friend amigo(a) 1

friendship amistad *f.* 15

frighten asustar 13

from de *prep.* LP.

front desk recepción *f.* 17

fruitful fecundo *adj.* 10

fruit fruta 5

furniture muebles *m. pl.* 7

G

game juego 3; partido 14

   game show programa de concusos *m.* 14

garter liga 15

gas station gasolinera 1

gate puerta 16

generous generoso *adj.* 2

geography geografía 1

geology geología 1

geometry geometría 1

German (language) alemán *m.* 1

gesture gesto 2

get a suntan broncearse 13

   get along well llevarse bien 15

   get dressed vestirse (e→i) 6

   get hurt lastimarse 9

   get in line hacer cola 6

   get married casarse 15

   get near acercarse (a) 18

   get off bajar(se) (de) 9

   get on/in subir(se) (a) 9

   get sick enfermarse 18

   get up levantarse 6

gift regalo 6

girl chica 13

girlfriend novia 1

give dar 3

glass (for water) vaso 12

   glass (for wine) copa 12

gloves guantes *m. pl.* 8

go ir 3; lograr 12

   go back volver (o→ue) 5

   go bike riding montar en bicicleta 3

   go by plane ir en avión 16

   go canoeing pasear en canoa 13

   go horseback riding montar a caballo 3

   go off (e.g., an alarm) sonar (o→ue) 7

   go shopping ir de compras 3

   go to bed acostarse (o→ue) 6

   go to the movies ir al cine 3

godfather padrino 4

godmother madrina 4

good bueno *adj.* 2

   Good afternoon! ¡Buenas tardes! LP.

   Good evening! ¡Buenas noches! LP.

   Good morning! ¡Buenos días! LP.

   Good night! ¡Buenas noches! LP.

Good-bye! ¡Adiós! LP.

good-looking guapo *adj.* 2

gram gramo 10
grandaughter nieta 4
grandfather abuelo 4
grandma abuelita 4
grandmother abuela 4
grandpa abuelito 4
grandparents abuelos 3
grandson nieto 4
gray gris *adj.* 2
great bueno 1; estupendo *adj.* 14
   great-grandfather bisabuelo 4
   great-grandmother bisabuela 4
green verde *adj.* 2
greet saludar
groceries comestibles *m. pl.* 10
groom novio 15
growth crecimiento 13
guest invitado 15
guide guía *m./f.* 17
guitar guitarra 1
gymasium gimnasio 3

H

hair pelo 6
hair dryer secador de pelo *m.* 11
   hair salon peluquería 11
half mitad *f.* 10
ham jamón *m.* 5
hand mano *f.* 1
handkerchief pañuelo 14
hanging colgante *adj.* 13
happiness felicidad *f.* 15
happy contento *adj.* 4; feliz *adj.* 6
hardworking trabajador *adj.* 2
hat sombrero 8
have tener (ie) 2
   have a cookout hacer una parrilla da 13
   have a good time pasarlo bien 14
   Have a nice trip! ¡Buen viaje! 16
   have a picnic hacer un picnic 13
   have breakfast desayunar 5
   have fun divertirse (e→ie, e→i) 8
   have just acabar de + infinitive 6
   have lunch almorzar (o→ue) 5
   have supper (dinner) cenar 5
   have to tener que + infinitive 7
he él *pron.* LP.
head cabeza 18

headache dolor de cabeza 18
health salud *f.* 10
hear oír 7
help ayudar 10
hemisphere hemisferio 16
her su *adj.* LP.; su(s) *adj.* 2; la *pron.* 7
here aquí *adv.* 1
Hi! ¡Hola! (informal) LP.
high alto *adj.* 10
highway carretera 16
hike in the mountains caminar nor las montañas 13
hill cerro 13
him lo *pron.* 7
his su(s) *adj.* 2
history historia 1
holiday día festivo *m.* 9
home hogar *m.* 11
honest honesto *adj.* 2
honey (term of endearment) amor 15
honeymoon luna de miel 15
hope esperar 14
Hope so! ¡Ojalá! 14
hors d'oeuvres tapas 12
hot caliente *adj.* 5
hotel management hotelería 4
hour hora 1
house casa 7
how cómo *adv.* LP.
How? ¿Cómo? LP.
   How are you? (informal) ¿Cómo estás? LP.
   How are you? (informal) ¿Cómo está usted? LP.
   How interesting! ¡Qué interesante! LP.
   How many? ¿Cuántos(as)? LP.
   How old are you? ¿Cuántos años tienes? LP.
   How's everything? (informal) ¿Qué tal? LP.
hug abrazo LP.
   hug (each other) abrazar(se) 15
Huh? ¿Cómo? 5
human humano *adj.* 18
humanities, letters letras 1
humidity humedad *f.* 17
hunt cazar 17
hurt (someone) doler (a alguien) (o→ue) 18
husband marido 4

I

I yo *pron.* LP.
   I (don't) like (no) me gusta + infinitive 1
   I am (19 years old) tengo (19 años) LP.
   I know (it) lo sé LP.
   I wish you well. ¡Qué le vaya bien! 9
   I would like me gustaría 4
I'm (very) sorry lo siento (mucho) 9
ice hielo 12
ice cream helado 5
iced tea té helado *m.* 5
idiom modismo *m.* LP.
in en LP.
   in a little while al poco tiempo 13
   in case (of) en caso (de) que *conj.* 15
   in cash en efectivo 11
   in front delante de *prep.* 9
   in the afternoon de la tarde 1
   in the evening de la noche 1
   in the morning de la mañana 1
incredible increíble *adj.* 18
Indian indio(a) 17
indirect pronoun pronombre indirec to 5
inexpensive barato *adj.* 11
information información *f.* LP.
inn albergue *m.* 17
insist (on) insistir (en) 13
instructor profesor(a) LP.
intellectual intelectual *adj.* 2
intelligent inteligente *adj.* 2
interpreter intérprete *m./f.* 1
introduce yourself presentarse LP.
introductions (to someone) presentaciones LP.
intuitive intuitivo *adj.* 2
invite invitar 3
iron hierro 10
iron planchar 14
Isn't that right? ¿Verdad? LP.
It's (im)possible. Es (im)posible. 14
   It's a shame. Es una lástima. 14
   It's bad. Es malo. 14
   It's bad out. Hace mal tiempo. 6
   It's better. Es mejor. 14
   It's clear. Está despejado. 6
   It's cloudy. Está nublado. 6

It's cold. Hace frío. 6
It's good. Es bueno. 14
It's hot. Hace calor. 6
It's important. Es importante. 14
It's logical. Es lógico. 14
It's necessary. Es necesario. 14
It's nice out. Hace buen tiempo. 6
It's raining. Está lloviendo. 6
It's raining/snowing. Está lloviendo/nevando. 6
It's ridiculous. Es ridículo. 14
It's snowing. Está nevando. 6
It's sunny. Hace sol. 6
It's time to Es hora de + infinitive 7
It's windy. Hace viento. 6
it (feminine) la *pron.* 7
it (masculine) lo *pron.* 7
It rains. Llueve. 6
It snows. Nieva. 6
its su(s) *adj.* 2

J

jacket chaqueta 8
jam mermelada 5
January enero 3
jewelry joyas 11
jewelry store joyería 11
jog correr 3
jot down apuntar 12
Journalism periodismo 1
joy alegría 9
juice jugo 5
July julio 3
June junio 3
jungle selva 16
just solamente *adv.* 11
    just a minute un momento 9

K

key llave *f.* 17
kind tipo 3
kiss (each other) besar(se) 15
kitchen cocina 7
knife cuchillo 12
knit tejer 14
knot ovillo 14

know (a fact, how) saber 3; **(a person, place)** conocer LP.

L

lake lago 13
lamp lámpara 7
land terrestre *adj.* 18
language idioma *m.* LP.
languages lenguas 1
large grande *adj.* 2
last último *adj.* 9
    last minute última hora 9
    last month mes pasado *m.* 7
    last night anoche *adv.* 7
    last week semana pasada *adv.* 7
    last year año pasado *adv.* 7
later más tarde *adv.* 6
laugh reírse (e→i, e→i) 11
law derecho 1
lazy perezoso *adj.* 2
leader líder *m./f.* LP.
learn aprender 2
leave (go out) salir 3
    leave (behind) dejar 14
lechería dairy store (Spain) 10
lecture conferencia LP.
legs piernas 6
lemon limón *m.* 2
lemonade limonada 5
less . . . than menos... que 6
lesson lección *f.* LP.
let (allow) dejar 14
Let's see. Vamos a ver. 11
letter carta 2
lettuce lechuga 10
level nivel *m.* 10
library biblioteca 1
life vida 15
lighter (in weight) más ligera 5
like como *adv.* 3; gustar 5
listen escuchar 1
liter litro 10
literature literatura 1
little pequeño *adj.* 2
    little boat botecito 9
live vivir 2
living room sala 7
logical lógico *adj.* 14

long largo *adj.* 15
look for buscar (qu) 7
loud fuerte *adj.* 12
love querer (e→ie) 4; amor *m.* 15
low bajo *adj.* 10
luggage equipaje *m.* 16
lunch almuerzo 5; comida 5

M

made up arreglado *adj.* 17
main dish plato principal 5
make hacer 2
    make a stop (on a flight) (at) hacer escala (en) 16
    make one's bed hacer la cama 7
    make up (a room) arreglar 17
man hombre *m.* 4
manager gerente 17
map mapa *m.* 1
    map (of a city) plano 9
March marzo 3
marine marino *adj.* 18
market mercado 9
married casado *adj.* 4
marry casarse 15
mass misa 6
match (game) partido 14
May mayo 3
maybe tal vez 16
me me *pron.* 7
meal comida 5
meat carne *f.* 5
medical médico *adj.* 18
medicine medicina 1
meet (someone) conocer 3
merchandise mercancías 11
Merry Christmas Feliz Navidad 9
Mexican mexicano *adj.* 2
microwave oven horno de microondas 7
milk leche *f.* 5
million millón *m.* 8
minus menos LP.
mirror espejo 7
Miss señorita (Srta.) LP.
missionary misionero(a) 17
molest importunar LP.
Monday lunes *m.* 1
money dinero 8

monkey mono 17

month mes *m.* 3

monument monumento 16

more más *adv.* 5

    more . . . than más... que 6

mother & godmother refer to each other as *comadre* comadre 4

    Mother (Mom) mamá LP.

    mother madre *f.* 2

    mother-in-law suegra 4

motocicleta motorcycle 1

motorized motorizado *adj.* 17

mountain montaña 13

mouth boca 18

move (to a place) mudarse 7

movie película 14

    movie theater cine *m.* 3

mow the lawn cortar el césped 7

Mr., sir señor (Sr.) LP.

Mrs., ma'am señora (Sra.) LP.

museum museo 3

música music 1

musical (play) función musical *f.* 14

my mi *pron.* LP.; mi(s) *adj.* 2

    My name is . . . Me llamo... LP.

    My pleasure. El gusto es mío. LP.

mystery film película del intriga 14

myth mito 14

N

name nombre *m.* LP.

napkin servilleta 12

nasty antipático *adj.* 2

near cerca de *prep.* 9; cercano *adj.* 9

nearby cerca *adv.* 9

necklace collar *m.* 8

necktie corbata 8

need necesitar 5

negative expression expresión negativa 9

neither tampoco 9

    neither . . . nor ni... ni 9

nephew sobrino 4

never nunca 9

new nuevo *adj.* 2

newlyweds recién casados 15

news noticias 14

newspaper periódico 2

next próximo *adj.* 15

next to al lado de *prep.* 9

nice simpático *adj.* 2

    Nice to meet you. ¡Mucho gusto! LP.

    Nice to meet you. Encantado(a). LP.

niece sobrina 4

nine nueve LP.

    nine hundred novecientos 6

nineteen diecinueve LP.

ninety noventa 2

no longer ya no 11

no one nadie 9

nobody nadie 9

noise ruido 17

non-smoking section sección de no fumar *f.* 16

none ningún 9; ninguno(a) 9

nonstop (flight) sin escala 16

nose nariz *f.* 6

not any ningún 9; ninguno(a) 9

    not at all nada 9

    not . . . either tampoco 9

nothing nada 9

    Nothing else. Nada más. 10

noun sustantivo LP.

November noviembre 3

now ahora *adv.* LP.

nowadays hoy día 2

number número LP.

O

occur desarrollar 13

océano ocean 1

October octubre 3

of de *prep.* LP.

    of course cómo no 5

often muchas veces *adv.* 4

oil aceite *m.* 12

okay bien *adv.* 1; bueno 1

old viejo *adj.* 2

older mayor *adj.* 4

olive aceituna 10

omelette (Spain) tortilla 12

on credit a crédito 11

    on the dot en punto 1

once una vez *adv.* 11

one uno LP.

    one hundred cien 6

one million un millón 8

one thousand mil 6

one year ago hace un año 7

one-half medio 10

one-way ticket boleto de ida 16

onion cebolla 10

only solamente *adv.* 11

open abierto *adj.* 9; abrir 8

    open-air al aire libre 10

orange (fruit) naranja 5

orange (color) anaranjado *adj.* 2

order pedir (e→i) 5; pedido 12; decir (e→i) 13

other otro(a) *adj.* LP.

ought to deber (+ infinitive) 2

our nuestro *adj.* 2

oven horno 7

overcoat abrigo 8

owner dueño 17

P

pain dolor 18

painting pintura 1; cuadro 7

país country 1

pajamas pijama *m.* 6

pants pantalones *m. pl.* 8

paper papel *m.* 1

park parque *m.* 2

parrot papagayo 12

parsley perejil *m.* 10

part parte *f.* 6

party fiesta 3

passenger pasajero(a) 16

passport pasaporte *m.* 16

    passport control inmigración *f.* 16

pastime pastiempo 3

pastry pastel *m.* 5

    pastry shop pastelería 10

patient paciente *adj.* 2; paciente *m./f.* 18

pay for pagar 8

peach durazno, melocotón *m.* 10

pear pera 10

pedestrian sidewalk vereda peatonal 13

peel pelar 18

pelican pelícano 18

pencil lápiz *m.* 1

península península 1

people gente *f.* LP.

pepper pimiento 10

    pepper (spice) pimienta 12

    pepper shaker pimentero 12

perhaps tal vez 16

permit permitir 13

person from Valparaíso, Chile porteño(a) 13

personality personalidad *f.* 2

photo foto *f.* 3

    photo album álbum de fotos *m.* 11

photographic article artículo fotográfico 11

physical characteristic característica física 2

physician médico 18

pick up recoger (recojo) 16

    pick up (someone) pasar (por) 3

picture foto *f.* 3

piece pedazo 12

pill pastilla 18

pineapple piña 10

pink rosado *adj.* 2

piranha piraña 17

pitcher (for liquids) jarra 12

pity lástima 14

place lugar *m.* 6

plan on pensar (e→ie) 4

planetarium planetario 16

plate plato 12

play (a game) jugar (o→ue) 5

    play (an instrument) tocar 3

    play cards jugar (a las) cartas 3

    play tennis jugar (al) tenis 3

pleasant agradable 16

please por favor 1

plus más LP.

political science ciencias políticas 1

poop deck popa 9

pork carne de cerdo (puerco) *f.* 10

possessive adjective adjetivo posesivo 2

post office oficina de correos 9

postcard tarjeta postal 11

potato (Latin America) papa 5; **(Spain)** patata 12

prefer preferir (e→ie, e→i) 4

pregnant embarazada *adj.* LP.

preparar la comida cocinar 12

president presidente *m./f.* LP.

pretty bonito *adj.* 2

print film rollo para fotos 11

printer impresora 11

private privado *adj.* 17

problem problema *m.* LP.

professor profesor(a) LP.

profession profesión *f.* LP.

pronoun pronombre *m.* LP.

prosperous próspero *adj.* 2

provided (that) con tal (de) que *conj.* 15

purse bolsa 8

put poner 3

    put (in) meter 10

    put (in) meter 18

    put aside soslayan 14

    put on (music) poner 3

    put on (lotion) aplicarse 13

    put on makeup pintarse 6

pyschology sicología 1

Q

quality calidad *f.* 11

quantity cantidad *f.* 10

quiet reposado *adj.* 10

R

race carrera 3

radio radio 1

railroad ferrocarril *m.* 13

    railway station estación de trenes *f.* 9

rain lluvia 6

ranch hacienda 17

range (for cooking and baking) estufa 7

rather well bastante bien. LP.

reach lograr 12

read leer 2

reading lectura LP.

Really? ¿En serio? 14

receive recibir 2

recommend recomendar (e→ie) 13

recreation esparcimiento 13

red rojo *adj.* 2

    red wine vino tinto 5

reduce (in price) rebajar 11

reduced (in price) rebajado *adj.* 11

reduction (in price) rebaja 11

register registrarse 17

relative pariente *m.* 4

remainder demás *adj.* 17

remember recordar (o→ue) 7

rent alquilar 13

rented en arriendo 13

reporter reportero(a) LP.

request pedir (e→i) 13; rogar (o→ue) 15

reserved reservado *adj.* 2

resident of Santiago, Chile santiaguino(a) 13

rest descansar 1; demás *adj.* 17

retire jubilarse 10

return regresar 1; volver (o→ue) 5

review repasar 10

rice arroz *m.* 5

ridiculous ridículo *adj.* 14

right now ahora mismo *adv.* 13

ring anillo 11

river río 13

rock roca 17

roll panecillo 10

room (Latin America) cuarto 7; pieza 14; **(Spain)** habitación *f.* 17

roommate compañero(a) de cuarto 1

rosé wine vino rosado 5

roundtrip de ida y vuelta 16

rug alfombra 7

run correr 3

rust óxido 9

S

sad triste *adj.* 4

safety belt cinturón de seguridad 16

sail pasear en velero 13

sailboat velero 13

sailor marinero(a) 18

salad ensalada 5

sale (Spain) rebaja 11

salesclerk dependiente 8

salt sal *f.* 12

    salt shaker salero 12

saludo greeting 1

same mismo *adj.* 14

sandals sandalias 8

Saturday sábado 1

sausage salchicha 10

save (money) ahorrar 11

say decir (e→i) 5

    say good-bye despedirse (de) (e→i) LP.

scare asustar 13

schedule horario 16

school escuela 1

science ciencia 1

    science fiction film película de ciencia ficción 14

scientist científico(a) 18

screen pantalla 14

scuba dive bucear 13

sculpture escultura 16

seal foca 18

season temporada 3; estación *f.* 6

seat asiento 16

security seguridad *f.* 16

    security control control de seguridad *m.* 16

see ver 3

    See you later! ¡Hasta luego! LP.

    See you tomorrow! ¡Hasta mañana! LP.

sell vender 8

September septiembre 3

serious (medical) grave *adj.* 18

serve servir (e→i, e→i) 5

server (Spain) camarero(a) 12

set the table poner la mesa 7

seven siete LP.

    seven hundred setecientos 6

seventeen diecisiete LP.

seventy setenta 2

shake hands darse la mano 15

shame lástima 14

shave afeitarse 6

shaver máquina de afeitar 11

she ella *pron.* LP.

shellfish mariscos 5

shirt camisa 8

shoes zapatos 8

shop tienda 10

    shop window aparador *m.* 10

shopping mall centro comercial 8

short (in height) bajo *adj.* 2

shorts pantalones cortos *m. pl.* 8

should deber (+ infinitive) 2

shout gritar 12

show mostrar (o→ue) 11; **(movie)** poner 14; **(theatrical)** función *f.* 14

shower ducha 7; ducharse 6

shrimp gambas (los camarones) 10

sick enfermo *adj.* 4

sign firmar 15

sing cantar 3

singer cantante *m./f.* 14

single soltero *adj.* 4; sencillo 17

    single bed cama sencilla 17

    single room cuarto sencillo 17

sink lavabo 7

    sink into hundirse 10

sister hermana 2

sister-in-law cuñada 4

sit down sentar (e→ie) 12

situated situado *adj.* 16

six seis LP.

    six hundred seiscientos 6

sixteen dieciséis LP.

sixty sesenta 2

size (clothing) talla 8

    size tamaño 18

skate patinar 3

ski esquiar 3

skirt falda 8

sleep dormir (o→ue) 5

slide film rollo para diapositivas 11

slowly lentamente *adv.* 15

small pequeño *adj.* 2

    small flag bandarín 10

smile sonreír (e→i, e→i) 15

smoke fumar 12

smoking section sección de fumar *f.* 16

snack merienda 5

snorkel hacer el esnórquel 13

snow nieve *f.* 6

so así 9

    so (that) para que *conj.* 15

    So-so. Más o menos. LP.

soap jabón *m.* 17

    soap opera telenovela 4

soccer fútbol *m.* 3

socks calcetines *m. pl.* 8

soft drink (Latin America) refresco 5; **(Spain)** gaseosa 12

solamente only 1

some algún 9; alguno(a/os/as) 9; unos(as) 1

somebody alguien 9

someone alguien 9

something algo 9

sometimes a veces *adv.* 11

son hijo 4

son-in-law yerno 4

soon pronto *adv.* 6

sorry lo siento 9

soup sopa 5

souvenir recuerdo 16

Spaniard español(a) *noun* 2

Spanish (language) español *m.* LP.

speak hablar 1

specialty especialidad *f.* 12

spend (time) pasar 9

    spend (money) gastar 11

spoon cuchara 12

sport deporte *m.* 3

sports program programa deportivo *m.* 14

spring primavera 6

squid calamar *m.* 12

star estrella 12

start comenzar (e→ie) 4

stationery papel de cartas *m.* 11

    stationery store papelería 11

stay overnight trasnocharse 14

steak bistec *m.* 5

stepbrother hermanastro 2

stepfather padrastro 2

stepmother madrastra 2

stepsister hermanastra 2

stereo estéreo 7

still todavía *adv.* 7

stingy tacaño *adj.* 2

stockings medias 8

stomach estómago 18

stop parar(se) 9; **(travel)** escala 16; parada 18

stop over escala 16

store tienda 8

story cuento 12

stove estufa 7

straight ahead todo derecho *prep.* 9

strawberry fresa 10

street corner esquina 9

strong fuerte *adj.* 12

student estudiante *m./f.* LP.

study estudiar 1

style estilo 11

subway metro 3

suddenly de repente 9

sugar azúcar *m.* 10

suggest sugerir (e→ie, e→i) 13

suit traje *m.* 8

suitcase maleta 9

summer verano 6

sunbathe tomar el sol 13

Sunday domingo 1

sunglasses anteojos para el sol 8

suntan lotion crema bronceadora 13

supermarket supermercado 9

supper cena 5

surf correr las olas 13

surprise sorpresa 13; sorprender 14

sweater suéter *m.* 8

sweets dulces *m./pl.* 6

swim nadar 3

swimmer narador(a) 13

swimming natación *f.* 13

   swimming pool piscina 3

swimsuit traje de baño *m.* 8

Switzerland Suiza 18

synagogue sinagoga 8

T

T-shirt camiseta 8

table mesa 6

take tomar 1

   take (photographs) sacar 3

   take a bath bañarse 6

   take a shower ducharse 6

   take advantage aprovechar(se) 11

   take care (of oneself) cuidar(se) 18

   take off (clothing) quitarse 6

   take out sacar 12

   take out the garbage sacar la basura 7

   take place efectuarse 15; tener lugar 15

talk hablar 1

   talk show programa de entrevistas *m.* 14

tall alto *adj.* 2

tap (faucet) grifo 18

tape cinta 1

   tape recorder grabadora 11

   tape recording cinta 1

tax impuesto 16

tea té *m.* 5

teach enseñar 13

teacher profesor(a) LP.

team equipo 3

teeth dientes *m.* 6

telephone teléfono 1

   telephone booth cabina telefónica 3

tell decir (e→i) 5

   tell (a story) (about) contar (o→ue) 10

ten diez LP.

tengo I have 1

terrace terraza 7

test examen *m.* 1

textbook libro de texto 1

thank dar las gracias 9

Thank you (very much)! ¡(Muchas) gracias! LP.

that esa ese, eso *adj.* 5; esa (+ *f.* noun) 4

   that (way over there) aquel *adj.* 5

   that (way over there) aquella *adj.* 5

   that one ésa , ese *pron.* 5

   that one (way over there) aquél, aquélla *pron.* 5

That's all. Eso es todo. 10

the el, la, los, las 1

   the least el (la, los, las) menos 6

   the most el (la, los, las) más 6

theater teatro 14

them (feminine) las *pron.* 7; **(masculine)** los *pron.* 7

then entonces *adv.* 6; luego *adv.* 6

there allí *adv.* LP.

there is, there are hay LP.

therefore, so por eso 8

these estas, estos *adj.* 5

   these (here) éstas, éstos*pron.* 5

they ellas, ellos *pron.* LP.

thin delgado *adj.* 2

think pensar (e →ie) 4; creer 5

thirteen trece LP.

thirty treinta LP.

this esta, ests, esto *adj.* 5

   this one ésta, éste *pron.* 5

those esas, esos *adj.* 5

   those (there) ésas,ésos *pron.* 5

   those (way over there) aquellas *adj.* 5

   those (way over there) aquéllas, aquellos, aquéllos *pron.* 5

three tres LP.

   three hundred trescientos 6

throw tirar 15

Thursday jueves *m.* 1

thus así 9

ticket billete, boleto *m.* 16

time tiempo 3

tip (gratuity) propina 12

tired cansado *adj.* 4

title título LP.

   title used with a man's first name don LP.

   title used with a woman's first name doña LP.

to a *prep.* LP.

   to me me *pron.* 5

   to the left a la izquierda *prep.* 9

   to the right a la derecha *prep.* 9

   to us nos *pron.* 5

   to you (formal), to him, to her le *pron.* 5

   to you (informal) os *pron.* 5

   to you (informal) te *pron.* 5

   to you, to them les *pron.* 5

   to/for me me *pron.* 8

   to/for us nos *pron.* 8

   to/for you (formal), him, her le *pron.* 8

   to/for you (formal), them les *pron.* 8

   to/for you (informal) os, te *pron.* 8

toast pan tostado *m.* 5; brindis *m.* 15

toaster tostador *m.* 7

today hoy 3

toilet paper papel higiénico *m.* 17

tolerant tolerante *adj.* 2

tomato tomate *m.* 5

tonight esta noche 3

too (also) también *adv.* LP.

   too much demasiado *adv.* 17

torte torta 10

tortoise galápago 18

touch tocar 10

toward hacia *adv.* 9

towel toalla 13

town pueblo 8

   town square plaza 9

toy juguete *m.* 9

traffic tránsito 17

translate traducir 17

travel viajar 9

   travel agency agencia de viajes 16

traveler's check cheque de viajero *m.* 16

tree árbol *m.* 17

trip viaje *m.* 16

tripod tripié *m.* 11

try on probarse (o→ue) 8

Tuesday martes *m.* 1

turismo Tourism 1

turn (a certain age) cumplir 6

    turn (on a street) doblar 9

    turn on poner 14

turning aside volcando 14

turtle tortuga 17

TV set televisor 1

twelve doce LP.

twenty veinte LP.

twice dos veces *adv.* 11

twin gemelo(a) 2

two dos LP.

    two hundred doscientos 6

    two hundred thousand doscientos(as) mil 8

    two million dos millones 8

    two thousand dos mil 8

    (two) years ago hace (dos) años 7

type tipo 3

typewriter máquina de escribir 11

U

ugly feo *adj.* 2

umbrella paraguas *m.* 8

uncle tío 4

understand comprender 2

United States Estados Unidos *m. pl.* LP.

university universidad *f.* 1

unless a menos que *conj.* 15

untie desatar 10

until hasta *adv.* 6; hasta que *conj.* 15

up to hasta *adv.* 9

us nos *pron.* 7

V

vacuum pasar la aspiradora 7

    vacuum cleaner aspiradora 7

vegetable vegetal *m.* 5; verdura 5

vegetation follaje *m.* 13

verb verbo LP.

very often muchas veces *adv.* 11

Very well! ¡Muy bien! LP.

video camera videocámara 11

    video movie película de vídeo 3

videocassette player (VCR) videocasetera 7

videotape caseta de vídeo 11

viejo old *adj.* 11

view vista 16

vineyard viña 13

visit visit 3

W

wait for esperar 8

waiting area sala de espera 16

wake up despertarse (e→ie) 6

walk caminar 3

want querer (e →ie) 4

wash lavar 6

    wash clothes lavar la ropa 7

    wash the dishes lavar los platos 7

    wash up lavarse 6

watch reloj *m.* 7

    watch television mirar (la) televisión 3

water agua *m.* 5

waterski esquiar sobre el agua 13

wave ola 13

we nosotros(as) *pron.* LP.

wear llevar 8

weather forecast pronóstico 6

weather report pronóstico del tiempo 14

wedding boda 15

    wedding (Chile) matrimonio 15

    wedding cake torta nupcial 15

    wedding march marcha nupcial 15

Wednesday miércoles *m.* 1

week semana 1

weekend fin de semana *m.* 3

well bien *adv.* 1; bueno 1; pues 4

    well, fine bien *adv.* LP.

went fue 7

western film película del oeste 14

what ¿cuál? ¿cuáles? 2

What? ¿Cómo? 5

What? ¿Qué? LP.

    What's new? ¿Qué hay de nuevo? 3

What a shame! ¡Qué lástima! 14

What can I do for you? ¿En qué puedo servirle? 8

What do you think? ¿Qué te parece? 3

What else? ¿Qué más? 10

What time is it? ¿Qué hora es? 1

What would you like (to eat)? ¿Qué te apetece? 5

What's the matter with you? ¿Qué te pasa? 6

What's the problem? ¿Qué tiene usted? 18

What's the weather like? ¿Qué tiempo hace? 6

What's your address? ¿Cuál es tu dirección? LP.

What's your name? ¿Cómo se llama usted? (formal) LP.; ¿Cuál es tu nombre? (informal) LP.

What's your name? ¿Como te llamas? (informal) LP.

What's your telephone number? ¿Cuál es tu número de teléfono? LP.

when cuando *conj.* 15

When? ¿Cuándo? 1

Where are you from? ¿De dónde eres tú? (informal) LP.

Where are you from? ¿De dónde es usted? (formal) LP.

Where from? ¿De dónde? LP.

where? ¿dónde? 1

which one(s) ¿cuál? ¿cuáles? 2

while mientras *adv.* 9

white blanco *adj.* 2

Who? ¿Quién(es)? LP.

Whose? ¿De quién(es)? 2

why? ¿por qué? 1

widowed viudo *adj.* 4

wife esposa 4

wild boar jabalí *m.* 17

win ganar 3, 14

window (building) ventana 7

    window (plane, train) ventanilla 16

winner ganador(a) 14

winter invierno 6

wish desear 13

with con *prep.* LP.

    with me conmigo 3

    with you contigo 15

without sin *prep.* 9

without sin que *conj.* 15

witness testigo 15

woman mujer *f.* 4

wonderful estupendo *adj.* 14

word palabra LP.

work trabajar 1

    work (function) funcionar 11

world mundo 2

World Cup Copa Mundial 3

worried preocupado *adj.* 4

worry (about) preocuparse (por) 9

worse peor *adj.* 6

write escribir 2

Y

yard patio 7

year año 3

yellow amarillo *adj.* 2

yes sí LP.

yesterday ayer *adv.* 7

yet todavía *adv.* 7

yogurt yogur *m.* 10

You're kidding! ¡No me digas! 15

you usted(es), tú *pron.* LP.

    you (formal) la , las, lo, los *pron.* 7

    you (informal) os, te *pron.* 7

    you (informal, plural) vosotros(as) *pron.* LP.

You're welcome. De nada. 3

young joven *adj.* 2

younger menor *adj.* 4

your (formal) su(s) *adj.* 2; **(informal)** tu(s) *adj.* 2

youth juventud *f.* 17

Z

zero cero LP.

zoo parque zoológico *m.* 17

INDEX

PHOTO CREDITS

Unless specified below, all photos in this text were selected from the Heinle & Heinle Image Resource Bank. The Image Resource Bank is Heinle & Heinle's proprietary collection of tens of thousands of photographs related to the study of foreign language and culture.

pg. 2 Robert Fried/Stock Boston;   **pg. 10 (left)** Robert Frerck/Odyssey; **(center)** J.P. Courau/DDB Stock Photo; **(right)** Ulrike Welsch;   **pg. 21** David Simson/DAS Photo;   **pg. 22** Robert Fried/Stock Boston;   **pg. 44** Ulrike Welsch; **pg. 60** Robert Fried/Stock Boston;   **pg. 72** Cameramann/The Image Works; **pg. 93** Daemmrich/ The Image Works;   **pg. 94** Daemmrich/Stock Boston; **pg. 100** José Carrillo/ PhotoEdit;   **pg. 119** Erik Neuhaus/Stock Boston;   **pg. 139** Ulrike Welsch;   **pg. 170**   Ulrike Welsch;   **pg. 176 (top)** Ulrike Welsch **(center)** Rob Crandal/The Image Works; **(bottom)** Ulrike Welsch;   **pg. 169** Peter Menzel/ Stock Boston;   **pg. 220** D. Donne Bryant;   **pg. 230 (left)** Suzanne L. Murphy/ DDB Stock Photo;   **(right)** Bob Daemmrich/Stock Boston; **pg. 264** Robert Fried/DDB Stock Photo;   **pg. 270** E.R. Greenberg/PhotoEdit; **pg. 273** Mangino/The Image Works;   **pg. 281** E.R. Greenberg/PhotoEdit;   **pg. 315** Ulrike Welsch;   **pg. 316** James Marshall/The Image Works;   **pg. 319** J. Halber/DDB Stock Photo;   **pg. 338** A. Ramey/PhotoEdit;   **pg. 383** A.E. Zuckerman/PhotoEdit **pg. 384**   Robert Fried/Stock Boston;   **pg. 397** Ulrike Welsch;   **pg. 407** Robert Fried/Stock Boston;   **pg. 408 (top)** William J. Jahoda; **(bottom)** Ulrike Welsh; **pg. 409** Ulrike Welsch;   **pg. 417** Steven Rubin/The Image Works; **pg.431** Virginia Ferrero/DDB Stock Photo;   **pg. 432** Virginia Ferrero/DDB Stock Photo; **pg. 433 (top)** E.R. Greenberg/PhotoEdit; **(bottom)** E.R. Greenberg/PhotoEdit.

TEXT CREDITS

pg. 32 courtesy of *Editorial Televisa*, Mexico City;   **Pg. 67** *géminis* reprinted from *Coqueta*, año 12, no. 12, diciembre 1990;   **pg. 87** *Cineguía* reprinted from Excelsior, 25 octubre 1992, p. 3-E;   **pg. 133** *Lo positivo y lo negativo del café* reprinted from *Buenhogar*, año 23, no. 11, 17 mayo 1988, **pg. 165** pronósticos reprinted from *El Nuevo Día*, 9 marzo 1989, p. 2;   **pg. 174** photo and caption of dormitorio-estudio reprinted from *Buenhogar*, no. 10, 7 mayo 1985, p. 5C, courtesy of *Editorial Televisa*, Mexico City;   **pg. 188** FORMICA reprinted from

América del Sur

GUATEMALA
HONDURAS
DOR
NICARAGUA
COSTA RICA
PANAMÁ

MAR CARIBE

Barranquilla
Cartagena
Maracaibo
Caracas
R. Orinoco

Port of Spain
TRINIDAD Y TOBAGO

OCÉANO ATLÁNTICO

Medellín
Manizales
Bogotá
Cali
COLOMBIA
VENEZUELA
GUYANA
SURINAM
Georgetown
Paramaribo
Cayenne
GUAYANA FRANCESA

Quito
ECUADOR

ECUADOR

Quayaquil
Iquitos
PERÚ
Cajamarca

R. Amazonas
Manaus
R. Madeira
Belem

BRASIL

Recife

Machu Picchu
Lima
Ayacuchó
Cuzco
Arequipa
L. Titicaca
La Paz
BOLIVIA
Sucre
Arica
Iquique
Potosí

Salvador

Brasilia

Belo Horizonte

OCÉANO PACÍFICO

Antofagasta

PARAGUAY
Asunción
Salta
Tucumán
CHILE
Córdoba
Mendoza
Valparaíso
Santiago
Concepción

São Paulo
Santos
Rio de Janeiro

Porto Alegre

R. Paraná
R. Uruguay

Rosario
ARGENTINA
Buenos Aires
La Plata
URUGUAY
Montevideo
Río de la Plata

Bahía Blanca

TRÓPICO DE CAPRICORNIO

Puerto Montt

CORDILLERA DE LOS ANDES

ISLAS MALVINAS

| 0 | 200 | 400 | 600 | 800 millas |
| 0 | 200 | 400 | 600 | 800 kilómetros |

Punta Arenas
TIERRA DEL FUEGO
Cabo de Hornos
Estrecho de Magallanes